ORDE WINGATE

CHRISTOPHER SYKES

ORDE WINGATE

COLLINS
ST JAMES'S PLACE, LONDON
1959

" Ce qui donne du courage, ce sont les idées "

CLEMENCEAU

CONTENTS

7

CONTENTS

LIST OF PLATES

ACKNOWLEDGMENTS

The Author and publishers are grateful to the following for permission to reproduce illustrations : Miss Monica Wingate, Mr. Granville Wingate, Miss Enid Jelley, Colonel Rivlin, Mr. Wilfred Thesiger, the *Daily Mail*, the Imperial War Museum and the United States Air Force

LIST OF MAPS

PREFACE

THE STORY of Wingate must take his biographer into many places and interests. For that reason the necessary research has depended on the help of many people, and the writer is under deep obligation to Wingate's wide acquaintance, even more than may appear, for if every given fact and anecdote had been used the resultant book would have been so thick with matter as to make it hard to get through. First of all thanks must be offered to Mrs. Lorna Smith who placed all her late husband's papers at the writer's disposal. Sir Ronald Wingate likewise allowed him access to the papers of the late Sir Reginald Wingate, and these two collections provide the basic documentation for Wingate's life from the time of his early manhood till that of his death at the age of forty-one. For the details of his life before his entrance into the Royal Military Academy, the writer is chiefly indebted to Miss Sybil Wingate for an extended family memoir, and to Mr. Granville Wingate, Mr. Nigel Wingate, Miss Monica Wingate, and again Miss Sybil Wingate for lengthy discussion of their brother's private life and the family circumstance from which he came.

At the commencement of the undertaking Mr. Antony Head, then Secretary of State for War, gave the writer all help and placed him under a lasting obligation not only to himself but to many officials whom he met in the course of research. They often enabled him to find his way through dense paper jungles.

In 1956 the writer made some researches amid the scenes of Wingate's principal actions, in India, Burma, Ethiopia and Israel. The High Commissioner for India in London, Mrs. Pandit, and our High Commissioner in New Delhi, Mr. Malcolm Macdonald, supported the enterprise with the result that, under the ægis of Mr. B. B. Gosh, Under Secretary of State in the Ministry of Defence, and with the help of Dr. Srinanand Prasad of the historical section, the writer was able to consult many valuable Indian papers relative to Wingate's Burma expeditions. From New Delhi, and the hospitality of Mr. John Robb, the writer went to Rangoon where through the good offices of our ambassador Mr. Paul Gore Booth, and of Mr. John Baddeley, he was introduced to the Burmese Prime Minister at that time, U Nu, who took a liberal view of the writer's wish for travelling facilities. The result was a memorable journey, in the pleasant company of Mr. Cranley Onslow, then Consul in Maymyo, to the scene of the Chindit stronghold near Mawlu followed by a leisurely progress down the Irrawaddy to Mandalay. The latter journey was to a great extent made possible and productive by the Chief of Police at Katha, U Thein Ohn, and by the hospitality of U Sein Tun of Inywa who organised meetings with the people of Inywa, Henlu, and Tigyaing.

From Burma the writer travelled via Singapore to Ethiopia where our ambassador, Mr. Douglas Busk, arranged meetings with the Ethiopian notables who are mentioned as first-hand authorities in the book. He was accorded the privilege of an audience with H.I.M. the Emperor, and spent a day in illuminating discussion with Brigadier and Mrs. Dan Sandford.

The last episode of this journey was a visit to Israel. Mr. Eliahu Elath, at present Israel Ambassador in London, had recommended the writer in advance, and in consequence Colonel Rivlin, head of the archives section of the Defence Ministry, and Dr. Ben Zion Kounine took the writer under their protection and introduced him to most of the Jewish authorities mentioned in the text, and gave him access to State Records. Mrs. Weizmann, the widow of the august first President of Israel, helped with numerous personal recollections and gave the writer access to the Weizmann archives. He is also much obliged to the Prime Minister, Mr. Ben Gurion, the then Foreign Minister, Mr. Moshe Sharett, and General Dayan for giving him lengthy interviews at a time of national crisis.

The authorities mentioned above are only a few of those who made the writing of this book possible. It is customary at this stage of a preface to furnish an enormous list of names which is skipped by all readers except those watching for an omission. It has seemed better in this case to break with convention and leave the rest of the names of authorities, including major ones, to the footnotes and the story itself. Three people should be mentioned, however, because they gave general guidance such as cannot be adequately acknowledged outside a prefatory note. From Wingate's first days as a soldier Major-General Tulloch knew him as no one else did outside his family. During long sessions at Singapore, where he was commanding the garrison in 1956, and later in England, Derek Tulloch gave the writer detailed and invaluable accounts of Wingate as he was at different stages of his life. The most difficult piece of research was into the military situation of Palestine from 1936 to 1939. Sir John Evetts went to great pains to elucidate that tangled subject which apparently remains without official record. In the accounts of Wingate's last two years of life the writer is under considerable debt to Brigadier

PREFACE

Bernard Fergusson who acted as a frequent and hospitable consultant and introduced him to fellow-Chindits.

The available bibliography is small, varied and curious. There is only one biographical study of Wingate, a short and sensational book called *Gideon Goes To War* by Mr. Leonard Mosley. The writer of any biography is always under some debt to a predecessor because the latter has given him a whole picture, no matter how imperfectly coloured or ill drawn. In the case of *Gideon Goes To War*, however, the debt is less than might have been expected, as the book seems to have been written after insufficient study, so much so that the record of even the most discoverable facts, such as the location of Wingate's family home, is gravely at fault. Furthermore this author evidently suffered some bad luck in his researches, as when he quotes a first-rate authority such as Zvi Brenner he follows a hopelessly garbled version. But the worst blemish on the book is that it has given currency to a story that Wingate attempted to instigate a criminal proceeding at Haifa, a story for which there is no basis in fact. (This is dealt with at some length in an appendix.) Yet in spite of faults such as these Mr. Mosley's book has some abiding interest because the author knew Wingate in the days of the Ethiopian expedition, and the picture he presents does in all probability reflect something of Wingate's conduct at that time when he was going through a crisis of passionate embitterment. It should also be said that it gives one remarkably interesting historical fact, not recorded elsewhere outside official documents, concerning Sir Winston Churchill's patronage of Wingate after the first Burma expedition.

Apart from Mr. Mosley's portrait there are very brief biographical sketches in Charles Rolo's *Wingate's Raiders* and William Burchett's *Wingate's Phantom Army*, which both give some rough notion of Wingate's early life. Apart from Rolo's and Burchett's few paragraphs nothing is published outside *Gideon Goes To War* on the subject of Wingate's service in the Sudan between 1927 and 1933, except his own report, published in the *Geographical Journal*, of his Zerzura expedition in 1933. Of his Palestine career, which was the central episode of his life, the only references outside the books above-mentioned are in Arthur Koestler's *Thieves in the Night*, in Lorna Lindsley's *War is People*, and in Dr. Weizmann's autobiography.

With his appointment to Ethiopia in 1940 Wingate began to be exposed to authors, and thereafter his life can be followed to some extent in published material. The best book on Gideon Force is without doubt William Allen's *Guerilla Warfare in Abyssinia*, a little classic of military history now unfortunately out of print. Mark Pilkington's letters give an entertaining picture of the day-to-day life of those who had volunteered for service in the Ethiopian Emperor's personal troops, and there is a very good outline account of the expedition by Edmund Stevens, which was published in *Life* magazine. In general, however, the press accounts of Gideon Force are unreliable. The operation was not in the forefront of preoccupations and editors allowed themselves excessive freedoms.

In addition to what has been written on the subject itself of Wingate's guerilla operation in the Gojjam, " background reading " is necessary if Wingate's rôle as the Gideon Force commander is to be fully understood, since he took some political initiative in the restoration of Ethiopian independence. The whole course of Anglo-Ethiopian relations at this time is admirably and minutely described in Lord Rennell's book *British Military Administration in East Africa*, and many personal details on the same subject are to be found in Sir Philip Mitchell's *African Afterthoughts*. Mrs. Sandford's book, *The Lion of Judah Hath Prevailed*, is somewhat too courtly in tone to be considered as authoritative on its own, but it contains much not to be found elsewhere and takes its place as required reading.

With the Chindits the story of Wingate is voluminously if erratically documented in the Press. From the summer of 1943 he was a famous man. Despite much in Press treatment that certainly brought the blush of embarrassment to all members of the Wingate family, despite exaggeration and sentimentalism, most of the Chindit reporting can stand up to informed scrutiny. Journalists and information officers in India at that time evidently understood their business.

The first book to be published on the Chindits was Charles Rolo's *Wingate's Raiders* which came out in 1944. It is chiefly based on the first-hand accounts of John Jefferies and Robert Thompson. (To the latter the writer is under particular obligation for help in India.) A year after *Wingate's Raiders* Bernard Fergusson's classic *Beyond the Chindwin* was published, followed in 1946 by William Burchett's *Wingate's Phantom Army*. These three books are of prime importance to a study of Wingate and are all marked by a high degree of accuracy. In 1947 Phillip Stibbe's *Return Via Rangoon* was published. It has less than the others to tell of Wingate himself but gives a valuable account of the first expedition as this was seen by a junior not under his direct orders.

By this time books on the second expedition had begun to appear. One of the first was an American book *Back to Mandalay*, by Lowell Thomas. Though containing some rewarding detail this book is of minor interest and importance since it is in fact not the first-hand account by Philip Cochran that it artfully suggests that it is, and furthermore it is marred by an unworthy bias towards proving that

Wingate's second incursion into Burma was essentially an American operation. It needs to be and has been used with caution, but not without relish. The account of Wingate by Cochran is so plausible and amusing that the writer is tempted to suppose that it is not purely fictional. He has quoted it as a " reconstruction."

In 1946 Bernard Fergusson produced his second Chindit book *The Wild Green Earth*, an account of 16 Brigade in the second expedition. It is a worthy companion of *Beyond the Chindwin*, and the fact that much of it was written under a mistaken idea of strategy gives it a curious interest which is the subject of some comment and speculation in the present text.

Eight years after the second Chindit expedition Michael Calvert's book *Prisoners of Hope* was published. Though not expertly constructed, and not as easy civilian reading as a book ought to be, this is one of the best war-books of recent times, written by a man who took a bold part in many actions. As a description of Chindit life it is the equal of Fergusson. Calvert was one of the few men who lived on terms of easy personal friendship with Wingate, and his account of him would be extremely interesting for that reason alone. In addition he was one of the few subordinate commanders who served that exacting master with a natural understanding of his methods and aims. He understood the man and his purpose as no one else did, and thus he erected his book on firm foundations. The writer is under additional personal obligation to this authority. On the dispersal of the Chindits Calvert was appointed to the command of the S.A.S. brigade based in England. There the writer met him, struck up a friendship and first learned from him about the strange organisation and the strange commander under whom he had made a name for valour.

The major English memoir on the war in the Burma theatre is *Defeat into Victory* by Sir William Slim. It is a memorable work written with the skill of a born writer, but the student of Wingate must read it with perplexity. Throughout the record the Field-Marshal adopts a detached and modest tone, and his general picture of the defeat of 1942 and the subsequent Burma campaigns culminating in the reconquest seems to be impeccable, yet when the same man comes to write of Wingate he is at such extraordinary variance with the memories and opinions of others, and in contradiction with so much ascertainable fact, that it is hard to resist the impression that on this subject the Field-Marshal's mind is not wholly free of prejudice. Wingate made some serious misjudgments of men, notably of Brigadier Sandford, General Sir Alan Cunningham, and Sir Philip Mitchell. In all these cases he allowed pre-conceived ideas to distort his vision, even when the evidence was plain before him. By a singular irony, so it seems, he himself suffered injustice through the same process, at the hands of a man whom he greatly and rightly admired. The point to be made here is that in all that concerns the war in Burma and the formation, command and action of 14th Army, Sir William Slim's book has been used as a master document, but that in reference to Wingate and the Chindits it has not been so used except where it is supported by contemporary papers.

Lastly, mention must be made of Volume II of *The War against Japan* by Major-General S. Woodburn Kirby, in the official history of the Second World war. This appeared while the present biography was in the press, and therefore could not serve as part of the initial study. With a sense of gratitude to the author and his collaborators it has been used for purposes of correction and reference.

The writer must acknowledge a debt to Mrs. Dorothy Baker for much valuable literary advice, and to Mrs. E. H. Harris for producing typescripts.

CHAPTER I

BIRTH AND ANCESTRY

THE BIRTH of Orde Charles Wingate took place at Naini Tal in the United Provinces of India, on the 26th of February, 1903. His father recorded the event in detail in a letter written to his mother-in-law :

" Montrose "   *Naini Tal*
Tuesday night   3rd March, 1903

My dear Mrs. Orde-Browne,
  I am afraid that my telegram of the 26th February : " Boy (born to-day) and Ethel (has) hæmorrhage and desire prayer (for her) " must have made you all very anxious, but it was the least alarming I could think of in the stress of the moment, without defeating my object, which was to get prayer for her life. At the same time or between 6 and 7 in the evening of Thursday I telegraphed urgent to the Searles, to General Scott, to Mr. Biddulph, the Andersons at R. Pindi, the Greets at Meerut, the De Wintons at Aden, asking for prayer for her. I telegraphed also to A.E. to come at once from Lahore. The Doctor said she cannot arrive in time and of course I knew she could not reach Montrose at earliest before Saturday afternoon, nevertheless I felt then and now I did right to summon her to come if possible—I put in the words if possible—Everything had gone well. About 7 o'clock in the morning of Thursday, 26th February, Ethel told me she believed her confinement had begun. Nurse Carroll had been in the house since the 5th February. Simla being so far away, 3 days journey, I had persuaded Ethel to get her a little earlier but the 26th was a very late date—the 10th was supposed to be a likely date, and this was not merely by Ethel herself but also by Dr. Fayrer——
  The confinement itself was entirely favourable—the little chap came into the world in the right way, and as far as the labour and confinement it was considered by Dr. Fayrer as one of the easiest and quickest out of all those he had attended in Naini Tal. . . .
  At 20 minutes to 3 o'clock in the afternoon our little son was

born—an unusually fine large baby weighing 9 lbs. About 4 o'clock in the afternoon, Dr. Fayrer bade her good-bye for the present, and had got outside the house and was just going off when I heard Nurse Carroll scream from the top of the staircase (Ethel's bedroom is in the upper storey to get away from the Whooping-cough—Rae and Syb are segregated with their 2 Ayahs on the ground floor) " Doctor, Doctor, quick "—We flew upstairs —it was hæmorrhage—what happened in that room between then 4 p.m. Thursday and 8 a.m. next morning Friday cannot be described—but I will try and tell you something of it—The hæmorrhage was very severe—injections of Ergot were given with the hypodermic syringe under her skin, the continuous douche with hot, almost boiling, water was used, the agony of these injections of such hot water to Ethel was excruciating but of all the remedies tried that night it was I think *The* one that most helped to save her life. I had as one of my arrangements procured a coolie load of snow from the top of the mountains above Naini Tal, and this enabled icy cold water to be applied externally only——

By 6 to 8 o'clock in the evening I saw she was sinking—then it was I left the room for a few minutes at a time to send off my urgent telegrams for prayer—3 times during the night Dr. Fayrer gave her up—once he all but said the words to me she is dead— another time he took me to her side, and then walked away to the far side of the room meaning that last moments were for me alone. Every quarter of an hour Nurse Carroll would shout in her ear, " Rouse yourself, Colonel Wingate is speaking to you."—Nurse Carroll feared to let Ethel alone even for a few minutes. She was constantly putting her hand in front of Ethel's mouth to see if there was any breath—in appearance Ethel was like a corpse for many hours on that night—Nurse Carroll was constantly urging the doctor to try something fresh—and Dr. Fayrer had explained to me that in severe hæmorrhage he was not justified in not attempting everything he knew of as likely to do any good. But about 2 o'clock in the night I thought that all these active efforts were wearing out her last flickering strength. I drew Dr. Fayrer aside and told him what I thought—he agreed : he replied there is nothing left to try excepting a hypodermic injection of perchloride of Iron, but in her state it will perhaps be fatal. I answered that I would not consent to trying this—he said you are quite right.

I was glad it was Fayrer that night. He combines the best medical skill with common sense—it might so easily have been one of these impossible R.A.M.C. doctors. Nurse Carroll is a little deaf and she gets " gabraoed "—there is no English equivalent in one word for this Hindustani but it means showing your alarm in your manner—these are her 2 faults—and if she was all alone with a patient they would be serious—she does not lose her head—her suggestions were excellent and mostly acted on by Dr. Fayrer.

I was the only one of the 3 in the room who could catch what Ethel said—now and again I caught her murmur, " More air—more air."

I was fanning her face with a handpunkah—iced water hand-kerchiefs were laid across her brow—the window was open—it was a wild tempestuous night outside, one of the most boisterous we have had, and I thought this rickety house would be blown down—cold water was sprinkled on her face whenever she appeared to go off in a dead faint or to lapse into a state of unconsciousness—brandy and ether all these sort of remedies were used—gradually the hæmorrhage began to lessen. I never lost hope because I was relying on prayer—I prayed myself without ceasing for her life to be spared. At 4 o'clock on Friday morning I thought I saw a change and I knew then prayer had been heard. By 8 o'clock a.m. it was beyond doubt that she was reviving—Dr. Fayrer was very surprised. . . .

I have had a bad go of whooping-cough caught from nursing Sybil 6 weeks ago. It quarantines me a lot as regards the new born but I hope to shake it off shortly now—I read Psalm XXX[1] to Ethel yesterday. He can make our life a song of deliverances.

Your affectionate son

George Wingate

This letter, singular in so many ways, was typical of the man who wrote it and of the life from which he came.

George Wingate was a member of an old Scots family something of whose past was briefly outlined in a curious note written by his father, the Reverend William Wingate. " They are said to have come over with William the Conqueror in the 11th century from Normandy, their French name being Winguet. They were after-wards divided into two branches, one of which settled in Scotland, the other in England. To the latter, I hope, Euston Wingate belonged, who imprisoned John Bunyan. I had once a Latin book sent me written by a Wingate in Edinburgh at the Reformation period in the days of Knox. Ours are the Stirlingshire Wingates. My grandfather was William Wingate of Craiginghelt, Stirlingshire, and my grand-mother was Sarah Carrick, sister of the celebrated physician, Dr.

---

[1] The fifth verse is as follows : " For his anger *endureth but* a moment; in his favour *is* life : weeping may endure for a night, but joy *cometh* in the morning."

Carrick of Bristol. Both were earnest Christians, and he was an ordained Elder in St. Ninian's parish, for over fifty years."

The William Wingate who wrote this lived from 1808 to 1899. He was a very unusual man who may be said to have opened a new chapter of Wingate history. The family had come into considerable wealth in the course of the Industrial Revolution and William Wingate's father was an affluent merchant of Glasgow. The world had much to give to the son, and at the age of twenty-one William Wingate was not only a well-endowed partner in the family business, but a gay and popular young man " of good connection " in northern society. " He entered on commercial life," says his biographer, " with zeal and diligence, a leader at the same time in all sorts of sports, balls, dinners, parties, etc., and devoted to horsemanship, keeping generally one or two hunters, a member of the Harrier's Club, and joining often in the fox-hunt."[1]

This happy mundane enviable career was brought to an end by the beneficiary himself. His nature underwent a sudden change in the face of a personal disaster. When he was in his late twenties his wife died three years after their marriage. In his grief the young man turned to his religion and became aware of a vocation to a life of good works. He was for two years an Evangelical lay missionary in Glasgow. Then one day " when walking down Vincent Street, thinking of the various missions he assisted, it occurred to him that he did nothing for the Jews."[1] Thereupon he saw his way clear : he decided to devote his life to the conversion of the chosen people to Christianity. He now finally abandoned his business career, learned German and Hebrew in Berlin, and obtained an appointment to the Church of Scotland mission to the Jews of Hungary. He was ordained in Buda Pesth in 1842 and remained there converting numerous Jews till the mission was suppressed, with many other non-Catholic institutions, in the Austrian reaction of the early 1850's. He returned to England and continued his work there till his death at the age of ninety-one.

He was a man of unhesitating singleness of purpose, but this did not give him the harshness that goes with determined character. His strict piety did not make him narrow. He did not forget that he had once been a gay dog and in his later years it was often noticed that he was sympathetic to the troubles of scapegrace youth. After his death he was remembered as a person of persistent gentleness and his strange remark about Euston Wingate, if intended for *odium theologicum* against John Bunyan, was very much out of his normal character.[2]

[1] *Life and Work of the Reverend William Wingate* by the Reverend Gavin Carlyle. 1901.
[2] It may be that he meant to indicate contentment that the Scottish branch was innocent of this persecution.

In 1843 he had made a second marriage to Margaret Wallace Torrance from whom his descendants were born.

George Wingate was his second son. He was born in 1852 and entered the British army in 1871, being gazetted in October as a cornet. He was among the last to be granted a commission by purchase, but it was very soon to appear that he was far from the kind of officer who brought the purchase-system into disrepute by frivolity and idleness. Early in life he showed a spirit which was recognisably his father's, though differing from it in many ways.

Soon after he was gazetted he obtained a transfer from the 19th Foot, better known as the Green Howards, to the Army of India, and while in India, he underwent a religious experience similar to that of his father in the eighteen thirties. He also saw his way clear, but he did not find it, as others have done there, in a way that drew him from his own traditions and people. It may be said that so deep and diverse is the religious spirit of India that it can provide for character and temperament quite unfamiliar with its surroundings ; can minister to such things as the derivatives of British Puritanism, which are as far removed from its home ground as can be imagined. The fact in question is that life in India impelled young George Wingate to join the Plymouth Brethren.

Two Indian incidents tell us all we need to know about the depth and passion of the young soldier's spiritual convictions. One day when he was still a young man (in a town of India and on a date both lost) he came on a mystic or " Sadhu " undergoing a discipline known as that of the three fires. This meant that the holy man, conforming to a known practice, had seated himself between two substantial fires in the full glare of the sun, in which posture he gave himself to contemplation, offering his ordeal by heat to Omnipotence. On grasping the significance of what the Sadhu was doing, George Wingate was seized with a desire to " win him for Christ," and he tried to start a disputation. But the Sadhu, either owing to a vow of silence, or to test the young officer, indicated that the other must join in the ordeal before any communication could be held between them. It is said that on this occasion George Wingate was Orderly Officer for the day and thus wearing his full regimentals and a sword. What is certain is that he accepted the invitation and joined the holy man, the two sitting opposite each other in the sun between the fires. They sat thus in silence for a long time, how long it would be unsafe to say, but sufficiently long to convince the holy man of the other's sincerity, for in the end he consented to talk. Unfortunately at the climax nothing of great note seems to have passed between them, for in later years George Wingate had no wisdom or revelation to remember from this experience.

Such was one incident. The second is less dramatically arresting, but equally remarkable to modern ideas. In 1879, at the time of the disorders following the accession of King Thibaw of Burma, George Wingate, who was still a junior officer, was ordered to join a force assembled on the Indian frontier for a minor campaign, known after as the Naga Hill Expedition. The General Officer Commanding was waiting for George Wingate and his contingent but, whatever his impatience, and a commander on the eve of action may be impatient, he was obliged to wait twenty-four hours longer than he expected, the reason being that his subordinate had insisted on halting by the wayside with his men for one whole day, since it was a Sunday, and he would not invite Divine displeasure by desecrating the Christian Sabbath. What may strike us, who live in the age of efficiency, as strangest in this episode is the fact that George Wingate's high-handed and rebellious scrupulousness was perfectly understood by the General, and the younger man not only went unrebuked but received the campaign medal with clasp and was mentioned in despatches. Puritanism is an abiding force in British affairs. The story of Orde Wingate is one of many examples of its power.

George Wingate married late in life and under unusual circumstances such as attended most of his actions. While on leave in England when he was twenty-six years old he was taken by his commanding officer, Colonel Mitchell, to visit a certain Captain and Mrs. Orde-Browne who were living at Plumstead near Woolwich. Mrs. Orde-Browne was Colonel Mitchell's sister. The Captain and his wife had a family of six girls and one boy. George Wingate asserted afterwards that as soon as he met the eldest daughter Ethel, who was then only twelve years old, he made up his mind to marry her as soon as she was old enough to accept him. It is foolish to debate the causes of love at first sight, but it should be noted that one reason why George Wingate may have been attracted to the Orde-Browne family was that they belonged to his adopted religion, that of the Plymouth Brethren. He loved Miss Orde-Browne in separation for twenty years and married her in September, 1899, at the Gospel Hall, Woolwich. He was forty-six and had attained the rank of Colonel. She was thirty-two.

Mrs. Wingate is best considered in association with her father, Charles Orde-Browne, whose character and career show some resemblance, with considerable differences, to those of George Wingate. He came of a family belonging to " county gentry," as their class was then described. His father, Colonel Browne of Stout's Hill, who once commanded the Ninth Lancers, died early, and young Charles had inherited the family estate while he was still a boy. He obtained a commission in the army at the age of sixteen, and within the year he was sent East and saw active service in the Crimea. It was there, amid the stresses of war and at the most impressionable age, that he found his soul, and, to the exasperation of his family, he turned from the Church of England to the Plymouth Brethren. He felt called to a consecrated life, and when the war was over the young Captain resigned his commission in order to found a centre or " meeting," as the term is, of Plymouth Brethren in North Woolwich. He took charge of the centre, and in ordinary language may be said to have established a slum mission church in which he officiated as an unordained minister. He gave his life to the poor. In the earlier part of his missionary days, between 1865 and 1871, he met and made friends with General Gordon, then " Commanding Royal Engineer " at Gravesend. They had a common interest in religion and the rescue of the destitute, and for a time they worked in association.

The Browne family had a streak of extraordinary intellectual ability. Charles Browne's nephew, Edward Granville Browne, was to be one of the three or four greatest Oriental scholars produced by England, indeed by the world, and there can be little doubt that if Charles Browne had received a full education he must have attained to eminence and perhaps fame. As it was, though almost wholly self-taught, he was able to make of himself a proficient mathematician, and an authority on certain branches of engineering. He was chosen to represent the British Government at a conference held in Germany on ballistics and armour-plating (in the years before Tirpitz and Kaiser Wilhelm II) and, in a specialist capacity he accompanied an expedition to Egypt led by the Astronomer Royal. He needed to make money to provide for his growing family and he did this by lecturing on mathematics at the Royal Military Academy at Woolwich, and by contributing articles to specialist papers such as *The Engineer*.

He was a man of forceful character, and a little incident tells us something about that. Great numbers of tramps and beggars used to call at his back-door, and one day he found some hieroglyphics chalked on the wall, the advice of one outcast to another in their ancient code. When translated the message ran " charitable but sharp." In addition to some sternness, however, he was possessed of unusual charm, and he captivated the minds and hearts of his numerous children. His favourite was his eldest daughter. He treated her as a beloved companion and shared his intellectual and spiritual

25

life with her. He came to exert over her the fullest possible measure of influence that a father can over his child, and in after years Mrs. Wingate's children felt through their mother the same strong influence of the grandfather they had never seen. Through her they became familiar from the earliest age with restless intellectual curiosity and a wide range of interests from philosophy to music. From her they were taught, as though from her father, to know mathematics as an adventure of the mind. From her also they learned their grandfather's unfashionable but not valueless ideas about poetic composition. He had a taste for the arts, amused himself with painting and, this being in the years of the Gothic Revival, by turning his knowledge of metal-plating to the construction of model suits of armour, but his main æsthetic pursuit was in versifying. In this latter activity, however, he was out of step with the age of Tennyson, and clung to the ideas of the century before his own, being convinced that poetry was largely a matter of mechanical contrivance and craftsmanship and that every-one could and should express themselves through that medium. He obliged his daughters to write quantities of poetry, and the eldest daughter made his Wingate grandchildren toil in the same spirit for the sternest of the muses. She handed on to them Charles Browne's odd belief that only "vanity" prevented any literate person from expressing anything he wished to say in poetic form. The young Wingates were obliged, therefore, to bend themselves to the colossal task of composing poetry without having any poetic talent to help them. It is a hard way, but not a bad way of learning to write.

Colonel and Mrs. Wingate were well suited to each other, if we believe that happy marriages are to some extent based on contrast. They were united in their devotion to the religion in which they both had an absolute faith, but they were quite different in tempera-ment. While the piety of the converted husband was gloomy and brooding, that of his wife was worn more lightly, and in a way which did not mitigate her inherited gladness of spirits. He could never lose his independence of mind and for all the deep-rootedness of his faith he inclined to free-thinking. She was orthodox and never questioned the least part of the Brethren's doctrine. He was an emotional man guided by deep and hardly definable impulses. She was of a different sort. Though she was the reverse of shallow, she left the deeps to themselves. She was a person of continual mental activity such as wrought her consciousness to a high point. In a way both of them were possibly miscast for what they did in life. If in his early years George Wingate had met someone capable of grounding him in mystical theology he might have become a religious devoted to a life of spiritual exercises, renouncing the world, and marriage with it. If she had lived in an age which took the idea of a full education for women as a matter of course, she was likely to have become the principal of a women's college at a University, or to be known in some other way as a leading intellectual. She can (though not necessarily rightly) be considered as the victim of narrow prejudices concerning "woman's place." But if there was frustration in their lives it was not she but the man who showed it. He was grim. She was gay. In his face there was something of the fanatic, notably in the deep-set brilliant china-blue eyes, all the more noticeable from his white hair and white bushy eyebrows. She was spare and fragile in appearance, delicate in build with little wrists and ankles and the beauty of line drawing in her aquiline features. She was a very clever woman. He was not clever and had no wish to be thought so.

Some five months after the birth of their first son at Naini Tal Colonel and Mrs. Wingate returned to England with their two little daughters and the baby boy. They lived in rooms in Blackheath to be near Mrs. Orde-Browne, and after six months' leave returned to India in February, 1904, leaving the three children at Blackheath with their grandmother, at 11 The Paragon. In the next year, 1905 (after the birth of another daughter) a great change overtook the life of this family. Colonel Wingate had reached the age of 52 and in accordance with a recently introduced regulation, he was obliged to go on to the Supernumerary List, being granted the substantive rank of Colonel. This was in effect retirement, though not in fact so. He was among the last officers (perhaps the very last), to draw a handsome pension from " Reckonings," nearly equal to his pay on full duty. He was never obliged to retire. As he had entered the service, so this devout, virtuous and stern-living man left it, with the consolations and eases of an age when privilege was little questioned.

In October of this momentous year in the Colonel's life, the husband and wife returned to England for good. From here on to the end of their days they lived (with several changes of address) in the Southern Counties, never far from London. At the end of 1905 they went to their first English home, in Worthing in Sussex, first living in rooms and then moving to a house at 6 St. Germain's Place which they rented for two and a half years.

They lived simply, in less comfort than was to be expected from their means. The reason for this was that a great part of their income was devoted to the missionary enterprises with which they were associated. The Colonel served on the committees of several of these, notably one concerned with North Africa, another with " The Regions Beyond " (meaning Central Africa), one known as " John Groom's Crippleage," another as " The Rescue Society." But his love, among these passionate interests, was " The Central Asian Mission " of which he was the Chairman for many years. He had helped to found this particular enterprise during his years of service on the North-West Frontier, and in after years he referred to it as his " eighth child." To these and similar ardent institutions Colonel and Mrs. Wingate gave all that they could, not only a large part of their income but a large part of their energy too. They toiled at routine work, at regulating accounts, copying out agenda, editing the correspondence of missionaries for publication, proof-reading, posting and distributing pious magazines, composing requests for prayers and other circulars. Mrs. Wingate edited two publications, *Dawn in Central Africa* and *The Intercession Paper*. As they reached years of discretion the children were called on to help in carrying this large burden of sacred labour. One of them said in later years that sharing in the work led them from an early age to recognise the drudgery behind organisation and achievement, and also to take note of the distant places of the world.

Every Sunday, wherever they happened to be living, the family used to attend a " morning meeting " of the Brethren. At these the Colonel would often address the congregation. Many of his performances were not wholly to the taste of his hearers since he would prepare what he had to say with great precision, a practice considered " unspiritual " because, in the belief of the stricter brethren, the spoken word on such occasions should be as far as possible unfettered by mental exertion and be left to the care of the Holy Spirit alone. But occasionally he was able to satisfy the most exacting, and would speak as though he was inspired. It would seem then to his hearers as though something outside himself had taken possession of his whole being ; the expression of harsh fanaticism left him to be replaced by a rapt and tender look indicative of deep inward peace. His hands would tremble nervously as he turned the thin rustly pages of his Bible and, usually beginning with a quotation from his slender stock of mystical poetry, he would deliver a devotional address so different in character from his usual prosier style that it seemed as though it came from another man. The brethren used sometimes to say among themselves : " The Colonel has a gift for the ministry."

The family continued to multiply till 1911, by which time there were seven children, four daughters and three sons. Even so late as this the Colonel and his wife had not yet found a permanent home and some further changes of address should be noticed. In 1908 the family

went for a year and a half to a house called Hilden in God-
ington Lane, Orpington, in order to be near the Colonel's mother
living at Bromley. Two years later, in 1910, they moved to a
house called Marchworth in Furzefield Road, Reigate, where the
youngest son was born. By this time the subject of this book was
eight years old.

CHAPTER II

EARLY YEARS

MEN OF great talent rarely grow in accordance with the smooth routine of nature. Their childhoods are apt to fall into two categories, one in which the self-evident prodigy delights or dismays his elders by a brilliant display of qualities leaping into premature fullness, the other in which nothing in evidence of coming distinction can be seen, as though weighty preparations were being made at a deep level, out of reach of ordinary sight, even of the knowledge of the future man. Orde Wingate belonged to this second class. Throughout his childhood and youth he showed no extraordinary proficiency, no unusual alertness of mind, no sign of exceptional gifts. People who met him in his first years often noticed a childish reflection of the brooding temperament of his father, but none of them found reason to guess that he was to be anyone outstanding. He seemed to be one of hundreds of difficult little boys, singular only in the very singular circumstances of the family life from which he came. We have seen something of this from the point of view of the parent generation. Let us look at it again from the point of view of the children.

The home was a very bookish one in which the pressure of work and learning was such as we read of in the early life of Macaulay or John Stuart Mill. Compared to what went on in the Wingate schoolrooms the life of a public schoolboy at the time was one of leisure. A system was devised which went as follows : Mrs. Wingate taught the four eldest children the rudiments of reading, writing and elementary knowledge ; they in turn taught those younger than themselves, while a governess was imported to advance matters onward from a primitive stage. In addition, schoolmasters and mistresses from the local grammar schools called at the house to teach music, drawing, mathematics, French, Latin and Greek. At one time the children had seven different instructors, and some of the Reigate neighbours supposed (not unnaturally) from the sound of constant piano practice, the procession of masters, and the classroom noises of monotone or recitation, that this was not a family house but some sort of infant school. The impression was deepened after 1909 when the Colonel's elder brother, Sir Andrew Wingate, brought his influence on to the

30

training of his young nephews and nieces. He had strong views on education and he insisted that large maps should be hung in the rooms where the children worked so that they might be early acquainted with world geography, and he persuaded his brother and sister-in-law to enter them for public examinations suited to their years. He also proposed that the contributions to the missionary societies should be cut down so that the children might be given more becoming clothes, but no suggestion ever seems to have been made in this household that the hours of work should be reduced. The children worked full school hours every day, and though Sunday was very much set apart it was not a day of idle repose.

The morning of Sunday was taken up with religious devotions, and the afternoon with one of the main family interests, the study of the Bible. The children would assemble round a table for sacred reading and doctrinal exposition by the parents, followed by lighter readings from such publications as *The War Cry* (the magazine of the Salvation Army). Some rigidly circumspect diversions were allowed later in the day, and this usually meant that the children were encouraged to toil at the colouring of black and white drawings depicting episodes of Bible history. From these pious Sunday afternoons a family custom grew, part solemn part play, for the children to master a chapter of the Old Testament in the Authorised Version sufficiently well to be able to read it through and recite some of it by heart. When the test was passed to the satisfaction of the parents a copy of the Bible was presented.

It was found in the course of years that the little Wingates could gain a Bible by this feat of reading and memorising when they were about five and a half, but the eldest son had to wait until after that age. He could memorise but only with help from the others. He had already dislocated the educational regime of the household by his inability to learn reading from his mother, and he again showed himself behind the others in his slowness with the Scriptures. The others were quick at applying Biblical quotations to the events of their lives, and the story was long remembered of how the fourth child Monica had told the cook that it were well for her if a millstone were hanged about her neck and she was cast into the bottom of the sea because she had offended one of these little ones, the little one in question being a pet mouse to whom the cook had omitted to supply a meal. But there was nothing of this spirit with " Ordey." He remained perversely slow at his books, and it was impossible to guess at the deep impression being formed on his mind and soul by the splendours of the Word of God.

Then he learned reading suddenly, but not, as the Colonel and Mrs.

Wingate would have liked, because he thirsted for the Bible, but because he was being teased by his two eldest sisters, Rachel and Sybil. They were reading Grimm's fairy tales, and, in the fashion of little girls, they effectively maddened their brother by giving him hints of those marvellous stories but not the stories themselves. This feline behaviour exasperated him into literacy. He remembered afterwards that his first reading was Grimm, followed by *The Arabian Nights*, *Jock of the Bushveldt* and *The Swiss Family Robinson*. From now on he was able to rival his sister Sybil in learning passages of the Bible by heart, but this first signal of the later man could not be recognised for what it was. He still seemed rather a dull little fellow in mind.

An acuter student of psychology than the Colonel might have been consoled by the little boy's prowess in play. The children discovered for themselves a world of fancy, and like most such worlds it was full of the romance of war, conspiracy and battle. They called it " Lodolf," though whether this name signified an imaginary kingdom or a " way of life " would be, and always was, hard to say. Something of both. Its ruler was King Harold, a rôle violently filled by Ordey, who was compelled to share his throne, however, with two other crowned heads, King Alfred and King Leonard. The children were obliged to " double " many parts, among which only that of King Harold remained constant, and Lodolf became thickly populated. There were figures of pathos, like the abandoned Prince William, figures of eccentric valour like the Amazonian Lady Elfrida who rode to battle with her sovereign brothers, or of farce and contempt like the Lady Drusesla who burned all her furniture in a fit of extravagance and was of cowardly disposition. These notables, worthies, and royal personages were involved in adventures borrowed consciously or otherwise from Grimm, Scott, Mallory, Tennyson, *The Arabian Nights*, and every sort of child's book current at the time. After a visit to Edinburgh by the Colonel and Mrs. Wingate in 1910 and the presentation of Douglas kilts to Ordey and the second son Nigel, Lodolf was extended to embrace some Scottish history and " The Northern League " was formed.[1] Many bloody episodes of Douglas history were revived and put into a Lodolf shape, and a convenient hillside served for frequent performances of the Battle of Killiecrankie. Whatever the games, their continual theme was war and a struggle for power which raged through the Wingate shrubberies, plantations, gardens, schoolrooms and nurseries, in Orpington, Reigate, and later Godalming. The leader was Ordey, and years after he said that these games had made a lasting impression on him and had influenced his character.

Most large families invent worlds of escape for themselves, and

---

[1] Colonel Wingate was related to the Douglases through his mother.

Wingate's father

Wingate's mother

Wingate aged four

Lodolf was not unique territory. For all that it was of a rare order. Like the similar Angria and Gondal of the young Brontës it took a kind of reality from the intensity of the players, and this intensity, with the Wingates as with the Brontës, came from loneliness, from the felt lack of the real world. For the most extraordinary feature of the Wingate family life, which, in its merits and defects, belonged so entirely to the nineteenth century, was its insularity, and especially the segregation of the children from others. It has been calculated by one of them that for six years, from 1909 to 1915, they met hardly more than half a dozen other persons of their own age, notably the four youngest children of Henry Mandeville, a family friend of the Orde-Brownes, and a little boy called Frank Jones, the only son of an Anglo-Indian military man living at Reigate. Their only other meetings with other children, apart from Church, occurred when for a year, at Reigate, the four eldest went to the High School for drill. For the rest, there were no outings with others who were not of their family, no children's parties, no juvenile dances, no football and cricket, no sight of the human world beyond the family gates. This segregation was carefully planned, it being the belief of the parents that contact with people outside the faith would have a corrupting effect on the souls of their children.

It is probably true to say that all accounts of all family circles present pictures which are more or less horrifying. The act of growing up is rarely other than painful and the necessary tyranny of the best of parents must become to some degree odious to the most dutiful of children. The extraordinary Puritanism of the household in which Orde Wingate grew up is easily condemned as calculated to deform and fetter its members. But such a judgment is superficial. That the eccentricity and harshness in Orde Wingate's character was emphasised by the harsh eccentricity of his first upbringing, is probably true ; but it is also certainly true that from the world of piety and sincerity and submission to the Divine will, where his parents had their being, he drew strength for the rest of his life. Children have minds different from grown-up people, and grown-up people forget what it is to have a child's mind. It is difficult to know whether this was a happy home or the reverse. Those who belonged to it remember much joy and grief. The children certainly groaned at the long hours of study to which they were condemned, at the excessive church-going, and the forbidding of all luxuries of food. But they never knew the boredom of vacant days, in a house so full of the activity of the mind, and the delights of Lodolf stayed with them long after that fairyland's supersession. If they were locked away from the companionship of other children, they had the freedom of the countryside and from an early age were encouraged to explore it. In after years Orde Wingate said that his family circle seemed horribly dismal to people outside it, but was in fact not so to the children themselves. Not all of his family have agreed with this. Whatever the final verdict may be on this matter, there can be no doubt that the exacting character of the father weighed heavily on the house, and especially on the eldest son. It is not fanciful to see in this circumstance some beginning of his lifelong rebelliousness, a rebelliousness which in these early days, and after, was much qualified. He was an insubordinate and devoted son. He loved both his parents, but it was to his father that he gave his admiration, more than to the mother from whom he inherited his mental quickness and brilliance. We may be very faintly reminded of what Bismarck's English biographer has said of the founder of modern Germany : " He was the clever, sophisticated son of a clever, sophisticated mother, masquerading all his life as his heavy, earthy father."

In 1914 there was a last change of address, to " Summerhill," a large villa in Godalming. The purpose of this move was for the parents to be near their eldest son when it was time for him to be a schoolboy. It was their intention that Ordey should have the advantages of the best education but without the dangers attaching to residence in a public school, away from the Brethren. In so far as it was possible they wished to continue the segregation even after the first fearful separation of young life, and after he had become immersed in the herd-life of a British education. To some extent they succeeded. In 1915 he went to a private school in Godalming called Hillside ; a year later he commenced underdog at Charterhouse. He attended both places as a dayboy.

The school career of Orde Wingate need not occupy much space in his biography. Throughout it he was insignificant. If he was noted for oddity, he yet never rose from the crowd of other boys. He made little mark. One of his contemporaries[1] recalls him at his private school as a small uncommunicative untidy little scalliwag with a stooping gait. Another remembers " a little rat-like fellow," but adds " you could see even then he had a will."[2] He was known as " Stinker." Another contemporary[3], also a dayboy, remembers a characteristic conversation. It was on a Saturday. The two boys were walking home from Hillside through the streets of Godalming when Wingate's friend told him that next day his parents were taking him to a Sunday concert. Young Wingate was horrified. He told his friend he must

---

[1] Mr. John Hayward.   [2] Mr. Adrian Daintrey.   [3] Mr. Phillip Radcliffe.

not go to this abominable desecration of the Lord's Day, but the other was unconvinced, not even when the young zealot cried out in panic : " If you go you will bring your soul into danger of hell-fire ! "

In the great school of Charterhouse, that most splendid of Victorian conceptions, there is in the chapel porch a memorial to Orde Wingate which was unveiled in 1946 by a famous commander related to the Royal family. It is a fitting testimony to one of the most famous of modern Carthusians ; but in the days when he studied at Charterhouse, Wingate seemed an unlikely subject for such honours. It must have seemed as probable then that marble trophies or princely monuments were to be erected to celebrate the man who mowed the lawn or the boy who blacked the boots. Throughout his Charterhouse days, from September, 1916, till he left in 1920, Orde Wingate won no prize and distinguished himself in no branch of study or athletics. He did not rise above Lance-Corporal in the Officers' Training Corps.

Dayboys of Charterhouse are made members of houses, and Orde Wingate was given a place in the headmaster's house (known to Carthusian folk-lore as " Saunderites "). He seems to have made little impression on his house-mates and teachers. The headmaster in those days was the eminent and greatly admired Sir Frank Fletcher. When he came to write his memoirs he made no mention of Wingate. They were published in 1937 and by that time Fletcher had probably forgotten the irritating little boy from twenty years before who was soon to be a famous man. It is only by an effort of the mind that anyone who knew Wingate in those days can at all remember him as he then was.

If he was noted at all it was as a boy with an odd religious streak. Though he did not figure as a person of religious fervour in his home circle, in the profaner air of his school he did. Many years afterwards, when Wingate's name was known to the world, one of the masters of Charterhouse, a clergyman who had taught him, was asked what he could recall of the General's early youth. He could recall almost nothing except that on afternoons when the boys were free to amuse themselves as they chose, and when most of them turned to cricket or football, he would steal away to the chapel and give himself up to prayer. This was not looked on as wholesome.

So obscure in most respects was Wingate's Charterhouse career that, except in the monument, it is difficult to find substantial evidence of his having been there at all. The only other traces remaining after forty years are dry entries in official records, and the photographs taken every summer of the Saunderites grouped round Sir Frank Fletcher. There he is quickly picked out. An undersized boy with a large head, his face in childhood very much the same as in later life, and as in

35

later life with piercing glaring fierce eyes. For the photographs he has been tidied and brushed, but he is most often remembered when at all (with the customary effort), as untidy and ill-kempt, remarkably so even by the horrid standards of boyhood. He made few friends. Remembered more easily than this lonely angry child are the visits to Charterhouse of his father, Colonel Wingate. The latter was much worried as to whether attendance at Anglican services in the school chapel might weaken his son's allegiance to the Plymouth Brethren, and he would come and argue the question with his masters. On the latter he made a daunting impression and the sight of him walking up the hill to the school came to be somewhat dreaded by them. The Colonel's fears for his son were not imaginary. Having left home, even though only partially, Orde Wingate began to leave the religion of his parents.[1]

Of the little that can be ascertained of Wingate's school career one thing can be held as certain. He was wretchedly unhappy. He felt persecuted. There is no evidence that in fact he was. Charterhouse has humane traditions, and a school which was remembered with life-long affection by so sensitive a spirit as Max Beerbohm was no jail. But this need tell us nothing. Irrational misery, the grief that comes inexplicably from within, can be more tormenting because more elusive than one which follows a visible pattern of cause and effect.

A child knows nothing of the pains of growth, only that he is in pain. The unformed mind has no notion of what is meant by the frustration endured by oncoming talent ; it cannot possibly understand the elaborate inner process whereby an instinctive resentment is being brought into being against the neglect and arrogance of ordinary people ; it can only feel the bitterness of exclusion. With Wingate this bitterness was never to be lost, and if rebelliousness had a first origin at home, it had a second and more conscious one at school. The whole of his story from his early days to the end is one of conflict between the individual and the mass. In no action of his short life did he fail to assert the right of the exceptional man over the beliefs, conventions, expectations, hopes, and even the morality of " the herd," " the mob," as he came to think of all majorities. That long conflict in which all that was admirable in him was to show, and in which he was frequently to be mistaken, in which he was to be both wise and foolish, began, as he admitted himself, at Charterhouse, and with imagined wrongs. The conflict was probably inevitable.

To continue with this blankest page in the story. In November, 1920, when he was seventeen, he passed (with low marks) from his

[1] From meetings with Charterhouse masters, arranged by Mr. Richard Usborne.

public school into the Royal Military Academy, Woolwich. In keeping with the adventures of his family, this ordinary transition was marked by an odd irregularity. Having passed his examination, he received orders to report to the Royal Military College, Sandhurst. He returned the orders to the War Office and obtained correct ones. His father applied for a reduction of the Academy fees giving as his reason that " The Government profess to be anxious to help fathers of large familes. I have," the Colonel continued, " seven children all educating between the ages of nine and twenty. My Fixed Income, so diminished by the heavy taxation, is quite insufficient to meet these charges. I shall be, therefore, grateful for a reduction in the rate."

The application was agreed to.

The young cadet was examined by the medical authorities. They found that his health was sound, his height five feet six inches, his weight nine stone three pounds. He joined the Royal Military Academy on the 3rd of February, 1921. Without any promise of glory his military career began.

CHAPTER III

DISCOVERIES

FOR MORE than two years the dismal story of Wingate at Charterhouse was prolonged, with little modification, into a second chapter to be entitled Wingate at Woolwich. As a cadet officer in his first terms he appeared to most people as a contrary, unsociable and dislikeable young man. Though he had natural good looks, he contrived an appearance that was the reverse of pleasing. He was no more tidy than he had been as a schoolboy, making now something of a cult of slovenly clothes, well calculated to exasperate feelings in a military society. He did as little work as was possible without being sent away. His intellectual interest was music. He only showed a keen interest in two parts of the curriculum, shooting and horsemanship. He seemed a boorish youth with small hope of military or other success.

The changes in him, if significant, were not such as to soothe authority, or enable them to discern a great future. He was now a voluminous reader, but a reader apparently devoid of all ambition to improve his mind, a devourer of thrillers and such-like, of which he had a large collection. He had, however, become an unmistakably positive person. He was noticed ; and if he irritated the instructors and the more conventionally-minded of his fellows, he rallied some of the rebellious spirits. He found other companionship too. He was inevitably liked by those, always numerous among Englishmen, who shared a passion for horses, and he had a few friends who liked him on account of a taste for odd fish. Something of a clown, something more of a rebel, with an extraordinary natural talent for riding, he had a certain following among the juniors, but a larger opposition among the cadets generally. In the main he was unpopular. In his last year at Woolwich in 1923, his unpopularity was the cause of a humiliating and very important incident in his life.

There was a custom at "The Shop" whereby cadets who had egregiously misbehaved were "run" by the senior cadets, a practice of unofficial punishment in the same class as the Subaltern's court-martial of loathsome memory. As these things go, it was not a very cruel custom. After dark the miscreant was obliged to parade naked on a football field where the Senior Form were assembled in two lines, all armed with knotted handkerchiefs with which they lashed him as he ran the gauntlet. Having run the gauntlet the miscreant was hurled into a nearby tank of water for which reason " runnings " were more suited to winter than summer.

During his last winter at Woolwich the Senior Form decided to " run " Wingate. In the normal course of events he would himself have been a member of the Senior Form, but he had lost a term's seniority through illness. This might have counted against the decision to " run " him, but did not, an indication of how unpopular he had become. The misdeed for which he was condemned was nothing much, not heinous enough in the ordinary way to deserve this punishment, the worst and most ignominious known to the manners and customs of the Academy. It seems that this is what happened. Whenever he could he went out on horseback, and one afternoon he kept his horse out longer than was allowed, preventing someone else from enjoying a ride. Upon this not grave misdemeanour the vengeance fell. He was really being punished for his unconventionality and the horse was the excuse. The cadets of the Senior Form came to him in his room one night with the summons and he obeyed it.

Most people when " run " literally ran, and the episode usually ended in a bellowing chase and a resounding splash. Wingate was determined to show no panic, and all his contempt. He had one odd advantage in the situation : he was not embarrassed by being naked. Throughout his life he often embarrassed other people by wearing no clothes at unlikely moments, but never himself. So he was able to appear before the two lines of lashers with a disturbing composure. He asked them what they wanted. He was told to run the gauntlet. Saying nothing he walked slowly between the lines, looking, said one witness, " like a young bull, like a young rhinoceros," and fixing each of his enemies in turn with the full glare of his angry piercing eyes. He seemed to be signalling a message, said the same witness, that he could knock down any one of his assailants alone with ease, had any one the courage to take him on alone. The hail of blows did not fall, instead a few feeble flicks. He walked slowly to the end of the two lines, approached the tank, poised himself and dived neatly into the water, no one daring to push. The band of senior cadets dispersed, conscious that he had made fools of them, and that they had not made a fool of him.

The insult was quickly avenged. Wingate's term rallied to him and the next night rushed in a body to the room of the ringleader of the Seniors, broke up his furniture and pictures, and soused his clothes. The ringleader hid, until the riot was over. When the affair had died down people compared his conduct with that of his victim, and

Wingate was looked on with new respect by his friends and opponents. One of the senior cadets was called Derek Tulloch. He had hardly known Wingate before the " running." He admired his bearing on this occasion and wished that he himself had not gone with the crowd. The two men were to be friends for life. From an effort to crush him Wingate had scored a considerable moral victory.

Nevertheless the fact remains that this bullying prank left a deep wound. He told several people in after-life that it remained a hideous humiliating memory of which he could never rid his mind. It deepened his sense of isolation, confirmed his suspicion of men acting together, especially when they were in positions superior to his own, and such was the angry bitterness with which he would refer to this business that people were often left with the impression that he had been treated with abominable physical cruelty. One reason why this insult may have left so much abiding pain is that, at the time, he was involved in one of those deeply sentimental friendships which are common among young men,[1] and on the night of the " running " his friend had run away. Nothing in after-life can wound like the first betrayal. On the other hand it may only be that because this occurred at the most impressionable age of a man, it sunk deeper than it should have done, and too deeply for him to pluck it out, as we are advised to do with stings.

The episode had an astonishing sequel. A few days later, the Commandant of the Academy, Sir Webb Gillman, summoned Wingate before him and read him a severe schoolmasterly lecture. He told him that his work, his turn-out and his sense of discipline fell so far beneath what was expected or even tolerated, that unless he showed an immediate improvement he, the Commandant, would have to order him to leave Woolwich forthwith and obtain a commission in the army by some other means, as best he might. No doubt Sir Webb Gillman had said similar things to other young men, and no doubt he hoped for nothing much more than enough improvement as would allow him to keep the boy on the books. But in the event he caused a revolution.

The same day Wingate took his large collection of yellowbacks to a convenient place in the grounds and burnt them. He took to intensive study of military science, and devoted his leisure to serious reading for which he found a sudden and omnivorous appetite. He took a plunge into the classics of antiquity and the master works of modern philosophy, thought, history, fiction, poetry and economics. He conceived the enormous ambition of making himself as fully

[1] This is not to suggest homosexuality. Wingate, the subject of numerous myths and calumnies, is not even *alleged* to have had any homosexual character.

acquainted as a man can be with the whole thought and culture of his time. From now on his superiors, never without grievances against him (often justified), never needed to complain of any lack of application. He became and remained a prodigy of hard work.

What the Commandant thought of the vast and total change which his words wrought is not recorded. But it is known what Wingate thought. He told Derek Tulloch, shortly afterwards, that the " running " had filled him with a deep raging determination that never again in his life would he allow himself to be ordered about and insulted by a mob. The only way to ensure thoroughly against such a thing happening again, he decided, was to have power. His problem was how to get it. While he was angrily occupied with these thoughts, the Commandant's lecture suddenly opened his eyes to the fact that unless a man was educated, and not only ordinarily educated, but well equipped with mental furniture, he could never acquire and maintain ascendancy over his fellow men. So he decided, quite simply, to change his life. Instead of amusing himself with thrillers and romantic gush, and skimping his work, he would in future make himself thoroughly familiar not only with his professional studies, but with the writings of the master minds, reading whenever he could from early morning till late at night, and thus fortified, he would, by dint of heroic toils, rise to a foremost place in the army, and in the world. After that there would be no more trouble with the mob.[1]

The first fruits of the great reformation appeared in his conversation. It took on that belligerently learned character which is more often an ordeal to be endured at the hands of young Oxford than of young Woolwich. A friend of his later period at " The Shop," Richard Goodbody,[2] remembers long harangues centring round the teaching of Plato, Tolstoy, and Karl Marx, having for object the complete reformation of man and his environment. In his studies he became an argumentative but attentive pupil, and something of the grasp of strategy which was to make him a commander of note began to be faintly discernible. Not principally to the teaching staff. His friend Goodbody remarked it on a trivial but exciting occasion. He had a room next to Wingate and one night, when the two cadets were alone on their staircase, the occupants of an adjoining staircase, for reasons which are forgotten, decided to launch an attack. They laid siege and rushed in. There was instantly much smashing of furniture and other wreckage and they finally succeeded by weight of numbers in achieving their objective which was general havoc in

[1] Major-General D. D. C. Tulloch, C.B., D.S.O., M.C. A communication and an essay referred to later in the book.
[2] Major-General R. Goodbody, C.B., D.S.O.

all the rooms, but not before Wingate had resisted the siege for more than half an hour and had somehow contrived to isolate the back stairs by which he evacuated himself and his companion from the battle zone. His friend was impressed by the vigour and instinctive authority with which he took charge of the situation, the rapidity and skill of his disposition, and long afterwards he maintained that in this early action Wingate proved that he was a soldier of talent.

At the end of the summer term of 1923 he passed creditably out of Woolwich, not brilliantly for he had only taken to intensive work a short time before. He obtained a commission in the Royal Artillery, and on the 28th of August, 1923, he was appointed to serve in the 5th Medium Artillery Brigade at Larkhill near Stonehenge. In a sister-battery he found Derek Tulloch. Their friendship which had had little time to ripen at Woolwich deepened here into a lasting attachment, and again the strange fact may be noted that it had begun with an incident which was to haunt Wingate's mind with rage and indignation to the end. It was a lifelong characteristic of this man, remarked by everyone who knew him, that he rarely if ever bore personal grudges. The fact that Derek Tulloch had " run " him meant nothing to him whatsoever. He only minded that he had been " run."

He remained stationed in Salisbury Plain for three years, and there now opened for him a period of carefree joyousness such as he was not to experience again. The long frustration and dismal indolence of his childhood and youth were over ; his mind had taken on sudden strength and he revelled in its unaccustomed exercise ; he had made himself into a first-class horseman and he was living near some of the best hunting country in England. As soon as he was settled into the camp at Larkhill he gave himself up to horses, books, and music. It may seem odd, at first, that he did not give himself up in equal measure to the " profession of arms," but the time was one of military decadence. " I do not wish to suggest," writes Derek Tulloch in his essay on his friend, " that he neglected his military duties, but in those days these were not of an arduous nature. The system of all fatigues and camp duties being carried out by combatant soldiers, coupled with the shortage of men through continual finding of drafts for service overseas, shattered the military ardour of many young officers. On morning parades, except during the brief summer training season, the numbers of men who were left, after the fatigues and duty men had been marched off, could be counted on one hand. These were usually dismissed for weeding the garden, whitewashing the ropes round the huts, or some such innocent pastime. Senior officers were still suffering from the aftermath of the war, and young subalterns were left very much to their own devices."

Under these conditions serious soldiering was postponed, and as a result the course of Wingate's life can remind one for a space of a chapter in the novels of Surtees.

Though neither he nor his friend Derek Tulloch had any but the slenderest private means and lived on their pay, they decided nevertheless to indulge the most expensive of pastimes and follow hounds. For horses they had their chargers, and in addition they hired two nags which they lodged, with the hunters of many other officers of Salisbury Plain, in the hospitable stables of Pyt House, near Semley on the Dorset border. Neither of them had ever hunted before and the enterprise was one of more social daring than might appear to people who have never taken part in this ancient sport.

Thirty years ago the idea that certain people might and others might not hunt was very much alive among those who did. Civilians had an elaborate and hardly comprehensible set of prejudices to guide them, and their unwritten laws of the chase were reflected with full illogicality in the customs of military men. Officers in certain regiments were expected to hunt, while others in other regiments dumbly understood that such a pursuit was not for them. In the Artillery, officers in the Field Brigades hunted, but medium gunner officers did not, and when Orde Wingate and Derek Tulloch decided to follow hounds nonetheless, (for King's Regulations were silent on the subject), their fellow officers in the Field Brigade were affronted and treated these thrusters to disapproving and lordly airs. " All very childish," wrote Derek Tulloch twenty-five years later, " and we took offence fairly easily, which led to minor bloodshed later on."

They could not afford to dress in the correct splendours of scarlet and mahogany-tops and so on, and had to be content with what Derek Tulloch described as " Mr. Moss's second best," wearing (according to the inappropriate custom) black coats of clerical or undertaker appearance, and owning only one silk hat each. Fortunately they had both inherited good boots. They had little idea of how they were supposed to behave. " We knew enough," says Derek Tulloch in his essay, " to put our spurs on the right way up, and to put a point to our hunting whips. I personally wore my grandfather's white breeches, which, though of excellent material, were of curious cut. We were doubtful of how to make any hunting cries, which sound so different to the way they are written, so we wisely refrained from them until we had listened carefully and practised in private for some time." In the first week of November, not without qualms, they attended the opening meet of the South and West Wilts Hounds at Motcombe. No record of the day's hunting seems to exist ; it was not thought worthy of commemoration in *The Times* or the *Western Gazette*. It may be concluded that the sport was nothing remarkable, but Derek Tulloch recalls the mood of delirious exaltation in which he and his friend rode home.

The two black-coated sportsmen from Larkhill hunted as often as their supply of two horses apiece allowed. For a while they were not much remarked as they rode mildly in the wake of more experienced people, but before Christmas they had found confidence, and long before the season was out they were not only remarked but had acquired some local fame as hard riders to hounds. Wingate, early on in their enterprise, began to specialise in lone pursuit, and the single-handed dash with which he rode over the Dorset and Wiltshire country recalled the heroic age of Mytton. When running hounds turned left or right-handed at a difficult place, and " the field " were anxiously and angrily debating how best to catch up with them, Wingate would ride a little way away from the throng, and then taking his own line, make straight across country over yawning drains, " bullfinches," marshland, stout timber, wired fences, anything. He is remembered in many grotesque acts of valiance, as when once, when he was confronted by an iron bedstead filling the gap in a wall of brambles, he rammed his hunter at it and together they cleared the ditch on the far side, bringing the bedstead clanking over with them.[1] Once when the field was held up at some insurmountable obstacle in the shape of a high thick-growing hedge, Wingate noticed that there was one jumpable place but that the bough of a tree was hanging over and across it. He decided to chance it, and crying out : " It'll break," he spurred his horse over the hedge, striking the bough with his body, smashing it as he did so.[2] Hunting people may be over-addicted to convention, but they admire people who do this sort of thing, and so it followed early on in his hunting career that Wingate, for the first time in his life, found himself a popular man, and even held in esteem by the formerly supercilious officers of the fashionable Field Brigade.

His admirers were not wholly uncritical however. They had things to find fault with. They did not approve his mercilessness to his horses, and the ruthless way he drove them to the limit of endurance, nor did they look with favour on such continually spectacular performance. They said that he rode too much for show. Sometimes when galloping across country on his own he would be seen to deviate from a straight course and make for a gate, but not to open it and thereby save his horse, but to jump it. He had frequent falls.

During their first hunting days, the two friends were hard put to it to get from Larkhill Camp to the meet. Fellow-hunters, and the

[1] Mr. T. Brocklebank.   [2] Goodbody.

converts of the Field Brigade, would sometimes give them a lift, but for the most part they had to rely on their own transport which amounted to one Douglas motor-bicycle. On this the two of them would drive the twenty miles to Pyt House for their horses, and then ride on to the meet. A few weeks after the season had opened, however, the bottom gear broke. As they could not afford to have it mended this meant that the Douglas could no longer climb hills. When they came to steep ones they had to push the heavy machine, heavier at each hill, to the top and then start again. On gradual hills, however, this labour could be reduced by the pillion-rider getting off, the driver then making a rush for it, with luck reaching the top, where he would await the other pounding and panting up behind him in his boots. The two top-hatted figures would then change places and the same performance would be repeated, with reversed rôles, at the next hill. They came to look with special dislike on that long hill, over two miles from base to summit, which ascends from Wylye to The Bake. We sometimes marvel at the fortitude of the sportsmen of old who hacked long miles to the meet in all weathers, hunted a full day, and then hacked back home again in the dark, but these two heroes of our own time had to do more than half their journeys to and from the hunt on foot !

In the summer following their first season Wingate came into a legacy of £2,000 from a great-uncle, and he immediately invested the bulk of this sum in further horseflesh and a car. The horse was called " Tatters," and was bought in the most unorthodox fashion, without even a preliminary inspection. It happened that he heard a fellow officer tell in mess how his uncle in Ireland was trying to sell a horse which the nephew extolled, at a ridiculously low price, and fired by the account Wingate immediately arranged for his groom to go to Ireland and make the purchase. He gave him money for his journey and a hundred pounds in notes saying, " This is the address, Baronston in Westmeath. Go there and bring back a horse." The groom returned in a week with Tatters who was to become famous in the West Country. Unlike most such transactions, (which were untypical of Wingate), this one was eminently successful.

The purchase of the car was less successful. Unlike the horse it was expensive. It was a white flashy racing model of showy design, long past its prime and almost past its function, nor was it saved by expert handling, for Wingate was taught to drive it by Tulloch who had but recently learned himself, and hardly had he mastered the rudiments of the craft than he took to driving as fast as he could. Every account of Wingate from this time onwards tells of his passion for speeding to the hideous alarm of whomever was unfortunate enough to drive with him. He drove as he rode to hounds, the swiftest way, forgetting the hazards of the road in his preoccupation with the objective. The excitements were never greater than with this first car which in early stages lost the use both of its lower gears and the clutch, so that it could never be brought to a stop in traffic. To Wingate the car was a source of constant pleasure, but Tulloch, who was usually the passenger, called it a whited sepulchre.

But another thing needs to be noted about the use to which Wingate put his legacy. He parted with more than a hundred pounds to his fellow officers in loans which in most cases were gifts in disguise. This was not only the reckless generosity of youth but was characteristic of the man. He had the best sort of money sense. Throughout life he never let short means restrict his experience, yet he never ran into serious debt, and he was always as free in giving as he could afford to be. The grim strain did not come into his money dealings, and a letter of this time written on Larkhill notepaper and beginning: " Hullo you—— Just a line to ask you for £3. . . ."[1] tells all we need to know.

When autumn came round again the two friends were both better mounted than they had been in their first season. Wingate had two horses of his own, Tatters and Red-Hot, and Derek Tulloch had " a broken-down thoroughbred called Bachelor." They soon added to their already considerable reputations, and enlarged their experience of hunting country too. In this second season they took to hunting with the Portman in the country round Blandford in Dorset. The Master of these hounds was Colonel William Browne, known as Bill Browne, and he and his wife took a liking to the two young men and often had them to stay for hunting week-ends. The Portman country is difficult to ride over in many places because of the rivers, and this brought to light a curious thing in Wingate's powers of observation. There would often occur moments in a hunt when the hounds would be seen working up and down a river bank, till the leader would swim across, pick up the scent on the far side and then be followed over by the rest of the pack. The Master and the hunt servants and the field would thereon gallop to the nearest bridge (always far off) but when they caught up with the hounds again they would sometimes find Wingate hunting them by himself, having crossed the river on his horse. From his early rambles in the countryside and the battles of Lodolf he had acquired an extraordinary grasp of the signs of nature, and, a little to his own surprise, found that he knew how to locate fordable places by the colour and flow of the

---

[1] Wingate Papers I, the property of Mrs. Lorna Smith: W.P.I., so described to differentiate them from Wingate Papers II (W.P.II), the property of Sir Ronald Wingate, Bt.

water. When asked about it he used to say that he could not describe precisely how he did this, or what the differences in colour and flow were, it being a matter of hardly conscious knowing. Though he had his floundering moments, he rarely made mistakes on the rivers, and farmers in Dorset say that he discovered at least two forgotten fords across the Stour, and others across the Winterbourne and the Devil's Brook, and across the river that runs through Bere Regis. He got a nickname in the Portman country ; the hunting farmers used to call him " the otter."[1]

In later years, when Wingate's name was one of the most famous in England, Colonel and Mrs. Browne were often surprised at the accounts of their friend that used to appear in the Press, and in which he was compared to the fierce, stern, unsmiling commanders of the Cromwellian army. They remembered a gay young man with a passion for outdoor life, an entertaining talker, and one who, after a massive hunting tea, enjoyed nothing better than to play with the children and tell them wild stories.

By the spring of 1925, as the season drew to an end, the two sportsmen from Larkhill decided that the hour had struck for them to advance their sporting claims yet another step. " We found ourselves," relates Derek Tulloch, " full of trepidation (on my part) following a stout starter on a stouter cob to the line-up for the South and West Wilts Members' Race. No one fancied our chances much : Orde was a 15–1 chance and I was a 33–1 outsider." At the first fence someone crossed the 33–1 outsider, putting him temporarily out of the race, but Wingate challenged from the beginning, and, as amazed as anyone present, won the South and West Wilts Cup, the first race in which he had ever ridden, by two lengths. Derek Tulloch came in third. Before the end of the point-to-point season both Wingate and his friend had won other races, and for the next two years were to become well-known in the West Country as " gentlemen riders." Wingate's principal racing successes were not to the credit of Tatters, however, but to that of a horse called Clarence which he bought at a point-to-point meeting after seeing him bolt out of the race. Clarence bolted so fast that he convinced Wingate that here was a horse with that turn of speed necessary to victory. After some ruthless breaking in, Clarence, an iron-mouthed monster unemployable off the racecourse, won the Subaltern's Cup in 1926 and 1927. Wingate's success brought its personal problem. The swift evolution of a Plymouth Brother into a prominent steeplechase rider was not, as may be imagined, wholly in accordance with family ideas, but his mother found it difficult not to share in the

[1] Colonel Browne.

triumph. He used to keep his trophies at Godalming and Mrs. Wingate is remembered saying to a visitor : " I don't approve of racing, but Orde goes in for it now, and—well, there are the cups ! "[1]

The Army of that time was still horse-minded and believed that the sport in which, according to Mr. Jorrocks, there resides " all the glory of war bar its guilt and less 80 per cent of its dangers," served a purpose as subsidiary military training. Wingate's hunting and racing success received an early professional reward, and in the January of 1926 he was selected to attend a course at Weedon in Northamptonshire. This was the supreme military school of equitation in England, and it was to be expected that Wingate would be gratified by his selection, a privilege not ordinarily extended to medium gunners. If he was at all gratified he did not show it. As soon as he found himself in the society of fashionable cavalry men, all his old rebelliousness rose up in him again. He set out to shock, and succeeded. He made things difficult by bringing with him an Alsatian bitch who whelped in his room during his stay. He rebelled against the teaching. Weedon was a fount and model of classical riding and Wingate set himself from the first not only to defy the rules but to madden his instructors by excelling in performance at the same time. Early on in the course, when he was still supposed to be learning the rudiments of horsemanship, he asked if he might " go round the Olympia jumps," for he had seen that in one of the riding schools jumps had been made up to the full size required at a forthcoming Olympia horse-show. On obtaining permission he gave a demonstration of a personal style evolved by himself and Tatters in West Country show-rings. The classical method was (and is) to trot to within ten yards or so of the jump, then to move into a canter out of which the leap is made ; but Wingate preferred something like the style of the Viennese *hochschule*, never taking his horse out of a slow collected trot. To the admiration, and certainly the irritation of his instructors, he achieved a clear round of the Olympia jumps in this unorthodox and ungainly fashion.

January is the pinnacle of the hunting season, and he went out with the other officers of Weedon to follow hounds in the most fashionable sporting country in all Britain, his black contrasting with the scarlet of the others, his bruised top-hat and dishevelment with their well-groomed glitter, his angry manners and language with their conventional reserve, but, as in the South and West Wilts country, his daring soon won many critics round. In the thick-hedged and timber-fenced country of Northamptonshire, he specialised in jumping railway gates. He could easily have made friends in this horse-loving society, but he preferred to persist in opposition and invite un-

[1] Miss Monica Wingate.

popularity. It pleased him to extol the theories of Karl Marx to his cavalry audience, in long and sometimes far from enjoyable monologues usually delivered at meal-times, and when he improved his hunting dress he did so in a manner to provoke further disquiet. He acquired white breeches, but having only one pair, and hunting as often as he could, he feared they would shrink with frequent washing, so on returning from the hunt in the evening he would get his servant to scrub his breeches and pipe-clay them before he took them off. He further tormented the instructors by asking them questions informed by his new erudition and calculated to be incomprehensible to them. He would never give the orthodox answers prescribed by the text-books, and at his final examination when asked to define what is meant by rhythm with the horse, he replied, " This is best defined as simultaneous anticipation, a contradiction in terms but a suggestive one." The authorities found him a trial but acknowledged his merits. In July of 1926 they granted him the certificate of a qualified instructor in equitation. He received it with an ill grace. When asked by the Commandant at the end of the course what he proposed to do next, he said that he intended to study mechanised transport " so as to get rid of the smell of horses."[1]

A last hunting picture from the hand of Derek Tulloch. One week, while the two friends were staying at the Crown Hotel in Blandford, Wingate was at every meet from Monday to Saturday, riding in turn his charger, Tatters, Red-Hot and a hireling. On the Friday it was the hireling's turn, and Wingate went off to the meet alone. Tulloch, unable to hunt that day, remained in Blandford, and early in the afternoon was surprised to see his friend returning on foot, carrying his leathers and stirrups over one arm. Wingate looked depressed. He explained what had happened : in the course of a fast hunt with strong scent and hounds going well, the field was held up by a big barbed-wire fence. While the usual frenzied debate was going forward as to what to do next, Wingate solved the problem for himself in characteristic fashion. He took off his coat and laid it over the top strand, drew his horse back and leaped over the place where the coat was safeguard. No one followed him, a gate or gap elsewhere having emerged as solution from the argument. A less rash person, after leaping the wire, would have dismounted to recover the coat, but Wingate plucked it up again without leaving the saddle, laid his reins on the horse's neck, and proceeded to dress. The horse took fright and galloped off with the rider struggling Mazeppa-wise on its back with both arms entangled in the sleeves, till he slid down the hireling's hindquarters to a crash on the ground, dragging the stirrups

---

[1] Tulloch Essay. Goodbody. Colonel A. Simonds O.B.E.

from their moorings. According to Derek Tulloch the horse was not found for a long time.

In this life of hunting and racing, wild parties and violent guest-nights, of an attempted moonlight steeplechase, of hunt-balls and show-rings, and all the delights, charms and absurdities of a little country society, serious intentions were growing and taking shape as will become clear later. Throughout Wingate never left his books for long. We must imagine him often coming back to Larkhill from a long day in the saddle to spend hours of massive reading, usually in philosophy and political theory, these ardent sessions being some-times diversified with gramophone concerts devoted to the music of the great composers, chiefly Beethoven, Mozart and Wagner. He never forgot his vast aim : to master the learning of the world, to make of himself a modern Kalos Kagathos. The friends of his Larkhill days would often notice that in the midst of the fun his eye was cold, and he seemed taken up with secret thoughts.[1] After the sudden transformation at Woolwich he was not a man who changed greatly. But in these three contented pleasure-seeking years, if there was evidence of a deep current of serious deliberation, there was little sign of that overmastering passion to bend all men and things to his will, the sleepless ambition which was to carry him to a great place in the world. Youth is its own ambition.

[1] Goodbody.

CHAPTER IV

PORTENTS

DURING THESE hunting years, Wingate postponed serious soldiering, as noted. But he did not forget it. He was promoted from ensign to lieutenant in 1925. He was described as "promising, keen, hard-working." In the next year 1926 he took the first part of his examination for promotion to Captain with success. He did this in the form of an essay on "Strategy in Three Campaigns," the three in question being the German invasion of France in 1914, General Allenby's Palestine campaign in 1917, and the Russo-Japanese War of 1904. The purpose of the essay was to combat the then orthodox preference for the strategy and tactics of "envelopment," inherited from the First World War, and to urge the superior value of a strategy of concentrated effort, the argument running that the latter type of manœuvre was apt to preserve swift interior communications. None of the principal ideas in the essay were to remain with its author so there is no need to examine them in detail. More interesting is the boldness with which he expressed himself. For example he ended his introduction as follows: "Although it may be possible to derive special advantages from exterior lines, yet he who deliberately divides his forces in order unnecessarily to assume them, is a pedant with little knowledge of war." Wingate was to use such language again, not in academic essays, but in official reports.

The paper was corrected by Major-General Sir Louis Oldfield who gave him 78 per cent marks. This was a disappointment as it missed the percentage needed for a "special" or distinction by two points. His military career was still progressing at an ordinary pace.

His family life was undergoing familiar transformations as the elder children grew up and dispersed. The eldest daughter Rachel had followed family tradition and was now a field worker in the service of the Swedish Mission in Chinese Turkestan, and had left home to take up a post in Kashgar. "She must often be lonely, poor darling," wrote Mrs. Wingate to her son on one occasion. "Tho' nothing, I am sure would so compensate her for what she has done as seeing converts of the splendid old plucky quality of those at Kashgar." Monica, who was nearly two years younger than the eldest son, was an undergraduate at Newnham College, and in October of 1926 the second son, Nigel, went to Pembroke College, Cambridge. During one long vacation Monica wished to go to a meeting of the University League of Nations Union in Geneva, and her brother Orde gave her £10 towards her expenses. When Nigel went to Cambridge his brother gave him a present of £20. " I hardly know," wrote Colonel Wingate to Orde, " how you can spare this money. I hope it does not mean that you will have to scrape and starve yourself between now and Christmas." It did mean that, more or less.

Shortly before Rachel left for Central Asia, in 1925, Mrs. Wingate had suffered a break-down in health. She recovered but remained somewhat weaker for the rest of her life. This episode contains one of the ironies of her son's story. A quotation from a letter written by her to him at Blackheath in June tells us what is necessary to know.

> " Dr. Eric Lacey came over on Monday and Tuesday, meeting your father here also on Tuesday. He found my heart ' very tired ' and one or two subsidiary troubles but not of the nature of which the ' intense ' gentleman at Godalming spoke. . . . Finally it was decided I should go to Sir Thomas Horder (at the top of the tree alas ! a 4-guinea wallah) and this I have done to-day. I was anxious to hurry on because Ray is D.V. home to-day and her days are fast running out. Sir Thomas's report is very encouraging and we must thank the Lord for His goodness to me. Sir T. finds a tired heart like the rest of them, but says *he* would be worried with heart trouble if he gave his heart the work to do . . . that I'm giving mine. . . . Eventually please God I may expect to get back where I was before—really. The Lord is good. How He does answer our prayers."

The name of Sir Thomas Horder is to occur again in the story.

From the beginning of his life at Larkhill Wingate had thought about equipping himself for service overseas, and, probably influenced by the example of his cousin, Sir Reginald Wingate, he told his father that he wanted to study Arabic at the School of Oriental Studies in London. His father was not averse to the plan but for some reason (perhaps the delights of the hunting field) it was not acted on till more than two years later, in 1926. There is a letter on the subject written by Colonel Wingate to his son as early as January, 1924.

> " I don't quite understand what you write about Arabic in October. That is a long way off. Some would be ready by October to take a first examination. I know I passed the Government Lower

Standard exam, in Oordoo and in Hindi within 12 months of my landing in Calcutta, but perhaps you mean that in October you will be given leave to attend Finsbury Circus for a Course in Arabic. That will be very good and meanwhile you can mug Arabic as hard as you like."

In the autumn of 1926 Wingate made the first move in the direction of his later career. It seems likely that though he still wildly enjoyed his horses and racing, and life with the South and West Wilts and Portman Hounds, he was, at the same time, growing tired of these things, and perhaps saw a danger, despite his books and music, of decaying into a happy vacant state of constant sportsmanship. In his young days he often used to dilate (sometimes at excessive length) on what he described as " the tragedy of unfulfilled gifts." At all events in the autumn of 1926 he persuaded his Commanding Officer to apply for him to attend a War Office course in Arabic conducted by the School of Oriental Studies. The application was successful and he attended the school from October, 1926, till March, 1927. For his first two or three months as a student he lived in a garret in High Holborn with two fellow officers who shared his studies.

They formed a very odd trio : the three friends were as unlike each other as can be imagined. The eldest of them was a flashy young man with an extravagant and indeed quite abnormal interest in matters of sex. Outside his work his chief preoccupation was the seduction of almost every member of the opposite sex with whom he came in contact, exploits which he did not hesitate to describe in detail to his wondering companions, and from which, despite the frequent irruption of fathers, husbands or more honourable rivals, he contrived to emerge unscathed. Strangely enough this member of the trio was the best scholar among them.

Wingate's other companion belonged to a very different category. He was a youth of slow and ponderous mind with no aptitude at all for the complexities and puzzles of Oriental speech. He had found his way to the School of Oriental Studies through lead-following hero-worship of Wingate, and the pied piper used to watch the results with some dismay. Wingate told afterwards how when the three of them used to devote an evening to study, the sight of this unhappy dullard wrestling with his task sometimes literally frightened him, for the young man would groan over his books, Wingate said, as though in actual pain. Nevertheless he did not abandon his self-enforced struggle with Arabic grammar but held valiantly on till he achieved something of a tortoise-victory. None of them had any money beyond their pay. They were forced to live with the utmost frugality (a tribute to the skill of the Don Juan among them) and yet they contrived to have much fun. Sometimes this took rowdy forms and before long they were haled before Lord Ruthven, then General Officer Commanding the London district, on a charge of chasing one of the students of the school (a fellow officer) up the down-escalator of Piccadilly Underground Station. They were rebuked.

Sometime early in 1927 Wingate left the garret for lodgings in Camden Hill. If High Holborn was in the style of Trilby, the next address provided a study in the manner of Jerome K. Jerome. Wingate's landlady on Camden Hill enjoyed some local fame from a widespread belief that Horatio Bottomley had made wrongful advances to her daughter. She used to relate how she and her child had been admitted to that famous man's presence, " sitting behind a table looking larger than life with a smile all over his face," and that on their saying farewell to him the magnoperator made an affectionate gesture towards the daughter, whereat, the landlady would tell :

" I said : ' None of that, Mr. Bottomley, if you please. I think I know what gentlemen in Parliament will do if they get the chance,' and I walked out very dignified with my daughter behind me."

The other lodgers were a commercial traveller of Byronic aspect known as " the dancing master," two Indians whom the landlady extolled as models of decorum, and a technician addicted to drink who used to belabour his wretched hideous little wife whom Wingate took under his protection. From the beginning of his residence the landlady treated the young artillery officer as her special pet. This was for two reasons : she was pleased at having a member of the upper classes for a tenant, (she tolerated his untidy habits and clothes as aristocratic eccentricities), and she had a regard for his family because, as she expressed it herself to Wingate : " I once made dresses for your dear mother."

Here Wingate lived till the end of his time at the School of Oriental Studies, but the final phase of his association with his landlady ill became the happy opening stages. By the time he left he had offended her mortally because when she had suggested that he should take out the daughter whom she had preserved from Horatio Bottomley, he did not respond. She pent up her rage till the moment of his departure, and as he was about to get into his taxi and drive to Waterloo station she addressed him somewhat as follows :

" It is my belief, Mr. Wingate, that you are not what you say you are. If you are an officer where is your uniform ? I have been through all your clothes and you haven't got one. Oh . . . I don't say you weren't an officer *once*, but I should not be surprised if you had had to leave the army and are hiding from the police at this moment. I know your poor mother would break her heart to see you standing there, a disgrace to her. She was a great lady, but you are no gentleman."[1]

During these five months he attended the School of Oriental Studies every day except during the brief Christmas recess. He learned Arabic under Sir Thomas Arnold, the head of the faculty. His teachers were Mr. George Ehret Iles and Shaykh Goma'a Muhamad Mahmud. He was taught phonetics by Professor Lloyd James who, like Henry Sweet (immortalised in Bernard Shaw's *Pygmalion*) was something of a magician in that science. James once briefly examined the young man and deduced from his mode of speech that he came of Anglo-Indian stock, had lived in the South of England and been educated at Charterhouse. Wingate found the school a stimulating place, as did everyone who worked there.

In 1926 this eminent and recent institution was located in an eighteenth-century house (since demolished) in Finsbury Circus, and presided over by Professor Sir Dennison Ross, the first director. " Prof." (so he was known to all students) was the most genial and accessible of potentates, and as the devoted disciple of Wingate's maternal cousin, Edward Browne, and the friend of Sir Reginald Wingate, he must certainly have often summoned the young man to his study. There Wingate would have found Prof. sitting at an enormous heaped-up table surrounded by the most beautiful clerical staff in London, by Indian and English students of all ages, and very possibly by one or two higher-ranking peeresses seeking his advice on the study of Chinese or Tibetan, or what first footsteps they should make in Hindu mysticism, for it was Prof.'s astute policy to make oriental studies fashionable. The room would be filled with smoke and talk until the director would suddenly pluck out his watch and cry in a thunderous voice that he had a lesson (usually he taught Persian though he used to say he could teach any language given a twenty-minute start) whereupon everyone, including the peeresses, to whom he showed no favouritism, would be rapidly bundled out. The atmosphere was that of a club with a varied membership, and the scene was a house which, like many buildings of the eighteenth century, was a remarkable mixture of splendour and squalor. The library on the first floor was one of the best rooms in the Regency

[1] This account of Wingate's private life in London is drawn from a paper compiled in Edinburgh in which recollections of his own account of these years are set down. This is referred to elsewhere as " The Edinburgh Paper."

style to be found in London, but to go from it to one of the lecture halls often involved a journey down dark damp narrow passages in which artificial light was necessary throughout winter and summer. The lecture halls had a workhouse look about them. It was impossible to avoid the catching of colds. Despite all that, the school in those days, under a director who knew how to inspire a passion for study, was one of the happiest places of its kind in England. The work done was prodigious, and Wingate one of the prodigies.

In March of 1927, he took the preliminary examination in Arabic and obtained 85 per cent marks after only four and a half months of tuition. Sir Thomas Arnold was impressed by this performance and encouraged his pupil in the plan which he had begun to devise, namely to go abroad and live for a time somewhere in the world of Islam with the purpose of qualifying himself in Arabic for an interpretership.

It was during what may be called this " Finsbury Circus period " that the young man first met the best-known member of his family, his father's first cousin, Sir Reginald Wingate, known to the younger generation as " Cousin Rex." At this time Sir Reginald was sixty-six years old, had retired from the public service, and when in London (his home was in Scotland at Knockenhair, Dunbar) he lived in a flat in Queen Anne's Mansions. To him his young cousin confided his plan to work for an interpretership. Sir Reginald strongly recommended him to pursue his Arabic studies in Egypt and the Sudan where the name of the family was famous, he himself having been Lord Kitchener's successor as British Governor-General of the Sudan, and then High Commissioner in Egypt.

At first the plan misfired. On the 14th of March, as soon as he had the results of the examination, Wingate tried but failed to get the necessary leave. He called on his cousin and left a note for him.

> " Dear Cousin Rex. Sorry to find you out. I've called to say goodbye. I go to Fort Brockhurst, Gosport, to-morrow. Unfortunately my colonel, Leech, has refused to forward my application for leave on the grounds of my youth which seems silly."

But he put in for leave again in June, and this time he was successful. There was some muddle in the first official response and by a clerical error he was posted to the District Establishment of Aden. Eventually he obtained his six months' leave of absence in order to travel in the Sudan and learn the language. In September he went to Scotland (the only visit of this Scotsman) to stay with Sir Reginald, and there the plan was perfected. It was as follows. The young man was to go to Cairo where he would report to the Sudan Agency and ask for travel facilities to Khartoum. In Khartoum he would apply for permission to join the language classes attended by officials of the administration and while studying try to get himself " seconded " to the Sudan Defence Force. Sir Reginald wrote a letter for Wingate to present to General Huddleston, the Commander.

" He will not," the letter stated, " have completed five years' service until August, 1928, and unless exceptions are made with regard to length of service, I suppose any application he might make to join the Sudan Defence Force, could not be considered until he has completed the specified period."

This broad hint was to be taken.

The visit to Sir Reginald had been a success, and the foundations of the short formidable career which reached its climax fourteen years later in Burma were firmly laid at Knockenhair. It cannot be said, however, that on the personal side this success was wholly unqualified. Sir Reginald wrote in a second letter to General Huddleston :

" I may say that until I saw him in Dunbar when he stayed with us for a few days, I had little or no knowledge of him, and although I think he is a fairly strong character, I do not know that I was altogether impressed with his *savoir faire*, but then I am a bit out of touch with the modern young officer and perhaps he is only one of a type but I do believe he is a good sportsman and a hard worker."[1]

The life of Larkhill and the South and West Wilts and the Portman came to an end. Derek Tulloch had been posted to a Field Battery in India and the two friends did not meet again for several years. The hunters, poor overworked animals, were sold, Clarence having been disposed of some months before. The car appears to have been un-saleable and merely ceased to exist. Soon after his visit to Sir Reginald Wingate, he went to Godalming to say good-bye to his family. Before leaving he asked his sister Sybil to pray for him. She was surprised and said, not too solemnly, that she had supposed that with all his new learning and advanced notions he must have long ceased to believe in the efficacy of prayer. But he answered : " How could any of *us* ever be atheists? "[2] While it was still September he set out.

He had never been abroad in his life before, and he decided that though he had very little money to spare, he would not go the cheap way by sea but overland through Europe. He sent his baggage on to Egypt, and himself went by bicycle through France, Germany, Czechoslovakia, Austria to Yugoslavia, and thence by train to Genoa.

[1] W.P.II.　　　　[2] Miss Sybil Wingate.

Not surprisingly this journey has proved another assembly point for legends, and his arrival in Egypt and his posting to the Sudan are said to have been of the most fantastic and dramatic nature. He is pictured arriving at Ismailia or Port Said, bursting into the Consulate and announcing his name, pedalling to Cairo, seeking out the Sudan Agency there, and insisting as a Wingate on being transported to Khartoum, achieving all by a fiery display of personality. The truth is milder. He set out well supplied with letters of introduction from Sir Reginald to the Sudan Agent in Cairo, to the Governor-General of the Sudan, Sir John Maffey, and to General Huddleston among others. His gravest mishap was falling in with a Jewish pedlar with whom he made friends and who disappeared in Prague, after robbing him of some money. Shortly after reaching Khartoum Wingate wrote a full account of his adventures.

" 1st November 1927   Sudan Club

Dear Cousin Rex,

I have deferred writing to you until I had something definite to tell you. I had a most amusing trip through Europe—altogether I push-biked about 600 miles and trained about three or four hundred.

I found that I could average 70 miles a day on the road barring accidents. Consequently I developed a colossal appetite that has not yet left me.

I was robbed in Czecho-Slovakia, arrested in Vienna, and sold my bike for a fiver in Yugo Slavia. After which I took the train to Venice and thence to Genoa where I caught the Sitvar boat to Alex.

When I left Vienna I found I had just enough money to take me to Genoa if I went direct and biked the greater part of the way. On the other hand I wouldn't get anything for my bike in Italy where they are as common as dirt.

If, however, I adhered to my original plan and crossed the Loubl Pass into Yugo Slavia I should, in the event of finding it impossible to sell my bike at very short notice, be reduced to biking the whole way to Genoa as I wouldn't have enough money for the railway fare and that would mean missing the berth I'd booked for the 6th October.

I decided to chance it for the sake of seeing Yugo Slavia. After all I could always put in a month as a waiter or agricultural labourer or something in the event of being held up by funds.

As it happened I was so fortunate as to meet a good Samaritan in Neumarkt just the other side of the frontier who not only showed me round but bought my bike for a fiver although it could be of little use to him, living, as he did, on the side of a mountain.

I was always taken for one of the proletariat in Central Europe. Consequently I found the common people always ready to help but the officials somewhat brusque and of course in the case of Slavonic countries, terribly dilatory, stupid, ignorant, self-important and inefficient.

However Slavonic countries have their compensations. They're very cheery and always seem to be laughing about something. I saw more good-looking women in Praha than anywhere else in Europe. But the country's poor and under-developed and the people age quickly and soon lose their adolescent beauty. I travelled third in the Sitvar line and was so lucky as to find another gunner whom I knew well set down in the same cabin with me.

There were six of us in the cabin but on the whole we were very comfortable and well fed. In fact I see no advantage to a batchelor (*sic*) in travelling second commensurate with the additional expense involved. We knew several of the people in the second class and when our food seemed inadequate we used to receive surreptitious food through the window from them. We always sat on the 2nd class deck and used their accommodation. In Cairo I stayed ten days with my friend, Jim Woodford. He is living in 1 Sharia Walda just opposite the residency. We had all our meals with Boulanger of the National Bank who lives just overhead. I don't know whether you remember him.

I made the acquaintance of several Egyptian officers and used to go over and watch them at work. In fact had I stayed in Cairo I should have had enormous facilities for learning Arabic but I felt that it was much better to put the primary object of a job in the S.D.F. first and come to Khartoum.

In Cairo I went and looked up Ibrahim Bey Dimitri who lives in Heliopolis, and delivered your letter.

He couldn't have been kinder or have taken more trouble to help me had I been his own son. He appeared to be only too glad to do anything for you. He introduced me to a number of Syrians who had served under you and they all said they would never forget you and sent their salaams to yourself and Cousin Kitty.[1] I ascertained as many names as I could in case they might interest you."

There follow three paragraphs giving the names with some details. The letter continues :

[1] Lady Wingate.

" I got a quarter fare to Khartoum thanks to your letter to the Sudan Agent who incidentally was not there but was replaced by Ryder who gave me dinner and was genuinely helpful. . . .

Sir John Maffey is also away and is not due to come back until the middle of this month so I've still got your letter to him. Huddleston is here and I have already dined with him. He thinks he can give me a vacancy by April 1st next. I have put in an application accordingly. Meanwhile I do not like Khartoum as a residence for the student of Arabic. There are no classes on at present that I could attend and living in the clubs as I do I hear scarcely any Arabic spoken. I employ a Gordon College teacher to come in and talk every other day but that's not nearly enough. . . .

I have talked it over with various people and they all agree that my best plan is to get some D.C. if possible to take me in for a few months.

Consequently I am writing to a fellow I met on the way up called Vicars Miles who is stationed at Rashad in the Nuba Mountains asking whether I can come and stay with him. . . ."

While travelling on the steamer between Wadi Halfa and Khartoum, Mr. Vicars Miles had noticed among the passengers a strange-looking person who in spite of his untidy clothes, his tousled hair and untended chin, was unmistakably English. He also noticed that he seemed to be unwell. He approached him, asked who he was, and whether anything was wrong. Wingate told him who he was and that he was suffering from toothache. Mr. Vicars Miles who, like all tropic-living men, had medicines with him in abundance, applied first aid with success. The two men fell to talking and in the course of the journey they made friends. From the first the older man liked Wingate and decided that this odd stooping gloomy young man was a stimulating companion. While they were still passengers on the boat, he put it to him that a good way of learning Arabic was to settle in some remote district away from the club life of Khartoum, and added that he would be welcome in Rashad. As related in the letter to Sir Reginald, Wingate took up the invitation. He went to Rashad early in the new year, travelling the last part of the way by camel.

Mr. Vicars Miles found that his new friend was a very strange fellow indeed. The young man proved to have extraordinary ideas and extraordinary habits, notably a disconcerting way of lying on the sofa in the drawing-room for hours at a time, sucking at a sugar cane when he was not chain-smoking and tossing the stub-ends of his cigarettes on to the floor. He had novel theories about health and bodily needs in tropical climates, of which interest his sucking of sugar was a lesser manifestation. One day Mr. Vicars Miles found his guest sitting in the fierce midday sun with his head and torso uncovered. He asked him in some irritation what he supposed he was doing, and Wingate replied that he was conducting experiments in endurance and ascertaining the point at which sunstroke might be expected to supervene. In no way mollified by this answer Mr. Vicars Miles ordered him to go indoors. As a result of his self-imposed ordeal Wingate was very badly burned and did not recover for some days. He was, all his life, a man who took no theories on trust, no matter how soundly tested they might be.

After dinner, night after night, the two men would sit talking and drinking whisky together, and Mr. Vicars Miles sometimes found himself driven to extremes of exasperation by the provocative and often insolently conceited nature of his companion's talk of which he would be given voluminous spates between spells of brooding silence. The young man's ideas were devoid of all reverence for the world's establishments, and such ideas could not be congenial to a minute society of officials charged with the maintenance of rule. Sometimes in the course of conversation Mr. Vicars Miles found himself in a state of such anger with the saucy young eccentric as turned to active and strong dislike. And then, as he was to tell many years later, there would come the unexpected moment of reconciliation. When the young man had shown a particularly galling turn of revolt and desecration, all expressed in the aggravating terms of new-rich learning, then unexpectedly, he would break into a boyish smile, as though to confess that he knew he was intolerable, and knew that there was wisdom on the other side ; as though to confess that, more than his uncertain convictions, he found argument for its own sake irresistible fun. Then Mr. Vicars Miles would have no regrets that he had invited this whirlwind into his house, and at the end, and after other meetings at a much later stage, he could say that, greatly as he disagreed with much that Wingate thought and did, he could only think of him as a friend, and a great friend.

It was otherwise with the two young subordinates who composed Mr. Vicars Miles's staff. They found the visitor an insufferable bore, a monstrous addition to the burden they were called on to bear. They frankly hated him and with them there were no reconciliations. Throughout life Wingate was in easier relations with those older or younger than himself. Apart from a few close friends, he was often on awkward terms with people of his own generation and often made mistakes about them.[1]

As mentioned, the letter from Sir Reginald Wingate to General

[1] Mr. Vicars Miles.

Huddleston achieved its purpose. The Kaid (as the commander in the Sudan was called) wrote immediately to the War Office in the young man's favour. A reply came that Wingate might be made available to the Sudan Defence Force in April of 1928 thus allowing him to transfer before the completion of his five years' service in August, and without the inconvenience of having to return to England at the end of his leave.

The Sudan Defence Force was a curious organisation, unique in the annals of British arms, and typical of them. It had been formed by General Huddleston only three years before, in January of 1925, following the expulsion of the Egyptian army from the Sudan, one of the terms of reparation imposed on the Egyptian Government by Lord Allenby after the murder of Sir Lee Stack. The Force was re-cruited from many different clans of the Sudan and neighbouring countries, and from Arabs settled in this part of Africa. The officers were mostly British, with the number of Sudanese officers increasing yearly. The *lingua franca* being Arabic the titles of the force, following a lazy fashion, gave a misleading impression that here was a little Arab Army. There were four principal units : a Motor Transport and Machine-gun Battalion, the Camel Corps, the West Arab Corps, the East Arab Corps. The use of the term " Corps " was the subject of much military merriment while the force existed, for in effect the whole concern was the size of two brigades under strength, numbering about 4,500 in all.[1]

Wingate was posted to the East Arab Corps which had head-quarters at Gedaref, and its principal stations at Kassala, Singa, Roseires and Gallabat. Soon after joining, he found himself in Gedaref in the " island of Meroe " (so called because it is surrounded by the Blue Nile and the perennial Nile tributaries of the eastern banks). The life was that of the typical outstation. Like others Wingate soon found himself forced into new interests. Lonely posts in the first months of service were the secret of Sudan administration. Newcomers were never posted to Khartoum. Most men, when separated by many miles from any Western company except a gramophone, found the treatment effective, and if only as a remedy for the pains of solitude, identified themselves with the life around them. Wingate spent all his six years' service with the East Arab Corps, serving at Gedaref, Kassala and Gallabat. For his first year he remained a subaltern.

In the summer of 1929 he returned to England on leave to sit for the official examination held by the School of Oriental Studies on the 18th of June, and there he obtained the first-class interpretership

---

[1] These figures appear to have remained constant until 1940 according to Sir Harold MacMichael's two books on the Sudan and its administration.

which had been the original object of his setting out. He applied for the language grant attaching to the distinction, and from the 23rd of July he could count himself richer by £120 a year so long as he was serving overseas in the Arab-speaking world. He returned to the Sudan in September and in the following March he obtained his first Company command, the happiest moment, as has often been said by soldiers, in a military career. He was Captain Wingate henceforth, though for long only of a temporary or local kind ; under the irksome conditions of gradual promotion then obtaining in the British Army, he was not to be gazetted Captain for another seven years. By the odd constitution of the Defence Force his Company or " Idara " was in fact nearly the size of half a British battalion. He was given the local rank of Bimbashi which may be translated as Major. He was twenty-six.

Meroe is a country of prairie and open forest, parched except in the brief and violent rain seasons, for the most part hot thorny jungle split by numerous river-beds, dry through most of the year but containing many constant pools where the animals of the wild come to drink. It is a paradise for a young man such as this one who delighted in adventure and exploration. He claimed to have taken his men to places where no European had been before (but this was not very difficult) and he learned by patient watches by the pools the process of that extraordinary *jus gentium* of nature by which the animals at their drink are immune from each other's aggression. His original turn of mind led him to make of his military exercises wild games suited to the primitive character of the men in his charge. He organised platoon competitions for rapid unloading and assembly of guns, giving to the winner a prize of a sheep which would be eaten amid carousal at nightfall. For target practice he was not content with conventional equipment but had an enormous silhouette of an Abyssinian horseman and his slave cut out in sheet metal, and these figures were then mounted on a wooden wheeled frame and drawn rapidly by lorry across the field of fire. His men found more interest in shooting at this object than at a blank square.

He was now for the first time an administrator. In common with many other young inexperienced officers in the Sudan he found himself in a position of substantial authority, and in this situation he formed many ideas which were to remain with him for life.

" In my Idara," he related, shortly after this time, " (there were) three hundred first-class Sudanese fighting men. It was my business to train them in the art of warfare and to administer their domestic affairs. They were nearly all Moslems and they were drawn from the tribes of the central and eastern Sudan with a sprinkling of Beggara

63

Arabs and a few pure-blooded Somalis and negroes. Their women-folk were like themselves. I lived and moved among these people. ... They were delightful and I would have been perfectly happy to concern myself with their affairs indefinitely. I ruled them by means of certain powers. According to the regulations I was allowed to administer maximum punishment of twenty-five lashes with a rhinoceros hide whip, thirty days' solitary confinement or thirty days' cut of pay. These were maximum inflictions and within their scope came every sort and kind of minor disciplinary power. If I cared to make a man's life intolerable, I could drive him to suicide, or, on the other hand, I could become to him a guide, philosopher and friend. All the squabbles of the married quarters were brought to me."

He told as follows of how he dealt with a case of homicide, a matter outside his province. " I ought not, of course," he said, " to have dealt with the murder, but I did. I saved the murderer from hanging. Two private soldiers quarrelled about a woman. On a hot afternoon one of them went to sleep in a hut and his enemy came in to have it out with him. Finding the man asleep face downwards on the ground, he lifted his stick which was shod with steel, and brought it down sharply on the small of the other fellow's back. No doubt all he intended was to wake up his enemy in a sharp unpleasant way. By chance the blow split one of the man's kidneys and he died soon afterwards in frightful agony. Of course, it was manslaughter and not murder. But the fact of the quarrel ... would have meant a long term of imprisonment. ... My thought processes were quite simple. I said to myself : ' Here is an ignorant peasant. His mind is quite uncomplicated. ... Since he is a man he is capable of showing great virtues, as I know, and he is also capable of suffer-ing mental distress. ... To inflict on such a man the hardship of prison for a term of years, to shut him away from his natural surroundings, would be in my opinion a crime greater than this particular manslaughter.' When I arrived at these conclusions, I talked to the prisoner and told him I was not going to send up his case."[1]

His views on punishment and its correct application came from his Sudan experience and changed little. They were very precise. He had a great horror of imprisonment, of its slow and certain destruction of a man, and its lack of connection with the cause and effect of crime. He had no hesitation in ordering the lash on occasion, but he was careful as to whom he condemned to this punishment. His own memory of receiving corporal punishment at home and at school had

[1] The Edinburgh Paper.

A day with the Portman Hunt. Wingate is the second from the left, and Derek Tulloch is on the right

Wingate with Miss Enid Jelley at a tennis party

Wingate aged about 30

made him unconfident of his own ability to resist any form of torture.[1] His bold excursions into philosophical reading had already taught him the enormity of the problems presented by the facts of violence and pain.

While he was posted in Gallabat he made friends with Ethiopians, with traders who used to cross the frontier to attend the market. He began to study their life and tried to understand something about the religion in the region beyond, the strange Christianity which in the Middle Ages was one of many springs contributing to the legend of Prester John. He often found occasion to cross the border and on Sundays he was sometimes taken by his new friends to attend Mass in a little white-domed church on the far side. From many such occasions, there began Wingate's interest in Ethiopia and its people. There was as yet no sign of where that interest was to lead.

At a slightly later date he described in some detail his then feelings about these new companions. His duties were largely concerned with the prevention of elephant-poaching, and the offenders were for the most part men from the interior of Ethiopia, often acting for themselves but more often hirelings of illicit ivory merchants. His instructions were to track these men down, surround them if he could and bring them to justice, or, if that was not possible, to chase them away. Wingate said that when he first had to do with them, he came to feel for these courageous and lawless folk the love of the hunter for his quarry ; admiration mysteriously heightened by exasperation. But graver emotions followed, he said, when he came to meet civilised Ethiopians and understand something of their life. He grew to believe (as many believe) that this mixture of races represents the highest nation of Africa, and that these people, the only Africans to devise a written language such as can stand comparison with Asian and European scripts, had a historical part to play in the world. He said moreover that he was convinced that the reason for this high Ethiopian character and destiny was that alone of the peoples of Africa they had chosen a true religion.

One day, on a patrol led by Wingate against the elephant poachers, his men surrounded a lawbreaker who tried to dash to liberty through the bush, failed, and was shot dead. Immediately, as a matter of routine the men reported this to the patrol-leader and took him to the place where it had happened. Wingate had never seen a dead man before, and he who in life was to witness so much of death, and to inflict it on many people, was appalled by what he saw now. By his own account he was utterly overcome by a crushing sense of terrible

---

[1] He confided to several people, including Dr. Kounine, that he dreaded capture in war as he was not confident of his power not to tell all he knew if tortured.

responsibility. He looked long and hard at the corpse and remembered years afterwards that it was dressed in a ragged native gown over which the living wretch had pulled an old khaki jersey, a piece of abandoned British Army wear. The dead man had no other visible belongings. Wingate said afterwards : " He only possessed one thing of any value or importance, and that was his life, and we took it away."

In the course of his duty he was more often than not the only European in his station, and he obtained a new nickname among his Sudanese junior officers and men, " His Honour the Judge." One of his Sudanese troop-leaders, to whom he was much attached, was a tall majestic Arab, remarkable for a gloomy and haughty air. One day the two of them were talking about the days before British rule, and Wingate got out an old photograph. He showed it to his friend and explained that it had been taken by his cousin Sir Reginald. It was a photograph of the Caliph and his Emirs lying dead on sheepskins in November 1899. The Sudanese examined the photograph looking, said Wingate, " rather green." He handed it back with the words, " I am the Caliph's youngest son."[1] Wingate was deeply confused. But the friendship persisted despite this disastrous coincidence. He rarely wanted for response to his growing powers of leadership. The life of the Sudan suited him and he suited it.

Among his own people whom he would meet at Corps Head-quarters and in Khartoum, Wingate made his way with more difficulty. Sir Terence Airey, then a young officer in the Sudan Defence Force, knew Wingate in these years. He remembers opposing impressions coming from the contradictions in Wingate's character. As a bearer of the most honoured name in the Sudan, the young officer had naturally been well received, but his unaccommodating manners soon chilled some people. As during his months of probation at Rashad, he half purposely, half by the unconscious pressure of great energies still wanting outlet, caused barriers of hostility to form around him. The correctitude of British deportment in places under British rule overseas has been exaggerated and caricatured, but at no time, and in no place in the Empire, were official colleagues likely to regard, without some perplexity and protest, such a being as this inconsiderate young man who held all the conventions in contempt, including sometimes the wearing of clothes, cast doubt and scepticism on every accepted belief, and seemed to take pleasure in wearying and exaspera-ting his fellows by forcing on them every opinion that they were likely to resent. In this conservative-minded society he gave most people who met him the impression that he was a Communist.[2]

[1] The Edinburgh Paper.
[2] Lieutenant-General Sir Terence Airey, K.C.M.G., C.B.

He went to such lengths in annoying his brethren of the service that at one moment he even put his future in some jeopardy. This is what happened. A senior officer summoned him to his office and addressed him in some such words as these :

" You've been talking too much. A young officer of your age is meant to be seen and not heard. I don't like the things you say and I don't like you. I am going to give you a choice. Either you shut up and keep your ideas about Communism and so on to yourself or I shall have you returned to your regiment—with a bad mark against your name." Wingate's first reaction was a feeling that to obey would be a degrading renunciation of his right to free speech. For a moment he was utterly at a loss for words. Then, deciding (as he told much later) that whatever he said would be misunderstood by this fool, he said, "Very well, sir," and went to his quarters. He took the lesson to heart and moderated his behaviour, but when recalling these years at a later time of life he would recall too with how much bitterness and sense of humiliation he met again in this man his old enemy of Charterhouse and Woolwich, the tyranny of the dull mind.

It would be a mistake, however, to consider that here in the Sudan Wingate was at any time an object of general dislike to his compatriots. He was never friends with all men in any circumstances, but he had more friends than enemies during these first African years. The suspicion with which people regarded him dissolved when they found that the eccentricity was not mere pose, or, if there was pose, that the acting expressed what was real. As at Weedon his courage won him friends, less in the hunting field than in polo-games, and on one astonishing occasion when he successfully tried out a theory (correct given adequate nerve) that the way to deal with a charging buffalo was for the hunter to charge *it*—thus giving it less opportunity to turn—and shooting it in the flank as man and beast passed one another at thirty miles an hour or so. The seriousness and determination with which he worked at his language studies were respected by members of a service which prided itself on high standards of Arabic. His continual seeking out of opportunities to share the life of Sudanese and Ethiopians was also well esteemed by people who belonged to a tradition of Government which (whatever British faults may have been in other territories) placed a high value on knowledge, through experience, of the ruled. But in addition the first hostility went because, once people recognised the genuine quality of the young man, they liked him for the very fact that he *was* eccentric. In the life of the Sudan monotony was the constant burden, the constant problem, and the least sensitive could sometimes feel the approach of the

" noon-day devil." In this life an undeniable break in monotony was offered by the great proconsul's unexpected Marxist kinsman. Wingate was an exasperating man but he was a cure for boredom.[1]

None of his colleagues, juniors, or superiors seems to have guessed that during this period of his life he was undergoing a grievous trial of the spirit. It was a thing he confided to only one person at the time, and to not more than six people in his life. The only thing he himself wrote on this subject is expressed in cryptic terms. It is contained in a journal he kept for a few days in April of 1931 and which he addressed to a girl in England, with whom he was in love.

" 12.4.31. I want to tell you my experiences and thoughts this afternoon. At first I found a phrase to comfort and strengthen me, ' Fear God not Death ' and ' Serve God not self,' but after a while I changed the form of it a bit, and I suddenly seemed to see the truth. It seems to me that if we feel with those around us and try to serve our Maker by serving them, to serve them as if we were serving our Maker, that then our personal life cannot weigh very greatly with us. Death is no respecter of persons and we should not live so that the death of another is the death of ourselves. I have I think loved mercy and justice, but I have yielded too much to my own desires and lusts because I wanted to. And to this extent my house is built on the sands of self. . . .

These thoughts have given me great comfort because I feel I can now cast aside this self-love—and that, should it please God to take my life, I shall know that my love for His creation lives on, and that my own self is a small part of me. If it should please Him to spare me—why then I hope that all my life after I may be more careful of God's creatures and less indulgent of self. . . .

14.4.31. These last months, instead of living where God has placed me, I have lived entirely in England. . . . The effect is as though my body in an English drawing-room were to see its stomach wandering among African forests, and about to be torn in pieces by wild beasts. The feeling is, ' What has *this* danger to do with me ? By what rule of common sense or common justice am I exposed to risks so totally unrelated to my whole way of life ?'

I must learn to love God's creation wherever I am, and not to shut myself up in a world of dreams that the world of reality can so pitilessly shatter. Not that the opposite creed of complete

[1] Airey.

avoidance of dreams will hold water. Not to dream is to slip back. The present is in this sense a dream, as is the future and the past—to live rightly is to achieve a proper blending of the three, or rather two, for the present in this sense does not exist. We call dreams for the future (so long as they are not merely dreams *of* the past, as is usually the case) ideals, and the dreams of the past realities. . . . What I mean is that we cannot wholly live either here and now or in an imagined future, but we must have just that touch with the ideal that will enable us to work with a blessing upon reality. . . .

15.4.31. Now right out in the wilds. No human being within an hour's march and civilisation's outposts four days away. We are between the Nile and the Dinder. There is no water either way for a day's March, and the way we are going for a day-and-a-half. . . ."

The entry on the 12th refers to his feelings on hearing of the sudden death of his sister Constance. By the 15th he seems to have recovered his spirits, and we might suppose that after some days of mourning he took up his life again. This is wrong. The journal gives only a small indication of what he went through. The first death to involve the younger generation in a family often comes to them as a stupefying shock, far greater than they could guess from imagination. Wingate experienced something more than this. He found himself confronted with an unreasoning conviction that he himself was now fated to die, and at the same time he became obsessed by a delusion that all creation was a chaos, without hope, without purpose, in which only evil had abiding reality. For the first time, perhaps, in his life he really felt the need of prayer, and for the first time, perhaps, he knew his debt to his family because they had taught him how to pray. He described his sensations as those of a man losing consciousness and sinking into death, and being able to hold on to life by repeating a few words affirming his faith, short simple words, almost literally clutching them.

This horrifying experience might nevertheless have seemed part of the normal routine of life if it had happened only once, as one fearful reaction to a fearful personal grief ; but it was to recur. At a distance of time when he might have expected the pain of his sister's death to become part of the accepted order of things in his mind, he was again suddenly overwhelmed by dreadful forebodings, as though, seeing through delusion into truth, he could recognise that all life and creation was a howling lava-wilderness of unmeaning. He found in the depths of this descent into despair that he was physically affected, that he began to shake in his limbs, and by instinct he found that he needed to seize some steady object, a tree or post or piece of rope, and hold it fast with his hands, repeating words of faith till the horror passed. He needed to use short sentences which he could see in a second. In his journal he recorded some of the words he used : " Fear God not death." On another occasion he said over and over again : " God is good, God is good."

The experience was not restricted to his life in the Sudan ; it was not a consequence of loneliness. It once overcame him amid the most improbable and gregarious circumstances. While he was on leave in London about this time (but at a date not remembered) he went to a cinema with the girl to whom he had addressed the diary, and to whom he was then engaged to be married. The film they saw was of no great merit but it so happened that the hero of the story had been given the name of " Wingate," and this coincidence, which ordinarily would have meant nothing to him, made him restless and worried. The story ended in the hero's violent death. By this time the authentic Wingate could stand no more and muttering, " Let's get out of here," made a hurried departure. Outside in the street his companion noticed that he was looking drawn and pale. They went to her flat, where he looked so ill that she became alarmed. Presently he found relief in vomiting. He could not explain why he was ill and for the rest of the evening sat almost speechless. Once when she asked him what was the matter he murmured something about being sure that he too would " die like that."

She saw him all the next day, and he was still in the same wretched state, until the evening. Then he rapidly returned to his ordinary self again, and he told her something of what had happened. He said that he was liable to these fits of melancholy depression when he seemed to feel the imminence of death, and that they could be started by trivial things such as the coincidence of the name in the film. He told her that he was ashamed of this weakness but was powerless to overcome it. This fit had been mild, he said, as it had only lasted for twenty-four hours. His companion saw that it was painful for him to talk on the subject so she did not press him more. This is the only occasion, it seems, when there was a witness of what he went through when subject to the malady. It is not clear how often he fell into this state of mind, but from what little he recorded it would seem that its ambush never came on him with all its violence before the patrol described in the diary-letter, when he was brooding on his sister's death. In the only definite statement which he made on the matter, nine years after, he said that he had suffered these " attacks of nerves," as he called them, on four or five occasions. He said very little about them because they implanted in his mind a fear, which he was not to lose for nearly ten years, that he might go mad.[1]

In considering these extraordinary experiences, one may be reminded again of Wingate's father.

It has been astutely said that the Colonel was a mystic who never knew his vocation because of lack of opportunity. May not the same have been true of the son ? His wide reading was inevitably conditioned by the fashions of his time and he had probably never heard of " the dark night of the soul."

Wingate came home to England for three months every summer, but in 1932 he took his leave from February to May. The reason was that he was making preparations for an exploration in the Libyan Desert, his first essay in bold individual enterprise. His attachment to the Sudan Defence Force would terminate in April of 1933 and it was clearly his aim to finish his African sojourn with a grand finale which would give him some, perhaps enduring fame.

His first move was to find an object worthy of his exploration and, following his romantic bent, he began to study two of the more fabulous conjectures known to learning : the lost army of Cambyses, and the oasis of Zerzura.

The Cambyses project was the more unlikely to succeed and he appears to have studied it before the other. Herodotus relates that the Persian conqueror of Egypt sent an army to Siwa to destroy the temple, but that on the way a sandstorm overwhelmed this great host which was never again seen by the eyes of men. From this it has been supposed that somewhere an uncannily preserved multitude of dead Achmenian warriors lies in the Libyan Sea of Sand, and ardent souls have indulged the unlikely hope of discovering the site of the disaster and of an enormous haul, a whole museumful of ancient armour, weapons, utensils and such-like. But the story is feebly attested, and even if the army of the King of Kings was indeed suffocated *en masse*, the spoils are likely to have been removed many centuries ago, and not by archæologists. Wingate did not waste too much time on this crank-sport, abandoned Cambyses and turned his attention to Zerzura.

This oasis was, up to that time, of very doubtful existence. From the thirteenth century, Arabic writers had given currency to the story of an oasis far to the west of the Nile, a place of delectable sweetness

[1] A letter from the recipient of Wingate's journal mentions his premonition of death. He felt this premonition so strongly that he had even made arrangements for the journal to be sent to her in the event of death. The foregoing is from accounts given to the author including one from Miss Enid Jelley who witnessed the attack which began in the cinema. These accounts are precisely corroborated by G. W. B. James's deposition dealt with in a later chapter.

loud with the songs of thousands of fluttering birds, and containing a snow-white city full of treasure, the abode of a sleeping king and queen and of black giants who would issue from it on destructive raids. For all the unlikelihood of these and similar tales geographers, including Sir John Gardner Wilkinson, tended to treat them with respect, and the oasis of Zerzura was thought to be the likely prize of a future explorer. The Sea of Sand was among the least known places in the world, and no stories of what was to be found were yet to be dismissed. At this time, a reasonable explanation of the Zerzura story was put forward by Count Ladislaus Almasy, of whom more will be heard. He said that such tales of lost oases, of which there are many, are not invention but misinterpretation of real phenomena, and he cited several places in Libya where greenery has sprung up after abnormal rainfalls, giving a temporary appearance and indeed the amenities of an oasis for several years, after which vegetation withers for lack of moisture and a place of refuge becomes " lost." Then, so he argued, when desiccation has done its work, cameleers still remember stories of an oasis in such and such a place, seek for it in vain, and, after years of frustrated search, fall to telling weird stories of luxurious retreats which magically elude discovery. Almasy's theory was that periodical or "lost" oases have occurred, presumably may again, in the former North-South river-beds running from the recently discovered Gilf Plateau (450 miles due west of Aswan). Zerzura may have been a fabled account of mushroom-like growth here, or the legend may have attached to several places.

Wingate had probably not yet heard of this Almasy theory, but while casting about in his studies of the Libyan desert he made the acquaintance of another and older desert-traveller, a former member of the Sudan service, and this encounter had (much later) a very considerable importance in his life. The name of this man was Colonel Wilfred Jennings-Bramly. He lived at a place called Burg el Arab, about thirty miles west of Alexandria on the Senussi tribal frontier. His family had been associated with Egypt for three generations, from the time when Colonel Jennings-Bramly's grandfather, John Wingfield Larking, had become the confidant of Mehmet Ali. During the First World War the grandson served in Egypt where he discovered a lasting interest in the Senussi tribes. On his retirement from the Egyptian frontier force a few years later, he decided to devote his life to an undertaking whose purpose was to associate the Senussis of Libya with the necessities of civilisation. He used his influence with this nomad population to persuade them to build a small walled city known as Burg el Arab, to serve as a market centre and as the annual scene of an act of homage paid by the tribes to the sovereign of Egypt. At this time

Burg el Arab was still uncompleted. Wingate stayed with him there on two occasions in the latter half of 1932.

In August he wrote to Cousin Rex, evidently not the first letter on the subject, telling him of his preparations :

" The main thing now is to get hold of the necessary instruments as soon as possible so as to be thoroughly familiar with their use before Jan. next.

I have sent a list to the R.G.S. based on Ball's[1] recommendations which I should think carry weight with them. Meanwhile I am trying to borrow some from the Survey Department here. I shall have plenty of opportunity for practice after the rains.

I may take a wireless set. I can't afford one of course but might buy, borrow, or steal one ! But I may decide I am better without. I shall either go alone or with a trained surveyor, in all probability. Camels I hope to buy from the Amara and start from Halfa early next January. I'll send you all details later as I think you may be interested."

Sir Reginald was always interested in the career of his gifted, odd and pertinacious cousin. He was to help greatly in this venture.

By a curious coincidence another exploration party intent on the same prize sought his help at the same time. Towards the end of October a certain Dr. Bermann[2] wrote to Sir Reginald telling him that an expedition was preparing in Egypt with the object of seeking for lost oases in Libya, but had run into financial difficulties. The preliminary research had been promising. Six months before, Squadron-Leader Penderel of the R.A.F., and Count Almasy had taken photographs from the air in the middle of the Gilf Kebir and these, on examination, showed a wadi in which traces of plant and animal life, and ancient rock carvings, could be dimly discerned. This, they concluded, was surely the lost oasis of Zerzura. Penderel and Almasy had interested Prince Kemal ed Din and Sir Robert Clayton[3] in their discovery, and had obtained their agreement to finance an expedition by desert-travelling motor. Then in the summer both the Prince and the Baronet had died and the expedition was therefore left without supporters. No great sum was needed. The cars had been bought and were ready. Was no one interested ? Such was the gist of Bermann's letter.

Sir Reginald immediately thought of his cousin. After sounding

[1] At this time Dr. John Ball was Director of Desert Surveys to the Egyptian Government. He discovered the Gilf Plateau while leading a patrol in 1917.
[2] The whole of the ensuing Bermann-Almasy-Wingate episode is drawn from W.P.II.
[3] Sir Robert Clayton-East-Clayton, Bt., a cousin of the brothers Sir Gilbert and Iltyd Clayton.

various authorities, he wrote to him as follows on the 27th of October.

"My dear Orde,

Although I have not written to you very recently. . . . I have not been idle in the matter of your proposed journey in the Western Desert and things are developing in rather a curious and interesting way.

You will remember my speaking to you of Dr. Bermann who is an Austrian (*entre-nous* political correspondent in Vienna of the *Berliner Tagblatt* and a man of very considerable European influence) —he was a very staunch friend to my dear old friend Slatin up to the end of the latter's days, and he and I have been in constant correspondence.

Only yesterday I received a long letter from him a copy of which I now enclose and which shows that he is joining an Expedition which, to some extent, is a rival of your own and evidently he is going largely with the idea of writing a book. All this may be good from your point of view—for it means that whatever may be the success of the Expedition he contemplates, it will be given very wide publicity and this may be a good thing for you should you decide to join it.

Immediately I got Bermann's letter I sent it to de Lancey Forth post-haste as I wanted to lose no time in getting his reply (especially as he is leaving almost at once for Egypt to stay with Jennings-Bramly) and his views, for I look on him as quite the most reliable, trustworthy and experienced traveller in the Western Desert that I know and what he says is *absolutely reliable and invaluable* and please believe me, you cannot do better than be guided by his advice and I enclose a copy of his reply to me. In a matter of this sort it may be a question of life and death and therefore I would urge you to ponder very carefully over all he writes. I am inclined to think that it might be more advantageous for you and your future, to join this Expedition rather than go off on your own, but I must leave this entirely to your appreciation of the situation, only I would reinforce Forth's very serious warning that travelling in that illimitable desert sea is far more difficult than it looks and a far more strenuous business than my friend Bermann and his friends realise.

I am dictating this hurriedly as the mail goes to-day and there is not a moment to be lost in getting into touch with you and I think your best plan will be to communicate direct, as Forth suggests, with Bermann, whose address is given in the copy of his letter, but unfortunately I have no idea if he has a telegraphic address.

Now I will not say another word except to wish you the best of luck and may you be helped to a wise decision in a very important matter—indeed, I repeat my warning that you cannot be too careful in your ultimate decision and in the steps you take to carry out your project should you still intend to face the perils of the desert sea alone."

This letter was part of a five-cornered correspondence which opened between Sir Reginald and Orde Wingate, Colonel de Lancey Forth, Dr. Bermann and Count Almasy. It continued to December. Copies of all the main items were distributed to the participants by Sir Reginald, and before long the discussion showed a main party cleavage between those who believed in camels and those who believed in cars. Colonel de Lancey Forth led the camel party and declared : " the crossing of the sand area from Kufra *due East by car is impossible* and . . . if they *attempt it, as suggested, and stick to it with determination they will leave their bones in the dunes.*" Almasy led the car party and related how he " set out in 1929 and 1930 by car and drove all over that country. . . . Colonel de Lancey thinks that the Sand Area East of Kufra cannot be crossed by car, but then he has not been engineer in the testing department of a motor factory for the last 12 years and has not driven a car all over Africa including the Sud Region."

In this conflict between the old and venerated, and the new and mechanised styles of exploration, Sir Reginald Wingate, as shown by his letter, started on the conservative side, but found himself quickly converted by Almasy's argument, and thereon he recommended his cousin to join the motor expedition. Almasy was in favour of this and wrote to Doctor Bermann to say so. But Orde Wingate, rebellious man as he was, remained on the conservative side. He wrote to Doctor Bermann to say that the discovery of Zerzura was by no means his main purpose which he described as " a rough topographical survey over a portion of the sand sea." Wingate added that his camel contract was now concluded in Egypt so that "matters having gone so far as this," he did not feel able to change his plans at " this stage." He refused. There is no reason to suppose that the reasons he gave for refusal were in the least untrue, but there is cause to suppose that he did not give his deepest reason which was that he wished to conduct an expedition on his own.

In the middle of November things stood thus, that Wingate was preparing a camel expedition, and Almasy a car expedition, both hoping to obtain valuable geographical results, both hoping to go down in history as the discoverer of the lost oasis. Then things went wrong with both parties.

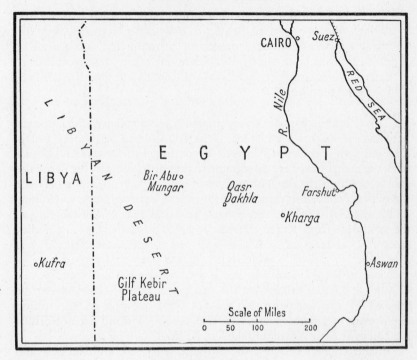

The Libyan Desert

On the same day as Wingate wrote to Dr. Bermann, Sudan Defence Force Headquarters refused to allow his proposed expedition on the grounds that they could not stand surety for the risks, and they refused to accept his personal guarantee. At the same time the Almasy expedition ran on the rocks too : with no new backers forthcoming, certain rapacious Egyptian authorities began to make claims on the fleet of motor cars assembled by Prince Kemal ed Din. Of the two frustrated expeditions that of Wingate found rescue first. As soon as he knew of the prohibition by Force Headquarters he once more appealed for help to Cousin Rex. The latter wrote a tactful letter to the Military Secretary, as a result of which a War Office telegram was sent to Khartoum approving the expedition on the terms Wingate had proposed, namely that he took personal responsibility for anything that might happen. On receipt of the telegram Force Headquarters raised no further objections, and the road ahead lay open.

It was understood that his main purpose was to explore the old Abu Mungar road to the Kufra oasis in Cyrenaica, as far as the Cyrenaican frontier, with reconnaissance north of the road for water. He was supplied with surveying instruments by the Royal Geographical Society and the Sudan survey department, and these included one unusual piece, a bicycle wheel equipped with a revometer for measuring distances. It was to be a source of great exasperation for many reasons and showed an error of $2\frac{1}{2}$ miles in 130.

Before leaving Khartoum (to which he was not to return till 1940) he sent his baggage for safe keeping to his friend of Woolwich and Weedon days, Richard Goodbody, who was stationed in Cairo. With the baggage he also gave him letters to be sent to his family, his girl, and a few friends, in the event of his never emerging again from the Sea of Sand. He told Goodbody that he was to keep the baggage and the letters for eight weeks, after which, if he had not arrived in Cairo, Goodbody was to sell the contents of the baggage and post the letters. The explorer would be dead.

On the 28th of January he left Khartoum for the north by train. A companion of this journey, Mr. Geoffrey Payne, a legal adviser to the Egyptian Government, remembers him as extraordinarily ill-kempt in a badly fitting uniform, and as a stimulating and talkative companion evidently in a state of wild high spirits. On the 1st of February Wingate left the train when it reached Oasis junction near Farshut, about three hundred and fifty miles south of Cairo. He travelled by motor lorry from the station to the Oasis of Kharga and thence to Qasr Dakhla. The latter townlet is a veritable outpost of the human world, on the edge of the Libyan and Sahara Deserts, with nothing but a few shelters between it and Kufra. Wingate described his arrival.

"It is customary in these cases, when approaching human habitation in a car, to depress the button of the electric horn and keep it depressed until the population is assembled to greet you, and to answer any inquiries you may wish to make. It struck me at first as discourteous, but I found that this was merely the prejudice of ignorance and that the kindly peasantry would be hurt by any omission of the popular practice. There is a real enchantment in the appearance of these huddled villages of mud brick. They are all, or nearly all, built on mounds formed, no doubt, of the remains of past villages, and they have a castellated effect that suggests knights in armour. In the dusk standards of size are somehow annihilated, and one receives the impression of a gigantic and labyrinthine castle standing on a hill, surrounded by Brobdignagian date palms and pleasant gardens with running brooks."

Here he met his thirteen camels and his four Arab cameleers, his companions for the next five weeks. The sight disheartened him. One of the Arabs was a child. Another was " lean lanky and feline." They all wanted to go home. Only the leader of the caravan, Es Senussi Abdullah of Kufra, seemed at all trustworthy. The camels were not the kind he wanted, the Maghrabi or Western breed, but Egyptian hill-camels. None of the beasts was trained for the ardours Wingate had undertaken and he was to tell later that " their leisurely and complaining progress was an unfailing source of irritation " to him. With diminished hopes of accomplishing anything, he set forth the next day.

The first objective was Bir Abu Mungar which they reached after a journey of four and a half days. The first stop was at Sheikh Maihub. Wingate recorded the clothes he wore on the expedition, a turban on his head, sandals on his feet, and a long Arab shirt over his shorts and bush shirt. Part of his object was to test his own endurance. He took 80 lbs of food for himself, consisting only of dried dates, " as hard as cardboard," biscuits, oranges, and cod-liver oil. He had water-skins capable of carrying 10 lbs of water. He miscalculated the blankets he needed and only brought three. As a result he was bitterly cold every night. He entrusted the wheel to one of his Arab crew and could only induce him to work it after the promise of a reward. The man seems not to have grasped the principle of this instrument and for the first march it was secured with other baggage on to the back of a camel. Later the man carried it like a rifle at the slope.[1] At length he learned the purpose of the wheel but even then " his methods were not reassuring." Wingate recorded :

" When he was not zigzagging like a snake he would be running off the track to head off a stray camel or to collect firewood. I decided to take the wheel myself and kept it till we returned to Qasr five weeks later. I soon grew accustomed to it, and for weeks after I had sent it back to the Sudan I used to feel as if I were improperly dressed when I went out for a walk without it."

From the first Wingate established a harsh and unfamiliar discipline on the caravan. The normal method of desert travel through the East is to rest during the greater part of the day when the sun is hot, to start towards sunset, travel through most of the night navigating by stars and then to halt an hour or two after sunrise. This is no way to observe country however and he insisted, to the woe of his men, on travelling throughout the day. " I did not unsaddle," he wrote after, " from dawn

---

[1] Neither of these two adventures of the wheel are mentioned in Wingate's article in the *Geographical Journal*. They were told to Major-General Goodbody and Colonel Simonds by Wingate.

to dusk ; a procedure which would scandalise the military experts of the camel corps. But nearly all such rules depend for their validity on the condition of the animal. Once get your beasts thoroughly hardened and you can ride roughshod over most of them (the rules)." He might have added, for the sake of perfect truth, that he preferred his method in some part just because it was unorthodox. He perhaps gave away more of his thought than he knew when he added to the above : " Government beasts are necessarily fat and scarcely ever hard, and must be treated accordingly."

At Bir Abu Mungar he established a dump of food and water, and then travelled westwards towards Kufra along the ancient road made in times when Nature had not laid her full curse on these regions. Wingate ably described what he saw :

> " The desolation of this high and ghostly waste of grey rock has a powerful effect upon the imagination. Suddenly to be translated here one would suppose oneself to be on the moon. Everything looked as if it had been falling to pieces for ever."

Journeying through this fearful place it has been plausibly conjectured that he sought the solace of Holy Writ, and that he amazed and impressed his cameleers by reciting the words of the Authorised Version aloud. This stirring picture is however contradicted by the known facts. The only book he carried with him on this journey was Hume's *History of England*, and he is unlikely to have sought to beguile his companions by readings from that profane and excellent work.

They laboured on into the desert. In the notes he made on the way the extraordinary eye for country which he had developed from childhood, and which had been admired in " the otter," and was to be a great part of his generalship, showed the mature strength of his powers of observation. Here is a note he made on the colour and character of sand.

> " When there are a number of grains on the surface larger than the prevailing size, and particularly when there is a purplish appearance, the odds are that the sand is soft. This purplish appearance is due to the colour of the large grains, but I believe it is only apparent when the size of the smaller grains with which they are mingled is smaller than the average size of grain in the sand sea. This gives them a whitish appearance, why I cannot say, but it is so, and this whitish hue emphasises the purple tint of the large grains, which do not normally show up from any distance. Thus when one sees a purplish patch one may say, firstly, that it will be soft,

and secondly that it consists of a mixture of exceptionally large
and exceptionally small grains."

They found no trace anywhere of the oasis of Zerzura. They
found the carcass of a camel, the skeleton of a bird, an egg, and a
prehistoric flint tool. They were caught in a sandstorm and one of the
cameleers declared that sandstorms invariably arose round the mysterious oasis when travellers approached. That was all the evidence they
collected and it added up to nothing. On the 18th of February, in
mid-exploration, an appalling thing happened. As they were journeying in the heat of the day Wingate discerned a black speck far away.
They changed direction and began to make towards it. As they
neared it, it took an odd shape. Slowly its true significance dawned
upon the approaching caravan. It was a motor car. When they drew up to
it they found it empty. Wingate got into the car, turned on the engine
and found that it started easily. Evidently someone was going to call
for it soon. Surely he must have thought of Almasy at this moment.
But there is no mention of such a thought in his record. In fact the
car belonged to Mr. Patrick Clayton, (not to be confounded with any
of his numerous namesakes), a member of the Desert Surveys Department of the Egyptian Government, who was conducting a separate
exploration of the same area. He had a camp nearby which the caravan
had missed. There are many perils and terrors, and hideous discomfort,
in explorations such as those of Doughty and Burton in whose footsteps Wingate was piously and humbly treading, but the worst calamity
of all is to find at the end of an agonising march of two weeks that
the whole road can be done in a day by car. True, Almasy's paper
must have warned him of such possibilities, but to be warned in such
a case is only to strengthen an inner utterance of " I told you so."
A small consolation for Wingate was that his caravan was by now
making homewards. Wingate was back in Qasr Dakhla in the middle
of March. He had established that Zerzura was not on the old Kufra
road. On his homeward route he had found interesting traces of prehistoric civilisation north of the road.

He arrived at Richard Goodbody's house in Cairo exactly eight
weeks after the date of his letter from Khartoum containing his precise
and sombre instructions to be followed in the event of death. He was
wearing an old suit and had not washed for a long time. He looked
thin and worn. He asked if he could stay and his friend told him that
he would be welcome for as long as he chose. He spent some days in
Cairo, resting and regaining his strength. He delighted his host and
hostess with stories of Arab ways and folk-lore, and sometimes entertained them with songs which he had picked up in the course of his

journey in the desert. They found him happy and assured, as they had not done before.

At this time all the indications were that his life's ambition was to become one of the company of the great English Orientalists. Like them he found the load of antique tradition in Eastern life the subject of never-wearying interest. Like them he disliked the semi-European culture of the great Eastern cities; from his first to his last visit he found himself repelled by Cairo, and he had been disappointed by a visit to Jerusalem.[1] But in the old, primitive, fierce yet graceful life of the country-dwelling and desert-roaming Arabs he found, as everyone must, the enchantment of wild poetry. When he wrote an account of his exploration for the Royal Geographical Society (not published till April, 1934) he concluded with the words:

" Others have achieved material results far greater, have made journeys more perilous and spectacular. But no one, going forth in the spirit of adventure, has found more joy and delight in the fulfilment of his enterprise than I did in the failure of mine."

It is perhaps not digressive to add a postscript to this chapter of African exploration since the reader is likely to wonder what happened to Almasy. In the end he and Penderel found backers among Egyptian and British notables, and his four-motor expedition, manned by himself, Penderel, Dr. Bermann, Dr. Kadar of Budapest University, and three Sudanese servants set out from the Kharga oasis on the 22nd of March. They spent two months exploring the still very imperfectly known Gilf Plateau. They were very successful. They discovered three wadis in which were traces of former vegetation. This was of considerable interest as the most reputable Zerzura story was the one recorded by Sir John Gardner Wilkinson in 1838 describing the fabulous place as composed of three valleys. No geographer will absolutely affirm that the wadis of Gilf Kebir cannot but be the oasis of Zerzura, but if there are discoverers of the truth behind the tantalising legend their names are Almasy and Penderel.[2]

Those who delight in the ironies of history may regret that Wingate and Count Almasy never met in spite of being so forcibly brought to each other's notice. Almasy resembled Wingate in one thing only, the extraordinary will with which he pursued his ambition. In all

[1] A letter about Wingate written by Miss Jelley suggests that he suffered an " attack of nerves " while in Jerusalem.
[2] The interested reader should consult *Le Desert Lybique* by L. E. M. Almasy, Cairo, 1936, and the record of the proceedings of the Royal Geographical Society for 8th January, 1934, reported in the *Geographical Journal*.

other respects he was as dissimilar as can be imagined. He was a smooth-mannered, intrigue-loving, frivolous-minded cosmopolitan Hungarian of the upper class, deeply and sincerely devoted, however, to the cause of experimental exploration, especially as regards the adaptation of motor-transport to desert conditions, a subject to which he contributed much of value. He was not particular as to who helped him or whom he helped, provided he was enabled to do the one thing he wanted : to cross and charter the unknown places of the earth. A little after this time, in the mid-thirties, he seems to have obtained financial assistance for his work from the Government of Hitlerian Germany, in exchange, it must be supposed, for information. But he was genuinely attached to Great Britain, having been partly educated in England, and at the outbreak of war in 1939, being in Cairo, he sought employment as a desert adviser to the army commanded by Sir Archibald Wavell.[1] Something seems to have been known or suspected in G.H.Q. of his Nazi connections, and the offer was turned down. Thereupon he left for Hungary but returned to Egypt two years later as desert adviser to General Rommel. Mysteriously the Germans reported him killed in action in 1942, but he was once more to be seen in Cairo, as a visitor, after the war. His change of allegiance and his association with the repulsive cause of the Nazi Reich did not, in all likelihood, distress him to any great extent. Outside his professional interests the affairs of the world lay lightly on his mind. He was a society man, a playboy who delighted to foster the reputation of a Don Juan. He was as amiable and entertaining and interesting as a man almost devoid of seriousness can be. What an improbable companion for Orde Wingate !

[1] The offer was made through Sir Thomas Russell, better known as Russell Pasha.

CHAPTER V

MARRIAGE, BULFORD, SHEFFIELD

By the time his exploration was finished Wingate was thirty-one years old, and had thus reached the distressful moment in life when a man ceases to be young, has accomplished little, and so has learned to doubt the abilities that he can now recognise in himself. Wingate at thirty was in no way free from the dissatisfactions common to that age.

Though his character was distinct, it was not yet settled. Though he had developed his mind and proved some of his capacity, he remained contradictory, more so than is usual at the time of life he had reached, even more so than most men in their formative years. In the old-fashioned psychological term he was " conflicted." Most persons of such sort show the effects of contradiction in some vagueness of personality, in indeterminacy, often in a quite fatuous variety, and " woolliness " of mind. What was remarkable in Wingate, and made him interesting to those who knew him, was the definiteness of the different ingredients of his being. He struck people with the force of a harsh and intended discord in music.

He was rarely an easy companion, and he was certainly not such at this time of his life. He was restless, and found none of the calm which sometimes comes with the loss of youth. It was one opinion that this was because he could never be a " whole man," and with this he seemed himself to agree. He would liken himself to Puck, saying that he was destined to circle the globe, had no fixed aim and habitation, was a rootless errant sprite, and, when there were arguments about himself, he seemed to concede sometimes that he was incapable of growing up into a fully resolved human being. A wandering soul, a lost child ! He would think of himself thus sometimes.

He had abandoned the outward forms of the Plymouth Brethren, but the religion of his early years had left a permanent impression on him. He felt the Divine presence and will everywhere and could have said with Blake that he saw God's forehead pressed against the pane. As with many people brought up within the large religious area covered by the Evangelicals, his attention was less fixed on Christ than on Jehovah, less moved (in this religion of the heart) by the wisdom of the New Testament than by the ecstasy and splendours of the Old. As a natural result, fear of the Lord rather than the love of God was at the deep centre of his never-unconscious religious feeling and self-communing. He remained throughout his life intensely pre-occupied with a sense of omnipresent evil and found nothing with which to disagree in the doctrine of original sin. Every impulse which he noted in himself or others he felt to be most probably a work of the devil, till proved otherwise. When arguing (and half of his life was arguing) about some line of action contemplated by himself, or suggested to him, or when discussing what was happening in the world, he would stop in the middle of what he was saying, or stop where he was as he walked with his hunched-up figure round the room, to ask suddenly : " Yes ? But does it make for *rightness* ? "

There was much in him (as has often been pointed out by others) of the seventeenth-century English Puritan, but such an idea must not be given more respect than it deserves. The classical Puritan character was a tyrannical one. Wingate, on the contrary, was almost obsessed by hatred of tyranny. He saw the slave-making instinct everywhere ; he declared that his early life had taught him the breadth, danger and iniquity of this common human failing ; he had seen it at home, he said, under his mysterious old father ; at school (where he was ignored), and among the cadets of Woolwich who had degraded him because he was different from others. He was a passionate violent libertarian, and in this he used sometimes to go to fantastic extremes. He would sometimes imagine tyranny where none conceivably existed. At this time he was engaged to be married, and sometimes he would violently accuse his fiancée, Miss Enid Jelley, whom he called Peggy, of tyrannical and cruel conduct towards him, only because she would not argue with him ! Throughout life he was prone to the error, common to masterful people, that it was tyrannical not to do what he wanted. (But he was conscious of the error and often corrected it.)

To return to his essential contradiction : as though to offset the intense seriousness of his mind, the other joyous side of his being, the part of him which Derek Tulloch knew best, the sportsman and merry-maker, the charmer with the irresistible smile inherited from his mother, persisted too. He could be as gay and foolish as any other young soldier on occasion and had a strong idiosyncratic sense of humour. He was not above playing the buffoon. On one occasion he was walking down a London street with a box of chocolates under his arm. Peggy was with him. In the crowd he noticed a somewhat dismal-looking gentleman, and having tapped him on the shoulder, he held the box out to him and said in his darkest and solemnest tone : " Would you like a chocolate, sir ? " The man, it seems, took a chocolate in some alarm and then made off quickly. If Wingate took himself with exaggerated seriousness, he knew how to laugh at the comedy this presented. As with many jesters his pranks were often the expression of a deep inner melancholy. A main cause of his melancholy was thwarted ambition.

Immense visions of future renown are common to many people in youth, to be discarded in the light of common sense at a later date. Wingate never abandoned his boyish resolve made at Woolwich to be one of the great men of his time. When he was grown up he remained in the thrall of that dream. He used to say at about the time of his thirtieth birthday : " I cannot be a nobody ! I cannot be nothing ! " He despised ordinariness, and the common search for security and happiness. At tennis parties and such-like occasions in England (where he would put on aloof airs, refusing to join in a set with, " Thank you, I don't play ball games "),[1] he is remembered muttering to Peggy : " Look at them all sitting smugly on their backsides with their wives. How do you expect me to be satisfied like *that*—with happiness ! It is a mean ideal." He used to say that he wanted a cause to fight for, and when friends suggested the various worthy causes of the day he would impatiently dismiss them. He wanted one that he could believe in, heart and soul. He used to say that he was fated " to lead a country," and would add (but sometimes with a burst of laughter) that " any country would do." He felt, he sometimes said, that there was a " vision of glory beckoning him," and his fear was that a man might miss his fate, and that, though he might seek for it, he could yet suffer the calamity of dying " unfulfilled."

His five years in the Sudan and his venture into the Libyan desert had shown him how great was his gift of leadership. He had long discovered that he had a far more active and capacious mind than the kind of people he knew as fellow-officers, and this sharpened his unrelenting ambition anew. But at the same time he was quick to recognise that his gifts were dangerous ones tending to that tyranny which he abhorred, and (to the end of his life) he was, for all his bold use of it, half afraid of the power which he had found in himself. Knowing that he had the means to achieve something of his ambition, if ever the opportunity came, he also grew suspicious of the ambition which never left him alone ; as he did of the arrogant cynicism with which, he knew, he could unsettle innocent minds. For there was another contradiction here : this pious man was a cynic.

He used often to say that he wanted peace, that he wanted to escape

[1] With the exception of polo in which, according to Sir Terence Airey, he was a bold but moderate performer, Wingate had no taste or aptitude for games. Once in the Sudan he was inveigled into playing in a cricket match during which he bowled five wides in a single over and one no-ball.

from his discordant self. In obedience to this impulse, he loved Peggy because she was so different from himself. He developed a deep affection for her great-uncle, James Murray, because again he found in this gentle, pious, and wise old man none of the weaknesses besetting himself. This friendship marks another contradiction. As noted already he was often at his best with people not of his own generation, but at the same time he remained at thirty often youthfully and unworthily intolerant of the old whom he would see as entrenched tyrants standing between him and his " fulfilment." Once when he had delivered himself of such ideas with unusual force, Peggy said to him : " You know, the trouble with you is that you have a secret inferiority complex " ; to which, to her surprise, he answered : " Yes, I have." After a moment he added, " Look, you know too much about me." And another time he said to her : " When you are in the room, I am at a disadvantage. I can't talk freely. You can see when I am being unreal, and when I am showing off, and when I am acting. You have the truth about me, and I don't like that."

He was convinced he was a dedicated being, though dedicated to what he did not know, and he lived in continual fear that he never would know.[1]

In the middle of March, 1933, he left Alexandria for England. He planned to get married soon after his return.

As already said, he was engaged to Miss Enid Jelley, to " Peggy." He had met her in 1927, in his Finsbury Circus days. They had fallen in love, and later they planned to get married, but throughout their long relationship Wingate often expressed doubts as to the wisdom and " rightness " of the proposed match. He told her many times that he felt he had nothing to offer her but the dull life of a garrison. She often said that she would welcome such a fate, for him, but whatever assurances she gave, he could never lay aside a feeling of uneasiness that in marrying her he would be condemning to a life of tedium someone fitted for lively and interesting society. So, as a result of such doubts and hesitations, the engagement was no confirmed till six years after their first meeting. They spent nearly all their time together whenever he was home on leave.

It may be permissible to tell something of his feeling for Peggy, not to reveal what should remain personal, but for the light that their association throws on Wingate's character. He told Peggy several times that she was to him a kind of mother, that she represented his mother's world, and this was the essence of his love for her. It would

[1] The foregoing is taken from the recollections of friends, chiefly of Miss Enid Jelley who knew Wingate better than anyone else between 1927 and 1933.

be a mistake to conclude from this that he was one of those men who throughout life seek only the maternal relationship from women (a dismal predicament). The case was more complicated. He told Peggy that though he felt for his mother all that a son should, yet, in a manner of speaking, he looked on her as his "enemy" because, unlike him, she was one who believed in the value of patience, of good-humoured argument, and understanding of the difficulties and weaknesses of people of a different kind. She was charming, his mother, and in his love for her, which was very great, there was to be found again his delight in people who were free from the faults of his own nature. But at the same time, he said, he knew that his mother's way of gentle charm, kindliness, and persuasion could never be his way which was more that of old Colonel George Wingate. If he followed his mother's way, and he said he was often tempted to, he knew that he could never realise himself, and would remain " unfulfilled." His mother's world was something he respected, needed and loved, but something he did not want as part of himself.

By 1933 it was agreed that the marriage should not be postponed longer, and a notice of the engagement appeared in the papers shortly before his return home from Egypt. Then the course of Wingate's life was changed when it seemed most predictable. At Alexandria he caught a P. & O. steamer, the *Cathay*, which was sailing from the Far East to Marseilles via Egypt. Among the passengers was a lady called Mrs. Paterson who was taking her daughter, Miss Lorna Paterson, back to England after a visit to Australia. The daughter was sixteen years old.

He and the young girl fell in love immediately, but at the beginning he showed a conscious reserve. This was not, as has been suggested, because his puritan upbringing had made him neurotically uneasy in the presence of women, but for the very natural reason that falling in love at this moment put him in a disturbing quandary. What puritanism had certainly done for him was to give him a strong sense of personal duty and honour. He dreaded giving pain and disillusion to one with whom he had spent so many happy hours.

He and Peggy arranged to meet shortly after his arrival in London, outside the Army and Navy Club in Pall Mall. When the time came, she was shocked by his appearance as he walked down the steps to her. He was haggard and miserable, " looking like death." She immediately guessed what had happened. After they had been walking a little way together she asked him, " What's the matter ? " He said, " Nothing." She said : " I suppose you have fallen in love." He did not answer " Yes " straightaway, but half agreed. He said that he was not sure, and that he was in a state of great perplexity. She insisted that he must have fallen in love, and at length he admitted to her what he probably had difficulty in admitting to himself. He told her that what she supposed was true, and that he had fallen in love. She said that in that case their own engagement ought to be broken off immediately. He was loth to do this, but she insisted that he ought to. They met several times during that spring in London, and at last after much discussion he came some way round to doing what she believed was the right thing. He told her (another strange confession) that he hesitated so much in breaking off the engagement because he felt that in doing so he was breaking with his mother, so before making a decision, he said, he would consult his mother and do whatever she advised. When he put his problem to Mrs. Wingate she said to him : " If there is any doubt in your mind at all, it is your *duty* not to go through with the marriage." Then the engagement was broken off.

Soon after this, in the summer, Peggy was parking her car near St. James's Palace, when she heard someone running up behind and calling her. It was Wingate. He said he had seen her drive past and had followed her. They walked up St. James's Street together but found that they were tongue-tied. When they reached Piccadilly she said : " Well, I go this way." He said : " I go the other way." Without any feeling of rancour on her part, they went their different ways. They never met again.[1]

Before telling of the rest of this episode, it may be as well to note the progress of Wingate's professional career, from 1933, the date of his leaving the Sudan Defence Force, till 1935, the year of his marriage. This was the least eventful and the least interesting part of his military life and the subject need not detain the reader for more than a page.

At the close of the year 1933 it was said that his service in the Sudan had left him somewhat out of date and out of practice in artillery theory and usage, but that he had remedied this rustiness.[2] From this it must be supposed that a great deal of his time was spent in technical studies. He was fortunate in rejoining the Artillery at a moment of change when everyone had much to learn for the first time. The 9th Field Brigade had recently been mechanised. Wingate was not the man to fool himself into the belief that somehow or other, and despite industrial progress, horses would continue to fulfil their ancient military functions with undiminished usefulness and glory, but he found the transition as distasteful as his fellows did. He regretted as much as any of them the vanished days when a gun was drawn by a team of eight Suffolk Punches, and when the blacksmith's forge made a pleasanter regimental centre than a garage. But if he was a

[1] Miss Enid Jelley.   [2] Information obtained at the War Office.

romantic he was not a sentimentalist. He set himself to mastering the new traction vehicles.

He was now stationed at Bulford Camp near Amesbury in Wiltshire, having been posted to the 9th Field Brigade in the same month as he arrived home. He was to remain in Bulford for over two and a half years. He was now back to " Mr." again, the authorities having stripped him of his modest rank of temporary Captain, according to military practice, rather in the manner of Mr. Sowerberry, as portrayed by Dickens, stripping the mourner of the shawl when the funeral was over. He was to remain Lieutenant for nearly two years. In those days ardent service and initiative could rarely of themselves accelerate promotion.

He was Senior Subaltern and Brigade Messing Officer. To the latter duty he brought a zealous spirit of reform which sometimes weighed heavily both on his fellow-officers and the men. He had discovered in the Sudan that mess bills could be reduced to a remarkable degree by the clandestine introduction of watered gin at a certain point of the evening, and he now imposed this unscrupulous but effective method of economy, and others like it, on the mess at Bulford. He went on a cookery course at Aldershot after which he reorganised the kitchen. He noticed that the taste of the men for meat, sausages, mash and chocolate pudding was bad for their health and he forced vegetables and fruit on them in a merciless nursery spirit. " It's no use," he overheard a man murmur one day, " it's no use leaving your prunes, because if old Mr. Wingate says ' eat them up ' you get nothing more till you do." It was one of his ambitions to undertake large-scale reforms of service conditions, but in his short career he never found the opportunity. He recorded some of his views however. His African experience had showed him that it was entirely possible to maintain military discipline while providing married quarters for all ranks. It was his belief that barracks, both at home and overseas, should be communal centres filled with thriving family life. To the obvious criticism that the building expense would be prohibitive, he would reply angrily that it was nothing compared to what had to be borne as a result of the existing system with its " wastage of good human material " by the refusal of trained men to re-enlist, and the squalid prevalence of homosexualism, brothel-visiting and venereal disease.

During his first months at Bulford he was, inevitably, in low spirits. The transition from a free adventurous life in the Sudan with good pay and some privilege of rank to the restricted life of a junior gunner officer with very meagre pay indeed was as depressing as he expected it to be. Bulford was a horrible-looking collection of tin huts and wooden shanties in those days ; it had something of the appearance of a penal settlement. Wingate lived with three others in one of the mean dwellings reserved for unmarried subalterns, a nasty little hutment whose veranda let into four sparsely furnished rooms separated from each other by canvas walls. There was so little privacy that one of the four lodgers complained that he was kept awake by the beating of Wingate's heart since every stroke was echoed on the defective spring of his mattress. A sense of humour was of little avail to him at first. Even his reading, which he pursued, sitting through afternoons and evenings on a hard chair in his un-curtained room, devouring books with all his accustomed passion, even this best-tried of all means of escape from the load of self could not bring him effective solace. His continual longing and regret for the life he had come from made him more lonely than he had ever been in the Sudan, and it is not surprising to learn that he had once more here to fight a dark mood of absolute despair which closed over him. But slowly his natural vitality reasserted itself and he came to terms with his circumstances. People can usually do that when they are in love.

The curiosity and delight in nature which he had kept from his youngest days, a most precious gift, came to his help now. He began to explore the austere beauties of Salisbury Plain, finding wonder in its continual contrast of wide wold and valley, with hidden glades and woods often elusive to search in this hill country. It would seem that he had not noticed that the Plain was a beautiful place in the old days, and did so now. One very curious predilection he brought with him from living in the desert, a sensuous enjoyment of water. Anyone who has lived in drought knows what loveliness can be found in the sight and sound of running streams, and it is often a custom in dry countries for parties of families and friends to sit at a water's edge by the hour in pleased contemplation. Wingate carried this delight with him for the rest of his life, and even into the humid climate and landscape of England. He continued the tropical habit of lying in a bath for a long time, often to the ruination of his books, but stranger still he continued to rejoice in the spectacle of water in this land of cloud and rain. When he looked at water people would notice an expres-sion of peace and joy on his face. He would sometimes stop his car when driving and walk across a field to look close at a pond or river, and on occasion he was even known to find interest in ditches. The car, it may be mentioned here, was a hoodless two-seater lacking in windscreen, horn, self-starter, and spare tyres. He had bought it for £15 and drove it as fast as it could be driven. To the surprise of his friends he had no serious accidents.

His greatest source of joy at Bulford, the main solace, it may be conjectured, in this scene of anticlimax was the revival of a friendship. Derek Tulloch, now married, had come home from India the year before and was stationed at Larkhill. There was a renewal of the jaunts and jollities of their first Army days. The mechanisation of the Artillery had somewhat illogically, but very rightly, left artillery officers their old privilege of maintaining one charger at Government expense. Wingate called his charger Hannibal. The latter was a large well-bred bay horse with a white star on his forehead, imperfectly broken in and with wild manners. A year before, when he was on leave from the Sudan, Wingate had bought a blood mare (cheap because barren) which had been kept for him by friends in Devonshire. Matrine, as the mare was called, was brought up to Bulford in the summer. When the autumn came round he had two horses in condition, and he and Tulloch went hunting with the South and West Wilts as of old, and " the otter " again enjoyed long wonderful weekends in the Portman country with Colonel and Mrs. Browne ; riding out to the meet from the kennels with the hounds ; relishing after five years with the African sun, the silver enchantment of English winter mornings when the breath of the horses is smoky, and when " the hedges look black," infallible sign of good scent. In the spring he rode Matrine in races during the hunt steeplechasing season but she was said to be " unlucky," and though she was often " placed," he won no race on her. This second foxhunting period lasted through the winter of 1933–1934 till the end of the next autumn. It was a time as full of homeric matter as the first : of achieved bullfinches, and swum rivers, of charges across country with the field watching amazed, but it can be doubted if the first rapture could be wholly re-won. There can rarely be a true return to past joys. The deeper preoccupations were elsewhere : in Wingate's profession, in his whetted ambition, in his new-found hope of marriage.

Nearly two years after their first meeting he and Lorna Paterson were married in Chelsea Old Church on the 24th of January of 1935. After a short honeymoon in Devonshire they went to their first home whose address was number 5 Sommes Lines in the married quarters of Bulford Camp. That military centre, as has been indicated, is not, by ordinary notions, the setting for an idyll. But such it became for these two.

Their house had the advantage of being on the edge of the camp with an open view on to the plain. It had been a hospital not long before, and its former purpose brought with it the added advantage of spacious size. It also brought a sinister annexe in the shape of a mortuary still equipped for use. They inherited the house in a state of dust-laden neglect, not made more tolerable by coils and strands of electrical wire left by a mechanically-minded predecessor, but they contrived to make of it a cosy and pleasantly furnished dwelling, canvas walls notwithstanding. Their life together in this place was described many years later as one of " books, Beethoven and irregular meals." They shared unconventionality, and the Bohemianism of the house in Sommes Lines was augmented by the presence of a baboon named " Bathsheba." It was widely supposed in the camp that this animal had been tracked down in Africa and seized by Wingate in some daring jungle venture and tamed by him later with exotic skill : in fact Bathsheba had been bought from Harrods's Pet Department. She proved no exception to the general reputation of baboons. She was early fascinated by strong drink, yet such was her temperament that alcoholism was reckoned among the lesser of her excesses. A goat was added to the household, but of the goat little is remembered probably because its mode of life was colourless by the standards of the baboon's.

The cares of housekeeping were thrust into the second place, or rather given over in entirety to the two batmen who acted as cook and houseman, leaving an open field for passionate discussion, for intoxicating concerts on the gramophone, and explorations in the master literature of the world. There was a fortnight when both the batmen went on leave at the same time, and they returned to find used plates and glasses piled to the ceiling. Household chores had not been allowed to interfere with the major preoccupations of this strange couple, even during this period of self-help, and it was said that they managed by eating off clean plates until they had exhausted their store of wedding presents, after which, had the batmen not returned in time, they were prepared to eat directly out of tins.

Derek and Mary Tulloch in nearby Larkhill used often to dine with Orde and Lorna Wingate in Bulford, and invite them back. In his essay Wingate's friend remembers numerous parties, sometimes with several other people, usually only the four of them, where the talk would begin long before dinner, persist throughout, go on into the night. " He would speak very fast indeed," relates Tulloch, " and sometimes would hold up a dinner party, though at other times he would talk and eat at the same time which could have disastrous results." He remembers that since Lorna " had very strong views of her own and was as well read " there would be spirited verbal duels between husband and wife. But there were contrasting and some-what perplexing departures or lapses from the habit of intellectual debate conducted at white heat. There were occasions, usually after a long and fatiguing day, when Wingate and Derek Tulloch would sit together by the fire with a whisky apiece, and then, like a pair of old squires, talk slowly, ponderously and without animation about different hunting countries, and the best breeds of hounds, and ways to break in a horse, and snaffles and curbs and York-and-Ainsteys and martingales and the most serviceable sorts of leathers and irons. Wingate would explain these transformation scenes by the enigmatic remark : " Derek and I know each other very well."

The horse-and-hound days were nearly at an end. 1935 was the last year in which Wingate rode in a race, and after this year he never again tied a white stock, " that emblem of sport " as he called it, round his neck. But to the last day at Bulford, till the change of scene which was to herald in the periods of his life which brought him fame, he remained intensely, one may say violently devoted to horse-mastery. A friend who saw him in the riding school set down impressions some years later. " It was an experience " runs this record, " to watch Orde breaking in a horse. He varied his methods, almost he changed his personality when he changed his horse. He hardly ever used a curb ; he rode even the wild Hannibal on a snaffle. . . . When he took in hand Airy Lover, a little thoroughbred weed, all nerves and no temperament, he was cold and ruthless. With the mare Matrine he was cheerful, gentle and sometimes he would even take advice from her. He respected her sense and courage. . . . But his favourite was Hannibal who was the best and most beautiful of all his horses, and not quite right in the head. He talked to Hannibal all the time."

The change of scene and experience came at the end of 1935. Adjutants were needed for two Artillery Brigades of the Territorial Army in the North of England, and the two officers selected were Tulloch and Wingate. The stations were York and Sheffield. They drew lots out of a hat and, with a groan of disappointment, Wingate drew the murky city of Sheffield. With the temporary rank of Captain once more, he reported for duty with the 71st Field Brigade of the Territorial Army on the 13th of December. He and Lorna went to Sheffield in low spirits but soon discovered there was much to interest them there. For one thing he found for the first time, a full outlet for his remarkable ability and passion for teaching. It is at Sheffield that he is first heard of lecturing with the aid of a sand-table.

His Headquarters, the Drill Hall in Edmund Road, which had been built of dark brick, in the days of Lord Roberts as response to the first patriotic enthusiasm for the Territorial Army, was not an object of architectural beauty. In the main room, the hall itself, the guns were kept in fixed order and well tended. On the first floor most of the space was taken up by the ballroom where the Christmas parties, the " Penny Readings," the socials, and Brigade dinners for the officers were held. There was a bar up here and next to it an apartment reserved for the more graceful scenes of life. This was an ante-room without windows, and furnished with a black carpet and two repellent black leather arm-chairs, where ladies might be given drinks. The adjutant's office on the ground floor is remembered as looking like the inside of an enormous rusty tin box. All was Northern hideosity built to last thousands of years.

The assignment was a difficult one. Though the steel trade was reviving at this time, Sheffield still showed a shameful scene of poverty, and, among the working classes, of mass-embitterment and hatred of authority, the prime cause of this angry frame of mind, here as elsewhere, being the continuing unemployment. By a freak of misunderstanding, the uneducated poor, main sufferers from the economic ills of the country, looked on the army with virulent loathing. They saw in soldiers a sign and symbol of the Government on whom they blamed their misfortunes, and following vague and muddled reasonings they had come to believe that it was the army that kept unemployment at high and intolerable levels. Soldiers in uniform were often insulted and even attacked in the more wretched streets. Early in his Adjutantship Wingate was involved in a trivial but interesting episode which brought home to him the strange prejudices which it was his professional duty to overcome.

One day he went to a Sheffield club for lunch and parked his car in the wrong place along with some others nearby. The police took notice and the offenders were in due coarse summoned to appear before a magistrate. The latter is remembered as a small man of ill-tempered appearance. There was no defence and a fine of ten shillings was imposed on each offender until it came to Wingate's turn. He alone was not represented by a solicitor and so, when the magistrate came to deal with him, this offender rose in person. He was wearing uniform, and the sight of his uniform set on fire his angry little judge. The man burst into a violent tirade against the military in general. " You damned soldiers," he is remembered crying, " think you can come here and do anything you want—a law to yourselves !—but I am going to show you," and so on. It was an unsavoury exhibition of a common human phenomenon : an educated person currying popular favour by voicing ignorant delusions. The frantic little magistrate inflicted a fine of fifteen shillings on Wingate (ten on the rest), presumably as a public humiliation and chastisement of the armed forces of the Crown. Wingate said nothing to the tirade or the petty injustice. Afterwards Lorna asked him why. He said : " The

man was prejudiced. There is no point in arguing with a prejudice."
He had found the incident instructive.

Patiently he set to work to disabuse working class minds of distrust. In this difficult and unfamiliar field he was suited to his task.
Northerners admire gloom and at the same time are addicted to farce ;
the mixture of brooding, religion, and occasional high spirits in the
Adjutant was to Sheffield taste, and he became on easy terms with its
diverse population. He would go down pits with miners and came to
know their life well. He said he loved their traditions of loyalty and the
way they took pride in their particular mines, rather as sailors do in
their ships. He found his work taking him into new worlds and
showing him that rousing good-heartedness which the mills of industry have not crushed out of Northern character. Slowly he found
himself able to raise the number of recruits to the Territorial Army
and merited the good opinion of the War Office.

As in all " special areas " (as the abodes of poverty used to be
called), necessity's sharp pinch had driven a great many people to
crime. There dwelt in the poorer parts of Sheffield in those days an
intimidating array of gangs armed with razors, broken bottles, and the
other weapons of the underworld. Wingate came to know a good deal
about Sheffield gang life through unwittingly becoming the object of
a gang's solicitude.

This is what happened. One hot summer's day the adjutant took
some of the men for an exercise and route march. There were about
fifty of them. On the march back he halted the men by a public-house
and sent two to ask for beer. The answer came back that the pub-
keeper " hadn't any beer for soldiers " and they " could move on."
Wingate flew into a rage and was about to go to the public-house
himself and make an angry scene when one of the sergeants suggested
that it might be wiser to let him, the sergeant, go first. Wingate
agreed, the sergeant went, and a minute later cases of beer were brought
out to the soldiers. Wingate asked the sergeant how he had done it.
" Oh," said the sergeant, " I told him that if he refused us beer I'd tell
the Tikes. And if I told Tikes, then Tikes wood smush poob." He
went on to explain that among the gangs of Sheffield the fiercest were
the Tikes and the White Boys, and you only needed to hint at Tike or
White Boy interest to get your way. Certain it is that after this public-
house episode there was never any difficulty about beer for soldiers on
exercises near Sheffield.

Wingate was never a very sociable man and in consequence he saw
relatively little of the business society from which most of his officers
came. But he could not avoid dinner parties and such-like altogether,
so he came to know and to enjoy the life led by the heirs of the

Industrial Revolution, a life of massive meals, plentiful drinking, mid-Victorian furniture and pictures, Nottingham lace curtains, and plate-glass windowed villas. He became part of this self-contained Northern English world which remembers him with affection and some special pride, but though he and it were congenial during this brief period, he did not look at it without his usual restless criticism. He used to say that he found the segregation of the sexes, practised here as in most English societies of conservative character, to be a feature of great oddness. He said that he wondered when some of his married officers saw their wives except in bed, meaning those who were at work by eight in the morning, and after attending the Drill Hall were often not back till late at night, and who at evening parties kept to the room reserved for the men both before and after dinner.

Strictly nineteenth century in character and informed by the non-conformist religion of Yorkshire, this society (to the surprise of the Wingates) was unexpectedly free in its conversation. Even at dinner parties in a few houses Wingate would occasionally wonder if he could have heard aright, while at the Penny Readings in the Drill Hall, the gunners and their families would sit on the benches rocking and howling with laughter at two favourite comedians, in clerical dress, whose turns were based on unprintable back-chat of the extremest kind. At the end of a particularly ferocious limerick at one of these entertainments a respectable elderly lady turned to Wingate with the words, " Weren't that champion ? " He found these manners and customs very perplexing and interesting.

Throughout their Yorkshire year he and Lorna lived twelve miles from Sheffield at Baslow, in a hotel called " The Peacock " kept by Mr. Webster who had a cast in his eye. Since the Territorial Army did its drill and training after the business of the day was over, Wingate had to keep pressman's hours. His work in his office usually began at five in the afternoon and was rarely over before one in the morning. On his return to " The Peacock," he would join Mr. Webster and some cronies in a nightly meal of pickled walnuts, cheese and beer. A regular member of this midnight company especially intrigued him, an old shepherd called Wilfred who worked for a miserly employer at a wage of twelve shillings a week. How he could live at all was something of a mystery to Wingate, until one night Wilfred brought two cockerels with wrung necks out of his pockets and handed them round for inspection. When their quality had been remarked on, Wilfred returned them to his pockets saying, " Fox bin among chickens again." Wingate would go up to bed after half an hour or so, leaving Mr. Webster and his friends to their gossip and beer. It was always a matter of surprise to him how little sleep they needed. He himself used to get up late in the morning and sometimes not till lunch-time. His contradictory character appeared in the way he would alternate between periods of extreme and exacting activity, and others, such as this in Baslow, in which he would give himself up to relaxation to an extent which made people who did not know him suppose that he was incurably lazy. He would spend whole days in bed, eating very little, drinking quantities of weak tea, having hot baths at intervals and then going back to read in bed, or to sleep. He believed, and perhaps he proved, that by such means a man can store up energy, and he saw no sense in taking pointless exercise. He held in contempt the British ideal of keeping fit by the playing of games.

" Organised games," he is remembered saying, " bear no relation to life. Whoever saw a wild animal wasting his time playing an organised game ! Left to themselves children play games, and very elaborate ones, but anyone who watches them will see at once that they are an imitation of some aspect or other of life itself. The truth of the matter is that most people's power to amuse themselves is utterly stifled in their childhood by stupid grown-ups and they have to play golf or cricket because they can't think of anything better to do. This is a good enough reason, but it is merely absurd to call it keeping ' fit.' It would be more accurate to call it keeping out of mischief. To keep fit most people would have to eat less and sleep more."

He had plans for hunting, but these came to nothing because the winter of 1935 to 1936 was one of exceptional hardness. His regime of physical inaction did not mean that he had no outdoor life in his leisure. He loved to drive to the moorlands for long walks, and his never-dormant romanticism led him to a little manor and a village of old houses bereft of human life. He wanted to buy the manor, but on inquiry he found that this low-lying habitation was condemned to extinction in one of the projected reservoirs. A frosty day is remembered and Wingate going into Chatsworth Park and watching the figures of ducal guests skating on the lake in a white scene. He is remembered watching them, as though wondering to himself what he might accomplish with their privileges, not guessing that the obstacles might be as many.

In general it might seem that during this time, while he was working among people whom he liked and who liked him, happily married, and with all the satisfaction to the mind of discovering new fields of experience, Wingate must have been passing through an enjoyable period of his life. This was not altogether so. Though he found this year very interesting he could never throw off a feeling of repugnance at the hideosity of the Sheffield landscape, its vast acreage of factory architecture and towering chimneys under an always smoke-cloudy and rainy sky, and what remains of its open countryside disfigured by the black pyramids of the mines, even the grass and trees darkened by soot. He and Lorna had moments when they wanted to escape from these dismal surroundings.

Release came in the late summer of 1936 under curious circumstances. During his Bulford-Sheffield days Wingate suffered two professional disappointments, one of which meant little to him, the other much. In June of 1935 he sat for the yearly examination in Arabic organised by the School of Oriental Studies. He hoped to " requalify." In the event he failed—honourably enough, receiving 100 marks out of a possible 150. He had regarded his chances as doubtful (having done little special study) and the setback did not bother him. In the next year, however, in 1936, while he was at Sheffield, he met a more serious failure which caused him much worry. It was now his set purpose to attend a course at the Staff College of Camberley. Entrance to this Military University proceeds by two stages : first the candidate is required to sit for an entrance examination ; if he passes, or " qualifies," he is then scrutinised by a selection committee for " nomination." Wingate sat for the entrance examination twice, in February and June, and at the second attempt succeeded in qualifying. Then, for some reason which remains obscure, he was instantly beset by doubts and premonitions that he would not be nominated. He had apparently no evidence that he would be rejected, and yet the thought that some well-spoken nonentity with good connections would be chosen in his place became a certainty in his mind, and the contemplation drove him to such a fury of indignant imaginings that he decided that the time had come for him to play again the trump card which had never failed him in moments of doubt. He once more asked Cousin Rex for his intervention. The letter in which he did so is most self-revealing.

" Peacock Hotel, Baslow, Derbyshire.   10th June, 1936
Proprietor : T. W. H. Webster.

Dear Cousin Rex,
    I have qualified for the Staff College. It remains for me to get there.
    If one is to believe what one is told, the nominations are given on a scrutiny of papers only—names not being mentioned. This is difficult to believe but, in any case, makes no odds because it is quite obvious that the arrangement of the facts and the emphasis laid on them will decide who get nominated.

I believe that I deserve a nomination on the following grounds :

(1) I have seen very varied service and held a position as Station Commandant, etc., whose scope and powers are greater than any that have ever been enjoyed by most of the qualifying candidates.

(2) I have, so far as I know, nothing against me and have always had very good reports.

(3) The extent of my reading and general knowledge is many times that of the average. (This cuts no ice, of course, but I say it to you.)

(4) I am a first-class Interpreter in Arabic and have travelled widely in the Near East and thoroughly know the character and conditions of Near Eastern peoples.

(5) I am now an adjutant and the T.A. offers more scope than the Regular Army. It is important too that future commanders should have had some experience of the T.A.

(6) I have at my own expense organised and carried out an exploration that was fully reported in the R.G.S. journal. (This to my mind would tell heavily provided it were put up. What I fear is the suppression of the fact on its way to the Army Council.)

(7) This is hardly a reason for consideration by the authorities but it affects me :—
In these days you either graduate at the S.C. or you never reach high rank. It would be false modesty in me to say that I have a poor opinion of my abilities. I have a very high opinion of them. Given the opportunity that is necessary to the use of my ability I see no reason why I should not reach the highest rank in the British Army. But if I fail now, in this my last chance, to get to Camberley, I shall not waste any more time in the Army. I shall regard it as a sign of failure.

Seeing that I have exceptional experience in the Near East and in infantry as well as artillery (having commanded an inf. Idara for years) ; that I have experience as adjt. ; that I have not only organised and carried out an enterprise of military value, but in such a manner as to justify my account of it being printed by the R.G.S. Journal ; seeing all this I believe I shall have a nomination.

The problem is how to have these facts presented to the Army Council in the right way.

So many people who, from a squalid ambition, determined to play for a nomination, have obtained footling little staff jobs and picked up a good word here and there from great names. These things count more than solid gifts and requirements.

Well, Sir, I show some audacity in again asking for the help you have so adequately and generously given me in my past enterprises. But if you would like to see me treading in your footsteps (somewhat tardily!) and the name of Wingate with fresh prospects of greatness in the service of the country; then I hope you may find some way to assist me towards this nomination—the turning-point in my life.

Lorna sends her love. I do hope you are both well. I am acting secretary of the Zerzura dinner club now and shall probably be in town in July. Shall you still be there?

Your affectionate cousin,

Orde Wingate "

And once more Sir Reginald intervened. On the 11th of June, the same day that he received the last-quoted letter, he wrote an energetic letter of recommendation to the Military Secretary. It is conceivable that this intervention, before the nominations were made, was a mistake, since the gesture could not be met by agreement without arousing a suspicion of undue family influence. At all events, the attempt wholly misfired, and Captain Wingate was not nominated. The blow was devastating. He was moved to write to his cousin a letter which can make the reader think of the History of Pendennis.

" Officers' Club, Catterick Camp, Yorks.   24th July, 1936

Dear Cousin Rex,

I see in to-day's *Times* that I have not got a nomination. There is nothing to be said but I think I will write in a complaint to the Army Council that their method of selection made it impossible to produce the relevant details of the Zerzura trip, or even a letter from Sir John Maffey while G.G., congratulating me on my patrol against poachers and bandits on the Abyssinian border.

I would word my letter diplomatically, and, seeing that I am now in a position where I have no prospects of winning much, it follows that I can't lose very much.

I hardly expect any good to come of it, but there's nothing like trying.

Again I thank you for all your kindness.

Your affectionate cousin,

Orde Wingate

P.S. The new C.I.G.S., Sir Cyril Deverell, visits us on 3rd

August but I could hardly approach him on the subject unless he asks me."

The heading and final words of this letter are worth further scrutiny. First the heading. The list of nominations appeared in *The Times* while Wingate was attending a Territorial Army Training Camp. The professional soldiers there would naturally read the list, and some of them would know that Wingate had been a candidate. The news had broken in a place and at a time when the humiliation of his failure was most public.

The postscript is very interesting. It is unlikely that when he wrote it Wingate had formed any particular plan of action, but by the time Sir Cyril Deverell arrived to watch the manœuvres, he had. On the 3rd of August, the Chief of the Imperial General Staff was standing on a hill commanding a wide prospect, attended by his retinue, when the angry jaw-jutting figure of Captain Wingate thrust itself into the midst of the Vernet-like group of senior officers. He went straight up to the central figure, saluted, and stood before him holding an old copy of a magazine in his hand.

" Well," said General Deverell, " what is it ? "

Wingate told him who he was and then went on :

" I believe, sir, that you are chairman of the Selection Committee for nominations to the Staff College. Is that correct ? "

" Yes," said the General, " and what of it ? "

" Although I qualified for the Staff College I was not given a nomination. Now," he went on—while the entourage reeled, " I want to ask you if you were aware of the fact that I conducted an expedition on my own into the Libyan Desert and obtained some results of value. You did not know that ? "

" No," said the General, " I must confess that I did not."

" Well," Wingate persisted, " I consider that selection committees should be informed of such things. Don't you agree ? "

The General said " Um," but before he could say more Wingate held out the magazine which was a copy of the Journal of the Royal Geographical Society for April, 1934. " It may interest you," he said, " to read the record I made of the expedition."[1]

There are stories that the interview concluded with Wingate silencing the C.I.G.S.'s expostulations with saucy witticisms, but such is wholly unlikely. The point of the episode is that the sudden irruption of the shaggy Artillery Captain into the inner circle of the supreme

[1] This account of the conversation is taken from Derek Tulloch's essay. He was present at the Camp. The same incident is recorded in similar words in The Edinburgh Paper.

British military commander impressed the latter favourably. General Deverell ordered the case to be examined. The result, as Wingate was told later, was a promise that he would be considered for the next Staff appointment suited to his rank, though he was warned that this was not likely to be to the Staff College where there was no foreseeable vacancy. The promise was kept. In September he received orders to report for duty as a Staff Officer overseas. Among his first actions on receiving the news was to write to his never-failing benefactor.

" Peacock Hotel, Baslow.   7.9.36
' Proprietor : T. W. H. Webster.

Dear Cousin Rex,
You will be interested to hear that I have just received orders to report to 5th Div. H.Q. at Catterick to proceed to Palestine as Intelligence Officer 5th Div. I got on to Catterick at once and they are sending my orders here to-morrow I hope.
I am very pleased indeed and shall try to make the most of my chances. I hope the order will be to sail at once, the sooner I can get out there the better.
I'm glad I haven't let my Arabic drop altogether and shall buy as many papers as I can in London to refresh my memory on the way out.
Do you think this is going to be a serious business or not ?
I will let you know how things progress with us.
Lorna is dying to go but I tell her she'll get no further than Cairo.[1]
Your affectionate cousin,
Orde Wingate "

He was relieved that the setback to his career had been overtaken, and doubtless he felt some pride that the result had been brought about by his own exertions, but he was not wholly satisfied. He told Lorna that he remained disappointed that he had not been nominated to the Staff College, small as his chances for this were. He got orders to be prepared to sail immediately.
A little before he started, on the 20th of August, while he was still at Baslow, he received a telegram from one of his sisters urging him to come to Godalming that day as his father was on the point of death. He arrived in the early hours of the next morning and was just in time to be recognised and to exchange last words. Colonel Wingate was in his eighty-fourth year and had been bent and infirm

---

[1] Lorna Wingate proposed to accompany her husband. He preferred her to wait in England till he had found accommodation in Palestine.

for some time. His end was expected, but expected death is also grievous. The end came on the 21st. When it was all over his eldest son acted in characteristic fashion, finding an anodyne to his violent grief through instant action. As soon as he had recovered sufficiently to do so, he telephoned to *The Times* to ask them to publish an obituary which he would dictate to them there and then. The people in *The Times* office said that they could not accept a dictated article but would publish as soon as they had a manuscript. Immediately he wrote an obituary and drove with it to London.[1]

In September he left for Haifa with 5th Division. He had no premonition of great things ahead.

[1] Miss Monica Wingate.

CHAPTER VI

DISCOVERIES IN PALESTINE

THROUGHOUT HIS life Orde Wingate had an extraordinarily acute and an extraordinarily imperfect political sense. A letter he wrote to Sir Reginald Wingate in January, 1936, on the Italian invasion of Abyssinia, is a model of reasonable opinion, yet the same man, during five years of service in the Islamic world, had never noticed the burning political issue of Zionism in Palestine, even though, as recorded, he had visited Jerusalem. He was to tell later of his first acquaintance with the cause which was to concern him so deeply. The introduction was made in the improbable surroundings of the hunting field. During a season with the Portman he became friends with a Jewish sportsman who told him how the Zionist movement first grew under the stress of persecution in the ghettoes of the Russian Empire, and was refounded by Theodore Herzl at the turn of the century and suddenly came to prominence in the world when, in 1917, Arthur Balfour authorised a declaration in the name of the British Government favourable to the establishment of a " National Home " in Palestine. He told him something of what this most singular of all irredentist movements meant to Jews living in the East and West, the scattered children of Israel. Wingate was interested, as he could hardly not be, but he admitted, when recalling these initiations, that at the time they meant little to him. He could certainly not have foretold then that one day he would be a Zionist himself.

He went to his new post as an Arabist qualified to deal with Arabic-speaking people. As such the authorities chose him, as such he accepted his appointment to Palestine.

Since Wingate was to leave a permanent mark on this corner of the world, it is as well for the reader of his life to have some handy notion of the situation there in the autumn of 1936. Very roughly it was as follows :

Since 1919 the country had been administered by the British Colonial Office acting as the trustee of the League of Nations. The charge was a difficult one. From the first the Balfour Declaration had been received by the Arabic-speaking world, by the Moslem majority in Palestine, and by the Christian, and even to some extent by the indigenous Jewish minorities, with anger and alarm. The traditional holders of the land in Palestine and their neighbours in Syria were aghast at a revolution in the structure of their society made without any consultation of themselves. Under the Government of the First High Commissioner, Sir Herbert Samuel, however, this natural resentment of the Arabs (as the Arabic-speaking Syrian inhabitants of Palestine are best called) began to die down. Palestine enjoyed a six years' peace due in part to government being in the hands of a first-class administrator who knew politics, due also to the moderation of the Jewish leader, Chaim Weizmann, to the latter's much-publicised agreement with King Feisal (an arrangement entered into for dubious reasons by Feisal in 1919 but reassuring to many Arab minds) and due above all to the fact that the immigration of Jews into Palestine proved to be not on the overwhelming scale first feared. But the peace was one of slumbering fires ready to break out into murderous conflagrations. This happened in 1928 and 1929. But in those years there was little general alarm at Zionism in the Moslem world at large. The tension remained local. In the early thirties, however, it was communicated again to the neighbouring countries. The reason for this was a radical change in Western destiny.

The Balfour Declaration had been given, and received, under a pardonable but enormous misapprehension. No one had supposed in 1917 that the *majority* of Jews from any European country would wish to undertake the arduous pioneering life of the Zionist settlements, because no one had envisaged then the possibility of Europe falling far away from the high standards of civilisation reached in the course of the eighteenth and nineteenth centuries. But such a turn in the affairs of men was manifestly possible during the rise of National Socialism, and it became an accomplished fact in January of 1933, when a long and heartrending Jewish exodus began from Germany and Central Europe to the National Home. The numbers of the immigrants began to leap from hundreds to thousands and to tens of thousands. The newcomers brought a novel and baffling social problem with them. The Jews wanted one thing above all : land on which to settle, and the more they obtained this, the more did they arouse the exasperation of Arab nationalists, though they did the former owners no legal wrong.

It was a common accusation against the Jews at that time that they inveigled Arabs into selling valuable land at low prices, and stories were told of Jewish profiteers carousing on productive estates bought by trickery or pressure from simple peasants ignorant of the land's real worth. Such stories could never stand up to investigation. The truth was very different. For one thing all land sales were subject to the scrutiny of the Jewish Agency and the latter body, sensitive to world opinion, dreaded the propaganda repercussions of any story likely to give colour to the idea that Jews were prone to swindling or to the unfair exercise of influence. This official Jewish sensitiveness put purchasers at an obvious disadvantage, but this disadvantage, considerable as it was, counted as nothing compared to that which came from the greater eagerness of the Jews to buy than of the Arabs to sell. On the Arab side land sales were for the most part business deals like any other ; on the Jewish side they were part of an attempt to build a nation and a homeland, an attempt informed by all the fervour of ardent, starved and sometimes fanatical patriotism. Since the Arabs knew their advantage they could usually sell the land at well above the market price. Exasperation did not come from rigged markets or financial twisting, but from the bad social structure of a former Turkish province.

A large proportion of the sales were between Arab small-holders and individual Jewish immigrants, and these simple transactions were not the real cause and certainly not a direct cause of rancour. The land problem of Palestine came primarily from something different : the sales, often of very large tracts of country, by absentee landlords to Zionist individuals and syndicates. A usual condition of such sales was that the tenants should be evicted, for of what interest to Zionists was the possession of Arab-tenanted land ? Then wretched people who had earned a living, sometimes for many generations, on the land in question, found themselves forced out of their homes and deprived without compensation of their only means of earning bread. Politicians took up their grievance, and their miserable plight was used to inflame an always easily roused anger against the Jews, but was rarely used to discredit conscienceless proprietors, members of the class from which the politicians were drawn. Evicted tenants, the real sufferers by Jewish immigration, were the essence of the Palestine problem.

They were a manageable problem before 1933, but thereafter, when their numbers began to grow great, catastrophe was a matter of time. Its beginnings were discernible in 1935. At the end of that year large numbers of arms were discovered to have been smuggled into the country, and an affray in the North of Palestine showed the authorities a new element of violence in the situation : armed bands of Arab nationalists prepared to make concerted and disciplined attacks on Jewish settlements. The extremists were rapidly gaining Arab leadership. The explosion was imminent. It shook Palestine (as expected) in 1936.

An attempt conducted by the High Commissioner, Sir Arthur

Wauchope, to arrive at a settlement by the formation of a Legislative Assembly had failed through Jewish objection.[1] This gave Moslem nationalism its cue. Preparations were made for a six months' strike which was declared in April. In the same month, on the 15th, an Arab campaign of violence began with the murder of two Jews. Anti-Moslem demonstrations at the funeral of these men in Tel Aviv were represented by Arab propaganda as Jewish aggression and an epidemic of Arab crime followed, its main feature being the assassination of defenceless people ; in one place a cinema crowd was fired on, in another nurses in a Jewish clinic were shot with their patients, and there were murders of Jewish children. In many places bands of Arab peasants used to set out by night to destroy the crops and orange-groves of the Jewish settlers. This was the beginning of that state of intermittent war which was to plague Palestine from that year to the present time. For what was happening was much more than a spasmodic popular rising. It was (on a still very small scale) a nationalist military campaign conducted in these opening phases with considerable and unscrupulous skill by a certain Fawzi Kawakji of Syria. He was fully alive to modern notions of ruthlessness and approved them. To his murders of Jews he added equally atrocious murders of his own people, the most notorious being that of the Mayor of Hebron, who was shot in his garden soon after he had declared his disapproval of a policy of bloodshed. It was known that Fawzi Kawakji enjoyed the support of Arab Governments outside Palestine and Syria. He was in secret league with the Mufti. The British authorities seemed powerless to master his campaign of ambush and though with the arrival of the 5th and 8th Divisions the garrison was raised to a total of 30,000 men,[2] it proved incapable of assuring the security of the roads and railways. This was in spite of the imposition of virtual martial law and repressive measures such as internment, the destruction of houses where rebels had sheltered, and collective fines.

Under a show of force the policy of the British Government was that of a divided mind. There was full realisation among English politicians at home, and among their representatives in Palestine, of the injustice done to Arab nationalist feeling by the Balfour Declaration, and much apprehension of what full support of Jewish irredentism might mean to the British position in Asia with its multitudinous Moslem connections. Amid threats and scenes of turmoil the govern-

[1] The Assembly was to have had an advisory function. It was to contain Arab and Jewish elected members at a ratio of two to one in Arab favour. The Arabs were prepared to negotiate on this proposal but Dr. Weizmann rejected it on the grounds that it condemned the Jewish interest to a state of permanent minority.

[2] *Annual Register.*

ment pursued a policy such as was to be described later as one of
" appeasement." For a time this policy seemed to bring some political
reward. In July of 1936 senior Arab civil servants of Palestine, supported by the Emir of Transjordan and the Iraq Foreign Minister,
presented a moderate statement of the Arab case to the High Commissioner. In the autumn the British Government chose the occasion
to repeat their offer of a full inquiry into Arab grievances. The six-
months' strike was thereon called off on the advice of Arab sovereigns.
A Royal Commission headed by Lord Peel was appointed to visit the
country before the end of a year. But hopes of a lasting reconciliation
were somewhat dashed when Fawzi Kawakji was given a triumphant
reception in Baghdad and formally received by the King of Iraq.

During this year of conflict, in which over three hundred people
lost their lives,[1] the Jews of Palestine behaved with extraordinary
restraint. This was due to the policy of their political chiefs and the
magnanimous leadership of Chaim Weizmann. He knew that to achieve
a permanent Zionist establishment he needed world sympathy and the
approval of the League of Nations. The latter institution, though it
had received its mortal wound, was still an imposing, respected, and
even powerful body, still enjoying a prestige not acquired by its
successor. This was still an age of pacifism, nowhere more so than in
America, and Dr. Weizmann knew the immense, and as it turned out
the decisive importance to Zionism of American goodwill. But
Dr. Weizmann's leadership involved the Jews in a policy of considerable complexity. In the course of the nineteen thirties they
organised a clandestine and illegal force known as " Hagana " : they
believed themselves impelled to do this because the Administration,
fearful of what would follow if Jews and Arabs came into armed
conflict, insisted that only the British Army should counter-attack the
Arab rebellion, and denied the Jews the right to defend their own
settlements. But Hagana, secretly drilled and secretly armed (very
feebly), never went over to the attack, not even in the smallest way.
The policy of self-restraint persisted, and in these vexed years no
ambush or murder of an Arab could be laid to the charge of a Jew,
in spite of the ceaseless provocation to which Jews were subjected.
The effect of Weizmann's policy was lasting in spite of its radical
reversal later. If ever the pacifist idea achieved a victory it was for
the Jews of Palestine during the years which saw the bloodiest of all
the persecutors of their race reach absolute power in Germany.

Such in crude outline was the situation in Palestine in the September
of 1936. Ever-growing Jewish immigration, ever-growing Arab

[1] Total casualties 1,351, including 187 Moslems, 80 Jews, 10 Christian Arabs, 28 British
troops and police killed. *Annual Register*.

resentment and violence, a repressive regime conducted by a Government inwardly puzzled in mind, a faint but tempting hope of a settlement by negotiation. Wingate began to study these things in Haifa, in a room in the Savoy Hotel which was now being used as a military headquarters.

He only stayed three and a half months in Haifa, and in that time he became a Zionist. It seems that the process began when his studies of the local situation showed him that he had been seriously misinformed about the Jews. Throughout life he had a passionate sympathy with the oppressed, and the little information he had about his new assignment had suggested to him that the Arab population showed a distressing case of the disinherited suffering ill-treatment at the hands of the rich. The Zionists had world-wide resources, were supported by millionaires, and enjoyed an enormous propaganda organisation, whereas the unfortunate Arabs of Palestine had only backward and impoverished neighbours to support them, and no voice in the places where the destinies of the world were determined and power resided. What hope for them was there in so unequal a struggle ? Only the guardianship of Great Britain stood between them and an annihilating exploitation. Such was a common British opinion in those days and it seems to have been Wingate's at the time of his arrival. But when he discovered something of the conditions under which the sales of land were conducted he began to reverse these ideas, and he rapidly came to suspect that it was not the Arab but the Jewish population which needed protection from exploitation. He discovered, so he believed, a particularly noxious form of swindle. Arab small-holders who sold land to Jews, against the exhortations of the Mufti not to do so, sometimes became victims of the terrorist bands. But this was not a consequence only of nationalism. For at the same time, a close relative of the Mufti was doing a brisk trade in precisely such allegedly criminal deals, but with a notable difference, for this person used to force sales from Arab small-holders at niggardly prices, and then resell to Jews at the usual exorbitant rates, and it was said (with doubtful truth perhaps) that unpatriotic small-holders were shot, not for unpatriotism, but because they got in the way of a large and lucrative industry.[1] When he found that his ideas about Arab grievances were at fault Wingate went hungrily in search of other ideas and found them. It would seem that he was a Zionist within a month. The first Jews who met him in Haifa found in him a man who shared their national convictions to the full.

He was so very much of a Zionist, so extremist even among

[1] Morris Marguiles. A letter describing his first meeting with Wingate published in *The American Zionist*.

extremists, even at this time, that many people, including some Jews, found his enthusiasm hard to account for. Some presumed that he was a Jew, either wholly or in part, a supposition which his aquiline features made plausible, but in fact Wingate had no Jewish blood either on his father's or mother's side. Others have pointed out that in an English society, such as he found in Palestine, and which was predominantly Arabophil, he could hardly fail, with his opposition-temperament, to espouse the Jewish cause. There is undoubtedly some truth in this. As a champion of the Arabs he would have been one of a crowd. As the champion of the Jews, he needed to follow the lone path suited to his strange combative character. But it is wrong to consider this delight in opposition as more than a little contributory factor to his Zionism, as more than something in his character which facilitated his sudden access of faith. He himself gave several explanations of his conversion. Wilfred Thesiger once asked him why he, a non-Jew, should be so wholeheartedly with Zionism. He replied somewhat as follows :

" When I was at school I was looked down on, and made to feel that I was a failure and not wanted in the world. When I came to Palestine I found a whole people who had been treated like that through scores of generations, and yet at the end of it they were undefeated, were a great power in the world, building their country anew. I felt I belonged to such people."

But he gave a more illuminating account to Frederick Kish. In his earliest days, he said, he had received an injection of the Bible, but the effect only appeared many years later.[1] Here we may remember again his occasional resemblance to the Puritans of Cromwell's day. Many of them became Zionists through much reading of Holy Writ. It is sometimes forgotten that the famous Rabbi Manasseh ben Israel was invited to London from Holland largely through the pressure of Zionist-minded Puritans who believed that if Jews were settled in England the " scattering " prophesied by Daniel would then be complete, so that the return of the people to Israel might be accomplished, a prophecy which, as no one seemed to notice, was actually fulfilled in 1917. But the fact was noticed in 1936 by this spiritual descendant of Protectorate England.

One of the most prominent Jews of Haifa was a man called David Hacohen, a former officer in the Turkish Army, and now the head of a large contracting company known as Solel Bouch. He was probably the first influential Zionist to meet Wingate. One of the British Intelligence officers in the Savoy Hotel, a sympathiser with Zionism, told Hacohen that he ought to meet a strange newly arrived colleague

[1] Mr. David Hacohen. A communication.

of his who was " trying to find out what was going on in the country," but who had as yet no first-hand acquaintance with the Jewish population. David Hacohen did not welcome the suggestion, especially after hearing the name of the new arrival. Like many Zionists at that time and after, he regarded Englishmen with disillusion (largely through underestimating their difficulties) and furthermore Hacohen found it hard to believe that a cousin of the famous Sirdar Wingate would not prove to be naturally drawn towards Arab sympathies. But Wingate's colleague persisted in his proposal and so the two men met alone in a little room in the Savoy.

Hacohen was impressed by his first sight of the man who was to be his close friend. " He had the looks of an ascetic," he recorded in an essay written at a much later time, " dressed as he was in simple and worn uniform which strangely became his emaciated and serious face ; his bright eyes, devoid of conventional smiles, were deep in their sockets and so penetrating that in his presence one seemed unable to hide the slightest movement or utter one superfluous word. His nose was finely formed, his hair dark and covering his forehead untidily, his conversation concentrated though fluent, to the point, sincere, straightforward and without formal politeness." Their talk began by Hacohen remarking to him that he believed that he was anxious to learn about Zionist achievement in Palestine. He asked him if he had met any of the Jews.

Wingate replied : " I have met few Jews in my life, but my sympathies are with Zionism."

Hacohen asked him what he had read about Zionism.

Wingate replied : " There is only one important book on the subject, the Bible, and I've read it thoroughly. Have you ever read the Koran ? "

Hacohen replied that he had read many passages of the Koran. In Arabic ? asked Wingate. Yes, he had read some of it in Arabic. " I have read the whole thing in Arabic," said Wingate. He then burst into a diatribe in the course of which he told Hacohen that the more you read in the Koran the more surely you saw in it little but a heap of pompous verbiage, found nothing but vapourings whose grandiose cloudiness gave a deluding impression of great mystical poetry, and he said that when you occasionally lighted on something better than this you might be quite certain that the fatal Arabian had lifted it from the Old or New Testaments. There could be no comparison between the Koran and the Bible, and no choice for any but a fool between a movement based on the Koran and a movement based on the Hebrew scriptures.

Hacohen was much surprised. While never yielding on political matters it was very much Zionist policy then to cultivate an attitude of polite respect towards Islam, and on hearing so unexpectable an attack, this Zionist put in some good words for the Koran and its author, all of which Wingate brushed impatiently aside. At the end of their talk, Wingate made to this man, whom he had never met before, what may be called a confession of faith. What he said was remembered by Hacohen as follows :

" This is the cause of your survival. I count it as my privilege to help you to fight your battle. To that purpose I want to devote my life. I believe that the very existence of mankind is justified when it is based on the moral foundation of the Bible. Whoever dares lift a hand against you and your enterprise here should be fought against. Whether it is jealousy, ignorance or perverted doctrine such as have made your neighbours rise against you, or ' politics ' which make some of my countrymen support them, I shall fight with you against any of these influences. But remember that it is your battle. My part, which I say I feel to be a privilege, is only to help you." He added, " Please, will you open for me the hearts of the Jews in this country ? "

Hacohen felt dazed as he went away from this interview with the new Intelligence Officer, and extremely elated. He hastened to tell his Zionist colleagues that " an extraordinary man, a friend who will fight fearlessly for our cause," had arrived in their midst. But his fellow-Jews were sceptical. Might not this be some well-planted spy, some more than ordinarily ingenious *agent provocateur* ? For all his advocacy Hacohen, a famous jester among other things, was not taken seriously. The very notion of an Englishman discharging Governmental duties and at the same time entertaining an active belief in Zionism, was something outside normal Jewish experience in Palestine.

One Jew, however, was not sceptical. He was an architect of Russian-Jewish origin called Emanuel Wilenski.[1] He was familiar with the association of Englishry and Zionism, having been a friend of Philip Orde Guy, the Scottish son-in-law of one of the founders of modern Zionism, Ben Yehuda. Through Philip Guy, Wilenski knew Wingate's Zionist colleague in the Savoy Hotel, the man who had brought about the meeting with David Hacohen. Of the Zionist colleague's devotion to the Jewish cause Wilenski had signal proof, since this officer had once not only warned him of an impending search by the police for Hagana arms but had advised him to let some of them be discovered, since the presence of some arms was certainly known. This man now invited Wilenski to a dinner, a " stag party," to meet the new Intelligence Officer.

So many people found in their first sight of Wingate an ill-kempt

[1] Since then Emanuel Wilenski has changed his surname to Yolan.

figure wearing tattered clothes, with unbrushed hair and unwashed hands, that it is a refreshing change to learn that when Wilenski first saw him he was smartly dressed in blues and presented an appearance of soldierly and thoroughly British neatness. As was his wont Wingate broke straight into serious talk and began a discussion of Zionism. Wilenski was impressed by the man's fervour, puzzled at finding this voluble and learned enthusiast in British uniform, and rather shocked and apprehensive at the extremism of his views. Wingate seems to have spoken somewhat in the same strain as he had done to David Hacohen for he is remembered quoting the Koran in Arabic and the Bible in Hebrew. (He had already begun to study Hebrew and, as said already, he was never a man to wear his learning modestly.) He has been represented as cornering Wilenski at this party and shouting at him that the Jews needed to take up arms and give battle and enter " a bloody struggle," and so on. This is an exaggeration ; there was a somewhat heated discussion, but the dinner party passed off quietly. At this time a demand was growing among younger Jews for a militant organisation which would break with the passive course of action followed by Hagana on instructions from the Jewish Agency, and there was some talk at the party about the fact that a few extremists were known to be secretly forming irregular military bodies for the furtherance of an aggressive policy. Wingate said that these extremists were in the right. Wilenski referred to the policy of self-restraint. Wingate with quiet but passionate insistence asserted that with the new turn in affairs a state of war now existed between Jewry and Islam and that the time had gone by when passive and merely defensive policies were practical. The need was for the formation of an army, and he declared in all seriousness that it was his ambition to lead a Jewish Army into battle. The discussion was long and Wilenski came away from the party with his ideas severely shaken. He found he could not sleep that night ; he could not banish from his mind the image of the small round shouldered officer with the penetrating gaze and the low insistent grumbling voice who seemed to talk not as people usually do at such dinners : to express whatever ideas, serious or otherwise, happen to be at the surface ; but from an inner compulsion. He formed the opinion, which he was never to alter, that Wingate was the most remarkable man he had ever met in the course of his life.

He went to his fellow-Zionists in Haifa and to his secret colleagues in Hagana (of which he was an Intelligence Officer) and declared to them that in the newly arrived Englishman Zionism had a staunch and valuable ally. As with David Hacohen on the same mission he was met with doubt and scepticism. It was impossible, the Jews said, for an Englishman to be a Zionist. Why should an Englishman be a Zionist? Great Britain had her widespread Moslem interests and commitments all of which were fatally disturbed by Jewish ambition. Why should that state of things be pleasing to a British official? The Administration had inherited the consequences of the Balfour Declaration and doubtless it could be trusted to safeguard the existing settlements, but did the Administration relish the prospect of these settlements growing to great dimensions, or could it look with approval on the unquestioned Zionist aim of founding a Jewish state in the land? Of course not. Perhaps Wingate was one of those persons who liked to dream about " ancient Judea " and " restoring the Kingdom " along with many other self-befuddlers, pietists and semi lunatics who from early times had infested this birthplace of religion? The Jews were tired of dreamers. As Wilenski pressed the claims of Wingate against such ideas he came to be regarded as something of a bore. " Oh you and your friend," people used to chaff him. From this Wingate got a nickname among Wilenski's acquaintances : " Hayedid Shelkha," " Your friend." It was used sarcastically then, but before long it became a kind of private title of respect among Zionists, " Hayedid," " The Friend."[1]

The conversion of the Haifa Zionists to confidence in " the friend " came about slowly, but a curious little incident is held to have marked the turning of the tide. It happened as follows. David Hacohen took Wingate to Deganiya for an overnight visit. This settlement is situated by the junction of the River Jordan with the Sea of Galilee and is the oldest of the communal settlements (the Kibbutzim) of Palestine. It is a religious foundation, one of those places in the re-covered land where the toil and burdens and joys of every day are shared in a spirit of ancient piety, resolved into a single harmony by a collective fervour ; such a place as must force the Gentile equally with the Jew to acknowledge the living force of Jewish faith. This was the first visit of Wingate to a Jewish settlement, and the first time that he found himself in the very midst of Jewish life. According to the custom of the Kibbutzim the presence of guests and strangers was not remarked, but with business-like attention the member on duty in the refectory put a supper of vegetables, cheese, cream, eggs and fruit before them. Wingate is remembered by Hacohen as looking in wonder all round and watching the table-customs of Orthodox Jewry, scrupulously observed here, things which he had heard of but had never seen before. That night after supper there was a merry-making to celebrate the end of a period of training for a group of young German immigrants, a noisy party in a little room with mouth-

[1] Mr. Yolan.

organ music and dancing. When the older people had left and the party still went on Hacohen asked Wingate if he was not tired of the fun and ready for bed. But he replied : " This seems to be the first time that I have seen young people dancing as they should dance. It is beautiful and gay, simple and civilised." He sat "as though nailed to his chair" watching the dance. But he could never be a passive spectator for long, and so when there was an argument between a mother and her son, she trying to stop the son dancing as he had strained his leg in the fields, Wingate must needs join in to assert that physical weakness should be overcome by spiritual fortitude, and that the son ought to prove the point by continuing to dance.

At supper Wingate had noticed that the bread of Deganiya was very good, and before he went back with Hacohen in the morning he asked for a freshly baked loaf to take with him. When he was back in Haifa he took the loaf to his superior officer and told him that this was the kind of bread that should be supplied to British troops. He said that the places that could produce such bread could produce much else for the soldiers in the way of fresh food, in the place of their customary tinned rations. It was this incident of the loaf of bread, strange as it may seem, which convinced the few Jews whom he had met so far that Wingate's Zionism was not of the sentimental order which some suspected, but was based on common-sense consider-ations.[1] Soon he made many Jewish friends in Haifa, but he still had to wait a long time before he was fully accepted and trusted by the Jews.

While waiting for Lorna to join him Wingate used sometimes to stay with the Hacohen family in Haifa. His extraordinary manners came to them as something of a shock. After dinner the household would be sitting round the fire or the stove, talking and arguing, when they would notice that Wingate was working one of his shoes off a foot as he talked, then working off the sock, then, as he went on talking, they would see him pull a pencil out of his pocket and with the aid of the pencil commence a thorough massage of his toes. On other occasions his disregard of the custom of wearing clothes would collide with the conventions of the house. One day Mrs. Hacohen knocked at the door which was immediately opened by an entirely naked figure who in confusion slammed it shut again instantly. He was not an ideal guest, but David Hacohen remarked that though his behaviour was often something of a trial, yet his bad manners were not those of a boor. He had the gift of sympathy, and a natural delicacy of feeling, both unmistakable under something of a pose of rugged *farouchete*. For, sincere as he was, he was never quite free

---

[1] David Hacohen and Emanuel Yolan. Communications.

of the posing habit. Like all men who have it in them to command, he was a gifted actor.

His Zionism grew apace, and, true to his masterfulness, he was soon ordering his Jewish friends about and telling them what they must do to be worthy of their inheritance, and what they must not do. One day he had a quarrel with David Hacohen over what may seem a wholly uncontroversial matter. The scene opened the eyes of his Jewish friend to the increasing intensity, almost the fanaticism of Wingate's new faith. This is what happened. Some Englishmen, including Wingate, were at a Jewish party and Hacohen entertained the company with a Yiddish comic story entitled *The Goat*. A man (so runs the story) who was depressed on account of his poverty and the wretchedness of his home, went to ask the advice of his Rabbi as to how he might discover some happiness in life. The Rabbi asked him if he had a cow, and when he learned he had, he told him to stable the cow in his house and report back concerning his state of mind on the morrow. When he reported back he said he felt more unhappy than before because a cow in the house was adding to his discomfort. So the Rabbi ordered him to take the poultry into the house as well and again report back on the morrow. When the man duly reported that he was suffering a further sinking of his spirits, the Rabbi ordered him to provide accommodation in the house for all his family and relations, and when the man was almost out of his mind with the overcrowding and squalor of his home life, then the Rabbi finally ordered him to take in a goat. When the man reported back the day after the in-take of the goat, the Rabbi began a reverse process ordering the removal day by day and one at a time of the cow, the hens, the relatives, and at last the goat by which time the man's spirits had risen to a state of almost delirious joy and he acknowledged that he knew now what the happiness of life could mean. Such was the story of *The Goat*, an innocuous yarn one might suppose, and when told by a master of Jewish buffoonery, apt to be exceedingly funny. His audience roared with laughter, all except Wingate who glared with disapproval. He went up to him and said, " David, I hate you for telling that story ! "

" Why. What do you mean ? " asked his friend.

" I mean this," growled Wingate. " Squalid stories of that kind give the Jews a bad name, and make them despised. Why don't you do away with that sort of folk-lore ? The whole purpose of the return to Israel is to stop the Jews being associated with that kind of story ! " and he went on scolding.

Often he used to revisit Deganiya, the settlement where he had first seen Zionism in action, and which remained his favourite place in the land.[1] One day, as he and Hacohen were driving back to Haifa through the valley of Jezreel, his friend noticed that Wingate was looking hither and thither with an agitated eye, muttering to himself, and evidently in a state of ungovernable excitement. Suddenly Wingate cried out : " But why was he defeated ? He ought to have won this battle ! The man was a fool ! "

" Who do you mean ? " asked Hacohen, trying to think back to the Allenby campaigns.

" I mean Saul ! " cried out Wingate, and then he went on somewhat in this style : " That man Saul had all his army *there* (pointing). I mean there, up there on the heights on Gilboa, south of his water supply which was there (pointing to the water course)—imagine the folly of that when his enemy was to the north *there*, in Shunem (pointing again), and why did he do it ? He could have brought his army over— he had freedom of movement—how do I know, because the night before the battle he went nearly all the way to Tabor to visit the witch of Endor—*there* (pointing to Ein-Dor). Do you know why he did it—the damned fool !—because he had brought all his women and all his furniture and his tents and his household with him. He didn't know how to travel light. He was a bad soldier."

" But do you think," asked Hacohen, " that it matters much now ? "

" What ! " shouted Wingate. " Matter ! Of course it matters ! By his folly, by his incompetence, Saul threw away his position and he held the greatest position a man has ever occupied or could ever occupy in history. He was King of the Jews ! He had been elected to rule over the most wonderful people in the whole world, the only people who had discovered God—and he threw it all away by his sheer damned silly incompetence ! Matter ! Of course it matters ! " And so on for a long time.

The reader may learn with a pang, but perhaps without surprise, that this Bible-enthusiast to whom the events related in the Books of Samuel were of immediate importance, found himself in time drawn towards one of the most singular and grotesque of all theological schools, that of the British Israelites, people whose central belief is that the inhabitants of Great Britain are descendants of the ten tribes of Israel who did not return to the land of Canaan from the Babylonian captivity. He studied, and was apparently impressed by the ingenious and laughable etymology and notions of race, and the numerology deduced from the pyramids, by which British Israelites attempt to fortify their enormously improbable beliefs.[2] But the reader may be

---

[1] Mrs. Vera Weizmann.

[2] Morris Marguiles. *The American Zionist.* Wingate seems to have expressed his transient interest in British Israelitism to no one else.

reassured. It would seem that Wingate's interest in this wild deviation of learned minds lasted for a very short time. It was probably a fleeting extension of that vein of fantasy which he was never to lose.

Against these scenes of pious frenzy and scolding and eccentricity remembered by David Hacohen, contrasting scenes are remembered by the Wilenski household. During the weeks in Haifa while he was waiting for Lorna, he stayed some of his time with the Wilenskis and his hosts came to know the side of him that was hidden from most. There were children in the house and, as with many men of active mind, he always loved talking to children and joining in their games. (His views about these have been noted.) There grew up a custom that whenever he was staying Wingate had to pull the little girl's foot in bed before she would go to sleep. They saw him relaxed and at ease, as he used to be when gossiping about dogs and horses with Derek Tulloch, or playing with the children of Colonel Bill Browne, or chatting in Mr. Webster's parlour. They became familiar with the smile inherited from his mother.[1] Not too much should be made of this, for his Palestine years certainly saw the final growth to maturity of a character astonishing for cold strength and fierce idealist dedication, but it is wrong to suppose that he was the least insensitive to the immemorial joys of everyday life.

In November Lorna joined her husband. She did so in circumstances which put his new-found Zionism to a sudden and severe test.

Wingate's friendship with Colonel Jennings-Bramly had continued since the days of his Libyan exploration, and when Lorna was making preparations to leave England the patriarch of Burg el Arab invited the two of them to stay with him in Egypt, the plan being that they should meet in Alexandria and then spend a few days' holiday together in the Burg before going to Haifa. Since 1932 Jennings-Bramly's great scheme had come to some sort of fruition. The town and his own castello were both completed by now. The descendant of John Wingfield Larking had succeeded in persuading the descendant of Mehmet Ali to support his venture, and King Fuad became so far interested in the plan for an annual act of homage that he even helped to devise an appropriate ceremonial. " The tribes," Colonel Jennings-Bramly recalled much later, " were to march in through the Town Gate . . . led by their Sheikhs and Omda, a flag with the tribal camel mark leading. When all were assembled in the square the Head Omda of all the tribes was to lock the Town Gate. I wanted the Arabs to feel for once that they were in a situation from which they could not escape. The Omda was then to give the Key to King Fuad who, having heard a recital of the year's happenings, would return the key, if he approved

[1] Emanuel Yolan.

of what had happened. King Fuad said he accepted this suggestion and seemed pleased. ' The key,' he said, ' will be presented by the Head Sheikh himself. It will be of solid gold.' I had to say : ' And how long does Your Majesty think your Head Sheikh will be alive ? ' King Fuad thought. He said : ' The key will be of iron, there will be an ornamental network of gold in the ring of the key.' "[1]

But before the ceremony could be conducted King Fuad died and his successor, King Farouk, was not a person to be interested in schemes of this kind. Nevertheless Burg el Arab fulfilled its main function in spite of neglect by those who had most to benefit from so much labour and devotion.

To this place, built by tribesmen from stone in the Ptolemaic quarries and the ruins of Græco-Roman villas, Wingate brought Lorna after meeting her in Alexandria. " When I saw the place," she recorded twenty years later, " on a freezing moonlit night I was stunned. A wall twenty feet high rose out of the flat silver desert. We passed through a gate twenty feet thick into an enormous square, slightly tilted, partly cobblestoned. Far away on the left wall was an arcade and the light of one candle burning behind it. There was nothing else except the icy black shadows on the sand." The house itself, part castle and part Italian villa, seemed an Aladdin's cave of inexhaustible delight and surprise. Whole walls were hung with splendid Venetian mirrors, the inheritance of Mrs. Jennings-Bramly. Among the treasures of the house was a faded blue ribbon of the Order of the Garter. It had been worn by Charles I on the scaffold.[2] Here was Lodolf in real life indeed !

At the end of their visit, on the very day, it seems, that the Wingates were about to leave Burg el Arab, Colonel Jennings-Bramly was moved to make a grave proposal to his guests. As a man of imagination, he felt all the marvel of the younger man's romantic personality, and he now asked Wingate whether he was prepared to make the little town his life-interest as he, Jennings-Bramly, had done. He invited him to quit the army and live there, as though adopted as an eldest son, working for the accomplishment of Burg el Arab's high purpose and to succeed to this unique property as the founder's heir. He turned to Lorna and said : " I will build you a house on the wall." Wingate, as is hardly needful to say, was deeply moved by so magnificent and magnanimous an offer, one that would take him out of obscurity, give him not only position and some modest wealth and prospects, but

[1] Jennings-Bramly. A letter to the writer.
[2] " The King Charles I Ribbon came to us from Colonel Tomlinson, to whom Charles gave it on the scaffold. His daughter married a Turysden and after that one of their family married a Style, and it came to me from my great-grandmother Dorothy Style."
—Jennings-Bramly.

minister to the deep-seated missionary spirit inherited from both his parents. It was an appeal to all that was fine in him. His Zionism was as yet a recent interest and it may be said that he was prevented by no reasons in the world from accepting the offer; but he divined reasons beyond the world why he should not accept it. He was moved but not tempted. He smiled and said that he must stay in the army. He refused the offer " with regret, but no hesitation." He and Lorna went to Haifa.[1]

Soon after their arrival in Palestine the Wingates were invited to dine with Sir Arthur Wauchope at Government House in Jerusalem. It was a large dinner party and the principal guests were Doctor and Mrs. Weizmann. (Wingate had already met the Governor through a letter of introduction from Sir Reginald.) After dinner, when in British fashion the men had had their moment with the port and brandy, and all the guests were together again in the drawing-room, Dr. Weizmann sought out his wife and asked her if she knew who Mrs. Wingate was. She said : " Yes, I sat next to her husband and I found him one of the most interesting men I have ever met." When the party broke up the Weizmanns asked the Wingates to come back to their house, and they sat down and talked till the early hours of the morning. It was the beginning of a friendship which was to have its influence on the history of the Zionist cause and the Jewish people.

The first episode in this affectionate, ardent, enduring and some-times stormy relationship was propitious. Toscanini was on a brief visit to Palestine, having undertaken to conduct a series of concerts by the newly-formed Palestine Symphony Orchestra. To all Zionists, and many others, this majestic protest by the greatest musician of his time against German persecution was a notable event. Never, it may be said, since the December day of 1813 in Vienna, when Beethoven conducted the first performance of the Seventh Symphony, can musical occasions have been so charged with emotion and meaning. Tickets were hard to come by. When the Weizmanns learned that their new friends were interested in music, and had failed to get places for themselves, they invited them to join their party. The concerts were given from the 26th of December till the 2nd of January.

Very shortly after this Wingate was posted to General Headquarters Jerusalem, still as an Intelligence Officer. By the time he reached his new assignment his mind had been made up on Zionism for some time, but it would seem likely that only after meeting the Zionist leader were his ideas finally clarified.

The time was one for decisions. The boldest and perhaps the best effort hitherto was being made by the British Government to reach

[1] Mrs. Lorna Smith. A letter to the writer.

a permanent settlement of the Palestine question. The Royal Commission headed by Lord Peel was the ablest body of men sent from England to the Near East since the Cairo Conference of 1921. It had been sitting in Jerusalem since the 12th of November and by the time Wingate reached Jerusalem it was holding its last week of hearings. Moved by the thoughts of the hour, and nothing daunted by the modesty of his rank and the brevity of his experience, Wingate felt that the time had come for him to express his convictions in full, and to press his advice on those responsible for the destinies of his country. He took a familiar course.

> " Hotel Fast,
> Jerusalem
> 12.1.37.

" Dear Cousin Rex,

I would have written long ago but the nature of what I had to say necessitated conveyance by hand and so I had to await a good opportunity—

It is as well that I did not write before as I have much more to say now that is to the point than previously. There are few men at home, I believe, in great places who are in a position to hear ' the low-down ' on the situation out here. It is, in my judgment, important that people in charge should not misunderstand the situation which is full of danger for England's future ; so I am putting on paper what I would otherwise leave unwritten.

I have now been four months in Palestine. I have ridden over the northern frontiers with the T.J.F.F.[1] I have stayed nights in Kvutzot. I have met many Arab and Jew notables.

I have met H.E. I have talked with most of the important Government officials out here.

The opinion which I now commit to paper I believe to be true and will engage to defend against all comers. As you know I am not ignorant of Arabic or the Arabs, nor prejudiced either for or against them.

Much of the information I give is known only to people out here and some of it is unknown to the R.C.[2]

The situation is then as follows :—

(1) The non-Palestinian Arab world is disposed for the moment to avoid any appearance of unfriendliness to Great Britain as they regard her as stronger than they were inclined to believe

---

[1] The Transjordan Frontier Force.
[2] The Royal Commission.

some months ago. Provided no deliberate insult be offered to Islam they are content (in the words of the Imam Yahya)[1] to leave the Palestinian Arabs to God.

(2) Islam in reality cares little for the Arabs of Palestine and, although concerned in the preservation of the Holy Places and finding the thought of Jews in Palestine distasteful, would be prepared to accept a *fait accompli*.

In any case Islam today has no strength. England continues to think it has the same influence as in pre-war days. That is a fallacy.

(3) The Arabs of Palestine are making a great song and dance about what they will do if the findings of the Commission are not 90% in their favour. Supposing they do all they threaten, i.e., rise *en masse*, we need only (*a*) arm the Jews, (*b*) proclaim martial law and arrest and exile every Arab notable ; to find ourselves able to master the revolt with no more than the eight battalions already here.

(4) There is a considerable risk that the Arabs of Transjordan will join in any revolt of the Palestinians. Although awkward for the moment, such a movement is really to our advantage. Transjordan is an integral part of Palestine, being no more than the east side of the Jordan basin and bound to share in any scheme for turning this basin into the market garden of the Mediterranean. Interference by Transjordan will provide the excuse for the removal of the corrupt and slovenly Abdullah and the reclamation of the country for Palestine.

(5) The military strength, past, present and future, of the whole Arab group is quite negligible, as I need not tell you.

(6) The potential military strength of the Jews, especially if we adopt my recommendations, is equivalent to at least two British Army Corps when trained and organised.

(7) Any claims the Arabs may allege over the Lawrence affair, are discussed and disposed of in the paper I enclose.[2]

(8) The administration of Palestine and Transjordan is, to a man, anti-Jew and pro-Arab. This is largely due to the fact that we seem to send only the worst type of British official to Palestine. They hate the Jew and like the Arab who, although he shoots at them, toadies to them and takes care to flatter their sense of importance.

The truth of the matter is, Sir, that the whole tribe of officials out here are third rate. I don't think you will get many

[1] Prince of the Yemen. The quotation has not been traced by the writer.
[2] This is missing.

whose opinion you can value to contradict that statement. The contrast between the civil service here and in the Sudan is startling. Hardly any of the D.C.s here know Arabic (or Arabs) let alone Hebrew (and Jews).

(9) The H.C.[1] although he has my sympathy and admiration for his fine qualities, is past his work by common consent and should be removed. He does not know what to do, asks and takes anyone's advice, pays his suit to the rebellious Arabs, begs their minor leaders to help him, and generally betrays that he has lost all grasp of affairs.

(10) The history of the last six months is a sad one indeed. The troubles started in such a way that we could have stopped them with half the force we had. Owing purely to the vacillation of H.E. and the pro-rebel sympathies of the entire civil service, what might have proved a mere riot developed into armed rebellion.

The Jews, who never broke the law and remained loyal throughout, had to witness their work destroyed, their families threatened, their blood spilt, and the blame for all laid on their shoulders.

(11) The Jews are loyal to the Empire. The Jews are men of their word—they have always been so—in fact it is the Gentile's main complaint against them. There are 15,000,000 Jews in the world.

Palestine will take well over a million within seven years. You can have no idea of what they have already done here. You would be amazed to see the desert blossom like a rose ; intensive horticulture everywhere—such energy, faith, ability and inventiveness as the world has not seen.

I have seen the young Jews in the Kvutzots. I tell you that the Jews will provide a soldiery better than ours. We have only to train it. They will equip it.

(12) Palestine is essential to our Empire—our Empire is essential to England—England is essential to world peace.

Islam is out of it. [We have] the chance to plant here in Palestine and Transjordan a loyal, rich and intelligent nation, with which we can make an everlasting treaty, and which will hold for us the key to world dominion without expense or effort on our part.

In event of war it is ten times more important to have a strong Jewish people here.

The Commission *appears* to be pro-Arab. It certainly meets

[1] High Commissioner.

no one but pro-Arab officials. In all probability it has no idea what to think or what to do.

But this is what it must do.

(*a*) Announce that a bad administration is to blame for the recent outbreak.

(*b*) Recommend that the Government assume full responsibility for protection of legitimate Arab interests : that the Government will settle all land disputes, with due regard to the rights of the Arabs as individuals : that the Government guarantees the economic future of persons of Arab race in Palestine : (All of which is too easy—ask the Jews).

Finally the Government will tolerate no dispute of its rulings whatever but will ruthlessly suppress any attempt at opposition.

(*c*) That the Government guarantees, to perpetuity, the preservation of Islam's holy places.

(*d*) That the Government recognises the right of the Jews to migrate to Palestine as the absorptive capacity of the country admits. (With a corollary to the effect that the late administration has grossly under-estimated that capacity.)

(*e*) That the Government recognises Palestine as the National Home of Jewry ; and its duty to advance the foundation of an autonomous Jewish community with all the means in its power.

(*f*) That the Government recognises the need to arm the Jews forthwith and will at once proceed with the raising of two Jewish Brigades to take over the defence of Palestine, internal and external.

If we do these things we will secure Palestine for the Empire and the Empire for the world. If we don't we shall have put our trust in the bruised Arab reed that, when we lean on it, will pierce our hand.

We are in for a war sooner or later—no hope now of avoiding that after the Abyssinian fiasco—for pity's sake let us do something just and honourable before it comes. Let us redeem our promises to Jewry and shame the devil of Nazism, Fascism and our own prejudices.

I look like staying here for some time. I have the job of I.O. on Comp. H.Q. Jerusalem. It is quite interesting but I'd sooner be raising a Jewish Brigade (under Govt. !) to defend our interests in the coming war! Lorna is here with me and is well and happy. We meet many interesting people, chief among whom is Dr. Weizmann; a truly great man, and, I am proud to say, our friend. We meet many of the pro-Arabs, anti-British, officials, of course, to whom I am not so explicit as here!

Jennings-Bramly, with whom Lorna and I stayed some days last month at Burg el Arab, asks me to remember him to you.

I feel Palestine is more important than Egypt henceforth and for evermore. I shall hope to identify myself with it.

Our love and best wishes to you both for 1937.

Your affectionate cousin,

Orde Wingate "[1]

This very singular document is worth some examination. The views expressed in it show an extraordinary mixture of perspicacity and prejudice. What Wingate said about the then lack of interest of Arab states outside Palestine in the latter's fate was probably true, and his implication that the Arab powers were kept active in this field by the undetermined nature of British policy, was probably true also. His contention that the rebellion could be mastered by arming the Jews and proclaiming martial law was almost proved in the course of the next two years. His idea that Transjordan intervention should be encouraged in the hope of wrecking the Hashemite regime is somewhat shocking and shows a vein of young ruthlessness which he was not to lose. The political notion here was fallacious. An extension of Jewish preponderance beyond Jordan was (and remains) an extremist idea and one which could not be followed without resulting in violent reactions of fatal result, above all to the Jews. Wingate was evidently ignorant of the fact that Abdullah, for all his faults, was a salutary influence for common sense. But his ideas on the value of Arab military strength and the latent military virtues of the Jews, though extravagantly expressed in this letter, have since been proved by the events of 1948 and 1956. His invective against the mandate officials was gross overstatement. Palestine was served by some admirable administrators, but the contrast he drew with the Sudan was valid. Palestine was never staffed by men who identified the needs of the country with their own. What he alleged about the personal pro-Arab bias in Palestine administrators was in the main true. It will be discussed later. His strictures on the High Commissioner, Sir Arthur Wauchope, are interesting. They are in line with much respectable opinion and are not easily denied. Wauchope was a military man of high character

[1] W.P.II : the letter has been somewhat shortened in this version, but nothing essential omitted.

who found himself out of his depth when he tried to carry out the confused policy of a Government which he was unable to influence. It is interesting to notice that what Wingate said about Jewish immigration figures now refers to something that has come to pass. It is another question, however, whether a million Jews could have been introduced into Palestine at any time without provoking bloodshed. He weakened his advocacy in this place again by urging impossibilities such as the establishment of a Jewish state beyond the Jordan as well as in Palestine. He never appreciated the dangers of extremism or the value of moderation. It was probably this that gave him such a false idea of what the Peel Commission was doing and was about to do. Nevertheless he inadvertently anticipated some of their findings when he wrote of " the foundation of an autonomous Jewish community." He completely overlooked the fact that no British Government of any party would have been able to carry through the kind of policy he was proposing. The main interest of this curious letter now is that it gives a full account of his opinions by a man who had thought deeply about a subject on which he could never be impartial.

When they moved to Jerusalem the Wingates lived in Talbieh, the Christian Arab quarter. They rented the upper flat of a two-storied building called Hallak House which they had chosen for its view and some pleasing ironwork over the door.[1] From the windows of the main room they could see, across the valley separating the new from the old city, the centre of that semi-mystical polity for whose realisation Wingate was ready to give his life. To one who does not readily share his devotion to the venerable land of Palestine, the passion which bore it on cannot be easily conveyed. There is no arresting natural beauty to help, none of the Mediterranean loveliness which surrounds the isles of Greece, in that harsh stony tract of land lying between the sea and the River Jordan. Except for the Dome of the Rock and the Turkish walls there is nothing of splendid architecture to mark out Jerusalem from other little Levantine towns. From the balcony of their flat the Wingates might see a corner of Mount Zion itself. The spectacle is not exciting. A fat graceless German church and a clock tower, both built in the coarsest style of nineteenth-century Norman, are the first objects on the skyline to catch the attention. Here on this hill lies the tomb of David. Here Jesus Christ sat at the Last Supper with the twelve. Here is a place sanctified by three thousand years of faith. To look at, it might be somewhere in Wimbledon. Palestine is only for those

[1] Mrs. Lorna Smith.

whose imagination is strong enough to do without what ministers to the eye.

The year 1937 was for Wingate one of prolonged study, thought and preparation. He made himself thoroughly familiar with the geography of the land by map-reading and travel. He mastered every available document and report on all recent military operations which had taken place there. He spent all the time he could in learning Hebrew till he achieved a moderate fluency. In the Headquarters building he shared an office with a friend, Captain Antony Simonds, and the state of disorder and litter in which they kept it was said to be remarkable. Wingate was never an easy colleague, with his habit of opinionated and unyielding argument, but at first he seems to have been on tolerably easy terms with his fellow-officers in the Jerusalem Headquarters, and with those set over him. He is found at this time earning a special word of commendation from his immediate superior, Group-Captain Buss, for the skill and efficiency with which he organised a course for Intelligence Officers. It is to be presumed that he was examined in Arabic again and that he " requalified " (thus obtaining his right to the language allowance) for he was appointed the official army examiner in the colloquial speech, a post in which he gained a reputation for severity. This was not a honeymoon with authority— for he could never be in love with it—but this was a year in which he and his superiors and colleagues lived together in relative quiet. Till the last months of 1937 not much happened in the country. Perhaps that was the reason.

He and Lorna spent most of their leisure in making themselves familiar with the life, inhabitants, and leading people of this part of the world, household chores being relegated to the background as at Bulford. It is a mistake to think that his partiality made him neglectful of the Islamic side of his duties for his fulfilment of which he earned some official praise. In a letter to Sir Reginald Wingate he tells of a visit to the Emir Abdullah in the spring. He knew George Antonius, the brilliant apologist of the Arab cause, the author of the best book by far on the subject of modern Arab nationalism,[1] and from this alone there is reason to suppose that he was fully acquainted with the strong Arab case against Zionism. But most of his time was spent in the little Jewish world which was to grow into a state within eleven years. It was at this time that they made an abiding friendship : with Moshe Shertock,[2] as he was then called, the most important man next to Dr. Weizmann in the councils of the Jewish Agency. He met David Ben Gurion (whom he underestimated),

[1] *The Arab Awakening* by George Antonius. 1939.
[2] He has since changed his name to Sharett.

and Advan Zazlani[1] who taught him Hebrew. Sometime in these days Wingate met another man destined to play some rôle in his life, and in that of the Jewish nation, Eliahu Epstein.[2] The meeting is remembered as occurring on a very hot day. Epstein had an introduction to him and called in the afternoon. Wingate was alone. He surprised his visitor by appearing at the door naked. He led him into the sitting-room. Immediately he began to talk of serious matters. "I believe," said the naked man, fixing his gaze on the other, "that you are an Orientalist. What is your special interest?"

Epstein replied that he occupied himself with Persian studies.

"Let me tell you," said Wingate, laying down the law as usual, "that the only really good books on Persia and Persian literature are those by Edward Browne. Have you read his travel-book, *A Year among the Persians*?"

Epstein replied that he was familiar with that classic.

"It is the only book about the Persians worth reading," said Wingate. "Don't bother with the others. Stick to Browne."

They then had a long talk about Zionism, where there was no laying down of the law, Wingate, questioning closely and increasing his knowledge. When it was growing late, the host, still naked, saw his guest politely to the door.[3]

Now that he had found a cause in which he could believe heart and soul (perhaps a country to lead) his character solidified and took its final shape. But this event did not mean, as it often means in the case of men finding themselves, a lessening of eccentricity. Rather did it mean the opposite. There was no abandonment of his White-Knight style of experiment. It was around this time that he took to the frequent eating of onions in the belief that physical nourishment could be maintained by their consumption alone. A curious first encounter with a young Jewish woman is remembered. She was staying the night in a friend's house where Wingate was expected for dinner. Her hosts were out, the husband at his business, the lady shopping late, when the bell rang and she opened the front door to a dust-whitened figure in shorts and a shirt holding a small conifer; small, that is to say, by the standards of the forest but enormous by domestic ones.

"Can you help me with this tree?" asked Wingate.

"Oh yes, I think so," she said.

They tried to move the tree into the house by the front door, and failing in this, tottered together with it round the outer walls to the

[1] He has since changed his name to Shiloah.

[2] Later he changed his surname to Elath and is, at the time of writing, Israel Ambassador in London.

[3] Eliahu Elath.

veranda behind. The effort was considerable, like that of moving a grand piano. When the tree was lodged in a place by the veranda the young woman asked Wingate what it was for. He sat down on the steps and explained in some detail that when he was in the Sudan he had found that certain natives held to a belief that a young tree could be made to grow in otherwise barren soil if the pit in which it was planted was first filled with ox's blood. The young woman asked him if that was his present plan and he said yes it was. She pointed out that their hostess was a sensitive person. He said that he had not yet made arrangements for obtaining the blood. Seeing how dusty and sweaty he was, the young woman suggested that he might enjoy a shower before dinner. He agreed and went to the bathroom. When he reappeared his hosts had returned. They asked Wingate if he knew the young woman. " Yes," he said, " we've known each other rather a long time." The further adventures of the tree are not remembered.[1]

Throughout the Palestine years the Wingates found their greatest friends in Dr. and Mrs. Weizmann. The home of the Zionist leader was at Rehovoth, south-east of Tel Aviv, and it became a home to these two unusual English people. The national leader of the Jews never lost his curiosity or his delight in the comedy of life, or his readiness to add new ideas to his own great store of them. He recognised in this man so much his junior a kindred spirit. They became intimate friends and the older man allowed the younger freedoms which he did not usually accord to others ; he was never put out by Wingate's intolerant disputatiousness and wild manners, not even when in a sudden mood of high spirits he seized the window-pole and danced round the room balancing it on end, nor when he arrived for dinner one night rather drunk and Dr. Weizmann felt called upon to apply drastic restoratives. Zionism is an enthusiast creed and Dr. Weizmann never doubted, as other Jews did, the authentic fire of this enthusiast's devotion to the cause. On Wingate's side, though nothing could now increase his Zionism, it would seem that his association with Dr. Weizmann rapidly emboldened it. In May he took an extraordinary initiative, the first of those steps in his career as a Zionist which was to leave him open to criticism and calumny.

To understand what happened the reader should have some knowledge of the further adventures of the Peel Commission. On their return to England in January, 1937, they heard the evidence of British people (notably Lloyd George), after which they prepared a report and presented it to the Government in June. Their main proposals, which were accepted in principle, recommended a division of Palestine into British, Jewish and Arab zones. The permanent

[1] Mrs. Bendor.

British zone (under mandate from the League) was to include Jerusalem, Bethlehem, Nazareth, the Sea of Galilee, and a corridor from Jerusalem to the port of Jaffa ; while a temporary British zone (its future to be negotiated) was to contain towns of mixed population, Haifa, Acre, Safad, Tiberias, and the Red Sea port of Akaba. The Jewish zone, which was to be a state, was to include the rest of Galilee, the plain of Esdraelon, and the coastal plain excluding the extreme south and the district of Tulkarm. The Arab zone was to comprise the rest of the country and was to be conjoined to the Emirate of Transjordan.

Before the publication of the report its main recommendations were discussed by knowledgeable gossip, nowhere more active than in the land it concerned. As an intelligence officer Wingate was inevitably well informed. On the 31st of May, while the terms of the report were still a State secret, he wrote as follows to Dr. Weizmann.

" Dear Dr. Weizmann,

I am most sorry to hear from Mr. Shertock that you have been unwell. I hope you are perfectly fit again. It would be a disaster for Zionism if you were not yourself *during these critical times*.[1]

Since you left I have gained a better knowledge of local conditions and personalities than I had a few months ago. I have learned about 1,000 milite lurit : and by heart some of my favourite passages, as ' Bi shev Adonaiyi shivat Teion . . .' and ' Anaki Adonaiyi alai yan masha Adonaiyi uti liua seyr anavia. . . .' It is a great pleasure to me to read the Old Testament in the original.

I hoped and expected you would be back in March, as you too had hoped, but I know that you are far more usefully employed at the centre of things. In my position I see a good deal of what is *going on, and I cannot but be aware that some solution on the lines of cantonisation is far from improbable*. You, of course, know more of that than I do. Supposing that some such solution will be adopted, I take it that the Government will grant you the *right of self-defence* ?

You may recollect my views regarding the rôle Palestine Jewry might hope to play in a *future world war*. The application of this to the problem of the *formation of a Jewish Palestine Defence Force* is that it must be efficient and (organised ?) in a special manner.

For this reason I conclude that you have considered the advantages of including in its ranks a small number of suitable

[1] The underlinings on the original TS. appear to be by another hand, probably Dr. Weizmann's. The letter is written on an old machine, and there are blots and erasures so that some words are doubtful.

British officers. I know the possible disadvantages of doing so, but my knowledge of military science (added ?) to what I have observed of the confusion and muddle that invariably follow the attempts of untrained, or partially trained, persons to conduct an undertaking, have convinced me that you will not get the forces you need without (such support ?) But my knowledge of the British military machine also informs me that, unless you specify to what persons you are willing to entrust the task, you are more likely to get officers who will be unsympathetic than not (for reasons that you well understand) and who will therefore prevent the result you wish and that is essential to you.

To justify these remarks I need do little more than mention that, so far as I know, I know more Hebrew than any officer in the British Forces and I know only 1,000 words ! . . .

In anticipation of the formation of such a Force I have given some study to the problems involved. I have further interested another officer who is in Jerusalem, and who has an unrivalled knowledge of Palestine.

I wish here to offer you, as head of the Zionist Movement, our services in case you should wish to accept them. Should you do so, then may I ask you further to inquire my views on this most important subject, as I have much to say ?

It is of paramount importance to look far ahead and avoid mistakes which cannot be corrected afterwards. I know that you could recognise the need of trained and friendly military advice.

My wife sends to you and Mrs. Weizmann her love. May God bless you and your work.

Yours sincerely,
Orde Wingate "[1]

Since this and similar communications were to lead to grave imputations on Wingate's character, it may be as well before going further to look at the ethics of the matter. There can be no question that the letter was thoroughly out of order. British officials in the country had strict instructions not to mix in Palestinian politics. Wingate cannot be defended on the grounds that he was innocent of insubordination and indiscretion. He was guilty of both.

But the charge against him weakens when it is realised that almost everyone else in his position was doing much the same thing, and often less harmlessly. There has never been a country more in the thrall of controversy than Palestine in the nineteen thirties and forties. It was like Ireland during the Sinn Fein troubles. Carefree simpletons could

[1] The Weizmann Archives.

escape the dilemma by seeing no one but their own kind. But people who were not simpletons, and who met the people of the country, could not be carefree and very few of them indeed remained neutral. Almost to a man they sided with the Arabs. What Wingate wrote to his cousin on that subject was hardly if at all exaggerated. The thing to remember here is the illogicality of that state of things. Arabs not Jews were in rebellion, yet Jewish loyalty to the British connection made far less impression than Arab propaganda. Mad as it may seem, Wingate's indiscretions would have been less censured when they were known if they had been in favour of Arab nationalism.[1]

His proposition to Dr. Weizmann was not so revolutionary as may at first seem. In making it Wingate was evidently influenced by a nearby precedent. Over the way in Transjordan the Arab Legion, still commanded by its founder, Colonel Peake,[2] was largely officered by Englishmen. Wingate seems to have calculated that, with the cantonisation plan accepted, the little new Jewish state would wish to raise a kindred body, and his anxiety was clearly to obtain an early footing in it, perhaps the command. None of this can be called reprehensible by the austerest critic. If Wingate had applied for an appointment to the Arab Legion (in the service of a prince moderately but openly sympathetic to the rebellion), no one would have seen anything sinister in the action. His transgression was in discussing State secrets. He was guilty of a lack of discretion in a country where the fever of ceaseless debate caused that dull virtue to be little practised.

No written reply from Dr. Weizmann survives. It is unlikely that there was one. They met very frequently and the matter was probably discussed by them in talk soon after. Since the question was not raised again it is most probable that Dr. Weizmann dissuaded his friend from any rash move. He esteemed enthusiasm, but with his never-failing political moderation he preferred friends at court to Quixotic swordsmen, at any rate for the time being. Neither of the two men could guess that the moment was not far off when the British would give Wingate what he was now asking from the Zionist leader. When that time came any question of a divided loyalty would be temporarily in abeyance.

In the course of his studies Wingate had familiarised himself with the books and letters of T.E. Lawrence and the literature about him. As a result he had become highly critical of that famous man, both as a

---

[1] In his " Complaint to the Sovereign " of July 1939, Wingate mentions an illuminating incident which occurred in the Jerusalem H.Q. " I remember well a certain superior officer whom I requested to record my knowledge of Hebrew asking me quite seriously whether I thought it would do me any good."

[2] Lieut.-Colonel Frederick Gerard Peake, C.M.G., C.B.E., better known as Peake Pasha.

soldier and a private person. He believed that Lawrence's military ideas were fallacious and he deplored the cult of which he was the centre. Shortly before he went to Palestine he had learned in the course of conversation with Sir Reginald Wingate that Lawrence belonged to the Chapman family to which Mrs. Wingate was related, so that it followed that Lawrence of Arabia was his distant cousin.[1] The news did not please him at the time, and even less now.

Soon he was to gain a new nickname which was not to his taste, " The Lawrence of Judea."

[1] Miss Monica Wingate.

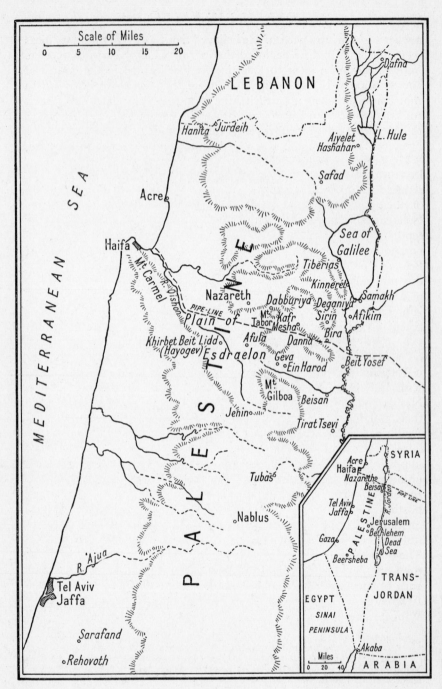

Palestine

CHAPTER VII

THE SWORD OF GIDEON

IN THE relative calm of late 1936 and 1937 the Palestine garrison was reduced from two divisions to two Infantry Brigades.[1] The semblance of peace could deceive no one. In the summer it began to break down. Isolated murder was answered by isolated reprisal in kind. When the report of the Commission was published it was clear that there must be another explosion. The general view of the time was that Lord Peel and his colleagues had made pro-Jewish recommendations, but this was not the opinion of most Jews and the report was criticised in America, and in left wing circles in England.[2] Nevertheless at the Zionist Congress the moderate party under Dr. Weizmann secured acceptance of the report as a basis of negotiation by a vote of 300 against 158. It was otherwise with the Arabs. All parties except one came down on the side of rejection. At first Raghab Bey Nashashibi was for negotiation on the basis of a partition policy but in the ensuing quarrel with Haj Amin el Husseini, who styled himself the Grand Mufti, Nashashibi found himself forced into a position more extremist than that of the extreme party. This turn of events was inevitable. The Arabs had blundered in their dealings with the Commission, and (after boycotting their proceedings till January) had asked for the impossible : a National Government without delay, no further immigration by Jews, all sales of all land to Jews to be prohibited. Instead of manœuvring Lord Peel and his associates into a bargaining posture by these tactics, they had only succeeded in losing the Commission's sympathy, and their rage at what they took to be a revengefully pro-Zionist bias in the result followed as a matter of course. The only voice of dissent to be heard in the Moslem camp was that of the Emir Abdullah. He and his small party continued to urge acceptance of the Peel Report as a basis of negotiation. No one listened. A renewal of clandestine war was delayed till September.[3] In it lay Wingate's chance and he seized it.

[1] *Annual Report to the Council of the League of Nations*. 1937. Colonial Office. H.M.S.O.
[2] At this time the Labour and Liberal parties were strongly pro-Zionist.
[3] On the 8th of September a Pan-Arab Conference at which all Arab States except the Yemen were represented, was held near Damascus. The recommendations of the Conference were the same as the submissions by the Arabs to the Peel Commission.

The Acting District Commissioner of Nazareth was called Lewis Andrews. He was an Australian and had been a member of the Administration since its beginning. He spoke Arabic and Hebrew and knew the country in detail. He was generally accounted the ablest man in the Palestine Service. Fatally for him, the Jews considered him to be a friend. On the 26th of September Andrews and his police escort were murdered by three Arab terrorists near the Anglican Church in Nazareth. The Arab Higher Committee (the Political Directorate of the Moslem Party in Palestine) gave formal expressions of regret which were not widely believed. (Their connivance at these murders was never proved however.) On the 1st of October the Administration retaliated on the atrocity by dissolving the Higher Committee and deporting those of its members whom it was able to arrest. The Mufti escaped to Beirut. A modified form of martial law (called " Military Control ") was proclaimed. But the Arab terrorist campaign persisted and Palestine remained in a state of quasi-civil war for nearly a year.

As before the Arabs were led by Fawzi Kawakji in a series of raids from across the northern border. Considering the superiority of the British troops opposite them, in numbers, training and valour, these raiders had enormous success. They caught their British opponents at a disadvantage which they knew how to exploit to the full : an army trained to meet another army in battle is often quite unable to deal with small mobile irregular columns skilfully avoiding direct combat. Wingate noted what was happening and later he gave an extremely vivid (if not entirely fair) account of the process by which the army failed to deal with their diminutive and cunning foe.

" Owing," he wrote, " to the number of roads in Palestine, to the high degree of mechanisation of the troops, and to the presence of an air arm, engagements with the rebels tended to take on a very definite form. A rebel gang would carefully choose a site commanding a road with a covered line of retreat and good air cover near at hand. It would then lie up and shoot up the first body of troops, police, or Jews, which it considered small enough to engage with impunity. In the case of troops the following would occur. The troops, invariably caught at a disadvantage as regards ground, would jump out of their vehicles and take cover. Thence they would open fire. Meanwhile an XX call would be sent for aircraft which would arrive within twenty minutes, and often sooner. On the appearance of the aircraft the gang would retire to its covered position usually among rocks and scrub, and, in spite of claims, very seldom suffered casualties from the subsequent air action. Since experience proved it dangerous for land troops to advance in close proximity to air action, the troops would usually remain where they were until the air action ceased or shifted. After this they might or might not make a reconnaissance in the enemy's direction, depending on their strength, the time factor, the urgency of the duty they were performing, etc. The engagement would be reported as a successful engagement of a gang. The truth was that a gang had successfully surprised a body of troops. . . .

". . . Another kind of engagement that occurred at times was when a large body of troops made a co-ordinated movement in an area in which large gangs were reported. Usually such movements produced no result, the gangs, warned by their numerous friends in good time, having become harmless peasants. But sometimes a bold gang-leader would deliberately lay wait for the troops. He usually regretted having done so, but there was never any question as to who had inflicted the surprise ; the gangs had."[1]

What is unfair in Wingate's account is that he makes no mention of the vigorous and successful patrol policy which was organised in the autumn of 1937. He makes no mention of the ingenious devices by which the troops were made independent of their mechanised transport and the roads, nor of the successful night operation on Mount Gilboa by the 2nd battalion of the East Yorkshire Regiment in October, 1937, nor of the larger operation commanded by Brigadier Evetts at Jenin in February of 1938 by which the rebellion was temporarily broken.[2] Wingate was writing for a purpose. He was justified however when he said later in this account that the army could never master the rebellion until it undertook night operations as part of its regular duty. The army did undertake this duty in 1938 and the initiative was Wingate's. This was made possible because by a fortunate chance the Commander in Palestine was a man who knew how to employ difficult subordinates. In September of 1937 Sir Archibald Wavell succeeded Sir John Dill. He gave Wingate his first chance to show what was in him. In the years ahead, after Palestine, he was to give the younger man all his other chances. The two of them were very different but it may have been that their association was facilitated by the fact that they shared something of the romantic spirit.

Wavell was one of the best and most curious Englishmen of his time. In appearance he was the expectable product of Winchester, Sandhurst and Scottish regimental tradition, a sound conventional gentleman not remarkable for imagination or liveliness of mind. In fact he was otherwise. He was always prepared to learn anew and to

---

[1] From a paper written for Sir Edmund Ironside in June, 1939. The circumstances in which this paper was written and presented are described later.

[2] Vide *Lord Wavell*, a military biography by Major-General R. T. Collins.

alter his ideas. He regarded military science as a useful rule of thumb for rough-and-ready guidance (no more) because he regarded warfare as something far outside regular calculation. He was remarkably free of prejudice. He seemed to live within himself more than most men, for which reason he was not communicative, yet he did not leave people in doubt of his grasp of affairs. Although he was sober in his conduct and orderly in his mind, although he was neither lecherous nor lachrymose, and very typically British, he could remind those he met of Kutuzov as that General is depicted by Tolstoy. He was tongue-tied in private and public and yet when he addressed troops he could fill them with a confidence they had not felt or imagined they could feel before. It would be a simplification to say that he was guided by intuition but he knew that there was such a thing and he let it influence his decisions. He seemed to regret the limitations of military life, and surprisingly enjoyed frivolous and chatterbox society, as though to seek relief from his own silent habit. He had a deep love of poetry to which he gave clumsy but sincere expression.[1] A facetious opinion declared him to be a model secretary of a golf club, but he was destined to master vast and calamitous situations in the second world war. He was a man who, by his ordinary bearing, invited derogatory judgments from superficial observers, but who himself searched for what lay beneath appearances. He was not likely to be roused to disapproval nor to be unduly impressed by Wingate's unconventional ways. When he heard complaints, as he surely must have done, that his Intelligence Officer was a rebellious misfit his impulse was not to send him away but to wonder how the man's energies could best be used. Wingate showed him how.

By early 1938 Wingate had come to some conclusion. His conception of a Jewish Legion similar to the existent Arab Legion did not remain idle in his mind. During the winter[2] he wrote a paper for Dr. Weizmann entitled *The Jewish State. Internal Security and Frontier Defence. Transition Period*, consisting of recommendations for the organisation of Jewish regular military forces. (He evidently assumed that the proposals of the Peel Commission would shortly be implemented by the British Government.) The most interesting thing in the paper, from the present point of view, is the section on the raising of a frontier militia. He envisaged this as a group of small armed bodies which in case of Arab attack could " render every homestead capable of defence for the short period that must elapse before the Regular unit can arrive." This in rudimentary form was the shape

---

[1] Vide his anthology *Other Men's Flowers*.

[2] The date of this paper is uncertain. It is marked 1938 and internal evidence suggests very strongly that it was written early in the year before the formation of the S.N.S. (see below) was at all clear in Wingate's mind.

of Wingate's next venture : the formation of patrol units drawn from the loyal sections of the population.

In his January letter to Cousin Rex, Wingate had already insisted that the Jews had the makings of first-rate soldiers. Since then he had been confirmed in his belief by his experience of the strict and conscientious defence discipline of the Zionist settlements. A small incident is supposed to have made a deep impression on him. He spent a great deal of his time visiting the Kibbutzim and one night he arrived late at one of these places. The gate was shut and barred and so he climbed over the wooden palisade. Arrived within he was confronted by a girl with a gun. He knew her, but she did not respond to his greeting.

" How did you get in ? " she asked.

" I climbed in," he answered.

" Then climb out," she said, " and I will open the door. Otherwise I will have to shoot you."[1]

He obeyed, approving the spirit of the order.

This little comedy was probably only one of many experiences which convinced him that contrary to conventional ideas, the Jews are a soldierly people. He had said soon after his arrival that his ambition was to lead a Jewish army. He began to see his ambition within his grasp.

His first move was to obtain the agreement of his superiors that he should go to North Palestine to discuss the possibility of establishing a system of military intelligence among the Jewish settlements. He went to Haifa sometime about February and presented himself to Brigadier Evetts, a man who was to play a considerable part in his Palestine career. At that time Evetts commanded the 16th Infantry Brigade. He and Wingate had met not long before, in September, when the Brigadier, and his Brigade Major, had paraded at Headquarters in Jerusalem to be examined in Arabic by the peculiar gunner officer with the lowering brows and piercing blue eyes. The Brigadier had passed, but the Major had been " ploughed." Now the three of them met again. The occasion was propitious. Evetts had received brief and comprehensive orders from Sir Archibald Wavell. " I look to you," the General had said, " to establish law and order in the north of Palestine, and if you get into difficulties come and ask me."[2]

Brigadier Evetts shared some characteristics with Wingate : extraordinary energy, a readiness to risk official displeasure, and some

---

[1] Zvi Brenner (see below) told the writer that at a discussion as to the wisdom of enrolling girls into Hagana Wingate strongly recommended such a policy and told this story.

[2] Lieut.-General Sir John Evetts, C.B., C.B.E., M.C. According to Sir John, Wavell gave written orders more rarely than is usual.

aversion to orthodoxy. He had none of Wingate's Zionism but he shared his impatience at the soft partiality of most Englishmen in Palestine for the rebellious party, and he admired the spirit of the Jewish pioneers. He readily fell in with the orders Wingate had obtained from Wavell. These were to the effect that he was to use his now considerable acquaintance in Jewish Palestine for the discovery of the secret tracks whereby smugglers and raiders came into the country from Transjordan, Syria and the Lebanon. He would begin therefore by watching the north-east and northern frontiers, taking up his quarters at first at a settlement near Beisan called Tirat Tsevi.[1] It is a little over twenty miles south of the Sea of Galilee, near the Jordan. He went there in February.

With the increasing unrest since 1936 the Jews had been allowed some measure of defence organisation, and like everything else in the Administration of Palestine, this was run on highly anomalous lines. A small body of what we would call Special Constables was raised by the regular police, and these " supernumeraries " became quite openly the legal centre of the large illegal military organisation, Hagana, to which a majority of the male Jewish population belonged. By the new system a selected number of Special Constables, after receiving weapon training from the police, returned to their settlements with the rank of Lance-Corporal and charged with the training of the "supernumerary establishment " of police allowed within the settlements for purposes of defence.[2] Their only weapons were rifles of which they were not allowed many, and the main reason for this niggardliness was that they were known to have other arms from the illegal Hagana. It is unlikely that the Administration ever wished this Jewish police to be a serious counter to the rebellion. It was probably intended as a Dogberry organisation, but, as already noted in Wingate's adventure with the armed girl, the settlers carried out their duties with seriousness and self-discipline. Wingate made their little police force into the beginnings of the Army of Israel.

At Tirat Tsevi he first put the results of many months of study to practical use. He had worked out likely paths of entry for the arms smuggling. He took out little patrols of the settlement police and watched these paths. He went to the Jordan frontier and once again " the otter " looked for fords. He found them. He would return to Jerusalem to verify observations and obtain more information and then go back to his round of the settlements. In these first explora-

[1] Lieut.-Col. H. E. Bredin, D.S.O., M.C.
[2] In 1937 there were 3,881 Jewish supernumerary police. In 1938 this figure had dropped to 1,268 (for reasons not explained). There was also a Jewish Railway Police which never seems to have been called out. *Annual Reports to the Council of the League of Nations.* Colonial Office. 1937 and 1938. H.M.S.O.

tions he still had Jewish suspicion to contend with, lively testimony
to the extent of the pro-Arab sentiment of the British in Palestine.
One of his visits was to the settlement of Afikim near the junction
of the Jordan and the Sea of Galilee, and one of the settlers, Zvi
Brenner, later made a record of his first encounter with Wingate.
" I had not yet heard anything about him," wrote Zvi Brenner,
" and I regarded him as one of those Englishmen who just came to
see our settlement. But the moment we got into conversation I
realised that he was a very strange person. He displayed no enthusiasm
about our achievements, but kept on asking questions about facts,
and always talked to the point, and as the conversation went on, I
felt that there was a marked difference between him and all those
Englishmen we had met before. He inquired particularly about our
arms and defence arrangements, and when we found out that he was
an officer of the Intelligence Service, we became all the more reserved
and cautious."[1]

When this brief tour was finished Wingate went to Haifa and put
a proposition to Brigadier Evetts : namely that he, Wingate, should be
given the task of organising night patrols recruited from the Jewish
supernumerary police with a " stiffening " of British officers and men,
these patrols to operate from the settlements. It was only by regular
night operations, he said, that the arms-smuggling and the entry of
raiders could be decisively countered : the rebellion was essentially a
night attack. Both the Brigadier and his Brigade-Major Arthur Dove
liked Wingate's plan and together the three of them drew up a scheme
in some detail. Among other things they decided that the kind of
patrol-force they had in mind should be known as the " Special Night
Squads." The next thing was to obtain the agreement of Headquarters.
For this purpose Wingate went back to Jerusalem.[2]

---

[1] A paper by Zvi Brenner given to the writer by Colonel Rivlin of the Archives
Division, Israel Ministry of Defence. The same paper is quoted, with many additions and
alterations in *Gideon Goes To War*. As noted Mr. Mosley seems to have consulted an
erroneous version.

[2] The reader must be warned at the outset that in tracing the origins and achievements
of the S.N.S. the writer has not been able to follow any full official record. The War
Diaries of 16 Infantry Brigade from 1937–1939 are no longer in existence. It seems that
no copies were retained at the War Office and that the originals were transferred from
Palestine to G.H.Q., Middle East, some time before 1942 and then lost in the destruction
of documents in the summer of that year when the Afrika Korps reached El Alamein.
The writer is mainly guided by the recollections of Sir John Evetts, Major-General Dove,
Brigadier Wieler, Brigadier Dudley Clarke Colonel Bredin, Colonel Antony Simonds,
Colonel Chaim Laskov, Colonel Israel Carmi, Mr Avram Akavia, Colonel Yeheskiel
Sachar, Mr. Avram Dekell, Mr. Zvi Brenner, Mr. Jose Hamburger, Mr. Dov Josef,
Professor Rattner and Mr. Ezra Danin. There is some documentation in Zvi Brenner's
paper aforementioned, and in a Jewish record called *The Saga of the Squad* a personal
recollection of life in the S.N.S., written in Hebrew and translated for the writer by Miss
Denman of the Zionist Organisation. Much light on the S.N.S. is to be found in Wingate's
Complaint to the Sovereign written in 1939, in a paper given to Sir Edmund Ironside in June

There was considerable objection at Headquarters. To allow Jews to take part in offensive military operations of any kind was to set aside one of the few stable principles of the regime, namely the avoidance of any line of action which could bring Jews and Arabs into armed conflict. It was not a senseless objection, but to Wingate, with all his obstinacy aroused, it was based on nothing but ignorance, prejudice and stupidity of the most hateful kind. He made his views abundantly and woundingly clear to his fellow-officers. He made enemies of many of them. They sneered at him and said that if he got what he wanted it would be because no one in Jerusalem could bear with him any more, and there is no doubt that he was very difficult to bear with. It must be supposed that he was tempted to frequent outbreaks of rage, and that at many moments of crisis he held himself in check to avoid an irreparable breach, for he was negotiating for something which in literal terms could be described as the ambition of his soul.

The manner of his returning to the north seems to have been very strange. It is believed on good authority (but the place and date are not certain) that Wingate obtained official approval from a personal interview with the Force Commander. Wavell was not, by the standards of generals, difficult of access, but Wingate found him so, and believed that to achieve a meeting he needed to employ extraordinary and almost violent means. The general usually visited posts by aeroplane, but one day he set out on a visit to one of the military stations by car. Wingate knew the road and the hour and was waiting for him. When the outriders of the escort had passed, and the general's car came in sight, Wingate stepped into the road and held up his hand. In those days in Palestine, when anyone in uniform held up his hand to a car it stopped. As soon as the general's car had stopped Wingate climbed in, told the driver to continue, explained to Sir Archibald Wavell that he had an important communication to make, and then with his fervour and eloquence, and perhaps with some of the charm he could use on occasion, he poured out all that was pent up in his mind—and his heart. He told Wavell what he had discovered in his recent tour of duty, and with the passion with which he was often to sway reluctant converts he put before him the plan for the Special Night Squads, for the formation and training of patrols recruited partly from volunteers in the Army under Wavell's command and partly

---

1939, in a letter to General Sir Robert Haining from Wing-Commander Ritchie written a month later, and in a letter of protest from Wingate to Brigadier Evetts of January, 1939. The authorities and documents are not meagre in quantity or quality but more margin of error must remain than would be the case if a precise record made at the time had been available. The evidence is often in conflict.

from the only friends which Great Britain had in that part of the world. Wavell was a fine judge of character; he could distinguish between valuable and worthless enthusiasm, between obsessed cranks and men driven forward by the power of irresistible ideas. It is unlikely that he had much sympathy with Wingate's Zionism, but he clearly recognised that it generated energy which he could use to some purpose. He was the last man to be annoyed by juniors jumping into his car provided that they had something interesting to tell him. He gave his assent to the scheme.

This success was not decisive. Between winning the support of the Commander and obtaining what he wanted there were still many obstacles to surmount, some expectable, some not. One of the first difficulties, and the least expected, was to get the co-operation of the Jews. As soon as he had official authority, Wingate went to Haifa to consult with Wilenski. He told his friend about the scheme he had planned with Evetts and Dove and the agreement of the Commander. He said he now wanted him to get into immediate touch with one of the principal military chiefs[1] of Hagana, Eliahu Golomb, and obtain an undertaking from him that the illegal Jewish army would supply the Special Night Squads with drafts of its best men. Wilenski and Hacohen had never ceased from their endeavours to persuade their fellow Zionists of Wingate's sincerity and value to their cause. They had succeeded to some extent but as Zvi Brenner's evidence makes clear there was still much misgiving among Jews about " Hayedid Shelkha." The suspiciousness which comes of long memories of persecution was not to be dissolved in a single year, and though Wingate's Zionism was accepted by many people for the genuine thing it was, his proposal that he should lead Jews into mass-service with the British was received with doubt and distaste. It was against the policy of self-restraint, and offended the belief of many Zionist leaders that one of their first objectives should be to reach a *modus vivendi* with the Moslem inhabitants. Moreover the odd situation of the Jews in Palestine would become positively sinister in its oddness if their illegal army became a recruiting ground for the armed forces of the British Crown! So, in spite of considerable negotiation by Wilenski, an answer was sent to Wingate in Jerusalem that Hagana personnel could not be made available for the patrols.

As was to be expected the recipient of this message flew into a passion of anger. His first act was to send a message to Zazlani that he could not have a Hebrew lesson that evening—strange expression of his displeasure with Israel! He decided that he must have the matter

---

[1] Hagana was commanded on a Committee basis. There was no over-all single commander at any time. E. Yolan and Professor Rattner.

out with someone at the head of Zionist affairs and asked for an immediate interview with Moshe Shertock. He was given an appointment at the Jewish Agency Headquarters in Jerusalem. He went in his best uniform, on fire with rage, but in full control of himself. He remained standing throughout the interview. Shertock confirmed the decision of Eliahu Golomb. The conversation was short and concluded with a well-calculated *coup de théâtre*. Timing his words well, we may suppose, Wingate said : " Shertock, why do you spend so much time flirting with your enemies and ignoring the help of your friends ? " Then he left the room.

The next morning in Haifa Wilenski received a long-distance telephone call from Shertock. The latter gave the other an account of the interview at the end of which he said : " Your friend shouted at me but all the same he impressed me. On reflection I am sorry that we did not take your advice about him." With Shertock's support added to Wilenski's the opposition gave way and instructions went out to Hagana that " Hayedid " Wingate was to be treated with full confidence. The decision to withhold Hagana personnel was withdrawn.

In the British part of the negotiation, ground which had been won was lost. In the first part of April Sir Archibald Wavell was transferred from Palestine to the Southern Command in England and was succeeded by Lieutenant-General Sir Robert Haining. There was no reason to suppose that the new commander would welcome Wingate's novel plans with the acclaim of his predecessor, and some reason to suppose that he might insist on a strict adherence to more orthodox methods.[1] The situation now was that Wingate was well supported in Haifa, but in Jerusalem (in part through his faults of arrogance) he lacked for allies. His immediate superior was an Air Force officer, Wing-Commander Ritchie, and it cannot be said that he and Wingate were in perfect accord. Wingate was rarely in accord with his immediate superiors, and in this particular case, there was the strain of a mystical loyalty to intensify the nearly inevitable conflict. In the result one must recognise Ritchie's fairness and patience. Wingate hardly considered himself a subordinate, and when he carried out the Wing-Commander's orders he did so in the most high-handed and independent fashion. He seems to have made little attempt to conciliate his superiors even now while the decision to organise the Special Night Squads was in suspense. In April Ritchie sent Wingate on a second tour of the north.

A month or so before this time, in March, a new agricultural

[1] This is suggested in a letter from Wing-Commander Ritchie to General Haining of 13th July, 1939.

settlement had been founded on the Lebanese frontier, about five miles inland from the Mediterranean coast. It was called Hanita. It was an outpost of more military character than others of the Kibbutzim, being situated in a danger zone. Children were not allowed to live there. It had ninety inhabitants and consisted of a group of pre-fabricated houses which had been brought in three hundred lorries and erected within forty-eight hours. Immediately on its completion, before the protecting walls had been finished, raiders had descended on the place. There had been a skirmish in which the special constable in charge, Yakov Berger, a Hagana commander of Jerusalem, had been killed. His place was taken by Zvi Ben Ya'akov, also a Hagana chief. A body of forty Jewish Supernumerary Police were sent with him to act as a protective garrison. It was a place whose life and atmosphere must have been similar to what our ancestors knew in the little Roman camps on Hadrian's Wall.

One day in April Wingate arrived. He was dressed in uniform but without any badges of rank, his only luggage being a rucksack. He had with him a collection of maps, a rifle, a couple of pistols, and a Bible. He had two requests: to see Ben Ya'akov immediately, and for his weapons to be cleaned.[1] As soon as he had met the chief of the settlement he demanded to know the plan of defence. Ben Ya'akov explained the disposition of guards round the walls. Wingate said: " Why are you defending this place from the inside and not from a picket-line outside ? " There was general puzzlement. It was ex-plained that it would be difficult to supply munitions to outposts. Wingate asked why. Because, said Ben Ya'akov, Hagana weapons were illegal and had to be kept underground thus making any but defence from within virtually impossible. Wingate looked puzzled in turn. The contortions and confusions of the mandatory policy could often surprise the most experienced. At length he said that defence from outside was essential and that he intended to organise patrols. It was agreed that he should do so, but not without reluctance. There was still some doubt as to his motives.[2] Among the settlers was Zvi Brenner who had been moved from Afikim to help in the defence of Hanita. His record of what happened during Wingate's visit is of considerable interest.

" My next meeting with Wingate was at Hanita. We regarded him already as a friend, but still an Englishman. Zvi Ben Ya'akov, the head of the settlement, told me about an Englishman, who had brought him a letter from Eliahu Golomb, asking us to show him everything, and not to be afraid because he was one of us. I was still against it, and decided to sleep in the same tent where Wingate stayed, so as to

[1] Mr. Jose Hamburger.   [2] Colonel Israel Carmi.

be able to watch his steps, which was a very hard thing to do with a man like Wingate.

" In those days no one was allowed to leave the settlement without the express permission of the commander, but Wingate used to disappear and return after a couple of hours. We had meanwhile searched for him in vain, whilst he had thoroughly explored the vicinity. The fact that Wingate moved so far away from our settlement and always returned safely, made many of our people sceptical as to his real intentions, and they suspected him of having some connection with the armed Arab gangs.

" One day Wingate asked me to come out with him for a walk, and I went to Zvi Ben Ya'akov and told him about it. In those days we never left Hanita without an escort of a well-organised squad, equipped with the best available arms, and Zvi said, ' Well, I shall give him about thirty men and let him go.' Wingate, of course, was far from agreeing to such a proposal, and after a lengthy discussion finally gave his consent for another man to join us.

" We moved far away from our base, and the farther we got, the smaller became our chances of ever coming back alive. Wingate walked all the time about a hundred yards ahead of us, and when we reached the hills, we stopped to have a rest. And then Wingate revealed to us the true aim of our military mission. He intended to move to a particular house, situated on the other side of the road. The house had served as a base for those Arabs who had attacked Afikim, and he wanted to go over and see what was in it. I felt ashamed to tell him how much scared I was, and suggested that we had better return to Hanita to bring up reinforcements, but Wingate said we should just stay here and wait, and he would go alone, and if he did not return within a certain time, we should set out on our way home. When the time limit had elapsed, we marched back to our settlement, and told the others what had happened. We assumed that he had been killed and gave up all hopes, and were deeply worried as to how we should explain the whole matter to the military authorities.

" We were just talking about the event, when all of a sudden Wingate walked in, and told us that he had searched the place for arms and that everything was O.K. He then advised us to change our tactics. Instead of defending the colony from inside, we should go out and meet the enemy in the open, near his villages. This was something entirely new for us, and we had still no experience in that kind of warfare.

" He was permitted to go out with a platoon, but objected, and picked out seven of our men. When we reached the Lebanese border, we sat down for a few minutes, and Wingate told us that he was trying to discover the routes on which Arab gangs infiltrated into the country. 'There are two ways to do the job,' Wingate said, ' one is to sit down and write a report, and the alternative is to go to the spot and obtain results,' and that was the way he liked to do things. We admired the way Wingate walked during the night, and his ability of finding always the right direction. Some of our people were born in Palestine and knew the country well, but they all agreed that they would never have found their way.

" During the march one of our boys fainted, and we had to carry him to the nearest spring for water, while two of us returned to Hanita to bring a donkey, but Wingate managed to bring him back to full consciousness. We had originally planned to be back at 10.00 o'clock in the evening, but returned instead at 7.00 o'clock the following morning, from what turned out to be the greatest military experience we ever had."[1]

The record politely obscures the fact that on this first reconnaissance Wingate did in fact cross over into the Lebanon.[2] From the first he taught the settlers the principle that defence must never be passive but adventurous, and in order to teach the lesson he took large risks. If the Jerusalem authorities had discovered that even before he had authority to organise patrols he was committing breaches of international law, the whole scheme would certainly have foundered on that alone. But they did not discover. They learned instead that while he was still at Hanita, on the 22nd of April, there was an attack in strength by Fawzi Kawakji's raiders. Two settlers were killed. Wingate took charge of the defence and in classic military style visited the improvised picket-line and heartened the men. These settlers knew nothing of field-craft and battle-drill except what they had discovered for themselves in hard experience. They had been taught how to handle and fire a gun, nothing else. Wingate found Zvi Brenner manning one post by himself. By his side lay a dead man. He was evidently in a state of nervousness. Wingate crouched by his side and put a hand on his shoulder. He said : " You are doing the greatest thing you can, and you are much stronger than they are. They are afraid to come near you." He was quite right. The Arabs, meeting opposition, called off the attack. This was not only Zvi Brenner's first experience of battle, but Wingate's also.

When he had completed a round of northern settlements and

---

[1] Zvi Brenner. The first sentence of the record has been edited for the sake of clarity, otherwise the original is followed. Israel Ministry of Defence Records.
[2] Hamburger and independently Carmi.

reported to Brigadier Evetts, Wingate went back to Jerusalem at the beginning of May. The situation was now favourable to what he wanted. General Haining had decided on new dispositions as follows : having only two infantry brigades (six battalions) and one armoured-car company as his ground forces,[1] the system of mobile columns which had kept the country patrolled was suppressed in favour of a system of pickets in the more populated areas. This was in accordance with orthodox theory in that the rebellion having been effectively countered here, a picket system would have the effect of re-enforcing success. In the meantime the " Tegart Wall " was being built in the north : a wire-entanglement fence equipped with subsidiary defence works and strong-points stretching along the eastern part of the northern frontier.[2] (This was being put up by David Hacohen using both Jewish and Arab technicians and labourers.) It was not yet complete. The irregulars led by Fawzi Kawakji had recently taken to a new and exasperating form of sabotage, namely wrecking the Iraq Petroleum Company's pipe-line by blowing holes in it at night at scattered points. Since the beginning of April hardly a night had passed without several and successful sabotaging raids. The plan to organise night patrols in the area of the pipe-line, though not liked by the Commander, undoubtedly fitted in with his general scheme.[3]

Yet even now there were obstacles to be overcome before the Special Night Squads were a fully accomplished fact, and an odd thing to be noticed here is that the last obstacle was of Wingate's own making. When he came back to Jerusalem with his latest reports on the clandestine movements of the raiders Wing-Commander Ritchie decided that he should be posted to the north, to Nazareth, where he would open and take charge of a military intelligence centre. Here Wingate would be in the area where he intended his night squads to operate ; he would be under 16th Infantry Brigade orders once more, and he knew that he could count on the Brigadier's support in the raising of his little force. It is natural to suppose therefore that the Wing-Commander's latest instructions must have been congenial to Wingate, but strangely enough he resisted them. Possibly he suspected that a further assignment as an intelligence officer doing general Intelligence work would give the authorities the means to drop his proposal for organising and commanding patrols ; possibly he preferred not to be burdened with orders which he had no intention of obeying in a literal sense. At all events he told his superior that he objected to the proposed mission on the grounds that he " refused to

[1] *Annual Report.* 1938. Colonial Office.
[2] Designed by Sir Charles Tegart, K.C.I.E., C.S.I., M.V.O.
[3] Evetts. Dove.

spy on the Jews." Ritchie over-ruled the objection and sent him to the
north. Arrived there Wingate immediately delegated all his Nazareth
duties to the Brigade Liaison Officer and bent his mind and all his
prodigious energy to the formation of the Special Night Squads.
As he knew he would, he received support from Brigadier Evetts
who expressed himself thus : " You chase them by night and I'll
chase them by day." Sir Robert Haining acquiesced in the situation.
In May he gave the long-awaited order for the formation of the S.N.S.,
with misgiving.[1]

Wingate made his Headquarters at a settlement called Ein Harod,
half-way between Afula and Beisan. It had the advantage of being
situated north of his water supply, the River Harod (for he remembered
King Saul's tactical error) ; it was conveniently near the pipe-line,
his main responsibility, and it also had the advantage of being only
twenty miles from Nazareth, for the fiction that his main concern was
the new Intelligence centre needed to be maintained. When the
organisation was completed he maintained two platoons in all the
S.N.S. posts. They numbered four including the Headquarters, the
others being at Geva, a couple of miles west of Ein Harod ; at Tel
Amal,[2] about ten miles south-west, and at Kinneret on the Sea of
Galilee. Except for Kinneret all these places are in the plain of
Esdraelon and near Jezreel, the capital of the ancient Kingdom of
Israel ; they are all in the country where in the days of the Judges
Gideon fought the Midianites and " the children of the East." The
River Harod is where Gideon chose his men from watching how they
drank.[3] There is no doubt that the thought of this saviour of the
Chosen People was constantly in Wingate's mind.

In May his second-in-command, Lieutenant Bredin of the Royal
Ulster Rifles, arrived at Ein Harod. He had no idea on what duty he
had been sent. Wingate, whom Bredin had never met before, did
nothing to dispel the mystery. He met him on the road near the settlement. " Are you Bredin ? " Wingate said. " All right. Come on."
With Bredin came three British officers and thirty-six volunteers from
16th Infantry Brigade. Hagana had given about eighty men. By
obtaining further men from the Jewish supernumerary police in the
settlements he was able to form nine patrols.[4] The month was taken

---

[1] Information obtained at the War Office.
[2] Now called Nir David.
[3] " So he brought down the people unto the water : and the Lord said unto Gideon,
Every one that lappeth of the water with his tongue, as a dog lappeth, him shalt thou set by
himself ; likewise every one that boweth down upon his knees to drink. And the number
of them that lapped, *putting* their hand to their mouth, were three hundred men : but all
the rest of the people bowed down upon their knees to drink water." *Judges* VII.
[4] The figures are taken from Wingate's paper addressed to Sir Edmund Ironside.—
W.P.I.

up with preliminary training, organising an administration, the choice and collection of equipment from 16th Infantry Brigade and other accessories from his Jewish friends in Haifa. He decided that the members of his force would be armed with rifles, (ammunition in bandoliers), hand grenades, and that they should carry a special torch he had devised, an electric flare affixed to the end of a pole to enable men to signal to each other over the scrub. The torches were manufactured in Haifa. For uniform he chose blue police shirts, linen trousers, light rubber-soled canvas shoes, and the broad-brimmed hat of the Australian Army. He relied on Wilenski to obtain much of this and surprised his friend by insisting on the hats being ordered from London. This was expensive and so, since the needed sum had to be found from the Hagana exchequer, Wilenski referred the matter to Moshe Shertock. Neither of them approved of spending money on such frivolities but Wingate insisted that this was the kind of detail which was apt to impress his countrymen favourably, and so the hats were duly ordered and sent out, Wilenski facing much renewed chaff about " Hayedid Shelkha." Wingate himself usually wore an old-fashioned military pith-helmet, a bucket-like thing such as might have crowned Lord Wolseley's head fifty years earlier. He had bought it in London before setting out for Haifa in 1936 and he developed a superstitious affection for the hideous object. He wore it (or its successor) on all his campaigns and more than one crude drawing of it is to be found in his note-books.

On the 3rd of June a Special Night Squad went into action for the first time. It is to be supposed that most of the squads, rough and inexperienced as they were, had been out several times before, but on this night there was something resembling an engagement. There is no detailed record. It is impossible to be sure of what happened, but it seems probable that Wingate went out from Ein Harod with seven of the Hagana members of his miniature force, and surprised a gang of saboteurs. Shots from both sides. The saboteurs bolted which meant advantage one way ; signs later that two Arabs had been wounded.[1] Enough to report. Back in Ein Harod the shots had been heard. Through the small hours before dawn the sentry on the tower awaited the return in wretched suspense. Then by the early light he saw the little patrol coming over the brow of a hill and he counted them one by one up to eight. It was a victory. But the fruits had to be waited for. They were satisfactory. For a couple of days there was no further sabotage of the pipe-line.

The first " battle " in which this strange little army took part

---

[1] The only mention of this engagement is in Wingate's letter to Evetts (31.1.39). W.P.I.

occurred on the 11th of June. Again there is no contemporary report, but it is possible to give the course of it with a tolerable degree of probability. Two mixed patrols, consisting each of one British officer and twenty men (ten soldiers from the Royal Ulster Rifles and ten Jewish constables), left Ein Harod at evening for the pipe-line to the north. Following Wingate's principle that " in Palestine someone is always watching you," the patrols left Headquarters after dark in civilian cars heading south-east for Beisan. Between Ein Harod and that town they dropped off the cars at intervals, assembling by arranged signals and going north across country. They had already evolved their classic march formation. First went two outposts armed with grenades marching twenty yards apart. Then came the scouts maintaining the same mutual distance. Then came the main body marching in single file. Wingate usually took one of the scout positions, as did most of his officers. On this night when they reached the pipe-line they marched along it in a zigzag path, crossing and recrossing, making wide sweeps over the area. They came to a little hamlet east of Afula called Danna. By a wonderful coincidence, as they neared this place a raiding gang cut the line, only about three hundred yards away. There was a violent explosion. The grenade-throwers ran forward under covering fire from both patrols, and chased the gang into Danna. The patrols surrounded the place and in the fight which followed two raiders were killed, three wounded, and six captured with their weapons.[1] Wingate had grown to suspect the claims for enemy casualties in official reports and he was determined that his own should be supported by proof. Before returning to Ein Harod in the morning he took the corpses to the police station at Afula for identification. It was his invariable custom in Palestine to bring bodies to the nearest police station after an affray. For some days again there was no sabotage on the pipe-line.

The attack was not allowed to slacken. Throughout June patrols were maintained every night over an increasingly large area ; training and operation were not sharply divided, indeed to a large extent the squadsmen were trained through taking part in operations. After a few days of instruction and practice by day the newly-joined recruit found himself on a night patrol, often in an engagement. It is the opinion of those who had experience of life in the little force that after three weeks under Wingate a squadsman was made a soldier. The original system of service in the S.N.S. was as follows : men were on duty for a fortnight at a time, during which they went on patrol on nine or ten nights ; then after their term of duty they were given

---

[1] Wingate to Evetts (31.1.39). The same action was described to the writer by Colonel Israel Carmi who took part.

a week's leave, after which they returned to camp for another fortnight. Of course, with sudden operational demands often coming
in, this roster was not always neatly followed. Wingate drove his
men hard. They said he was two men in one : on parade or exercise,
and above all on operations, he was a merciless tyrant who in fury
at a disregarded order, and especially at bad map-reading by one of his
Jewish recruits, new to military life, would not only upbraid the
offender with wrathful language but would strike at him. If a man
coughed or made any needless noise on night operations he would
hit him with the butt end of his rifle. A Jewish sergeant once drank
at a pool before his men. Wingate landed him a blow between the
eyes. Yet off parade this ferocious authoritarian entirely " laid aside
his greatness " and mixed with his Jewish soldiers (not so much
with his British ones) as an equal. Surnames were rarely used. He
was often called " Hayedid " by his men, but more usually
" Orde." There was a patrol every night, not only from Ein Harod
but on the northern frontier from two temporary S.N.S. posts,
one at Aiyelet Hashahar, four miles south-west of Lake Hula, the
other at Hanita. The patrols were in six engagements during
June.[1]

Two of these engagements are of peculiar interest. One at the very
end of the month, on the 28th, nearly ended in disaster. A patrol of
eight, consisting of four Royal Ulsters and four Jewish squadsmen
under a British corporal went by day to the tents of the Beshattwe
nomads encamped near the River Jordan where the pipe-line crosses.
Their task was to tell these Arab tribesmen that sabotage on the line
had started again and to warn them that if they were found to be
implicated they would be deported *en masse* to Transjordan. (It is not
clear what if any authority Wingate had for this declaration of
policy.) The patrol went to their task in lorries which stood by.
The camp was in two divisions. In the first the patrol only found
quantities of what Doughty called " their harridanish women." They
went on to the second camp which lay in a parched gorge of this dead
country. Their foolhardiness soon got them into trouble. While
they were looking for someone with whom to parley they found
that they were surrounded from the heights by sixty to seventy men
who opened fire. With perfect courage they deployed and moved
with stealth to behind one of the hills to the north and drove their
attackers from it. The lorries misunderstood signals and both left for
Ein Harod. By accurate fire the little patrol kept their attackers at a

---

[1] Wingate to Evetts (31.1.39). He reports five, but another very small ambush operation
at Aiyelet Hashahar is reported by Zvi Brenner and can be identified as taking place in
June.

distance inflicting a few deaths on them, suffering none themselves. They reached the Zionist settlement of Beit Yosef. The lorries returned to the Beshattwe camp in the night towards dawn with reinforcements who engaged the Arabs again, inflicting about ten casualties.[1] What was remarkable about this action was that the Jews involved were subjected to one of the severest military tests, an ambush attack by overwhelming numbers in country unfavourable to them, and yet by military skill they turned their disaster to success although none of them could have had more than a month's training. The Jewish N.C.O. was a man greatly esteemed by Wingate. His name was Israel Carmi.

The other operation took place at Hanita on the 17th of June, eleven days before the Beshattwe ambush. Wingate arrived in the evening to find a plan being prepared on information given by an Arab. He suspected the informer but pretended confidence, and then devised a new plan with his men in case of treachery. They set out at nightfall, three patrols composed of Jewish squadsmen and men of the Royal West Kents led by Lieutenant Grove. They made for the village of Jurdeih about three miles to the east. Their maps were faulty and they found other little unmarked hamlets near Jurdeih. They found a Bedu tribesman prowling in the dark. They seized him and he told them where a gang of fifteen were sheltering for the night. They did not take him with them because they saw he was being watched by a woman from the nearby tents, and they feared that he or she would give the alarm. They moved on to surround the rebel shelter, but before they were in position the Bedu had run off to the Lebanon side of the frontier screaming: " My brothers! My brothers! The children of the Jews are upon us!" They heard him answered by the warning screech of a woman. As the squadsmen came into Jurdeih the gangsters ran out, saw their enemies, fired wide, were headed off by Lieutenant Grove's men, and ran in disorder over the frontier leaving two of their number killed by grenades. The S.N.S. had not time to search the shelter before fire signals to alert the rebels shone from the Lebanon. They prudently withdrew and reached Hanita at six in the morning.[2] It had not been a very triumphant operation but it turned out to have been more successful than they might have immediately supposed. There was a remarkable sequel.

The Mukhtar or headman of Jurdeih sent a deputation of notables to the Hanita chief, Joseph Fein, proposing an agreement for peace in

---

[1] Wingate to Evetts (31.1.39). Carmi.
[2] A detailed account of the operation written by Wingate immediately afterwards. W.P.I.

the future. For many weeks after this the little threatened outpost of Hanita was free from raiders, and the local gang which had been discomfited on the night of the 17th never attacked Hanita again.[1]

At the beginning of July the temporary S.N.S. outposts in the North, those of Aiyelet Hashahar and Hanita, were withdrawn as unnecessary after a battalion at full strength had been brought into the frontier area. The Special Night Squads were back once more to their four original stations. They had proved themselves and were about to come into their own, but before giving some account of their next actions it may be as well to consider the life led by the squadsmen and their officers, the day to day routine from which they set out on their expeditions.

The stations were very unlike British military camps. Their character was much more that of the Kibbutzim on which they were centered. Despite Wingate's autocratic rule, they were run as democracies and accounts of them tell of numerous meetings, and lobbyings before the meetings, and the election of committees to inquire into grievances. For there seem to have been multitudinous grievances, all taken up and exploited with that habitual skill in complaint which the Jews had brought with them from their years of oppression, and which often turns happier people against them. They sometimes suspected that their British comrades looked down on them because they tended, not unnaturally, to live to some extent separately. They sometimes resented the better British rations and issues of clothes.[2] The administration of the stations was always haphazard due partly to the irregular nature of the force and perhaps to the fact that it was perplexingly supplied from two sources, from military Headquarters in Haifa, and from the still illegal Hagana (but legally), and also due to the fact that Wingate himself was as yet a very imperfect administrator, too intent on the major things, the acquisition of weapons and the planning of training and strategy, to concentrate equally on the humdrum details which are the secret of good organisation.[3] To a large extent he relied for provisions and such-like on a man called Noah Sonin whom he had met at Hanita. This man was one of the early pioneers, belonging to that rare generation of Zionists which had spent all its life in Palestine. He is remembered as a dark-haired bearded figure with the appearance and manner of a prophet of the Old Testament, and with eyes burning with a fanatic light. He seemed able to produce anything anywhere at the shortest notice : lorries, wire, drink, knives, anything. Nevertheless there seems to have been a continual shortage of clothing

---

[1] Wingate to Evetts (31.1.39).   [2] *The Saga of the Squad.*
[3] A. Simonds.

and tent pegs and other necessities, and, as aforetime, the people "murmured."

Under inadequate leadership the Special Night Squads would probably have melted away in failure. The Jews were prone to cynicism and the idea that they were being continually betrayed by the British was a fixed idea. Also they had an inner lack of confidence in their soldierly ability.[1] Wingate's vigorous leadership, skilful training, and the fact that he proved that Jews were superior in courage to Arabs gave the little force a sudden irresistible and dynamic unity, and in spite of all the murmuring, and the frequent breakdowns in discipline when "the Captain" and Bredin were away,[2] and their impatience (greater than that of ordinary soldiers) with the boredom of empty days in camp, the S.N.S. gradually became what Wingate secretly intended, the beginnings of a Jewish army. He himself set an example of work and energy beyond others' attainment. Long before reveille at 6.30 (unless he was out on an operation) he was about in the camp dressed in his ragged shorts and bush-shirt and his monstrous sun-helmet, and on a return from an exercise or an operation when all the rest of his party were too exhausted for anything but a collapse on a bed, he would inspect weapon-cleaning, look into the multitudinous complaints of the camp, take out his car for a visit to other stations or drive (at the usual nerve-racking speed) to Haifa for a conference with Brigadier Evetts, Major Dove or Major Wieler.[3] As men do when they are testing themselves he added gratuitously to the burden of toil and privation which was on him. A bath or a shower is the greatest luxury in a hot land but for some reason, probably following one of his experiments in physical well-being, he rarely had a bath at Ein Harod and preferred in his relaxed moments to lie naked on his bed in the little hot hut which he shared with his second-in-command, massaging his body with a brush. His passion for eating onions has been remarked. He had an equal passion for grapes. A couple of large bunches of grapes would sometimes be his meal for the day. Some of this was play-acting no doubt, but not to be confused with exhibitionism. Soldiers like a glitteringly well-turned-out leader. Equally they like a dervish. Of all men soldiers of the rank and file are the best judges of whether or no a man is authentic. These men, British and Jewish, never doubted Wingate.

With July, according to Wingate's own account, the Special Night Squads began their "really successful employment." From the

[1]Professor Rattner.   [2] The Saga of the Squad.
[3] Brigadier Leslie Wieler, C.B., C.B.E. He succeeded Arthur Dove as Brigade Major in Haifa in June, 1938.

Intelligence centre at Nazareth and the Jewish settlements they received abundant information which Wingate knew how to use. Meantime the conflict was preparing anew. The reverses suffered by saboteurs and the dispersal of gangs in June had infuriated rebel headquarters and the latter determined to strike again harder. The result was three main engagements between the S.N.S. and the gangs during July. In one of these Lieutenant Bredin commanded the squads, in the other two Wingate.

A little before midnight on the 5th, Bredin was leading a patrol of four Royal Ulster Rifles and five Jewish squadsmen around the pipe-line north of Ein Harod when they came to a hill near Danna, called Kaukab el Hawa on whose summit are the remains of the Crusader castle of Belvoir. Here they found a rebel force estimated at a hundred. The rebels saw them, opened fire and seriously wounded a rifleman and a Jew. Bredin immediately divided his own small force into two and initiated a pincer-movement up the hill. This was too much for the Arabs. They abandoned their impregnable position and ran away to safety.[1] It seems that when Fawzi Kawakji learned of this ignominious rout he made hasty preparations for a decisive stroke. Bredin's valiant escapade was the prelude to the largest engagement in which the S.N.S. took part. This may be called " the battle of Dabburiya." It was planned from known enemy intentions.

In the days after the dispersal of the gang on Kaukab el Hawa information came in from all sides of rebels on the move. They made an attack on Nazareth and were even able to hold it for one night, before being dispersed in the morning by men of the British battalion in the north. Wingate's car was spotted and fired on south of Beisan. Information came in that a large Arab force was secretly assembling between Dabburiya and Ein Mahil under a certain Shaykh Naif Zobi.[2] Wingate thereon decided to attack before the enemy.

Dabburiya is a little town about five miles east of Nazareth, immediately under Mount Tabor which is held by old tradition to be the place where Jesus Christ was transfigured before his apostles. Ein Mahil is a village about three miles north-west. There is a townlet called Iksal about two miles west of Dabburiya which should be memorised too. On the 10th of July Wingate called out the whole of his forces and placed them in siege round Dabburiya whither the rebels had gone for shelter behind a rough picket-line. With elaborate craft the movements of the squads were disguised. They left their stations in the short twilight, some travelling east, and Wingate's party travelling

[1] Wingate to Evetts (31.1.39).   [2] Wingate to Evetts (31.1.39.)

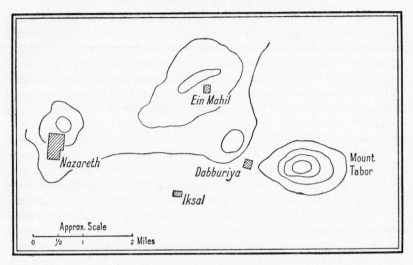

The Battle of Dabburiya

north to Tiberias with a party of girls in the car as further cover for
his intentions. Then after dark all the lorries travelled along the
Nazareth-Tiberias road, some going east, some west, dropping men
off at prearranged intervals, the lorries never slowing down. The
first object was to surround Dabburiya. A patrol of the Royal Ulsters
under Corporal MacConville armed with Lewis machine-guns went
with their trucks to a Jewish settlement called Mahanah Israel at the
foot of the Hill of Moreh about five miles south-west of the town.
A mixed patrol of the Royal Ulster Rifles and Jewish squadsmen under
Lieutenant Bredin stationed themselves in a copse near Iksal. Another
mixed patrol of Manchesters and squadsmen under Lieutenant Gray
approached Dabburiya from east of Mount Tabor and by the paths
south of it. (Zvi Brenner was among these.) Another mixed patrol
of Royal Ulsters and squadsmen approached from due south. The
main assault party under Wingate numbering about forty-five, and
including Royal West Kents, Royal Ulsters, and two platoons of Jewish
squadsmen, approached from the north. The rendezvous was for one
in the morning and was kept with a ragged punctuality which led to
trouble.

Much went wrong. The patrol from due south seems to have
attacked prematurely or to have approached too near Dabburiya. At
all events they ran into an ambush on the outskirts, found themselves
surrounded, were forced to go back. One of the squadsmen, Avram
Yoffe, was wounded and in the confusion a red Verey light was sent

up. This was the signal for help. Wingate saw it from the north and his party ran to their rendezvous with the Lewis gun party under MacConville. The latter was in position at a haystack half a mile or so west of the town. On nearing the haystack the Lewis gun party had found an Arab suspiciously crouched beneath it. They had shot him. The noise of the premature attack, of the shooting at the haystack, and the glare of the Verey light had alerted the rebels in the town. Surprise was lost. Wingate decided to open the assault immediately. He told MacConville to give him covering fire with the Lewis guns. He said : " Cover me in and cover me out." He then gave the signal for the attack from all sides, leading his own party first into Dabburiya. On their way, as they were rapidly marching to the assault from the haystack to the town, there was a further piece of blundering. Two of the Royal West Kents in Wingate's party had picked up Arab cloaks somewhere on the road and were wearing these for warmth. There was a cry among the squadsmen that Arabs were among them and there were shots at the two cloaked soldiers. No one was hurt but surprise was lost again. When Wingate and his men went into Dabburiya they were met by a volume of well-placed fire. The other columns moved in at the same time. The fight in the town was short and sharp and, because of the loss of surprise, Wingate's party soon found themselves nearly surrounded. They did enough for their purpose before going back, but they had to go back as quickly as they could to escape destruction. Corporal MacConville was waiting with his Lewis guns. He saw figures rushing towards him from Dabburiya. He took them for fleeing Arabs and opened fire. He killed one man and wounded another before he saw his mistake : these hurrying figures were Wingate's party in retreat. The fatal casualty was a squadsman, the wounded man was Wingate himself, struck in the right arm and both legs.

They carried him to the haystack and hastily bandaged him. Ten minutes or so later Lieutenant Bredin came back with his party from their assault. Wingate told him to take charge. Bredin urged him to go to hospital immediately in one of the trucks. Wingate would have none of that, told Bredin to get on with his job, and remained by the haystack, propped up in a sitting posture and in increasing pain. Bredin led a second assault, but by now the battle was nearly over. The Arab leader Shaykh Naif Zobi had fled and the gang were rapidly dispersing before daylight. Scared townsmen told of multitudes of wounded and dying carried away. Nine bodies were found in the Arab pickets.

As dawn drew near Wingate was still sitting by the haystack, tended by Israel Carmi and a British corporal. He refused to go till he knew more of what had happened. He was particularly worried about the column under Lieutenant Gray which had sent up the Verey light, for this party contained a large number of completely inexperienced Jewish squadsmen. In the first light Zvi Brenner was marching with a platoon of Jews from Mount Tabor to Mahanah Israel when he saw the group by the haystack and made his way there to report. Wingate asked him how he was.

" I'm all right," said Zvi Brenner.

" I heard that you'd all been wiped out," said Wingate.

Then, when he heard that in fact the column had suffered no casualties, he turned to Carmi and said, " Well now you can take me to hospital." But he did not mean what he said.

It seems that he was in that state of hectic nervous excitement that comes on a man after battle, especially after one that he has planned and commanded. Almost everything had gone wrong, as is known to be the case with all battles great or small, yet a fact inevitably emerged : the S.N.S. had been in their first sizeable action—and they had won it ! To retire from the " scene of victory," from the delights following, from the tumultuous discussions in mess, the interrogations which would show what had in fact happened, from the glad restlessness and chatter and bustle of men coming out of action, in order to go to bed in a hospital away from it all, was impossible for the man most responsible.

At first Wingate wanted to go to Ein Harod but was persuaded, with difficulty, that so long a journey was dangerous, and that with the long dusty drive his wounds might become septic. He insisted that instead he should go to Nazareth. Driven by his assailant Corporal MacConville he reached the Intelligence Centre early in the morning. There, it seems, he gave a first-hand report to his colleagues followed by another by telephone to the Orderly Officer at the Haifa Headquarters. He then demanded breakfast, not the plentiful dish of eggs and bacon and coffee that other returned warriors might have asked for but one of olives only, for olives, with grapes and onions, had become a favourite meal of this ever-experimenting dietician. Whenever hospital was mentioned he put the question aside with delaying answers. Breakfast over, he went to the map-room and began to plan further S.N.S. operations to follow up the battle of Dabburiya. He called for the most recent Intelligence reports and began to examine them. At length someone rang up Headquarters in Haifa and told the Brigade-Major that Wingate was wounded in three places, refused to go to hospital, and was otherwise behaving in a somewhat peculiar manner. The Brigade-Major said he would see to the matter and rang off. Shortly after this the telephone rang back at Nazareth.

Brigadier Evetts was on the line for Wingate. He told him that an ambulance was on the way, and when Wingate began to say something about Ein Harod the Brigadier told him that he was to go to hospital and that this was not merely a suggestion but a military order. That settled the matter.[1]

[1] This account of the battle of Dabburiya is based on Wingate's letter to Evetts (31. 1. 39.), and the records of Colonel Carmi, and R.S.M. MacConville, Colonel Bredin, Colonel Laskov and Zvi Brenner.

CHAPTER VIII

POLITICS AND THE SWORD
SHARPENED

WINGATE SPENT a fortnight in the Military Hospital at Sarafand, near Ramle, in reluctant and restless idleness, receiving numerous visitors, studying maps and reports, sketching out new plans and further operations, typing out memoranda and driving the nursing sisterhood mad. Lorna could not reach him before he left the hospital, being away in Scotland to escape the hot weather, and the only other person who might have quietened the patient, Dr. Weizmann, was also out of Palestine. (He sent a message through his sister, Dr. Anna Weizmann, urging Wingate not to expose himself needlessly in battle.) The fact has been remarked already that Wingate believed that health required men to intersperse active life with periods of lethargy; but this particular period of lethargy, coming enforced at the climax of a period of action, and causing him to lose precious training, could not be met so philosophically, and he spent it (as befitted the hot weather) in a state of tempestuous impatience.[1] The fortnight was not quite barren however. To occupy himself he produced among other written things a document of commanding interest in which he gave as fully as he ever did his views on the whole question of Palestine. It happened in this way. Just before the final establishment of the Special Night Squads, in May, Wingate had an interview with the members of the Woodhead Commission. When it was over he was asked by the Commissioners to submit what he had told them in writing.[2] This he now did. A point has been reached in the story where it may be convenient to consider again something of what was happening at large in the Mandated Territory of Palestine, and to record Wingate's brief appearance in the general political scene. (Later he expressed some annoyance that this appearance had been brief.)[3]

Between the 27th of April and the 3rd of August of 1938 the Palestine Partition Commission, the successor to the Commission

[1] Carmi.
[2] *Record of a Conversation between members of the Palestine Partition Commission and Captain O. C. Wingate.* Lent by Brigadier Leslie Wieler.
[3] Evetts.

headed by Lord Peel, held fifty-three secret and two public sessions in Jerusalem.[1] The Commission was charged with recommending practical steps whereby the Peel Report could be translated into action. They toured both Palestine and Transjordan. They heard a multitude of witnesses, but, as with the Peel Commission the Arabs held aloof. This time Arab tactics succeeded, and the 1938 Commission found themselves the prey of doubt and second thoughts. The chairman was Sir John Woodhead, one of the most eminent civil servants of his day. Like the majority of his colleagues[2] he had massive experience of administration in India; his lifelong task had been the maintenance of law against the claims of enthusiasm and fanaticism. It is not fanciful to say that the Woodhead Commission was bent on achieving a peace of prosaic reason in a situation which had been created twenty years before in a mood of exalted idealism reckless of the claims of common sense. Acting from the best motives they undid the work of their predecessor. The process was more or less inevitable. The Balfour Declaration had called on civil servants to carry out a policy that was radically against their training. Poets could grasp it more easily. Shakespeare, who seems to have gone along with the vulgar anti-Semitism of his time, and probably never met a Jew in his life, showed more understanding of Zionism than any Administrator or Commissioner when he made his villainous Shylock cry to the world : " An oath ! An oath ! I have an oath in Heaven ! Shall I lay perjury upon my soul ? No, not for Venice ! " This sort of language had never been to the taste of a British Government and was not understood by the ministry of Neville Chamberlain. Had it been so, they might not have failed as they did.

It is not quite clear whether Wingate was summoned to give evidence at one of the sessions, as the Commissioners did not give the names of individual witnesses. It seems most likely that he was introduced to the members of the Commission after an adjournment and given an opportunity to submit his views " off the record." An interesting fact about this meeting is that he was introduced by General Haining.

Wingate began, at the invitation of the Commissioners, by discussing the internal security of the country and he took the opportunity to enter a strong plea for the policy of combining British strategy with enlarged use of the Jewish supernumerary police ; he evidently

---

[1] *Annual Report to the League of Nations.* Colonial Office.

[2] Sir Alison Russell, K.C., Mr. (now Sir) A. P. Waterfield, C.B., Mr. T. Reid, C.M.G. With the exception of Sir Alison Russell, the members of the Commission were all members of the I.C.S. In the final report Sir Alison Russell and Mr. Reid put considerable reservations on record, Sir Alison in a pro-Zionist sense, Mr. Reid in protest against any plan for partition.

tried to obtain the Commission's support for the still debatable Special Night Squads, and in the course of doing so he summarised what in his view were the proper duties of District Commissioners, animadverting on the failure of these people to live up to them. This may sound as though he behaved in an intolerably pretentious manner but it is to be noted that his audience heard him with interest and encouraged him to tell all that was on his mind. He spoke as a Zionist apologist. At one point he said : " . . . such advance as the Arab has made since the granting of the Mandate had been principally in the neighbourhood of Jewish areas and colonies, [and] is the result of Jewish influence. . . . The most savage and ignorant communities, and most the prey of irresponsible agitation, are precisely those . . . furthest removed from Jewish influence. . . . These communities . . . have now gained the upper hand. . . . The rebellion of the past two years has resulted in the virtual stoppage of immigration and the arresting of the development of the Jewish National Home [and as a result] there is no longer any hope that more moderate [Arab] counsels will prevail. The Arabs are now ruled by either fanatical or cynical factions, neither of which have either faith [in] or affection for H.M.G." Like all partisans he gravely underestimated sense and sincerity on the other side.

During the course of this opening discussion, he gave, for whatever high motives, an absurdly misleading picture of himself to the Woodhead Commission. He concluded the first section of his account as follows : " I would like here to record the fact that, before giving my views on political or quasi-political subjects, I pointed out that, although it had been my duty for the past two years to study the political situation (I have been in fact the one officer in the country who has this duty) yet I had no title officially to speak on such matters other than to my own immediate superiors. This obligation I had always scrupulously observed and before making an exception I asked the Commission's permission to do so." He presumably made a very strong distinction between what he said as an official, and what he said " off the record, " but it would have been better to have said nothing. In January he had made the acquaintance of two prominent British Zionists, Mrs. Dugdale[1] and Victor Cazalet.[2] She recorded her first meeting and her diary may be quoted as a corrective to Wingate's improbable self-portrait. " January 23. . . . He (Wingate) told us that Ibn Saud's London representative had wired to Ibn Saud . . . that he understood a joint memorandum from all the Arab Kings on the subject of Palestine would be acceptable to H.M.G. This confirms

[1] Mrs. Edgar Dugdale, Arthur Balfour's niece and biographer.
[2] Victor Cazalet, a Conservative M.P. and Zionist.

Chaim's conviction of F.O. intrigue. . . . Lucky for us that Wingate's fanatical Zionism gets the better of his sense of duty as an Intelligence Officer. He is clearly one of the instruments in God's hand."

In spite of his parade of official delicacy the Commissioners asked Wingate about political matters only. They may have recognised that, whatever his views, this man had gained more experience of the people of Palestine in two years than most officials managed to do in a long career.

One of their questions related to the sentiments of the Christian Arabs of Palestine, and his answer shows all his shrewdness. They had, he said, "a slave mentality. That is to say that it does not say what it thinks, but expresses views with an ulterior motive. . . . Their greatest dread is that they will be again subject to a Moslem power. The measure of this dread is their determination to conceal it from the community they fear. . . . Simultaneously . . . they cherish a strong dislike of the Jewish community due to the fact that the Jews beat them at their own game of financing and developing the country. . . . What the Christian Arab desires . . . is . . . the British Mandate. Failing that what he most fears, and for that very reason is determined to conceal the fear, is his inclusion in a Moslem state. He would prefer to be included in a Jewish state. He would then be sitting very pretty. Firstly he could make a great outcry. . . . Secondly he could wait and see whether he were likely to acquire in the Jewish state a position flattering to his vanity. . . . All this time the value of his property in the Jewish state would be rapidly appreciating." These views are debatable but the forensic skill with which Wingate presented them and turned them to Zionist advantage is remarkable. One may suspect that he had in mind George Antonius, a Christian Arab of polished mind, by far the most able of the Arab propagandists, who exerted considerable influence on his wide circle of European friends. If Wingate intended to discredit Antonius the blow was delivered with cunning.

The next question was as follows : What would be the effect of including Galilee in the Jewish State ? This fairly set him off on a vigorous exposition of his ideas concerning the whole question of the establishment of a Jewish State. "I should prefer the question put the other way," he began, "since . . . the effect of not including it would be far more serious." Many of the views he expressed have been described already and others concern dead or forgotten issues and need not be recalled. What should be remembered, however, and to Wingate's honour and justification, are his prognostications of what would happen as a result of a policy of caution regarding Jewish immigration. To understand the point of his remarks it should be recalled that in 1935 more than 61,000 Jews had been allowed to enter Palestine as immigrants, but that by 1938, the time of the Woodhead Commission, when the Jewish need was yet more terribly immediate, these numbers had sunk to 12,868.[1] Here is part of what Wingate said :

" The Jew is continually conscious of facts that the servant of Government has continually to be reminded of. He remembers that his great experiment has been brought to something like a dead stop by the British Government in response to the murderous attacks upon the latter by the Arab community. He has been told to have faith in the Government and to wait. . . He believes that he has been promised a State that will at least include Galilee. Such a settlement he is willing upon conditions, loyally to accept. But there is a limit in time to his patience, a limit in extent to his endurance. There are [extremist] counsels now in the Jewish camp which are slowly gathering weight, counsels which find their origin in the reaction of the Government to the Arab rebellion. . . ." These remarks may sound like truisms to-day. At the time they did not. A persistent British error was to take Jewish acquiescence for granted.

When a member of the Commission stated his objection to forcible transfers of population, Wingate was roused to strong protestation. He said that if this scruple was accepted, " then it would be found to apply to every act of Government in Palestine. It would mean that simply nothing could be done. No railways could be built, no roads made. All these acts involved arbitrary procedure in the interests of those concerned. Ultimately what this argument amounted to was that the Government of Palestine should do what the Arab majority wished. Well, there was no doubt as to what that was. The Arab majority wanted to cut the throat of every Jew and to thrust the British into the sea. . . . We can always employ the democratic argument to justify any inactivity we favour."

There were further questions regarding transfer of population, and the discussion touched on the basic problem of evicted tenants. " The Arab landlord," said Wingate, " who will most certainly try to leave his peasants in the lurch, must be compelled to set aside a certain percentage of the purchase money for the purpose of providing employment either on his new lands or elsewhere." He added that remaining peasants " will become the responsibility of the Jewish State, which will, in accordance with schemes already in contemplation, arrange for their profitable employment if possible upon the lands they now occupy, but in any case upon contiguous lands." This is the weakest passage in the record, and it can remind a reader of the facile optimism to be found in Theodore Herzl's book *Der Judenstaat*.

---

[1] *Annual Reports.* Colonial Office.

Inevitably Wingate had taken on some of the less sturdy mental habits of Zionist propaganda.

Towards the end of the meeting the discussion returned to security and here Wingate seized the opportunity to make a forecast of what would happen with the alienation of the Jews. His estimate is astonishing in its accuracy. " Every Jew in this country," he said, " whatever his antecedents or traditions, realises that he will one day have to fight for his country. The Jewish community has imposed upon itself a tremendous self-restraint that has too often been mistaken by British officials for timidity. Should the time ever come when the Jews have reason to believe either that they have been betrayed, or that their best hope lies in a complete reversal of their policy, we shall find that we are facing something very different from the Arab revolt. . . . It will be as a community that the Jews will act and not piecemeal as the Arabs have done." The reply was long and repetitive, and no more need be given of it except a curious remark at the end. " I feel," said Wingate, " that I lay myself open to a charge of partiality. I repudiate this charge. Nowadays people seem to imagine that impartiality means readiness to treat lies and truth the same, readiness to hold white as bad as black and black as good as white. I, on the contrary, believe that without integrity a man had much better not approach a problem at all. I came here with an open mind and I testify that I have seen. I believe that righteousness exalteth a nation and righteousness does not mean playing off one side against the other while you guard your own interests." It is not known how the Woodhead Commission received this unusual utterance.

The last questions concerned the value of a Jewish state, to British interests and to the Arab world. He answered by giving an outline of one of his favourite theories : that a Jewish state equipped for heavy industry and supporting an army subsidised by Great Britain would supply a large, dependable and immensely valuable arsenal and garrison such as would make the position of the British Empire in the Mediterranean impregnable. (This plan was not originated by Wingate but by Professor Lewis Namier who had put forward a scheme to this effect two years before.)[1] " The best hope of the Arab world," he said, " lies in the speedy creation of a Jewish State." In these final answers his forecasts were weakened by the fact that he took no note of the all-conditioning factor of oil.

In the bed next to his at the Sarafand military hospital was a young man on whose life Wingate was to have some influence. He was

[1] Vide *In the Margin of History* by Sir Lewis Namier.

Lieutenant Archie John Wavell, the son of the General. Their friendship which began now had interesting results much later.

While Wingate was lying impatiently on his sick-bed there occurred two events of importance to his little army. Brigadier Evetts was due to go home on leave in July but, before he left, he drafted a " citation " for the award to Wingate of the D.S.O. " for gallant and distinguished service in Palestine." On the night of the 13th of the month, two days after the battle of Dabburiya, Lieutenant Bredin took two squads along the pipe-line. At a place called Bira they found a large gang, the remnants of Shaykh Naif Zobi's army. They advanced on them from two sides and sent them flying leaving fourteen of their dead behind. Bredin was wounded. This little action completed the work of Dabburiya. For the rest of the month the pipe-line was left alone. The S.N.S. had by now learned their task and were proving that they were effective. People who had suspected that Wingate was an unbalanced fanatic changed their view of him. It was now that he began to be nicknamed in the half-joking half-respectful English fashion " The Lawrence of Judea." Success was coming his way at last.

He returned to Ein Harod on the 30th of July and was welcomed back with a feast prepared by the settlers and presided over by the Kibbutz chief, Wingate's closest friend there. At the end of the supper there were toasts and lengthy speeches in Hebrew and English which Bredin described as the " Jewish national sport," and to which the British troops present, thrust into the unfamiliar life of the settlements, listened with bewilderment and the enormous boredom to which British people are especially prone.[1] The last speech was by Wingate. He is remembered as saying that Britain as the Mandatory power had a sublime duty laid on her to be true to the Bible and the Holy Land ; by accepting the mandate England had accepted a great honour and a great privilege. He said in Hebrew : " God give it to us to slay the enemies of the Jews, for the enemies of the Jews are the enemies of all mankind."[2]

In the morning Corporal MacConville had orders to report to the Captain. The huge Irishman was dressed in his best. He attended the orderly room in a state of some apprehension. Wingate had said nothing to him about Dabburiya but there was no doubt that even if he had not known the facts of the case from the beginning, he knew them now. When the moment came MacConville entered, saluted, and stood ready to receive the outpourings which he had learned to expect from this wrathful man. Wingate looked up at him with his fierce blue eyes. He said : " MacConville, at Dabburiya we all made a great many mistakes. The needful thing for us is to learn from our

[1] Laskov. Carmi. MacConville.   [2] Ephraim Dekell.

mistakes." There was a pause. MacConville saluted and left. The matter was closed.

That night Wingate led all the S.N.S. on an operation in the country south-west of Beisan. This was not a pipe-line operation, according to the usual S.N.S. form, but a manœuvre to surprise caravans of smugglers from over the Jordan. "The otter" had by now a very full and accurate idea of the fords, and he calculated that the smugglers were likely to make for a place called Um Mejada'a in the Wadi Tubas, a valley which leads from Beisan to Nablus. To reach the hamlet they needed to cross some of the most difficult country in Palestine, not only over hills but across marshes in the plains, sometimes wading deep for what seemed long distances. After every wading through the marshes Wingate needed to change his bandages. A hot sand-bearing wind was blowing hard from the south so that when the squadsmen were not undergoing the ordeal by water they were wracked with the thirst which comes intolerably with the dust clouds. By accurate timing and perfect march discipline they reached Um Mejada'a at three in the morning. A few minutes before their arrival the smugglers, carrying arms and drugs on a string of camels and donkeys had moved into the village. The S.N.S. took up ambush positions. Before the first light the caravan, accompanied by about forty-five men, moved out. There was an ambush attack followed by pursuit and exchange of fire in the hills. Eleven smugglers were killed and four prisoners taken.[1] By the time this operation was over Wingate was unable to walk and had to be carried to the lorries on the main road. He could hardly speak. This is the only occasion when he is remembered to have broken down before physical strain while on an operation. He was just out of hospital, in poor training.[2]

The engagement at Um Mejada'a had a tragic consequence. It provoked the Arabs to a new ruse. For long they had mined the main roads. They now took to mining the little roads and paths and tracks leading to the fords. This led to a calamity which moved Wingate to grief and rage beyond his control.

The chief of the Kibbutz at Ein Harod was called Chaim Shturman. He was a pioneer belonging to the days when the first Jewish settlers came to Palestine from the Russian Empire ; he was one of the " Hashomer," the old-style watchman-guards from whom Hagana derived, romantic knights-errant comparable to the " Indian fighters " of American history. He had opposed the setting up of S.N.S. Headquarters at Ein Harod, had not much liked the whole venture when he first heard of it, dreading that it would result in Arab-Jewish warfare

---

[1] Wingate to Evetts (31.1.39) and Carmi.   [2] Carmi.

or at the very least in a permanent hostility between the two peoples. But when he met Wingate and recognised the ardour of his Zionism he changed his mind. They became closely attached. In the evenings they would be seen walking idly together, often saying nothing. Wingate is remembered saying, " Shturman's silence is better than other people's talk." The old pioneer was extraordinarily useful to him. He knew almost every single human being inhabiting the plain of Esdraelon and the valley of the Jordan. To the end he counselled moderation in all dealings between Jews and Arabs. In accordance with his piety he insisted that Arab prisoners kept in his settlement should be decently housed and fed and treated as guests. To him the Arabs were " the strangers in the land " and he remembered the admonitions in Leviticus, " Ye shall not vex him. But the stranger that dwelleth with you shall be unto you as one born among you, and thou shalt love him as thyself." One day Shturman and three friends were walking on a rarely frequented track south of Beisan. They saw figures looking like armed rebels lurking around. As they walked one of the four trod on a mine. Shturman was killed instantly with two of his companions. The survivor was able to find a car on the main road and drove back to Ein Harod.[1]

When the news came Wingate was lecturing in the main hall of the settlement, with Israel Carmi translating for him. The survivor told what had happened. At first the news seemed incomprehensible to Wingate, but when he understood he showed the immensity of the shock he had received. He said nothing for some moments, as though about to break down. Quickly he collected himself and shouted out orders that all squadsmen at Ein Harod were to fall in for action instantly. Men were scared for they had never seen him like this before. Within minutes all available squadsmen were piled into the lorries, ready to go. They were in Beisan within half an hour of the news arriving. They drove south, not bothering about any feint to hide what they were doing. They came to the place. Wingate's orders were that rebels in the neighbourhood of the crime were to be rounded up, and shot if they tried to escape. They were wild unconsidered orders made in the heat of the moment, and as a result some innocent loiterers were shot among fleeing rebels who returned the fire. It was a sudden unprepared raid, a mistake on Wingate's part, uncharacteristic of his teaching and practice.

It must be stressed that this was the only occasion in the career of the Special Night Squads when Wingate is known to have disregarded his own frequently given orders that the Arab population were to be scrupulously differentiated from the rebels. If it seems undeni-

[1] Dekell.

able that some bad things to the contrary happened in the S.N.S.,
it is equally undeniable that Wingate, except on this occasion, was
throughout an influence of restraint on the more reckless spirits
among his squadsmen, and insisted, even at peril, on humane conduct.
Many allegations were made against him, sometimes by shocked
Jewish followers who came from the decency of civilian surroundings.
None of the allegations, except those regarding the indiscriminate
shooting south of Beisan, can withstand scrutiny, and experience
shows that unidentifiable events are usually imaginary ones. Wingate
had many enemies in Palestine who (not without goading from him)
tried to discredit him. But when they came to make definite accusa-
tions they made none of the kind indicated here. He had many faults,
and he had a streak of harshness that occasionally played him false
as after the murder of Shturman, but the dark and perverted impulse
from which springs " man's inhumanity to man " was nowhere
in him.

To return to the story. With the success of the S.N.S. now established Wingate decided to enlarge his force for which purpose he bent
his energies towards new projects. In all the operations to date he had
succeeded in his surrounding manœuvres but not often in pursuit. He
decided to add a cavalry wing to his army, his intention being
apparently to conduct his operations in the last hour of night so that
in the visibility of breaking dawn his horsemen, fanning out suddenly,
might gallop after fleeing rebels and capture the remnants of discomfited gangs. He decided to raise this cavalry with the help of his
Jewish supporters. A liaison officer went to Ein Harod from the Jewish
Agency in order to conduct the negotiations. He was called Ephraim
Krassner,[1] whom Wingate, slow to memorise foreign names, always
called " Crashner." This man found Wingate, as most people did at
their first meeting, untidily dressed, not military in appearance at all,
looking " more like a professor than a soldier." Krassner had arrived
on a day when Wingate was receiving visitors. Chief among them was
Isaac Sadeh who had some fame among the Jews of Palestine as the
organiser of the " Plugot Sadeh " : the Sadeh patrols, a portent of the
S.N.S., which had operated against Arab insurgents around Jerusalem
at the beginning of the troubles. Joshuah Gordon, a prominent
Zionist politician and publicist, and Avram Ikar, chief officer of the
Jewish Supernumerary Police, were there too. After a while Wingate
drew Krassner aside to discuss business. He told him that he needed
thirty horses with saddles and bridles. Krassner was empowered to
agree. While they were discussing the matter Wingate peered at
Krassner " like a bird." He asked him whether he was a member of

---

[1] He has since changed his name to Dekell.

Hagana. Krassner said that he was. With some asperity Wingate asked him why he had not told him straight out instead of waiting to be asked. While Krassner expressed confusion Wingate said to him : " You do not trust me."

The thirty horses arrived and strenuous efforts were made to train cavalry, but the venture was abandoned after a short time. He had few fully taught horsemen and he found it took too long for practical purposes to train horses to lie down in battle so as to afford a ramp on which the rider might rest his gun for shooting. The cavalry never went into action. Concurrently with this abortive effort, went another in which the fantasy of his nature made a brief and astonishing appearance.

It will be remembered that his hero, Gideon of Ophrah, finally routed the Midianites and the children of the East through stampeding them by the unexpected use of torches and trumpets, as recorded in the seventh chapter of Judges: " So Gideon, and the three hundred men that were with him, came into the outside of the camp in the beginning of the middle watch ; and they had but newly set the watch: and they blew the trumpets, and brake the pitchers that were in their hands." (The pitchers concealed torches.) " And the three companies blew the trumpets, and brake the pitchers, and held the lamps in their left hands, and the trumpets in their right hands to blow withal: and they cried, The sword of the Lord, and of Gideon. And they stood every man in his place round about the camp : and all the host ran, and cried, and fled. And the three hundred blew the trumpets, and the Lord set every man's sword against his fellow, even throughout all the host : and the host fled. . . ."

Wingate decided that this ruse should be tried again by the Special Night Squads. He ordered Krassner to obtain ram-horn trumpets such as are used in Jewish ceremonial. Krassner found this mission beyond him. Ram's horn ceremonial trumpets were not manufactured in large quantities, and were only obtainable from synagogues whose clergy had none to spare. So instead of ram-horns he brought a consignment of bugles from Haifa. Wingate was furious. Krassner was puzzled by the whole business and went to ask Bredin for an explanation. Bredin threw up his hands and said that as far as he could make out, the Captain, after a deep study of Holy Writ, wanted to have some ram-horns to blow round the walls of a village where the gangsters sheltered. More than this he did not know. Krassner went back to Wingate and said that he must either make his experiment with bugles or abandon it altogether. The clergy were not in a position to supply ram-horns even to the smallest military unit. It seems that the bugles were used on one or two operations, and then the scheme was dropped. But Lodolf was to reappear again before the end of Wingate's career as a military commander.

The more serious of his plans succeeded : to open a training course at Ein Harod with the object of doubling the size of the Special Night Squads. During all August he was at work obtaining the agreement of Force Headquarters in Jerusalem, of the Jewish Agency, of the ruling committee of Hagana, and, as at the beginning of S.N.S., the difficulties did not always come from the expectable places. Force Headquarters were compliant. Wingate had proved himself ; the General had underwritten the Brigadier's recommendation for the D.S.O. ; the authorities seem to have agreed readily to what he wanted. But it was otherwise with the Jews. No people is more wedded to democracy and parliamentary ways, and the building up of an Anglo-Jewish force by Wingate, albeit to the advantage of Zionism, had provoked a political conflict. The Zionist parties were numerous but they admitted of a rough division into Left and Right. The strongholds of the Left were the Kibbutzim which were all run on communal lines and contained some communists. Their aggressive socialism, their class-consciousness and Leftist prejudice irritated many Jews who cherished a traditional and individual way of life, and the difference between Left and Right took on something of a conflict between townsman and countryman. When the request came to Hagana for a hundred more recruits to the squads there were loud complaints on the Right accusing the Left of monopolising the opportunity to give Jews military training. The Right suspected a plan for imposing an extreme socialist system on whatever Jewish state should in process of time come into existence, and it was a fact not to be denied that the great majority of the squadsmen had been drawn from the Kibbutzim.[1] The result of the consequent party wrangling was that the decision to select and send new recruits to Ein Harod was held up pending the outcome of party negotiations. Someone had to tell Wingate about these developments. The lot fell upon Professor Rattner, a Jew of Russian origin and a former officer in the Imperial Russian army. Holding a responsible and illegal position he preferred to mix only with Jews, for which reason he had never met the central character in these disputes. He was chosen, rather than Hacohen or Wilenski, so that the expected explosion should not mar a friendship. Also he was chosen because, belonging to the military directorate of Hagana, he could take a decision on the spot if necessary.

He drove over to Ein Harod and broke the news with the delicacy

[1] Colonel Yeheskiel Sachar, at present Chief of Police, Tel Aviv, in 1938 personal secretary to Dr. Weizmann. A communication.

natural to his pleasing Russian manners. As predicted, Wingate flew into a rage. He inveighed against the folly of party bickering at a moment when great Jewish success was within reach. He said that he had had much difficulty in persuading the British to agree to the extension and that this delay would prompt them to second thoughts. He heaped abuse on the Zionists of Haifa. Rattner listened patiently. The storm blew itself out harmlessly because the emissary, having an imperfect knowledge of English, was not able to follow the denunciations in detail. When Wingate had recovered his calm he proposed that he and Rattner should drive over to Haifa to put the matter straight there. Rattner agreed.

As they drove along the plain of Esdraelon from Ein Harod to the western shore, Wingate, as was his custom, spoke of the Biblical significance of the places they passed through. His unconventionality often appeared in the rapidity with which he treated those he met as established friends, and Rattner found himself talking to this man as though he had known him for several years and not since that very afternoon. The Professor was not a devout man and he had some difficulty in hiding the fact that his knowledge of Holy Writ and Biblical geography was superficial, but Wingate talked so much that the gaps in the other's sacred learning were not noticed. Then, as they drove together through the late afternoon, Wingate remembered his rage again and stormed anew at his frustrations. He told Rattner that he found an appalling discrepancy between the miraculous achievement of Zionism and the utterly flat and second-rate character of the men who directed the movement in Palestine. So much so did he feel this, Wingate went on, that he doubted whether he had in fact met the real rulers of the regathered nation. Only one of the men he knew was worthy to be called a prince in Israel, he went on, and that was Dr. Weizmann. For the rest—he had come to believe that there was a conspiracy of distrust, a stratagem to keep him out of acquaintance with any Jewish personage of importance. What had Professor Rattner to say to that ?

The Professor thought a moment and replied : " Then perhaps, Captain Wingate, you are one who believes in the Protocols of the Elders of Zion ? "

At this remark Wingate's mood changed. Something in the way the Professor spoke the last words tickled his sense of humour, and for several miles he drove on, chuckling silently to himself as was his wont when highly amused, and hardly able to speak for his mirth. At length he managed to say : " Perhaps all Gentiles are prone to have silly ideas about Jews." All the way to Haifa he went on laughing to himself and when they arrived Wingate had won a new ally in

Rattner. He received his hundred men. They arrived in the first days of September.[1]

Meantime during August the patrols were out every night and there were some operations though none of first-rate importance. After the battle of Dabburiya there came somewhat of a lull in banditry in the area of Ein Harod. At the end of August the pipe-line had been breached only three times in eight weeks. But this relatively tranquil state of affairs was not typical. Elsewhere in August the rebellion grew yet more violent. There were derailments, bank robberies, telegraph sabotage, murderous hold-ups on the roads, frequent murders of Jews by Arabs and more frequent murders of Arabs by Arabs, but only one of these crimes, the assassination of three Englishmen in Jenin, occurred in the area of the Special Night Squads. This did not mean, however, that the rebels had withdrawn from the fight. They were planning to leap back into Southern Galilee, as they did, with fearful results for the Jews and themselves, in October. But for the moment the story is with the now enlarged S.N.S. in September.

With the arrival of the new recruits the system of training at Ein Harod was somewhat altered. It remained idiosyncratic, practical and ruthless, as was to be expected of any Wingate venture. The courses followed short cycles of eleven days : three days of lectures round a large sand-table, with drilling and exercise in and around the camp, then four days' patrol work, then four days' leave. Within only a week now, man could find that he had made the transition from the seemliness of civilian life to participation in battle.

Wingate's notes for eight lectures have survived.[2] They are precise, brief, to the point, and mainly technical. They are also curiously self-revealing. Numerous touches suggest unconscious self-portraiture. " Great soldiers were serious and diligent in their youth," he said, " and many of them were people of outstanding moral character . . . a coarse and savage man makes a very bad soldier." His impatience with his chosen occupation is clearly visible when he warns against taking the professional soldier as a model. " Learn his discipline and calmness " he said, " but don't imitate his brutality, stupidity and drunkenness." His assertive self-confidence appears in his orders regarding the proper way to attend to what he had to say : " If you will thoroughly study and digest the lectures you will hear from me,

[1] Professor Rattner.
[2] In order they were on the following subjects : 1. The Nature of War, the War-machine, Infantry tasks and " Soldiers' Commandments." 2. The Infantry Platoon in battle. 3. Infantry in Defence. 4. Infantry in Attack. 5. Leadership and military vices. 6. The tasks of different forces. 7. Field Artillery in support of Infantry in the field. 8. The tasks of Engineers and cavalry. The last three lectures are on a single theme, " The tasks of different forces." Israel Ministry of Defence Records.

you will have something on which to base in future your study of the art of warfare. I don't want to see anybody taking notes. Notes are made to be forgotten, and their taking down will inevitably prevent you from receiving the impression . . ." The impression of him himself. When he came to deliver his " Soldiers' Commandments" his Biblical and Puritan background was in clear evidence. He gave his men Cromwell's exhortation : " Know what you fight for and love what you know." When he came to instruct them in the duties of commissioned and non-commissioned officers he expressed himself thus : " Show restraint in the fulfilment of your needs. Out of ten thousand candidates Gideon chose three hundred who were not gluttons. Place the welfare of your comrades before your own." There is an Ironside ring again in the following injunction : " Use your equipment only in fulfilment of your duty, and use it sparingly. Abstain from cruelty and brutality. Always behave with respect towards the bodies of wives, children and individuals. Always keep your body and equipment in good condition." It is allowable to wonder whether he turned an inward smile on himself when he laid down the following : " Carry out every proper order of your commanding officer with speed and understanding. Accept his leadership with faith, and don't ask permission to add your explanations to his words and instructions." It cannot be said that Wingate was ever scrupulous about obeying this important injunction, unless the word " proper " is to be forced into much extra duty.

His second-in-command for the course was Yakov Dori, a Hagana leader and an able organiser. He sometimes helped as translator at the lectures, the system being that Wingate spoke in English, often giving a few phrases in Hebrew, but most of the time relying on an interpreter. His usual translator was Israel Carmi. One day there was no translator available for a lecture and Wingate asked for a volunteer. One of the youngest of the new recruits offered his services, a bolder move than might appear, for Wingate was known to be hard on slow or halting translators. The young man performed admirably and Wingate often used him after. His name was Avram Akavia. This was the beginning of a close friendship.

Faulty memory is sometimes as indicative of truth as the most precise. Many men who attended these training courses at Ein Harod have a clear recollection of Wingate opening his introductory address by saying : " Our purpose here is to found the Jewish army " ; they seem to remember him laying down with the utmost clarity that the Jewish members of the S.N.S. were to look upon themselves as a cadre from which the military force of Israel would grow in due time. Wingate, politically reckless as he often was, never made so indiscreet a statement in public but the fact remains that the squadsmen were indeed the cadre of an army, and they undertook their tasks consciously in that spirit. Wingate never said anything to contradict such an idea which was unquestionably his too, and he said much to encourage it in private. Zvi Brenner remembers him in a day-dreaming moment saying that the Headquarters of the Jewish Army should be at Mount Carmel and that the remains of Herzl should be laid to rest in the same place. From his first days in Haifa till the end of his life he dreamed persistently of leading picked men of Israel into battle. He was picking them now and teaching them to bear arms for a cause identical with Gideon's. The squadsmen understood this. So did he.

The school of training had hardly begun at Ein Harod when the Special Night Squads conducted the most successful operation of their whole career. This took place at a little village called Khirbet Beit Lidd[1] in the centre of the plain of Esdraelon. News came that a large gang commanded by a man called Abu Durra, one of Fawzi Kawakji's lieutenants, had collected forty strong in the tents of a certain Shaykh Tahir, which were pitched around the village. Sabotage on the pipe-line had begun again, and this assembly was the reason. Following their old procedure the S.N.S. took up their posts in movements concealed by the usual elaborate deceptions, and a small operation was conducted elsewhere on the pipe-line to draw attention away. Under such cover five squads marched to positions which encircled the village and the encampment. Last minute reinforcements were drawn from the nearby Kibbutz of Sared. A little before first light the assault went in led by Wingate. The surprise was complete. The gang hardly rallied but scattered in the dark in all directions. Prisoners were taken. Fourteen Arabs were killed in the mêlée including Shaykh Tahir. In the captured baggage there were found all the Shaykh's written instructions with the names of some hitherto unsuspected leaders.[2]

As after the battle of Dabburiya, Wingate could not rest. As soon as the action was over he went to Haifa. It was still very early. He woke up Major Wieler and gave him a full account of the action at Beit Lidd. " He arrived in my bedroom thoroughly dishevelled," the Brigade-Major told many years later, " and gave me an account of his evening's work and concluded by saying : ' I've left the captured rifles in the guardroom and now I must get my leg tidied up.' " It seems that in the course of the action one of his leg wounds had been re-opened. As soon as the leg had been bandaged, and as soon as

---

[1] Now called Hayogev.
[2] Wingate to Evetts (31.1.39). Carmi. Laskov. MacConville.

Evetts was up Wingate went to the Brigadier's house to show him the documents he had captured. Among these was the appointment book of Abu Durra, and the latter, with extraordinary lack of foresight, had recorded a forthcoming visit to the Arab mayor or Mukhtar of Tantura (about twenty miles south of Haifa) in order to collect some arms expected by caique on the 4th, that is the next day. Wingate wanted and obtained permission from the Brigadier to arrest the Mukhtar and intercept the caique. Then, while they were making out the contents of the tell-tale engagement book, and discussing what should be done, Wingate was suddenly overcome by exhaustion. He collapsed on to the sofa and stayed there half asleep the rest of the day. He could not even get up to eat and had to be fed in nursery fashion by Mrs. Evetts.

Next day Wingate went to Tantura with a picket of squadsmen to secure the Mukhtar. Of what then happened no record survives. It seems that after the squadsmen had surrounded the village Wingate and a small guard went in to seize the guilty man. It seems that the latter was not known by sight, and that several suspected people were rounded up and led outside the village for identification. Then while Wingate was going down the line examining the prisoners one of them dashed away and fled and was instantly shot by a squadsman. Wingate flew into a rage, heaping abuse on the squadsman for what he had done. The dead man was the Mukhtar. The affair was hushed up.[1]

As soon as he could Wingate returned to Ein Harod and the training course.

Again there was relative calm in this part of Galilee. Again the rebels withdrew, after having been thrown off their balance at Beit Lidd just as they were about to spring back for revenge. For the moment they confined themselves to surreptitious murder and sabotage. But at the end of the month there were signs that the conflict was about to flare out into battle again. On the 23rd of September there was another engagement on the scale of Dabburiya and Beit Lidd. Hussein Ali Diab and Naif Zobi had both returned from Syria and were reassembling a gang near Danna. Information came to Ein Harod about these movements and once again Danna was surrounded. Again the gang was routed with twelve men killed including Hussein Ali Diab.[2]

The wretched little town where this happened typified the miseries of the ordinary people of Palestine. Two years before it had been a prosperous market-place by the bare standards of Levant rural life; now half its population had fled and some of its houses had been

[1] Carmi, confirmed (though not as to details) by authoritative evidence.
[2] Wingate to Evetts (31.1.39).

torn down as official punishment for harbouring gangsters and rebels, and fields lay untended. By the end of the rebellion it was scarcely a human habitation, and since those days it has vanished from the map. The people still dwelling in Danna in the summer of 1938 lived in constant fear of being rounded up for interrogation by the squadsmen, and in equal fear of assassination by rebels suspicious of betrayal to the squadsmen.[1]

By October the state of the rebellion was more dangerous than it had been for some time. The Arab party were filled with a new self-confidence which had grown throughout the European crisis which ended at Munich. Showing a political acumen not typical of Arab minds, the rebels saw the phases of the Czechoslovakian disaster as a succession of victories for Nazism. The German Government had taken the exiled Mufti under secret patronage, and the Nazi-Fascist Axis had for long been giving open encouragement to the rebel cause. When the unfolding of the crisis seemed to prove that the Arabs had chosen their supporters well, they renewed their work of destruction and murder. In September the number of people killed by Arab gangsters rose to a hundred and eighty-eight, with a hundred and fifty-six wounded.[2] The climax of this procession of terror and bloodshed was reached on the 2nd of October.

It so happened that on that date General Sir Edmund Ironside, Governor of Gibraltar, and Commander-in-Chief Designate of the Middle Eastern Theatre, was in Haifa staying with Brigadier Evetts. On the evening of the 2nd he was dining with his host in one of the Haifa hotels. Major Wieler and General Haining were the other guests. In the course of conversation Sir Edmund declared himself sceptical about the Palestine situation. He could not see, he said, how with the substantial number of troops in the country, and the feeble armament of the rebels, the situation could be as serious as the authorities claimed, and he even went so far as to say that he thought that the amenities of the Mediterranean climate and a desire for medals had led to a great deal of official exaggeration. " Well, sir," said Evetts, " I can only hope that something unpleasant happens while you are here to alter your view."

As the party was breaking up there was a telephone call for Evetts from Wingate. The latter was on an operation and he was ringing up to tell the Brigadier that he had just received information that rebels had entered Tiberias. That was all he knew. When he was back with his party Brigadier Evetts suggested that he should conduct General Ironside to Tiberias early in the morning. This was agreed.

What was happening in Tiberias was an attempted massacre of the

[1] Ezra Danin.   [2] *Annual Reports*. Colonial Office.

Jews. Under well-preserved secrecy, and following a careful plan, a large gang of rebels had infiltrated to selected points in the town. The Jewish population of Tiberias was relatively large and to a considerable extent composed of pre-Zionist settlers, people often out of sympathy with Jewish nationalism. The massacre, though apparently well organised, was not as successful as might have been expected by Fawzi Kawakji's administrative staff. Nineteen Jews, of whom ten were small children, were murdered. Many of them were killed by being burned alive after having been stabbed.[1] The massacre might have been on a larger scale if the assassinating party had not given themselves up early to looting and carousal. What made the incident doubly disgraceful to British rule was the fact that on the very night of the attack a British battalion (not under Brigadier Evetts) had arrived at Tiberias and taken up quarters in a Turkish fort serving as barracks. They had so little notion of conditions of guerilla warfare as to settle therein without establishing a picket-line, and as a result of their carelessness they were effectively surrounded by a few brigands with automatic weapons. Police and men of the Transjordan Frontier Force from Samakh on the south shore came to the rescue too late. The battalion had been kept within the walls till the massacre was over and the gangsters out of the town.[2]

During this bloody night Wingate had ordered the main part of the squads to surround a gang reported to be settled in a hamlet called Sirin ten miles south of Tiberias, but by good fortune he himself was leading two squads (presumably from Kinneret) on a similar mission to a place called Kafr Mesha, a little way west of Tiberias. The latter town was out of the S.N.S. area, perhaps as a result of the dispositions which had sent the British battalion there. Nevertheless at the moment, and after, Wingate bitterly reproached himself for the disaster saying that since the S.N.S. had taken on the task of ambushing infiltrators from the north he ought to have been able to prevent the gangsters reaching their goal.[3] Whether or not he was to blame (and it is difficult to see that he was) he made good any deficiency by what he did now. He took his two squads out of the Kafr Mesha operation and led them to Tiberias. Somehow or other he obtained information as to the movements and intentions of the brigands within the town, and with his few men (not more than twenty) laid an ambush.

The little hot stone-built town of Tiberias lies on the side of a steep hill where the Jordan rift meets the water of the Sea of Galilee far below Mediterranean level. Two roads lead out of it, one northwards

[1] *Annual Reports.* Colonial Office. Wingate to Evetts (31.1.39), also photographs shown by Sir John Evetts to the writer.
[2] Field-Marshal Lord Ironside.
[3] Zvi Brenner.

along the shore of the sealet, the other to the west up a steep-climbing zigzagging course till it reaches the level plain. It is not clear whether Wingate laid one or two ambushes, but it is certain that the main one was on the westward road climbing the hill. They did not have to wait long for their enemies. Foolishly overconfident after their discomfiture of a whole British battalion, careless and weary after their success, and many of them the worse for drink, the bulk of the murderous horde straggled up the westward hill an hour or so before dawn. They walked straight into the trap laid for them.[1]

Meantime General Ironside had revised the views he had expressed the night before at dinner. His drive from Haifa to Tiberias had opened his eyes to the appalling state of this little British-protected country. He had seen overturned pylons, blown-up bridges, ruined police posts, and other outward signs of two years of strife.

When he reached Tiberias he was confronted with the spectacle of the charred corpses being carted away from the wrecks of buildings, and he heard with indignation the dismal tale of how the British battalion had failed in its task. (He dismissed the commanding officer on the spot.) Full of anger he began on the westward journey back to Haifa. Near the top of the hill leading out of Tiberias he encountered a grim-looking man in an antique sun-helmet superintending the laying-out of robed corpses and the piling of captured weapons.

" And who are you ? " asked General Ironside.

" I'm Wingate," was the reply. The General looked at him curiously. The younger man had spoken as though his name must inevitably be known to the other as that of a famous person. General Ironside asked for some explanation and this was given to him. Wingate told him about the S.N.S. and explained how he had laid the ambush and collected six bodies, adding that he calculated that he must have accounted for forty.[2] The General questioned further, discovered the Captain's relationship to the Sirdar, and heard some details about the work of the little Anglo-Jewish army led by this unusual commander. When he was back in Gibraltar Sir Edmund, amid many new impressions of the civil and military administration in Palestine, retained a lasting memory of the grim Captain on the heights over Tiberias. He noted that he had commanded the only force to meet, fight and punish the assassins on that night of slaughter. He decided that his name was not one to forget.

The day after the Tiberias massacre Wingate led the Special Night

---

[1] Wingate to Evetts (31.1.39). Ironside. Evetts.

[2] Field-Marshal Lord Ironside. Wingate to Evetts (31.1.39). Wingate gives 40 as the probable number, the relevant *Annual Report* gives 50. The latter number is more likely to be accurate. Again it is not clear if one or two ambushes accounted for these numbers, but the language of the *Annual Report* suggests two.

Squads into action for the last time. He was at Sirin with squads who seem to have camped in the village after drawing blank on the night of the second. On the morning of the 4th he was driving from Sirin to Nazareth when he spied two taxis. At the sight of him the occupants drove off, one towards Jenin, the other towards Dabburiya. With his extraordinary ability to identify faces at long range Wingate instantly recognised Abu Durra and Naif Zobi. By luck the two squads who had ambushed the massacring party from Tiberias appeared at that moment driving towards Nazareth in lorries. Wingate led them in pursuit of Naif Zobi towards Dabburiya and Mount Tabor. The gangsters went up into the mountains pursued by the squadsmen. The latter were equipped with wireless and Wingate sent out a call for R.A.F. support which was rapidly forthcoming. Being an unprepared operation ground signals were misread and the danger from bombs was greater to the squadsmen than to their enemies. Of the latter fourteen were killed, the action ending with a sharp-shooting duel between Lieutenant Bredin and Naif Zobi on a ledge of the monastery attached to the Church of the Transfiguration.[1]

Unfortunately for the drama of history this final appearance of Wingate at the head of his little force ended in anticlimax. Since the squadsmen numbered less than twenty there could be no pursuit and the majority of the gangsters escaped with their chief.

[1] Wingate to Evetts (31.1.39). Carmi.

CHAPTER IX

FORTUNE AND MEN'S EYES

BY THIS time Wingate was beginning to show signs of strain. On two known occasions (and probably on others) he had suffered something like prostration after action. One such incident has been noted after the affair of Beit Lidd. Another occurred after an attempt on his life at Haifa. He was staying with the Wilenskis after a night patrol. While driving in the town in the afternoon an Arab threw a—defective—bomb into his car, then fled. Wingate stopped the car, leaped out, pursued the would-be assassin till he lost him in little side streets. He showed his usual courage during the assault and pursuit, but when he was back in the Wilenskis' house, he suffered a reaction which left him hardly able to move and in the throes of a trembling fit.[1] He was in need of rest and leave.

It is to be doubted, however, whether he took his overdue leave in any spirit of therapeutic self-care. During all the period of the formation, training and enlargement of the Special Night Squads he had been mixing ever deeper in the politics of Palestine. He had written a paper for Dr. Weizmann on *Zionist Policy and the Partition Plan* in which he urged Jewish acceptance of the Peel recommendations so as to facilitate the formation of a Jewish Army. (Always the dream of a Jewish Army with himself commanding it; though he did not mention himself on this occasion.) His thesis was that with an army at its disposal the new State would be able to play a part in a second world war such as would leave it at the end of hostilities master of Syria, Lebanon, and Transjordan.[2] On 10th October a prominent Zionist of Palestine, Dov Josef, wrote a letter to Dr. Weizmann in England, indicating the extent to which Wingate was concerning himself with Jewish affairs. In reporting him the writer caught Wingate's style of expression with accuracy.

"You will be interested," his correspondent told the Zionist leader, "in the following conversation I had with one of our mutual English friends in the Service. He wished to warn us against making the fatal error, at this critical moment, of treating with H.M.G. on the same basis as we have in the past. Any doubts we may have had

[1] Yolan.
[2] Weizmann Archives. 1938 papers.

on the subject should have been dispelled by the experiences of Czechoslovakia. It was clear that the fate of this country was now being decided. Unless we took the right line at once we could lose out completely. We must not rely on the fact that we regard the British as friends who would treat us fairly.

" I interrupted to say that our views on this matter were not based merely on surmise. We knew that Dr. Weizmann had seen Mr. Chamberlain a few months ago. I understood that Mr. Chamberlain had been quite friendly and sympathetic. To this he replied that one could be gentle to a sheep before leading it to the slaughter. He continued : ' If I were Dr. Weizmann I would make it my business to get in to see Mr. Chamberlain somehow, booking my passage to Palestine beforehand. I would say to him : ' You have just finished off Czechoslovakia and you apparently think it would be a good thing to deal with the Jews in the same way. We know that you are considering settling your problem in Palestine at our expense. If you believe that you will be able to succeed in doing so you are greatly mistaken. We know now that we cannot trust you any longer and we do not propose to let you sacrifice us to make things easy for you. We shall resist by force any attempt to deprive us of our rights and shall fight you to the finish. In the future we shall rely on ourselves and God. Good day.' I would turn about and walk out of the room. I know that what I am saying to you may appear dramatic and even fantastic, but I assure you that I know my countrymen. I know my countrymen, and I am sure that if he (Mr. Chamberlain) does not call Dr. Weizmann back before he leaves the room he will certainly send for him to return to London before he has gone very far on his way to Palestine. You people,' he went on, ' make the mistake of regulating your political conduct on the basis of logic and your understanding of justice. You think that because logically and on grounds of justice you should be treated in a certain way that H.M.G. will act accordingly. What is the good of all your logic and your attempt to persuade the British by reasonable argument that they should treat you fairly if they have no interest in your logic and reasoning, if they do not care at all about you and are only concerned about their own convenience ? Let me illustrate by an example. Supposing you had a horse and told me you wished to sell it. I offered you £80 for it and you asked £100. If you really had a *bona fide* intention of selling the horse there might be some point in my putting forward all sorts of logical arguments to convince you that you should accept £80 instead of £100 you were asking. But supposing on the other hand, you had no intention of selling the horse but were merely playing about with me and I found this out, would there be any sense in my going on trying to convince you on logical grounds that you should accept my offer? What I ought to do in such circumstances is to say to you I have found out that you have no intention of selling your horse, you are just making a fool of me and if you think you can do that you are greatly mistaken. I would not buy your horse for £100 or anything. I shall tell all your friends that you are a scamp and I would turn my back on you and walk out. If you acted in the way nine men out of ten would in the circumstances, you would be so taken aback by my blunt reproaches that you would immediately begin apologising and express your genuine readiness to sell the horse, whether you had really intended to or not. You must realise once and for all that the present British Government does not care one bit about you. It does not want any more worry and trouble about Palestine and fully intends to arrange things at your expense so as to have peace and quiet here.'

"I remonstrated with him that it would not be an easy matter for us to break with the British, that they were one of the few peoples who had been friends to us, and that we had a sense of loyalty to them, and what was more, the position of world Jewry to-day was so precarious that it would be a very serious responsibility to break off relations with H.M.G. in the way he suggested. Their reaction might be such as he thought but there was always the possibility of a different reaction. To this he replied that no one could expect to succeed who lacked the courage to dare to do what he should. 'You have everything at stake now,' he said, 'I am convinced that your only chance is to act as I suggest.' "[1]

In the light of this candid report, the reader may deplore afresh Wingate's assurance to the Woodhead Commission that he never discussed political matters except in the strict course of his duties. But a reader who knew the Palestine of those years might feel less inclined to pass judgment. One could find Wingate more blameable perhaps if so much of what he said had not been true, and if the warning he conveyed had been less needed. It seems likely from this and other evidence that he had information on the forthcoming Woodhead Report.

During his last days in Jerusalem before sailing for England he and Lorna entertained Zvi Brenner as their guest in the little house in Talbieh whence Zion was visible. The young Jewish settler was impressed by the great number of Wingate's books, and he noted with approval a large Hebrew section. One day Wingate took Zvi Brenner with him to Force Headquarters where he had an appointment not

---

[1] Weizmann Archives. The substance of the letter is very briefly given in Dr. Weizmann's account of Wingate in *Trial and Error*, p. 490.

expected to last long. Zvi Brenner waited for him outside, and when Wingate joined him again, he looked distressed. He said : " A gang of anti-Jews sits inside there." The decision when to leave was apparently taken in a hurry. Zvi Brenner came in one evening to find the household all packing. He asked Wingate if he was leaving for England. Wingate said Yes he was. London, asked Zvi Brenner. Yes, London. Zvi Brenner asked him why he was going to London. Wingate said he was going for personal reasons. Zvi Brenner asked him what personal reasons could take him from Palestine at such a moment. Then Wingate took him into his confidence and told him that Dr. Weizmann had cabled for him to come to London on which account he had asked for leave. He had told the authorities that he had urgent personal affairs to attend to.

It is always dangerous in army life to take leave if there is any doubt about the security of the post from which the leave is taken. Wingate had an uncertain place in Palestine administration. The golden opinions he had earned from authority were mixed with much disapproval. It will be remembered that General Haining had had reservations about the wisdom of the S.N.S. policy from its beginning, and his doubts had not been soothed by the independence with which Wingate discharged his duties, or by the way the S.N.S. commander gave his superiors a minimum of information about his intentions and turned blind eyes and ears to any instructions with which he did not agree. At one moment in the summer the General had even considered the possibility of dismissal. He summoned Captain Dudley Clarke of the Operations Department and addressed him somewhat as follows : " Here is a fellow Wingate who makes no secret of the fact that he only obeys orders which suit him. Whether he is right or wrong in his criticisms of orders, if he won't obey them I cannot retain confidence in the man. If you lose confidence in a junior, then, whether the junior is right or wrong, you had best get rid of him. I want you to go to Wingate and tell him that." Dudley Clarke went to Ein Harod from where he was directed to a cave in the valley of Esdraelon. A patrol was in camp here and Wingate (commanding the patrol) was out when his visitor arrived. Presently he came in looking, so Dudley Clarke recalled long after, " like a caveman who has killed a beast for the cave family supper." Dudley Clarke delivered the General's message which Wingate took calmly. In return he promised to amend his behaviour in the matter of obedience. The incident contained an obvious and ominous warning, one of several similar ones which he had received in the course of the year. His political activities had not gone quite unnoticed. He was rash to leave Palestine, but Dr. Weizmann's message left him no alternative. In a fateful hour for the future of Zion and Jewry he wanted to do what he could to influence the men in power.

The worst Jewish fears of what the Woodhead Commission intended were realised in the event. Their report was published on the 9th of November. The main difference between the new recommendations and those of the Peel Commission lay in the proposed dimensions of the Jewish State. From it all Galilee was excluded and retained under the Mandate together with the Negeb. Jerusalem was denied to both parties because it could not be partitioned without injustice. The rest of the country outside the Jewish and Mandated territories was to form an Arab state, and the possibility of Jewish expansion was to be anticipated, and prevented, by a prohibition on all land transfers from non-Jews to Jews in Mandated territory except in Jerusalem, Haifa and Tiberias. This prohibition was to remain in force for ten years when it would be " reviewed " but not withdrawn or relaxed unless the Arabs so wished. It was known what happened to Arabs who did wish such things against current political trends. In the almost uncultivated south there was some alleviation of these stern conditions. Some guarded encouragement was given to the pioneering spirit of the Jews. Virgin desert could be obtained and exploited by Jews if the Government agreed, but more promising land could only be bought and occupied by Jews after they had met the wild Bedouin in committee and reached agreement, and it was stated that in such negotiations the right of refusal must remain with the Bedouin in consideration of their great poverty. The inducements held out to the Jews by the Woodhead Commission were not substantial. In return for submitting to discriminating laws against them under the flag of England ; in return for agreement to forget Jerusalem, the Jews were offered complete freedom to live as they chose in an unexpectedly small pale of settlement. The proposed boundaries extended from Tantura to Tel Aviv on the Mediterranean shore and only a quarter of this distance inland : the new state would contain about four hundred square miles, being about forty miles north to south by ten miles west to east. It is difficult to believe that the Woodhead Commission or the Government of Neville Chamberlain intended this document for acceptance, and did not merely wish to provide an occasion to continue the Mandate. But it must be recalled also that this was the year and season of " Munichism " when sloth, alarm and idealism in conjunction produced many strange and sincere aberrations. It was an abdication-time and the Jews were invited to abdicate.

The recommendations were debated in Parliament later in November. The Secretary of State, Mr. Malcolm Macdonald, introduced them on the 24th in a speech of extraordinary Parliamentary skill, in spite of which he was not well received. He paid a considered tribute to the tremendous Jewish achievement in settlement and reclamation ; he rightly stressed the essential cause of the Government's difficulties : the pressure of immigration on Palestine from European persecution, and he claimed that the British promise conveyed by Arthur Balfour had been concerned with small numbers and manageable conditions and should not and could not extend to the abnormal situation caused by a German relapse into barbarism. Mr. Macdonald further gave a precise and fair description of the Arab situation, and told of both the villainy of their politics and style of combat, and the undeniable fact that their cause was just and " moved by a genuine patriotism." He laid stress on the fact that though few Arabs had immigrated to Palestine from neighbouring territory, yet their numbers had risen from 600,000 to 990,000 in sixteen years owing mainly to the survival of more children in a land where Western facilities, in this case thanks mainly to Jewish initiative, had provided doctors and hospitals. The speech was as fair as it could be, and it was also a logical speech until this last passage about the material benefits which " the Arabs in Palestine had gained." Here, true enough, the Minister might have indicated that even for so goodly a mess of pottage the Arabs could not barter their birthright ; he might have urged political restraint on the part of the Jews, but he went far beyond anticipation in this direction, indeed beyond most Arabophil argument when he proceeded to disown the recommendation of the Peel Commission on the ground that the Jews had made the pottage too well. Under partition, he said, closely following the Woodhead Report, " the Jewish State would have a great surplus on its budget every year, but year after year the budgets of the Arab State and the Mandated Territory would show a great deficit." He agreed with Zionists that this was " a remarkable tribute to the achievement of the Jews," but for the very reason that the achievement was so remarkable, for the reason that the Jews were not as lethargic and incapable as their neighbours, they were to be confined for fiscal convenience to a territory of less size than that of an average English county. He hoped, he said, for early negotiations between Arabs and Jews and the Government. He concluded on a note of personal emotion. He felt awe and reverence before the subject of Palestine, and " I cannot remember," said Mr. Macdonald, " a time when I was not told stories about Nazareth and Galilee, about Jerusalem and Bethlehem where was born the Prince of Peace." According to unconfirmed gossip of the day, at the mention of the Prince of Peace the Right Honourable Member for Epping was heard to murmur : " I always thought he was born in Birmingham."

Not for the last time Wingate returned to harbour after distant and valiant deeds to find that the deeds had gone unnoticed. In the autumn of Munich there was little public thought to spare for the woes of Palestine, as relief turned to recrimination, and as the fears of sceptics were widely shared when news of the November pogroms in Germany came in. Hitler was immediate, Palestine far away, and the connection between the two could only lead to further disgust with a beautiful gift turned bad. In a more ordinary time the avenger of Tiberias might have been greeted with acclaim. As it was most people had heard of the massacre, to forget it under closer preoccupations. The news of the disaster had come in only four days after Neville Chamberlain's return from the Munich negotiations. The arrival of the avenger three weeks later was unremarked.

He and Lorna spent their leave in London living in furnished rooms in Welbeck Street. It was to be a time of failure with one splendid flash of near-success prophetic of great successes ahead. Immediately Wingate set to work to meet persons of political consequence with the object of bringing them to the belief that, only through a Zionist policy, could the British Government find a road to permanent tranquillity in Palestine. He was always adept at meeting whomever he chose, but by his skill he now added to his growing reputation for intrigue. That he got such a reputation is not surprising, but it must be stressed that he was without the intriguer's furtive character. He brought many of his troubles on himself by the open way he advocated and sought otherwise to help causes he believed in. He began his present campaign by again asking for the help of Sir Reginald Wingate. The relations of the two men had become somewhat less close. The old Sirdar, one of the last Empire-builders of the classic school, was inevitably critical of his cousin's suddenly found Zionist faith, but this did not mean that he lost any of his affection or any of his abounding confidence. He recognised the patriotism of Orde Wingate's aim (even though he disapproved of the form) and helped him as he had always done and was always to do.

The first question was whom to meet. Wingate remembered that in 1933, while staying in Cairo with Richard Goodbody, he had been taken to a garden party at the British Residency. In the course of this entertainment he had been introduced to the High Commissioner, Lord Lloyd, who already knew of Wingate from his relationship to the old Sirdar, and from his exploration in the desert. Lord Lloyd took a liking to him, held him in conversation and asked him in detail about his adventures in the Libyan Desert and the Sudan. Now, five and a half years later, Wingate, through the intervention of Cousin Rex, wrote to Lord Lloyd reminding him of this meeting. He received a reply indicating continuing interest and giving him an appointment. Lord Lloyd was at this time a frequent and forceful speaker in the House of Lords on matters relating to the Islamic world. He was President of the British Council, but the vigour of his personality often made people suppose that he was a Minister, and he undoubtedly contrived to give to his partly official post (which he had founded) something suggestive of Government.

David Ben Gurion was in London during this November, greatly distressed at the intensity of Arabophil opinion in England. He and Wingate consulted with Dr. Weizmann and it seems that the three men worked together at a new scheme of partition which they thought might conceivably recommend itself to the still uncommitted Colonial Office. By this plan the Zionists would surrender all Galilee and the port of Haifa and in compensation take full possession of the sparsely inhabited south, down to the Gulf of Akaba, and a substantial share in the more fertile centre east of Tel Aviv.[1] The scheme asked less for the Jews than had been recommended the year before and was perhaps put forward as a last attempt to salvage something from the Peel Commission's wreck. Its authors decided that their first objective should be to obtain Lord Lloyd's support so that the scheme might be transmitted to the Colonial Office through him and with his approval. Wingate and Ben Gurion made this their mission. They saw Lord Lloyd together but took from him very different impressions.

Lord Lloyd was incapable of Anti-Semitism but he was a settled opponent of Zionism, regarding the Balfour Declaration as a disastrous aberration of policy. But he was a fair-dealing man, always prepared to listen with an open mind, and he gave the new scheme close attention. Only one point in it he completely refused to admit as reasonable : the formation of a Jewish army. This he saw as nothing but a further provocation in an already provoked situation ; he said that if war were to break out he would be in favour of the formation of one Arab and one Jewish battalion, but no more. Regarding the rest of the scheme—he listened but said nothing to compromise himself. He readily agreed to transmit the paper to the Secretary of State. Ben Gurion came away from the meeting in a glow of optimism. Wingate felt otherwise. He was dismayed by an impression that Lord Lloyd

[1] These details were given to the writer by Mr. Ben Gurion.

was a firm and tenacious opponent of Jewish nationalism, and the fact that Wingate admired him and had pleasing memories of his first meeting made his disillusion the more bitter. There is no doubt that Wingate judged the better of the two. Lord Lloyd remained an opponent of Zionism to the end of his life.[1]

Wingate also obtained an interview with Mr. Malcolm Macdonald. To him as to the Woodhead Commission he put his view in full and he was met by sympathetic politeness. So far as his career was concerned this interview with the Secretary of State was an extremely rash move. It could not fail to become known to the authorities in Palestine and could not fail to irritate his superior officers, the distrustful Haining and the long-suffering Ritchie.

The plan to influence the great was persisted in, but seemed to achieve nothing except meetings. There was one with Jewish businessmen (unnamed)[2] from which he learned that Jewish capital amounting to thirty million pounds might be invested in Palestine if, but only if the British Government announced a policy encouraging Zionism. There was a luncheon to which Wingate was invited so that he might give his account of Palestine to members of the British Press. He expounded his views to an audience which included Geoffrey Dawson, Chamberlain's devoted publicist, and the most influential propagandist of the appeasement policy. It may be concluded that on this man (and so on *The Times* of which he was editor) Wingate made no impression, for the appeasement of the rebellious Arabs (who had much justice on their side) was then considered an integral part of that policy of general appeasement whose grand purpose was to soothe men who openly cared nothing for justice at all. But from this luncheon Wingate at least took something : he was encouraged to meet the last of the great Press Barons.

In the popular sphere the *Daily Express* was doing similar work to *The Times* in support of the official policy of the day. On the Palestine question this most widely read of papers took up an attitude of candid British self-interest ; whether or not the directorate or staff had knowledge of the Woodhead Report before its publication the *Daily Express* prepared the minds of the British people for its proposals. The accounts of Palestine written for the paper by Emrys Jones, Tom Driberg and Sefton Delmer gave their readers little notion of the Arab atrocity and criminality and persecution behind the rebellion, or of the stoic self-restraint of the Jews. This is not to suggest that they reported amiss but that they reflected the prevalent British view

[1] This account of the meeting with Lord Lloyd is drawn from an interview with Mr. Ben Gurion. As regards Lord Lloyd's anti-Zionism Dr. Weizmann gave some account in his *Trial and Error*.
[2] Wingate to Ironside (7.6.39). W.P.I.

which could forgive much to the rebel party because their patriotism, unlike that of the Jews, was uncomplicated and of a familiar kind. The *Daily Express* said openly what others said with circumlocution. The leading article of 13th October was typical of many when it declared : " The Arabs must recognise the right of those Jews at present in Palestine to dwell among them. The Jews must consent to a cessation of Jewish immigration." This was the real wish of the Government in concise form. The moving spirit of the *Daily Express* associated himself closely with the paper's policy. " It is a lie," said Lord Beaverbrook in a personally signed message to the paper, " it is a lie to say that Britain is breaking any pledges to the Jews in Palestine. The strife in that unhappy country arises out of a faithful and comprehensive fulfilment of these same pledges to the Zionists. Those who hate this country and work to do an injury to the British people spread stories at home and abroad that Britain has broken faith." It should be said that despite ungenerous advice concerning British policy towards Jews in this fearful moment in their history, the Beaverbrook Press did repeatedly urge that Lord Samuel should be given charge of a definitive mission to settle the question, a proposal more constructive than most.

On the 9th of November Mr. Bruce Lockhart arranged a meeting between Wingate and Lord Beaverbrook. It was not a success. It may be that, weary of the polite and sympathetic discouragement he had met in his efforts so far, he decided that now was the time to employ the fierce tactics he had recommended to Dov Josef the month before. At all events, when they met, these two very different descendants of Non-Conformism did not discover the instant comradeship of strong men, but rather its opposite, and it seems that when Wingate saw that he had failed to impress on the champion of Imperial solidarity the idea that the Zionist movement was of value to the well-being of the British Empire, he found his temper rising and began to speak the more loudly and the more violently, the other listening in " silence and cold anger."[1] Lord Beaverbrook let him have his say until there was a pause whereat he began : " I have decided——" but Wingate interrupted him by crying out : " It is not you, but God who decides ! "[2] The encounter lasted about a quarter of an hour. When Wingate strode out of the room he was not called back, and no shift in the policies of the Beaverbrook Press followed. Four days later the *Sunday Express* published an editorial which concluded thus : " Here is a word of advice from a newspaper which has always been sympathetic to the Jews and is anxious for their safety now. Beware of Zionism. It is an issue which divides this country. There is no reason

[1] Sir Robert Bruce Lockhart. A letter to the writer.　　　[2] Bruce Lockhart.

why political controversy should be stifled or the divergences of
opinion reconciled. But in your zeal be restrained. Beware above
everything of catchpenny agitation stating the Jewish case in violent
and offensive terms by men who really give no allegiance to Zionism
and the Zionist cause but who merely embrace it for the sake of its
advantage to themselves."

Among people who tried to help Wingate in his mission was Mrs.
Israel Sieff. She was told by Dr. Weizmann that this valuable witness
to Zionism was having difficulty in obtaining a hearing, and he suggested that she should invite Wingate to her house to meet further
possible converts of influence. She did as he asked and at Brook
House near St. James's Palace, where she and her husband then lived,
Wingate met yet more people of eminence, mostly the editors and
correspondents of leading newspapers. At Brook House he had another
meeting with Lord Lloyd of whom the Zionists still cherished hopes.
It is unlikely that, in the then state of opinion, this second offensive
would have obtained results, but in fact it was brought to a premature
end. Wingate was informed by someone in the War Office that his
meeting with the Secretary of State for the Colonies, which had been
reported back to Palestine and commented on, was not considered
a correct initiative for a person of his rank to have taken, and he was
urged, though not ordered, to abandon any political programme he
might be engaged on. Wingate communicated the news to Mrs. Sieff,
asking her not to waste her time on him further. He said : " What it
amounts to is that I have been forbidden to speak, and perhaps the
best way I can now speak is to let as many people as possible know
about the prohibition." He added : " I have been ordered to shut my
mouth and I intend to shut it as noisily as I can."[1] He had achieved
one important thing. He had a new ally in Mrs. Sieff and her friendship
was to be of value to him later.

As things fell out he had one notable and gratifying opportunity
of opening his mouth before returning to Palestine. It happened in
this way. He had had some communication with Mr. Winston Churchill
through Captain Liddell Hart. The latter had read a memorandum
given to him by Wingate on his S.N.S. theory and practice, and had
subsequently transmitted this to Mr. Churchill who had expressed
interest.

Then, in November, Lord Rothschild, whom Wingate had met
through Dr. Weizmann, found a way to arrange a meeting. There was
a family custom whereby Mr. Churchill's birthday on November 30th
was celebrated every year by a dinner party given by Mrs. Venetia
Montagu, the widow of the eminent Jewish statesman, Edwin

[1] Mrs. Rebecca Sieff.

Montagu. These parties were serio-comic in character, much merriment and chaff being mixed with grave political discussion, and there had been occasions when the debate at the table had grown heated. At one of these dinners a young and distinguished Oxford don, on another occasion Mr. Duff Cooper (a regular attendant), had been subjected to Johnsonian maulings at the hands of the eminent guest.[1] Lord Rothschild, as a close friend of Venetia Montagu, arranged for the Wingates to be invited for the celebration of 1938, the last of its kind to be held.

All parties went well under the stimulating direction of Mrs. Montagu, a woman who combined ready wit and humour with the formidable beauty which goes with tall stature, prematurely grey hair and piercing eyes. The birthday celebration was, as usual, a mixture of frivolity and ardent discussion held together by the guests having been chosen for distinction, animation and " clubbability," and this year the evening passed without turmoil. Wingate did not make any particular mark on the company (not easy to do with such a chief guest there) until the end of dinner. It was then that Venetia Montagu drew him into conversation with Mr. Churchill on the subject of Palestine.

The talk of the others died down. What started as a conversation gradually turned into a monologue, as Wingate told Winston Churchill of the present state of Palestine, the threatened Kibbutzim, the continuing achievement of the settlers, and the soldierly character which he had found in the Jews. He told him of the formation and success of the Special Night Squads, and as he went on he found himself in the strange position of being listened to in silence by the most eloquent man then living in the world. It seems that Wingate talked about Palestine and its problems and his own adventures there for about ten minutes. At the end of his discourse there was a brief silence which was broken by one of the ladies. She said : " Well, that's that." Mr. Churchill was not pleased by this comment and he turned on her, as Lorna remembered later, " slowly, like the gun-turret of a tank." He said : " Here is a man who has seen and done and been amid great actions, and when he is telling us about them you had better be quiet." The rebuke was not too serious, was replied to with suitable sauce, and the party went forward again with general talk and the accustomed jollity of the anniversary.[2]

About this time, at the end of November or the beginning of December, he received orders to return to Palestine. He had put himself at a disadvantage with his superiors as in his hurry to respond to

[1] Lord Rothschild.
[2] Mrs. Lorna Smith. Lord Rothschild. Mr. Granville Wingate.

Dr. Weizmann's appeal he had taken his leave before formalities had been completed, and the summons to return was somewhat threatening in tone. He was not in a position to resist any part of his instructions which were of an unwelcome kind : he was to return not to Ein Harod but to Force Headquarters at Jerusalem, the command of the Special Night Squads having been given to Lieutenant Bredin. Wingate reported for duty in Jerusalem on the 12th of December. On the same day the camp at Ein Harod was dispersed.[1]

The decision to remove him from the little force that he had raised meant what it appeared to mean. The authorities were " apprehensive of the lines on which the S.N.S. organisation was developing," by which they meant that Wingate " was chiefly concerned with the political object of associating Jews to the greatest possible extent with offensive operations against the rebels, although he was well aware that this was contrary to policy. . . ."[2] The wider purpose was to reduce the S.N.S. " to a passive rôle " such as the Jewish supernumerary police had played before the spring of 1938. The moment was propitious for these changes. When the Munich crisis was over massive reinforcements had been sent to Palestine amounting to ten infantry battalions, two regiments of cavalry and a battalion and detachment of the Royal Horse Artillery. There were now in all eighteen infantry battalions in Palestine.[3] So heavy a concentration could restore rule by sheer weight and the rebellion began slowly to die down. There was no longer the former urgent need for Wingate or for his S.N.S.

He had gone to England to find himself and his deeds a matter of indifference ; he returned to Palestine to find himself an object of embarrassment. Less than three months after his action at Tiberias he found himself in disgrace with fortune and men's eyes. The extent of his political interests was now becoming known, and reports of his meetings in London had confirmed any remaining doubts. Shortly after his return Wing-Commander Ritchie told him that he " had acted improperly as an officer serving in Palestine in obtaining an interview with the Secretary of State for the Colonies." Wingate replied that he had expected such to be the " service view," but that his own view was that he had a higher loyalty to his conscience.[4] In January an event occurred which brought home to him the full meaning of the new course.

---

[1] *The Saga of the Squad.*
[2] Letter of comment by Wing-Commander Ritchie (13.7.39).
[3] The total number of units was as follows : 18 Infantry battalions, 2 regiments of cavalry, one battalion and detachment R.H.A., one regiment and one company A.F.V., the Transjordan Frontier Force, two squadrons R.A.F. *Annual Reports.* 1938.
[4] Ritchie (13.7.39).

Though the camp at Ein Harod was no more, though the sand table had been broken up and its contents poured back into the desert, no final decision had been taken as to the future of the Special Night Squads. But on the 23rd of January an initiative was taken towards their abolition. On that day a Divisional Conference of Intelligence Officers proposed recommendations to Force Headquarters among which was the following: " The conference is generally opposed to the dressing up of Jews as British soldiers ; in particular it is considered undesirable to have a proportion of Jews in S.N.S. detachments : these should be entirely British. In this connection it is noticeable that the pipe-line has remained unmolested . . . since the S.N.S. left the area. In short, if it is desired to conciliate the Arab, we should not provoke him by using Jews in offensive action against him."[1]

The paper came to Wingate in the course of his duties. As was to be expected, he did not accept its contents in a meek spirit. His first move was to go to his superiors and ask that he might be allowed to visit the Division in question and put the facts of S.N.S. as he saw them, to its Headquarters. He was told that this was not desirable as Lord Gort was on a short visit to Palestine and that in consequence the people whom Wingate wished to see would be too busy to spare him time. Being in a weak position he had to accept this snub.

When Wingate was cornered he always did the same thing : he wrote a memorandum. He did this now, and now as always he wrote what he did from the heart. He addressed what he had to say to Brigadier Evetts.

He pointed out that the wording of the recommendation showed serious misunderstanding of the facts since the S.N.S. were even at that moment operating in the pipe-line area, while the pipe-line itself was still the object of sabotage raids, but his main purpose was to defend his men. The S.N.S., he said, employed " the loyal section of the population against rebellion . . . and men of whatever race or creed who fight bravely under British officers against rebels should not be described by any officer holding His Majesty's Commission as ' dressing up as British soldiers.' " By using offensive language about the Jews of Palestine the Intelligence Officers had weakened their not feeble case by putting themselves in the wrong. Wingate did not spare them.

The longest part of this memorandum was devoted to a record of the origin, development and achievements of the squads. It has already been said that when Wingate expressed himself in writing he

[1] Wingate to Evetts (31.1.39).

usually erred on the side of prolixity, and certainly in this memorandum he was not as brief as he might and should have been. One may regret, however, that he did not give his literary vice freer rein. What he wrote was to have an importance he could not foresee : with the destruction of official documents in the Second World War his draft, kept among his private papers, remains to-day the only detailed official record in existence of the deeds of the anomalous little Anglo-Jewish force which he brought into being. He ended what he had to say with one of his dramatic and sombre flourishes : " If we in this country pursue a policy of favouring our enemies at the expense of our friends, what fate may properly await us ? "

Thanks to the inept phrasing of the offending minute, Wingate won a paper victory. General Montgomery, who well knew the work of the S.N.S., saw the memorandum and sent a message to Wingate saying that he disapproved of the language used by the Conference, and would moreover make amends to the Jews by recommending certain squadsmen for decorations.[1] Some men might have been mollified by such notice, but Wingate could only estimate every event by its consequence to the cause to which he had dedicated his being. When he saw great misfortune coming to the people with whom he had identified himself he wanted much more for them than gratitude for services rendered. He remained embittered.

The moment was felt by the Jews to be tragic. True, the Woodhead recommendations, together with their proposed little pale of Jewish settlement, had been abandoned by the Government, but the debates both in Parliament and the British Press had shown more understanding of the undoubtedly strong Arab case than of the Jewish one, and in the atmosphere engendered by such a tide of opinion a conference of Arab and Jewish leaders had been proposed and agreed to. It was to take place in London early in 1939. It was clear that the Arab delegations would demand total suppression of Jewish immigration,[2] and not clear that the British Government would resist them. Inevitably the Zionists in Palestine were in a state of restive pessimism in which their continuing loyalty to the Administration began at last to appear doubtful, and Wingate was known to be in their councils. The matter worried General Haining and Wing-Commander Ritchie. They conferred and the General authorised the Wing-Commander to withhold from Wingate any information likely to be the subject of an indiscretion.[3] Aggrieved allies can be more dangerous than understood enemies.

[1] *Complaint.*
[2] The Pan Arab Congress of October, 1938, held in Cairo had unanimously agreed on this. *Annual Register.* 1938.
[3] Ritchie (13.7.39).

Wingate did not know of the interdiction[1], but he may have suspected it. What is certain is that in this period of anticlimax, disappointment and indignation, he began to ruminate on his future and nearly took a bold and disastrous step. One day he sought out his friend David Hacohen and the two men had a long and earnest discussion. Towards the end of it Wingate said somewhat as follows : " You know, the British Empire believes that it can only survive by letting someone down regularly once a fortnight. It is an absurd belief. The British Empire is something much finer than that ; it need never let anyone down. It is up to you Jews to explode this ridiculous myth." Hacohen, used as he was to the other's violent mode of expression, was puzzled by these words. Wingate told him more of what was in his mind. He said : " The time for self-restraint, for open and legal opposition, for the co-operation of the Jews with the British Government is past. You will have to go underground. I will come with you. I will send in my papers and become one of yourselves. This," he said, pointing to his D.S.O. ribbon, " this does not matter, nor does my future as a British soldier." Hacohen asked him why he told him this. He replied that he needed advice. Without hesitation Hacohen advised him, and advised him very strongly indeed that what he suggested was mad and could do no good to Zionism or to himself. He besought him utterly to dismiss any such plan from his mind. Wingate was impressed by his words. After consulting with other of his Jewish friends and receiving the same advice he did what they urged, forgot the plan and never reverted to it again.

It was a foolhardy plan. The advice against it was without question wise and speaks nobly for the good sense of his Jewish friends at a moment when such outbreaks and protests were tempting. But it must be stressed that for all his temerity Wingate had proposed nothing which was not within the rights of men as these are normally understood, even though he may have been tempted to take extreme and blameworthy advantage of those rights. It needs to be stressed because from this episode (kept secret but darkly hinted at here and there) a story arose much later that he was a secret traitor. The story has no more solid foundation. It is nonsense.

This is the time to consider what became of the Special Night Squads. The paragraph may be brief for by January of 1939 their end was near. After the closure of the camp at Ein Harod the main body moved to the north to the country above Lake Hula. The borderland above the lake was marshy and sparsely inhabited then, and in that dismal country the S.N.S. fought against some of the last of the

[1] In the *Complaint* he says he was given access to all documents.

organised gangs. From the little that is recorded, their operations seem to have been successful and conducted with harshness. At the same time as this move to Hula, a rump of the Ein Harod unit moved to a place called Kadurie, a very small Jewish settlement about a mile north-west of Mount Tabor. The Kadurie squads were joined by the remains of those from Kinneret. They operated for the most part in the Hula district but at the same time they continued to patrol the pipe-line, with success, it would seem, from the absence of incident. The policy of " dejudification " was continued and, according to Jewish diaries, with a display of tactlessness truly British. Inexperienced young men were put in charge of Squads and they seem to have treated the Jews with ungracious discrimination, assigning menial tasks to them so as to relieve the British soldiers of their more irksome duties. By March most of the squads were wholly British in composition, though the Kadurie group, with mixed British and Jewish membership, continued in their patrol-duties right into the summer.[1] In the meantime the founder of the S.N.S. was condemned to the routine of Staff duty.

" At Force Headquarters," Wingate was to tell later, " my work was primarily to study the political situation. I am very much better qualified for constructive military work than I am for this kind of purely academic work." In vain he tried to arrange for employment which would take him back to Galilee. He noticed that the official machinery for supplying officers in the field with the military intelligence they needed was cumbersome and resulted in dangerous delays. He remembered how on S.N.S. operations he had devised methods of obtaining information rapidly from the Intelligence Centre at Nazareth, and he now proposed that he should be given some kind of roving commission to establish efficient liaison between Headquarters and forward troops. He put the report in writing and received no answer. When he pressed the matter he was told to remain where he was. In March he tried to escape again. Sometime in the year before he had been to Damascus where he had met people who told him about the organisation of the Palestine rebellion. He now suggested that he should go to Damascus for further exploration and was told again that he was to remain in Jerusalem.[2] He had tried all means of escape in vain. He remained therefore in Jerusalem.

During these days he met an American journalist, Lorna Lindsley, who left an account of him. She visited his house several times and

---

[1] *The Saga of the Squad*. Wingate to Evetts (31.1.39) (where some of the later history is very briefly dealt with). Bredin. Zvi Brenner.
[2] *Complaint*.

in her racy journalistic book, *War is People*, she gave a vivid if slightly inaccurate picture of him in his private life at this time. " There were comfortable chairs in the room," she wrote, " but Captain Wingate had an aversion to them. He had spent his childhood in the Orient and he liked a low couch on the floor, covered with a rug. The tables were low too, to match the couch ; there were bowls of flowers and fruit in the room and the walls were lined with books, a great part of them in the Hebrew language. Like all men whose lives are passed out of doors, he looked vaguely out of place even in his own library. He was a small spare man with a compelling face ; his eyes were like the blue far-sighted eyes of a sailor. . . . I was struck by his resemblance to Lawrence of Arabia. . . .

" Lorna Wingate was beautiful ; her black hair and eyes made her look oriental. . . . She too believed in the nation that was being formed anew in Palestine : she had been enthralled by the mysticism of Jerusalem, captured by its tragedy. They both loved Judea so much that any other land would have been an exile.

" Captain Wingate was blunt about John Bull Humpty-Dumpty. He laid the responsibility for what went wrong in Palestine squarely on the Foreign Office in London.[1] Whitehall was at the bottom of the mess. It was full of bureaucratic officials who did not know conditions. . . . . British policy in Palestine was too often shaped by officials who had no local historical knowledge, and it was too often enforced by military men who were ignorant of the Oriental mind, officers who had avoided meeting Jews from the days when they wore the old school tie, and whose admiration for the Arabs was founded only on the fact that they were a horsey race who rode their mounts well."

Lorna Lindsley gave a brief account of the S.N.S. which need not be repeated, except for a pleasing Wingate story not recorded elsewhere. In the early days of the squads Wingate said to one of his Jewish friends : " They are excellent soldiers, these boys, but do all Jews talk so much ? The amount of talking these boys do in a week is more than British boys would do in a year."

At the time she met him she described him as " more or less sulking in his tent." She continued : " He hated inaction, he hated to be called off his quarry, he didn't like to be told he could go so far but not *too* far. He felt his Jewish soldiers had been let down too ; they were all good soldiers, so let them fight. He told me ardently that Jews were good fighters, capable and ready to defend themselves ; why

[1] It was a popular error that the Foreign Office ruled Palestine. Miss Lindsley clearly remembered Wingate's words wrong. The reader will have noticed her mistake about Wingate's childhood, and is about to notice another concerning old school ties.

in heaven's name not let them do it ? As for those chaps in London, they were so anxious to conciliate everybody that they ended in conciliating nobody.

" We had heard in Palestine that the Grand Mufti was being paid £10,000 a year by Berlin—H. R. Knickerbocker had dug out that bit of information—but I had also heard a rumour that the British Government had offered him £5,000 to call off the attacks of his Arab gang. . . . I asked Captain Wingate if there was any truth in this story. He shook his head ; it was only a rumour. But he looked as if he thought that, this tall story aside, Whitehall was capable of any form of appeasement.

" I went to Wingate's house again just before I left Palestine. I found Wingate lying on his couch listening to the Bach B Minor Mass played on his gramophone ; the floor was strewn with other Bach records. At the same time he was reading the Old Testament in Hebrew. He put the book down and stopped the record, saying that he never tired of Hebrew literature nor of Christian Church music."

In May of 1939 the Palestine Mandate entered the last phase of its melancholy inter-war history. Jewish and Arab leaders had assembled in London in February but the proposed Round Table Conference never took place because the Arab delegation refused to meet the Jewish one. There followed instead two separate conferences, a British-Jewish one and a British-Arab one, both of which failed through the refusal of Jews and Arabs to accept the British proposals. In March the Jews led by Dr. Weizmann declared that they could not negotiate further and they were soon followed by the Arabs. The British Government then let it be known that failing any agreed policy they would impose one. There was little doubt as to what the terms of this would be ; in general they would follow those already laid before the two conferences, and which had been rejected by the Arabs because they did not annul the Balfour Declaration, and by the Jews because they limited immigration drastically and forbade the free transfer of land. April and the first fortnight of May were spent in anxious waiting and wondering. Shortly before the publication of the White Paper many Jews of Palestine were dismayed by a piece of news which seemed to portend calamities ahead : Hayedid Wingate, " the friend," was under orders to go.

The first intimation that he was to be given a new appointment came to Force Headquarters from the War Office in the first week of May. Details were sent on the 10th : he was to serve as Brigade Major in a newly formed Anti-Aircraft Brigade with headquarters at Uxbridge. He was to leave at the end of the month.[1] He had no doubt that his transfer was due to official disapproval of his political interests. He was right : General Haining had for some time been requesting the War Office to transfer him.[2] When he had the news Wingate made a last request to his superiors : that he might go once more to Galilee, collect his belongings and say good-bye to his friends. In an interview with General Haining before going north Wingate pointed out that with his unusual influence with the Jews it would be well if he took the opportunity of this last visit to Galilee to urge moderation on the exasperated Zionist community. The General agreed to this.[3]

Wingate kept that promise, as is shown very clearly by closely detailed accounts of his behaviour while in Haifa, but being the man he was, impulsive in his dealings, and dedicated to a great cause, he forgot his discretion on one occasion. At the S.N.S. station of Kadurie he addressed the assembled British and Jewish squadsmen in English, urging them to maintain the spirit of co-operation they had learned, but then he added in Hebrew : " I am sent away from you and the country I love. I suppose you know why. I am transferred because we are too great friends. They want to hurt me and you. I promise you that I will come back, and if I cannot do it the regular way, I shall return as a refugee."[4] Or so his words were remembered, and unfortunately the gist of the report prompted a paragraph in the Jewish Press, and the paragraph was reported to the War Office.

Having collected his belongings at Ein Harod, having said good-bye to his friends there, and in the other Kibbutzim in the course of a long last tour of Galilee, he went to Haifa arriving about the 15th of May. It was while he was there, on the 17th of May, that the British Government issued their statement of policy.

It was precisely what had been expected. The idea of partition was rejected. The aim was the formation of an independent Palestine in ten years in preparation for which boon Jews and Moslems were to be more closely associated with administration. The Jews were to be allowed to introduce 10,000 immigrants a year for five years in addition to 25,000 refugees from Central Europe. At the end of five years, when the number of the Palestinian Jews would have been increased by 75,000, and when the Jewish community would form a third of the

[1] It seems that at first Wingate was not fully informed as to the nature of his new appointment. The following perplexing telegram was sent on 12th May from the Jewish Agency in Jerusalem : " Following from Captain Wingate for Weizmann and Shertock quote offered immediate transfer good staff appointment if refuse risk being sent anywhere stop will accept your views as to action unquote address reply Zazlani." The reply has not been preserved. Weizmann Archives.

[2] Information obtained at the War Office.

[3] Israel Ministry of Defence Records.   [4] Zvi Brenner.

population of the country, no more Jews were to be allowed to settle " unless the Arabs of Palestine (were) prepared to acquiesce in it." The High Commissioner was to be given powers " to prohibit and regulate transfers of land." The White Paper was based on a supposal (for which there was no evidence of any kind) that the Arabs and Jews felt a common patriotism towards Palestine for whose sake they could and would both sink their differences. To the Jews acceptance would mean that they submitted to permanent minority status in the Promised Land. The Arabs had won the great prize for which the rebellion had been fought : cessation (under conditions which they at first resented) of Jewish immigration.

It seems that Wingate (probably through Divisional Headquarters in Haifa) received advance notice of the terms of the White Paper. His immediate reaction was to buy some bottles of whisky which he presented as a gift to the Wilenskis. They were surprised at this generous extravagance, and they asked him (while thanking him) for some explanation. They were laughing but he was serious. " I got that whisky for you," he said, " because in the next few days you are going to need all the whisky you can get."

The next day, the day on which the White Paper was made public, the Wilenskis had arranged a farewell dinner party for Wingate who was due to sail for England in ten days. They invited several of the leading Zionists of Haifa including Eliahu Golomb, Yakov Dori, and Emanuel Wilenski's brother. Everyone present was a member of Hagana, some of them of considerable influence. This circumstance excited rumour. The party has formed the subject of a widely accepted libel on Wingate's character, so it is necessary to set down the facts with as much precision as possible.

According to the book in which the story appeared Wingate, on arrival at this party (represented as a secret meeting in defiance of the law) immediately harangued his Jewish friends on the need " to declare war on the English," telling them that he had come to obtain the declaration and to plan the first attack. And then, so the story goes on, he seriously proposed that with their agreement he would secretly lead Jewish forces into the great oil refinery at Haifa and destroy it.[1]

None of this is true.

When the dinner party assembled at Wilenski's house Wingate appeared looking pale and restless.[2] He felt the disaster to the Jews as keenly as though he himself were of their number. While all was rumour, even though the rumour was of a dispiriting kind, there had

[1] See Appendix A for details of the story and the grounds of refutation.
[2] Yakov Dori.

still been hope ; now all was plain and in the White Paper the hopes of the last years were extinguished. Despite the grief of the moment, the dinner party went forward in an ordinary way until the end when conversation became more serious. This phase began with Eliahu Golomb asking Wingate if it was really true that he was about to leave Palestine.[1] "It is true," answered Wingate, whereupon Golomb addressed him at some length expressing his own and the general regret that so staunch a friend should be leaving them at so grave a time. Under the stress of their preoccupations the host and guests began to talk of Zionism in general terms and Wingate, as he was apt to do, began to convert the conversation into a monologue to which everyone present listened with interest. He spoke at some length. It seems that he felt that the occasion was historic and he gave what may be described as a valedictory discourse on the subject of the Zionist movement, its history, its meaning and its threatened future. From this the talk turned again to the White Paper and the need for a more active and stubborn Jewish policy. Among the horrors of the Jewish persecution in Europe at that time was a traffic in Zionism whereby German agents used to charter unseaworthy vessels, overload them with Jews fleeing from Nazi rule and send the masters off with orders to get rid of the passengers by any means so long as they were not brought back to Germany. The great majority of these " coffin-boats " deposited their cargoes secretly on the shores of Palestine. At that moment there was a group of illegal immigrants, as the Jewish victims were called, in Haifa awaiting deportation. Wingate insisted that on no account must the Jews of Haifa allow this deportation to take place. He regarded the fate of these immigrants at this moment as a test of Jewish firmness. The Jews, he said, must go to all lengths to stop such an abomination as the handing back of these wretched people into the hands of their tormentors.

This began a debate as to what kind of methods the Jews ought to adopt, and here Wingate put forward definite views. He said that in urging a more aggressive policy he must not be understood to urge a policy of violence. He had in mind campaigns such as those organised by Mahatma Ghandi in India. He became insistent on this point and said somewhat as follows : " At the moment you may be in the mood to think bitterly of England and the British Government, but I assure you that there are hundreds of thousands of English people who feel much as I do about Zionism and our cause. We have abundant goodwill in England and this is going to be of immense value to Zionists in the future. I warn you not to jeopardise that goodwill. If you ever resort to violence, if you kill one British soldier

[1] Yolan.

or one British policeman you may so shock people in England, who think better of you, that you may throw away a great and precious asset."

After this the discussion turned to the subject of the new provisions concerning land-transfers and their effect on the present settlements and their protection. Not much is remembered of this part of the conversation, and there is some conflict in the evidence as to whether it preceded or followed the more heated scene during which the company considered the fate of the illegal immigrants. The evening is remembered as one of affection and melancholy rather than one of drama. There was no mention at any time of an attack on the Haifa refinery.[1]

Soon after this Wingate and his wife went to Jerusalem together for the last time. Among the friends whom they saw there was George Antonius whose remarkable book, *The Arab Awakening*, had been published earlier in the year and had probably done much to influence British opinion towards sympathy with Arab nationalism. One day the three of them were walking round the vast stone piazza in the middle of which stands the blue-tiled mosque of the Haram a'Sharif. In the middle of their stroll Lorna turned impulsively to their friend and said : " You know, George, you and we are now on opposite sides. You may shoot me first but I would try to shoot you first." He took the assault with good humour but then answered : " No, Lorna, if we get what we want and turn the British out of Palestine I won't be shot by you or Orde but in the back by one of my own people." He was a sincere nationalist but he had no delusions.[2]

There were other farewell parties among the Jews. One was at the house of Dov Josef. He had known Wingate since the year before and had fought in the S.N.S. He assembled about fifty friends one evening a few days before the departure. Towards the end he presented the chief guest with a certificate of his enrolment in the golden book of the grand synagogue. Wingate acknowledged the honour in a formal manner, speaking in English till, moved by a sudden impulse, he took an oath customary among Jews when leaving their venerated homeland, raising his hand and uttering the words in the Hebrew language : " If I forget thee, O Jerusalem, let my right hand forget her cunning. If I do not remember thee, let my tongue cleave to the roof of my mouth, if I prefer not Jerusalem above my chief joy."[3]

They left on the 26th of May travelling by train to Port Said where they embarked on the troopship *Dorsetshire*. By a confusion not without precedent in Army administration, the Transport Officer at Head-

[1] Emanuel Yolan. Mrs. Yolan. Yakov Dori. [2] Mrs. Lorna Smith.
[3] Dov Josef.

quarters had overlooked the fact that the troopship was to sail to Haifa from Port Said before making west for Gibraltar and the journey home, so, shortly after embarking, they found themselves back in Palestine for a day. But this touch of farce and anticlimax resulted in a fitting last scene. They heard from Wilenski that the venerable mother of Dr. Weizmann was in Haifa and Wingate went to pay his respects and say good-bye. When the moment came for him to leave the old lady pronounced a blessing on him in the Jewish fashion, laying her hands on his head.[1]

[1] Yolan.

CHAPTER X

RECOVERY INTO THE DOLDRUMS

By the time the troopship was halfway across the Mediterranean Wingate had begun to plan his future afresh. He knew well enough that he was under a cloud of official disapproval and he believed that the fact was known on the troopship. Yet during this journey Wingate gave no sign of his embitterment or anger. He was at his most amiable, in part perhaps because a long tension had been relaxed, in part perhaps because he had recourse to his usual anodyne. Soon after sailing from Haifa he began to write a memorandum twenty-seven pages in length entitled *Palestine in Imperial Strategy*.

He wrote it not only under the stress of a great emotion but of a great ambition which was nothing less than to change the whole direction of British policy in the East, and as on other occasions he unknowingly drew a self-portrait. Following a sound forensic technique he began by first presenting the proposition to which he was opposed, in apparently favourable terms. Then, having discussed Pan-Arabism, Palestine relative to Islam, and the Jewish character, all in an Arabophil sense, he proceeded to demolish the arguments to which he had given substance. He was not successful throughout. Like others who have pleaded on one or other side of this debate he sometimes fell into the error of endeavouring to show as simple a question that was essentially hard of solution because it was complicated. But when he relied less on theory than on his own observation he made what he had to say extremely convincing. He insisted that policy was largely influenced by mistaken notions of the Arab character. " That unfortunate masterpiece," he wrote, " *The Seven Pillars of Wisdom*, joined to the combined efforts of a number of distinguished Britons who found it amusing and convenient to live among and write about the Arabs, has given the British public a quite false notion of the value of the Arab as a man of war. The Arab is lazy, ignorant, feckless, and, without being particularly cowardly, sees no point in really losing his life. He will take a certain risk for the sake of loot." He referred also to " George Antonius whose eloquent and inaccurate book . . . had no small share in smoothing the way for the White Paper."

Among these disparagements of the Arab character and national cause, he interspersed contrasting passages which dwelt on the loyalty and energy of the Zionist movement. " No one," he wrote, " who has not thoroughly inspected the Jewish settlement in Palestine can readily believe the extent of the achievement," but, remembering his audience, he resisted his tendency to rhapsodical expression and there were no quotations from the Bible. Throughout the paper he was suggesting the need for a Jewish army. He found a strong argument to the effect that those who had pioneered so valorously in Palestine were its natural defenders. " I shall presently prove," he said with a characteristic touch of his self-confidence, " that the only way to provide local security in Palestine is to employ the Jews," and this led him inevitably whither trains of reasoning often led him in his memoranda—to " A brief account of the formation and employment of the Special Night Squad organisation in Palestine during the 1938 rebellion."

The most interesting thing in the paper came at the end where he made a forecast of what would happen as a result of the White Paper. It is interesting because of its accuracy. He foresaw that the Government's decision of policy towards Jews and Arabs must lead in the end to armed conflict with the Jews, and that such an unnatural state of things must fatally weaken the British position in the world. Anyone who reflects on subsequent Palestinian history must be impressed by the vision which enabled Wingate to read the meaning of tumultuous events, in which he was involved, with such masterly precision. But, as with many men of keen vision, he mistook the time-factor. He assumed that this weakening of the British Eastern position would come about immediately. In fact it did not, and in Palestine the policy of appeasement was in large measure successful. Pro-British persons in the world of Islam took heart at what they felt to be a change of mind, and this was to be of considerable value in the war. Zionism sank from the first place in Arab preoccupations ; the rebellion slowly faded away in Palestine ; the German conspiracies in Syria and Iraq failed to a large extent because of the presence of friends to the Allied cause within those countries. King Ibn Saud gave the Allies the support of his moral prestige in the worst days of defeat. Egypt proved a tranquil base for the Middle East Forces. The Zionist has to recognise the unpleasing fact that in preferring to soothe the rebellious party rather than rally the loyal population of Palestine, the British Government reaped a plentiful and immediate political reward. A heavy price for this doubtful transaction certainly had to be paid, as was accurately foreseen by Wingate, but it had to be paid much later, not at once.

The ship was sailing towards Gibraltar on the evening of the day when he finished this paper. He sought out the officer commanding the troops on board and asked him whether the ship was going to make a stop there, and for how long. The officer replied that the troopship would arrive early in the morning and would stay but a few hours. "There will be no shore-leave" he added ominously, or as the other thought ominously. Wingate appeared indifferent.

At dawn the next morning when the troopship arrived Wingate was up and dressed smartly. To his dismay he found that the troopship did not berth alongside a quay but alongside a cargo boat berthed between her and the mole. Yet in a way this was an advantage since the difficulties of reaching the shore were such that the authorities had not troubled to mount a guard. Wingate soon found a place where he could leap from the troopship to the cargo boat, and once he had achieved that feat, he had no difficulty in reaching the shore down a gangway. On landing he was saluted not questioned. He walked into the town until he found someone to drive him to Government House. Arrived there he naturally found no one astir except a few of the servants and the officer on duty. He approached the latter and told him that for urgent reasons he must request an immediate interview with the Governor, explaining that he had little time to spare. The officer took his name to the Governor's bedroom.

There must have followed for the intruder some minutes of anxious waiting. But the message came back that he was to present himself in the Governor's dressing-room immediately. As luck would have it Sir Edmund Ironside was obliged to get up unusually early that day in order to do the honours to a visiting admiral. He did not receive the request for a dawn interview in any choleric spirit. He had not forgotten the name of the fierce Captain he had met on the heights of Tiberias on the morning after the massacre, and he still held his anomalous post of Commander-in-Chief Designate for the Middle East. He was anxious for any first-hand report on Palestine which he could get. He received Wingate, despite the uncomfortable hour, in a friendly way and asked him what he wanted. Wingate presented the memorandum and said that he only wanted Sir Edmund Ironside to read it. Sir Edmund promised that he would do so. The meeting was short, both participants being pressed for time, and nothing of note seems to have been said. Before leaving Wingate left his London address.[1] One would like to know more about his departure. Was he offered an official car back to the harbour, and did he willingly or unwillingly indicate at all why he would rather be without this embarrassing convenience? What is known is that he returned to the mole where the ship lay, walked back on to the cargo boat (had he made

[1] Ironside.

sure it was not to leave ?)—and found a safe moment for the counter-leap. He was back on the troopship about nine o'clock in time for breakfast. He was in a state of high elation.

He was right to be pleased with what he had done.

The *Dorsetshire* arrived at Southampton on the 13th of June. He reported to his new Headquarters at Uxbridge and then he and Lorna spent a short holiday till the 23rd, staying at the Kensington Palace Hotel. Their rooms overlooked Kensington Gardens and they feasted their eyes on all that greenness with the pleasure which only those who have lived in sun-burnt lands can know. One day Wingate received an interesting letter.

" Government House, Gibraltar   June 8th

My dear Wingate.

I am in complete agreement with your paper. I had a good deal to do with that unfortunate charlatan Lawrence in the Rebellion in Iraq in 1920. He was such an impossible creature that I cannot understand how this wretched myth has sprung up around him. In the end, of course, he became egotistical and impossible. Had it not been for men like Liddell Hart he might have been forgotten.

I have the profoundest admiration for what your squads did in Palestine . . . to hear that these activities have ceased is sad.

If the crisis in September had developed I had made up my mind to arm the Jews and to withdraw most of the troops.

I do not know the Jews except under the worst conditions of oppression in Russia and Germany, but I must confess that I have been a little frightened of the strength and sincerity of Zionism. To see Jews in such numbers is somewhat terrifying. I must confess that Tel Aviv was an extraordinary experience. I wondered what would happen were the country to become very prosperous— as I am sure it would under the Jews. I wondered if the Jews would not radiate once more from their new home in Palestine back into the world of Gentiles. Would that be good for the British Empire ? It is very perplexing. There is no absolute guarantee that the finance of industry established in Palestine would remain properly controlled. I do not think it is possible to establish heavy industries in Palestine without great difficulty. Where are the raw materials ? They ought to be close by. We have had so many examples of failure in Russia when the Soviet tried to place the industries uneconomically. But I am very ignorant about the whole thing.

Come and see me in London. I should like to hear what you have to say about it.

Yours sincerely,
Edmund Ironside "

When their leave was up Wingate went to Uxbridge and Lorna moved to rooms in the Cumberland Hotel. He often came up to London and sometimes would stay a few days with a Jewish friend, Arthur Louri. A curious thing happened during their first days in England. An officer whom he had known in Palestine wrote to ask him for the loan of a hundred pounds, if possible immediately, offering him his fruit farm in Hampshire as a security. The two men had not been close friends in Palestine, if anything rather the opposite, and this fact made Wingate realise that the man must be in very dire straits indeed to have written such a letter. His reaction was typical. He wrote to his bank for a statement of his account and the bank answered that his credit stood at £105. Wingate immediately sent his fellow-officer the £100 he asked for. Lorna asked him if he was going to accept the offered security. " Oh no," said Wingate. " He must need his fruit farm more than ever now."

In the meantime, during the last weeks of pre-war summer there opened a strange chapter in his life.

While he was on leave at the Kensington Palace Hotel he received copies of the annual Confidential Reports made on him by his superior officers, in this instance Wing-Commander Ritchie and General Haining. The two reports were in agreement and were both adverse. Ritchie said that Wingate was a remarkable man of distinguished mind and abounding courage, but that being an enthusiast by nature he tended to use his undoubtedly great gifts in the service of causes to which he felt dedicated, rather than in the service of the administration to which he was bound. In Palestine, said the Wing-Commander, Wingate had given his sympathies so unreservedly to the Jewish cause that he became unable to fulfil the neutral functions of an Intelligence Officer, and he was now recommended for regimental rather than staff employment. The General endorsed this opinion while paying additional tribute to Wingate's qualities and achievement, but at the same time expressing a yet sterner view of the ill-effects of his enthusiasms on his duties as an impartial public servant.[1] Anyone who has followed the course of Wingate's career so far, and who has recognised the extent of his political activity, will probably agree that these restrained

[1] The writer has been asked not to quote the reports verbatim as being contrary to the spirit in which such things are written.

reports were wholly justified. But to Wingate himself they seemed monstrosities of injustice, and he immediately took the strongest measure open to him in self-defence. He appealed to the King for the reports to be withdrawn.

This is another of those points in the story of his life around which absurdities have clustered. Wingate has been represented as demanding an interview, telling the Army Council in session that it was an ignorant body, then rushing out into Whitehall, leaping into a taxi and driving to Buckingham Palace with the offending documents. He is said to have scribbled a note to the King in the hall of that famous residence in answer to which he received a gracious message conveyed by an equerry, and so on, in the style of an old-fashioned film.[1] But in fact the sequence of events was very different and much more interesting.

As soon as he had the report and had satisfied himself on his right to appeal under section 42 of the Army Act, he wrote a fifteen-page memorandum which he had completed by the 27th of June. Its title was " Complaint to the Sovereign by Captain O. C. Wingate, relating 1. To the contents and manner of the rendering of a Confidential Report by Wing-Commander Ritchie, A.F.C., G.S.O., " I " of Force Head-quarters Jerusalem on Captain O. C. Wingate, D.S.O., R.A., for the period 1.10.38 to 30.4.39; 2. To the Absence of any Confidential Report from Brigadier J. F. Evetts, C.B., C.B.E., M.C., both for a portion of the above period and for the period of equal length, as regards actual service, of 1.6.38 to 13.10.38 during the whole of which time Captain Wingate was in fact serving under the direct orders of Brigadier Evetts although technically only lent for a portion of the time ; 3. To the absence of any recognition for services since 11.7.38 " The title shows clearly enough the main line of counter-attack : to establish that Wing-Commander Ritchie was not in a position to know the real facts, and to obtain from Evetts an official report likely to be favourable.

The Complaint was immediately lodged with the War Office. Wingate had to wait till Christmas Day for the answer.

The procedure followed three defined stages. The Complaint was to be considered by the Army Council who would examine the case in full and make their recommendation on it. Their findings would then be conveyed to the Secretary of State for his guidance. When the Secretary of State had reached his decision he would convey the Complaint to the King with his advice. All these steps, except the last, were followed in the case of Wingate, while he, in the meantime, continued as Brigade-Major to the 56th Light Anti-Aircraft Brigade,

[1] *Gideon Goes To War*, p. 81.

often coming up to London to meet his Zionist friends and take part in their political discussions.

The Complaint is an odd, diffuse, ill-constructed document, of rare interest because of the frequent autobiography in it. He wrote it under the considerable disadvantage that he had few papers with him, and so for the most part he had to make his case from memory. He laboured under another disadvantage. He could not fail to realise at any time that the very moderation of the reports made them difficult to answer. He was not accused of disloyalty or intrigue or indeed of any offence, he was only said to possess faults of temperament. As he wrote the Complaint he may often have wished that his superiors had said something worse than they had said.

He began by arguing that if his enthusiasm was held to have vitiated his work as a member of Force Headquarters then his work in suppressing the rebellion was likewise put in doubt. Only Brigadier Evetts could give a definitive opinion on this subject for which reason he, and not the Wing-Commander, should have written the report. He added that if the Brigadier's report still left the question in doubt then the supreme Commander, Sir Edmund Ironside, should be invited to give an opinion. " In order," he said, " that facts rather than opinions should speak, I propose here to describe what I did during the eleven months anterior to this report." There followed another brief account of the Special Night Squads, not given in chronological order but in the form of a résumé of their various achievements. In the course of this account he raised the question of his D.S.O., pointing out that he received no recognition for the far more valuable work which he and the S.N.S. had accomplished after the battle of Dabburiya. He expressed himself unfortunately here. He was not asking for more medals but for promotion.[1] " I must maintain," he concluded the first section, " that in my work I displayed the following qualities : creative ability ; judgment of men, military problems, and political realities, without which I should early have met with disaster ; tact, without which my relations with the various officials I had to deal with would not have been as friendly and successful as they were." The assertion of tact in this thunderous document may not command full agreement.

In the next section he told of his service in Jerusalem from December 1938 to the time of his departure. He stated that in spite of his friendship with Jews he remained without bias, and he enlarged on the frustrations he met with. He ended the section : " I would remind Wing-Commander Ritchie that I am the fifth consecutive gener-

[1] Mrs. Lorna Smith. In fact (a point not mentioned anywhere during the subsequent discussion) he had been mentioned in despatches in April, 1939.

ation of my family to serve in His Majesty's Army, and the suggestion that I could become useless to the Crown as a result of sympathy with aliens needs strong proof."

There then followed an " Analysis of the Report " in which he made the same points as he had done already in closer detail and with reference to particular words and phrases. One quotation will suffice to give a notion of this part : " My public and private support of the Jews was obligatory," he said. " They had always been loyal to me and to Great Britain. I would state here that neither I nor my wife, nor any member of either of our families has a drop of Jewish blood in their veins. Experience has taught me that one gets better results, to put it on no higher ground, by consistency than by trimming one's sails to suit the wind. Is it ' emotional ' to have a sense of honour and to defend your men when they are attacked ? "

The last section was entitled " My Rôle in Palestine." There was nothing in this part of the Complaint which he had not said before, until the last very curious paragraphs in which he took his auto-biographical habit farther than usual. This is what he said :

" A man who possesses creative ability tends inevitably to form his own original opinions. Unless he is very fortunate the value of his opinions will not be apparent to his superiors unless there is some acid test to which they can be put. In most professions there is such a test. In the Army in time of peace there is as a rule no such test. But I maintain that if such a test takes place, and if the opinions suspected of unsoundness receive triumphant vindication, then nothing could be more unfair than to fall back upon opinion in order to justify disagreement with the man with creative abilities.

" There have been no less than three such acid tests in my life. The first was in the Sudan where, on the first occasion in my life when I had an independent command, I planned and carried out a wide sweeping march through country held to be impassable and not previously traversed, which resulted in the complete surprise of numerous groups of Abyssinian and Sudanese bandits. The second test was when on leaving the Sudan in the Spring of 1933 I planned and carried out a march right across the Sand Sea from east to west at right angles to the line of dunes. I did this alone and at my own charges. I surveyed the whole journey with a theodolite and took scientific observations. The whole is reported in the *Geographical Journal*, Vol. 83. . . .

" The third acid test occurred in Palestine and has been described by me here. This was a case in which my judgment was vindicated and my theories justified. It is not to be thought that the creation of the Special Night Squads by me was the bright idea of a moment. For the previous two years, against the opinion of my superiors, I had been advancing the theories that I afterwards successfully applied. It is these judgments and theories that Wing-Commander Ritchie regards as based on distorted judgments and emotions.

" I submit that where acid tests exist opinions are of no value unless in accordance with the results of these tests. I claim that I have given proof of the abilities and qualities of a commander. I state and can prove that by making a successful contact with Jews I was able to be of considerable service to the Crown, although personally I only suffered from the connection. I further claim that future developments in Palestine are likely to render my services there again of potential use, and that they should be employed there."

The document ended with a formal recapitulation of the grounds of complaint and an expression of regret that it should have " occupied so much space, and that the nature of it has necessitated so much self-praise."

The Army Council communicated the text of the Complaint to General Haining and Wing-Commander Ritchie for their comments. Their answers were received in Whitehall on the 20th of July. Neither of them was moved to withdraw anything said in the reports, nor to recommend further reports. " I do not intend," wrote General Haining, ". . . to do more than to say that the work done in the field by Captain Wingate was, in my opinion, adequately recognised by the award of the D.S.O., that his request for a report by Brigadier Evetts and General Sir Edmund Ironside seems singularly pointless as he has been on the staff of G.O.C. British Forces Palestine and Transjordan since January of 1937 during which period his confidential reports were rendered normally in 1937 and in 1938, the latter by me ; and that I consider the report rendered by Wing-Commander Ritchie is a very fair and indeed generous one."

The reply from the Wing-Commander was longer. It is a document of much interest as it gives many details of Wingate's Palestine career as seen from an official point of view. (They have been given already in the course of the story.) He paid renewed tribute to Wingate's " great ability and courage," and insisted with the General that the award of the D.S.O. was an adequate recognition. Against Wingate's argument that his practical achievements proved the blamelessness of his official way of life, he asserted that in the later stages of his command of the squads, Wingate, contrary to instructions, had been concerned with political objects. Of Wingate's last Palestine phase he said, " I have received information since which leads me to believe that during the last few months of his service in Palestine Captain Wingate was tendering advice to the Jewish leaders here on political and other matters. Although in so doing he was ostensibly acting in a private capacity, I consider that in view of his official position and known access to official information and opinions Captain Wingate's action was not merely indiscreet, but definitely improper, whatever the nature of his advice." He declared himself puzzled by Wingate's references to Sir Edmund Ironside and ended with a reassertion of the views contained in the report which, he said, he was not willing to withdraw or qualify.

General Haining's reply (but not Wing-Commander Ritchie's) was communicated to Wingate who was immediately moved to write a new memorandum. This took the form of an " Annexure . . . to be attached to a Complaint to the Sovereign . . . made by Captain O. C. Wingate, D.S.O., R.A." It is a repetition (with more autobiographical touches) of what he had said in the Complaint. In the latter and now again in the annexure he strove in every paragraph to remove the debate on to more favourable ground for him : his service with the S.N.S. which had in fact hardly been questioned. His two superiors were shown the annexure and remained insistent that the debate should be confined to the specific and not severe strictures contained in their reports. After this the matter was referred with Haining's and Ritchie's comments to the Army Council for definitive consideration. But the time was now August ; the Army Council had other matters on its hands, and the case was postponed awhile.

In the meantime there had been important changes in high military appointments. These were to prove advantageous to the petitioner. Sir Edmund Ironside had relinquished his post as Commander-in-Chief-Designate for the Middle East and Governor of Gibraltar, and was now Inspector-General of Overseas Forces in Great Britain. Wingate was not slow to obey Sir Edmund's request for him to visit him in London, and in the course of various meetings he told the General of his present troubles. He added to the good impression that he had first made. While his appeal to the King was awaiting discussion Sir Edmund wrote to the Director of Military Operations and Intelligence as follows :

" August 22nd.   Office of the Inspector-
                                              General of Overseas Forces,
                                                        Thames House,
                                                             S.W.1.

Dear Pownall,

    Here is a paper by one *Wingate*,[1] a gunner Captain, who was working with the Jews in Palestine. I believe that he got a bad mark for being too Jewish. He is a most remarkable soldier and

---

[1] The paper was called *Appreciation of the use of Jewish Forces in the war.*

leader of men. He infused glory into his Jewish squads. If we get into this war we shall want all we can find. In September '38 I made up my mind as Commander-in-Chief Middle East to arm the Jews. Here is the beginning of an Organisation of which you should not lose sight. It taps Jewry in the U.S.A. and South Africa. A man who might take on a job of running such a business is Brigadier Evetts, now in India, a very able soldier.

Don't answer this. But, don't forget that you have Wingate in this country as Adjutant 56th Light A.A. Brigade R.A., Duke of York's Headquarters, Chelsea.

Yours sincerely,
Edmund Ironside "

On the declaration of war Sir Edmund Ironside was made Chief of the Imperial General Staff. Sir Archibald Wavell became the Middle East Commander. Wingate's position, to apply a frequently used military expression, was serious but not desperate.

On the bright Sunday morning on which the Prime Minister made the fatal announcement, Dudley Clarke was driving down St. James's Street to the War Office in Whitehall. On his way he saw a short purposefully striding figure in khaki uniform, a large pistol swinging from the belt. He recognised Wingate and considered, then and later, that this was a fitting first sight of the men and events which were to occupy the years ahead. Dudley Clarke had left Palestine the year before at his own private request, having found the strain of maintaining neutrality in mind and action intolerable.

On the 6th of September the Wingate case came up for review and a minute was written to the Military Secretary asking whether " owing to present conditions this appeal should go forward to the King or be held in abeyance and the officer in question be so informed." An answer was returned three days later from the Military Secretary's office : " We consider that the appeal must go before His Majesty. Under section 42 of the Army Act no one can prevent an officer from exercising that right. May we have a statement of the case please." The British view was the Roman view : " Hast thou appealed unto Cæsar ? Unto Cæsar thou shalt go."

The Army Council reached their decision at the beginning of October : their advice to the Secretary of State was that the reports should stand and that the request for additional reports by Brigadier Evetts and Sir Edmund Ironside should not be granted. (The question of inadequate recognition seems to have been dropped for the moment.) This decision could only mean that unless the Secretary of State was to dispute the Army Council's guidance (and there was no reason to suppose he would) the Complaint would be communicated to the King without Ministerial advice to " issue any special instructions." The appeal would have failed. This would not help Wingate's future career. It could even kill it.

He was always prone to believe that authority was conspiring against him, but at this moment in his life authority conspired to rescue Wingate from the consequence of his over-confidence. Again one may be reminded of St. Paul's adventures with Roman officialdom. " And when Paul had thus spoken, Agrippa rose up, and Festus, and Bernice, and they that sat with them. And when they had gone aside they talked between themselves saying, This man doeth nothing worthy of death or of bonds. Then said Agrippa unto Festus, this man might have been set at liberty, if he had not appealed unto Cæsar."

Sir Edmund Ironside was determined that if possible Wingate should be dissuaded from appealing unto Cæsar so that he might be " set at liberty " to give his services in the widest measure. When he conveyed the recommendation of the Army Council to the Secretary of State he attached a skilfully worded minute.

> " Captain Wingate is a very valuable officer now employed as Brigade Major 56th Light Anti-Aircraft Brigade. I think that the facts are these. Captain Wingate was serving under an officer of the R.A.F. who was charged with the Intelligence duties upon General Haining's staff. It is always difficult to check any tendency, which is considered doubtful, in a subordinate, but it is doubly difficult for the officer of another service.
>
> Had Captain Wingate been handled better, I think that he might have stopped his supreme crime of favouring the Jews too much. General Haining, in command, doubtless realised this and dealt with it.
>
> I consider that the appeal should not be allowed. I feel that there is nothing in the report which prevents Captain Wingate being employed for the good of the Army. I think that he can rest assured that his merit is thoroughly known.
> Edmund Ironside, C.I.G.S., 3.11.39."

Though evidence cannot prove the point, it is nevertheless not fanciful to infer that this minute obtained additional force from being addressed to one who was himself a Jew. At all events Mr. Hore-Belisha marked the last twenty-five words of Sir Edmund Ironside's minute with a red marginal line and a cross. He then wrote as follows to the Adjutant-General :

> " In view of C.I.G.S.'s comment should not Captain Wingate

be informed as at X (saying that this is the opinion of the Army Council after consideration) and asking whether in the circumstances he wishes to pursue his appeal ? What is the right procedure ?—H.B. 4.11.39."

The Adjutant-General replied that there was no reason why a letter in the sense indicated by Mr. Hore-Belisha should not be sent. He then circulated this reply with the Secretary of State's proposal and all other documents of the case to his colleagues of the Army Council, laying stress on the fact that in the event of Wingate insisting, his appeal must nevertheless go to the King. He pointed out that Wingate would be " well advised not to insist as he has clearly failed on all four counts that he pleads. Moreover, it is highly irregular . . . for an officer personally to plead for recognition of his own services." The members of the Council agreed to the proposal without dissent. So on the 25th of December the following letter was sent to Wingate from the office of the Military Secretary :

" Sir,
    I am commanded by the Army Council to inform you that after careful examination of your appeal under Section 42 of the Army Act, dated the 27th of June, 1939, against the terms of the confidential report rendered upon you, they have decided that the reports shall stand and that further reports shall not be called for. Your appeal to them therefore fails.
    I am to add that the Council feel that there is nothing in the report which prevents your being employed for the good of the Army and you can rest assured that your merit is thoroughly known. In the circumstances I am to inquire whether you wish to pursue your appeal to His Majesty the King.
    I am, Sir, your obedient servant,
                            G. W. Lambert "

The C.I.G.S. told him privately where his interest lay.[1] On the 28th of December Wingate answered the Military Secretary, acknowledging receipt of his letter. " Under the circumstances," he added, " I do not wish to pursue my appeal to His Majesty the King." The case was closed.

In following the Complaint to the Sovereign the story has been brought to the end of 1939. Other things had been happening meanwhile in Wingate's life. Once more he was busying himself with the

---

[1] Ironside.

destinies of Zion, in particular giving vigorous help to Zionist leaders in their endeavours to raise a Jewish army.

The twenty-first Zionist Congress had taken place in Geneva during August, 1939, under the shadow of impending war and of the disappointment of all Jewry at the announcement of British policy in the White Paper. The Conference refused acquiescence in the policy but offered the services of the Jewish nation to the struggle against Nazism. At the end of the month Moshe Shertock was sent to London by Dr. Weizmann to negotiate whatever he could of this offer with the British military authorities. He saw General Pownall, but without achieving anything. He decided to go back to Palestine and booked an air passage via Berlin and Warsaw. The night before he was due to leave he went to the house of Arthur Louri. There, in Louri's house in Church Road, Hampstead, he met Wingate again, and they talked together. When Wingate heard that the other proposed to travel by Berlin he could hardly believe that Shertock was serious. He implored him to change his mind, pointing out that it was misguided patriotism for a national leader to expose himself to arrest, and the horrors of Nazi imprisonment which could only end in his disappearance. But Shertock was firm. Since he had received no encouragement from the British authorities in London he was convinced that his presence would be of more value in Palestine. War was threatening hour by hour and the Warsaw route was the short one. Wingate then had an idea. Would Shertock stay behind if he, Wingate, could arrange a meeting with General Ironside ? The latter, at this time, was still Inspector-General of Overseas Forces, and as such the most important person from whom a prospective raiser of overseas armies could seek help. Shertock was non-committal. At this Wingate telephoned to Sir Edmund Ironside and asked him to see Shertock. Sir Edmund wanted to know precisely what post was held by Mr. Shertock in Palestine. The intricacies of Zionist organisation momentarily baffled even Wingate. " Oh," he said, " he's kind of head of the Jews in Palestine." Sir Edmund Ironside gave an appointment ; Shertock was obliged to accept it ; and the future statesman of Israel was perhaps saved by this means.[1]

But the purpose of the interview was not accomplished then or at any time. Sir Edmund Ironside always favoured the idea of a Jewish army, and subsequent history has proved his military wisdom. But he was overridden. It seems that ten days or so after his meeting with Shertock he put forward a plan for a " Jewish Legion " to the Secretary of State. What is certain is that Mr. Hore-Belisha turned it down " for the present."[2] This was the first move in a long negotiation for

[1] Sharett. Ironside.   [2] Dugdale Diaries.

the raising of a Jewish army which lasted nearly till the end of the war, and in which Wingate took a considerable part during the first year.

About this time, in the summer when war began, the Wingates made friends with a man of strong Zionist conviction who was to play a considerable part in their lives. He was a Jewish doctor called Ben Zion Kounine. They had first met him during their leave in October and November of 1938. He now became their frequent companion, in whom they confided much. He returned their affection, loving them both, and finding in Wingate, as many people did, a fascinating and enigmatic study. He felt sure that here was a man who would accomplish notable deeds because of the absolute intensity of his will and the formidable association in him of egocentricity and selflessness. As said, Wingate changed less than do most men in the course of life. As strongly as in his youth, when he used to tell Peggy that he knew he was dedicated to some cause, he knew not what —Wingate still believed himself to be an instrument of fate. He was capable of Napoleon's utterance : " *Je ne suis pas un homme, mais une chose.*" Men who feel thus are either deluded or great. Kounine believed in his greatness. He noticed that he was not free from the weaknesses of his state : a tendency to fantastic dreaming of what he could achieve ; and an opposite tendency to despairing moods when he contrasted the hopeless feebleness of one man against the seemingly immovable establishment of the world, and would dwell on his impotence to achieve anything of merit at all. But Kounine could recognise that in Wingate there was an essential base of common sense which kept the conflict within disciplined limits. He was impressed by the prosaic hard work behind Wingate's imaginative theorising. He discussed with him the odd experiments he had made in dieting during his Libyan exploration and he came to the conclusion that Wingate was extraordinarily well versed in medical science, was by no means the amateur crank that he often appeared. In the difficult time that was ahead of him Wingate was to draw great and invaluable strength from this friend, Ben Zion Kounine, who never lost sight of endurable qualities sometimes obscured by reckless enthusiasm.

On the 30th of September the Headquarters of the 56th Light Anti-Aircraft Brigade moved to Sidcup in Kent. From his first day with them Wingate had thrown himself into his work with all the ardour of escapism, and as usual, when he wanted to escape, he found relief in memoranda. Of the many able technical papers that he wrote from the Drill Hall, Half-Way Street, only one retains some interest to-day. He believed that anti-aircraft theory was fallacious in that it was concentrated on an objective impossible of attainment, namely the destruction of all invading aircraft before they had been able to drop any bombs. He pointed out how in the artillery action dependent on this theory anti-aircraft guns tended to open on enemy aircraft prematurely under unfavourable conditions, thus allowing them to get through in force to the defended area. He proposed a Wellingtonian policy of holding fire, and of assuming that in every sector some invading aircraft would reach their target and drop some bombs. Defence was not to be found in idealistic plans for warding off all bombers but in exacting such punishment from the raiders as to make their raids impractical. " How is this damage to be inflicted ? " he wrote. " By deciding on that zone or belt within which enemy aircraft must fly when dropping bombs and immediately after, and then siting guns to command this zone." Whether or not this memorandum influenced events, there can be no doubt that he previsaged something of later strategy.

On visits to London Wingate would often talk over his troubles with Dr. Kounine, and the latter remembers a walk with him on a winter evening in Kensington Gardens, and Wingate confessing to him all the unconquerable wretchedness in his heart at the turn his life had taken. He had sought through his youth and first manhood to discover whither he must go to fulfil his destiny. He had found the way only to be turned from it. The authorities might show him kindness now, but theirs was the kindness people show to a discredited man because such a man is the feeblest and least dangerous of beings. He was forgotten, he said ; he was finished. His friend could only counsel him never to abandon hope.

Wingate confided such feelings to very few. He gave no sign of distress or inner conflict to his fellow officers, and he was on very good terms with both the Brigadiers whom he served. His manners and habits continued to be extraordinarily unconventional, but he showed a gracious side on occasion too. Sometimes the wives and families of officers would come to the mess, and sometimes they were shy at finding themselves in a social milieu which was unfamiliar to them. He would take trouble to put them at their ease, and he often showed that, when he wanted, he could be as smooth as a courtier, though incapable at any time of courtier-like insincerity.

Only in one respect did he cause some exasperation to his fellow-officers, and that was in the way he used to dispose of the comfortable illusions of the hour. He used to say : " I tell you the French are no good at all ! The Germans will break through them as soon as they attack——" and he is distinctly remembered as pointing to Sedan on the map. " The British," he would go on, " will suffer the greatest Corunna of all time. There is no hope at all that we will win the war in France. It is in the East that everything will be decided." He used to list the British and French Generals and explain their incapacity in detail. All this made distressing listening, but not so much so as to disturb his easy relations with his companions. There was only one quarrel which is remembered, and that was with an anti-Semitic officer on whom Wingate used to turn with annihilating wrath.

To one officer in the Headquarters, and to no one else, he told something of his deeper preoccupations. He was Lieutenant Alan Abraham Mocatta.[1] They became friends, as people often do, from a grotesque incident. The aforementioned Anti-Semite asserted one day in mess that the Secretary of State for War " was no good because he was a Jew." Mocatta said that as a Jew himself he resented the remark and called the fool to order. Wingate was not present but he liked the spirit of Mocatta's protest when he heard of it. They never talked Zionism because they differed on the subject, but they often talked about Wingate's ambitions and hopes, and sometimes discussed the more interesting of the memoranda. The Headquarters chief typist, Miss Pocock, found herself, possibly to her surprise, typing memorandum upon memorandum addressed not only to his military superiors, but sometimes to members of the Government.

It so happened that there existed a strong link between the 56th Light Anti-Aircraft Brigade and Zionist Headquarters in London. One of the battery commanders in the 16th Light Anti-Aircraft Regiment was Victor Cazalet. It seems that at this time he used to meet Mrs. Dugdale and some of the Zionist leaders every week or fortnight in a room at the Dorchester Hotel, and it followed as a matter of course that he often took the Brigade-Major to these conferences. From the full diary kept by Mrs. Dugdale (a political record of extraordinary interest) it appears that after Hore-Belisha's refusal to support the formation of a Jewish Legion, in which he was joined by Malcolm Macdonald, this committee bent their minds to a similar though less radical proposal. Encouraged by Mr. Winston Churchill's support, which he conveyed to the Zionist organisation by Mr. Brendan Bracken, Dr. Weizmann put forward two proposals, one for the establishment of an arms factory in Palestine, and the second for the bringing over of two hundred Palestinian Jews to form the cadre of a Jewish army. The first of these proposals was " well received " by the Minister of Supply, Mr. Leslie Burgin, but no discernible action followed, while the second languished for nearly a year when it sprang to a semblance of life. Both the proposals are so similar to those

[1] Alan Abraham Mocatta, O.B.E., Q.C. The writer is indebted to him for personal recollection of Wingate in his Sidcup days.

which Wingate had made to General Ironside that it is likely that his memorandum had acted as a strong formative influence.

Then these two proposals took second place when the committee became more exercised over forty-three Hagana members who were condemned to long terms of imprisonment after having been found drilling. Their defence, which was not open to doubt, was that they were drilling so as to fit themselves for military employment in the war against Nazism. Many of them were former S.N.S. men. Among them was Moshe Dayan.

This scandalous case exercised Cazalet's committee for a long time and the offensive seems to have been opened on November 1st. Mrs. Dugdale says that on this day she went to the Dorchester to the weekly meeting. "Wingate there," she recorded. "We discussed the harsh sentences of the forty-three boys who were drilling with arms for Hagana. Victor and Wingate beside themselves with rage. It was settled that V. should talk to Lord Halifax about it and failing that, it should be raised in the House of Commons. We have a cast-iron case about these boys, regarding intention." Two days later Cazalet was at least able to get an assurance from Malcolm Macdonald that the sentences would not be confirmed, and on the 14th General Ironside identified himself with the protest. He called the sentence "savage and stupid," and told Dr. Weizmann that he had telegraphed to Palestine in that sense, adding "the idea of condemning one of Wingate's boys to imprisonment! They ought to have given him a D.S.O." The C.I.G.S. told Dr. Weizmann on the same occasion that as far as a Jewish force was concerned he remained in full support. The case of the forty-three was not settled till February of 1941 when Malcolm Macdonald's Anti-Zionist successor, Lord Lloyd, authorised their pardon on his deathbed.[1]

Wingate often used to go over to dine and sometimes spend the night at Victor Cazalet's country house near Tonbridge. Mr. and Mrs. Dugdale were there on the 5th of November, and she recorded in her diary : "Captain Wingate arrived to dine and sleep. Edgar saw the likeness to T. E. Lawrence, was rather scared by his fanatical earnestness. He is a very forcible character." A somewhat similar impression was made on another of Cazalet's friends, Mr. Harold Nicolson. He also saw the likeness and was left with a feeling of uneasiness. One day during the winter of 1939 to 1940 Victor Cazalet invited Wingate to meet a man who was to have a decisive influence on his life. He was Leopold Amery.

After Mr. Churchill had joined the Government in September,

[1] Dugdale Diaries. Entries of 7th, 20th, 30th September, 2nd October, 1st, 3rd, 5th, 14th November, 1939, and 5th February, 1941.

1939, Mr. Amery was by a long way the most influential private member in the House of Commons, and it was as certain as such things can be that he would hold office before long. This powerful and brilliant man was from the first favourably impressed by Wingate. He felt an instant conviction that here was a man of extraordinary and masterful ability, a man of genius maybe. He was puzzled by something familiar in the piercing blue eyes till he, like Edgar Dugdale and Harold Nicolson, remembered Lawrence. Wingate would not have been pleased to know that he reminded so many people of his distant kinsman, but some resemblance was undoubtedly there and it stood him in good stead now. Mr. Amery already knew from Dr. Weizmann of the achievements of the Special Night Squads, and now he asked Wingate to give his own account. Wingate talked long, as he always did, and the other listened. Back in London Mr. Amery made up his mind that Wingate must somehow or other be used to advantage in the war.[1] A few months later when there had been great changes in the Government, largely brought about by himself, Mr. Amery was in a position to act on his determination.

But for the moment, in spite of the meetings of Cazalet's committee in the Dorchester, and its excitements of political lobbying, all was continued doldrums, so far as Wingate was concerned. It seemed that this ambitious man who believed himself to possess supreme powers of leadership might spend the whole of the Second World War as an anti-aircraft officer on the outskirts of London. One day he went to David Hacohen. At this time there was a secret plan (unconnected with the Jewish Legion project) to recruit Jews from Central Europe for the purpose of carrying out demolition raids on oil refineries supplying the German Army, and on locks on German waterways.[2] Shertock had been approached by veiled authorities for the co-operation of the Jewish Agency, and he was in communication on the subject with the office in which David Hacohen worked. Wingate may have been told about the plan by his Jewish friends, but however that was he said to Hacohen : " David, I cannot go on doing nothing. Can you arrange for me to come and work with you ? " Hacohen said that he must consult his superiors. He did so and there followed a departmental meeting at which Wingate was present. He spoke and one of his listeners recorded after how he came to understand from this encounter " Wingate's power to win men's hearts."[3] It was agreed by the committee that in the event of the plan being accepted Wingate's

---

[1] The late L. S. Amery. A communication.
[2] Sharett. Hacohen. Possibly another origin of the Haifa legend. See Appendix A.
[3] *Magen Baseter* (Secret Defence) a Hebrew book published in Israel of which passages have been translated for the writer by Miss Denman of the Zionist organisation. It contains interesting details of Wingate's Zionist career.

A typical S.N.S. patrol

At Chaim Shturman's funeral. Shertock is on Wingate's left

Ein Harod, 1939; a cartoonist's impression. Bredin is on the left

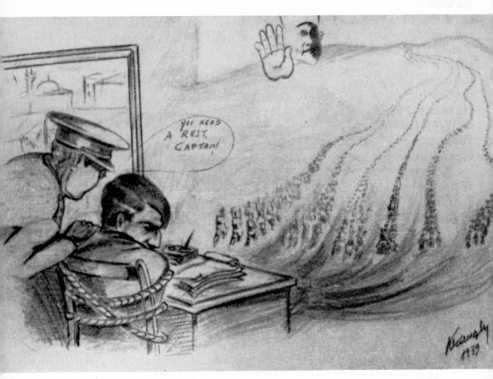

Wingate under strain. The face and hand are those of the Mufti

advice would be sought again. It seems that the plan, which included the formation of a Jewish reserve of agents, was accepted in principle shortly after this, and Wingate was invited by one of the Jewish principals to take command of the operations.

And now Wingate was thrown into a state of indecision. He talked over this new offer with Lorna. Here at last was the Jewish army for which he had striven since his conversion to Zionism in 1936, and with himself moreover as its leader. And yet here was the dream fulfilled in a doubtful and even malign form. As he argued the thing out with himself he liked the prospect less and less, and he put his conclusions in somewhat this way: " The Jews need an army that will give them something to be proud of, that will give them self-respect. But an army of secret agents gives no one self-respect and indeed would give point to the story that the Jews are an untrustworthy secret intriguing people. And I don't want to be a secret agent myself. I am a soldier and I want to lead Jewish soldiers." But the alternative was Sidcup and unfulfilment.

The problem was solved by Sir Edmund Ironside. One of the Jews working on the scheme went to Sir Edmund to ask whether it would be possible to release Wingate for these proposed services. The General answered somewhat as follows : " If Wingate wants to go with you he can. But I would not advise him to do so. In a war on this scale there are many opportunities for people like him and he only needs to be patient for one to come his way. If he goes with you, he will never become what he might become ; a great and famous soldier. He will be of great help to you if he goes, but your asking for him if he accepts, will be of no service to him personally." Later the General called for Wingate and put these arguments to him himself. He said that for a regular soldier " to separate himself from the regular army " was always fatal to his career. Wingate agreed to practise the virtue of patience yet further.[1] With that resolve went the last chance ever to come to him of leading a Jewish force into action.

It was now spring of 1940. While the storm accumulated and broke, Wingate remained with his Anti-Aircraft Brigade at Sidcup. In all his life there can have been few more dejecting moments than this. What he had done already as a military commander was little by the scale of great wars, and here was a great war being fought almost within sound, and this soldier of proved ability remained in part charge of silent batteries not needed in the action. In one of his novels Disraeli wrote : " View the obscure Napoleon starving in the streets

---

[1] Ironside. Shertock. Hacohen. *Magen Baseter*. In the absence of documentation there is a conflict of evidence as to who approached the C.I.G.S. It was not Hacohen or Shertock.

of Paris ! What was St. Helena to the bitterness of such existence !
The visions of past glory might illumine even that dark imprisonment ;
but to be conscious that his supernatural energies might die away
without creating their miracles : can the wheel or the rack rival the
torture of such a suspicion ? " If the cases were not similar, the
predicaments were.

It was during these days that David Hacohen, one of his first
friends in Palestine, met him for the last time. This happened in Arthur
Louri's house where Hacohen was living. " On his free nights," he
relates, " Wingate would come to stay with us, spending most of the
time talking at length and with bitterness about the weakness of the
Allies and the lack of faith in his country's leadership. Chamberlain
was still Prime Minister at the time. The signs of national decay and
treachery in France were no secret. The German invasion of Norway
was astonishing in its success and the retreat from Narvik was a
shameful defeat. Wingate ground his teeth at the emptiness of his
work ; he used to sit with us, gloomy and disappointed. He was sure
that worse was to come, that the Germans were still to conquer the
whole of Europe. This is what he used to tell us : ' There, across the
channel, they will sit safely with their guns towards London. All France
will be vanquished and that ally on whom we now rely will be dead—
a corpse ! The belief that at the last moment the French nation will
arise and conquer is nonsense. Nevertheless England will win in
the end, not because of " traditions " or cheap boasts that England
always wins the last battle, but because deep down in the heart of every
Englishman there is a feeling of guilt about his own share in the war,
a feeling that he must pay for the errors he made in his desire for peace
at any price. Every man in the street knows that he has to make the
utmost effort, even sacrifice his life for victory, if his people are to have
any future. He knows that he must do this rather than look for
guilt in others.' We listened together to the wireless report of that
historical Parliamentary session after which Chamberlain resigned
and Churchill took over."

Hacohen says nothing of Wingate's continual preoccupation with
the formation of a Jewish army. The prospects for the realisation of
the project were not bright now. The new Prime Minister was an open
friend of the Jewish national cause but the new Colonial Secretary was
Lord Lloyd, the last man likely to encourage a policy of armed Zionism.
Nevertheless when Dr. Weizmann went to call on Lloyd on the 24th
of May he was well received, and that most astute judge of men told
Mrs. Dugdale that he believed he had made " a dent " on the Minister's
mind. Subsequent events suggest that Weizmann was not indulging
in wishful thinking. Then at this moment, on the very day it seems

of Weizmann's interview, Wingate did an extraordinary thing. He sent a memorandum to the Prime Minister on the subject of Palestine in which he passed serious strictures on the administration of the country and on Government policy, by implication on the new Colonial Secretary.[1] The story went round the Zionists that he had " accused the High Commissioner of being a Fascist," and Mrs. Dugdale was moved to write in her diary " Wingate is an able man but an irresponsible lunatic."[2]

In fact he had not written anything so foolish as that Sir Harold MacMichael was a Fascist, but he had been guilty of a lack of tact through inexperience of political procedure, and it may be that this ill-considered step, reminding the official world of his reputation for political busybodying, cost him his life's ambition to lead a Jewish army. This becomes clearer later on.

On the 27th of May, Sir Edmund Ironside, at his own request, ceased to be Chief of the Imperial General Staff. He was succeeded by the Vice-Chief Sir John Dill who appointed General Sir Robert Haining as the new Vice-Chief. Sir Edmund Ironside himself was appointed Commander-in-Chief of the Home Forces. These changes suggested to Wingate a new escape-route from Kent. The outcome of the battle of France and the approach of the battle of Britain were both becoming horribly clear. In the last week of May Wingate discussed his latest plan with his commanding officer Brigadier Hunt, as a result of which he went to London on the 1st of June for an interview with Sir Edmund Ironside in his new Headquarters.[3]

The plan was as follows : in the event of a German invasion of the British Isles Wingate was to lead " a special type of unit to deal with penetration of (by ?) enemy units behind (British) lines, either by tanks, by parachutists, or airborne troops." Two successful forms of German tactics were making a deep impression on military thinking : the penetration of Allied lines by small armoured units followed by attack from the rear, and sabotage attacks within defended country by German Fifth Column agents, a ruse whose extent and achievement was greatly exaggerated at the time. What Wingate was proposing was that in a land battle of Britain he should counter these two forms of attack with a unit similar in character and intention to the Special Night Squads. Sir Edmund listened to his proposal, gave it his approval,

---

[1] The paper might be one of two : *Palestine 1940*, or more probably a second version of *Appreciation of the use of Jewish Forces*. The papers borrow from each other and both contain the strictures. W.P.I.

[2] Dugdale Diaries. Entries of 24th, 25th May, 1941.

[3] A diary kept by Wingate, 1st–21st June, 1940. W.P.I.

and arranged for him to give details of his scheme to a member of his staff Colonel Daubuz. The latter asked how soon he could be ready, and here is Wingate's account of how he replied : " Wingate said *if* necessary orders given he could assemble and train unit in little over one week. He also sketched to Daubuz the events in France which have since happened and said that at worst we had some weeks."

On the 4th of June he was ordered to fly to Northern Ireland. There he met General Huddleston who received the proposal as favourably as Sir Edmund Ironside had. There was much talk in those days of a repetition of what might be called " Operation Casement." Wingate flew back to London on the 5th. He recorded the next move : " Wingate held conference with selected personnel at H.Q. 56 A.A. Brigade at Sidcup. All volunteered and Brigadier Hunt personally spoke to the Regimental Commanders and stated that in the interest of the Army he approved the transfer of ten officers and 150 other ranks selected out of a total in the Brigade of some 120 officers and 4,000 other ranks, should they be required by G.H.Q.H.F." Then Wingate ran into trouble again.

On the day of this Brigade conference, the 6th, he reported to Sir Edmund Ironside's Headquarters, and what occurred there is again best conveyed by the hurried and vivid jottings of the notebook. Wingate continued to record his doings in a Cæsarian third person singular. He related that on the 6th, he " was present at a telephone conversation between General Paget and General Anderson, A.-C.I.G.S. W.O., in the course of which General Anderson appeared to tell General Paget that General Haining had strong personal objections to Captain Wingate (who had complained of his treatment to himself and his men to the Sovereign). General Paget then asked Wingate what had been his relations with General Haining and, after replying Wingate stated that General Ironside had for months been fully conversant with every particular."

There was a second conference in the War Office at which General Beaumont-Nesbitt, the Director of Military Intelligence, was present. Wingate spoke in defence of his plan, and again his own account conveys the scene : " No objections were raised except on the grounds that the I.R.A. might be annoyed and thus hostilities precipitated. Wingate replied that General Huddleston considered that the effect of the employment of the proposed force would be the opposite of that suggested. The impression given to Wingate was that the decision to dispose of the scheme on personal grounds had already been arrived at."

Next day he learned at Home Force Headquarters that so far as

Northern Ireland was concerned the plan was turned down as he had expected. He persisted in his belief that the decision was influenced by spite rather than valid considerations of policy, as the diary makes plain : " Wingate then saw General Ironside to whom he complained of the personal attack on himself as improper. He pointed out that apparently it was suggested that he was proposing to use Black and Tan methods whereas, as General Ironside knew, the methods employed by Forces under Wingate's command in Palestine had been the exact opposite of these, and that a high standard of soldierly conduct and compassion to foes had been the rule. This had been necessary, even if not otherwise desirable, in view of the numerous enemies he had had in Palestine as a friend of the Jews. . . . General Ironside said that he supposed that General Haining was nervous that movement in Northern Ireland might start something and that he thought Wingate more likely to do this than anyone else. He did not suppose the objection was purely personal. In any case he fully intended to employ Wingate's force."

His suspicions regarding General Haining seem to have been without foundation and the plan was saved for the moment. An accommodation was reached with Northern Command where General Forbes Adam[1] was in full accord with the proposal. Sir Edmund Ironside wrote to Wingate on the 9th of June.

" My dear Wingate,
    It has been decided to employ your posse in the southern portion of the Northern Command. General Adam will take you on with enthusiasm and I am sure you will get a chance. As far as I can see, there has been a rumour of 5th column in Lincolnshire for some time, but no actual discovery. It is a very likely place in which to land.
    Will you see that you have an efficient 2nd in command so that you may send him off to another area for a similar duty or leave behind if you move away.
    The best of luck to you. Let me know from time to time how you get on and establish yourself at the earliest possible date.
                                    Yours sincerely,
                                    Edmund Ironside "

On the 10th of June Wingate was posted to the Northern Command. He went to York on the 11th. On the 21st the scheme in final and fully detailed form was submitted to the War Office by Home Forces Headquarters. And there the story may be left incomplete. This attempted dash out of the doldrums came to nothing

[1] General Sir Ronald Forbes Adam, Bt., G.C.B., D.S.O.

because (as the reader may remember) the Germans did not after all invade the British Isles, and Wingate and his " special unit " had therefore no opportunity to show their valour.[1] At the same time other and more fruitful plans for him were under discussion. On the 10th of June Italy had declared war on Great Britain and France. In the course of the next month Wingate's name was remembered again by Sir Archibald Wavell and Mr. Amery.

It would seem that the initiative was taken by Mr. Amery, who by now had become Secretary of State for India, at a meeting of the Middle East Committee of the Cabinet in July. He suggested to General Haining that in the war with Italy " the ideal man " to lead insurgent forces from within the Italian African possessions was " a certain Captain O. C. Wingate."[2] Remembering the occasion later Mr. Amery said that he considered Wingate to be " a much more virile and solidly balanced Lawrence, but with much the same sort of power of inspiring others,"[3] a description which in all likelihood reflects what he said on his behalf to the Committee. The suggestion was conveyed to the Middle East Commander, Sir Archibald Wavell. He replied in terms of enthusiastic acceptance[4] to which however he added a condition, and this condition brought to Wingate lasting and agonising disappointment.

It so happened that at this moment of his life, when he was on the brink of great opportunity, Wingate was involved in a coincidence of a very painful kind. Nothing could divert his interest from Zion, and throughout these days of hurry and conference, and of course yet more memoranda, as he organised his new unit, he yet contrived to attend Victor Cazalet's Zionist Committee at the Dorchester. Since the White Paper their meetings had more often than not been melancholy occasions to discuss nothing better than their fading hopes, but now, in the late summer of 1940, the political fortunes of Zionism suddenly brightened. The prospect of raising a Jewish army drew near as it had never done before. On 15th July Dr. Weizmann had a successful interview with Haining as a result of which the General promised to telegraph to Sir Archibald Wavell

---

[1] In his interesting book, *Invasion 1940*, Mr. Peter Fleming asserts that General Andrew Thorne was the originator of " Auxiliary Units," as these guerilla formations came to be called. It is clear that Wingate anticipated him, but it would be futile to organise a competition for first prize. The idea probably occurred to several people at the same time.

[2] This appears from a letter from Mr. Amery to Sir Alan Brooke of 7th January, 1942. " My dear C.I.G.S. When the Middle East Committee of the Cabinet was considering the possibility of operations in Abyssinia in J. of last year, I suggested to Haining that the ideal man to lead Abyssinian insurgents would be a certain Captain O. C. Wingate. . . ." It would seem that " J. of last year " means July, 1940.

[3] Amery to Sir Alan Brooke (7.1.42).

[4] This may be assumed from the terms in which Lord Wavell referred to the transaction in his preface to *Wingate's Raiders* by Charles Rolo.

urging him " to get on with the training of cadres of Jewish officers and N.C.O.s."[1] Mrs. Dugdale added her own comment : " So the walls of Jericho fall at last, with not much blast of trumpets after all ! " Wingate spent what time he could spare in furnishing the project with a detailed strategic programme. This was for assembling the army in the Tibesti mountains and striking northwards against the Italians in Libya.[1] Then there was a setback.   General Haining had second thoughts, but after the Prime Minister had renewed his support of the project to Dr. Weizmann on the 6th of September,[1] it seemed as though it could not now fail. The Secretary of State for War, Anthony Eden, came out in favour, and, what was most surprising, he was joined by Lord Lloyd. The moment of highest optimism was well recorded by Mrs. Dugdale : " 13th September, Friday—and yet a lucky day ! A great day ! For to-day Chaim met Lord Lloyd, Anthony Eden and Mr. Bagally of the Foreign Office and heard from them that all our demands are granted. There is to be a Jewish Fighting Force of 10,000 men, of whom three or four thousand are to be recruited in Palestine, and national status and recognition granted as to Poles and Czechs. The walls of Jericho have fallen, fallen ! I looked in at the Dorchester about 5 p.m. and found Chaim just back from this interview, elated and solemn. He said : ' It is almost as great a day as the Balfour Declaration.' Orde Wingate was there too, radiant. It may be the beginning of a great future for him too."

" 14th September. At 4 p.m. I went to the Wingates' flat where was Lewis (Namier). Orde explained his scheme for the recruitment, training and future use of the Jewish Fighting Force. He said, without conceit, that no one could carry out these ideas except himself ; failing himself General Evetts. He lost his temper very badly when he thought Chaim had failed to be straightforward with him about making an appointment for him to see General Dill, and nearly smashed the tea-cups. Afterwards he apologised, but he is a most ungovernable character."

It is possible that Dr. Weizmann knew something about Amery's negotiation with Wavell, whence his hesitation to arrange the interview with Dill. However that was, the moment for which Wingate had longed since his first Palestine days seemed imminent. He was instructed to make over the command of his " posse " in Lincolnshire, and to report personally to the C.I.G.S. on the 17th. He was in the dilemma of Lord Curzon in May 1923, exalted by false hopes based on solid evidence. He was quite certain now, and with reason, that the past no longer counted against him, and that he was to command a Jewish army. But when he went to the War Office he and Sir John

[1] Dugdale Diaries.

Dill seem to have talked at cross-purposes for a while. When Wingate put forward his plans and ideas, Sir John Dill showed some perplexity, and then explained that " the idea had rather been to send him in to the Abyssinian side."[1] Wingate came back to 49 Hill Street, where he and Lorna had a flat, to find Mrs. Dugdale and Lewis Namier. Mrs. Dugdale wrote in her diary : " I hope he (Wingate) has put this right, for certainly without him the whole thing would be a flop." She was correct in her last judgment. The whole thing was a flop after this. The Jewish army was never raised.

On the next day, the 18th of September, Wingate went to the War Office for details of his new appointment, and there he learned something that caused him grief to the end of his life. He was told that he was to " proceed " to Cairo where he would report to a department of General Headquarters called G (R) with a view to ultimate employment in operations against Italian East Africa. His instructions included a prohibition against his going to Palestine for any reason whatever, either on duty or on leave.

When the interview was over he drove straight to the Zionist headquarters in Great Russell Street, where he found Weizmann, Louri, Kounine and Mrs. Dugdale. He stormed and raged. He asked Dr. Weizmann to intervene with the Prime Minister, but Weizmann replied that this was impossible. Wingate insisted that he should. Weizmann, who still felt complete confidence in the new pro-Zionist policy, said something as follows : " Go out and win fame in another field. Even without you, we will have our army." But such words could not calm Wingate at that moment. Ben Gurion met him the same day and said that anyone who befriended Jews was liable to misfortune, and he told of a Russian whom he had once known, and who, because he protested against Tsarist Anti-Semitism, found himself the subject of the " blood-accusation."[2] But Wingate would take no consolation. His Jewish friends advised patience till they found their own taxed to the limit. One reason, it may be assumed, for the violence of Wingate's desperation was the knowledge that he was helpless. He must have known in his heart that the authorities would never revoke the prohibition and could support it with strong arguments. He knew too that in wartime a soldier cannot refuse an appointment to an operational theatre. He believed that the prohibition came from people in the War Office who wished to revenge themselves on him. He seems never to have known that in fact it came from Sir Archibald Wavell.[3]

[1] Dugdale Diaries.
[2] Ben Gurion. The " blood-accusation " is an old anti-Semitic legend that Jews employ Christian blood in the making of unleavened bread.
[3] Ironside.

Later Weizmann saw Sir John Dill who explained to him that Wingate's appointment to G (R) had been arranged long before the Jewish Fighting Force plan came into recent discussion, and quite independently of it.[1] But when told of this Wingate remained bitter and angry. He may even have been exasperated by Weizmann's action. He was showing increasing disagreement and irritation with him and before they parted they exchanged bitter words. Shortly before Wingate went away to his new post, he called on Dr. Weizmann alone and again urged him to intervene. He had by now come to believe that the decision to debar him from Palestine was part of an official manœuvre to dispose of the Jewish Fighting Force. (Here he was probably wrong but things did fall out as he foresaw.) Again Weizmann refused to intervene and Wingate in answer went to such lengths of protestation that he even accused the other of moral cowardice. At one moment in the course of the argument Weizmann said: "Suppose what you say is true, what action would you propose?" Wingate answered: "You ought to go into Winston's room and *demand* a Jewish Army! You ought to bang the table! Why don't you do that?" And Dr. Weizmann answered: "I could do as you say, and I might even achieve something by doing it, but I could only do it once, and I want to see Winston Churchill many times."[2] But Wingate, with his soldierly impatience of the craft and delicacy and tedium of political manœuvre, could not see the difference here between caution and timidity, and they parted in anger.

A little after, it may even have been the same day, Dr. Kounine came to dine with the Wingates in Hill Street, and Wingate told his friend about his quarrel with Dr. Weizmann and defended his behaviour. He said that Zionists must not shrink from harsh tactics because only by bringing pressure to bear on British politicians could British policy be purged of its faults, and he reminded his friend that even at that moment members of Hagana were in Acre jail serving long sentences. This, he said, was what came of Weizmann's gentlemanly approaches to the British Government! He talked on, and in his impatience at Zionist moderation he began to abuse all Zionists in general, and the Jews, exclaiming: "They are not a people! No—that is the trouble with them—they are *not* a people!"

Dr. Kounine presently suggested that Wingate should put his views to Ben Gurion who was then living in Hampstead. It has been noted already that Wingate underestimated this able Jewish statesman. He shook his head and said: "Ben Gurion is not a leader."

[1] Dugdale Diaries.   [2] Mrs. Weizmann.

Kounine replied : " That is not the point. He is at present a man in office.[1] For that reason you ought to see him."

After some discussion Wingate, his wife and Dr. Kounine set out for Hampstead, in the blackout, in Dr. Kounine's car. Since the 7th of September the " Blitz " had begun, and that night, even before they started off, London was subjected to heavy German bombardment. Through the crash of high explosive and the thunder of anti-aircraft guns they drove from Hill Street to Hampstead, and it can be confidently surmised that Wingate's thoughts were not with his former comrades in arms in Kent, not with the prospect of sudden death, but only with the destinies of Zion. Up at Hampstead the three of them were temporarily removed from the inner cauldron of the attack. Dr. Kounine went to Mr. Ben Gurion's door and, as he expected, found him studying Greek as he usually did in the evening after work.

For some reason (probably because the house was in disorder through furniture-moving) Mr. Ben Gurion did not invite his visitors in but preferred to come out to them in the car. It was (very oddly indeed) decided that he and Wingate should conduct their discussion in the car driving round Hampstead Heath while London glowed beneath them. Then in a long monologue Wingate told Ben Gurion all that he had told Dr. Weizmann, expressing himself with a wild eloquence which made Kounine think of him as a prophet in his frenzy. He finished this discourse by telling Ben Gurion that it was a Zionist duty to rouse American opinion to demanding a Jewish Fighting Force as a condition of help. Ben Gurion said nothing, merely shook his head vigorously. Wingate then used insulting words such as he had used to Dr. Weizmann, and told him that he was a traitor to his people. Ben Gurion reddened, looked all his anger but said nothing. By this time they were near his home again. He got out of the car, walked up to his door and went inside with never a word.

Dr. Kounine and the Wingates then drove back in silence to Hill Street and the blitz. The bombardment was now at its climax, but remembering that evening many years later the doctor could assert that the tempest of world war without, seemed less violent than the silent tension within the car. When they were back in the flat Wingate asked Kounine whether *he* would be prepared to go to America on such a mission as he had proposed to the two leaders. When he in turn said no he was likewise accused of treachery.[2] It may seem strange that after such scenes Wingate could still retain the confidence of his

[1] Mr. Ben Gurion was then Chairman of the Executive of the Jewish Agency for Palestine. He was in conflict with Weizmann at this moment and the two met as rarely as they could.
[2] Kounine.

Jewish friends, but the indisputable fact is that he retained not only their confidence but their affection. These quarrels all passed as if nothing had happened.[1]

At about the same time as he received orders to embark he received other orders which would once have been marvellously welcome. An early hope was fulfilled. Even so late as his Sidcup days, when he had the S.N.S. to his credit, he was still apt to grumble that he had not been nominated to Camberley.[2] He could now put that grumble aside. He was called to the War Office and told that he had been nominated to the fourth Junior War Staff Course to be held at the Military Academy. He signified his inability to comply with the order in abrupt fashion.[3] On the 19th of September he left England by boat for Cape Town from where he went overland to Egypt. In his pocket diary he noted only four events of the journey : the stop at Ascension Island on the 1st of October, and at St. Helena on the 3rd, the arrival at Cape Town on the 7th, and at Cairo on the 17th. While the British nation rallied to its supreme act of defence Wingate was forced to undergo the doldrums for the last time.

[1] "I knew in what spirit his reproaches had been made. My wife and I both loved and revered him." Dr. Weizmann. *Trial and Error.*

[2] Mocatta.　　　[3] Tulloch Essay.

CHAPTER XI

VOCATION TO ETHIOPIA

CAIRO IN the first two years of the war was dominated by the personality of Sir Archibald Wavell. History may pronounce favourably or otherwise on his merits as a general, but there can never be doubt of his merits as a leader. In his untalkative and deceptively conventional manner, Wavell could rouse the spirits of the defeated as effectively as Winston Churchill did by the use of an openly dramatic character and majestic eloquence. The rally in the Middle East owed to Wavell everything that it did not owe to the voice of the Prime Minister. He was in the singular position of being loved equally by the ordinary soldiers and officers, by his senior commanders and by his staff. In the summer of 1940 he was almost without critics. An officer known to be esteemed by the Commander-in-Chief, arriving in Cairo then, was in a good way to find his opportunity. Wingate seems to have added to his advantage by letting something be known about his ministerial connections. G.H.Q. gossip, and later Khartoum gossip made these the subject of awestruck rumours which Wingate, with a pardonable lack of scruple, did not contradict.[1]

When Wingate arrived in October he reported to Colonel Adrian Simpson, head of the department of General Headquarters known as G (R). Though he had been recommended for guerilla employment in Ethiopia by the Secretary of State for India, only vague instructions to that effect had descended from the Commander-in-Chief, and by the time he arrived, moreover, he found that all the appointments for an Ethiopian rising had been booked many months before. All this was characteristic of the Middle East Command, perhaps of any distantly situated one : many other G.S.O.2 officers beside Wingate were sent to Cairo to discharge duties which had been apportioned to others, and it was a rule worth learning quickly that on the junior levels Middle East employment was largely a question of initiative.

---

[1] In evident confusion with episodes of the second Burma campaign it has been said that Wingate enjoyed direct access to the Prime Minister at this time. If he did enjoy access to a Minister it would have been to Mr. Amery. There is no evidence that he ever availed himself of the privilege, but much evidence that he took advantage of an absurd piece of gossip in his dealings with his superiors.

" What would you like to do ? " commanding officers used often to ask of the newly-arrived. Wingate replied that he would like to write a memorandum. He reverted again to his plan for an attack on Libya from the south and he occupied himself in his first Cairo days by writing a detailed paper for Colonel Simpson. The memorandum itself has not survived, but eight thousand words of comment have done so, and from these it is not difficult to reconstruct Wingate's first appearance on the stage of the Middle East theatre.

The Tibesti scheme came to nothing. It is only interesting because it shows certain of Wingate's master ideas which were after to influence the deeds of his fame. The S.N.S. had taught him the military value of raiding in a small area and he was now applying the lesson to a large area. He remembered Ein Harod and the importance to S.N.S. of establishing a separate raiding Headquarters away from regular Headquarters and as near as could be to enemy territory. Carrying the idea into the different context of vast spaces and long distances he was proposing that in the Tibesti Mountains a large military base should be formed, a rallying point and a fastness supported by a detachment of the R.A.F., situated as near as could be to the Italian lines. It was estimated that the necessary private army, as such organisations came to be called, would number 10,000 British troops, 1,000 R.A.F. personnel, and a large but unspecified contingent of Nigerian native troops. They would be generously equipped with desert-faring motor transport. Here it is evident that Wingate had learned from Almasy's success over him in the search for Zerzura. He now took it as axiomatic that, as he had written in his account to the Royal Geographical Society in 1934, the desert is " as open to cars as the ocean to ships." His belief was true but it did not wholly accord with facts. The Germans had been quicker than the British to take advantage of Almasy's experiments, and the Tibesti scheme probably came to nothing because at this time there was in existence no type of British or American vehicle capable of surviving the exactions of the desert for long periods.

" Came to nothing " is the right description of the scheme's part in Wingate's life, but it may have had posthumous life on its own. It was received with respect and minute study. It has been plausibly suggested that it gave guidance to General Leclerc for the famous march of his force from Lake Chad. If this was so it would have been a consequence of the memorandum circulating from department to department in the Headquarters. It may have given something to the remarkable achievement of the Long-Range Desert Group. None of this can be known for certain.

Ethiopia

The memorandum had one surprising characteristic. The suggested recruitment for the force was from the United Kingdom, and no suggestion was made for seizing this opportunity for the formation of a Jewish army. With what bitterness may be imagined, Wingate had forced himself to accept the condition on which he was to be employed anew. While the memorandum was going the rounds he received a summons to Khartoum on the 2nd of November. He was to concern himself with a guerilla campaign in Ethiopia after all.

The situation of Ethiopia four and a half years after the end of the Italian war was disheartening from the point of view of both vanquished and victors. Graziani's reign of terror had been replaced by the more civilised administration of the Duke of Aosta, but this desirable development occurred too late to make much difference to Italian fortunes. The conquerors lived in disillusion. Not only were they surrounded by hatred but they found that the new Roman Empire did not pay. An authoritative estimate well described the material causes of their growing dismay. " Naboth's vineyard viewed from within was not what it had seemed to be from a distance. Minerals which could have justified the lavish expenditure on sea bases, public works, roads and bridges, had not been found in quantities that would repay the cost of the necessary machinery ; the expected discovery of oil had not been made ; trade was negligible ; public security was non-existent and revenue from agriculture could not be collected in consequence ; nor did these conditions tend to attract foreign capital in spite of strenuous efforts by the Italian Government in this direction."[1] When Italy declared war on Great Britain and France on the 10th of June Ethiopia was a plum ripe for the picking.

Strangely enough, very little of this situation was known to Imperial Italy's British neighbours in the Sudan. The victor, with his other gains, obtains a propaganda ascendancy, and Mussolini saw that the advantage was followed up. By the " Bon Voisinage " agreement of April, 1938, between Great Britain, France and Italy, the British and French governments withdrew diplomatic representation in Addis Ababa and the remaining consulates were deprived of the services of an " Oriental Secretary " or specialist officer. As a result Italian policy was triumphant in the field of propaganda. The newspapers of the Western Alliance, starved of better material, followed Fascist guidance, and " informed circles " in Khartoum unknowingly did much the same. The fateful balance in appreciation might have remained

[1] Report by R. E. Cheesman.

uncorrected to the last if it had not been for the valiant efforts of three spies. Their information arrived just in time.

The French, unlike the British, took the "*Bon Voisinage*" agreement for what it was, and had no scruples about organising "intelligencers." One of their men was called Colonel Monnier. He arrived in Khartoum from an extensive and clandestine journey in the interior of Ethiopia at the end of July of 1939. Soon after he died of malaria. He had had a companion on his arduous travels, an Ethiopian of high character and distinguished record, who was known at this time as Walde Mikael, elsewhere as Thompson, and correctly as Lorenzo Taezaz. After Monnier's death Taezaz went to Cairo to be examined by officers in the Middle East General Headquarters. He gave them a full account of his own and Monnier's discoveries. The third spy was a man called Paul Langrois, an Italian exile to France, who had a record of gallantry in the Spanish Civil War. He arrived in Khartoum in early 1940. He had the same tale to tell as his two predecessors: that owing to the internal state of Ethiopia the Italians could not make war on the Sudan from their Empire, howsoever war might be declared in Rome. They were agreed on another matter too: the focus of the irrepressible patriotism of the Ethiopians was to be found—whatever Italians might say about an array of sponsored Perkin Warbecks—in the exiled Emperor, Haile Selassie.

These were strong testimonies, and they formed a party of optimism in the British camp, but they depended on the observation of only three men and were, for that reason alone, not strong enough to sweep away the misgivings of the more cautious (and rightly cautious) party. Chief among these was the British Military Commander in the Sudan (traditionally known as the Kaid), Major-General Sir William Platt. Before the outbreak of war he had declared that British resources in the Sudan should be devoted primarily to defence. He approved in principle the idea of raising revolt in Ethiopia in such a way as to keep the patriotic ferment in being but, he said, he did not approve proposals "to launch a mere thousand soldiers, armed with rifles and one or two machine-guns to a company, in two or three packets, into the mountains of Abyssinia, against a European-led enemy vastly superior in the air, in ground numbers and armament, on nebulous information with no known local chieftains to rely on for support and insurrection."[1] In broad outline General Platt unwittingly described in this paper what was to be successfully attempted in the second year of the war.

Sir Archibald Wavell belonged to the optimist party. Before the outbreak of war in September, 1939, he had taken an important

[1] March, 1939. Information obtained at the War Office.

initiative on the advice of his Intelligence staff; he sent for a certain Daniel Arthur Sandford, who was at that time acting as treasurer of Guildford Cathedral. Sandford had longer experience of Ethiopia than any other European. He had been consul at Addis Ababa in 1914, and he had lived as a farmer and occasional adviser to the Ethiopian Government from 1920 to 1936. Palmerston once said that if you wished to be misinformed about a foreign country you needed to seek the advice of an Englishman of long residence. Sandford proved a remarkable exception to this rule. From 1939 onwards his advice on Ethiopia never seems to have been at fault on any important matter. He was convinced of two things : first that the Emperor Haile Selassie was worthy of the fullest possible support, being not only without serious rivals for the Ethiopian throne but capable of commanding the devoted allegiance of his former subjects ; secondly that the patriotism of the Ethiopians was a powerful force. He maintained that stories of large sections of the population being reconciled to Italian rule were empty propaganda. In October of 1939 this energetic and far-seeing man drew up plans for raising an Ethiopian rebellion which formed the basis of all that followed.[1]

Between then and the autumn of 1940 there followed long and elaborate manœuvres around the subject of a British Ethiopian policy and these need not be recalled. The party conflict in Khartoum was eventually stilled into uneasy truce by the liaison officer between the War Office and the Middle East Command, Colonel Elphinstone. In October he obtained agreement to a proposal for a census of the Ethiopian refugees in Khartoum, and for the establishment of arsenals on the Sudan-Ethiopian frontier. From these proposals grew the Frontier Battalion of the Sudan Defence Force. This unit was to play a great part in the events of the next year.

There followed a long period of preparation by Sandford and his supporters and helpers. They were always working against the discouragement of sceptics in power. But by the spring and early summer of 1940 they had achieved something. There was an Ethiopian Intelligence Bureau operating in Khartoum under Robert Ernest Cheesman ; the Frontier Battalion had been organised into five companies under the command of Major Hugh Boustead of whom more will be heard ; Sandford had toured the Ethiopian frontiers in Somaliland and Kenya and made tenuous contacts with notables in the Ethiopian interior ; the Ethiopian refugees in Khartoum had been indexed so there was some notion as to what Ethiopian fighting men would be available for a campaign. The sceptics drew strength for their arguments from the fact that the refugees were split into two

[1] Information obtained at the War Office.

parties which sometimes assaulted one another in the streets. The optimists might have been defeated but for the testimonies of the three spies which received dramatic confirmation. An agent of Sandford stole an Italian postbag and brought it to Khartoum for inspection. The contents were private letters which told a long tale of despair and homesickness.

When Italy declared war on the 10th of June Sandford was in Cairo. The Commander-in-Chief called him to a meeting of senior staff officers and formally instructed him to undertake the raising of an Ethiopian rebellion. Sir Arthur Longmore, the Air Commander-in-Chief, was present and he promised R.A.F. support. After the meeting Sir Arthur spoke to Sandford privately and said something like this : " Look, Sandford, I have no aircraft and you know it, but if you really need air support let me know personally and I will see that you get it. But I trust you never ask for it unless you simply cannot do otherwise."[1] Meanwhile the plans that Sandford and Cheesman had laid were allowed to go forward in Khartoum. Arms and ammunition were distributed to nine chieftains within Ethiopia. Then on the 25th of June an event occurred which took all parties in Khartoum by surprise. The Emperor arrived in Alexandria.

He was accompanied by his second son, by Lorenzo Taezaz and another secretary, and by Mr. George Steer. He travelled under the name of Mr. Strong. The enigma was really quite simple. Within a few days, as was obvious with the fall of France, it would be impossible to fly direct to Egypt from England. So the Emperor had been given a passage to Africa by flying boat, in case he was needed. The Foreign Office left any problems to be solved by the authorities on the spot. The problems proved enormous.

Two days after his arrival at Alexandria the Emperor was despatched by flying boat to Khartoum with Mr. Edwin Chapman Andrews, the assistant Oriental Secretary at the Embassy, added to his entourage. The first sign of official Khartoum reaction occurred on the southward flight. The aeroplane was diverted by signal from Khartoum to Wadi Halfa where in the discomfort of intense heat and makeshift accommodation the returning sovereign was obliged to spend a week. Chapman Andrews in the meantime flew on to Khartoum to urge the Emperor's claim to residence there, urged it on an opposition headed by the Governor-General and the Kaid. He returned with Sandford. The Emperor was moved to hear from this valiant friend about the efforts made by him on behalf of his cause, but he was disappointed when he heard of the small quantities of arms allotted to his followers and hurt to find Sandford in agreement with the official prohibition

[1] Brigadier D. A. Sandford.

against his immediate return to his native land.[1] But at least the prohibition against the Emperor's proceeding southward had been overcome by Chapman Andrews. The Emperor was assigned a pleasant shady residence at Jebel Aulia twenty-eight miles from Khartoum. He went there on the 2nd of July under the name of Mr. Smith.

When news of the Emperor's arrival became known to his subjects refugee recruits flocked to Khartoum in such great numbers that they rapidly became a new major problem of the Administration. There were no large enough barracks or houses, no arms to spare for them, no instructors to train them. (To provide them with a commanding officer a Sudan policeman was decorated with N.C.O. stripes.) At the same time, in the desperate situation of the Sudan where British forces were outnumbered by Italian by twenty to one, with British Somaliland and Forts Kassala and Gallabat surrendered, the unfortunate Emperor was so closely guarded for the sake of security that he was more a prisoner than the sovereign ally of his British hosts. He submitted to the vexations of his state with the resignation and kingly dignity which marked the whole of his exile. But his restricted freedom could not but add to his irritation when he found greater cause for complaint.

A little more than a month after the arrival of Haile Selassie Sandford entered Ethiopia to promote the rebellion. He led the advance party from Doka and on the 18th of September he reached Faguta (about thirty-five miles south of Lake Tana) in the Sakala district. He made this his Headquarters, and from Faguta he succeeded, against all the difficulties of inadequate supplies, doubts in Khartoum, and of Ethiopian war-weariness, in reviving the once fierce enthusiasm of Ethiopian patriotism. His major difficulty was in the rivalry of two main chieftains Dejasmach Mangasha Jambare of Mecha (a place near Addis Ababa), and Dejasmach Nagash Kabada of Burye. He planned a revolt led by these two men whose purpose was to open the area of Gojjam to further invasion from the Sudan. But the mutual jealousy of Mangasha and Nagash brought the plan to nothing beyond a skirmish between Nagash's forces and Italian troops east of Burye. Among his many vexations Sandford was continually alarmed by the indiscretion of all the Ethiopians he could rally, but in fact this military vice of his allies stood him in good stead. Their boastings and exaggerations, increasing by compound interest as they spread, reached the Italians and depressed their low morale further. Then at the end of October the whole prospect of the rebellion changed anew owing to political events in Khartoum.

[1] Chapman Andrews.

The relations between Haile Selassie and the British had become strained.[1] The Emperor complained that his people were receiving far fewer rifles than had originally been promised; that he himself was given no say in how and to whom these few weapons should be distributed; that his bodyguard was not being trained and equipped; that plans were made for operations within the frontiers of his own kingdom without any reference to himself; that an armed battalion of Eritreans, which had deserted from the Italian army during the Italo-Abyssinian war was being kept in internment in Kenya instead of being sent to him in Khartoum.[2] He demanded, as he had done from the beginning, the status of an independent sovereign in alliance with Great Britain, and as earnest of British good intentions he now said that he wished them to negotiate with him, immediately, a long-term treaty of friendship and alliance.

By raising questions of political gravity Haile Selassie, not for the first or last time, proved himself a statesman. He threw the Sudan Administration into a state of perplexity and the result was that they requested a ministerial conference. This took place on the 28th of October in Khartoum. The British Government was represented by Mr. Anthony Eden, at that time Secretary of State for War. He was accompanied by Field-Marshal Smuts, Sir Archibald Wavell, Mr. Michael Wright as representative of the Embassy in Cairo, Lieutenant-General Dickinson and his successor in the command of the East African forces, Lieutenant-General Cunningham and, among other staff officers, by representatives of G (R). In three days of meetings described as " stormy," agreement was reached between the Emperor and the British on the main questions in dispute. This was because Anthony Eden espoused anew the cause which he had defended before the League of Nations in 1935. He asserted Haile Selassie's right to rebellion; he persuaded the Sudan Government to look on the existing rebellion as a war of liberation. This was the great result in which Wingate's fortunes were to be closely concerned.

The decisions of the conference, though negotiations for a treaty were refused, were all in favour of Haile Selassie and the optimist party. Chapman Andrews and Lorenzo Taezaz were to go to Kenya to clear up the confused situation of the Eritrean battalion; a large supply of Springfield rifles and Bren guns were to be given to the Ethiopian rebels (known henceforth at the Emperor's request as " the Patriots ") ; an assurance was given by Anthony Eden that the

---

[1] The narrative follows here an account by Sir Edwin Chapman Andrews.

[2] This incredible state of affairs was due to reports (which proved fallacious) that the Eritreans were not willing to fight for the Ethiopian Emperor or cause. In this incident Italian propaganda probably achieved its greatest triumph.

transport difficulties of Mission 101 were to be overcome regardless of monetary difficulties; "operational centres" commanded by British officers and served by British N.C.O.s were to be recruited from the whole of the Middle East with the object of training the patriots and leading them in military operations in the interior; two Regular Army officers were to be sent to Khartoum to act as liaison between the British military authorities, Mission 101, and the Emperor; they were to keep Middle East Headquarters informed of Ethiopian requirements, and to supervise the collection, enlistment and training of the Ethiopian patriots. The two officers selected for this last duty were Major Tuckey of the Deputy Quarter Master General's department, and Orde Wingate. That was how Wingate came to lead guerilla forces in Ethiopia. He arrived in Khartoum on the 6th of November.

He had met the Emperor once some years before, in Brown's Hotel in London.[1] Nothing of note seems to have passed between them on that occasion but the Emperor had not forgotten a favourable impression of a strange and gifted man. Wingate left his own account of his initial meeting with Haile Selassie in Khartoum. "I found the Emperor depressed," he recorded. "He said that nothing had been done yet towards making the patriot campaign practical politics, and was evidently afraid that he himself was merely being used as a pawn. I told him that the liberation of Ethiopia was an indispensable part of the British war aims; that it was also of the greatest importance that the Ethiopians themselves should play a leading rôle in the coming campaign, and, finally, that he should take as his motto an ancient proverb found in Gese: 'If I am not for myself, who will be for me?' and trust in the justice of his cause." It seems that Wingate had already made up his mind how to accomplish his great purpose for, as the Emperor told Chapman Andrews later, at this first meeting he impressed the other not only by his energy but the sweep of his strategic concept. At the close of this first audience Wingate told the Emperor that he was certain that he himself could bring the Ethiopian cause to success if the Emperor would "grant him one thing."

"What is that?" asked the Emperor.

Wingate answered: "Your Majesty's complete trust and confidence, without reservation, at all times."[2]

It will be seen that Wingate's new post was not in theory a very authoritative one. His rank was still only that of Major. An un-

[1] H.I.M. The Emperor Haile Selassie. A communication to the writer at an audience in Addis Ababa. H.I.M. could not be certain of the date beyond the fact that it was some time before the war.
[2] Chapman Andrews.

ambitious man or one who was careful not to exceed his instructions
would have left the rebellion to Sandford and Boustead and confined
himself to administration and liaison duties. It is curious that when
Wingate turned his appointment into a command he was not resisted.
But the time was an odd one ; heroic, generous, irresponsible in one
sense, and exaltedly responsible in another. The war was lost to all
appearances but the British people were determined not to admit
defeat. In such a time any man who believed, and could convey his
belief that he knew the way out of the disaster into victory was sure
of a respectful hearing, and was more likely than at any other time to
obtain a following. This circumstance was soon to introduce a
remarkable complication into the Ethiopian campaign, as appears
presently.

Before leaving Cairo, Wingate had obtained a million pounds
credit for the Ethiopian rebellion. Strengthened thus he set about his
new-broom task with violent innovation and energy, and his first
business was to obtain transport in accordance with the terms of the
Eden agreement with Haile Selassie. There was an irremediable
scarcity of motor transport and there were too few horses and mules
in the Sudan to solve the problem that way ; but there was abundance
of camels. So with characteristic logic and directness Wingate bought
camels in the vast numbers that he needed for the transport of war
equipment from Khartoum to the Ethiopian frontier. He was given
authority to buy up to 25,000 camels and according to his transport
officer, the eminent scholar, William Allen, he bought 18,000. Of these
(according to official records) 15,000 were used in the campaign. Not
one of the unfortunate beasts that went into Ethiopia survived more
than six months.

The first Ethiopian battalion (as it was called) arrived from Kenya,
the second (after Chapman Andrews's investigation) was being prepared to follow it. Ten thousand Springfield rifles were delivered from
the north, and every day British volunteer officers and N.C.O.s came
into Khartoum to report for duty in the " operational centres."
The Ethiopian refugee volunteers, the patriots, had for some weeks
been assembled in a camp at a place called Soba near Khartoum. This
was from the first to last a very makeshift uncomfortable and untidy
place by British Army standards,[1] but now it began to take on something of the appearance of a military cantonment, with a Camp
Commandant, an Adjutant and a Quartermaster and similar amenities.
Despite continuing misgivings among the great, the rebellion was now
being undertaken seriously. This was Wingate's first and very considerable achievement.

[1] The diary of Mr. Neil Maclean, M.P.

Immediately after his arrival in Khartoum he decided to meet Sandford as soon as possible. The first proposal was that he should be dropped at Faguta by parachute, but this scheme was quickly abandoned because it would mean a long absence while the parachutist found his way back to Khartoum. It was decided in the end to attempt the visit by air. At Faguta there was a flat space on a table-land just sufficient for a skilfully controlled landing, and, conceivably, for a very skilfully controlled take-off. All around were precipices and ravines. Wingate found an airman, Flight-Lieutenant Collis, prepared to make the attempt. They set off on the 20th of November taking two Ethiopians with them, Ato Getahun Tesemmra and Dejasmach Makonnen Desta. On the outward flight, as he looked down on the frontier landscape (his first sight of Ethiopia since the days when he served in the Sudan as a young officer who had never heard of Zionism) Wingate decided that when the time came for the Emperor to return to his country he would take this route. What impressed him was the fact that this was ideal country for compass-marching independently of roads. No guides were necessary here because Mount Belaiya, standing forth independently of the plateau, was visible for far around: here then was a gap in the defences. Behind the mountain was another gap, a way up the escarpment discovered by Cheesman and not known to the Italians.

The perils and discomforts of the flight were increased by rainy weather. Nonetheless they did not fly straight to Faguta but first over the garrison towns of Danghila, Engiabara and Burye, rightly calculating that they would not be observed during the siesta hour. They arrived at Faguta, with a perfect landing, early in the afternoon, and the two main organisers of the revolt met for the first time. They were soon to be bitter rivals, not through Sandford's fault. Their first introduction to each other passed off happily. Four years later Wavell wrote : " I should like to have seen the meeting between Sandford and Wingate when the latter flew in to an improvised landing strip in the heart of Abyssinia. Few people looked more like a fiery leader of partisans than Wingate, few looked less like one than Sandford—solid, bespectacled, benevolent—who was in his way as bold and as active as Wingate."[1]

They went into conference. Sandford had a sad story to tell of half-hearted support from Khartoum and neglected opportunity. He had received only a thousand rifles and inadequate ammunition ; he lacked for money, high explosive, machine-guns and mortars. A supply convoy of a hundred and fifty camels was on its way from

[1] Foreword to *Wingate's Raiders* by Charles Rolo.

Roseires and that was all the help he knew of. He had been told in outline of the Eden conference and its results but this was not the first time that he had been told of encouraging decisions, and he was sceptical. Then Wingate in turn told him in detail about the new course and convinced him that the rebellion, which gave some sign of perishing through discouragement before the Eden conference, was now a large and vigorous undertaking to which the British Government was irrevocably committed. He told Sandford about the organisation of the operational centres which were to be composed each of a British officer in charge, five British N.C.O.s, and about two hundred Ethiopians. Three such centres were already fully manned and were expected to leave the Sudan for Ethiopia in three weeks. All this was joyous news to Sandford. The two men had only one disagreement at this first meeting. Wingate wanted all stores and equipment to be handled by the operational centres under his command. Sandford, not unnaturally, preferred to continue with his own method. The first convoys of arms, however, would need to be met at the foot of the escarpment in accordance with Sandford's existing arrangements. The disagreement was for that reason not serious because it could be postponed, but it presaged worse ones to come. They were in agreement over all else, especially that the Emperor should enter the country as soon as his bodyguard could be formed and trained.

The camp at Faguta was situated near one of the numerous sources of the Blue Nile, a place adorned by an Ethiopian shrine known as the Gishe Abai Mikael (the church of St. Michael's spring). Before returning to Khartoum Wingate and Dejasmach Makonnen Desta made the four hours' ride from Faguta to this venerable geographical wonder. They did the journey in a sight-seeing spirit but came on good political fortune at the same time. There was a little crowd of people at the Church and Makonnen Desta told them about Wingate's mission which, he assured them, heralded the return of their sovereign, that " sign " (as it was called) for which men in Ethiopia waited with religious awe.[1] The news, with the usual wild exaggerations, spread quickly and far.

On the 22nd Wingate and his party left for Khartoum leaving Makonnen Desta behind to help Sandford to organise the reception of operational centres. If the landing on the little table-land had been hazardous, the take-off was a nightmare. Collis reckoned that he had just and only just sufficient runway to enable him to climb into the air before the precipice. The take-off was only possible at all because the aeroplane was of an old design quicker to get airborne than

[1] Dejasmach Makonnen Desta.

more modern and powerful machines. Twice Collis drove forward and then raced the machine aside, unconfident of flying speed. At the third attempt the machine rose and cleared the ravine a few yards before its edge. It should be remembered (greatly to his honour) that Wingate's natural courage did not extend to flying, and he always suffered from bad nerves in the air even on the safest journeys.[1]

He spent a week in Khartoum before reporting back to Cairo. He lived in the Grand Hotel at Khartoum. His days were taken up with the work of administration and organisation.

At this time, and during the whole of this Ethiopian chapter of his life, he became like a caricature of himself. The reason seems clear. Though he never said so in plain words, the evidence is strong that the order against his re-visiting Palestine inflicted so deep a wound that during many months after his sentence of exile (for it was that) he lived in a state of utterly self-injurious embitterment. His many attractive qualities went into eclipse, only appearing fitfully, while at the same time the harshness, the impatience, the angry intolerance and the play-acting became emphasised as never before or after. He inspired devotion in many of his youngest officers, but for the rest he made few friends and many enemies. He is only understood at this time if it is remembered that he was passing through a dark period of the mind and spirit, and it tells much about his authentic strength that his suddenly prominent faults of character never seriously threatened his enterprise.

At other times of his life the element of eccentricity in his character would out despite himself, but now he seemed to emphasise his strangeness purposely. Among many extraordinary affectations he took to wearing a miniature alarm clock strapped to his wrist so that he could time his interviews exactly by the ringing of the bell. He took again to brushing his body instead of bathing and caused much amazement to some people with whom he had business by receiving them naked in his room in the Grand Hotel, brushing himself thoroughly the while.[2] If most people could bear easily enough with such-like " odd tricks which sorrow shoots out of the mind," it was otherwise with the new and extreme rudeness that went with these fantasies. His rudeness now went to utterly grotesque lengths, both in business encounters, when charges of pro-Italianism were frequent, and on private occasions when he took perverse delight in taunting expressions of views such as were sure to infuriate whom he was talking to.

[1] Mrs. Lorna Smith.
[2] Colonel Jack (veterinary officer to Gideon Force). Chapman Andrews.

Captain Dodds-Parker, the principal G (R) liaison officer, who also had a room in the Grand Hotel, used to breakfast at the smallest table he could find so as to avoid having to share that meal with Wingate and being provoked into a quarrel. On one occasion he took his cantankerousness so far as to accuse two of his staff officers with cowardice, saying that they had sought their appointments in order to avoid the dangers of battle elsewhere. Goaded beyond endurance they both said that they could not work longer with a man who accused them of such things and that they must resign their appointments forthwith. Fortunately the logical end of the scene could be averted. Dodds-Parker was in the room and he intervened :

" Wait a minute, Orde," he said, " if X and Y are accused of cowardice and are obliged to resign, the same applies to me. I'm in their kind of position, and I take your remarks as applying to myself too, so we'll all three resign."

Then Wingate laughed at himself and good humour was restored. But as a rule there was no one there to shake him thus out of his black moods, and the black mood was the most frequent one. He needed friends and kept all men at arm's length.

As can be imagined, his relations with his superiors were even more harassed, and everything that General Haining and Wing-Commander Ritchie had had to endure was exacted of Sir William Platt. There were moments when the Kaid asserted that he would not meet Wingate again, and Wingate, storming in his hot room in the Grand Hotel, asserted that he would not meet Sir William Platt again. The peace would then be patched up by Dodds-Parker or Brigadier Scobie, leaving murmurs of the storm still audible.[1] Such incidents and scenes had their influence on the conduct of operations and Sir William Platt was heard to say : " The curse of this war is Lawrence in the last."[2]

He lost affection by his treatment of colleagues ; he unnecessarily complicated his mission by the extremes to which he went in defying authority ; it seems that, in the days ahead, he occasionally showed excessive severity in his handling of those under him. Once, after this time, when an interpreter failed to give a correct translation, he gave way to ungovernable rage and knocked the man down with blows of a hide whip. On another occasion, also later, he was inspecting Ethiopian soldiers, and on noticing a man wrongly turned out he struck him down where he stood in the ranks.[3] There are other stories of the same kind. They are probably much exaggerated. It was a rough life in a rough world where physical violence was part of the

[1] Douglas Dodds-Parker, M.P. [2] Thesiger. [3] Eye-witness accounts.

accepted order, and some of Wingate's closest companions in arms throughout these African days deny absolutely that he showed needless cruelty,[1] but what is certain is that his reputation for harshness ran higher than at any other time of his life, and less is remembered from these days of his frequent, instinctive and impulsive generosity. The Ethiopian chapter, though not inconsistent with the rest, stands alone. Impatience and embitterment sometimes came near to destroying him.

One day in the week after his meeting with Sandford he met Wilfred Thesiger, already known as an explorer of Ethiopian experience, and now an officer in the Sudan Defence Force. He was to play a notable part in the campaign. He found Wingate in the camp at Soba. He introduced himself.

Wingate said : " Are you happy ? "

Thesiger wondered how to reply and then said : " Well, yes, I suppose I am—reasonably so."

Wingate said : " I am not happy. But then, I have been thinking, probably no great man ever was really happy." Of course this was said in farce, but even when he jested, he did so in a sombre and disquieting manner.

On the 2nd of December a conference was convened in Cairo for the purpose of settling military policy against the whole of Italian East Africa. It was attended only by senior commanders, and was presided over by the Commander-in-Chief. There was some question as to whether a person of such junior rank as Wingate ought to join the discussion, but Sir Arthur Longmore strongly recommended that he should, so Wingate was admitted for a short session. He was instructed by Sir Archibald Wavell to address the meeting for ten minutes on the subject of the patriot rebellion and his plans for a guerilla campaign. He did not keep to these instructions and gave one of his most remarkable performances.

For his allotted ten minutes he told the conference of his preparations in Khartoum, the state of things within Ethiopia as reported by Sandford, and his plans and theories for the future. He laid his strongest emphasis on the fact that the revolt would only succeed if it was led from within and associated with high moral purposes. " Hitherto," he wrote later of what he said, " we had made the mistake of appealing to the cupidity and self-interest of Ethiopians by offering them money and poor quality war material. These qualities were all on the side of the Enemy. Courage, faith and self-respect, these were the qualities

[1] W. Allen. Mr. Takle Rora, formerly a captain in the 2nd Ethiopian Battalion.

we could appeal to successfully because they were on our side. We had first to convince the Ethiopian . . . of our *bona fides* . . . He must see us fighting not by his side but in front of him . . . (we) must convince him that . . . we are not only brave soldiers but devoted to the cause of his liberties." He demanded that British propaganda to Ethiopia should take the story of David and Goliath as its main theme. " I pointed out to Generals Wavell, Platt and Cunningham," he recorded later, "(that) it was vital to our cause that we should make it plain to the world that we were being generous as well as just to Ethiopia. For early evacuation of Ethiopia to be practicable it was necessary to support the Emperor's authority and provide him from the first with an army."

His ten minutes were soon up, but he went on speaking, departing from his brief and entering the realms of grand strategy. The Italian offensive against Greece was then in progress and he urged on the conference that they should withdraw the bulk of British troops from Kenya and the Sudan thus enabling the Middle East Command to sweep the Italians from the whole of North Africa after which they could and would meet the Germans in Greece and the Balkans. (He made no tactless mention of a Jewish army but this was in his mind.)[1] Meantime if they left only sufficient troops in the south to keep Ethiopia in a state of siege he " would cause the Italian Empire to waste away from within." He was confident, he said, that under that strategy he could bring about an Italian surrender in May. (Here his judgment was at fault for it was to take till May to defeat the Italians with two British armies operating in Ethiopia.)

He had spoken for half an hour. In spite of the fact that he had occupied enormously more than his time at a conference of which he was the most junior and least welcome member, he made a deep and favourable impression.[2]

The main results of the Conference, so far as Wingate was concerned, were these : that the Emperor was to enter Ethiopia with his bodyguard as soon as possible making his first Headquarters at Belaiya at the foot of the escarpment ; that a company of the frontier battalion was to take post there as garrison ; that the second and fourth Ethiopian battalions were to be brought from Kenya to form the nucleus of the Emperor's bodyguard, the first Ethiopian battalion being divided among the operational centres ; and that the rebellion-effort was to be concentrated on the province of Gojjam and not

[1] Dodds-Parker. See below.
[2] General Sir Alan Cunningham. A communication to the writer. Dodds-Parker. In *Gideon Goes To War* Wingate is represented as scattering insults to the assembled generals, and the writer has heard this tale from other sources. Such behaviour then would have been quite fatal to Wingate's prospects and is not remembered by witnesses.

dissipated. The official despatch said : " The ultimate object of the plan was to seize an Italian stronghold in Gojjam, preferably Danghila, install the Emperor nearby, and from this centre to widen the area of revolt and desertion."

Wingate returned to Khartoum on the 7th December and took up the work of reorganisation and training again.

In the same month there occurred in this part of the world a very odd incident which had little effect on the trend of affairs, but caused some stir at the time. It had an influence on Wingate's mind greatly out of proportion to its weight.

This is what happened. One day in the first half of the month a retired game-warden of the Sudan arrived in Cairo from London, sent by some veiled authority or other, for these things were growing fast, on a mission which, evidently, enjoyed some small degree of official approval. He was called Courtenay Brocklehurst. His mission was directed to the Galla people in the south of Ethiopia. These tribes are somewhat analogous to the Hazara descendants of Timurlane's soldiers, who are still to be found as separate people in Afghanistan. Like the Hazaras the Gallas are conquerors who have been conquered themselves. In the rude civilisation of Ethiopia the animosity of the conquered Gallas towards the ruling Amharas persisted, but, with the vagueness that goes with primitive society, there were opposite tendencies to forgetfulness and even to amalgamation at the same time. There was and is no racial barrier between the Amharas and the Gallas. (The Empress herself is of part-Galla descent.) But it followed as a matter of course that there were more malcontents among the Galla than among the Amhara.

Brocklehurst had a plan which he believed would heighten the intensity of the revolt, and he placed it before Sir Archibald Wavell. He proposed that he and his two companions should enter the Galla country and tell the tribes-people there that if they rose on the side of Great Britain they would make themselves free not only of Italian tyranny but of Amhara tyranny as well, and from a British victory they would obtain autonomous rule with guarantees and protection against all oppression of the centralised government. Brocklehurst argued that by this means he could bring over to the British side those parts of the Ethiopian population which had smallest interest in our victory. Sir Archibald listened to the plan which seemed to have much to be said for it. His likeness to Kutuzov has been mentioned, and it came out very much in those days when there was no way to victory and only time and patience in great quantities could turn fortune's wheel. He had abundant sympathy with men of imagination and energy, and he was more inclined to agree than disagree with novel proposals. He knew little about the internal affairs of Ethiopia, and so when Brocklehurst put his ideas forward, not only with the assurance of home support,[1] but with all the stimulus of a remarkably charming and impressive personality, Wavell told him "to go ahead" and make his arrangements in Khartoum. (He ought of course to have consulted his experts but he had much on his mind.)

The plan seems to have come to the Emperor's knowledge through Sirak Herouy, the son of an Ethiopian foreign minister.[2] If he had heard about it from British people his suspicion might have been a little less. As it was, he was thrown into a state of alarm and indignation. This was immediately and violently shared by Wingate. He saw the Brocklehurst mission as part of a large and sinister design whose aim was the denial of independence to Ethiopia and its reduction to protectorate-status under the British flag. His suspicions were not groundless. There is little doubt that many people among the white population of Kenya, and a few in the Sudan service, hoped that Ethiopian independence would never be restored. Brocklehurst may have been helped and influenced by such people. Their philosophy was not ignoble. They wanted civilisation to spread and were disgusted by the squalor, injustice and occasional atrocity inseparable from primitive independent rule. Following African precedents, their idealism was not unmixed with greed. Sandford had already had his difficulties with the protectorate school. One of the members of Mission 101 was a young man who used to write regularly to his father, a rich Australian businessman, about the exploitation-possibilities of Ethiopia, encouraging parental hopes that Haile Selassie might not be able to unite the country or re-ascend his throne. Sandford had checked the young man who henceforth obediently put aside commercial thinking. Sandford did not ignore the portent but he refused to let it disturb him much. He was a more experienced politician than Wingate. He recognised the strength of the Emperor's position. When he heard about the Brocklehurst mission (some time later), he hardly

[1] That Brocklehurst had at least partial official support is suggested by the following from *Hansard* of 18.12.40 : " Mr. Manders asked the Under Secretary of State for Foreign Affairs what was the present position in Abyssinia and whether all steps are being taken to treat that country and its Emperor as allied in the fullest sense. Mr. R. A. Butler : Information as to conditions in Abyssinia is naturally difficult to obtain but the movement of revolt against the Italians appears to be making progress. It is the policy of His Majesty's Government to extend to the Emperor Haile Selassie, *as well as to all elements within Abyssinia willing to bear arms against the enemy*, all possible assistance in their fight for freedom." Author's italics, cf. the unequivocal statement of Mr. Eden on 4.2.41 given on page 266.

[2] *New Times and Ethiopia News*, Jan., 1942 ; three articles on the Patriot rising which seem to owe something to Wingate. See below.

gave it a thought.[1] Wingate gave it abundant thought, both then and for long afterwards.

For the Emperor and his supporters the immediate need was to get the mission turned back before it could do any harm.

The Emperor consulted with Wingate and they decided to send a telegram from the Emperor to Sir Archibald Wavell for transmission to Mr. Churchill protesting against the mission, requesting its recall, and pointing out that the Emperor's " reluctance to admit the mission did not in the least alter his intention to institute a reasonable degree of local autonomy."[2] If this should fail they intended to appeal to President Roosevelt.[3] The result of the telegram was an assurance from the Commander-in-Chief to the Emperor that the mission would be withdrawn. Sir Archibald Wavell had been fully persuaded of its unwisdom by Chapman Andrews, and it appears that he acted on his own initiative before sending the message to the Prime Minister.[4] The Brocklehurst mission's brief day was over.

It was withdrawn. Its supplies of arms were made over to the troops of General Cunningham. Important backing could not save it, and probably never tried to, once opposition was met in Khartoum.

The mission represented a lost cause. In the age of nationalism and when the Emperor Haile Selassie was an admired figure in England and America (and when memories of the Hoare-Laval fiasco were recent) there could be no hope of success for a policy of dividing or reducing Ethiopia. And this is what Brocklehurst's plan meant in effect, if not in intention. The country was far too primitive for its people to grasp the subtleties of unrebellious opposition, and the idea that these rude Galla tribes were capable of the political balancing act of fighting the Italians on behalf of a country to whose sovereign they would meantime preserve an attitude of strict but peaceable protest in accord with the finest traditions of the Mother of Parliaments, was too ludicrous to be entertained by anyone who stopped to think for one moment. On the other hand the idea of provoking civil war within Ethiopia, on the argument of dividing and conquering, was not only far too cynical for the taste of the British voter (and soldier) in that moment of exalted patriotism, but was extremely danger-

---

[1] Sandford.   [2] Draft Report. W.P.I.   [3] Mrs. Lorna Smith.
[4] The following from *The Second World War, Volume II* by Sir Winston Churchill may suggest Wavell's rather than the Prime Minister's initiative in the fate of the Brocklehurst mission : " (Action this day) Prime Minister to Foreign Secretary and General Ismay, for C.O.S. Committee, 30.12.40. ' It would seem that every effort should be made to meet the Emperor of Ethiopia's wishes. We have already, I understand, stopped our officers from entering the Galla country. . . .' "

ous. Italian morale may have been low but with their gigantic superiority in numbers and material the Italian army could not be dismissed as of no account. The battle of Keren was to show that Italians were prepared to fight manfully, given a substantial chance of victory. An Ethiopian civil war might give them just that chance.

These were general and theoretical considerations against the merits of Brocklehurst's mission. There were other objections too. If Brocklehurst's ideas had been well-grounded in fact it would have been one thing, but there was evidence that they were entirely at fault. A large proportion of the patriot recruits to the Ethiopian battalions who had rallied to the Emperor were Galla, so that the first fruits of the missions were likely to be a mutiny at Soba. Furthermore it was known that since October Sandford, through Nagash Desta, had been in promising negotiation with Galla chiefs.[1] It seems not to have been recognised that Brocklehurst's judgment was extremely biased; that he was filled with a personal detestation of the Emperor such as blinded him to all facts that stood in the way of his preconceived notions. It was his conviction (held with honesty) that the Emperor had no claim to the throne and could have no large following among the Ethiopian people.

When the mission's plans came to be examined in Khartoum they found no friends.[2] In Cairo meanwhile Sir Archibald Wavell had appointed Sir Philip Mitchell as his chief political adviser on all matters relating to Italian-held territory. Sir Philip was later to find himself in conflict with the Emperor on questions of Ethiopian independence, but he seems to have had no hesitation over condemning the Brocklehurst mission.[3] It rapidly went the way of many other mad ventures.[4] It was of no importance except as a danger signal marking an obstinate

[1] Information obtained at the War Office.

[2] Sir William Platt appears to have been persuaded by George Steer of the danger of separate approaches to the Galla as early as October, a fact which suggests that Brocklehurst or the organisation he represented had anticipated the Commander-in-Chief's approval. Sir Alan Cunningham expressed himself in terms of decisive disapproval of the Brocklehurst mission in a comment on Wingate's Ethiopian report.

[3] " At the time when Brigadier Sandford and Major (later Major-General) Orde Wingate were organising the revolt in the Gojjam province of Western Ethiopia, which the Emperor was to lead later in person, a retired Sudan game warden and two companions arrived alleging that they had authority to start another rebellion, with independence for the Galla tribes as its objective—independence which meant nothing if it was not independence from the Emperor, and which must therefore mean war with him ! There were others preparing to promise all sorts of unachievable things to the Somalis. . . . There was even . . . a gallant Belgian officer who sounded me secretly, through an intermediary with a view to ascertaining what help he could expect in a revolt against his own Governor-General ! All he really wanted, as did many brave men at that distressing time, was to fight somebody. . . ." Sir Philip Mitchell. *African Afterthoughts.*

[4] Dodds-Parker.

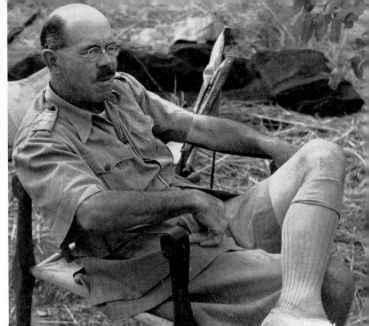

D. A. Sandford

The Emperor with
Wilfred Thesiger

Dambacha, April 1941. Wingate inspects a soldier of the
2nd Ethiopian Battalion

and supposedly obsolete way of white thinking about Africa. The mission would not be worth considering in such detail in this book, were it not that long after its dispersal it continued to haunt Wingate's mind and became an obsession.

The next month the revolt began.

CHAPTER XII

THE CAMPAIGN OPENS

ON THE 18th of January the Emperor, accompanied by British representatives and his entourage, left Khartoum by air for Roseires. On the 20th he was flown to a little place called Um Idla near the Ethiopian border. The next day he was the centre of a modest and dramatic ceremony. Thirty miles within Ethiopia, a guard of honour of the second Ethiopian battalion was drawn up for the Emperor's inspection. Then, when he had arrived and greeted his followers, the Emperor, with his own hands, hoisted the Ethiopian flag while the troops presented arms. Chapman Andrews stepped forward and read an address of congratulation from the Kaid while all present remained standing to attention. Wingate stood immediately behind the Emperor, and a photograph shows him with an expression of rigid solemnity under the monstrous sun-helmet which he had worn in Palestine and was to wear throughout this campaign. While the address was being read Italian aircraft could be heard distantly, and some who were present believed that they could discern the hum of the enemy machines being answered by the roar of lions in the bush, and took it for a good augury.

The entry was well timed. Two days before, on the 19th, General Platt had begun the advance into Eritrea with the 4th and 5th Indian Divisions.

The next part of the programme was to convey the Emperor to his Headquarters at Belaiya. The Frontier Battalion had already assembled there during December, escorting large camel convoys of provisions in arduous cross-country marches, making their way through bush and thorn-scrub country and over broken lava soil split by ravines. Many beasts had been lost on the way already. While this movement had been going forward, there had been a small action which had interesting results. To divert attention from the progress of the first convoy and a company of the battalion, a platoon and sixty Sudan police had entered the Gumz country to the south of the convoy's route. They had distributed arms to the negro population there, and endeavoured to hold the Italian garrison at Gubba fixed to their post. The diversion had succeeded, and was followed by R.A.F. raids on Gubba while

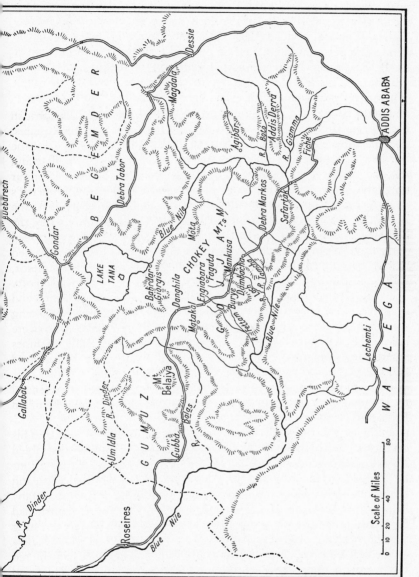

Western Ethiopia

the armed negro peasantry kept the garrison in a state of increasing alarm. Unnerved, the Italians withdrew from this isolated forward post a week or so before the Emperor's arrival on the frontier. This meant that the road to Belaiya from Roseires was now open. Nevertheless Wingate decided that no chance must be taken with the Emperor's personal safety, and he ordered that his onward movement to Belaiya must be made across country, marching by compass bearings. This caused much exasperation and protest to which Wingate only answered with grim anger that he understood compass-marching better than most men and he refused to change his orders. He owned after that he was wrong. He was too much under the influence of preconceived ideas formed in Palestine and he overlooked the fact that marching on compass-bearing was one thing in well-mapped country, and another in country for which the maps were unreliable.[1] He wore out his men, beasts and machines unnecessarily.

Wingate set out, the day after the entry, going eastwards towards Belaiya to reconnoitre the route to be followed by the Emperor, his bodyguard and entourage, and the second Ethiopian battalion. His party travelled in two trucks and included his Jewish secretary whom it may be convenient to introduce now. Some time back Wingate had asked through Brigadier Iltyd Clayton in Cairo for the services of one of the former squadsmen, preferably Carmi. The latter was not available already being usefully employed in the British army, but Avram Akavia was free, and he joined Wingate in Khartoum shortly before he left for Roseires. Wingate explained to him why he wanted Jews associated with him now. The war in Ethiopia, he told Akavia, was a war to liberate a country from unjust oppression, and as such similar to the Zionist struggle.[2] Once in Khartoum he confided to Dodds-Parker more of what he meant : that after a successful Ethiopian campaign led by himself he hoped to be in a strong enough position to ask for what he wanted : the command of two Jewish divisions. With these he would meet the enemy on the plains of Magido (Armageddon) and thereafter—all his Zionist ambition could be fulfilled.[3] He once said to Akavia : " Whoever is a friend of Abyssinia is a friend of the Jews. If I succeed here I can be of greater help to the Jews later on. You are here for the sake of Zion." At the same time that he asked for Akavia's services he asked (again through Clayton) for Jewish doctors in Palestine to serve with him as medical officers. Twelve had volunteered. They had not arrived but were on their way. Throughout the whole of the campaign, and in the period immediately after it, Wingate never lost sight of his

---

[1] Thesiger.   [2] Akavia : *With Wingate in Ethiopia*—published in Israel.
[3] Dodds-Parker. A similar statement about Wingate's aims is found in *Magen Baseter*.

ultimate aim; to achieve an overwhelming personal success which he could put to the service of Zion. This did not mean that his devotion to the Ethiopian cause was qualified, but that he found himself ardently devoted to two causes which he saw as closely related.

In the first part of his reconnaissance journey Wingate found the going easier than he had expected. On the 27th he sent back word to the Emperor that the country was passable for trucks, and he urged him to set out forthwith. The Emperor did so. This was a mistake. Wingate had acted too quickly. The defective maps which he and his party were using did not show the hilly country of Abu Wendi between the bush and the mountain, nor the gorge-broken lava area. It is difficult to understand why Wingate on reaching this place did not send back again and alter the course, unless we remember the extraordinary intensity of his determination. If he saw his objective he went to it the shortest way with ruthless directness, regardless of what it might cost him or others. He had determined to go straight to Belaiya, and he stuck with violent obstinacy to his original decision. He had to abandon his trucks and complete the journey on foot. So faulty were the maps of that remote part of Ethiopia that he found himself marching towards the Headquarters area with an error of twenty miles to correct.[1] He arrived on the 31st.

The Frontier battalion under Boustead had made a thorough reconnaissance of Mount Belaiya and had come to the conclusion that the natural fortress of the mountain itself was too inaccessible for a Headquarters. They chose instead a place in the foothills, a river bed in whose walls they dug a bomb-proof shelter for the Emperor and his entourage. Nearby on a piece of flat ground they were completing a landing strip. Wingate only stopped a night and a day and then started back with mules to meet the approaching Imperial party. Guided by his own traces and his skill in direction he found them on the 3rd of February about forty miles from the end of their journey. He was in a state of extreme fatigue, wanting both food and sleep. The heat was overpowering. The Emperor and his little force were in the thick of the chasmous lava region west of Belaiya. They had lost animals and trucks, and the endeavour to preserve the Emperor's own truck had often meant manhandling it down gorges. Everyone, and the Emperor himself, toiled at making some sort of a road. On the 4th of February they covered only six miles. They found easier country the next day and covered thirty miles. The scene through which they passed was fearful in its natural desolation and to this was added the spectacle of dead and dying camels in great numbers, wretched beasts of burden unused to this kind of ground, and hurried

[1] Thesiger.

through it by men who in most cases were ignorant of camel-management and had sometimes never handled their kind before. The reeking corpses with the occasional abandoned truck, lay like markers along the path.[1] On the 6th of February, mounted on one of the few mules which Wingate could bring to his succour, the Emperor rode into the Headquarters camp at the foot of Mount Belaiya.

Two days before, on the 4th of February, in the south, the small army of three divisions commanded by General Cunningham had invaded Ethiopia from Kenya.

It is a most curious fact that up to this moment there had been no definitive decision as to the military command of the revolt. Wingate still held the rank of major and was still only a liaison officer with additional functions. The first moves seem to have been organised on a committee basis and Wingate had in effect commanded the expedition to Belaiya because he could dominate the committee by the force of his personality. But now that he and the Emperor and the two battalions had reached the Gojjam border, and action was imminent, the position had to be regularised, all the more so as among those assembled at Belaiya to greet Haile Selassie was Sandford, the founder and head of Mission 101. The decision of Khartoum Headquarters was received by radio signal on the 6th of February, the day of arrival. It followed the classic English pattern of compromise. Wingate was appointed " G.S.O.I. to Mission 101," with the rank of Lieutenant-Colonel and his function was " commander of the British and Ethiopian forces serving with the Emperor in the field " ; Sandford was appointed political and military adviser to the Emperor with Chapman Andrews as his assistant. Wingate was to consult the Emperor through Sandford and obtain the adviser's agreement on all military projects. It was a most unfortunate arrangement such as could hardly have worked even with born committee-men. It never began to work with these two. Inevitably they encroached on one another's functions from the beginning to the end. The first and longest sufferer from this unhappy attempt to reconcile irreconcilable positions and claims was Major Donald Nott, the chief administration officer of the force, who received conflicting orders from both parties until his own position was in turn regularised, an event which did not occur till the end of March.

When Wingate was confirmed in his post, his first act was to give

[1] In *Gideon Goes To War* there is mention of fainting camels having fires lit under them to make them continue, the smoke being visible and the stench offensive at distance. This horrible detail of the march is not confirmed by any witnesses interviewed by the writer. It seems to be a confusion with the common cameleer practice of rousing obstinate camels by prodding them with a lighted brand, and a later occasion, recalled by Ato Gabre Maskal, when a number of dead camels were burned to avoid smell and infection.

a name to the little brigade of slightly more than three battalions (counting the bodyguard and the operational centres as one and a third) that had been drawn together to compose the Emperor's forces. He discarded the prosy appellation of Mission 101 as he may—no ! as he must have once wished to discard the prosy initials S.N.S. He called the little army Gideon Force.

Five days after the arrival at Belaiya, the landing strip having been completed by now, and an aeroplane having flown in at a signalled request, Wingate and Sandford went to Khartoum for a final conference with General Platt. Brigadier Lush, the chief political officer on the Kaid's staff (Sandford's brother-in-law) and Major Airey, Wingate's former fellow-officer in the Sudan Defence Force, now representing G (R), were present with the General. There the objectives of the rebellion were defined : to harass Italian communications between Gondar and Debarech and along the Setit river and from Gondar to Dessie, in the north ; from Addis Ababa to Asmara in the centre ; and on the main east-west road passing through Lechemti to Addis Ababa in the south. The roads were not to be destroyed. The purpose of this strategy was to keep as many Italian troops as possible occupied in the defence of the Ethiopian capital, thus relieving pressure on the armies attacking in Eritrea and the south. These plans were not carried out in any detail, but they influenced the direction and character of the guerilla campaign. In the circumstances of the time and place the plans could hardly have been intended to do more than this.

During the conference Sandford pressed for the immediate seizure of Danghila. On his way to Belaiya from Faguta he had intercepted a message to the Italian commander there, Colonel Torelli, urging him to get out of Danghila while he could. Wingate successfully opposed the plan. In the event Danghila was evacuated within a few days of the conference, as soon appears. It is difficult to say who gave the right advice on this matter. But Sandford and Wingate both urged that the Emperor should enter Gojjam as soon as possible, and this was agreed.

Further and more precise efforts were made towards a satisfactory demarcation of the Wingate and Sandford functions. Wingate was to have the rank of Colonel, the control of Mission 101 and the undisputed command of Gideon Force. Sandford was to have the rank of Brigadier. While Wingate was to direct operations, Sandford was to handle propaganda and all communications with Ethiopian leaders. General Platt would correspond directly with Sandford, and Sandford with Platt on political matters, and directly with Wingate, and Wingate with Platt on military matters, copies of all letters to each being sent to the other, while liaison officers were to keep Sandford and Wingate yet further informed of each other's activity.[1] And so on. It was an attempt to tidy a muddle. It would have been better to have removed the muddle altogether.

When the conference was over Sandford flew to Cairo, and Wingate flew back to Belaiya. There the movement of Gideon Force from the hot waterless plains to the plateau by way of an immediate ascent of the Gojjam escarpment had already begun.

Before and around the time that the leaders were in conference in Khartoum, a curious thing had happened which changed the drift of events, and showed for the first time (what Sandford had guessed from the beginning) that the decay of Italian morale was near putre-faction point. Colonel Boustead ordered one of his companies to take up defensive positions on the Balas River which flows between Belaiya and the escarpment. Of this company he then ordered a platoon to accompany Bimbashi Harris on a mission up on the plateau to make contact with the tribes of Tumha and Zarzur. By arrangement Harris met Tafara Dori, the Zarzur chief, at the foot of the escarpment on the 6th of February. The chief endeavoured to escort Harris up to the plateau but at the first attempt they had to turn back, after an exchange of shots, because Italian troops from Danghila were in a strong position at the height of the pass. Dori and Harris then tried another ascent with success, but by this time the Italians guarding the pass had withdrawn to Danghila. This meant that at the very moment when preparations were beginning for one of the most hazardous feats of the whole campaign those who could make it most hazardous, even impossible, ran away. But this was not the end of the incident. Harris met the Tumha chief and persuaded him, with difficulty and a show of force, to declare himself for the Emperor. This roused the spirit of the people, and though there was nothing the people could do, the fact was enough. As Sandford had discovered, the Italians were not anxious to remain in Danghila. Harris's sortie decided them. Believing that a British division had arrived, they abandoned that strongly fortified area,[2] and this was a first step in the abandonment of Western Gojjam.

If a platoon could effect this much, what could not Gideon Force do acting together?

In one respect and one only the Italians gained and held an advantage over Gideon Force. They denied them transport. There was only one economical way of moving baggage and equipment up the escarpment and that was by mule, and almost every mule in Western

---

[1] Minutes of the Conference.
[2] So described by W. Allen in *Guerilla Warfare in Abyssinia*, referred to later as Allen.

Ethiopia had been requisitioned by the Italian army. Sandford had tried and failed to get mules. Throughout the campaign men tried to get mules, by cajolery, bribes and threats, and always they failed because there were next to no mules to get. So the ascent was made with camels. The escarpment is a cliff-like rampart rising over three thousand feet from the plain. To take camels up its precipitous paths, not easily scaled by men, is as appropriate as to take cart-horses up marble stairs; but there was nothing else to do, and Wingate had already taken the bold decision. They had one piece of luck. About the time of Wingate's return from Khartoum, one of Boustead's company commanders, Bimbashi Johnson, rediscovered the pass east of Matakal, which had been discovered by Cheesman five years before. This meant that the movement could go a little more quickly and with fewer camel casualties, but nonetheless it was a slow proceeding and many wretched beasts, ill-tended by inexpert cameleers, died of exhaustion on the way. The ascent took from the 15th to the 20th[1] of February. The last to leave Belaiya was the Emperor. Sandford rejoined him on the 17th, and he left with his personal retinue and guards (in all over 500 men) on the 26th and reached the plateau on the 4th of March. The folly and pusillanimity of the Italians in allowing the movement is hardly credible.

A disquieting political event had occurred during the Emperor's sojourn at Belaiya. While he was daily receiving homage from multitudes of his subjects who had made their way to his obscure court, Brigadier Lush, flew to Belaiya to communicate the plans which had been made in Cairo for the administration of Ethiopia after liberation. Sir Philip Mitchell, assisted by Major Francis Rodd, and in consultation with Sir Archibald Wavell, had drawn up a plan for a form of British military rule. It was to be known as O.E.T.A. (Occupied Enemy Territory Administration), a title once chosen by Allenby. Sandford saw at once that plans made for the rule of Haile Selassie's kingdom, without a word to the sovereign, would inevitably provoke his distrust anew. To lessen the gravity of this diplomatic maladroitness Sandford held a long discussion with Lush and " went at it hammer and tongs for a whole day sitting under a tree on the banks of the stream there. As a result Maurice (Lush) flew back and was instrumental in getting necessary changes that would make the plans more workable in Ethiopia and more acceptable to the Emperor."[2] The damage could be diminished but not undone. It was necessary to tell the Emperor the bare facts of

---

[1] The majority but not the whole of Gideon Force went by the Matakal Pass. No. 3 Company of the Frontier Battalion under Bimbashi Harris took a route to the north.
[2] Sandford.

O.E.T.A., and this was done by Chapman Andrews. Haile Selassie was not pleased.[1] It would have been remarkable if he had been. In fact the political objectives of O.E.T.A. were governed by a directive issued by Mr. Eden (by now Foreign Secretary) which left no doubt of an honourable British purpose to restore Ethiopian independence and the Emperor's sovereignty.[2] But although Mr. Eden had made a public statement in London concerning these British intentions,[3] all that the Emperor knew in Belaiya was that arrangements for British rule in Ethiopia were in train, and that he had not been consulted. Furthermore these arrangements were being made by a Colonial governor. It is not surprising that he connected this political move with the Brocklehurst mission of less than two months before and began to feel again all his angry suspicions. Sandford was in sympathy with his distress. When he was told about these things in turn, Wingate (need 'it be said) was in sympathy too, and remembered not only his indignation against the Brocklehurst mission but all that he had come to believe in Palestine about official double-dealing. Writing about the affair long after, Sir Philip Mitchell regretted that he did not fly to Belaiya himself and consult the Emperor.[4] He would have saved misunderstandings if he had done so, and, incidentally, he would probably have altered the course of Wingate's story.

Still unaware of the size of Gideon Force and believing the wildest

[1] Chapman Andrews.

[2] The text of Mr. Eden's instruction is quoted as follows in Sir Philip Mitchell's book, *African Afterthoughts* : " 1. The policy of His Majesty's Government for Italian East Africa has been laid down as follows : (i) His Majesty's Government would welcome the reappearance of an independent Ethiopian State and will recognise the claims of the Emperor Haile Selassie to the throne. The Emperor has intimated to His Majesty's Government that he will need outside assistance and guidance. His Majesty's Government agree with this view and consider that any such assistance and guidance in economical and political matters should be the subject of international arrangement at the conclusion of peace. (ii) In the meanwhile the conduct of military operations by Imperial forces in parts of Abyssinia will require temporary measures of military guidance and control. These will be carried out in consultation with the Emperor and will be brought to an end as soon as the situation permits. 2. At a later stage the (above) statement made in Parliament will need clearer definition. For the present and as a working assumption, ' Ethiopian State ' may be taken to mean Ethiopia as it was before the Italian conquest, subject to any minor boundary alterations the Italians may have made. The first stage will be a period of active military operations. 3. It may therefore be assumed that the Emperor is engaged in a joint enterprise with us for the restoration of the independence of Ethiopia and of himself as ruler of it.—8.2.41."

[3] As indicated, the first paragraph of the instruction was given as a statement made at Question Time in the House of Commons on the 4th of February, 1941.

[4] " I often wished afterwards that I had sent the Emperor a copy of (Mr. Eden's) instructions ; and, particularly, that he and I had had a week together in camp, as I had intended, before he entered his capital and we both became involved in all the consequences of that fateful event." Sir Philip Mitchell—*African Afterthoughts*.

exaggerations on the subject, alarmed also at the news of British advances in the north and south, the Italian commander, Colonel Torelli, hurried on the withdrawal from West Gojjam during the second half of February. On the 16th he left Danghila preparing to follow this stroke by the abandonment of the next military post on the Addis Ababa road, Engiabara. The Italian intention was to give up Burye as well, then to hold Bahrdar Giorgis on Lake Tana in the north, and in the south to defend the approaches to Addis Ababa by taking up positions on the Tamcha River south of Dambacha. As appears later, these decisions might have had good results for the Italian army if they had been carried out and not bungled through panic. But at the moment, from the point of view of Gideon Force, all that was visible was the panic.

Wingate was in camp on the edge of the escarpment overlooking Matakal, when he heard of the evacuation of Danghila and rumours of the impending evacuation of Engiabara. This sudden enemy retreat gave him ideas, but for the moment he was involved in negotiations with the chieftain of the Matakal area, a man called Fitaurari Zalleka Birru. The latter had enjoyed Italian favour and had proved himself their useful ally and friend, but his eyes had recently been opened to the advantages of patriotism by Sandford and Mission 101. Wingate needed this man's help now, not only to ensure a tranquil base at Matakal, but also because he wanted patriot reinforcements, and the prestige of an outstanding Ethiopian figure, in order to give strength to his northern mission of which more will be told presently. With Bimbashis Harris and Johnson and the commander of the second Ethiopian battalion, he went to Zalleka's village to parley with the chieftain. He demanded a pledge of loyalty from him in the convenient shape of twenty mules. Zalleka Birru said he would do what he could. They left him, for in the meantime Wingate had called a conference of Boustead and the junior commanders, to meet him at the top of the escarpment, so that he might explain his new ideas and plans.

The short-term plan agreed hitherto was simply to harass the Italian retreat in co-operation with the four thousand strong patriot force under Mangasha, and in the north Bimbashi Jarvis had actually begun to follow this plan, pursuing Torelli's forces to Bahrdar Giorgis. But Wingate saw that the sudden Italian retreat coinciding with the rediscovery of the Matakal pass offered opportunities of greater scope, and so he now proposed that instead of merely harassing the retreat Gideon Force should compel the Italian army to turn and fight a forlorn battle with an invisible foe. His new plan, he said, was " by attacking secretly, often, and from as many directions as

possible to create in the minds of the garrisons . . . the same erroneous impression as to our strength as had led Colonel Torelli to
evacuate Danghila." He added that in the kind of attack he had in
mind, " twenty men is a good number to work with, but fifteen
is better than twenty, and at night ten is better than fifteen."[1] As
in Palestine he was following precisely the stratagem of Judge
Gideon.

When the conference was over Wingate gave his force a rendezvous
east of Engiabara and returned to his negotiations with Fitaurari
Zalleka Birru. The latter produced six mules which he assured the
British Commander was the sum total of all he possibly could produce
in that line. In addition to this service the Fitaurari promised to march
with reinforcements to the aid of the northern mission. With this
agreed the negotiations were concluded.

The Bimbashis and Major Boyle and a mixed escort of Ethiopians
and Sudanese accompanied Wingate as far as Engiabara which they
reached on the 22nd, two days after the flight of the Italians. From
here Wingate and Akavia went on alone to Faguta, Sandford's old
headquarters. There, on the same day, the 22nd, Wingate found
Major Simonds in charge and with him " the Propaganda Section "
which George Steer had organised in October before Wingate's first
arrival in Khartoum. Wingate immediately despatched Major Simonds
to take command of the northern mission. He then turned to the
propaganda section. Holding the prestige of a founding father of the
revolt this section had tended to act independently. Wingate now
asserted his authority over it and set it to work on a proclamation to
all men in Ethiopia who accounted themselves patriots. The English
translation read as follows : " Do you want to owe all the liberties
which the friends of humanity, now fighting the totalitarian powers
by land, sea and air, and which they have promised you—do you want
to owe these to their helping hands alone ? My Headquarters are
established in Gojjam whence I shall drive the enemy. You may
inquire after me from any of my troops. Bring your mules, your food,
and your armed men, and I will direct you against the enemy."
The section had a portable printing press, and they knew by
practice how to distribute things such as this proclamation over
large areas.

Before leaving Matakal Wingate had already issued another
proclamation to his own people in the form of an order of the day to
Gideon Force. He took his style from the young Napoleon. The order
read as follows : " The comforts which we now lack and the supplies
which we need are in the possession of our enemies. It is my intention

[1] Wingate Report. W.P.I.

to wrest them from him by a bold stroke which will demand all your energies and all your devotion. I expect that every officer and man will put his courage and endurance to the severest test during the coming decisive weeks." This preceded the rendezvous east of Engiabara. But before considering what happened there the northern mission should be briefly described.

The name of Antony Simonds will be remembered as that of Wingate's colleague in Force Headquarters Jerusalem in 1937. Their close friendship was revived when they found themselves colleagues again in the offices of G (R) in Cairo. When Wingate returned to Cairo for the December conference he asked Simonds to come with him and act as his second-in-command. He agreed with enthusiasm and obtained a transfer. Soon after the Emperor's arrival at Belaiya, however, Simonds ceased to be the second-in-command and instead, with the new appointments of Wingate and Sandford, filled Sandford's former post and became commander of the still separately existing Mission 101. But events baulked him of this assignment too when, as just related, he was sent from Faguta to the north. His orders were to join Bimbashi Jarvis and his frontier battalion company. He was then given command of an organisation comprising Jarvis's Company, an operational centre, and patriot forces, and this came to be known as Begemder Force after the Begemder province east of Lake Tana. Though under Wingate's orders Begemder Force (inevitably in the circumstances) acted almost independently most of the time. Their task was to prevent Torelli's men reorganising in the north of Gojjam for a flank attack on Gideon Force. They persisted in this difficult undertaking in spite of frequent failure to obtain the co-operation of their Ethiopian allies. They had begun with a setback before Simonds's arrival. They had intended to harry the retreat of the Italians all the way from Danghila to Bahrdar Giorgis but in the first stretch from Danghila to Meshenti, the man on whom they relied, Fitaurari Ayalu Makonnen, failed to provide guides in time and then feared to go into action because he heard that other patriots, hostile to his men, were also on the march against the Italians. These patriots were the forces of Mangasha, advancing from Sakala under their chief who was accompanied by Thesiger. They likewise feared to go into action while other bodies of patriots were at large. After Simonds's arrival Jarvis and his company had some success in harrying the second half of the retreat. Nevertheless the Italians reached Bahrdar Giorgis in safety. In the last days of February Zalleka Birru arrived to join the mission. He came with five hundred patriots of whom four hundred and fifty immediately deserted.[1] In spite of

---

[1] *Letters of Mark Pilkington.* Privately printed.

such disappointments Simonds and Jarvis somehow succeeded in ful-
filling their mission.

Gideon Force had many hardships before them and many under-
takings which demanded the courage of a few men against hosts. The
wonder is that they could find the needed physical and spiritual
energy, but amazement lessens when it is remembered that after the
ascent to the plateau, the labours of the climb were immensely and
immediately rewarded by finding themselves the inhabitants of a
pleasing land, in which torrid heat is unknown, in which streams and
lush grass and trees are plentiful. The chief dangers to health, insidious
sun-stroke, continual heart-strain, and malaria, appear nowhere on the
surface and the men of Gideon Force found themselves filled with
new exhilaration. It was otherwise with the camels. Those bitterly
suffering creatures fared worse now that they were out of their natural
climate and surroundings and without their accustomed diet. Their
already high rate of mortality rose from now on.[1]

By the afternoon of the 23rd Gideon Force had assembled outside
Engiabara. With Jarvis's Company away with Begemder Force, most
of another Company remaining in the forward base at Matakal, and
another Company under Bimbashi Campbell permanently detached,[2]
the main force consisted now of two companies and a platoon of the
Frontier Battalion, and the complete second Ethiopian battalion, with
a mortar section, a signal section, and the aforementioned propaganda
section. This small force proposed to rout an Italian army. Their
first objective was the fortified area comprising the town of Burye
and the village of Mankusa to the south. The march began at sunset on the 24th.

This may be a convenient moment to say something more about
personalities since they were to play some part in what immediately
followed. Gideon Force was lucky to have as its transport officer a
writer of ability who left a memorable record. William Allen's
first meeting with Wingate was not marked by cordiality. Wingate
asked him what regiment he came from and on being told that the
other came from a cavalry regiment, he went on in his surliest
manner:

" So you're a cavalry officer. I didn't want to have any cavalry
officers with me."

Allen replied : " Well in that case you make a big mistake. I'm

[1] Allen.
[2] Bimbashi G. T. H. Campbell's No. 5 Company was detached for operations at
Shogali, Asosa, and Afodu to the south of Belaiya. It never rejoined Gideon Force in
Gojjam.

your transport officer and a cavalry man is much more likely to understand the job than any other sort of officer. He's been taught how to
look after animals."

Rather surprised at this refusal to be bullied, Wingate added :
" What do you do in peace-time ? "

When Allen replied : " I'm a writer," Wingate looked at him with
different eyes.[1]

No one has bettered Allen's description of Wingate as he was in
these fierce African days.

" Tired men have short tempers and Wingate was scarcely the man
to conciliate a following. Crowds of flies round the bully stew would
provoke bitter questions as to how many dead men go to make a
Lawrence. . . . I think he had a thirsty passion for battle as others
have for gambling. His pale blue eyes, narrow set, burned with an
insatiable glare. His spare, bony figure with its couching gait and the
hang of an animal run by hunting yet hungry for the next night's
prey. Some demon chased Wingate over the Gojjam uplands ; perhaps
towards what is called greatness, perhaps towards that failure to inte-
grate which is called unhappiness.

" My prematurely grey beard must have given me a certain
immunity. In the evening he unbent a little. He held the most
pronounced Zionist views and was a Hebrew scholar well read in the
scriptures. His big nose and shaggy beard could recall, as he proclaimed the glories of Israel, the ghost of some harassed hill prophet ;
but the bony structure of the face, the thin high-ridged line of the nose
and the gleam of the blue eyes declared some old Norse blood soured
through Covenanting centuries. . . ."[2]

In every detail of character, essential and superficial, Hugh Boustead
was in contrast. He only resembled Wingate in the adventurousness
and unconventionality of his career, and the peculiar nature of the
headaches he had caused to the authorities. In 1915, when he was a
youth of twenty, he deserted from the Royal Navy, in which he was a
sub-lieutenant, because he was overcome with fear that in an African
station he would never be in warlike action. He eluded search,
joined the Gordon Highlanders as a private, and saw service in the
East and in France. He was commissioned without exciting notice,
but the award of the Military Cross brought his name into enough
prominence for naval authorities to spot the long-lost deserter. From
this coincidence he became the recipient of the King's decoration and
the King's pardon at the same moment of time. After the war (and

[1] Allen. A communication.
[2] Allen. They met at a later stage in the campaign but the quotation is given here
for convenience.

after having served with General Denikin in South Russia) he entered the Sudan service in 1924. He was serving under General Huddleston, sometimes in the Camel Corps, sometimes as a staff officer in Khartoum, during Wingate's " Sudan period," but they never met. In 1935 Boustead (after having endeavoured to climb Mount Everest in 1933) retired from the army to the Sudan political service. In 1939 he was District Commissioner of Western Darfur. Fearful once more, in his graver years, of losing the opportunity of action in war he often went to Khartoum and continually pressed his claims to military employment on the Governor-General and the Kaid. When Colonel Elphinstone in October of 1939 obtained agreement for the raising of the Frontier Battalion of the Sudan Defence Force the command was immediately confided to Major Boustead as he then was. Allen describes him with precision :

" Slight, wiry and nervous he had the quality of the rapier in his character. His looks, his movements, and his mannerisms belonged to the eighteenth century. Put a tricorn hat on that lean and wrinkled face, add a sparse pigtail and a high tight collar, and he might have been one of Clive's or Nelson's officers. . . .

" ' Action consumes,' they say, ' Rest destroys.' Guerilla war was burning fast enough the slight form of Hugh Boustead . . . yet he was not consumed by Wingate's hungry demon. In the field Boustead was a desperate driver of men and an eater of himself. But his eighteenth-century spirit savoured the amenities of life and he had that exaggerated modesty which is characteristic of so many fighting men. . . . His tastes were generous and humane. He ranged happily in conversation like an excited terrier, from Stevenson and Saki to Spengler and Bergson. An experienced African traveller, he kept a good table as soon as he could set up his tent in one spot."

It would be an unfair simplification to say that Boustead and Wingate did not get on together for the same reason that two great prime donne appearing in the same opera, or two great comedians sharing the same music-hall, sometimes fail to appreciate to the full each other's qualities. It would be very prudish, on the other hand, to say that there was nothing of this character in their uneasy relationship. Boustead was the older and more experienced soldier ; he resented the young Colonel's arrogant disregard of the notion of a chain of command, and he had no patience with Wingate's dramatic pronouncements and sense of mission, all of which he regarded as show-off play-acting. Wingate found Boustead's care for good living contemptible if not offensive to his puritan spirit, and in turn he regarded the other's dandyism as play-acting. Their latent hostility came to the surface and broke out in the first action fought by **Gideon Force**, in the country between Burye and Mankusa.

On the first night of the march from Engiabara they went about fifteen miles to where the River Fettam crosses the road. The bridge had been demolished by the retreating army so Gideon Force camped on the western bank. Wingate had said that there was to be no waiting for straggling beasts and that the column was to keep in close order, but with the frequent breakdown of camels, and the slipping of loads fastened by inexpert hands, these instructions were feebly carried out and the column which was two miles long at the start had spread over four miles of the road by the time they reached the Fettam. This confusion was of help, as mistakes often were in this campaign. The Italians had their observers and the enormous length of the column confirmed them in their preconceived belief that there was a large force in the field against them.

Gideon Force resumed the march the next afternoon, that of the 26th, by which time the bridge was in enough repair to get some camels across. Then from here to their rendezvous east of Burye they marched across country. After dark the way was shown by beacons lit by Wingate's leading party who would then leave two soldiers tending the flares. But this plan also went wrong when an Ethiopian soldier in excess of zeal started a heath fire illuminating the whole countryside and showing to anyone who cared to look the whereabouts of the movement. This was another chance for the Italians to break up Gideon Force but they neglected it, as they neglected them all, and stayed in bed in the forts of Burye. Thereafter beacons were given up in favour of whistling posts a few hundred yards apart. Before midnight Gideon Force was at the rendezvous and under cover in a deep thickly wooded ravine five miles north-east of the forts. It had been Wingate's original intention to attack the Italians in their base that same night but he was dissuaded. So he allowed his troops to rest, but first he made a disposition which (not through his fault) was to have bad results later. He sent the Ethiopian battalion eastwards under their commander (keeping back one of their companies) with instructions to make contact with Mangasha and Thesiger, and then to harass the enemy retreat between Burye and Debra Markos, the major town south-eastwards on the Addis Ababa road. They left in the middle of the night. In the early morning before light the rest of Gideon Force moved out of their shelter to their first action.

The intention was to make spasmodic attacks on the Burye garrison from the west but this was changed when news came in that two Italian battalions were moving northwards towards the ravine where the force had sheltered for the night. A new plan was adopted, namely

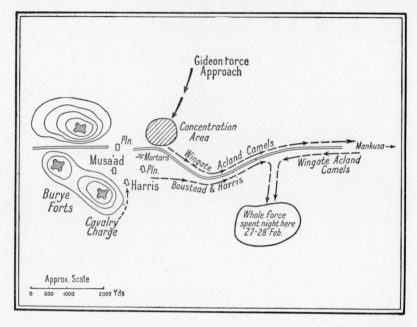

The Battle of Burye, 27-28 February

to raid the garrison from the east. Boustead held the main body of eight platoons in a defensive position in hills north-west of the three forts east of Burye, while Wingate went forward with three platoons of the Frontier Battalion. He approached the easternmost fort from the north-east under the cover of wooded country from which he sent a platoon to reconnoitre the hill in front. The platoon found the hill strongly occupied. They were fired on and held where they were. This part of Ethiopia has open country broken only by gradual hills and occasional coppices; for that reason, though there is thorn and bush for men's concealment, it is a difficult place in which to conduct a raid in daylight.[1] When Wingate saw what had happened he sent another platoon forward to rescue the first, and sent his third north-west to guard against a counter-attack. He then sent a message to Boustead which reached the latter at two in the afternoon. Boustead had heard at half past ten that the Italian movement had ceased and he had thereon gone forward southwards, moving very slowly, with his camels held up for a long time crossing a ravine. He now made his way to Wingate bringing reinforcements which consisted of the

[1] Allen.

274

remaining three platoons of his battalion, leaving the Ethiopian company to guard his camp. The boldness of this gamble, in which about four hundred and fifty men engaged in their fortified area a far better equipped enemy numbering about seven thousand[1] can hardly be exaggerated.

The reinforcements did not reach Wingate till four o'clock in the afternoon. Boustead sent his mortar section to a position north-west of the easternmost fort, and at the same time sent a platoon armed with anti-tank rifles to guard the road. In front of the mortar section he put a platoon under Bimbashi Harris. The fire of the mortar roused the Italians in the fort and on the hill to violent but ineffectual retaliation. The whole available Italian artillery seemed to be employed in a cannonade for about half an hour. Then the besiegers heard wild howling cries and a body of fifty Eritrean cavalry charged them from the southern spur of the hill. In the thorn and bush the horsemen only saw the most westerly of the sections (commanded by Shawish Hassan Musa'ad) and at one moment they had him completely surrounded. But the section under their courageous Sudanese commander stayed firm, and when the cavalry had lost three men and ten horses they galloped off. Soon after this it was dark with no moon. Boustead withdrew his men and set off towards Mankusa to join Wingate. He left one platoon behind under Bimbashi Johnson with instructions to march section by section round the forts at night shooting an occasional random shot at them. This simple manœuvre caused the Italians to waste further quantities of ammunition in repelling imagined counter-attacks. What they wasted in their fast-dwindling morale cannot be calculated.

As has been remarked by all respectable authority, battles in description seem to be neatly shaped events, but in experience bewilder by their disorderly incoherence. This odd battle of Burye was no exception. Messages were missed, no one seemed to know where anyone else was, and the baggage train was for some time reckoned lost for ever. The confusion increased rather than diminished as the battle went from the first phase in Burye to the second in Mankusa. At nightfall no one could find Wingate. He was in fact looking for and rescuing the baggage train. He had sent the camels out of the battle down the road towards Mankusa with orders to camp off the road but they went too far and about two and a half miles from Burye came under the fire of Mankusa fort. Hearing the noise Wingate and Akavia galloped off on mules to see what was amiss. The length

[1] 5,000 is the approximate figure given for the Burye garrison on the 5th of March. This figure evidently excludes Mankusa. The prisoners on the same authority can account for another 2,000. The evidence as to Italian numbers is often in conflict and conservative estimates are given.

of the train made it so unwieldy that when wandering in a fortified area it could hardly not lurch into danger and trouble, and it was no easy task to turn it about without propelling it ultimately into some opposite disaster. In the dark its control was a baffling undertaking. Somehow or other during the night Wingate managed to pull back the long procession of camels from Mankusa and bring them down to a camping site about three miles south of the road. Throughout the operation he tried to make contact with Boustead, and Boustead with him. They did not meet till about three in the morning when the whole force settled around the camel-camp. Here they stayed, though still within the field of fire of the eastern Burye fort, till the night of the 28th. Then Wingate ordered his camel train with a platoon for its defence to a place five miles south of Mankusa, and at the same time he moved the main body of Gideon Force to a ridge about fifteen hundred yards east of Mankusa fort. He led them there personally. It was now the 1st of March.

Many things happened on that day but nothing decisive. One of the first things was the arrival from the north-east of Nagash's chief military commander, a man called Zalleka Desta, leading a force of patriots and accompanied by Thesiger. Wingate now formed a plan for the next attack, as follows : Gideon Force would subject Mankusa fort to machine-gun and mortar bombardment, thus forcing the garrison out into the open, whereupon Zalleka Desta and his braves would swoop to the attack. The first part of the programme went according to plan. The mortar section was introduced to a place north-west of the ridge about a thousand yards from Mankusa fort. (The mortar was operated by Sergeant Body under the direction of Harris who, very oddly indeed, was unfamiliar with mortars and needed to be instructed for an hour or so by Wingate.) The fire of the mortar set buildings within the fort ablaze, and, as calculated, enemy troops came out on to the hillside where they were shot down by the men on the ridge. But the swoop by the patriots did not, to use the accepted phrase, " materialise." However Zalleka Desta did fulfil the useful task of covering the road between Mankusa and Burye and so prevented the garrisons joining one another. On this same day the R.A.F. bombed the forts of Burye with three Wellesleys. This was the only time that Gideon Force received support from the air.

On the next day, the 2nd of March, there was no movement by either side. The men on the hill kept up continuous fire while members of the propaganda section approached the fort and harangued the Ethiopians in the Italian garrison by means of loud-speakers, urging them to desert the lost cause, and as a result many did desert from the *bande* to Zalleka Desta. Then on the morning of the 3rd of March spies came to Gideon Force with great news. The Italians were preparing to abandon all the forts of Burye and Mankusa.

Wingate made a plan to meet this turn of events : an hour before midnight the main Gideon Force under Boustead was to move north of the road where Wingate would meet it in the morning with three

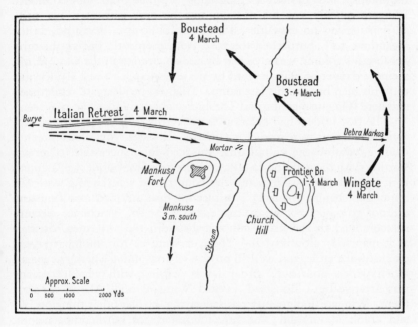

Actions around Mankusa, 1-4 March

platoons, in order to harry the rear of the retreating column. The plan misfired. After Boustead had left, the Emperor's liaison officer, Azazh Kabbada, urged on Wingate that if Gideon Force was not seen to occupy Mankusa fort the local population would be adversely affected. Wingate liked the advice and remained south of the road with his platoons. This might not have mattered if another thing had not gone wrong.

Wingate had a reconnaissance patrol out towards Burye to warn him of Italian movement, but this patrol had lost touch with both parts of the force by the time the movement began at the break of day. Allen records the scene : " An hour after dawn on the 4th of March the whole Italian strength in the Burye area came milling out in full force. With truck-loads of infantry and a few armoured cars, cavalry and artillery and swarms of *bande* fleeing the Emperor's wrath."

Wingate, unwarned, was surprised with his three platoons, and here again, as at the first action at Burye, his tenacity played him false. He could have taken the platoons to safety, according to his plan with Boustead, but instead he stayed to fight. They were a hundred against thousands, and moreover thousands who enjoyed air-protection. Wingate quickly saw his mistake but he only extricated his men, albeit suffering no casualties, with great difficulty. Boustead, in the meantime, had approached the road from the north, but very slowly because his column was attacked by Italian aircraft all the way. Then, seeing a danger of being cut off by the enemy cavalry and artillery, he took his men back to his last camp. This was an alternate rendezvous and here Wingate met him and Thesiger at about midday.

The two leaders had been on worse terms than usual during these actions, and they were ready for a quarrel. Boustead found in Wingate's latest adventure the culminating misdeed in a succession of errors starting with the decision to take up a position in front of the Mankusa fort, instead of vanishing into the countryside, and ending with the impulsive change of plan. The meeting was strained and Boustead did not go out of his way to make it any less so. A chance circumstance added to the usual contrast between the two men. Strange as it may seem Boustead and Thesiger were at this moment seated on chairs at a table, and were in process of consuming a neatly prepared lunch which Boustead's orderly was serving with what ceremony was arrangeable. Boustead invited Wingate and Akavia to join them. Wingate indignantly refused saying he had other things to do and think about and was not interested in luncheon-parties at the moment. He asked Boustead why he had not joined him and his three platoons in battle with reinforcements, and Boustead with exasperating calm said that his orders were to meet Wingate north of the road, and he had no notion that the other had changed his plans. How could he know without a message ? And this question led on (so the accounts seem to tell) to tactical argument with Boustead, the latter all coolness with his advantage of having adhered to plan, Wingate all fury without the advantage. He raged that because he had been denied support the whole Italian garrison-column had gone through unhurt, to which Boustead said something such as : " That's all right, old boy. They'll go down the road to Dambacha and we'll get them there," concluding with a renewal of his invitation to lunch. Wingate refused angrily again and plucked a roast chicken from the dish borne by Boustead's servant. While formal lunch proceeded course by course at the table, he sat silent on a rock, furiously divided the chicken with Akavia, and satisfied his hunger in campaigner's fashion, not bothering with proffered knives and forks. The tension persisted.[1]

Then plans were made for the next move with the intention of harrying the retreat so as to drive on the Italians in new worse fatal disorder. Bimbashi Harris's company was chosen for the principal rôle ; he was to start instantly and the operation was to begin that night with Boustead in command. The next action was at the place on the road from Burye to Addis Ababa where it meets the Lach river. The course of the action need be only briefly indicated because at the same time as these dispositions were being made Wingate was called back to look into the affairs of the Emperor, and in consequence he had no part in the ambush on the River Lach. This took place between dawn and nightfall of the fifth of March. It was full of its own muddles and desperate escapes but because Gideon Force now understood their rôle a little more easily, the action went forward with something resembling flow and smoothness. The Italian retreat to the east went on. Their army was by now more damaged, more perplexed, more in despair. Gideon Force continued the pursuit.[2]

Before telling of Wingate's next adventures, his part in this battle of Burye-cum-Mankusa ought to be looked at. It was Gideon Force's first battle, and Wingate's first attempt at sizeable command in action. His critics have found much to find fault with on this occasion.[3] They point out that he was guilty of four military errors : a tendency to carry out most of his movements in daylight ; keeping his force and his baggage-train operating as a single body (therefore open to annihilation as a single body); inadmissible rashness in committing almost the whole force in the daylight attack on the Burye forts ; remaining too long in one place (with all chance of the bluff being called) in front of Mankusa. The critics do admit, however, that these faults were not repeated in any later actions under Wingate's command.

A defence (and one that Wingate would probably have scorned) is certainly to be found in the mere fact that this was Wingate's first engagement as the commander of trained troops in action against other trained troops. The greatest soldiers have been known to show ineptitude in such circumstances. He may well have been experiencing, in all its benumbing terror, the fearful gap between the drawing up of plans and theories, and what Henry James once called " the dear little deadly question of how to do it." It is difficult otherwise to

---

[1] Thesiger. Boustead.
[2] Allen. Boustead. Information obtained at the War Office. *War Diary* by Akavia.
[3] Information obtained at the War Office.

understand how a man of such quick imagination and grasp could have allowed his unwieldy baggage train to wander in absolute vulnerability around the battle area, endangering itself and hampering the mobility of his fighting troops. The long pause in front of Mankusa is perhaps in the same class of mistake.

But the main charge is one of rashness and against this there is surely a wholly satisfying defence to be found in the peculiar nature of this kind of warfare. From first to last Gideon Force was an essay in deception. It was never an essay in common sense. The boldness of this entry into Gojjam had already convinced the Italians that a formidable number of troops were against them. It was of the essence of Gideon strategy to keep the Italians to that mistake. It is true that Wingate showed inconsistency : that he issued instructions on how the aim was to be achieved and then, in the heat of the moment, so it seems, followed a quite opposite method. In only one respect did he keep to the detail of the original plan ; he kept up the attack with unflagging persistence. It may be that in refusing to give the Italians time to think Wingate did the same to himself. But the point to be seized is that, whether Wingate acted as he did by accident or design, he achieved abundant success. There was no better way of making the enemy believe that British reserves were at hand than by behaving as if they were. By committing in daylight all the troops he had ; by following (blindly for the moment) a policy of " *de l'audace, et encore de l'audace,*" he made the false Italian estimate doubly credible. If he had acted otherwise, if he had followed here the cautious policy he taught from the beginning and put into effect later, his deception might have been discovered.

The first round had gone to Gideon Force but it was only the first round. The Italians were not yet defeated. As they withdrew eastwards they had large reinforcements at their disposal and short lines of supply. There was no reason why with a swift and thorough reorganisation the Italian army should not recover all that it had so foolishly lost.

CHAPTER XIII

VICTORY IN ETHIOPIA

THE SITUATION of Gideon Force after the fighting round Burye became alarming. The little army's supply problem had been saved by the Italian blunder of not thoroughly destroying their stores before retreating, but in the first week of March, Wingate's administrative machinery had utterly broken down. For this reason he was summoned back to Burye when Boustead went forward towards Dambacha.

The main trouble was the line of communication. Between Roseires and the forward posts at Mankusa, there lay two hundred miles of direct distance which was over three hundred miles measured by the roads ; and most of this distance had to be covered as regards supply by ill-adapted means of carrying, the slow-moving and fast-dying camels of the Sudan. Wingate's organisation depended on radio signal communication and for this he had deficient equipment. He was also working in a field where there was little precedent to guide him. The administration of Gideon Force never showed the masterly quality of Wingate's later achievement.

On the 5th of March Brigadier Sandford met him on the road between Burye and Mankusa. He was with Akavia and a few men, and at the moment of meeting asleep on the ground near the road with a sentry watching. He was tired and in a state of depression about all that had gone wrong and all that looked like going wrong in the actions ahead. He and Sandford went to Burye.

The next morning Wingate went to pay his respects to the Emperor whom he found gracious, but not so much so as to conceal a certain degree of irritation. In spite of his ardent (and entirely sincere) protestations of devotion, Wingate had not kept the Emperor informed of the course of events since his departure from Belaiya on the 19th of February. He had not sent him a signal since the 25th. Though defective signalling equipment accounted for much, Haile Selassie, who had grown weary of British failure to consult him, felt the need of further explanations notwithstanding. His displeasure was fleeting. Whatever his dissatisfaction, he had cause to be gratified by the achievements of Gideon Force to date. In two weeks Wingate had given him the beginnings of a second Empire.

Then Wingate and Sandford began long discussions on the state of Gideon Force's administration and rôle. Sandford told Wingate that his line of supply and reinforcement from distant Roseires was so lacking in direction and command that on his way from Belaiya he had found camel-trains and reinforcements, which included eight of the ten operational centres, wandering eastwards on the plateau with no clear idea as to where they were supposed to go. He insisted that a thorough reorganisation must be undertaken and Wingate agreed. A signal was sent to Colonel Airey in Khartoum requesting a conference. Airey answered that he would fly out to Burye on the 11th of March.

Sandford was not only critical of Wingate's administration but in disagreement with his main plan. He reminded him of the original conception of what part the rebellion was to play in the defeat of Italy : to contain the Italians *within* Gojjam, to keep them pinned helplessly to the ground where they would receive the *coup de grâce* from the armies commanded by Generals Platt and Cunningham. The present plan, Sandford insisted, could only result in chasing the Italians from Gojjam, a movement which would enable them the more easily to reinforce the Italian armies confronting the British invasions from the north, west and south. He wanted Wingate to include in his future plans two flying columns, one to operate against the Dessie-Addis Ababa road the other against the Wallega-Addis Ababa road, so as to restore as far as possible the classic rôle of the campaign. Wingate met Sandford's objections on one point only : he agreed to organise a flying column of patriot irregulars under Dejasmach Mangasha Aboyne (a Wollo chief) to operate against the Dessie Addis Ababa road. In fact, little came of this because events were to move too fast. Sandford's ideas were logical but his criticism overlooked what he had insisted on before all others : the fatuity of the Italian Army in Ethiopia. He underestimated the consequent speed of Cunningham's advance from the south. He also underestimated Wingate's capacity and the skill he was to show, such as in the last action of this campaign, by which, following improvised methods, he achieved all that he and Sandford had promised.

While they were discussing these things on the 6th March calamitous news came in from Dambacha. Gideon Force had continued the pursuit the day before, and taken the fort of Jigga, but this success led to the worst disaster suffered by the Force in the whole of the campaign. This is what happened. As the main Italian body hurried towards Dambacha it came on the 2nd Ethiopian Battalion which was astride the road without sentinels or defence positions. They had heard nothing about the flight of the Italians from Burye and so the " milling mob " took them by complete surprise. The Italians hardly deployed but crashed through the sudden opposition. The Ethiopians fought with fierce bravery for a short while, then broke and fled.[1] It was the first considerable combat between the armies of Mussolini and of Haile Selassie since 1936. Poetic justice was denied and the Fascist army inflicted, for the last time, a shattering blow on their victims, though they did this at a heavy price. When all was over two hundred of the Italian force lay dead on and around the road, and it was found after-wards that their wounded numbered near a thousand.[2] But the attempt was fatal to the Ethiopian battalion. They lost a quarter of their strength. For practical purposes they were of small value during the rest of the campaign. The fault was not theirs, much more that of the incompetent leadership of their battalion commander. Various parts of the battalion fought with distinction after, but they never again operated in battle as a unit.

While the disastrous action was in progress Boustead's men came to ineffective rescue. There was a moment when the classic situation for which Gideon Force continually strove came about : an Italian garrison caught between an opposing and a pursuing force, but nothing could be made of it : the Ethiopian battalion was already broken, the pursuers too weary and undernourished to fulfil their rôle. In the afternoon of this same day, the 6th of March, Boustead lost one of his best officers. Bimbashi Harris was badly wounded outside Dambacha and could take no further part in the deeds of Gideon Force.

Sandford was with Wingate when this news came to him at Burye. It should be clear by now that by circumstance and conviction Sandford was Wingate's sternest critic, but his impression of him at this appalling moment, then and after, was of his fortitude. An ordinary man must have been shattered by this new and sudden danger and the prospect of annihilation : defeat in front and a failing administration behind. But Wingate's instant reaction was one of resilience. He waited impatiently for Airey and the conference so that he could go forward again and command on the spot.

As a result of the conference on the 11th March Sandford was given charge of all the quartermastering of the force ; Burye was turned into the administrative base under Major Nott. The tenuous line of com-munication was at that time in process of being a little strengthened by the enterprise and skill of Bimbashi Le Blanc and Captain Tim Foley. They succeeded in getting twelve trucks up the escarpment.

[1] Information obtained at the War Office, modified by a communication from Sandford.
[2] Allen. Wingate's Report.

How they achieved this is beyond lay imagination: judging by photographs they and their men seem to have carried the trucks a large part of the way. Yet despite such fine efforts, the line of communication remained Gideon Force's weakness to the end. William Allen arrived in Burye shortly after the decisions of the conference had been put into effect and he described what he saw of the new Headquarters.

" The fort," he wrote in his book, " was a grim and dismal place. . . . Made up of stone huts giving on to a barrack yard—the whole surrounded by a wall. Trenches, dugouts, wire, dead mules, rubbish and dung, human and animal, covered the hill-side. Flies were myriad. In the afternoon violent dust storms . . . enveloped the countryside, and when the wind dropped the dust hung in the air like a fog. Burye fort had become the temporary base of Gideon Force; all questions revolved round the imperturbable person of Donald Nott, a major in the Worcestershire Regiment who had won the M.C. in Palestine. . . . He lay in bed with a badly poisoned foot—somewhat painfully treated daily by a Syrian doctor named Haggar who himself was a mine of anecdotes on the gynaecological history of the different royal families of the Middle East. Racked with shooting pains, Donald would lurch over to his table to cope with the supply problems of Wingate in Dambacha or Jarvis and Simonds at Bahrdar; or he would hobble out into the barrack yard to still a dispute between Sudanis and Abyssinians or master the intricacies of some crisis which had arisen in relation with the patriot leaders. Donald's . . . principal henchman was the equally imperturbable Sergeant Rees who, I was glad to find, had all financial questions well in hand so that my destined rôle as Paymaster lapsed into oblivion.[1] There was a young signaller whose sight was giving way from the sheer exhaustion of long hours by the light of a hurricane lamp. There was Johannes Abdu, the interpreter, a mild diminutive half-Arab landowner from Gore who had been on the staff of the northern Abyssinian Army during the campaign of 1935-1936 and who had chosen now the . . . most useful duty he could find. I fitted myself into the picture as a sort of general handyman and was soon occupied with Bill Maclean[2] on working out a defence scheme for the Burye area."

The last words refer to the changed situation. On the 8th of March the Italians evacuated Dambacha and continued their flight to Debra Markos, but after the events of the 6th they recognised at long last that they were the victims of deception. Wingate's bluff had been

[1] Allen joined Gideon Force as paymaster but at Debra Markos was appointed Transport officer. His interview with Wingate on that occasion has been recorded earlier.
[2] Neil Maclean, M.P., M.C.

called. The Italian field commander, Colonel Natale, was ignominiously removed by the General Officer, a man called Nasi, and his place filled by a soldier in whom the troops had confidence, Colonel Maraventano. Italian prospects began to look brighter. Their forces in Debra Markos numbered twelve thousand men and they enjoyed also some reasonable hopes of support from the population. These hopes rested on their ingenious use of a remarkable Ethiopian personality whose position should be briefly described.

His name was Ras Hailu. At this time he was sixty-six years old but great corpulence had already given him a very elderly appearance which a black curled wig did not much mitigate.[1] His character could remind people of the imposing and treacherous feudal lords who confounded Highland politics in the days of our Jacobites. He was of royal descent, being the only surviving son, albeit an illegitimate one, of King Takla Haimanot of Gojjam and Kaffa, a tributary prince under the Emperor Menelik. Long before the Italian invasion he had been on bad terms with Haile Selassie. He had acted a double-faced part in the troubled reign of Lij Yasu, the apostate Emperor,[2] and after Haile Selassie's accession he had intrigued for Lij Yasu's restoration, provoked into this treason, perhaps, by a fine of 300,000 dollars for corrupt practices. He had been condemned to death, reprieved, pardoned, and then much later ordered to accompany Haile Selassie on his flight from Ethiopia in 1936. But he had found opportunity to slip away from the Imperial train and thereafter gave his services to the Italians. These services were not of an edifying kind and a certain Ras Kassa, who appears later in Wingate's story, blamed on Ras Hailu the murder of his sons by the Fascist Government. In February this man had been put forward by the Italians as the rightful King of Gojjam. It may be asked how anyone with such a record, (and there was no question of misunderstood innocence), could command any respect among his hoped-for subjects. The answer is that Ras Hailu commanded a great deal, and the Italian move was astute. To understand how this could be the English reader must remember his own Norman and Angevin past and the unconditional respect that a deeply royalist society can feel for the representative of a great house, even though bastard, even though in rebellion against an acknowledged sovereign.

To return to the story then; the Italians under a new and supposedly vigorous commander were now concentrated in Debra Markos in great numbers, well armed, and enjoying the local support of Ras

[1] Allen.
[2] This youthful and inept reformer-Emperor reigned from 1911 to 1916 when he was deposed at the age of twenty after an ill-considered attempt to convert Ethiopia from Christianity to Islam.

Hailu followed by several thousand of his armed braves. Gideon Force at the same time had spent the first tide of their initial impetus, and had suffered a defeat. They were hungry, weary, and in rags.[1] Furthermore, the fact that they were a little force was now beyond disguise. In these circumstances General Nasi harangued his troops in Debra Markos and announced an immediate counter-attack on a large scale, the object being the recapture of Burye. So it came about that Captain Allen and Lieutenant Maclean found themselves preparing a defence scheme for the little fort-ringed town which was now the forward base of Gideon Force and the headquarters and court of the Ethiopian Emperor.

As soon as the conference with Airey was finished Wingate went forward to Debra Markos and to the longest and most difficult action in which the main body of Gideon Force was involved. Here more than anywhere else a false step could bring annihilation on the whole Gojjam rebellion. Wingate rose to the height of that challenge.

There was only one thing for Gideon Force to do in their present situation, and that was to reverse it. The bluff had been called, therefore it must be reimposed. Gideon Force had to look big again, and above all things, it was necessary not to allow the initiative to pass into Italian hands. None of this was easy and the task was made more difficult because time had to be passed inactively before supplies could come forward, and at the end of that time the Italians did take the initiative. A little more than twenty miles north-west of Debra Markos there was a military strongpoint called Fort Emmanuel which the Italians had left when they retreated. On the 19th Italian forward troops recaptured the fort, the British suffering two killed and four prisoners.[2] But on the same date Wingate also was ready for action. The initiative did not stay with the Italians for more than a few hours.

Wingate's plan for Debra Markos was not carried out because things went otherwise, but it should be indicated because it gave a shape to the events of the battle. He was always a quick learner and he had recognised that in this sort of warfare close command of all units could diminish mobility, so on the 13th he divided his force into two parts, the first consisting of two Frontier battalion platoons under Wingate, the second of the remainder under Boustead. The Boustead men were to attack around and in Debra Markos, provoking the Italians to a further retreat, while the Wingate men (temporarily known as Safforce), were to move to the south-east, to Safartak, and there ambush and destroy the fleeing garrison. "*Toujours de l'audace !*" remained the principle. The two parts of the force met on the 14th at a place called Amba Mariam, about twelve miles north of Debra

[1] Allen.   [2] These prisoners were later murdered by the Italians.

Markos. There they heard news that Ras Hailu had taken his final political stand and done battle with patriot forces led by the most loyal of Haile Selassie's followers Lij Hailu Balao.[1] This had happened in the hilly country to the north which is known by the Lear-like name of the Chokey Mountains. He was now descending from the mountains to the plain of Debra Markos and was only two miles away from Amba Mariam and Gideon Force. The latter, numbering a little over three hundred, were now caught between two large armies. Wingate responded to the situation by sending a message to the treacherous old princeling by an Ethiopian intermediary calling on him to acknowledge his liege lord and surrender. Ras Hailu declined the invitation in polite terms and presently moved his army to Debra Markos. Now Wingate changed his plan. While Ras Hailu's men were around in the country north of Debra Markos he could not leave for Safartak without the danger of being cut off from the main force. He delayed departure till the 17th and by that time had taken a fresh decision, namely, to keep Safforce at Debra Markos for the time being and to send Thesiger and Foley (the hero of the manhandled trucks) to Safartak with orders to make contact with Lij Belai Zalleka, the ablest military commander among the patriots,[2] and to arrange for him to ambush the retreating Italians.

Meantime he and Boustead and his other officers spent the time between the 14th and the 19th in detailed reconnaissance preparatory to the siege. It may sound mad to speak of three hundred men besieging twelve thousand, but this they did. Debra Markos was found to provide good terrain for the use of guerilla forces. Copses and woods are in plenty and skilled guerilla warriors such as those of Gideon Force could move wherever they wanted, and attack from wherever they wanted, always (it must be remembered) at the price of little sleep and great exertions, and fatigues which often seemed impossible to bear. Wingate drove them to the limit of their strength.

The first action was preceded by a reconnaissance of the forts north of Debra Markos on the 19th, the day Fort Emmanuel was lost, and opened at three o'clock in the morning of the 20th with an assault on the northernmost fort of Abima. It was delivered by three platoons of the Frontier battalion under Bimbashi Johnson guarded by two platoons under Bimbashi Acland. It succeeded. Drawing near to the Italian posts on the slopes from the fort, Johnson's men grenaded their enemies out of their picket line, and then at a green flare signal shelled

[1] At this time he was fifty-two. He was chief of the Amhara Saint district east of the Blue Nile. He never surrendered to the Italians and lived throughout the Fascist occupation as a *maquisard*. Sandford had made contact with him in November.

[2] Thesiger.

the interior of the fort with mortars,[1] causing the inmates to rush out for safety and abandon the place. At four in the morning lights were sent up in the colour of green, yellow and red (the colours of the Ethiopian flag), signalling withdrawal. The attackers had come invisibly but they went a little later than they should have done. When daylight broke they could be seen to the west by the men of an Italian

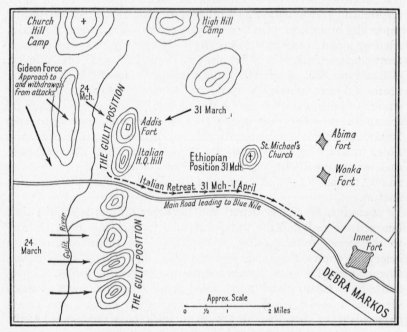

Debra Markos and the Gulit Position

gun position and they were shelled, without result however. The Italians immediately began to question the correct estimate they had made as to the numbers of their enemies.

The force sheltered at a place which they called " High Hill Camp " due north of Debra Markos, and thither Johnson's men withdrew reaching it about midday of the 20th.

Between the 19th and 24th there was no major action by Gideon Force but there was continual small action, and by this means the main

[1] According to Dejasmach Makonnen Desta, Wingate himself was in charge of the mortar on this occasion. Conflict of evidence suggests that this may be a confusion with a later incident.

purpose was gradually achieved : the Italians were soon convinced again that they were faced not by a small lightly trained agglomeration of brave men and adventurers, but by a division at least. Every night small parties advanced into the picket lines of Debra Markos. These parties usually numbered between forty and fifty, sometimes less. They approached along ways reconnoitred by day. They would get near to enemy camp fires and shoot at the Italian soldiers round them with light machine-guns. Soon the enemy got to know this technique and prepared for it, so another, more bloody, was organised. The Gideon men would creep by night to within ten yards or so of positions and then carry them with bayonet rushes after flinging grenades. They would always vanish before first light.

What part Wingate himself took in these actions is hard to say because his own reports do not tell and personal memories are often fallacious. What may be taken as certain is that he often led in person. Writing near to the time as an eye-witness Allen said : " He never spared his own body, and other critics would complain that he thrust into every action to gain credit for himself." Dejasmach Makonnen Desta has a curious memory of a reconnaissance expedition. Wingate and two officers drew near to an Italian position, having first posted a sentry to give them cover if they should be spotted and attacked. They moved nearer to get a better view and the sentry hearing them thought they were Italians and fired. A bullet went through the hat of one of Wingate's companions. The other one judiciously ran off. Wingate never moved, shouted to the sentry to mind what he was doing and called loudly for the officer to come back, which he did somewhat embarrassed. Then it was decided that since the Italians were now probably alerted, the operation must be cancelled. What impressed Makonnen Desta was the way that sudden danger in a help-less position never deflected Wingate's interest in the reconnaissance. He continued making notes and comparing the scene before him with his map as though on the most peaceable occasion. Strange that such a man should have sometimes thought of himself as deficient in natural courage.[1]

In one night action when Wingate was handling the mortar helped only by Makonnen Desta, Italian guns began shelling them with increasing accuracy. As the shells began to land near he cried : " Get out of it quick ! " to Makonnen Desta. The latter hesitated to obey. Wingate repeated the order angrily and so the other went, leaving the

---

[1] In Palestine a Jewish friend who disapproved of blood sports once told Wingate that he was disappointed to find him such an enthusiastic follower of hounds. (He used some-times to go jackal-hunting.) Wingate replied that he understood his friend's point of view but that he himself needed the slight dangers of riding to hounds as without such exercise his courage could easily grow rusty and even disappear.

commander firing alone till his ammunition was finished. Afterwards he explained his action to Makonnen Desta saying something as follows : " If you were killed you would be a great loss to your country because in Ethiopia there is a shortage of well-educated men, but if I am killed it is another matter. There are plenty of people in England to take my place."[1] Even in extreme danger he was prone to take an impersonal view of the situation.

From the 21st evidence came that Gideon Force was proving itself again. There was a continual stream of Ethiopian deserters from the Italian Army. They told of weakening spirits. In addition they could give precise information as to Italian dispositions, and this was added to by spies from the patriot bands of Balao and Zalleka, and numerous deserters to them from Ras Hailu. Then, on the 22nd, news came in from such sources that the Italians were about to move in strength against High Hill Camp which they had located. Immediately the whole force was moved northwards. The Italians came out, invaded the camp, and finding it empty, returned to the safety of the town and the forts. This and the recapture of Fort Emmanuel on the 19th were all that the Italians were to realise of General Nasi's counter-attack. Gideon Force had learned never to give battle on ground or at a time of the enemy's choosing, never to cease giving it in opposite circumstances. On the night of the 24th the besiegers put in one of their largest attacks.

On the morning of this day they moved down from the hills to a place a mile and a half north of the Italian defence line which lay west of the town, and was known as the Gulit position. A reconnaissance was made in the afternoon, and after dark the main body of the force, consisting of two companies, put in the first of three attacks on the posts established on four hills standing east from the gorge of the Gulit river. The main hill was called Addis Height and the assault here was led by Bimbashi Acland. The attacks were well synchronised. The familiar technique was followed: the men approached to within throwing distance and then charged in with grenade and bayonet. All the hill positions were penetrated from the east, the Sudanese "creating havoc,"[2] then withdrawing before the defenders could rally. Acland had the most difficult assignment, the machine-gun post on Addis Height being only approachable by a narrow ridge between precipices. Three of his men were killed by falls. He himself was wounded and took no further part in the campaign.

Despite all this, Acland's section of Gideon Force, like the others, succeeded in harrying the enemy position in front of them. The withdrawal of all the attacking parties was covered by the mortar section which kept up a bombardment of the enemy's main camp till well after the action was over. It may have been on this occasion that Wingate remained alone with the mortar after he had sent Makonnen Desta back to safety.

Gideon Force withdrew to their camp north of the Gulit position where Wingate granted them needed rest.

It would seem that some time during the 25th Wingate had an encounter with a patriot chief which epitomised what might be called his political theory of guerilla-campaigning when conducted by the " liberation forces " of a foreign power, a theory, as he often pointed out, which was in antithesis to those of his kinsman Lawrence. It seems, as he told in his report, that shortly after his arrival at Debra Markos " the local Baron " appeared, " ready to offer to fight, subject of course to my meeting his large demands for arms and money." When Wingate told the Baron that the latter was no soldier, and that Gideon Force were in charge of that side of the business, the Baron went away silent and bewildered. He was back at Wingate's camp after the Gulit action. The dialogue that ensued with the local Baron is best given in the words of Wingate's own account. The Baron speaks first.

" I hear you attacked the enemy at Gulit last night."

" Yes."

" Was it successful ? "

" Very."

" Why didn't you let me know ? I could have helped."

" Well, you are not a soldier."

" What ! I who have fought the Italians these five years ! "

" Anyway, you haven't the arms and ammunition, and we have none to give you."

" I *have* arms and ammunition. Let me bring them ! To show you ! "

" Well, if you really want to fight for your flag come with me to-morrow and I will give you a task."

Wingate added that later this man became a most trusted lieutenant.[1]

Gideon Force's next attack was scheduled for the night of the 27th of March, but before then Wingate received orders from General Platt to go back to Burye to reorganise the line of communication once again. The reason for this urgent and unwelcome summons was that the mutual positions of Sandford and Wingate had led to a new difference (to describe the thing mildly) between them.

This is what had happened. On the 19th of March Sandford in

[1] In his report Wingate did not date the episode but Akavia's *War Diary* indicates the 25th.

Burye had received a telegram from General Platt for Wingate instructing the latter to take all possible measures to prevent Italian reinforcements from Begemder reaching Keren, for which purpose he requested him to strengthen Major Simonds's force which was still laying siege to Bahrdar Giorgis on Lake Tana. In Eritrea the moment was a critical one. In the first part of February two attempts to turn the defences of the natural fortress of Keren, held by thirty-nine battalions and thirty-six batteries, had failed, and it was clear that only a frontal attack could succeed. This frontal attack had opened on the 15th March. By the 19th the relatively small but terrible battle of Keren was in its first indecisive phase. Sandford tried to forward the message to Wingate but, with Gideon Force's feeble signalling, the message did not get through.

At Burye they were not only ignorant of Wingate's whereabouts, but of what was happening at Debra Markos about which they heard some alarming reports. On the 21st Sandford decided to find Wingate in person, and so he rode out on horseback in the morning. He returned to Burye the next evening, having failed.[1] So he took the initiative. He ordered Number 6 Operation Centre under Lieutenant Walsh to go north to join Major Simonds. He sent forward another message telling what he had done. This message did reach Wingate, and when he read it he was beside himself with rage. He had already sent messages to Burye demanding more men and more guns and had been answered, so it seemed, with the weakest response. At one moment, on the 13th, he had even ordered Nott (on whom the administration of the line of communication depended) to come forward to Debra Markos, and Sandford had cancelled the order. Now that a valuable operational centre containing an officer and five British sergeants fully trained was denied him at the height of the most critical battle of his campaign, he found Sandford's action beyond all bearing, and he sent a messenger to Burye with a letter of protest couched in insulting terms. Sandford in turn found *this* beyond bearing. He signalled Khartoum saying that the present dual-control system was unworkable and requesting that a senior representative of the Kaid should fly out to Burye, or that he should be flown in to Khartoum so that the matter might be clarified and settled once and for all. Sir William Platt's answer was to order the force commander to go back to his base and organise his line of communication.

Major Nott recorded Wingate's arrival: "Burye. 27th March. Orde suddenly appeared without warning and looking as though he was out for blood. However, his magnetic personality dominated and

---

[1] Brigadier Donald Nott, D.S.O., M.C., O.B.E., who kept a diary which provides authority for much of the following. Sandford.

dispelled all disgruntled thoughts, although he was very critical of the way things had been sent forward from here. The trouble about forward movement is that there are no mules as yet, and the camels are tired, but above all, the camel drivers are refusing to go on, and so where are you ? " In great wrath Wingate asked Nott why several of his orders had not been obeyed, to which Nott replied : " For the very good reason that some of your orders can't be obeyed." Wingate asked him for an explanation of his words and Nott gave it, telling him in detail of the difficulties of administering an extended line of communication with few men and no serviceable transport. Wingate saw that he had in some measure blamed his base headquarters unjustly. But he was still in a rage.

After he had paid his respects to the Emperor he went into conference with Sandford. The meeting was stormy. On his side Wingate demanded to be told how it came about that Sandford had presumed to interfere in the conduct of operations, sending off needed men, cancelling an order to Nott, and other exasperating actions of the like kind. Sandford on his side demanded of Wingate how he expected him to act otherwise but on his own initiative when communication was severed between the front and the base for days on end, and when urgent orders came from the highest authority, and when the base was kept in absolute ignorance of what was happening so that all the news they had were the defeatist rumours of terrified Ethiopians. The explosion was protracted. It went on for several hours. It had the common effect of explosions, of affording relief by the letting off of steam. For the next nine days Wingate turned the whole of his attention to his administration and the reorganisation of his lines. He moved his own Headquarters, with a company of the 2nd Ethiopian Battalion, two operational centres and the advance supply group of the Frontier Battalion, to Dambacha. Major Nott went with him as his Staff officer. It was agreed that in future this long-suffering man was to receive orders from Wingate alone.

During these Burye and Dambacha days Wingate saw more of William Allen than of anyone else. It might be an exaggeration to say that they became friends, for friendship played less part in Wingate's life at this time than at any other, but they had an easy relationship, perhaps the only easy one he enjoyed here. Allen was not a respecter of persons and he did not hesitate to respond to Wingate's solemn harshness with flippant chaff such as is often welcome to a person labouring under heavy preoccupations. When Wingate once asked Allen why he bothered with his comforts and his food and could not be content with eating dates as he was, the other replied that wherever he was he liked to enjoy all available consolations. "If I was in Sing-Sing," he said, "I would make friends with my warder and see to it that whatever luxuries are obtainable in Sing-Sing ameliorated my hard lot." By such words he would provoke a reluctant smile. Being a man of wide education Allen could afford the other an opportunity for his favourite recreation : long arguments on learned subjects. Allen enjoyed these occasions likewise, though he sometimes found the other's dissertations on his current intellectual passion, Motley's history of the Netherlands, something of a trial.

In Dambacha three of the twelve Jewish medical officers recruited from Palestine arrived to report for duty. They were unloading their camels when Akavia came up to them, and said : " Colonel Wingate wants to see you straight away." They protested that they had not yet washed, but Akavia said that the commander did not like to be kept waiting and they must come. After their long and wearisome journey to serve in Gideon Force they were at first a little dashed at their reception. They were shown into Wingate's hut where they found him naked. His first words to them were : " Once again I have to see Jewish medical officers who are not serving in a Jewish army." He invited them to sit down and began to talk, but not on the expected subject. He said nothing about the present situation of the force, nothing about the siege and battle down the road, nothing about what had been achieved since he and his men had climbed the escarpment a month before ; he talked about his numerous and frustrated efforts to form a Jewish army earlier in the war, illustrating what he had to say by quotations from the Bible. He repeated what he had said to Akavia and indicated to this surprised audience the deducible connection between an Ethiopian success and the realisation of the hopes of Zion. This, he said, was why he had called for Jewish doctors to act as his medical officers, though there was another reason too. He realised, he said, as others did not, that Palestine was an ideal recruiting ground for such officers because since the great immigration from Germany there were more doctors in Palestine than the country needed. One of the medical officers, Doctor Beham, who had never met Wingate before, was impressed by the strangeness of this man, and for a long time he could not shake off the memory of his fierce piercing bright blue eyes.[1]

Wingate remained in Dambacha, with one visit to Debra Markos, till the 6th April. In the interval the battle which he had planned and begun was brought to its end. It was the critical battle of the campaign, more decisive than the men who fought it may have known at the time. Its last phases should be briefly outlined.

[1] Dr. Beham.

Whatever resolution General Nasi had been able to put into his troops was fatally diminished by the news which reached Debra Markos on the 27th. From the south General Cunningham commanding three divisions (the 1st South African, the 11th African, and the 12th African), had advanced one thousand and fifty-four miles in thirty days.[1] On the 26th March he received the surrender of Harar, the second city of Ethiopia. On the 27th General Frusci, commanding the great fortress of Keren, surrendered to General Platt after a siege of fifty-three days. From now on the resistance of the army at Debra Markos visibly weakened.

During the 27th of March Boustead led Gideon Force westwards to a camp in forest country behind Fort Emmanuel. Next day he reconnoitred the country to the south of Debra Markos and then prepared an attack from the south on the Gulit position. In the course of reconnaissance he had discovered a ridge dominating the Italian picket line from only three hundred yards, and which this inept enemy had not occupied. Up this hill went two platoons, with a mortar section, under Bimbashi Johnson, and at eleven o'clock at night they opened fire with mortars and machine-guns, obtaining accurate aim from the camp fires, and bombarding the whole length of the position. The next night the mortar section under Lieutenant Turral bombarded the position again from the north-west. On the 30th deserters told of sixty-eight casualties suffered in the lines from these two bombardments, and in the course of that day clandestine contact was made between Boustead and senior non-commissioned officers of the Italian Colonial battalion in the Gulit lines. These men sent messages that they wanted to come out and surrender and gave Boustead to understand that they spoke for the great majority. That night Makonnen Desta and Azazh Kabbada led patriot forces in a night attack on the inner fort guarding Debra Markos, a place called Wonka. The next day the Italians retreated from Fort Emmanuel, losing twenty-three men when two lorries were destroyed by land mines. In the evening news came that the enemy were preparing to abandon the Gulit position and retire on Debra Markos. This could only be a prelude to an abandonment of the whole area and with it there came a chance to finish the whole campaign.

The chance was missed owing to two failures, one to be expected, the other surprising and extraordinary. The plan was for two platoons of the Frontier Battalion to attack the Gulit position from the east on the night of the 31st and for a company of the 2nd Ethiopian Battalion to lie in ambush for the Gulit garrison on their road to Debra Markos the next day. The attack went in soon after midnight on the main post.

[1] General Sir Alan Cunningham. Report of Operation.

It was carried out in the accustomed style and with the accustomed success, but in the course of it the officer in charge, Colin Macdonald, was killed.[1] Then, in the early morning before sunrise, the whole Gulit garrison numbering about two thousand began to make their way across the plain eastwards to Debra Markos. This was the moment for the Ethiopian company to fall on them and destroy them. But they did not move. Their rout on the 6th March at Dambacha was still fresh in their minds, and at the sight of these great numbers of enemy soldiers the whole company was paralysed with fear. Their British commander exhorted them in vain.[2] They believed themselves to be surrounded and refused to open fire. The garrison went to Debra Markos, and temporary safety, unharmed.

This was a setback but a minor one. The real *coup de grâce* was scheduled to take place at the crossing of the Blue Nile at Safartak twenty-five miles to the west. Bimbashi Johnson was sent with Azazh Kabbada's patriots to join Thesiger and Rowe in their task of strengthening the large patriot ambush force at the bridge. There they waited from the 31st to the 4th of April, with every hope of victory.

During the next days Italian movements in and around Debra Markos became confused and this probably evidenced their indecision. Some evacuation, chiefly of European troops, began on the same day as the Gulit garrison joined the main force ; yet two days later, on the 3rd of April, reinforcements approached Debra Markos from the east and were ambushed and turned back by Bimbashi Johnson, (a remarkable action for which he received the D.S.O.). It seems that at the end the Italians could not bring themselves to admit so shameful a defeat : they retreated and rallied at the same time. They abandoned an inner fort, Wonka, but then tried to hold the outer fort. Of their two tendencies that towards flight was the stronger, and the main Italian movement was one of gradual evacuation performed under the harassment of frequent incursions by Gideon Force into the areas of the outposts.

On the 4th of April the Italians were out. The news came to Wingate at Dambacha and was followed immediately by a surprising overture from Ras Hailu. The latter sent his smart Alfa-Romeo limousine car driven by a liveried chauffeur to Wingate's Headquarters with an invitation to him to drive in style into Debra Markos. Wingate declined the use of the car with thanks and drove to Debra Markos in his own truck. There then occurred an incident of memorable comedy.

[1] Allen pays high tribute to him in his book.
[2] He was Sergeant Clarke. He was exonerated of all blame and later commissioned.

He drove directly to the central fort where he received the surrender from a captain in the Italian Medical Corps. He found the compound well stocked with provisions. Nothing had been sabotaged. While he was making a tour of inspection a telephone began ringing in one of the offices. Among Wingate's party was Mr. Edmund Stevens, the war correspondent of the *Christian Science Monitor*. Wingate turned to him and told him to come along. " You speak Italian," he said to Stevens ; " take the call."

" But what shall I say ? " asked Stevens.

" Say that you're the doctor," answered Wingate. " Tell them the British have captured Debra Markos and that a division ten thousand strong is heading for the Blue Nile crossing."

Stevens picked up the telephone and gave this message to an Italian Army switchboard operator speaking from one of the Nile posts. The operator was appalled. " Who shall I tell this to ? " he could be heard shouting at the other end.

" To your commanding officer of course," said Stevens in his fluent Italian, " and if you want my advice and value your skin, you'll pack up and get moving."[1]

The ruse was entirely successful. The Italians abandoned their defence positions on the Blue Nile and made for the crossing. This conformed perfectly with the plan for the *coup de grâce* at the Safartak bridge. Wingate then returned to Dambacha confident that the evacuating troops would be ambushed and that the task of Gideon Force would be brought to an end. But things fell out otherwise, and the battle of Safartak never took place. The story of this second and wholly unexpected failure is a curious one.

As said already, Lij Belai Zalleka was the ablest soldier among the patriot leaders. He was the only one with a professional understanding of military tactics, the only one who could impose regular military discipline on his column : he was the only irregular commander capable of moving his host from place to place in secrecy and silence.[2] He was Gideon Force's most promising ally. Unfortunately he was prone to a common human weakness. He was a bit of a snob. Knowing this, Ras Hailu rendered a last and considerable service to the Italians who had raised him to his rickety kingship. The Ras sent to Zalleka to say that if he allowed the Italian Army to pass unscathed over the bridge at Safartak he, Ras Hailu, would give him his daughter in marriage. Zalleka was of bourgeois birth and the prospect of marrying into royal circles, even the most discredited, was more than his social

---

[1] Mr. Edmund Stevens.
[2] Thesiger. He relates that any unnecessary noise by any of his men or by camp-followers of both sexes was punished with instant flogging.

instincts could resist. He drew off his men. Bimbashis Johnson and
Riley were able to maul the Italian rearguard, but their achievement
was little in comparison with what had been prepared. Too late,
Boustead arrived at Safartak with the main body on the 5th of April.
He found that the last Italians had passed over the gorge by the bridge
which they had attempted to destroy before leaving. The planks were
still smouldering. Zalleka enjoyed social eminence for a pitifully short
while. When the campaign was over, he was shot for mutiny by the
Emperor's order.

In the meantime Debra Markos, after suffering the woes of siege
and battle, became on liberation (as did many other places later), a
scene of political confusion. Ras Hailu loved his royal position so
dearly that he did not leave with his patrons but remained in his
Gojjam Kingdom. The usurper showed not only courage but astuteness
in staying behind, for when they came to take over Debra Markos and
its manifold problems Gideon Force found that they needed him. It
has been remarked that the principal objection to the Brocklehurst
mission was that it was likely to provoke a civil war. To have flung
Ras Hailu into gaol might have had a similar effect now. Wingate,
before leaving for Dambacha, instructed Boustead to obtain Ras Hailu's
surrender, leaving the details of the arrangement to his discretion. A
rendezvous was arranged, and the Ras, dressed in the uniform of an
Italian general, and showing a serene dignity,[1] received Boustead in
the main building of the town. He offered to be responsible for
order and security and could promise a cessation of looting. Boustead,
like Zalleka, (but not, it may be assumed, for snobbish reasons),
found it impossible to resist the propositions of the old Ras. For the
eminent wretch was not merely a doubtful sovereign but the effective
proprietor and feudal overlord of Debra Markos, and many thousands
of its surrounding acres. No man was more interested in the restoration
of orderly circumstances in which trade might flourish again, or more
capable of achieving them. Boustead therefore agreed to him becoming
a sort of unofficial civil Governor of Debra Markos. Though Ras Hailu
held this appointment for a very short time, the very fact of his
holding it at all made it difficult for the Emperor to punish him as he
deserved. He had played his cards very cleverly.

On Sunday the 6th of April Haile Selassie drove in triumph into
Debra Markos. He rode in the front seat of one of the trucks which
had been driven, dragged and hauled up the escarpment, and his driver
was Bimbashi Le Blanc in person. Within the truck, and hanging on
to its sides, were his chief officers, including Sandford and Wingate,
and the chief men of his court and of the Imperial bodyguard. An

[1] Boustead.

enormous crowd packed the streets, but despite the excitement of the hour they did not greet the Emperor with royalist delirium but with a decorous clapping of hands only. To the shock of long battle was added a feeling of general bewilderment at the quasi-recognition of the bastard King of Gojjam. On the same day the troops of General Cunningham enforced the surrender of Addis Ababa. The campaign was nearly finished.

The modest official ceremonies in Debra Markos included the hoisting of the Ethiopian flag by the Emperor in person, an Imperial address to the population, a durbar at which by ancient custom patriot braves ceremonially swaggered before the sovereign uttering boasts of what they had done on the field of battle, and a more modern form of court reception at which " the Emperor invited British officers into his stuffy reception room in the main building of the citadel to drink Italian champagne."[1] All these little junketings and acts of state went forward smoothly except for the speech. Wingate, (somewhat presumptuously it would appear), drafted what he considered a fitting Imperial greeting and, under the impression that the text had the Emperor's approval, he gave it in advance to the Press correspondents who duly reported it to their papers. But when the moment came for Haile Selassie to speak he used an entirely different text of his own composition. Wingate's version breathed grateful piety and Christian charity, the speech which the people of Debra Markos heard was a stern reminder of duty and more in keeping with doctrines of hell fire.[2] The disparity was not immediately discovered.

In the meantime, as soon as he could arrange it, Wingate, looking as dark and angry as he felt, summoned Bimbashi Thesiger and asked him to explain the failure of the well-laid plan at Safartak, and why he had not acted independently of the turncoat and taken the lead somehow. Thesiger explained that he and Rowe and their men and patriot followers had been in Zalleka's power, depending on him for their food. Though Wingate could hardly contain himself for rage, he accepted the explanation. He recognised that Thesiger had been placed in an impossible position.[3] Later in the month he showed the high degree of confidence he retained in this remarkable man.

Wingate's anger on this occasion was natural enough but (to be wise after the event) unreasonable. The escape of the Italian garrison from Debra Markos caused him and others to look on the battle as a missed opportunity, as a half-success. This judgment was surely at fault. It is easily forgotten that here the Italians enjoyed the best opportunity open to them in the whole course of the libera-

---

[1] Allen. [2] Akavia. [3] Thesiger.

tion of Ethiopia to launch a large and successful counter-attack. That Wingate's offensive ended in a large humbled garrison fleeing for their lives was, on any calculation at all, an astonishing military feat and in fact it was a decisive feat. All that came after it was epilogue.

With the Emperor's arrival the question of Ras Hailu needed to be, and was solved, of course in strange manner. The miscreant was required to do homage at a place outside the town, in full view, out of doors. Wingate attended the ceremony which he described later in some detail.

The dethroned usurper's last act of defiance was to keep the Emperor waiting for twenty minutes. Wingate noticed that Haile Selassie was angry at the slight, but said nothing and waited on a little knoll with the patience of his long-sighted self-control. Then at long last Ras Hailu arrived in his Italian car under guard. He got out some way off and approached on foot. He was wearing a black cloak enlivened with jewels, and gave the impression that the escort who led him under guard were a servile retinue. He walked up to the Emperor. Wingate said after that he never knew till that day what could be meant by "the grand manner." For all his premature age and his fatness Ras Hailu had the strength of a young man and a courtier-like grace which might have won the approval of Louis XIV. When he was at a fitting distance he bowed until his head almost touched the ground at the Emperor's feet and then returned to an upright posture all in one sweeping gesture. He then stood before Haile Selassie with the confident bearing of one king in conversation with another. Wingate said that the presence and dignity of the old villain were overpowering. The situation was difficult for the Emperor : he needed to show his deep displeasure but not so as to provoke the latent conflict of patriot and Hailuite. The conversation was cold and the Emperor showed his rancour by his manner rather than his words. Ras Hailu dropped hints that he had contributed to the Italian flight. The Emperor presently indicated that the audience was at an end. Ras Hailu repeated his Versailles bow and went back "with a graven scowl on his face."[1] The ceremony achieved its purpose. A little later the whole of Ras Hailu's army did homage to the Emperor. Afterwards, when he had recovered his composure, Haile Selassie expressed considerable amusement at the Ras's claim to have acted a loyal part in secret.[2]

There occurred now, for the first time in Gideon Force's campaign,

[1] George Steer : *Sealed and Delivered.*
[2] The Edinburgh Paper. Steer. Allen. Ato Gabre Maskal. Wingate's narrative (not written down by himself but from memory by others) is the main one followed.

a long lull in their activity, a time for rest such as the officers and men needed, and their commander who was suffering from a bad attack of influenza. But this was not what Wingate wanted either for himself or his men, and it only came as a result of further angry differences of opinion between him and his superiors, differences which were to have a strong and excessive influence on his ideas. To understand the story, it is necessary once again to look at the general scene.

The position of the Emperor dissatisfied himself and bothered and perplexed his British allies. At the beginning of March Brigadier Lush had visited the Emperor in Burye and had there reached a temporary agreement which he believed, and everyone else believed, would meet Haile Selassie's claims while safeguarding the responsibilities of the British command. It was agreed that Haile Selassie alone had the right to issue an "Awaj" or State proclamation, the British never to proceed beyond the issue of a "public notice." Ethiopian cases at law were to be confined to Ethiopian courts and no death sentences to be executed without the Emperor's signature. Foreign litigants or accused persons were to be tried by British courts. The British authorities undertook to consult the Emperor on all appointments of Ethiopians to Ethiopian posts, unless the exigencies of the moment made this impossible. All was for temporary conditions, and all was expressed in terms of high courtesy, but some claws appeared under the velvet. When giving advice British political officers would always seek adjustment with the views of the Emperor, but in the final issue their advice must be accepted by him.[1] The Emperor agreed on the supposition that two months at least would elapse before final decisions were taken on these matters. But in the event there was no time to negotiate further. General Cunningham found himself the victor of half Ethiopia and in possession of the capital within less than one month. After the surrender of April the 6th the Emperor wished to enter his capital forthwith. General Cunningham vigorously opposed him. The Emperor was grievously hurt and angered. General Cunningham thought the Emperor was most unreasonable.

By the surrender of Addis Ababa Sir Alan Cunningham was confronted with a frequently recurring problem of the Second World War: that of ruling and administering a large territory after an unexpectedly swift conquest. The O.E.T.A. organisation for Ethiopia was so far from ready that the General had to administer law and justice without the assistance of one legal adviser, and with only five

---

[1] Lord Rennell of Rodd: *British Military Administration in Africa*, 1941–1947, afterwards referred to as Rodd. At the time of these events Lord Rennell as Major Francis Rodd was chief deputy to Sir Philip Mitchell.

divisions in this huge country for garrison and police duties. This second difficulty led General Cunningham to a mistaken policy, as he himself candidly admitted in his despatches. There were large numbers of Italian civilians, including many women and children, in Addis Ababa, and in the terms of surrender General Cunningham insisted that the Italians should leave a sufficiency of armed men to protect this population from reprisals. The Italians left the needlessly large number of ten thousand fully equipped troops in the town and outer forts. General Cunningham had no adviser of the experience and quality of Sandford, and, commanding an army largely drawn from Kenya, he was usually given, when he sought authoritative guidance, opinions which took a low view of Ethiopians. Sandford had said from the beginning that, given adequate leadership such as the Emperor's, Ethiopians would be no more disposed to indulge in barbarous reprisal than Europeans, but his opinion was so much at variance with that of most white men in Africa (unconsciously tinged by Italian propaganda), that this eminently sensible man came to be looked on as a crank in love with a foreign country. Sandford was justified by events, and in an appalling manner. Despite their numbers the Italian troops in Addis Ababa gave way to the cruelty of hysterical panic. There were two bloody incidents, one in which the Italians opened fire on the inmates of a prison and injured or killed sixty-four people,[1] and the other a street affray in which they killed seven people and wounded fourteen. Even under such provocation there were no similar atrocities by Ethiopians on Italians.[2] After these incidents a policy was pursued of disarming the Italians and replacing them by Ethiopian police (of whom there were few) and by patriots after brief training by the few British officers and non-commissioned officers who could be spared from the continuing campaign. General Cunningham was under instructions to restore the Emperor to his capital as soon as possible but he delayed to do this until he was satisfied with the security arrangements. He was overcautious.

To the Emperor the delay was not only insulting but dangerous. The position of a sovereign returning from an enforced exile, no matter how honourable the exile, is delicate, and Haile Selassie knew that if he was excluded by a foreign army from his capital for any length of time he would suffer a fatal loss of prestige. The Emperor sent frequent messages of protest to Cunningham, always to be met by the same refusal. In desperation he declared that he would march to Addis Ababa regardless of Cunningham's wishes.

[1] Cunningham. Supplementary Report.
[2] " The Ethiopians behaved with admirable restraint, and except for minor instances of looting, no major incidents on their part took place." Cunningham. Supplementary Report.

He remembered the Brocklehurst mission, and wondered whether, under cover of liberation, the British plan was not a Colonial one after all.[1]

Sandford as before was sympathetic to the Emperor's distress, and urged firmness and moderation. Wingate was more than sympathetic, he was inflamed with anger, and he, too, remembered the Brocklehurst mission. He believed that General Cunningham was under its influence,[2] recalling that its stores of weapons and material had been made over to the Southern Army and not to Mission 101. (He seems not to have known that as a result of his own and other people's representation against the mission, Brocklehurst had been denied a Middle East post and had been sent to India, a bitterly disappointed man.) He began to imagine a conspiracy against the Emperor, the patriots, himself. In O.E.T.A., he perceived, or thought he perceived, the herald to an Ethiopia protectorate as it had been to the Palestine mandate at the end of the First World War. He came to believe that the reason that he never received air support after the battle of Burye was because the British command did not wish Gideon Force to succeed too rapidly and thus allow the Emperor to enter the capital before General Cunningham's army.[3] It is doubtful if he ever gave expression to these ideas to the Emperor in person but he told them to several people and through Makonnen Desta they surely came to the Emperor's ear. But he seems to have taken great care that Sandford should not know of his political interests. News of them, however, perhaps strengthened by memories of his pre-war tussles with authority, reached Cunningham.[4] From now on Gideon Force, very gradually at first, began to be broken up.

In these days of agitated idleness at Debra Markos Wingate's brooding spirits were probably not raised at receiving a letter from Khartoum.

31 March, '41

" Dear Wingate,

I have just returned from Keren which, as you know, we have taken after a particularly stubborn battle. The Italian positions were tremendously strong and they fought extremely hard. Never-

[1] " I had some difficulty with the Emperor on this question (Security in Addis Ababa), and he appeared distrustful of our future intentions towards him." Cunningham. Supplementary Report.

[2] Simonds.

[3] Makonnen Desta. Simonds.

[4] H.I.M. the Emperor and Brigadier Sandford have both told the writer that Wingate gave an impression of strict political correctness. That his political attitude was not " correct " is confirmed by every other witness. The fact was known to General Cunningham as the writer had suspected from reading his comments on Wingate's report, and as the General confirmed to him personally.

theless, our Commander and troops stuck it longer than they did and we inflicted very large casualties on them, at no small cost to ourselves.

When I returned to my Headquarters I found that I had to spend a large proportion of the very few hours available to me in sorting out the differences of opinion, squabbles and friction which had arisen in the Gojjam between you and Brigadier Sandford. I need hardly say that I found the state of affairs presented to me to be regrettable. Your rôle, and Brigadier Sandford's, were clearly laid down in the Minutes to a Conference held at H.Q. tps in Sudan of 12 Feb 1941, and it should be quite possible for both of you to carry out your respective tasks without these constant clashes provided you both have *the will* to co-operate.

I want you to realise that we are all fighting this war on the same side, and that these quarrels must cease. You really must for instance not address to Brigadier Sandford provocative letters some of which I have seen.

While I have every confidence in you in your allotted rôle I expect you to take every step to avoid further friction and to realise that, however much you feel the fault is not with you, it is your duty to go out of your way to put things right.

A comparison of what my troops in Eritrea have endured in the last few weeks in the way of heat, strain and casualties, might well be made with the conditions and climate of the Gojjam and should help you all to preserve a sense of proportion.

Finally, I will ask you to consider what would have happened in the last few weeks if my divisional commanders and L. of C. Commander had squabbled and written rude letters to each other instead of displaying the team-work and loyalty which ended in our victory at Keren.

Good luck to you to continue your good work.

Yours sincerely,

William Platt"

Wingate sought permission from General Cunningham to reassemble his force and move against the troops of General Nasi at Gondar, but this was refused, and Wingate again suspected the worst motives.[1] Gideon Force, he was told, was not to embark on new ventures. This

---

[1] Without saying so he strongly suggested in his report that General Cunningham made this decision because he did not wish the Emperor to gain too much prestige from the victory.

still allowed Wingate some initiative : he decided to send what remained of the Frontier Battalion to Mota, sixty miles north of Debra Markos. This place was the last Italian-held fort of Gojjam. Allen relates how he was enjoying an after-dinner conversation with Boustead on such various subjects as the Duke of Windsor, the Church hierarchy and life in the nineteen twenties, when an emergency operation instruction reached them from Wingate telling them to prepare for instant departure to the north. Next day a force of three incomplete companies[1] under Boustead set out with the few available mules and a train of sixty camels for the Chokey mountains. Though they had to go through blizzards on the high passes they only lost six camels on the journey. And then, hardly were the besiegers collected at Mota in the neighbourhood of the fort, when a wireless message came from Wingate in Debra Markos for them all to return except one platoon of Sudanese, a mortar section and two Operational centres. Those who stayed (roughly two platoons in strength) were to remain under Boustead and, in conjunction with local patriots, enforce the surrender. The fort was manned by a battalion armed with a mortar and eighteen machine-guns. In twenty-four hours Boustead had the surrender.

The rest of this wing of Gideon Force returned, cursing Wingate, to Debra Markos which they reached on the 26th April. Then they heard the explanation of their apparently senseless orders. It was connected with the dispute between the Emperor and General Cunningham which had at last reached climax and decision, by the Emperor's initiative. This curious episode had opened shortly after Boustead had left for the north.

It began on the 22nd April, sixteen days after the fall of Addis Ababa, with a telegram conveying instructions to Wingate. He was informed that General Cunningham was still not ready to receive the Emperor in the capital, and might not be ready till the 9th of May. As a result, (the telegram continued), Wingate was instructed that " the Emperor will be delayed from starting by persuasion and every means short of force until 2 Division confirm that the road is safe, which they will do," and further that " if the Emperor starts in spite of your efforts you will keep East Africa forces informed and provide adequate protection."[2] This was to put Wingate in an embarrassing position, had he been a man prone to embarrassment. It was to confront him with a painful conflict of loyalties, had he been in the least unclear as to the nature of his allegiance. But on this he was quite clear : he had asked the Emperor to give him unreserved trust, and while the Emperor was the ally of his country, he regarded himself as his loyal servant.

[1] Allen.   [2] W.P.I.

When Haile Selassie was informed of the further delay imposed on him he had no more patience. He declared that he could not accept the General's proposals and that, as the undisputed sovereign of Ethiopia, he would set out for Addis Ababa as soon as possible, instantly. He met no opposition in Debra Markos. Sandford and all the other British people in his confidence believed him to be in the right and did not hesitate to tell him so. Wingate was impassioned in his support, and felt anew all his resentment at what he believed to be the Emperor's wrongful treatment. There was only one thing he could do to strengthen Haile Selassie's resolve and he did it. Regardless of the risk of a defeat at Mota, he called back the greater part of Boustead's force so that, by the terms of his instructions, he could " provide adequate protection " on the road. Also, with sound political sense, he wanted as many as possible of Gideon Force to take part in the historic parade in Addis Ababa. General Cunningham was then informed that the Emperor was not responsive to persuasion, and the Imperial party, escorted by the troops commanded by Wingate, set out from Debra Markos on the 27th April.[1] On their way to Addis Ababa they met lorry loads of Italian prisoners of war from Mota.[2]

As Wingate's instructions had clearly implied, there could be no effective opposition to this move. The state entry into Addis Ababa took place on the 5th day of May, on the fifth anniversary of the day when an Italian army had entered as conquerors. Wingate was in charge of the procession and he did not forget the claims of Lodolf. He procured a white horse from somewhere and besought the Emperor to ride through his streets mounted on its back.[3] But the Emperor was weary of riding and was moreover a stranger to the romantic impulse. He preferred to drive in a smart open car, such as was now available after recent captures of Italian material. In consequence the white horse was ridden by Wingate at the head of the first contingent of troops, in great discomfort. He was unable to find riding-breeches or boots so he was obliged to endure the anguish of attempting elegant horsemanship wearing a pair of shorts. Conspicuous in the old-fashioned sun-helmet which had accompanied him from Palestine, he led the procession at the head of the 2nd Ethiopian Battalion, Akavia marching directly behind him with the leading officers. The Emperor's car followed leading a string of other cars in which sat his chief men

---

[1] *Akavia War Diary*. The details of the Emperor's departure from Debra Markos are not documented beyond the telegram of 22.4.41 and this diary. The episode was nowhere recorded by Wingate in writing. The account given here is drawn from recollections of verbal accounts given by Wingate to his friends, and from independent recollections of people who were in Ethiopia at the time.

[2] Allen.

[3] Akavia.

and some of the officers of Gideon Force. Last came men of the Frontier Battalion. The streets were lined by patriot fighters under Ras Ababa Aregai. The populace of Addis Ababa greeted their sovereign with violent acclaim and numerous prostrations. When the procession reached the town palace the Emperor was ceremonially greeted by Sir Alan Cunningham and a guard of the King's African Rifles. He then delivered a long and grave speech to his subjects in which he recalled the events of the last five years, describing their happy termination in words which gave no hint of recent disagreements. " While my troops," he said, " were cutting the enemy's communications and pursuing him beyond the Blue Nile. . . . I heard the happy news that the formidable armies of Great Britain had occupied our capital. . . . The army of the Sudan had smashed the enemy's strong positions at Keren. I therefore gathered my men who were scattered everywhere in pursuit of the enemy, and I am in my capital to-day." When he had retired to his personal dwelling, the new palace outside the town, he said to those about him : " *Vraiment, j'ai été très émotionné.*"[1]

The campaign was not over. The victorious two platoons of Mota were sent north to join Major Simonds's Begemder force. They arrived too late to take part in the protracted siege of Bahrdar Giorgis from which the Italians fled on the 28th of April. Instead they took part in the subsequent operations east of Lake Tana at Debra Tabor, but before their conclusion they were ordered to go farther east to Dessie to combine with the operations of the 1st South African Brigade.[2] After Mota they pass out of this story. Not so Safforce, the detachment of the Frontier Battalion under Bimbashi Johnson which continued the pursuit of the Debra Markos garrison.

The latter had an obvious objective : to reach the Italian garrison at Dessie, but the surrender of Addis Ababa left them without a road. They now had two courses of action to choose from, to go to the south-west or the north-west. They chose the second alternative and it became clear that their plan was to move by way of the well-stocked forts at Addis Derra and Agibar to Magdala which lies about a hundred and forty miles north-east of Debra Markos. From here they would have a good chance of joining hands with the Gondar garrison under General Nasi. They travelled very slowly, labouring under the difficulty of taking with them a multitude of two thousand Ethiopian women with their children in flight from patriot reprisal, and eight hundred sick people. In the panic of retreat they had provided themselves with insufficient rations for long marches. Allen described the

[1] Mrs. Christine Sandford : *The Lion Of Judah Hath Prevailed.*
[2] Cunningham. Supplementary Report. Information obtained at the War Office.

movement as a " retreat from Moscow in miniature," with Johnson and his men, who only numbered a hundred and fifty, playing the part of Denisov and his Cossacks, tormenting the retreaters with constant harassing attacks, but suffering from difficulties almost as great as beset their enemies. They were in a situation which recurred in the adventures of Gideon Force and was to recur in Wingate's subsequent campaigns : an enemy reduced to weakness pursued by avengers reduced to almost equal weakness by the boldness of their undertaking. At the end of April Major Nott took command of Safforce. Besides Johnson the officers were Bimbashis Thesiger and Riley and Lieutenants Rowe and Naylor.

For a month Safforce pursued, both the hunters and the hunted moving only a few miles a day. At the end of April, when Nott took over, the Gideon prospects brightened as the new commanding officer brought with him Ras Kassa and two thousand armed followers, but the advantage was quickly taken away. For reasons of internal politics the Emperor forbade the Ras to cross the Giamma river, and so for the moment he abandoned the fight. This was serious for the pursuing force, as the country north of the river was inhabited by a Moslem population who were on relatively good terms with the Italians. (It had been part of Fascist policy in Ethiopia to divide and conquer by favouring Moslems at the expense of Christians.) Here was one of the few places where the Italians had the favourable local conditions usually enjoyed by the liberating armies. There followed a very difficult action at the river crossing, with the Italians strongly entrenched by Addis Derra on the plateau and Nott's hundred and fifty in the gorge below. Nevertheless, Nott succeeded in harassing the Italian camp in a night attack, and finally rescued his little force from their weak position by counting on Italian unwillingness to come down and give battle. He lit camp fires in the gorge for the Italians to shell by night and while they were doing so he led his men up the escarpment. It was now the 30th of April.

By May it looked as though Gideon Force had tried to do too much, had at last attempted a gamble which they were not to win, and on the 3rd of May the Italians were stung into counter-attacking. They were thrown back by Nott, but two days later when Thesiger attempted an attack on the right flank the Italians repulsed him by successful use of their cavalry. Some patriot bands came in to help the force led by two brothers Balambaras Hapte Mariam and Balambaras Bezabe Banjo, and others led by Fitaurari Kibra Selassie and Kenyasmach Redda. On the 12th a co-ordinated attack, one of the few Gideon-Patriot actions which adhered to plan, was attempted by Riley and Kenyasmach Redda. It failed. There seemed no way of dislodging the Italians from their positions at Addis Derra. At the same time it became obvious to the men of Gideon Force that the enemy had again taken their measure and were determined not to be bluffed a second time. The pursuers were running out of food and short of ammunition. Their spirits began to sink. There was talk of abandoning the effort.

At this moment, on the 14th of May, Wingate arrived with the news that, as a result of his representations to the Emperor, Ras Kassa was coming up behind him with three thousand armed patriots and abundant provisions. Showing his extraordinary power of leadership suddenly in its natural vigour, he changed the spirit of the little force instantly. The men and officers forgot their miseries, their peril, their recent failures, and recaptured again all their old confidence that Gideon Force could accomplish miracles.[1] Those who had things to forgive Wingate, forgave him now, and some said that not till this moment in the campaign did they recognise what manner of man it was who led them. One who was there seemed to recall, years later, that he arrived riding a white horse—then corrected himself, seeing that this was a confusion with photographs of the State entry into Addis Ababa, but the mistake was eloquent. Wingate's dispositions appear in the course of the story. His immediate achievement was to throw his own fire into a dispirited force. Even though a large part of the new rations were useless to the Moslem Sudanese, (they were tins of Coptic bully beef), even though the situation remained radically the same, by the 15th of May Gideon Force was what it had been in the Debra Markos days. This was the fitting prelude to Wingate's most spectacular single achievement in Ethiopia.

Then, on the eve of action, on the 15th, orders were signalled to Wingate from General Cunningham which, if obeyed, meant breaking off the pursuit altogether. Wingate was to go to the north to join Boustead and Simonds, Nott was to go to Addis Ababa, the force itself was to go under Johnson to join the 1st South African Brigade at Dessie, avoiding battle on the way. Wingate summed up his reaction to this order later when he came to write his report : " In war," he said, " the greatest difficulty is to get the troops to the right place at the right time. It must be seldom that when this has been achieved they are then ordered away without fighting."[2]

He decided to nullify his orders by stalling. In his first reply he asked for the message to be repeated, claiming that the code groups he had received appeared to be corrupt. By a happy chance the repetition

[1] Thesiger. Nott.
[2] The reason for General Cunningham's order was that he wanted to reinforce Amba Alagi in the north and his forces in the lake area to the south, both at the expense of the 1st South African Brigade. Comments by General Cunningham on Wingate's report.

really was corrupt so he gained more time while a second repetition, duly requested, was on its way. To this he replied in a long message with which Akavia, temporarily in charge of signals, filled twelve foolscap pages of code groups. With calculated verbosity Wingate pointed out that the orders he had received were strategically unsound since the slender advantage of reinforcing the British troops at Dessie by a hundred and fifty would have to be paid for by leaving the Italians free to reinforce Dessie or Amba Alagi or Gondar, in the north, by fourteen thousand. (One may wonder why he did not see to it that some of his own messages were corrupt.) He concluded this enormous signal by assuring the General that he could guarantee to put the force opposite him out of action in ten days.[1] To this he received a reply from the General telling him that he must obey orders. Wingate then sent the last item of this remarkable correspondence referring Headquarters to his former message, and asking them to study afresh what he had said there before issuing a definitive instruction. After this ultimatum he found it politic to close down wireless communication. By now he had gained sufficient time for his purpose and was in the thick of his last action in Ethiopia, the battle for Agibar.

Wildly exaggerated news of an enormous invasion by patriot forces reached the Italians soon after Wingate's arrival, and on the 16th they evacuated Addis Derra and made for Agibar, thirty miles to the north. At four o'clock in the afternoon Gideon Force occupied the abandoned town. "From the summit of the fort," Wingate wrote afterwards, "I watched (the Italian) column, nearly eighteen miles long, disappear into the 5,000-foot canyon, and climb the far side." The pursuit was undertaken immediately.

The fort of Agibar and its subsidiary fortlet of Wogghidi are situated in a landscape of grotesque fantasy. The tributary rivers of the Nile, that is the Ghenneli, Yasum, Boto and Uolaka, and their extinct fellows, have fashioned the earth's surface here into a strange pattern of gorge and highland, tablelands separated by deep canyons and sometimes joined by slender ridges at their own height. These are usually not more than a few hundred yards across. The action was dominated by this nightmarish geography and all the natural advantages were with the defenders.

On the 17th Thesiger was sent forward with a hundred men of Gideon Force and three hundred of Ras Kassa's patriots with instructions to get behind the Italians as far north as he could and then attack. Wingate meanwhile would lead the rest of the force with Johnson in a

---

[1] The gist of the message as remembered by Thesiger and Akavia conforming with information obtained at the War Office.

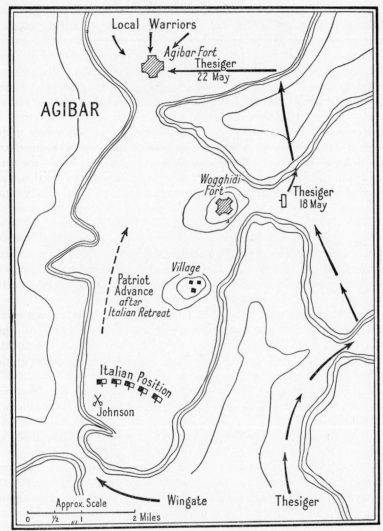

Local Warriors

Agibar Fort
Thesiger
22 May

AGIBAR

Wogghidi
Fort

Thesiger
18 May

Patriot
Advance
after
Italian Retreat

Village

Italian Position

Johnson

Approx. Scale

0   ½   1   2 Miles

Wingate   Thesiger

The Battle for Agibar

synchronised attack from the south at the southernmost end of the
five-mile long tableland below Agibar. At two in the morning Thesiger
set out with only two days' rations and no transport. He was attacked
by hostile Gallas in Italian service on the way but reached the ridge
due east of Wogghidi by the evening of the 18th.   On the

19th he sent an ultimatum to the Galla garrison in that fort (they numbered twelve hundred), and the same day he found it deserted and occupied it.

In the meantime Wingate, starting five hours after Thesiger, had moved to a southern position. He had with him the remains of a Frontier Battalion company under Johnson, a mortar section, an Ethiopian mortar platoon, and twelve hundred of Ras Kassa's patriots. Though the difficulties of rapid marching through this country were extraordinary, so much so that it took them five hours to descend into the Boto river bed, he and his men were on the main escarpment (south-west of that on which Wogghidi stands), by the night of the 17th. Before dawn of the 18th Johnson was on top of the Wogghidi tableland, exchanging shots with Italian patrols before first light.

With day the southern and main Italian position on the tableland could be seen in detail from Wingate's camp. Between him and them was a ridge or " panhandle " as they called the joins, beyond which, about a mile and a half within the tableland, the Italians were deployed in a mile-wide crescent. Wingate's plan was to attack this Italian forward position at nightfall, Johnson and his company with three hundred patriots to get round the left flank, while two other patriot forces closed in simultaneously on the right and the front. Ras Kassa's braves seem to have fought with more resolution than others of the irregular armies, but they had little training and attacked or retreated as the mood took them. Their attacks on the right and the front could do little in the face of Italian machine-guns and their spontaneous charges and rushings hither and thither often blocked the Sudanese line of fire. They put Johnson and his men under a crippling handicap. But they showed sustained courage and this had a decisive effect on what happened.

In the daytime of the 18th the Italians counter-attacked but they foolishly went against the strongest point, where Johnson and his Sudanese company opposed them. In the confusion caused by patriots in flight and running they knew not whither, Johnson could do little, but the Italians did not succeed in doing what they wanted, driving their attackers down the gorge or forcing them into the panhandle where they were at the mercy of machine-gun fire.

By nightfall of the 18th the Sudanese were exhausted and Wingate took them out of the battle. The patriots had taken up such haphazard and untraceable positions by now that nothing could be done to extricate them.[1] They lay hidden around the Italian lines, sometimes

[1] During this action Johnson's casualties were 1 killed, 40 wounded, and the patriots' 40 killed, 100 wounded.

within three hundred yards of machine-gun posts, and there they stayed throughout the 19th. There were patriot sniping attacks on the Italians all that day but no counter-move by the Italians. On the 20th the Italians had gone.

Wingate ordered a general advance. Before his part of Gideon Force could reach the Wogghidi tableland, the patriots had caught up with the northward-bound Italians and they attacked them fiercely, and in their usual disorganised way, throughout the 20th, suffering more than a hundred and fifty killed and four hundred wounded. For the moment the situation looked bad again. On this occasion Italian withdrawal had not been merely another panic flight. This time they had a purpose : to demolish the northern wing of Gideon Force under Thesiger.

Wogghidi fort which Thesiger had occupied the day before was not easily defended from the west, south or north, as it faced the eastern panhandle and was designed for defence from eastern attack. So he moved to a village a mile and a half to the south standing on high ground. Here the Italians put in a large-scale attack, their last attack on Gideon Force. Having shelled the village they charged in from the south-west and the south and threatened the eastern side with their cavalry. Thirty-six of Thesiger's patriot force were killed and both officers wounded, Thesiger lightly but Lieutenant Rowe seriously. He was forced back across the north-eastern panhandle to his original position of the 18th and the Italians recaptured Wogghidi fort. Among those taken prisoner was Rowe. But this setback was already being offset by the ingenious initiative of Wingate.

The German theory that war is the continuation of diplomacy by other means is well known. In the difficult and confused situation of this action Wingate decided that diplomacy must now serve as the continuation of battle. Through his wireless he received no more messages from his superiors, as said, but he did hear the news, and the events of the 19th suggested a new course of action to him. On the 20th he sent a letter to Colonel Maraventano under a flag of truce. He found a peasant to act as his messenger and counted out a hundred Ethiopian dollars into his hand and promised him the same again if he should return.[1] The letter read as follows :

"19th May 1941.
To the Commander of the Italian Forces between Addis Derra and Agibar.
From the Commander, British and Ethiopian Forces.

[1] Wingate Report.

1. Since our last encounter at Debra Markos I have been engaged on the difficult task of organising your ex-Colonial troops into guerilla brigades. One of these, led by Ras Kassa, I have brought with me from Addis Ababa. Two more are on the way from Fiche.

2. In addition to these guerilla forces, a patriot contingent two thousand strong has just reached me from Bichena, accompanied by a Sudan unit under British officers.[1]

3. As you are no doubt aware, the Duke of Aosta and his army have surrendered to-day to the British Forces at Amba Alagi.

4. I have been ordered to withdraw all British personnel from your neighbourhood during the rainy period, leaving the conduct of the operations against you to the very considerable guerilla forces under Ras Kassa and the Crown Prince who are now assembling round you. W/T sets will be left to call for air support when this is available. This is likely to be sooner than we expected owing to the fall of Amba Alagi.

    I linger here for perhaps twenty-four hours more only in the hope that you will decide not to sacrifice needlessly the lives of so many brave men who have been in the field for so many months suffering privation. If you refuse this last offer, control passes out of my hands.

5. If I receive no reply from you within twelve hours I shall know what to think.

O. C. Wingate. Colonel."

The answer arrived on the same day.

" To the Commander, British and Ethiopian Forces.
From the Commander, Italian troops between Addis Derra and Agibar.

1. The Duke of Aosta surrendered after heroic resistance as your forces were much superior to his.

2. I have picked up one of your officers[2] who was badly wounded. I have not got the necessary bandages and medicines for his proper treatment. Will you please send us the necessary medicines and bandages for treating wounded.

3. Until all my ammunition is exhausted and only one round is left there is no question of surrender. As you too are soldiers you will understand what I mean.

---

[1] It is impossible to trace these reinforcements.
[2] Lieutenant Rowe.

4. As regards the brigades that you said are coming, please note that before retiring we will fight them fiercely, even if they are superior to us. Danger, privation and fatigue we Italian soldiers will bear for the honour and grandeur of our motherland.

5. As I cannot surrender without the permission of my superior Commander, I will send your letter to him by W/T. He is the only man who can order me to surrender. If I get an answer from the supreme commander I will send it on to you. Will you please send the same messenger to-morrow, the 21st.

Saverio Maraventano. Colonel."

On the 21st Wingate sent as follows :

"To the Commander, Italian Forces between Addis Derra and Agibar.
From the Commander, British and Ethiopian Forces.

1. I have received your reply to my letter and note that you are referring its contents to your superior officer for his decision.
With regard to the point you raise relating to the duty of a soldier to fight to the last round, that is, of course, thoroughly appreciated by me and my officers. Commonsense, however, must be applied, and, in the circumstances, you may well be described as having arrived at the point where surrender not only implies no disgrace but is the duty of a commander who has the welfare of his troops at heart.

3. Continuing to hold out after I and my officers have handed over the command to the patriot forces I referred to would not be to perform a service to your country. The guerilla forces which I have referred to will remain in the field regardless of what happens elsewhere, and, as you can well believe from your knowledge of this country, the majority of them are not employable in other regions. Thus your continued resistance will merely make you the prey of these forces without in the least assisting the resistance of your fellow countrymen in other parts of Ethiopia or elsewhere. The troops that we can use elsewhere will, in any case, be used elsewhere It has been part of my duties to secure this.

To sum up, your continued resistance is not only of no use to your country but will be cruel and inhuman to the men who have fought so long and so bravely under your command.

4. As regards detailed arrangements for your surrender and accommodation, should such be authorised, we can arrange these by wireless or by runner the moment the main point is decided on. Until I hear from you to-morrow I do not propose to make any major attack upon you, provided I receive a definitive answer from you by 1500 hours.

O. C. Wingate. Colonel.

P.S.—Reference medical comforts for the wounded officer you refer to, I will, of course, supply these if you will state the nature of his injuries and his name."

The real situation was very different from what Wingate conveyed to Maraventano. The only patriot forces still keen for battle were some of the local Moslem people to whom the Italians had in desperation issued seven thousand rifles and who, after the news from Amba Alagi, began to turn against them. But the numbers of the Ras Kassa patriots had dwindled through desertions since the actions of the 19th and 20th, and they were nearly at the end of their ammunition. At the same time there was no further effort by the patriot leaders who had joined at Addis Derra. Kibra Selassie and Redda seem to have faded out of the story with Hapte Mariam and the gallant Banjo. Wingate's letters were the most stupendous bluff of this campaign of bluff.

In conformity with the promise contained in his second letter, Wingate sent Riley to Thesiger on the 21st telling him not to undertake any offensive operation but to guard the eastern panhandle. An answer came from Agibar.

"From the Commander of the Italian forces between Agibar and Addis Derra.
To the Commander of the British Forces of the same area.

The High Command has allowed me to cease hostilities.

In order to avoid further shedding of blood on either side, as proposed by yourself, I will discontinue the fight on the conditions that the terms are honourable, and worthy of the troops who have fought bravely and victoriously to the last moment.

Since there are many points to be discussed and on which to form a mutual agreement, I pray that you will let me know the place, the day and the hour for our representatives to meet.

S. Maraventano, Colonel."

There were two negotiations in neither of which Wingate took part personally. One was conducted by Nott with Colonel Nuovo, the other by Thesiger with Maraventano. Both were ultimately successful. The surrender took place on the 23rd.

The whole number of people who came over numbered ten thousand, of whom two thousand (except for one European) were Ethiopian women and children.[1] Wingate told afterwards that this was the most alarming moment of the battle, for now at the last moment the bluff might be called by the whole of this Italian army assembled in the presence of the minute and weary force which had tricked it into surrender. It seems that they came out to surrender passing from the tableland across the eastern panhandle, delivering their arms where it meets the main escarpment. The description Wingate gave is remarkable. (Allowance has to be made for faulty statistics as he was writing before they could be accurately compiled.) " Across a level plain," he related in his report, " sloping towards a hidden valley, the Italian commander and his staff of thirty officers advanced on horseback. Behind them came eight hundred Fascists, and then phalanx upon phalanx of Colonial troops (who did not want to surrender)[2] with their two hundred and fifty Italian officers, and their guns, mortars, machine-guns and three million rounds of small arms ammunition. Altogether 14,000 men marched in order of battle, while to receive them stood thirty-six Sudanese. These formed five lanes through which the enemy poured laying down his arms in heaps, reformed in units, and passed on over the edge to the valley where they found myself with Ras Kassa and a few patriots ; but their arms already lay piled under guard of our Brens." As the commander and his staff arrived at the surrender point a guard composed of ten men " did a ragged present arms."[3]

The first care was to send Lieutenant Rowe by car to Addis Ababa hospital. He was still alive when he reached there but died of his wounds very soon after. On the 24th the ten thousand prisoners began the first stage of their journey to the Ethiopian capital, and the events of that march, or rather its uneventful progress, are greatly to the credit of the Ethiopian guards, and of Wingate himself. This was one of many occasions when he showed that his leadership was not only that of the battlefield. For on the day that the long procession set out, he first issued a solemn order and appeal to the patriots, reminding them of their duty as Christians to treat their prisoners with

[1] 1,100 Italian troops, 7,000 Colonial troops including muleteers and servants, 2,000 native women and children.
[2] This is very doubtful judging by the amount of desertion throughout all theatres of the campaign.
[3] Nott.

forbearance and humanity, and this order was obeyed scrupulously. Bimbashi Johnson and his company led and Wingate and Nott and thirty men brought up the rear, but inevitably the main duty of the guard devolved on Ras Kassa's patriots, and they vindicated those, like Sandford, who had long asserted that the Ethiopians were not a barbarian people. Desertion from the patriot hordes was easy, and difficult to detect, and when they had left the Wollo highlands, the Italians were obliged to go through country where they had made their name execrated. Yet in the march of nearly two hundred miles from Agibar to Addis Ababa there was only one bad incident, and this incident was in no way the responsibility of the patriots with Gideon Force. Two Italian stragglers were murdered by peasants after the column had passed down the road. In a national campaign of liberation, such as was conducted in France three years later, such calamities became so commonplace as to be hardly noticed.

They reached Addis Derra on the 26th. The next day the column was joined by Bimbashi Thesiger with the last prisoners rounded up from the neighbourhood of Agibar. On the 29th they reached Fiche where those entitled to bear arms had to relinquish them, and the column paused for a rest of five days. The Emperor insisted that the prisoners must march past him as he sat on a throne. Colonel Maraventano and his European officers protested against this debasement but they were told that it was not against any term of surrender agreed on, and that they must obey. Before this impressive and repulsive ceremony took place, however, Wingate left Gideon Force and drove to Addis Ababa with Major Nott on the 1st of June. At three o'clock that afternoon they attended the funeral of Lieutenant Rowe. Afterwards they reported to General Wetherall who was in command of British troops in the capital. The General had grave news for Wingate. Gideon Force no longer existed. Its troops were to be dispersed and used as opportunity offered. It could no longer claim a staff. Wingate no longer had a command.[1] He was under orders to fly to General Cunningham's Headquarters at Harar the next day, or as soon as there was a place in an aeroplane, and from there he would be sent on to Cairo. All success is an anticlimax but this was something beyond expectable experience.

He took his disappointment in good part—at first. He presented himself to the Emperor to say good-bye. Haile Selassie placed a little house at his disposal and later sent him gifts by the hand of his secretary; a gold chain collar, his signed photograph and for Akavia a watch with his embossed monogram ; also a case of champagne. The Imperial secretary showed some emotion. " This," he said in a voice choked

---

[1] Information obtained at the War Office.

with tears, as he pointed to the gifts, "this is not what the Emperor of Ethiopia would wish to give to Colonel Wingate in return for all that he has done, but in the present distressed state of the country this is all he can give."

The Emperor's gratitude showed a true understanding of what Wingate had done. Without Gideon Force to bestow on it a victorious character, Haile Selassie's return to Ethiopia might not have terminated in the undisputed restoration from which his country was to obtain great benefits. The military brilliance of Wingate's achievement has been sufficiently indicated already. Its difficulties would have been enormous even had he been furnished with the pick of the army and been allowed to act within a sensible administrative framework. As it was, he accomplished what he did with soldiers of whom many were unfitted for this kind of task, with defective equipment, with the worst of transport, and with the disadvantages of divided authority and no air support. The strain imposed by these circumstances was enough to break any man's spirit, and it nearly broke his.

He said good-bye to Chapman Andrews and to Sandford. His last words to Sandford were : "The fighting is over. My job is finished and I'm off. It's your turn now."[1]

When he said good-bye to Nott he told him that he was going to take a few days' rest in Harar and then report to General Headquarters in Cairo as soon as he could. He said that once in Cairo he intended to worry the authorities into allowing him back into Palestine with the object of raising a Jewish army.

The next day Wingate flew to Harar where he was ordered to present himself to General Cunningham. The latter demanded an explanation of his disobedience at Addis Derra. He gave it, and it was accepted.[2] As things had turned out Wingate had been perfectly vindicated and Cunningham acknowledged the fact. Nevertheless, the General was anxious that Wingate should go away. This was not, as has been said, because he was frivolously irritated at Wingate's independence of mind, or at the disregarded order, or at his unorthodox soldiering, but because he had been told that Wingate was prone to political intrigue and had some evidence of it from the events of Debra Markos in April.[3] On the 11th of May there had occurred the "affair of the seven ministers" when the Emperor as a display of independence (and a highly successful one), appointed seven ministers without reference to British authority.[4] It was believed that the Emperor's British advisers had encouraged him. It is unlikely that Wingate was involved in this particular matter, or he would surely

[1] Sandford.   [2] Wingate Report.   [3] Cunningham.
[4] Rodd. Mitchell.

have said so at some time, but the incident had served to arouse authority anew to their perennial dislike of political enthusiasts outside political professions, and Wingate was precisely such a man as they disapproved.

He left Harar for Khartoum and flew to Cairo arriving there in the first week of June. He took a room in the Continental Hotel.

CHAPTER XIV

DISASTER AND A RETURN
TO LIFE

No ONE who saw Wingate receiving the surrender of the garrison at Agibar could have guessed that he was on the edge of the most calamitous month of his whole life, of a period when failure seemed to close on him for ever.

On the 31st of May Hugh Boustead wrote a letter which followed Wingate to Cairo. In the course of saying good-bye Boustead reminded the other how, at the senior commanders' conference in December, he had prophesied a German attack on Greece, and that this had since come to pass, while at the same time an Axis effort from within was reported from all the Middle East countries. Boustead, who had evidently not heard of Wingate's orders to report to Middle East Headquarters, went on to tell his commander (who was never his friend), that his duty now lay outside Ethiopia.

"Come out," he wrote, "of these mountain fastnesses where all of importance is over, as fast as you can get, and go to where your services and experience and other qualities will be of the greatest value to the Empire and the Army. Time is short, the blitz is swift and these moves against Palestine, Syria, Egypt and Iraq are already in process of their swift and detailed preparation of which the Germans are absolute masters. So do not delay in what is now a minor theatre here, or you will be too late and the hurricane will already have swept over the real Middle East before you reach it."

The letter indicates plainly enough one reason why Wingate was not loudly acclaimed on his return to Cairo. The British cause lay under terrible defeat. The Germans had invaded Greece and Yugoslavia on the 8th of April, four days after the fall of Debra Markos to Gideon Force, two days after the fall of Addis Ababa to Cunningham. These achievements in Ethiopia counted as nothing beside what followed the Nazi attack on the Balkans. By a stroke of political genius according to some, by an act of incredible military and political folly according to others, a British army landed in the Balkans, and there followed a disaster comparable to and (according to some) more ruinous than that of Dunkirk. The loss of material put back any possibility of an allied recovery, let alone victory, by many months. All our gains in the Western Desert were sacrificed to the Greek venture, and the Germans obtained an airbase in Crete. Men who had lived through the retreat from France in a spirit of defiant exaltation began to believe in the possibility of Britain losing the war now. It is not surprising that at such a moment the victor of distant, paltry, unknown Agibar should have been little noticed when he returned.

On reporting to his head office in General Headquarters he was welcomed with an instruction to revert to the rank of major. As for an account of his stewardship no one seemed in a hurry to have that. In the press of other preoccupations relatively few people in G.H.Q. outside his department had heard the bare name of Gideon Force, and within the department there was not the eagerness he expected for details of the little devoted band which had precipitated a revolt and vanquished an army.[1]

On the 16th of June Wingate was joined in Cairo by Major Simonds who brought with him his own considerable grievances. Little has been said of the able and energetic campaign of Begemder force for it lies outside Wingate's own experience. In its last stages it had received orders similar to those which came to Addis Derra. On the 17th of May Simonds supported by Boustead and a force of five thousand patriots was on the verge of capturing the garrison of Debra Tabor. On the 18th of May Simonds was told to hand over to Boustead and go at once to Cairo, by way of Dessie, in order to take up an urgently needed staff appointment in General Headquarters. Two days later Boustead was ordered to go with his men of the Frontier Battalion to Dessie. The orders were obeyed. The patriots lost heart and the battle for Debra Tabor was abandoned. On arrival at Cairo Simonds was told that the staff appointment to which he had been called had been filled in the meantime. He and Wingate found themselves trudging the corridors together, going from office to office of G.H.Q., on fruitless errands. They felt that they were not only unwanted but objects of dislike. They were both ill. Simonds was recovering from jaundice and Wingate was in the first stages of an attack of malaria.[2] Both diseases have devastating effects on the mind and feelings.

Wingate was in the mood to dwell on his grievances of the last eight months. Many of them were just. He remembered the obstruction he had encountered when he first took up his appointment to Mission 101, the negligent distribution of arms, and an unforgettable truck

---

[1] Simonds.
[2] Simonds. A communication and his *Brief Narrative of Begemder Force*.

issued to Simonds in Khartoum without tyres or spare parts. He remembered how after Burye he had never been given air support, and Simonds came to remind him how the same thing had happened in the north throughout the campaign. He brooded on the orders which had nearly robbed him of his most spectacular success, and had robbed Simonds of victory at Debra Tabor. He had a new and oppressive grievance in the present. Against familiar walls of correctitudinist obstruction he was trying, so far in vain, to obtain monetary awards for his men in compensation for the hardships they had undergone. These "hard-lying allowances," as they are called in Army language, were being refused on the grounds that the claims had not been put in at the appropriate time, and that the hardships of Gideon Force had been no severer than those of other troops operating in Italian East Africa or the Mediterranean theatres. The first argument was an intolerable instance of fussy clerical ungenerosity, the second was contrary to the honourable traditions which govern the employment of volunteers in irregular tasks. It was entirely against the facts. Sometimes in the short lulls following the evacuation of Italian towns Gideon Force had lived in plenty and even luxury, but more often they had lived on "food and drink that rot the guts," and never on the rations that were their due and were usually a hundred miles behind the men, loaded on slow-moving and stricken camels. Often the men had undergone long marches without food of any kind. One day in Headquarters Simonds was informed that the claim for hard-lying allowances was "inadmissible," since Gideon Force, having operated *behind* the enemy lines, could not be classified as a "unit *in* the field." Wingate began to suspect a conspiracy against himself and everything he represented.[1]

It is difficult to say precisely what turn his ideas took for he gave contradicting accounts about this part of his life, but it seems that in these days of frustration and disappointment, he gradually came to the idea that he was being persecuted because he stood for Ethiopian independence against a deep-laid plot to incorporate that country within the British Empire. He never forgot the Brocklehurst mission; he continued to connect it in his mind with the maladroit diplomacy of O.E.T.A., and with the sneers at "native Empires" which he had heard from Kenya men—to form a grizzly and irresistible picture of a vast betrayal. It has been noted that in the early days of the Ethiopian campaign he made military mistakes because he applied too many Palestine lessons too literally to another terrain. It seems probable that he began to do the same thing in the sphere of politics.

[1] Wingate Report, June, 1941. Correspondence, Wingate-Airey, September 1941. W.P.I. Simonds.

For Ethiopia he read the National Home, for O.E.T.A. he read the Woodhead Report. He believed that he had abundant evidence for all his supposals.

By the time Simonds arrived Wingate had nearly finished writing his "appreciation" of Gideon Force's operation. Simonds helped in its completion and added an appendix of his own on Begemder Force. The whole thing was done by the 23rd of June. This report became famous or at least notorious.

It is not a wild coarsely-worded document, as has been made out; on the contrary, it is direct, factual, well-argued in the main, superior in this respect to some others of his many memoranda. But it contained sufficient injudicious matter to allow Wingate's many enemies to burke all its recommendations. It was a moment for tact, but in his boiling indignation Wingate had no time for that. He wrote in a rage, and as enraged people do he sometimes became illogical and put himself in the wrong.

In shape the report was thoroughly unconventional. The main paper was not a narrative but more in the nature of an essay on guerilla-force theory. He opened with a brief statement of Gideon Force's achievement in which he estimated his prisoners with fair accuracy at sixteen thousand three hundred and twenty. This was followed by a section of about two thousand words on his general theory in which he contrasted the Lawrence technique of distributing as many arms as possible to potential insurgents, with his own theory of withholding arms from men until they had proved themselves. His theory was illustrated by the Gulit episode,[1] though here he put it forward as an illustration without much suggestion that it really happened. It was in the middle of this section that there occurred the first of those passages that gave the report half of its bad name. He wrote "Given a population favourable to penetration, a thousand resolute and well-armed men can paralyse, for an indefinite period, the operation of a hundred thousand. But the qualities of both men and commander must be of the highest. It is useless to select the scum of an army, as was done in the case [of Gideon Force]." There can be no doubt that some of the personnel of Gideon Force had joined not as volunteers but as victims, and not respectable ones, of regimental purges, and Wingate was right to protest against such methods of recruitment. But to do so by using such language as this was not only unfair to the force as a whole, but made nonsense of much of his subsequent argument.

This section ended with three well-written paragraphs which are of particular interest as they are the only ones in this version of the report

[1] See page 291.

to express his besetting, fallacious and generous political ideas.

" Cynicism in this war will defeat us, but it is very prevalent in our councils. Neither the Eritrean campaign, nor that of East Africa Force could have succeeded without the patriot support. In fact, at least double the forces would have been required, and the progress would have been much slower. This statement is capable of proof in detail.

"We owed this success to the fact that Ethiopians believed our propaganda. They now begin to think (and their change of opinion is the consequence of our action) that we deliberately deceived them for gain. That so long as it was advantageous to us, we preached liberty to the captives, and that now that there seems something to be gained by offering to replace the chains we can see no objection to doing so.

" If Ethiopia, always suspicious of white Imperialisms, thinks this to-day, the world will find cause to think it to-morrow, and we shall lose at one blow the potential support of millions. The enemy foretold the present apparent trend of our policy. He was not believed. To-day he is believed ; not only when he says that we are equally prepared to annex Ethiopia, or hand it back to him as appeasement, but when he says that our cause is merely that of an Imperialism weaker than that of the Axis. Righteousness exalteth a nation."

Though he was careful to represent British Colonial ambition in Ethiopia as an enemy allegation, he made it clear that he believed the allegation was true.

The next sections were called " Modus Operandi," " Preparation," and " Commands and Staff." In them he considered in another two thousand words the selection, training and composition of such a unit as Gideon Force, with frequent reference to its purpose and objectives. He very justly complained of the absence of all effective liaison with the R.A.F. He made no allowance for the fact that in the desperate war situation of that spring there was a shortage of aircraft which jeopardised every British campaign, but there can be no doubt that he was right to emphasise the lack of combined effort which, in great actions and small ones, remained a British weakness till late in the war. Gideon Force never needed much air support, would certainly have got less than they asked for, but deserved to be given something more than nothing. Longmore's promise to Sandford was made before the calamity in Greece. By now Longmore had gone.

He complained, again with justice, that he was ill served regarding radio signal equipment. It was a common complaint in the army, and his statement (in an appendix) that the first transmitting set supplied to Gideon Force had a broken transmitter key, no petrol reserve, and no distilled water for the batteries, will find an echo in many memories.

He followed this up with bitter criticism of his signalling staff and expressed indignation anew at the way his officers and N.C.O.s had been selected. Yet in a later section he was to plead vehemently for hard-lying allowances and an immediate award of decorations, adding a strong protest against the dissipation of the force. William Allen justly remarked of him: "The same fervour that made him goad men . . . insisted later that their courage be recognised." Unfortunately people in authority, unfriendly to Gideon Force (and there were many such), found it only too easy to contest these pleas on the grounds of what Wingate himself had said about the scum of an army.

After the three sections on selection, training and composition, he moved to a consideration of weapons and material. (This has little interest for a general reader to-day.) After this came a section on " Tactical Employment " with two sub-sections, one on the correct military relationship of regular and irregular forces, and the second one unexpectedly, but logically, on the subject of propaganda. He had a good understanding of propaganda, and with perspicacity he pointed out the mistakes consequent on forgetfulness of his sound rule that propaganda to Ethiopia should have been based throughout on the story of David and Goliath. Though he had some cause for dissatisfaction here, this section was written with moderation and even good humour. The paper concluded with a proposal for the formation of a large guerilla brigade. This, he suggested, should have its own R.A.F. wing, and be based either on the Tibesti mountains for operations against Libya, or on Palestine for operations against the Caucasus. (He made only a light, hardly noticeable reference to the possible employment of Jews.)

Attached to the report were six Appendices of which the first was a narrative of the main force's adventures under Wingate's personal command. In a normal despatch this would have formed the principal item. It is very brief, and, considering that it was written from memory, reliable. Its merit as a historical record must have been considerable before it was superseded by William Allen's book. He was unduly grudging in his praise of others. In the whole of his report he singled out for personal tribute only Boustead, Harris, Johnson, Akavia and Regimental Sergeant Major Grey, and that very briefly. For Sandford he had nothing but implied contempt for inefficiency. But though he glossed over some mistakes (not only his own), he nowhere misrepresented the course of events. Nor did he indulge in even the most permissible vanity. Without ornamenting facts he could have made much more of his brilliant success at Agibar. He always believed himself to be acting impersonally as the instrument of fate.

He made the mistake of putting in witticisms. Some of these were of a high order. On the subject of the military tendency to respect theory rather than the lessons of experience, he wrote: " This is natural in a profession which rarely practises, and whose commanders learn most of their art in dummy operations which are in war what dummy operations would be in medicine: fruitful sources of false doctrine and orthodoxy." But others were mere schoolboy abuse. Of the dispersal of Gideon Force he wrote: " To dissipate such a military organism after it has been created and while the need for it still exists, or to suppose that you get equal results from the employment of equal numbers in sporadic operations, is the mark of the military ape."

When the report was finished, but before it had been sent in, Wingate met a friend of Palestine days, Dudley Clarke, who was in charge of a department in General Headquarters. It may have been that Wingate had gone to the stencilling office to collect copies, but at all events they met one morning when Wingate had copies with him. He gave one to Dudley Clarke and asked him to read it and give an opinion. That evening Dudley Clarke called at the Continental Hotel. He found Simonds who told him that Wingate was in bed feeling too ill to come down. Dudley Clarke gave Simonds his opinion: that the report would be badly received both in G.H.Q. and the War Office because of the excessively personal tone in which it was written. He strongly urged that it should be revised with this in mind. The advice was not taken, but it proved sound.

The report was not at all well received in G.H.Q., but it reached the Commander-in-Chief without delay. It seems that the main paper and some of the appendices were sent in on the 18th of June, the rest to follow. Sir Archibald Wavell recorded the occasion: " When it [the Gideon Force expedition] was all over he [Wingate] sent to my headquarters a memorandum that would almost have justified my placing him under arrest for insubordination. My staff were, to put it mildly, pained at its tone. I sent for Wingate and had out with him as man to man the grievances he had voiced. Some were misunderstandings, a few were real and could be remedied, some more were imaginary. That was the last time I saw him in the Middle East—he bore evidence of the great strain to which he had been subjected."[1]

The subsequent events have been represented as a struggle between authority and a rebel. Such they were but their course was not simple. While Sir Archibald Wavell was irritated by the abusiveness of the report, and told Wingate so, he was impressed by the revelation it contained of negligence and incapacity in certain fields. At their interview, he went through all the points that Wingate had raised, in full detail, and then, with regard to those matters which were of

[1] Wavell. Introduction to *Wingate's Raiders* by Charles Rolo.

continuing importance, he ordered inquiries to be made.[1] It can readily be imagined with what anger it was learned in the quarters concerned that Wingate's improperly worded report had become the starting point of a post-mortem inquiry likely to be of a damaging kind. It cannot be shown that there was an instinctive drawing together of imperilled seniors in a common purpose to defeat the inquiry, but such would be the way of a General Headquarters, and the evidence of later events points strongly to this likely happening. Wingate's enemies had an advantage which he had given them. Owing to its " explosive " nature the report was not given the usual wide circulation of such papers, and was thus only known to a few people in a few departments.[2] Then, before the inquiry was under way, the enemies obtained a decisive advantage. The days when Sir Archibald Wavell was without critics had long since passed; rightly or wrongly he had many now. On the 21st of June he was told by the Prime Minister that he was to be replaced by Sir Claude Auchinleck. In less than a fortnight he left Cairo. In the commotion of the change and of the assumption of his duties by the in-coming General, the inquiry died a natural and rapid death. Even the one question on which Sir Archibald Wavell had given a ruling, that of the hard-lying allowances, was shelved in the hope that it would lapse.

All this time Wingate was ill with malaria. He would not go for treatment to any doctor in the Royal Army Medical Corps. He feared that once on an official sick-list, he would be taken off the strength of G. (R.) and, in strict accordance with King's Regulations, put into the reserve " pool " of officers, doubtless to be sent away on recovery to some remote staff employment out of harm's way. As the authorities could only take such a measure after twenty-eight days of illness, and as G.(R.) would certainly and effectively have intervened in his favour, his fears were somewhat fantastic, but they served, unfortunately for himself, to make him act in keeping with his irremediable distrust of all authority. Then, on the 27th of June,[3] he did an ill-advised thing. He went to a local civilian doctor who seems to have been a practitioner of outstanding incompetence, for having diagnosed malaria this man gave Wingate a large supply of atabrin without warning him of the dangers of that powerful drug. Wingate found the atabrin effective in lowering his temperature and took it unheedingly and to excess. By now he spent most of his day in bed, at times rousing his strength to get up and find his way painfully to hated G.H.Q. He was often to be seen walking through the hall of the Continental Hotel, pale, much

[1] Simonds.
[2] Airey. This seems to be the origin of a legend mentioned in *Gideon Goes To War* to the effect that the report was burned.
[3] Report by G. W. B. James.

thinner than in any later photograph of him, gloomy beyond description, but with the glare of the blue eyes quite undimmed.[1]

Among the officers often to be found in the hotel there was a man whom Wingate knew slightly through Chapman Andrews. He was called Colonel Thornhill. He was a lifelong friend of Sir Archibald Wavell and very much a character of G.H.Q. In the Turf Club or the Continental he was a familiar evening spectacle, bustling hither and thither armed with an enormous knobkerrie, invariably attended by the tall monocled moustachio'd figure of his Staff officer Major Metherell, and more often than not occupied in loud-voiced argument while dispensing cocktails and whiskies to his wide circle of friends. He was a very amiable, garrulous, indiscreet person. He had a curious weakness: an indefatigable busybody, he was ever inclined to do other people's work for them, and sometimes seemed to prefer it to his own. He was one who literally could not resist being " in " every event that came his way, and the idea that he sometimes interfered where he had no business was one that never crossed his mind. His weakness was to prove of the utmost value soon. He lived at the Continental Hotel, and had the room next to Wingate.[2]

In these hot days of wretchedness three bitter thoughts dug continually into Wingate's mind: the injustice to his men, the injustice to Ethiopia, and the ingratitude and neglect of himself. He described his feelings later. " Things had often been difficult in the past, but I always believed that nothing could blot out real achievement, and that good work done in a spirit of truth could never utterly be cast away. When I went to Cairo I was quite confident that what the Patriots had succeeded in doing, and I with them, would ensure for us both, justice and a fair field for our endeavours. It was not so. I watched arrangements being made to deprive Haile Selassie of his self-respect and large parts of his country; and as for me, nobody knew or cared what became of me."

As his thinking became confused in illness, and then began to enter a stage of fantasy under the influence of atabrin, he began to brood more and more on what he believed was the British betrayal of liberated Ethiopia, and from this a strange chimera began to take shape in his mind: that he had a duty to lay down his life as a sacrifice to insulted ideals. He expressed it thus himself: " I thought our treatment of Ethiopia cold and tyrannical, and our talk of liberation miserable cant. . . . I thought that my death by my own hand would provide a point, a punctuation mark, in a story of faith betrayed; and that it would make people pause and think."[3] This was evidently not his only

---

[1] Personal recollection.   [2] Personal knowledge.
[3] Narrative of events, May to November, 1941. W.P.I.

incentive towards self-destruction, but it would seem to have been the chief one.

The tragedy of it was that this agony of spirit regarding his country's honour was a waste, and if only he had unburdened his mind to Chapman Andrews or anyone else who knew the facts (as he surely would have done if he had been himself), he would soon have discovered the extent of his mistake. The restoration of Ethiopia by Great Britain was a transaction of which there is nothing to be ashamed. Without doubt there were plenty of improvident men, and perhaps some bad men, who liked the idea of a protectorate, and may still like it to-day. They were a potent factor in forming opinion in the armies of Kenya, and influenced some of the Press correspondents, notably of *The Times*; but for all that, people who held such views never came near to forming a policy. The very notion of a protectorate or its equivalent had been ruled out from discussion four months before in February.[1] The only question of policy was as to the duration and conditions of the temporary military regime, and there was agreement that this duration must be not only temporary but short. To have denied or limited Ethiopian independence permanently was quite impossible and quite unwished from the military or the political point of view.[2] The commercial temptations to do so nonetheless were negligible.[3] The evidence for dishonesty was all superficial, though it was certainly of a kind to impress. Wingate had heard much unworthy talk of putting Ethiopia in her place, and had found a cynical disposition in many people in authority. But none of this was policy, as he imagined in his disordered state; it was a matter of manners, and not worth the sacrifice of too much peace of mind, let alone a life. Even in his state of illness he might have come to see this, and have resisted his impulse, if a last and terrible burden had been spared him.

In the end week of June and the beginning of July he felt himself sinking into that state of helpless despair which had tormented his early manhood and which he had not experienced since the distant days of anticlimax at Bulford Camp. Those who have suffered this devastation of the spirit know that one of its pains is fear of its return. Slowly he had lost that fear in eight years of freedom. He had come to believe himself permanently liberated, and now to his horror found that this was not so. He found himself overcome

---

[1] At a conference in Cairo attended by Mr. Eden, Sir John Dill, Sir Archibald Wavell, and Brigadier Lush.

[2] Rodd.

[3] Lord Chandos. A communication. He and the late Mr. L. S. Amery have told the writer that no policy contrary to Ethiopian independence was ever considered at Cabinet level.

by the withering delusion that God had turned away from him for ever.[1]

At three o'clock in the afternoon of July 4th he took his temperature and read that it was standing at 104 degrees. He had no more atabrin left. He got out of bed, made his way downstairs and out into the street, and tried to walk to the doctor's house. He could not find it although he had been there more than once. He became terrified. He now believed that his loss of memory was the beginning of madness.[2] In his weakness he had to hold on to the walls as he made his way back to the hotel. In his confusion and despair he had now made up his mind.

In the bedroom corridor he found the floor-waiter who used to bring him his meals. He said something to him, thanking him for his services. The waiter noticed something odd in his behaviour, followed him to the door and waited outside it. Wingate wanted to lock the door, but feared to increase the waiter's suspicions, so he half-locked it and waited till the man had gone. Then he took out his pistol and saw that it had not been cleaned for a long time and was still choked with Ethiopian sand. It was empty and he could not find the ammunition. (In fact Akavia had forgotten to pack it when Wingate left Addis Ababa.) He put the pistol away and took out a hunting-knife which a friend had given him. He went to the mirror above the washbasin. He held the knife in his right hand and thrust into the left side of his neck. He found the effort of cutting through greater than he had guessed. He saw that he must try again and suddenly remembered that the door was not locked. With the knife still in his neck, and drenching blood from the wound he went to the door and locked it, went back to the mirror, plucked out the knife, and taking it in his left hand, thrust with all his force at the jugular vein on the right, then fell unconscious on the floor.[3]

He would have died within the hour, but rescue came quickly. In the next room Colonel Thornhill was enjoying a siesta. He heard unusual sounds through the wall. They gave him an idea (though there was no shout or cry) that something untoward was happening. He decided that he had better look into it. He gave his reasons afterwards. He said: "When I hear a feller lock a door, I don't think anything about it, and if I hear a feller fall down, that's his affair, but when I hear a feller lock his door and then fall down—it's time for action." He pulled on his clothes quickly, went out into the corridor and knocked on the door. There was no sound that he could hear. He

[1] Narrative. W.P.I.   [2] James.
[3] Personal recollection of Thornhill's account. Mrs. Mary Newall. Narrative. W.P.I. Medical Case Sheet.

shook the handle and pushed. He ran to the lift, went down, rushed to the manager's office for the master key. He and the manager and others ran back, swept up to the corridor, and forced the door because the key was in. As they burst in, Wingate came back to partial consciousness. He remembered after that it seemed to him that he was dead and in hell. Colonel Thornhill applied first-aid and Wingate was taken to the 15th General (Scottish) Hospital. Wingate never knew who saved him.

He was operated on immediately and with some difficulty because an attack of vomiting reopened his wounds. He was in a state of confused rambling utterance, and when he was heard repeatedly crying to God for mercy the nursing sisters called for the help of the resident Anglican chaplain. The good man's ministrations were of no avail, but later that night, when Wingate was calmer, the Catholic chaplain, Father Blount, paid him a visit. He sat by Wingate's bed and said who he was. Wingate asked him to tell him if he was damned. The priest was silent for a few seconds, then laid his hand on Wingate's forehead, and said: "God will forgive you." The words brought relief. This moment was the beginning of a slow, painful, and ultimately victorious return to life.[1] It is strange to remember that after such an encounter Wingate retained to the end his puritan disapproval of the Roman Catholic Church. The personal meant nothing to him compared to any question of principle, even at such a cross-roads.

In Cairo the news of what had happened spread quickly, and at a time when people wanted distraction the Wingate story became the topic of the hour. Rumours began to spread, some fairly near the truth, some far away. Colonel Thornhill was besieged by questioners but he knew little about the case, although, with his way of plunging his fingers into every pie, he was among the few who had read the report. The two stories most widely accepted at the time were that Wingate had attempted suicide because his recommendations for a new guerilla brigade had been turned down by the late Commander-in-Chief, and secondly and equally fallaciously, that he was disappointed at lack of recognition and so had staged a sham suicide to draw attention to himself.[2]

His enemies are reliably reported to have rejoiced odiously at the disaster. "Now we've got him!" a Brigadier is remembered saying, "It's either a court-martial or a lunatic asylum and either way he's finished."[3] And indeed it looked as though Wingate's career was utterly at an end and that the common man had triumphed over him.

[1] Narrative. W.P.I.
[2] Personal recollection. The allegation of a sham suicide is wholly inconsistent with the facts reported in Wingate's medical case sheet.
[3] Narrative, W.P.I. and *Gideon Goes To War*. Personal recollection.

But the common man was overconfident. In interesting contrast to the unnamed Brigadier's exultation was the truer reaction of one of Wingate's most serious rivals for fame. Colonel David Stirling was at that time attempting to organise the first Special Air Service unit in the face of all the opposition that had confronted Wingate from the beginning. It had been suggested to him, in good faith, that he and Wingate might usefully combine since they shared many ideas. But Stirling was quite as much of an individualist as Wingate and for this reason he resisted the suggestion, so much so that he had even avoided meeting the other. Now, with many others, he heard the account that Wingate had attempted suicide because his plans were rejected, but he was not moved to glee or derision, rather to added respect. He recognised a formidable man in one who could face voluntary death for his beliefs, and he determined for his own professional sake to avoid him all the more.[1] As for old Thornhill, he used to say, "I don't know what the feller was up to at all."

After a few days in the hospital, Wingate was well enough to receive visitors. Among the first was Simonds to whom he said (disclosing part of his reasons): "I did it to call attention to our wrongs." Chapman Andrews was in Cairo and he and George Steer went together to the 15th General Hospital. They found Wingate in a state of uncommunicative brooding, as though wanting to talk and not able to. At length Chapman Andrews, feeling that Wingate needed to get the matter off his chest, hesitantly asked him why he had " done it," but Wingate could not answer. "Was it private trouble? " asked his visitor, "things going wrong at home? " He answered: "No, thank God, there's nothing wrong there." Chapman Andrews pressed him to tell him more, for he seemed to want to speak, but Wingate told him nothing. Then, suddenly looking round the ward, Wingate told him, not of his reasons for attempting suicide, but for failing in the attempt. He explained that to cut your throat with success you first needed to relax in a hot bath, otherwise you found that your neck muscles were tensed and that the effort was beyond you. He had not studied the operation first, for which reason he had failed. His visitors listened in some disquiet as he illustrated his meaning with graphic gestures. Chapman Andrews said something about being glad he had failed, to which Wingate answered, " That shows that I am destined for great things."

As they went away from the hospital George Steer remarked that Wingate had lost a certain dangerous look in his eye.[2]

Akavia arrived from Ethiopia the day after the disaster. He went to the Continental Hotel where he was only told that Wingate had left.

[1] Colonel David Stirling. A communication.   [2] Chapman Andrews.

He went to the G.(R.) office in General Headquarters where the news was broken to him. He was also among Wingate's first visitors at the hospital, but before going to see him he told the Cairo office of the Jewish Agency that Wingate was seriously ill in hospital as the result of an accident, and the Cairo office informed their head office in Jerusalem. As a result Shertock came from Palestine with a Zionist colleague Doctor Sireni.[1]

A day or two after Akavia's visit, Shertock and Sireni went together to the hospital. After a while Wingate said that he wanted to talk to Shertock alone. When Sireni had left them he asked Shertock what he knew about his reasons for being in hospital. Shertock said he knew nothing, whereupon Wingate with deep emotion said that he and Weizmann and Ben Gurion and the Zionist leaders must know what sort of man he was, because he was destined, he believed, to play a part in the redemption of Israel, and he told him that he had tried to kill himself. Shertock asked him why he had done this, and Wingate told him in reply, and without trying to justify his deed, that he had been depressed by his personal failure and wanted at the same time to protest against British policy in Ethiopia. With the ever-present generosity of his character Shertock said that men who achieved such things as Wingate had, brought themselves under the load of terrible problems, and he assured him that what he had done did not diminish Zionist confidence in him.[2] A little later Ben Gurion called on him, received the same confession, and gave the same assurance.[3]

It seems (from what Wingate said himself afterwards), that when he returned to his right mind he entertained no illusions about the merits of his deed, and acknowledged that he had done wrong. He humbled himself enough to say: " Such an act was not justified by the circumstances. Whether or not it is ever justified, I have not . . . made up my mind. Probably not."[4] George Steer's remembered remark is worth taking seriously. Wingate was reconciled to himself as men are in repentance. He needed to be reconciled with the world. This took time and effort.

There was one hideous scene in the hospital. A prominent officer of Gideon Force, who need not be named, came to see him. The visit began in a spirit of benevolent politeness, then suddenly degenerated into recrimination. It happened like this. The conversation touched on Wingate's report and his visitor asked to see it. Wingate had it with

---

[1] Sireni was of Jewish-Italian origin and had been physician to King Victor Emmanuel III. At the age of 56 he was parachuted into Italy. He was captured by the Germans and removed to Buchenwald where he disappeared.
[2] Sharett. [3] Ben Gurion.
[4] Narrative W.P.I.

him. His visitor read, at first placidly, then with growing disquiet, until, by the time he reached the Force Commander's hard criticisms of his officers and men, those angry paragraphs which Dudley Clarke had urged him to remove, he was so consumed with rage that he forgot himself unworthily. He flung the papers to the ground, and in his fury was driven to taunt the other, too weak to be able to answer, heaping abuse and insult on him; and as he left the ward, he stopped for further abuse at the door, as though not yet content with what he had done. Then he rushed out and they never met again.[1] It was like Wingate that he bore this man no ill will afterwards.

On the 22nd of July Wingate was examined by the senior official consultant in psychological medicine, G. W. B. James. It was to him that Wingate confided what has already been related here: the descent into the pit of despair which decided him to do what he did on the 4th. There is no record that he told anyone else, except his wife, about this; the subject, it would seem, was too horrible in his mind for further utterance. James gave a report on the case to the effect that Wingate was not responsible for his act of attempted self-destruction, which, he said, was the consequence of a depressed state to which he was prone and had been aggravated by malarial fever and the unsupervised use of atabrin. He affirmed his belief that he was no longer suicidal, had recovered his mind completely, and should be sent back to England for a long convalescence.[2]

Under good care Wingate began to get back his strength. There was a veranda outside his ward and he used to take a little exercise up and down it in the evenings, walking with his hands clasped behind his back and deep in his thoughts. This rapt figure was often seen by another patient in a private ward. She was called Mrs. Newall. The sight intrigued her and she asked the nurse (who happened to be Wingate's nurse too) who he was. The nurse told her that he was a suicide case. One day when he was at his evening exercise Mrs. Newall called out: "Colonel Wingate!" He stopped and came to her door. She said: "Colonel Wingate, come in here. I want to talk to you. I am so tired of seeing you walk up and down outside."

He came just within the door and she said boldly: "I have been told that you tried to commit suicide. I want to talk to you about that." He looked as one might expect, all hostility, for a few seconds. Then he came into the room and asked her what she meant. She told him that she had known a suicide tragedy in her own family, and that if he had anything on his mind, and which he felt he needed to say, he could say it to her. He came in and sat down by her bed. He told her that

---

[1] A first-hand account by the officer in question, supported by a second-hand account.
[2] James. Information obtained at the War Office.

he had led a campaign in Ethiopia and had come back to headquarters to find neglect and ingratitude for which reason, in a moment of folly, he had tried to kill himself.[1]

It is a common experience that, at a critical moment of life, a man seems to meet by chance, but as though by the design of fate, the companion he needs. Attractive, and in sympathy with the pains of his particular disaster, Mary Newall was in addition a vivacious sociable person. Her room was often filled with visitors and through her Wingate met people again in an easy way, and he slowly began to come out of that cave of brooding into which misfortune throws men. A friendship sprung up between them, informed on his side by the unchangeable seriousness of his nature, on hers by a gay disposition which lightened his burden of unhappiness. He used to sit talking to her for long hours about what the Zionists had achieved in Palestine, and with Ben Gurion he drew her into a scheme (which came to nothing), for raising a Jewish Women's Service Corps. Often he used to read the Bible to her and the nurse would come in to say " Now then, now then, it's long past bedtime, you know," and Mary Newall would say, " Oh, let him work it off, it does him good." One evening he read almost the whole of the Book of Job to her. He interrupted himself to say, " Isn't that magnificent! " to which she answered, " I've been asleep for the last half-hour so I really couldn't say."[2] This kind of chaff was exactly the right treatment for him then, and with the renewal of his spirits he began to plan the remaking of his shattered career.

If he had enemies in G.H.Q. he also had friends, such as Colonel Airey who had stood by him throughout these events. James's report was taken as sufficient reason for not holding a court-martial on the case. Wingate appeared before a medical board on the 18th of August by which he was classified in Category D as regards health and ordered to remain in hospital pending further instructions. These came shortly after and were that he was to sail for England.[3] His passage was booked for the first week in September.

In the meantime he took a skilful initiative; he brought himself to the notice of the recently arrived Minister of State, Mr. Oliver Lyttleton. The latter had been appointed in the first days of July about the same time as the change in Army Commanders. Wingate got to know something about the new establishment from his visitors, and the visitors he met in Mary Newall's room, and he decided that the opportunity must not be neglected. He sent a copy of his report to Oliver Lyttleton's military secretary who pressed it on his chief. It is not extraordinary, considering how little on the subject had

[1] Mrs. Newall.   [2] Mrs. Newall.   [3] Airey-Wingate correspondence.

been published privately or publicly, that Mr. Lyttleton had heard nothing about the guerilla campaign. When he had read the report he was filled with curiosity to meet the man who had led Gideon Force. He made inquiries which resulted in an invitation to Wingate to dine.

By a generous arrangement the Minister of State lived in the luxurious country house of Mr. Chester Beatty, situated not far from the great pyramids. On the night in question, at about eight o'clock, the Minister's wife, Lady Moira Lyttleton, was on the veranda sitting in an alcove formed by curtains as protection against the sudden cold of the night wind. As she sat alone reading, the curtains on one side were suddenly parted and a haggard face over a high stock of bandages suddenly looked in with burning eyes. She experienced considerable shock, and then said, "You must be Major Wingate." He may have said, "Yes," but if so it was the only word he spoke. This was his first encounter with ordinary life since the 4th of July, and he was not in the mood to ease it. His hostess naturally was. She made him welcome; she tried numerous conversational openings, in vain: he had nothing to say so he said nothing.[1] When the Minister came in he had no more success, and during a large part of dinner, at which there were a few members of the staff present as well, Wingate remained silent despite continual attempts to draw him into the talk. His strange guest reminded Mr. Lyttleton of a "porcupine with every hackle up." Seeing the ineffectiveness at this juncture of his conversational agility the Minister relied on the social powers of champagne alone.

Then towards the end of dinner the tied tongue was suddenly unloosed. A chance remark about guerilla war or the Ethiopia campaign gave Wingate a cue and he was roused to put forward his ideas. He spoke with hardly an interruption for about an hour, exerting on his audience all his old power of obtaining, holding, and fascinating the attention, and with all the old ease. His main theme, as remembered afterwards, was what might be called the "exclusive" theory of liberation, as opposed to the usual theory that the more arms are distributed to a friendly populace the swifter and more massive is the uprising. Oliver Lyttleton was impressed by Wingate's ideas which were new to him, and when the evening was over he was left with a conviction, as others had been, that this man must not be wasted. He took the next convenient occasion to bring his name to the notice of Mr. Churchill.[2]

Wingate's last days in Egypt were occupied in trying to right the wrongs of Gideon Force. A foolish and possibly well-meaning

[1] Lady Chandos.   [2] Lord Chandos.

attempt was made to bribe him into quiet. A hard-lying allowance was paid to him personally, but to no one else. He returned the money, except for ten pounds which he said he had spent in official entertaining. He wrote: "If this is regarded as a personal emolument I will return this too.[1]" He went back to his struggle for justice, and in the very long run he succeeded in getting most of what he asked for. In the end all the hard-lying allowances were paid, but not in the full measure he asked for, and only after long delays. Some of the men were not paid till nearly three years after.[2] In the matter of decorations the claims were ultimately met to an honourable degree except one. Major Simonds had been recommended for a D.S.O. which as the commander of Begemder Force he had abundantly earned. It will be remembered that he had been closely concerned in the composition of the report and the damning appendices. He did not receive the D.S.O. and was forced to be content with a mention in despatches. It is difficult to resist an impression that some men in authority contrived this as a makeshift revenge on Wingate.

The hospital ship in which Wingate sailed from Ismailia was called the *Llandovery Castle*. His journey occupied a little less than ten weeks, seeming longer. The first stage from Ismailia to Durban was a time of renewed wretchedness. One of the people in charge seems from accounts of him to have been exactly that kind of silly martinet distrust of whom had led Wingate to avoid official doctoring in Cairo. This self-important person appears to have been guilty of spiteful indiscretions about Wingate's case. Towards the end of September the boat reached Durban. Here the patients on board the *Llandovery Castle* were landed and put in a convalescence camp at Orubi, and Wingate, in common with his fellow-travellers,[3] found himself a prey to visions of months, or perhaps even a year or two, of lingering at this halting place. It was a thing that sometimes happened to men in transit. Did he imagine a deep-laid G.H.Q. plot to ship him to South Africa and keep him forgotten there? What is known is that he took extraordinary pains to convince the medical authorities at Durban that he was totally sane. Whether it was these efforts which saved him or not, he embarked with the majority of the *Llandovery Castle* patients, after three weeks or so at Orubi, and sailed from Cape Town on the troopship *Empress of Australia* on the 9th of October. He had favourably impressed the members of the medical board by whom he was examined. "He has completely recovered," wrote the Chairman, "and is eager to resume his duties."

---

[1] Narrative. Wingate-Airey Correspondence.   [2] Akavia.
[3] Lieut.-Colonel B. M. Franks, D.S.O., M.C. He was a fellow patient with Wingate through the journey and his account is mainly relied on.

The second stage of this long journey was happier than the first. In the course of these blank weeks Wingate showed the most amiable part of his character in an act of charity which must cancel the memory of many faults. He had the instinct to redeem his own state by helping others. His first effort to do so had been a failure. Among the patients on board the *Llandovery Castle* there was a Jewish boy in a state of hopeless insanity. Wingate used to sit with him and try to make some sort of rational contact with his mind, but the poor lunatic was beyond any such help and on seeing another person in his cabin would tear at himself and scream.[1] Another opportunity offered on the *Empress of Australia*. Wingate found among the people he met one patient who had been a Captain in the army and who was being shipped home after a nervous breakdown which had resulted in partial paralysis. As often happens with men suffering thus he was filled with shame at his weakness, and in consequence had lost all confidence in himself. Wingate made him tell his story and then argued him out of despair. He told the other that if he had things to be ashamed of, he, Wingate, had worse ones, and he described how in similar affliction he had given way and tried to kill himself. He made the other see that he was not alone, and that even after a man has been so vanquished by wretchedness as to try to throw away the gift of life, he may still struggle back to hope and the will to achieve afresh. He rescued the man, and for the short time that remained of Wingate's life the two of them were friends.[2]

He shared his cabin with an officer who was a fellow-patient, suffering from septicaemia contracted from desert sores. His name was Captain Brian Franks. He had served with a cavalry regiment in Palestine and so the two of them often talked about the places they knew. To him Wingate propounded his Zionist faith in frequent sessions, and his belief that the right British policy in the Middle East countries was one of wholehearted support of Zion resulting in a fully equipped modern polity inalienably bound to the British Empire. Brian Franks was sceptical but impressed. He and Wingate struck up a friendship marred only by one unserious but memorable difference. One evening as the passengers were going down the interior gangway to dinner Franks, apropos of a Palestine subject, thoughtlessly said something about "those bloody Zionists." Wingate lashed out with a heavy kick, causing exquisite pain on the other's shin. The assailant then withdrew to another part of the dining-saloon and remained angrily away from Franks the rest of the evening. But Franks refused to take offence so the quarrel was made up with chaff. Often in Wingate's story one notices that his dark mood could be dispelled by some appeal

---

[1] Narrative W.P.I. [2] Letters in W.P.I. Kounine.

to his sense of humour. It is a pity that so few people made that appeal. Certainly he did not encourage it.

He told Franks of his plans for the future: how he intended to organise influence in London for the formation of a guerilla force to operate from the Tibesti mountains against the Axis troops in Libya. Before the ship berthed in Liverpool he urged his new friend to come with him in this projected private army as one of his officers, but Franks unhesitatingly refused. Wingate asked him why. Franks said: " I don't want to be shot." Wingate received this unsoldierly confession with incredulous surprise. " Oh," said Franks, " I don't mean being shot by the enemy; I meant being shot by you."

The *Empress* berthed in Glasgow on the 14th of November. The senior medical officer on board wrote a report in which, after reviewing the case in detail, he asserted Wingate's recovery and recommended that he should be given six months' leave with permission to apply for a medical board any time after three months. He said it would be unwise to confine him in hospital any longer and urged that his leave should start immediately " as soon as he arrives in the U.K. especially as he would return to a wife and family to whom he is devotedly attached." He concluded by saying that " the unusual experience and achievements of this officer . . . make his return to combatant duty in the field most desirable from a national point of view."

One thought had troubled Wingate throughout the journey; he had not told Lorna what had happened, and he had no idea what she knew. She did in fact know that something terrible had happened, but no more than that. On the 18th of August Ben Gurion had written to her on arrival in England saying he had seen Wingate in hospital. " He has had some trouble with malaria," he wrote, " apparently picked up in Abyssinia—but when I saw him he seemed completely recovered."[1] A few days afterwards he saw her and happened to let slip a remark which suggested that there was worse than malaria in the case, and then hastily tried to cover it up. She saw that something was being kept from her. She tried to find out what had really happened, without success. Few people knew and those who did would not tell. When Wingate at last saw her again in their flat in Hill Street, he had to tell her himself. She asked him what had happened. He looked at her with the utmost tenderness, with no trace of the old arrogance, and said slowly and deliberately: " Don't you know? . . . I tried to kill myself." She took his hand and said the first thing that came to her, and her words of consolation expressed the same idea that Shertock had conveyed to him when he saw him in hospital. She said the disaster was a penalty such as came with living in the forefront of history. People whose fate

[1] Weizmann Archives.

it was to live so had to face the despair that he had faced, and the same temptation. Smaller people might sneer and disparage, but not men who had shouldered great responsibilities. She ended by saying that he should think of Clive who attempted suicide three times.

For some moments he was too moved to speak. He took her hand again. He said: "I forgot about Clive."[1]

[1] Mrs. Lorna Smith.

CHAPTER XV

RESCUE

SOON AFTER he was settled into the flat in 49 Hill Street, Wingate fell ill again with septic tonsilitis, probably contracted from the wounds in his throat. He was looked after by Ben Zion Kounine and nursed by Lorna whose conduct at this crisis in their lives earned the doctor's lasting admiration. Long after he described her as an Alcestis. She was helped by his sister Monica. The family had been told the facts of the case by Wingate and they proved the depth and nobility of the religious enthusiasm which informed all their lives. None of them had a thought of reproach and all of them an abounding trust in the mercy of God.

The relapse was short, and Wingate was evidently in health again early in December. Monica noted the moment of recovery. She slept in the same room and one night in the course of talking before putting out the light she happened to say that she had no good word for any dictator whatsoever, and then went on to commit the offence of classifying the great Napoleon with Hitler and Mussolini. This drew forth a long and passionate defence of Wingate's hero (to whom in his emaciated malarial state he bore some facial likeness), in the course of which Monica fell asleep and presently awoke to hear the tirade still in flow. She told him she was tired and persuaded him to drop the argument, for the time being anyway. But as she thought in the dark, she joyfully recognised that unless his throat was cured he could never have talked so long and loud and raspingly.[1]

Never for one moment on the journey or since his return had he lost sight of the need to remake his career, or of the possibility that he had lost it for ever. He had been granted leave in accordance with the senior medical officer's recommendations, but a three-months' wait was too long to be endured by this impatient man, and long before the end of that time he had successfully rallied influence to promote him to fresh and worthy employment. He was driven on not only by a sense of his own peril, but by a sense of duty, for, more now than at any previous time in his life, he was certain of great abilities that he could put to great use. He summoned all hands to the pumps to rescue a

---

[1] Miss Monica Wingate.

vessel that was sometimes floating better than he knew, and that was sometimes most in danger from his own indiscretions which were always in the cause of his ideals.

But before setting about his own rehabilitation he remembered the Captain whom he had helped on the journey. He and Lorna consulted Kounine and proposed at first that arrangements should be made for him to spend leave in the peace of the country. For some reason this proved unpractical, but instead Kounine obtained an appointment with a first-class psychiatrist so that a cure might be directed along profitable lines. Wingate paid for the consultation.

As to his own affairs, he was quite clear as to his immediate requirement; he wanted to appear before a medical board without delay in order to establish the fact of his sound mental and physical health. He talked it over with Kounine, explaining that when he did appear before a board he wanted to be absolutely certain in advance of a favourable verdict, all of which he looked to Kounine to arrange. The doctor pointed out more than once that his friend was asking for the impossible, but Wingate insisted, and as often happened when he insisted, a way was found. One evening as the two of them were discussing the matter Kounine suddenly stopped in the middle of talk and said: " I've got it! ", but he refused to tell more for fear of causing disappointment. Next day he acted on his impulse. He went to see Lord Horder, and in full detail Kounine told him the story of Wingate's attempted suicide, of his remarkable recovery to mental stability and of his wish to return to service immediately. He prevailed on him to see Wingate and judge for himself. Horder gave two appointments for the purpose.

At the first of these a very strange thing happened. Wingate's future depended on the outcome, but for that very reason, it can be supposed, he felt a challenge to his pride. He was evidently determined not to appear before the eminent physician as a suppliant, and he avoided that rôle by a sudden and perhaps unpremeditated display of the puckish humour that was a rarely visible but essential part of his character. Kounine was in the consulting-room when Wingate was shown in. His new patient walked straight up to Lord Horder, shook his hand, and opened conversation somewhat as follows: " You know, all men of extraordinary ability are liable to try to kill themselves— Frederick the Great did it, and Clive of India—three times—and of course Napoleon." The feelings of Doctor Kounine who saw his devoted and careful work of persuasion being recklessly destroyed by the beneficiary may be imagined, but in the event the moment passed without reverse. Lord Horder was agreeably rather than otherwise impressed by this wild show of spirit, and he proceeded to an examination.

To make doubly sure, however, Kounine organised a second way to Horder's good opinion. Dr. Weizmann was in London then and Kounine, having told him about what had happened on the 4th of July, urged him to join his voice with Kounine's and Wingate's own. Within a few days of his return Wingate had met Weizmann. The memory of the quarrel had passed, and when Weizmann heard that this valiant fighter for Zion was in trouble, and calamitous trouble moreover, he did as Kounine asked; he went to Lord Horder and pleaded for Wingate with the eloquence that could change history. He told the other that Wingate was a strange and eccentric man, intolerably so at times, but that this must never be allowed to obscure the fact that he was one who could truthfully be described as a man of genius. It would, he said, be a tragic thing if through lack of confidence such a man were wasted at such a time; for all his wildness and moments of folly, he said, Wingate was not a mentally unstable man. Dr. Weizmann ended by saying that he was prepared personally to guarantee his mental stability.

Lord Horder had evidently not made up his mind on the case, and at Weizmann's offer of a personal guarantee he asked: " In spite of the fact that he tried to kill himself? "

Weizmann said: " In spite of the fact that he tried to kill himself."[1]

Horder talked with Kounine after his second consultation, by which time he had come to a favourable conclusion. He said somewhat as follows : " You must realise that I have no official position, but it so happens that the other day the new D.G.M.S. came and called on me as a matter of professional courtesy and said he hoped he could rely on my help and so on. I was very touched by his action, and before he left I told him that I promised never to bother him unless the case was a really grave one . . . so I think I can do something for Major Wingate."[2]

This is to bring the story forward to the end of December. In the meantime Wingate had found supporters. The British climate had become claustrophobic after two years of siege, and men, such as he, who had seen service overseas were made welcome. He found himself in demand. Before his relapse he had met Arthur Hinks, the imposing secretary of the Royal Geographical Society, who invited him to lecture on the " Geography of the Ethiopian Campaign," an invitation he immediately accepted (though in the end nothing seems to have come of it). He was invited a little later to be the guest of honour at a dinner of the Royal African Society. He was asked to lecture to troops and when he was over the relapse he gave several lectures with remarkable success. One brought him a eulogistic letter of thanks from

[1] Mrs. Weizmann.　　　　[2] Kounine.

Eastern Command, another an offer to publish a book by him from Messrs. Duckworth. There was no question of his having to suffer in England the indifference and neglect that had met him in Cairo in June. By force of circumstances he was again coming to the notice of people in influential society, and he was not the man to neglect the advantage. Mrs. Dugdale recorded a meeting with him soon after his arrival. " Dined at Dorchester with Chaim and Vera. Lewis (Namier) there and John Gunther, the American journalist, a *very* nice and intelligent man, also the Orde Wingates. Orde, by our desire, held the floor all night. His description of the Abyssinian campaign, his handling of the natives, etc., quite brilliant. He is obviously a guerilla leader of genius. But he is so pro-Abyssinian as to be *almost* anti-British. I suppose it is part of his power to identify himself with the bands he leads. Altogether a very memorable evening of talk.[1] "

The entry shows plainly enough how Wingate was still clinging to his haunting vision of a martyred Ethiopia liberated and then deceived by a predatory British Government. The extraordinary thing is that at this time, when he was committing his worst political mistake, he was so much better informed than he knew. In mid-December Sandford wrote to him as follows from Cairo:

" I hope the terms of the Agreement between H.M.G. and Emperor, when published, will seem to you to be satisfactory. I think myself they are on the right lines and that barring unforeseen difficulties, they will be workable. The general scheme of things is naturally not quite like anything we have done before. We are going all out for setting up a completely independent state and are asking for no " quid pro quo " in return for the help we are giving. We hope that the Emperor will listen to his advisers and give them sufficient power of supervision to ensure that money is not wasted. I believe myself that he will, and that—given a fairly smooth first year—he will succeed in establishing a stable and reasonably good administration. I don't anticipate a bed of roses for myself and the other advisers![2]

"I don't know how soon the future ' lay-out ' of Eritrea and Italian Somaliland is likely to come up for practical discussion, but when I hear about this I will let you know. I imagine that now Japan has come in against us, we shall have less time than ever to give consideration to treaty making. . . ."

Wingate never understood the man whom he succeeded in Mission 101. Sandford was too prosy for him, and Wingate persisted in his own more dramatic ideas. For the moment he did little about those ideas, but he did not forget them, and unfortunately he did not allow Sand-

[1] Dugdale Diaries.
[2] Sandford was appointed Principal Adviser to the Ethiopian Ministry of the Interior.

ford's letter to alter them in the least. It is hard for a man to throw over any part of an idea for whose sake he has suffered.

On the 11th of December when the relapse was over, he and Lorna entertained Sir Reginald Wingate to lunch, and the host gave their guest an account of the campaign. "I do indeed congratulate you most heartily." Cousin Rex wrote the next day, "You may be sure we are all proud of the lustre you have so honourably and so gallantly added to the family name. Go on and prosper and 'more power to your elbow.'" The old alliance was re-established and was to prove as fruitful as it had done in the past. Sir Reginald spread the account he had heard.

Wingate went to see Mr. Amery who a little later recorded the meeting. "He . . . came to see me and told me a great deal that I found immensely interesting, not only as evidence of his own leadership and of the remarkable results achieved, but also from the point of view of future operations of a like character in other countries which we might hope to liberate from the enemy. He told me that he had gone down with a very bad malaria immediately afterwards and had only sent in a very brief note of his doings at the time, and did not know to whom he was to report now or if anyone wanted a report. I thought it very undesirable if the story were not fully available . . . and told him that if he would only write a full report I would take it on myself to act as unofficial channel. . . ."[1]

This was substantial help. It meant in effect that a senior minister was prepared not only to undo the affront Wingate had suffered in Cairo (the virtual cancellation of the report), but to show it to people who would probably not have seen the original if it had enjoyed a normal circulation. But Mr. Amery did not throw his discretion away. Perhaps because he knew something of Wingate's tendency to offend his superiors he offered to correct his draft. During the last two weeks of December Wingate worked at producing a second version of the report.

It must be said that this second version, though free of some of the blemishes of the first, is not its equal. A man can rarely write a second time what he has well written once, and Wingate's second Ethiopian report lacks the literary energy of the first one. There is a bad tradition of tendentious writing in military despatches with which he fell in on this occasion, and as a result the second report, though accurate in outline, is not in the same class as its angrier predecessor, judged as a record of events.

Mr. Amery knew nothing of the Ethiopian campaign and judged the report on its merits. In spite of what has been just said, these were

[1] Amery to Sir Alan Brooke (7.1.42).

not slight : the argument was lucid and firm, the general picture simply and convincingly drawn, and there was no dwelling on actions difficult to follow. Mr. Amery decided to press the report forward, but first he asked for revisions. He wanted certain passages removed as redundant, notably one on the Brocklehurst mission which, a year after its complete ruin, still deeply distressed Wingate's mind. The mission had not been mentioned in the first version at all, but in the second it occupied, in draft, two lengthy and disconnected passages. On Mr. Amery's advice Wingate reduced these to one, suppressing some offensive innuendo. The notorious " ape " paragraph was retained word for word in the draft. Mr. Amery thought it unwise. " The passage at the bottom of page 18," he wrote to him, " would suggest that you looked on General Cunningham as an ape, and would certainly create the impression that your normal attitude towards the high military command is one of contempt. This would certainly not encourage the authorities to entrust you with the kind of organising work that you want. . . ."[1] Wingate made all the proposed alterations.

The corrected draft was sent to Mr. Amery at the India office. There the Secretary of State arranged for a sufficient number of copies to be typed and then sent to Sir Alan Brooke with a tactful letter. At the War Office it was given a distinguished distribution: to Brooke himself and his vice chief, to the Directors of Military Operations, of Military Intelligence, of the Supply Department and of Motor Transport ; to Colonel Yule (for the War Cabinet Office), and to Brigadier Gubbins of the Ministry of Economic Warfare. A little later Wingate gave copies to Sir Reginald who sent one to Sir Hastings Ismay with a request that he would show it to the Prime Minister, and another to Brigadier Sim who, he explained to Orde, " has great weight in various directions." How could there be any question of neglect now?

At the turn of the year the rally showed some first results. On the 30th of December, the same day as Mr. Amery sent the corrections to his draft, Wingate appeared before a medical board. Lord Horder fulfilled his promise to Dr. Kounine generously, sending a statement to the Director General of Medical Services for him to show to the board if he wished.

" I have now had two consultations with Major Wingate, and have come to know his views, both of the ' incident' in retrospect and of his future work and ideals.

I am personally prepared to sponsor him in respect of any post of responsibility which the authorities may give him on the

[1] Amery to Wingate (30.12.40).

recommendation of the Director General of Medical Services that he is mentally and physically fit for active duty.

I believe that Major Wingate would not repeat the act which led to his present suppression from military service to however great a strain he might be subjected, and I have confidence that he may be trusted not to let down the men whose lives might be confided to him.

Horder, M.D., F.R.C.P."[1]

Kounine was asked to submit his own opinions to the board and he stated that "Major Wingate is now in good physical and mental health . . . in every way fit to resume active and combatant duty."

The board gave Wingate a cautious manumission. "There is no evidence," they reported, "of any mental depression. He talks freely of his illness and has good insight. . . ." They considered in conclusion that he could in all probability be classified as "Category A" in six months. It seems from what followed that this finding was accepted as sufficient to justify his immediate re-employment. All the same, the board's favourable judgment might have had no immediate consequence, if it had not been that in the course of January, Mr. Amery wrote or signalled to Sir Archibald Wavell reminding him that Wingate was once more available to serve under him,[2] and Wavell responded with a request for his services. The clouds had lifted, the career was saved, a happy ending had been brilliantly contrived, and yet Wingate remained suspicious of what the future held. He remained obstinately ignorant of his good fortune, and nearly undid it.

Though his most effective patron was the Secretary of State for India, Wingate did not entertain any ambition or wish to serve in the Far Eastern theatre. He was still preoccupied, (and harmfully to himself), with Africa, and so far as his military future was concerned, he remained committed in mind to his original plan for a guerilla force which would operate from the Tibesti Mountains. Judging from what he wrote, he insisted that no other offer of employment was acceptable. Strangely enough, he does not seem to have written anything new on the subject of this plan till he was asked to do so in the middle of February. Instead (judging by undated papers), he wrote a memorandum—possibly for Mr. Amery—which he called "Notes

[1] Kounine Papers.
[2] Amery. In 1955 the statesman in the course of a long and amusing conversation told the writer that he did not wish to claim more than his deserts in the matter, but that he believed that he obtained both Wingate's appointments overseas in the war : certainly the appointment to Ethiopia, and probably the appointment to Burma, though in 1942, as he pointed out, Wingate was so much better known than in 1940 that other patrons may have acted before him.

relating to possible employment." These notes are another plentiful source of biographical matter, and tell a good deal of how Wingate appeared to himself at this time.

"I served the first nine months of the war," he wrote, "as a Brigade-Major in Light AA Artillery. In this capacity I developed and enforced the theories of light AA defence which have recently been reluctantly adopted. . . . I planned and organised the Ethiopian campaign of Haile Selassie. I got the plans past a reluctant staff. I found the entry to Ethiopia and introduced the Emperor before either of the other campaigns had started. As his commander-in-chief I was in sole and undivided charge of the successful patriot campaign which is described in my Report. . . . I am prepared to attempt the repetition of the exploit elsewhere." He told of a disheartening lack of interest in the War Office where he had not been questioned or interviewed by any department. "Either they had never heard of me or Ethiopia," he said of those he had met in Whitehall, " or else they think I am not a person nice to know, for they passed me straight to A.G.6—the purely routine treatment of any officer on the medical list: not even an inquiry as to whether I knew anything of interest." He complained that after eighteen years' service and some achievement to his name he was still kept to the rank of Major. His constructive proposal was that with the rank of lieutenant-colonel he should be given the task of training and organising in England "a force of the type contemplated." When giving details of what he contemplated, he used, for the first time it seems, a phrase with which his sudden fame was to be associated. He described the kind of military operation which his force was to carry out as " Long Range Penetration."

There is an omission to surprise a reader of this revealing document. He said nothing about his S.N.S. record, and nothing about any plan for the recruitment of Jewish soldiers. Did this mean that he had by now, perhaps only momentarily, forgotten Zion? Never; but he had the tactical sense not to do battle for two distressed causes at the same time, and it was during this January that he again occupied his mind with his ideas about Ethiopia. He threw all his energy into renewed advocacy on behalf of Ethiopian independence. He followed the same methods by which he had tried to influence Palestinian policy two and a half years before; his aim now as then was to meet men in leading positions and bring the facts (as he saw them) to their notice. He asked Mrs. Sieff for her help, and as before she gave it.[1] His papers show that he met and entered into correspondence with Mr. Patrick Munro, Mr. Attlee, Lord Wedgwood, Professor Harold Laski and Lord Noel Buxton among others.

[1] Mrs. Rebecca Sieff.

One of the most strange things about Wingate, and one which comes out at every turn of his story, is that he was never a careerist, not even in the most blameless sense, and when he is described as ambitious that must always be remembered. His ambition was always for a cause and the cause always took precedence over the career. He had come near to throwing away his prospects in Palestine for the sake of Zion, and now in his zeal for Ethiopian independence he became again utterly forgetful of his own interest. As was to be expected his advocacy was as intemperate as ever, but even had he gone about his self-ordained duty in a conciliatory manner, the very fact of his conducting any sort of political campaign at all was bound to irritate authority. He had a reputation, a fatal one in military life, for political busybodying, and he was abundantly adding to it at a time when others were remembering it. General Cunningham sent his comments on the second version of the report to Sir Alan Brooke, and his last comment was this: "I am uncertain to what extent his attempted suicide in Cairo has upset him, but if he is back to the man I used to know, I would gladly accept him myself as a guerilla leader. I would, however, be chary of allowing him too much rein politically. It is along political lines that he appeared to me most unbalanced." Men in or near to power enjoy an inevitable freemasonry of their own. General Cunningham's opinion could not fail to become known among those whose influence Wingate was seeking. It would have been one thing if the General's opinion had been a frivolous expression of prejudice, but it was manifestly a true one, so far as Ethiopia was concerned.

If Wingate had contented himself with lobbying influential men he would have endangered himself enough, but in keeping with the most bitter phase of his life, he went furiously beyond this. At that time there was a weekly London paper called the *New Times and Ethiopia News*. It had been founded by Miss Sylvia Pankhurst five and a half years before with the object of keeping alive the memory of what Ethiopia had suffered, and urging help for the victim of Italian aggression. It was a vigorous publication which maintained the heat of indignation over the years. The four numbers occurring between the 10th of January and the 7th of February, 1942, are of peculiar interest to Wingate's story. They carried as their main feature a series of articles called "Ethiopian Mystery," the first three by Miss Sylvia Pankhurst herself, the fourth by "a well-informed correspondent." The Editor sounded the war-note in her first paragraph. She wrote: "Only a few know the frantic atmosphere of greed and cupidity, the lust for territory, the dire intrigues which surrounded the re-entry of the Emperor Haile Selassie into his native Ethiopia, to fight for her freedom after five years of exile." Wingate had provided Miss Pankhurst with much of her material, and through her highly-coloured writing the angry ring of his besetting ideas and even of his style of expression can sometimes be heard. The chief proposition set forth was that the victory over the Italians in Ethiopia had been mainly the work of Gideon Force, and that this turn of events had run counter to a grand conspiracy for colonising the liberated territory. It was not long before the name of Brocklehurst figured in the series, and with it a new idea about his mission, namely, that Sir Philip Mitchell had been a member, possibly a clandestine one, of the original team of dividers and conquerors. She referred to him as "the high priest of anti-African sentiment," and sketched his recent history with inaccuracy and dash. "This ex-Colonial Governor," she wrote, "now Major-General, held the view that before the Emperor Haile Selassie was allowed to re-enter Ethiopia an agreement should be signed whereby he would make various desirable concessions to British advantage. The Sudan would like to have Lake Tana with its flood waters, Kenya would be interested in the Lake Rudolph area for the benefit of her white settlers." In a supporting article describing "Causes of Friction" in Ethiopia, the plot was further particularised. It was darkly suggested that, as Brocklehurst had chosen Sir Philip as his agent, so the latter in turn had chosen an agent to operate for *him* in the field. The name of this surmised double-dealer may come as a surprise: it was that of Dan Sandford!

The last instalment of the series was devoted to a refutation of an inept account of the rising in Gojjam which had appeared in an Aberdeen paper. The offending article was a marvel of misreporting in which Sandford's initial pioneering had become confused with the battle of Agibar. This piffle was now massively counter-blasted and treated as though it had been a deeply considered move in the conspiracy to belittle the patriots and thereby load Ethiopia the more easily with Mitchell's chains.

Thus ended the "Ethiopian Mystery" series, and the same number of the paper in which the concluding article appeared contained a piece of news which must have added to the perplexity of the paper's readership. On the last day of January an Anglo-Ethiopian Agreement had been signed in Addis Ababa, and in the terms, which Miss Pankhurst faithfully published in full, there was no vestige of a shadow of the ghost of Brocklehurst.

The *New Times and Ethiopia News* did not enjoy a large circulation. Nevertheless, it is most unlikely that these Press attacks on Mitchell and Sandford and on British good faith in Ethiopia had gone unnoticed in the War Office. For all their extravagance they were well informed, and it could not be doubted that Wingate had had some part in them. It is not open to proof that a decision was thereon made to relegate him to humdrum employment out of harm's way, but things did fall out precisely as though exasperated officialdom took this course. On the 7th of February Wingate received news that made it appear as though his personal cause was finally lost, and the rally had been in vain. A letter came from the Adjutant-General's Department of the War Office, which read as follows: "Major O. C. Wingate, D.S.O., R.A. (27013), is posted . . . to 114 Fd. Regt. and will be instructed to join not later than three days from the date of receipt of this U.M. This order will not be varied in any respect unless express authority has been previously obtained from this department." It was followed next day by a letter from the Royal Artillery Depot saying, "You are posted to 114 Field Regiment, R.A., Wimborne, Dorset, and will proceed to join that unit on receipt of this memorandum. . . . Railway Warrant from London to Wimborne is attached."

On the day he received the first of these letters he saw Dr. Weizmann and it would seem that they discussed the continual struggle for a Jewish national army to fight against Nazism, and the continual frustration of that purpose. The process of encouragement followed by second thoughts had remained constant for a year. Precisely what manœuvre in this long game of British political double-think the two men discussed together seems unidentifiable:[1] it was probably a relatively minor matter, but reflection on it prompted Wingate to a needed act of reparation. On the evening of the 7th he wrote to Dr. Weizmann:

"My dear Chaim,

What you told me to-day made me sad indeed, malice and incompetence can go no farther; and it is no consolation to reflect that nemesis is already upon us.

Since with my relegation to Wimborne and your departure to the United States we may not meet again I would like to put on record a few of my views relating to our association in the great work of building the Jewish National Home in Palestine. As you know, we have differed—at times vehemently—as to the right policy to pursue from time to time. I have at times said and thought hard things of you, and I want you to know now that I have come to see that our differences were of temperament only and not of heart, and that I have come to realise the measure of your greatness, both in spirit and in work, and my own unworthi-

[1] Mrs. Dugdale's diary throws no light here but an entry on the 19th of February conveys the political tone of the moment. "Had tea in the House of Lords with Lord Davies to talk to him about the forthcoming debate on the Jewish Fighting Force, but he talked most of the time about his own forthcoming book."

The Emperor returns. Chapman Andrews reads General Platt's address. Wingate is on the Emperor's left

Wingate leads the entry into Addis Ababa, 5 May, 1941

The Emperor and Wingate

The pursuit to Agibar. Johnson's force

ness to criticise as I have sometimes done. At the same time I have always recognised the greatness of your contribution to Zionism even when I disapproved your present policies. I no longer disapprove them. I have grown to see the difficulties and also to comprehend the nobility of your patience and long suffering. This is the greatness of the Jews.

I write this letter—it is possible to write it—because this is a moment of disaster both for you and me personally and for Zionism. I want you and the Agency to know that I shall feel deeply affronted if there is ever any service I can render the Jews and I am not asked to render it. I shall not feel affronted if I am not chosen to fill positions for which I am not deemed capable by those responsible. I wish, however, to remain in contact and to do whatever I can in my humble position to help.

In a way I am more unfortunate than you. Your great work done during the prime of life will endure and be remembered whatever Hitler or enemies nearer home can do. My frustration comes too early. However, these personal matters are unimportant, but it must be a satisfaction to you to remember that you have done what cannot be undone.

God bless you in your American tour and bring you safe home again.

Yours with love,

Orde"

He did see Dr. Weizmann again, and he only spent one night at Wimborne. His predicament was not nearly so desperate as it looked. The championship of those who believed in him, in spite of opposition brought on sometimes by " the surfeit of his own behaviour," had had results which could not be thwarted, and though a last energetic effort at the pumps was made, this was in fact superfluous : the career was assured and could now float triumphantly into greatness. The story of the next weeks can be followed from two points of view: that of the official records, and that of Wingate himself who kept a diary of his mid-February adventures.

The official records show a dramatic coincidence. On the 7th of February, the day on which Wingate received his devastating summons to Dorset, Sir Archibald Wavell signalled the War Office requesting that Wingate should be sent to Rangoon as soon as possible. This signal was repeated two days later. Then, two days after that, Harold Laski wrote to Mr. Churchill telling him that Wingate had been posted to Dorset and urging his claims to more valuable employment. The

[1] Weizmann Archives.

Prime Minister sent a reply, through General Ismay, that Major Wingate had already been appointed to a Far Eastern post.[1] Before this reply reached Laski Wingate had received orders from the Military Secretary to be ready to fly to Rangoon at short notice. In the middle of these stirring events a bewildered note sounded from Woolwich. Wingate had left Wimborne, and the Depot Commander inquired, " May I be informed of this officer's situation please? "

Then when the new appointment was settled, there arose some competition for Wingate's services. There was a department called the Special Operations Executive which was directed by the Ministry of Economic Warfare and was concerned with Resistance movements. S.O.E. could offer tempting employment to Wingate but not such as could give him the opening he sought, a fact already pointed out to him in similar circumstances by Sir Edmund Ironside in the first winter of the war. At all events, nothing came of the proposition which was turned down on the grounds that Wingate was " difficult to work with."[2] But the episode had a sequel. After the proposition had been made and rejected it came to the knowledge of the Minister, Dr. Dalton, who inquired from Sir Alan Brooke, whether in his Far Eastern post Wingate's services were not still indirectly employable by S.O.E. This inquiry seems to have had the effect of increasing War Office curiosity as to Wingate for he was ordered to report for an interview on the 19th of February. He was seen by one of Sir Alan Brooke's deputies who told him what he could of the new appointment. This was not a great deal since Sir Archibald Wavell's answer to a request for details had not yet arrived. It came on the 24th and announced that Wingate was to be given a post on the Commander-in-Chief's staff for operational and liaison duty with the Chinese in Burma. Fitting rank would be accorded later.

Most officers would have been relieved and pleased and flattered at so much attention from men in commanding positions, especially when it came, as this did, immediately after a threatened eclipse. Not so Wingate. His diary shows the sequence of events which has just

---

[1] " My dear Professor, 13.2.42
    " The Prime Minister has asked me to thank you for your letter of the 11th February, and to tell you, for your personal information, that it had already been appreciated that Major Wingate's talents might be of great value in the Far Eastern theatre of war.
    " General Wavell, who is of course fully aware of Wingate's achievements in Ethiopia, was informed some time ago that Wingate could be sent out to him if he so wished ; and he welcomed the offer. Arrangements are therefore being made to send Wingate out by the fastest route at the first opportunity.
    " With kind regards,
        " Yours very sincerely.
        " H. L. Ismay." W.P.I.

[2] A first-hand account.

been recorded, seen through his own eyes. There can be few famous men who received their cue to history so reluctantly. His own account begins on the day after the railway warrant for the journey to Dorset had reached him.

(1) 9.2.42. Professor Laski wrote Churchill, explaining grounds for thinking the General Staff was discriminating against Wingate on political grounds. Churchill sent a verbal reply to the effect that he would see that justice was done.

(2) 11.2.42—9.30 a.m. Wingate rung up politely by Military Secretary's department and told posting to battery at Wimborne cancelled. He would receive an appointment on Wavell's staff forthwith. A special messenger was on the way with the order to stand by to emplane for Rangoon. He would be told nature of appointment later.

(3) Wingate makes preparations for flight.

(4) 17th February—still no word of appointment (unusual). Arrangements complete, seat allotted. Wingate meets Randolph Churchill and mentions Tibesti Plan for conquest of North Africa as only remaining chance. Churchill takes him to Ismay who takes little interest. Churchill asks Wingate to put proposals in writing and promises to pass them to the P.M.

Later Wingate meets Jebb of Ministry of Economic Warfare who is interested in his appointment as it bears on his province. Wingate expresses doubts as to its bona fides, pointing out that it is highly unusual to appoint a regular officer of standing to a job of any importance and not even to bother to send a clerk to see him. The curious absence of any definite appointment was also unusual and disquieting. The Military Secretary's department, from having at first been informative and affable had become indifferent and hardly polite. It was the more curious that, in view of all this indifference, Wingate had been allotted the very fastest way out of England. After this conversation Jebb, on his own, spoke to the Chief of the Imperial General Staff on the subject.

(5) 19th Feb. Wingate called to War Office at 7 p.m. to see C.I.G.S. At 7.30 saw a deputy who was very affable. He started by saying he wanted to explain Wingate's appointment. Wavell had been given full latitude and had asked for Wingate, among others. He had not, however, stated the nature of the appointment he wished to give Wingate. Therefore Wingate must go out as an unattached Major without appointment of any kind, and Wavell would fit him in when he got there. Was Wingate

satisfied with this? Wingate said that to send an officer to the Chinese to organise irregular warfare was like sending coals to Newcastle. The Chinese and Russians were probably a great deal better at that than we were. To this the general replied that Wingate might very well never get to China but remain in India or Burma. Wingate said there seemed little point in sending an officer who was an expert on the Middle East to Burma or India. He then gave a brief résumé of his thesis on modern war. The general had not apparently ever heard of him in connection with the campaign in Ethiopia where he was in command. He knew that he had once been in Palestine. Concluding his remarks Wingate summed up the position in the Eastern and Western war zones, pointing out that the most and the least we could do was to open a Western front, and that the only possible way to do this, in view of existing shipping limitations, was by a central thrust through Africa. The general nodded in apparent agreement but evidently did not wish a frank discussion. He remarked that he thought that the Far East was the place where " things were going to happen." The interview then came to an end with polite expressions on both sides.

It should be remembered that this general holds what is perhaps the most important military position in the State, that he devoted a quarter of an hour to say nothing to a major without a staff appointment, and that he could scarcely thus have wasted his time without an adequate motive. At this moment a major, in our army, ranks much the same as a junior clerk in one of the Government Departments. For this general to see Wingate in the manner described is much as if a Principal Secretary of State were to interview a junior clerk for a quarter of an hour in order to tell him exactly nothing.

It is of course possible that when Wingate arrives somewhere in the Far East he may be given some Staff Appointment should one be vacant. This is not very likely as all available locally are normally snapped up the moment they occur. What is much more likely is that Wingate as a supernumerary Major will be thrown into the first so-called irregular job that offers without rank or power to do anything, or apply any of the principles learned in Ethiopia.

Comment

In the history of war great soldiers have, without I think an exception, enjoyed, and to a large extent depended upon, the support of some at least of the political leaders of their nation.

During the past two centuries there have been few great captains—Frederick the Great, Clive, and Napoleon alone come into that category. In the last war, waged as it was on both sides by great military bureaucracies, no great soldier emerged. Allenby's claims are easily disposed of. He outweighed his enemy by three to one. It was not that there was no great military talent. It was that a great vested interest had been created in all belligerent countries, which everywhere exerted itself to guard its own interests—those of the professional military bureaucrat. England to-day is still in this state, but not so our enemies, still less Russia.

A Government machine is created to perform a given purpose. In course of time and easy conditions it begins to mistake means for ends, to exist for itself. It recognises only one loyalty—to the machine. When this happens—and it is bound to happen from time to time in all states—the leaders of the nation must be vigilant to correct the evil. This has not happened in Britain. Here our statesmen allow themselves to be fobbed off with any excuse by the permanent officials, of whom they have long learned to stand in awe.

Let us take the case in point. The Commander of the patriot forces in the most successful campaign we have had in this war is, for political reasons, reduced to major from full colonel at its close. He becomes ill and is invalided home. There he writes a report considered important enough to be read by several members of the Cabinet, evolving a new theory of modern war and asking leave to apply it on some scale, however modest. His report, although in the hands of the War Office, is ignored by that establishment. He is not asked to see a solitary staff officer. Finally, immediately after his being noticed as still interesting himself in the affairs of Ethiopia, he is ordered away to a job derogatory to his military qualifications and seniority, in an artillery regiment. The Prime Minister is told of the injustice and folly of this treatment, and engages to set matters right. And what is the result of this intervention by the nation's leader? Instead of being sent out to the Far East—an unsuitable theatre—as a major commanding a battery, Wingate is sent out as a supernumerary major without staff grading—the supposition being that he may get such grading on arrival. In other words the representations made have been ignored, but an unconvincing show has been made of doing something. Because a highly placed official passes on Wingate's query as to why no one in authority has seen him, one of the highest military officers sees him—but not to learn anything, nor yet to tell him anything; just to see him, with the view, one is justified in assuming, of saying that he has been seen.

When the permanent officials go their own way regardless of the leaders of the nation, that nation is on the down grade.

N.B.—The War Office is not dependent upon Wavell for giving Wingate suitable powers. Many of his contemporaries are colonels, and there is no valid objection to giving him brevet rank as Colonel.

In the course of this crowded and tempestuous winter, Wingate took up again his oldest and most devoted friendship. He and Derek Tulloch had not met since the days of Sheffield and York and of the fateful meeting with General Deverell at Catterick. In early 1942 Tulloch was an Army Staff officer at Fighter Command Headquarters, and sometime in February Wingate and Lorna went down to Uxbridge to visit Derek and Mary Tulloch. One result of the reunion was that shortly after this, in the second half of February, Wingate gave a lecture on the Ethiopian campaign (the last, it may be assumed, of this time), to officers of Fighter Command. In his essay Derek Tulloch has this to say : " I remember the occasion well ; he (Wingate) was looking very thin and fine drawn, dressed in a nondescript mufti suit with an odd hat he had found somewhere. He played down his own part in the operations, but even so it was a stirring story. . . . He stressed the importance of encouraging local support by example and not by gifts, and also the importance of retaining the initiative and never letting the enemy have a rest. . . . He had learnt . . . the value of silence as opposed to noise and the value of bluff. The R.A.F. officers listened spellbound . . . a scrap of humour here and there but mostly a dry recital of facts and reasoning. It was hard for them to believe that this quiet, unassuming, ascetic-looking man had been involved in such affairs."

The same week Derek Tulloch went to dine with the Wingates at 49 Hill Street. The time was around the 20th when the War Office was offering Wingate Far Eastern employment and he was still trying for Middle Eastern employment. Tulloch found him in the throes of doubt as to what to do, and himself gave the opinion that he should seize the offer from Wavell and forget his suspicions. He urged him to meet Chiang Kai-Shek and do with Chinese guerillas what he had done with Ethiopians. After dinner they continued the debate, and Wingate sat in a chair with an enormous geographical globe between his knees which he turned slowly as he talked, glaring down at it as though wondering which part of the earth's surface he should strike next. He told Tulloch that at one time he had almost persuaded Wavell to adopt a new Middle East strategy, attacking Libya from the south rather than from Egypt, and he was loth to give up this plan in which he believed and over which he had thought so long. Tulloch remembered him saying something as follows: " The L. of C. in M.E. is like the rim of a wheel and is vulnerable everywhere. That is because it goes the wrong way. It should run from the hub, up the spokes. One of the principles of war is to have your L. of C. behind you. How often we neglect this! " But Tulloch remained insistent that he should forget the Tibesti scheme, seek his fortune in the Far East, and " raise and train a vast army of Chinese troops and create havoc amongst the Japanese."

They met again the next day and Wingate showed signs of coming round to his friend's good advice. When they parted outside the Berkeley Hotel Wingate said, " I'll ring you up in a couple of days and let you know." A couple of days later he rang up Tulloch to say, " I've taken your advice and am flying to Chungking the day after to-morrow. Good-bye for the present."[1] He did get to Chungking in the end.

He left London by air for Rangoon on the 27th of February.

His biographer must needs record a fact which should be prominent in the record of a military man. In the course of these London days Wingate, in recognition of his services in Ethiopia, had been awarded a bar to his D.S.O. The fact was gazetted in the same week as he left. He seems to have made no comment on the subject to anyone, or at least none that anyone remembers.

[1] Tulloch Essay.

CHAPTER XVI

OPPORTUNITY IN DEFEAT

At the end of the winter of 1941 and 1942 the Western Allies suffered their last great defeats of the Second World War. The British unconditionally surrendered Singapore on the 15th of February and abandoned Rangoon on the 7th of March. By this time the Japanese were masters of all South-East Asia except Upper Burma, and after the loss of Rangoon the loss of all Burma was inevitable. But the speed of the Japanese advance was by now diminishing and for some weeks after the Rangoon disaster endeavours to stabilise the Burma front still seemed worth while, though disillusion always came swiftly. It was to a dismal scene of weakening hopes and increasing menace that Wingate was sent to organise a new Gideon Force.

His journey was not the rapid one he expected, and he was held up for more than two weeks in Cairo, before receiving his air passage in the third week in March. He flew, not to Rangoon, which was lost by now, but to New Delhi. On the 19th he was received by General Wavell who gave him orders; he was to fly to Maymyo and report to Army Headquarters with instructions to take command of all guerilla operations in Burma. He was given the temporary rank of Colonel. Maymyo is about thirty miles East of Mandalay and might be described as the Burmese Simla. Wingate arrived there on the 22nd of March and explained his mission to General Hutton.[1] The latter was not encouraging. He told Wingate in some detail of the state of the army, of the shortage of men and the increasing shortage of aircraft. As regards Wingate's mission he could only recommend him to make himself known to an existing guerilla organisation called " The Bush Warfare School " whose headquarters were also at Maymyo. In his own words, Wingate " moved into the Bush Warfare School " that same day. He had the right to take charge and displace the commandant. But things fell out otherwise.

Something should be said about the Bush Warfare School for it played a part in what followed. It was a secret organisation whose purpose was to promote demolition and ambush attack in the rear of

---

[1] *Record of an Attempt to Organise Long Range Penetration in Burma During April, 1942, by Colonel O. C. Wingate.* W.P.I.

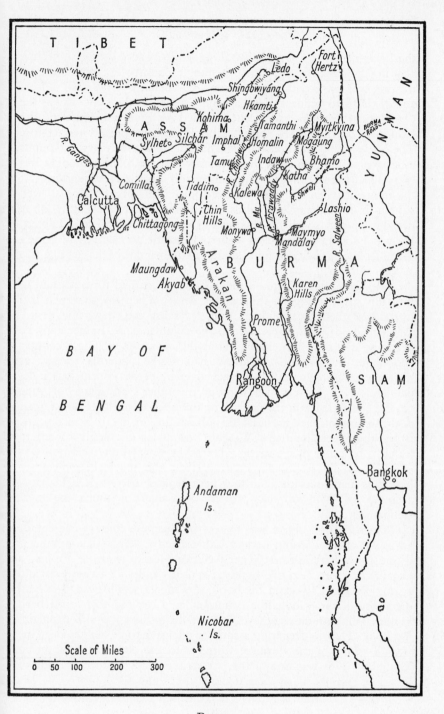

Burma

the Japanese Army. Its name was designed to mislead since its objective was not to attack the Japanese in jungle country but in China. Its mission was to provide a professional " stiffening " of British officers and N.C.O.s to Chinese guerilla bands,[1] much in the same way as the Operational Centres had been designed to give coherence to the Ethiopian patriots. The term " school " was purposely inexact too. The organisation was not so much an academy with lectures, and pupils as a fighting unit, much in the same way that the S.N.S. school at Ein Harod had been both a training centre and a battle Headquarters. At the moment when Wingate " moved into " this organisation so well suited to his talents and ideas, the commandant was away on a demolition raid south of Maymyo. He was called Michael Calvert. He was a soldier of first-class ability. He made no claim to Wingate's formidable originality of mind but as a commander in the field he was at least his equal.

Two days after Wingate's move Calvert returned from his raid to find this grim stranger sitting at his desk. When the two men had introduced themselves Calvert said, " Excuse me, that's my desk." Wingate yielded the place back to the commandant. Immediately he began to question him closely about the character of jungle country and about his methods. Calvert had studied guerilla warfare as intensely as Wingate and had reached many of his conclusions independently, but he was still without the other's advantage of wide practical experience in the field. The two men found they had a great deal in common, not the least an unhesitating dislike of staff officers. It has often been said that Wingate was an egotist easily roused to jealousy by other men's merits. He never showed any such jealousy of Michael Calvert; on the contrary, from the first he determined to have this man's services, and they became close friends. Of the many accounts of Wingate, that written by Calvert is much the most sympathetic.

Wingate's first object was to see the Burmese country. A day or two after their meeting, he and Calvert and a " lady stenographer " drove from Maymyo to General Slim's Headquarters at Prome, a distance of more than two hundred and fifty miles. " Every now and again," relates Calvert in his book, " Wingate would lean back and dictate something about the countryside. I realised that I had been looking at it with unseeing eyes." Sir William Slim was still maintaining hope. He was preparing a counter-offensive to be delivered by the two divisions of the Burmese Corps with the object of recapturing Rangoon. This was one of the last serious plans to turn the tide of invasion, and like all of them it came to nothing.

[1] *Prisoners of Hope* by Michael Calvert, D.S.O., referred to subsequently as Calvert.

When they arrived at Prome the two guerilla leaders had some difficulty, according to Calvert's account, with "a rather poisonous Staff officer," before they could gain admittance, but they succeeded in the end. The younger man introduced Wingate to the General and then left the two of them to a long talk alone.[1] They were to be much in each other's lives during the next two years. At this first meeting they both took to each other. Later, Slim was to have mixed feelings about Wingate, feelings which he never seems to have resolved. In the afternoon of the same day Slim's two visitors returned to Maymyo.

Wingate had two urgent problems, one of which he knew how to solve, while the other was insoluble; he needed to establish his authority, and he needed men. As regards the first problem, Michael Calvert never challenged Wingate's rights but other commanders did. The Bush Warfare School was one of several guerilla cadres and organisations run by veiled authorities, and, not surprisingly, the men in charge who had borne the heat and burden of the day, and enjoyed much independence, were not pleased to find themselves suddenly made subordinate to a new arrival who knew no more about Burma and the jungle than the next man. One of them refused openly to take any orders except from the Commander-in-Chief.[2] (It is strange how disaster does not modify the love of position.) In less desperate circumstances Wingate would soon have imposed himself irresistibly as sole and undisputed leader, in accordance with Wavell's orders, but the situation in Burma in early 1942 was empty of opportunity. Daring patrol operations were all that was possible in the line of guerilla war; there could be no long range penetration attempt with the Air Force weakened and part destroyed by the abandonment of Rangoon; and after the routs in Singapore and Malaya there were no men to spare. And then, just at this time, the few men from whom Wingate might have assembled a patrol force were reduced in numbers by an appalling reverse on the Irrawaddy, suffered by a hundred of Calvert's men. They were surprised at Padaung on the 29th and cut to pieces by the advancing Japanese. There were only eleven survivors.[3] There was no way of making good such losses and though Wingate struggled to obtain a force and make his command effective, it seems that he did not struggle with his old tenacity and strength. He was involved in one of the great defeats of history and he was evidently prepared, for the first and only time in his life, to admit a military situation utterly beyond him. This was common sense.

In the disaster there remained, however, just one faint and slender

[1] Calvert.　　[2] *Record of an Attempt.* W.P.I.
[3] *Appreciation of Chances of Forming Long Range Penetration Groups by Col. Wingate,* Maymyo. 2.4.42. W.P.I.

hope of obtaining troops in adequate quantity. A number of trained men had already been sent to China by the Bush Warfare School in accordance with its original plan. To these Wingate had a shadowy claim and he decided to press it before giving up. Circumstances helped him. General Alexander took over from General Hutton in Maymyo at the end of March, and in the first week of April General Chiang Kai-Shek flew from Chungking to confer with him. Wingate obtained authorisation to fly to Chungking to see General Bruce, the head of the British Military mission, and with Calvert's help he was given a seat on the aircraft carrying the Generalissimo. They flew to Chungking on the 6th of April,[1] Wingate introducing himself and enjoying a frank or apparently frank and cordial conversation with the Chinese leader, the frankness and cordiality not disturbed by the storm-tossed path of the plane as the pilot took evasive action from Japanese fighters, the while Madame Chiang vomited with elegance into a paper receptacle.[2]

It is tempting to follow a likely course in Wingate's mind. He was never a man to lose the sense of a continuous thread, and as Palestine influenced what he did in Ethiopia, so Ethiopia did the same to his Far East assignment. It is legitimate to suppose that as he flew northwards from Maymyo he indulged imaginings of Chiang Kai-Shek as a new Haile Selassie, and himself leading a new Gideon Force to the disruption of Japanese might from the heart of China. But there was no opening along such lines. The Gideon appointment (a ruinous one) had already been made in favour of the American Army, in the person of General Stilwell. As for troops, General Bruce explained to Wingate that for political reasons alone, if for no other, he could not transfer the Bush Warfare men from Chinese command at such a moment of disintegrating solidarity.[3] Wingate did not resist the argument. He was in a new world and he was learning.

He flew back to Maymyo on the 15th of April to find that while he had been away he had lost not only the few men he could command in Burma, but his authority. Calvert had tried to protect his interests and had failed. He put the failure down to staff conspiracy[4] against Wingate, but this is to be doubted. The Japanese had renewed their offensive, defeated the Chinese in the north, and were moving successfully against Prome and Mandalay. The remnant of the Air Force had been finally put out of action by ground attacks. In exactly a month's time the British Empire in Burma was to suffer total military defeat. The High Command had seen the inevitability of a retreat to the west of the River Chindwin since early March, and General Alexander's staff in Maymyo could have had no delusions on the subject. In such

---

[1] *Record of an Attempt.* W.P.I.   [2] Wingate quoted in Calvert.
[3] Information obtained at the War Office.   [4] Calvert.

circumstances there was neither the time nor enough men to attempt a new strategy for which only a handful of men were trained. So the men of the Bush Warfare School were used as a general reserve while Wingate and Calvert were put off with excuses and circumlocutions and lies. In the atrocity of war such dishonesties should not count for much.

Nor is there evidence that Wingate counted them for much. On his return to Maymyo he wrote a protesting record of his effort and its frustration but in moderate terms, as though his purpose was to register his claim, rather than to demand a revision of policy. He seems to have recognised that this was not his moment. He was now virtually unemployed and there was no reason for him to stay in Burma, but before leaving he seized one opportunity which was not to recur. He took a car, presumably from the Bush Warfare School, and made a " good long journey "[1] around Burma. It was the last chance he ever had of reconnoitring from the ground, and in relative calm, the place where he was to achieve the greatest of his deeds. The journey was made in the week following his return and before the week was over he had flown from Maymyo back to New Delhi.

This brief Burma interlude may appear as a clear episode in Wingate's life. If so, the biographer has been too solicitous for the reader's comfort. It was a very complicated and confused episode in which no man saw his way beyond a short distance; a sequence of cluttered-up days in which numerous plans were proposed and some-times part-organised, all against a background of complex and some-times conflicting secret organisations and authorities whose inter-relation would take much space to elucidate, and which was rapidly made obsolete by the simple and terrible fact of Japanese victory.

The retreat of the army from Burma to Assam was completed by the 17th of May, but for more than three weeks after this date, stragglers, lost groups of civilians, and rearguard parties made their way westwards by the little jungle roads to the Chindwin. They laboured under increasing difficulties and suffered increasing casualties, mostly through exhaustion. Several of the rearguards were drawn from the men of the Bush Warfare School, and in the fate of one of them, one of the last military units to attempt evacuation, a name already familiar in Wingate's story appears again. This rearguard was led by one of the Lieutenant-Colonels commanding detachments under Calvert. He was Courtenay Brocklehurst. In the confusion of the time he probably never heard that he had come under Wingate's orders for a brief period. Throughout March and April he had been away from Maymyo on a mission to the north. When disaster came he was slow to begin

[1] Calvert.

retreat, insisting, with typical bravery, on accomplishing all he could of his allotted task before seeking his own safety. After hairbreadth escapes he got his men across the Irrawaddy though the whole river was now held by Japanese. His detachment dispersed thereafter into small groups and he and his own party struggled north-west towards the Chindwin in the last days of May. In this attempt he was killed. His end was seen by no one but it seems that in trying to cross one of the northern tributaries of the Chindwin his raft was overturned in the rapids and he was drowned.[1] He never met Wingate. If he had done so it is difficult to believe that the two men could have been friends: too much of mutual distrust and prejudice was between them, and too much injury. They were fated to be enemies; a strange thing when it is remembered that Brocklehurst was loved by everyone who knew him. No one had more advantage in natural charm of address, in " gladness of character," than this courageous and handsome man who in middle age lost his life in performing duties which belong to the vigour of youth.

Wingate's first move after leaving Burma is easily guessed. Arrived in New Delhi he set himself to ensuring that his appointment was not lost with many others in the landslide of the disaster. He began immediately to plan for the future. There is record of him attending a meeting called by the Director of Military Operations as early as the 24th of April. He showed a new astuteness in manœuvre. He did not ask, as he had a right to do, for the command of all future operations behind the Japanese lines. He drew a distinction between guerilla units and long range penetration groups, and only wanted command of the latter. He guessed, in all probability, that what he would achieve by the long range method would so overshadow what others did, that he would become the effective centre of interior operations in any case. He may have guessed too, that under the ferocious tyranny of Japanese occupation an ordinary guerilla campaign, such as that conducted by the Ethiopian patriots, would be unable to achieve anything.

In detail his plans did not yet bear much resemblance to what was to happen. He proposed to train his men around Balasore (near the East coast of India half-way between Cuttack and Calcutta), so that he and they could cross by sea to Akyab whose capture he assumed to be his objective. In the event, training grounds were chosen far from Balasore; both his expeditions entered Burma overland from Assam; he was never entrusted with any attempt on the port of Akyab or the

---

[1] This account is drawn from records of the time lent to the writer by Sir Philip Brocklehurst, Bt.

Arakan coast. He asserted at this meeting that he could train men for jungle work in eight weeks.[1] It took longer than that.

He lived in a room in Maiden's Hotel, and of course his next business was to write a memorandum, one of many which he was to compose during that summer of discontent. He addressed this first one to the Commander-in-Chief and followed it up by frequent visits to a room in G.H.Q. where maps of Burma " papered the walls in untidy tapestry."[2] The inhabitants of this room were the Joint Planning Staff who had been ordered by Sir Archibald Wavell, even while the defeat was in progress, to study the reconquest of Burma. Among the officers who worked here was Major Bernard Fergusson, and in the account which he wrote two years later he gave a dramatic record of how the Long Range Penetration scheme was gradually forced on the notice of himself and his colleagues.

" Many people," he says in his book, " came into our office with plans for the reconquest. Some of their ideas were useful : these were carefully noted, and filed away for future reference. Some were fantastic and foolish : these we made a pretence of noting, and bowed their originators out of the room. . . . Only in one direction did there seem any prospect of action in the near future. It lay in the person of a broad-shouldered, uncouth, almost simian officer who used to drift gloomily into the office for two or three days at a time, audibly dream dreams, and drift out again. When in Delhi, he would make his headquarters in the G.H.Q. library, from which he would borrow a dozen books at a time, to the distress of the librarian. . . . We used to look on this visitor as one to be bowed out, as soon as it was possible to put a term to his ramblings ; but as we became aware that he took no notice of us anyway, but that without our patronage he had the ear of the highest, we paid more attention to his schemes. Soon we had fallen under the spell of his almost hypnotic talk ; and by and by we— or some of us—had lost the power of distinguishing between the feasible and the fantastic."

Bernard Fergusson had met Wingate in Palestine and again in Cairo after the Ethiopian campaign. He knew little about him. Gradually in the course of the summer he decided[3] to join his fortunes with those of this man who " was here in India, soberly plotting wild adventures in Burma."[4] Wingate's plan, like all his previous plans, was arrestingly simple. Fergusson thus described it :

[1] *Minutes of a Meeting held in the D.M.O.'s Office on* 24.4.42. W.P.I.

[2] *Beyond the Chindwin* by Brigadier Bernard Fergusson, D.S.O., M.C. The book is referred to subsequently as Fergusson I.

[3] He asked the advice of Sir Archibald Wavell who said : " If you were married I would advise you not to go with Wingate, but unmarried, as you are, I wouldn't hesitate." Fergusson. A communication.

[4] Fergusson I.

"Briefly, his point was that the enemy was most vulnerable far behind his lines, where his troops, if he had any at all, were of inferior quality. Here a small force could wreak havoc out of all proportion to its numbers. If it should be surprised, it could disintegrate into smaller prearranged parties to baffle pursuit, and meet again at a rendezvous fifteen to twenty miles farther on its route. Supply should be by air, communication by wireless: these two weapons had not yet been properly exploited. His proposal was to cut the enemy's supply line, destroy his dumps, tie up troops unprofitably far behind the line in the endeavour to protect these vulnerable areas, and generally to help the army proper on to its objectives."

Wingate spent May and most of June in the opening phases of a long wrestle with authority. His danger now was not rejection, but of being accepted on stultifying terms. The Director of Staff Duties, whose task is to allot troops to agreed operations, raised several telling objections to Wingate's first proposition. He pointed out that the example of the Ethiopian campaign was misleading because the native population had been united on the Allied side whereas the Burmans were not; that formations such as the Long Range Penetration Groups, as they had come to be called, should depend not on the direction of regular units, as Wingate wanted, but, in accordance with Army tradition, on the raising of volunteers; that the scale of the proposed groups was excessive, and instead of three thousand their total should be thirteen hundred.[1] Against these arguments Wingate counter-attacked with forensic skill. As regards the Ethiopian precedent he made strenuous play with the episode of Ras Hailu, from which he pointed the questionable conclusion that the difficult interior situation of Burma was much the same as he had found in Ethiopia. When he came to the matter of volunteering he artfully omitted to mention that Gideon Force had been composed of volunteers but, forgetting the hard things he had once said of them, drew unflattering comparisons between their achievements and those of the volunteer-commandos in the Middle Eastern theatre. As regards numbers he defended his proposal for three thousand by saying that rather than follow the D.S.D.'s. reasoning, " it is sounder to make an estimate of the weight of the punch you want to deliver, and thus arrive at the desired total and stick to it." Adding in a subsequent paragraph, " The man who uses (the groups) should decide their composition and strength in the light of requirements."

Wingate's struggle with the Army of India was rarely relaxed, never broken off, and when he had thrown one opponent he usually found that another was quick to replace him. The weeks in Maiden's

---

[1] *L.R.P. Groups. Comments on note of D.S.D. by Colonel O. C. Wingate.* W.P.I.

Hotel were not easily endured, for in spite of his increased confidence in himself and his ideas, his position was still so feeble that he often had to face the possibility that by the sheer force of circumstances nothing at all would come of his endeavours.[1] Of all the virtues that of patience was the most alien to his character, and now patience was forced on him. There are signs that he learned something of its practice by distracting his mind in strenuous mental recreations. A letter written to Lorna in April soon after his return from Burma tells, among other things, how he occupied himself between memoranda and arguments.

"I have just read a life of the unfortunate Nietzsche—whom I have never been able to like and still dislike; but what a Götter-dämmerung of a life! Nietzsche is too German, too humourless, hysterical and prancing to be acceptable. Besides neither he nor anyone else knows what he was trying to say. But as a critic he is often valuable and powerful.

I am amusing myself by writing a Charter for Humanity which might be used in an expression of war aims. My interest in it is more academic than practical as I greatly doubt whether any gospel is ever accepted without a long incubatory process. In drawing up this war aim I find it necessary first to define liberty of conscience—and that takes one to the root of things where one must beware of error—and then nationality—the terms of the latter definition being the arbiters of any international settlement, and therefore meriting meticulous care.

The Chinese are a charming people. Their dominant charac-teristic is cheerfulness. Under conditions which would reduce Europeans to a gloomy despair, smiles of pure joy break out constantly over the Chinese face. Esme Barton's friend[2] is a beautiful and vivacious person. I have not yet had more than a casual contact with them.

Tell mother Nigel is safe and well in Palestine when I last heard of him. . . . Mary Newall left (Cairo) on the day of my arrival and I never saw her. She was coming back later. I could write you a full and interesting account of the war, but in this mealy-mouthed era must not do so. I have on the whole been singularly free from my particular curse and hope to remain so. . . .

People here generally have not grasped the significance of this war. They have learned few if any of the lessons taught. Nor is it possible to change them or convince them that this is so. 'They hear not Moses and the prophets.' God bless you and bring us

[1] Calvert.   [2] Madame Chiang Kai-Shek.

together again. I flew over the Mountains of Israel to land on Gennesaret. They were more beautiful than the mountains of prey. How lovely it would be if you and I could be there now working to defend Ha aretz. (The Land.) Let it happen, please God."

The reference to his "particular curse" is interesting. He meant his fits of despair. After the calamity of the 4th of July he was never seriously afraid of this affliction again.[1]

Some time at the end of May Calvert arrived in India from Burma. He had had many adventures in a rôle similar to Brocklehurst's, and only by luck less fatal. At the beginning of the retreat General Alexander had coalesced the men of the school with others, described as the "odds and sods of Maymyo," into the "Bush Warfare battalion" which Calvert commanded in rearguard actions during the retreat. After the dispersal of this makeshift unit, when the army had reached Assam, Calvert and the remains of his school had returned to Burma for a last guerilla operation. When this was accomplished, Calvert and one of his officers, Captain George Dunlop, made their way to India, ill and exhausted. When Wingate heard that they were alive in Ranchi, he sent for them immediately. At this time the Bush Warfare School was still the only unit which he could (doubtfully) claim to command. Calvert and Dunlop went to Delhi and Wingate asked them if they would come with him in the new venture. They both said they would, and added that they could answer in the same sense for most survivors of the school. Wingate told them to go on leave and recover their strength. They did so.

At last, after a few weeks that may have seemed to Wingate like a few months, after much negotiation, and intrigue, and in the face of hostility which was never to be overcome, Wingate got what he wanted, and troops in the numbers he had asked for were allotted to him. The authority of the Commander-in-Chief, who despite misfortune maintained his extraordinary personal hold over the army, was on Wingate's side and this fact ultimately proved irresistible so far as the principle of the new venture was concerned. So, with the misgiving of many people, troops were directed to undergo training in the Long Range Penetration Groups which were now given a formal military title: the 77th Indian Infantry Brigade.

The composition of the new brigade was most unusual and ought to be looked at. Shortage of man-power was already becoming a British military problem and the choice of troops was consequently extremely unconventional. The nucleus of the brigade came, of course, from the men of the Bush Warfare School and these were

[1] Mrs. Lorna Smith.

formed into what was described as Number 142 Commando Company. They neither trained nor operated as a single body of men but were distributed in specialist teams throughout the eight columns into which the brigade was divided. The " Bush Warfare " officers and men were all volunteers from infantry regiments and from the Royal Engineers.

Of the units directed to the new brigade the most difficult from the point of view of command was a composite battalion of the Gurkha Rifles. This was a wartime unit so short of specialised officers that only one had experience of active service and only two a thorough knowledge of the Gurkhali language.[1] The difficulty did not lie only or mainly here, however, but much more in the fact that this was the only component of the brigade which belonged in the strict sense to the Army of India, and the Gurkhas brought with them some of the scepticism of the India authorities strengthened by a fallacious sense of superior knowledge. The Gurkhas had their own traditions of jungle training and tactics and some of their officers remained convinced that Wingate was an amateur who had nothing to teach them. Wingate believed, and Calvert believed that senior officers in Delhi and the depots encouraged their tendency to insubordination. It may have been so. What is certain is that the Gurkhas paid dearly afterwards for their conservatism.[2]

Wingate's other Oriental regiment, the second battalion of the Burma Rifles, knew the Burmese jungle better than he could ever hope to, but their reaction to their new Commander was quite different from that of the Gurkhas. Their detailed knowledge made them all the quicker to recognise that Wingate was a man out of the ordinary, and with them he had easy relations from the beginning. Their officers were British with few exceptions and came for the most part from the trading houses and families of Rangoon. The N.C.O.s and men came from many different parts of Burma and included Karens from the Irrawaddy Delta and the Karen hills, Chins from the Chin Hills in North-West Burma, and men of the widespread Kachin tribes. Wingate found them the easiest of his men to train and he continually learned from them.[3] In his account of them he praised them as he praised no others who served under him at any time, and it is not extravagant to detect in his admiration delight in a realised dream. Here were the Patriots again, but in a form in which he never saw the braves of Ethiopia: in a well-disciplined and perfectly suited military formation.

The most improbable component of the brigade were the officers

[1] *Report on the Operations of 77th Indian Infantry Brigade in Burma, February to June*, 1943, *by Brigadier O. C. Wingate*. W.P.I. Referred to subsequently as Wingate Burma Report.
[2] Calvert.　　　[3] Calvert.

and men of the 13th Battalion of the King's Liverpool Regiment. They had come to India at the end of 1941 with no anticipation of great military exploits. They were also a wartime unit and had been raised in 1940 and 1941[1] from men of Glasgow, Liverpool and Manchester. Few of them were young by modern Army standards, and most of them were married. They had spent the last months of 1940 and nearly the whole of 1941 in coastal defence in Britain. In December of the latter year, when invasion of England was no longer believed in, they were sent to India for garrison and security duties. In June they were directed to Wingate and on arrival at the training camp " showed a marked lack of enthusiasm."[2] But they soon discovered a high spirit of adventure. In the opinion of their commanding officer, Lieutenant-Colonel Cooke, their staid character was no disadvantage in their novel and fearful employment because " they knew what war meant."[3] In only one respect did their high age-average prove a handicap : many of them had passed the time of life when they could be trained in the rigours of jungle fieldcraft and battle drill. Two hundred and fifty men, including their Colonel,[4] were lost to the brigade for this reason, and were replaced by drafts from military depots how and when these were available. The battalion was not one which would have been chosen in circumstances of plentiful man-power, but there can be no doubt at all that this body of town-dwellers, trained and intended for far less daunting military tasks, gave weight and valiance to the jungle campaign.

In his Transport Company Wingate met a familiar problem in a new shape. Here, in contrast to Ethiopia, there were mules, but there were no muleteers, and the search for men with military training and sufficient knowledge of beast-management remained obstinately difficult. The problem was solved in part by giving the Company command to the veterinary officer, Captain Carey Foster, a massive breach of the rules, while the muleteering itself was given in the main to Gurkhas who never mastered that difficult craft.

There were in addition to the components described above a Brigade signalling section which ought to have been at least twice its size,[5] and an R.A.F. section to direct, organise and advise on supply by parachute. The Brigade was at first organised into eight columns, later reduced to seven[6] owing to the large number of men, chiefly of

[1] From a cadre consisting of Warrant Officers and N.C.O.s of the King's Own Scottish Borderers, the Royal Welch Fusiliers, and the Royal Ulster Rifles. Information obtained at the War Office.
[2] Wingate Burma Report.
[3] Major-General S. A. Cooke, O.B.E. Information obtained at the War Office.
[4] He was then succeeded by Lieut.-Colonel Cooke.
[5] Wingate Burma Report.
[6] Number 6 Column was suppressed.

the King's Liverpool Regiment, who were rejected in the course of training.

Such in brief was the force which Wingate came to command in the summer of 1942. Its formation and purpose were kept absolutely secret, so much so that until it had accomplished its mission no one outside the small official world, which Wingate continued to hate and distrust, was aware of what was being prepared or achieved. This was an inestimable service to the brigade and was rendered only at the cost of much self-discipline by the inhabitants of the aforementioned small official world who in turn hated Wingate as heartily as he hated them.

After much study and consultation a training area was chosen in the jungle country around Saugor. This is at the north-westerly tip of the Central provinces, south of Gwalior. The conditions here were the nearest that could be found to the dry zone of Upper Burma, and though the resemblance was not precise, it proved enough for the training except in one respect : there was no river of the formidable breadth, swiftness and treachery such as the brigade had to cross and recross during the expedition. In his choice of area Wingate had remarkable luck in one respect. Saugor and its neighbourhood came under the Central India Command and here Wingate found in Major-General Wilcox a superior who believed in him enthusiastically. Of course he often grumbled about the General during training, but when he came to write his report he found himself obliged to acknowledge a considerable debt to him and his staff. These passages, to anyone who remembers Wingate's usual rebellion against those set over him, make somewhat strange reading.

The training began in July but the work of assembly was so slow, especially regarding the mules, that full-scale exercises did not begin till the autumn. The rule was merciless severity throughout : to make men able to bear privation and fatigue up to the very limit of human endurance, and far beyond what men thought they could endure. Wingate followed the wise rule of military preparation that the best way to learn to combat a human enemy is to take arms against natural forces, and accounts of life in the jungle camps record almost every ordeal under nature except ice and snow. The men had to outdo our earliest ancestors in power of survival ; if they collapsed under the stress of heat in long marches with full loads they were revived with no more comforting equipment than the shade of trees and makeshift fans ; when the monsoon broke they were forced to continue the exercises in mud and incessant rain with no allowance for rising rivers and unpassable grounds ; they had to carry out heavy tasks on light rations; they had to ignore thirst;[1] they had to learn to bear midges and mosquitoes and leeches by will rather than protection; and they were virtually forbidden to go sick. This last discipline was the harshest but among the most necessary. " The first thing," Wingate wrote in his report, ". . . when setting out to train a L.R.P.G. is to root out the prevailing hypochondria. . . . I had the full, although sometimes misgiving co-operation of the medical officers. . . . Within three weeks of entering the jungle in the monsoon 30 per cent of the King's were either in or trying to enter hospital. Four weeks later their sick parade reached the peak figure of 70 per cent of their strength. With the co-operation of the doctors certain measures were taken and the sick parade numbers rapidly fell till towards the end of training they were less than 3 per cent. . . . [In the expedition] the man knew that sickness meant capture or death. He therefore did not only not go sick, he did not even feel sick." Except in the case of grave illness, he insisted throughout the training on all invalids being treated medically by the platoon commanders since this rough and ready method would necessarily be followed in battle conditions.[2] It is wonderful what men can live through.

Although under the stress of such living his officers and men often cursed him for a tyrant, he was on good terms with them, as he had been with the squadsmen, as he had never been with the majority of Gideon Force. Again it is allowable to wonder whether the calamity of the year before had released by violent means some inner constriction of the spirit. There is some evidence to suggest such a thing. Calvert, who joined the Brigade in August and became chief instructor, says this of him : " He tried out theories and discarded them. He liked people to tell him if they thought that he had taken the wrong turning in his training, He liked a true critical spirit among his officers. . . . (He) liked his comforts. He liked his whisky, and many a time have some of us become extremely gay with him over a bottle of whisky or rum. . . . He knew that he liked a party, and so, on the whole, steeled himself to avoid such frivolities." Calvert's picture is as well observed as William Allen's, and very different.

There is a small self-portrait of this time too, written under

---

[1] By a curious oversight Wingate seems never to have discovered the military value of chewing gum. It is nowhere mentioned in his training notes.

[2] Information obtained at the War Office. Calvert. *Wingate's Raiders* by Charles Rolo referred to subsequently as Rolo. The following quotation from a letter from Wingate to a member of General Wilcox's staff is of interest : " I am at last getting Platoon Commanders to be their Platoon Physicians for minor ailments and treatment. I never allowed this to interrupt our marches or operations. Gordon said, ' A man is either his own physician or a fool at thirty.' On this standard a great part of our nation must be classified as fools. I do not sit and take that as an unalterable fact, but set out to alter it, and I hope I succeed in doing so." (15th August, 1942) W.P.I.

somewhat curious circumstances. Before Calvert joined Wingate in the Central Provinces, he spent some time in Delhi as part-representative of the Brigade at General Headquarters, and (not to mince words) part-spy, both in an unofficial capacity. On the 6th of August, a few days before joining, he reported some hostile Delhi gossip to Wingate, notably that at a senior conference one of the Generals had said that Wingate was not fit to command a unit of brigade size. In the course of his long answer Wingate wrote : " Before I took command in Ethiopia people were saying exactly the same things they are reported as saying now. If there is any difference, I am a good deal more moderate now than I was then, having learned some valuable lessons in the interim. The personal attacks cannot be answered by argument, but they can be, and are, answered by the facts. It is because I am what I am, objectionable though that appears to my critics, that I win battles."[1]

As with the Special Night Squads, as with Gideon Force, the brigade was held together as a firm whole from the first by Wingate's astonishing gift of leadership. From the days when he first showed it, when he cowed his tormentors at Woolwich, to his last days in Burma, his use of this gift varied little : it had shown the fullness of its strength from the beginning. He was aided by two natural advantages, a clear carrying voice and handsome looks, but this was all he had in common with the more conventional exercise of this rare ability. Most commanders who can compel the devotion of their men do so by being able to convey a sense of close sympathy, by appearing in some sort as a big father or brother, by appearing essentially the same, in larger version, as the men they lead. Wingate belonged to a different and older fashion. When he addressed his men he seemed to speak from a different world. If he entered into small humdrum details of administration, discipline or equipment, he would as often as not relate them to principles of war, to the virtues of the cause for which his men were fighting, to the historical implications of the hour. A more dangerous method can hardly be imagined of exhorting British soldiers, always prone to philistine cynicism and a laugh at authority. Wingate never failed in seizing and dominating the attention of his audience. He never indulged in comfortable assurances. He was capable of telling men outright before an operation that not a few of them were likely to meet their deaths soon, and when he did this he did not lower their morale but strengthened it. He could always convey all his own self-confidence. One man, remembering a particularly grim address of the 1943 days, added that after hearing it he would " have followed Wingate to hell and back." This was not an exceptional reaction. His sincerity always struck home with the same telling response. There is no evidence that

[1] W.P.I.

he carefully trained himself in speaking or in the arts of theatrical "timing." His gift was spontaneous, from within, often used without any preparation.[1]

To return to the training. Fergusson, who joined the brigade in October as commander of number 5 Column, described a peculiarity of the Wingate regime not recorded elsewhere. "Every movement, from stand to stand, was done at the double : it was one of Wingate's fads that British officers thought it undignified to run ; and he saw to it that this particular form of false dignity did not obtain in his brigade. When he wished to move to another viewpoint, he ran there, and jolly fast too : arrived at the new spot, he would wheel round, and woe betide anyone who was not there to hear the first words that fell from his mouth."

In the course of Fergusson's first day's training Wingate, running from place to place as usual, led a party of officers to a river in order to reconnoitre a crossing. He invited opinions as to the best crossing place, and to all suggestions asked, "How do you know?" "It became apparent," says Fergusson, "that what he wanted was someone to say that you could not tell without reconnoitring the far bank ; so again I found myself swimming."

From his Sheffield days he had been an enthusiast for sand-table exercises, a procedure known in army jargon as the "tewt" meaning Tactical Exercises Without Troops. The normal equipment is a table of large but household dimensions fitted with a sand-filled tray. Wingate's belief in this method of tactical training had for long found expression in ever more enormous sand-tables : that at Ein Harod was remembered for its bigness; that at the Soba Camp was evidently bigger and better ; this one in the Central Province was as easily measured in acreage as in furniture terms, reaching proportions of twenty by twenty yards. He wanted "every hill, tree, river and gun emplacement . . . built in, exactly to scale—a hundred yards to a foot—and . . . every movement timed with stop-watch precision, so that an officer lying down in the sand-pit could visualise the operations as a whole."[2] The realisation fell short of what he wanted, not surprising with the day-to-day weariness of men under his training, and though many of those he led reported afterwards that his sand-table exercises had wonderfully prepared them for what they found in Burma, he himself made contemptuous remarks later about the laziness that had prevented him employing the method more fully and to greater advantage.

[1] This is drawn from numerous accounts including those of Calvert, E. Jary, Chit Ken, Christopher Perowne, Fergusson. See also *Safer than a Known Way* by Ian MacHorton and *With Wingate in Burma* by David Halley, referred to subsequently as Halley.
[2] Rolo.

If the life was grim it had its occasional delights too, such as are never distant in conditions of physical fitness and wild scenes. The life also had its moments of comedy. There was a strange occurrence with the milch buffaloes kept at Brigade Headquarters. On one occasion they all fell ill with a disease that none could diagnose, and neither the professional attentions of Carey Foster, nor Wingate's own White-Knight experiments with blankets, Flit, and whisky could relieve the buffaloes of their mysterious weakness. It seemed as though they would all pine away, when a local wizard, hearing of the matter, made his way to the camp and, in Wingate's presence, moved by unknown impulses, branded the beasts on the crutch, flanks and one shoulder, after which torture they instantly recovered. No one could speak the wizard's language so Wingate and his party were left to their awful perplexity. They used to tease him about the wizard at Headquarters afterwards and he enjoyed them doing so.[1] Again this is in contrast with the Wingate of Ethiopia.

By the end of September he had two thousand of his men under training and he considered that the time had come to put his force to the test of a large-scale exercise. General Wilcox provided umpires. The Commander-in-Chief came from Delhi to watch in person, a singular mark of his esteem. For all that, the exercise was not an enjoyable occasion for the brigadier : it seems that more things went wrong than is usual on manœuvres, so much so that Wingate reacted in a way to surprise the student of his life. At the end of the practice he was suddenly filled with doubts and second thoughts about the whole venture, and he confided a lack of confidence to Wavell. In his own words, he questioned " whether we could do the work the Commander-in-Chief had destined us for." But Wavell was of another mind. He never doubted Wingate's ability at any time, and now he urged this usually extravagantly confident man to put his misgivings away and persist in the work he had begun.[2] Though Wingate never allowed any suspicion of his fears to become known to his followers,[3] and though he was stimulated by the Commander-in-Chief's words, he could not entirely dismiss his doubts for some time yet. He never underestimated the enormity of what he was undertaking. He never hid from himself the fact that whereas his former successes had been against weak enemies, he was now opposed to a fierce people with whom long and modernised civilisation had done nothing to lessen their primitive brutality and primitive courage. After the exercise he ordered the brigade back to the training, of which one of the men said

[1] Calvert.
[2] Wingate Burma Report. Information obtained at the War Office.
[3] Fergusson. A communication.

afterwards : " Compared to what he put us through, the operation was a piece of cake."[1]

Some time in these training days Wingate was joined by two Burman officers. One of them was Aung Thin of Rangoon, the other, who was called Sao Man Hpa, came from the Shan states. When they reported to the brigadier in his jungle camp south of Saugor, they found him deep in study dressed only in shorts and sandals, but as soon as they had been brought up to him, Wingate, to mark the gravity of the occasion, crowned his head with his sun helmet, (the same bath-like object he had worn in Palestine and Ethiopia), before shaking hands. He turned to Aung Thin and said, " I am glad to have you both here. You are to be my Burmese experts." This came as a surprise to the officers and Aung Thin hastened to explain that they had both been educated in the West, Aung Thin in England, Sao Man Hpa in the United States, and though they could both speak the Burmese language imperfectly, only one of them could write it. " No, no," said Wingate. "You are to be my experts." And they found that they had no choice.[2]

One day some weeks later Wingate endeavoured to obtain specialist advice from Sao Man Hpa. He explained that he was looking for a name for the brigade. He wanted the name of an animal. " What is the supreme animal of the Burma jungle? " he asked.

" The elephant," replied Sao Man Hpa.

" Oh, that's no good," said Wingate, " What's the next animal? "

" They say there are lions in the jungle still."

" What do they call them? What's the word for lion? "

" *Chinthé*."

" Chindit ? "

" No, *Chinthé*."

" You are sure you can't say Chindit for lion ? "

" No, *Chinthé*."

" That wouldn't make sense in English. I must think of something else," said Wingate and appeared to forget the matter.[3]

In November Wingate began the final reorganisation under which 77 Brigade entered Burma. He went to the Headquarters of the Eastern Army at Imphal and arranged for the establishment there of an Advance Headquarters under Major Jefferies, the officer commanding 142 Commando Company. He met the Army Commander, Lieutenant-General Irwin, and the Commander of 5 Corps, Lieutenant-General Scoones, on whose front the entry was to be made. He had a con-

[1] Rolo.
[2] Brigadier Aung Thin, D.S.O.
[3] Sao Man Hpa. A communication. As in Persia the lion is extinct but is still believed in by good patriots.

ference with Scoones on his plan of operations, and, after some modifications by the General, he arranged the date and the route of the brigade's transit through the Corps area, and the siting of staging camps on the Manipur road. In both the Army and Corps Commanders he again found men who believed in him, and who strove to help him to the utmost. He said so after, not omitting to grumble at the same time about the cumbrous staff machinery with which they were surrounded.[1] Then before returning to Saugor he found a last opportunity to look at Burmese country at some leisure, this time from the air. He was taken as a passenger in a Blenheim bomber during an R.A.F. operation (probably their November raid on the Irrawaddy town of Katha), and he saw the hills, valleys, forests and rivers across which he was to march soon. Before the end of the month he was back in the Central Provinces.

He now had his full complement of men, three thousand all ranks. The training was to end with two full-scale exercises, the first lasting five days and held round Saugor itself, and concerned chiefly with signalling, the second taking place in the jungle country in the north and ending with a mock capture of the railway and key installations of the town of Jhansi. The first exercise passed off well, but the second one showed him that the brigade still suffered from many defects. He noted with irritation and disappointment " an undue number of faint-hearted stragglers," some breakdown of discipline, and much incompetent handling of mules. The exercise had not been set by himself but by Central Command and erred, according to Wingate himself, " on the side of severity," so it may be assumed that for the men taking part it was hell on earth. And then, at the end of it, Wingate was again seized with doubts as to whether he ought to lead his imperfectly trained followers into the difficult operation he had planned. Again he was persuaded, this time by General Wilcox,[2] to forget his misgivings, and this time he seems to have put them away for good. They are not heard of again. 77 Brigade was committed to its task.

In January of 1943, Wingate's last full year of life, he and his men went by rail and river to Dinapur whence they marched a hundred and thirty-three miles by road to Imphal. They covered the distance in eight days. How they did it and what they saw was to be memorably described by Bernard Fergusson.

" None of us could tell you much about the famous Manipur Road, for we marched up it at night. By day the long motor convoys went grinding up and down it, and we had to leave it free; but it was too dangerous for night driving, and then it became our property. The

[1] Wingate Burma Report.   [2] Wingate Burma Report.

stages varied in length from seven to eighteen miles. We would start the march at dusk, have one halt of an hour sometime during the night ... not till nine or ten in the morning would we wake up to see whither our night's march had brought us.

"Sometimes the view which thus burst on us was enough to take one's breath away. Huge mountains rose across the valley, and mists curling up from far below betrayed the line of the streams. Sometimes one would be minded of the West Highlands. ...

"Frequently we came to places where the engineers were at work on bridges, or clearing landslides, or hollowing away more of the overhanging cliffs. Their great arc lights lit up the dripping sides of the hill, while the bulldozers and angle-dozers jerked screaming to and fro, shoving slithering tons of earth over the edge and down the hillside. Like ours, their work began when the traffic ceased.

"At last, the summit far behind us, we came out, one cool clear morning, on to the Imphal plain."

During the course of the march Wingate was riding one morning after daybreak with Aung Thin when they passed a Buddhist pagoda whose entrance was adorned by two statues of griffin-like beasts. It was such a shrine as may be seen all over Burma and occasionally in Assam. Wingate wanted to know exactly what the little temple and its carved monsters signified, and Aung Thin told him what he knew, saying that the griffins were revered as symbols of everlasting guardianship. Wingate wanted to know more about the griffins, and asked what they were called in Burmese. Aung Thin said:

"We call them lions—*chinthé*."

"Chindit ? "

"No. *Chinthé*."

"Hm. That's no good," said Wingate, and they rode on.[1]

In the Advance Headquarters of 77 Brigade in Imphal there was one very striking feature, namely the "operations room" set up by Jefferies. Wingate described it in his report: "A large room twenty-five foot square was papered over all walls and floors with maps of all scales and air-photograph mosaics of all objects. On the floor a complete set of 1 inch to the mile maps provided means of running over the rôle of the columns in detail with all officers in turn. This was done for as long as twelve hours a day for five days."

After all they had endured, his men may have hoped for some relaxation before the strife, but Wingate would have none of that. "In order that the troops might not be softened by the cinema at Imphal," he arranged for them to be bivouacked seven miles to the north of the town, and they were only allowed to make visits to the local Babylon

[1] Aung Thin.

for the purpose of attending his long and concentrated lectures in the big map-papered square room. They were denied last pleasures and instead put through last exercises.[1] They may have cursed him anew in the camp for his harshness, but they probably did not do so when the operations had begun and every man needed every ounce of strength that he had gained, and was grateful for any power of resistance that he had been able to build up within him.

Absolute secrecy surrounded them, but they knew that they were to move out of Assam into Burma and across the Chindwin within a few days.

[1] It was not till the brigade's arrival in Assam that full-scale supply-drop exercises could be undertaken in conjunction with the R.A.F. Wingate Burma Report.

CHAPTER XVII

THE CHINDWIN

The expedition of 77 Brigade was originally designed as part of a large offensive movement converging on Burma from the north and centre. Roughly the plan was this : that while 77 Brigade moved forward into the middle of the country, 4 Corps would open a limited offensive in the centre against the Chindwin towns of Sittaung and Kalewa, while concurrently the Chinese forces at Ledo which were commanded by Stilwell, together with the Chinese Army in Yunnan, would move down from the north and north-east respectively as far as Myitkyina,[1] Bhamo, and Lashio, with the object of reclaiming North-East Burma and reopening the land route to China. During these operations a further one by 15 Corps was to end in the recapture of Akyab and the Mayu and Arakan districts. This Arakan operation was actually in progress in early February. It had opened in mid-December and had done well till early January when there occurred, in Sir William Slim's phrase, " an unfortunate pause."[2] Thereafter it fell on evil days. It was to end in failure though this was not evident till March. But at the time of the brigade's assembling at Imphal at the end of January the general prospect was encouraging : a large offensive movement was in initial stages with every hope of success, and the rôle of the Wingate Expedition was envisaged as similar to that of Gideon Force during the Cunningham and Platt offensives.

In the first month of the new year the plan began to fall to pieces and soon nothing of it remained except the already operating Arakan expedition, and the Wingate expedition. It happened thus. First the Sittaung and Kalewa projects were deferred owing to lack of road-making labour and material, and lack of transport. Then hardly had the forward movement by 4 Corps been cancelled when news arrived

---

[1] Burma, having come late into the sphere of European interests, has proved an orgiastic hunting-ground for Orientalists with a taste for the fantasies of learned trans-literation. In consequence accepted European spellings are often a feeble guide to pro-nunciation. The pedant's masterpiece is Myitkyina which, as no one is likely to guess until told, should be pronounced Mitchina. Other unexpected pronunciations will be indicated to the vulgar in the course of the story. Rangoon, Mandalay and the rivers Chindwin and Irrawaddy received their European spellings in more primitive times, and can be pronounced exactly as written.

[2] *Defeat into Victory* by Field-Marshal Sir William Slim, referred to subsequently as Slim.

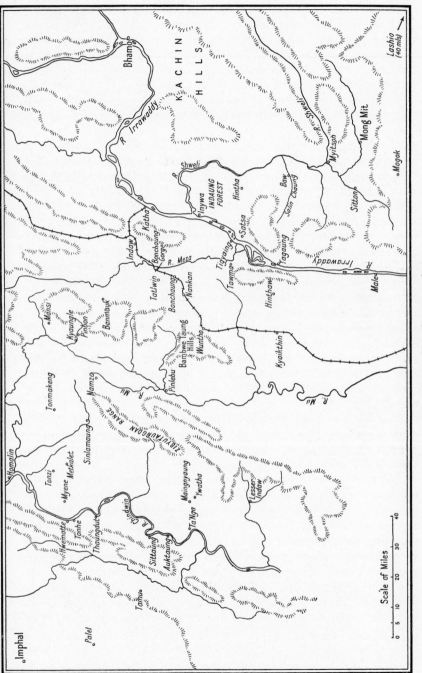

The First Chindit Expedition

from Stilwell that Generalissimo Chiang Kai-Shek would not sanction the agreed advance by Chinese forces. This put an end to any hopes of reconquest in 1943. With so much of the plan in ruins, strong reasons appeared for abandoning it altogether and organising afresh. Many people still believe that this should have been done. It was clearly the logical thing. On the 3rd of February Wingate was told that on the Commander-in-Chief's instructions the advance by 77 Brigade into Burma was indefinitely postponed. Already the feeling in the camp was one of restlessness because, in the odd telepathic way of armies, the officers and men had become vaguely aware that something was amiss.

On the 5th of February Sir Archibald Wavell arrived in Imphal with Lieutenant-General Brehon Somervell of the United States Army. He had made it known that he had come to cancel Wingate's expedition, but, being the man he was, he would not take a final decision before hearing the arguments on both sides. Wingate spared him no argument that he could think of. They conferred for two hours.

Wavell's reasons for cancelling remain obvious: to dispatch Wingate's expedition without any offensive to follow it was not only to jeopardise the whole brigade but to render useless whatever they might accomplish, because such a plan must leave the Japanese time to repair all damage. The sacrifice of many lives, perhaps of all the lives of these men, might be in vain. Against this reasoning Wingate brought, according to his account, six objections, and it can be assumed that he put them forward with all his accustomed passion. When he came to summarise his arguments later he listed them in an unexpected order.

His first was that if the expedition was cancelled " the vast majority of Staff officers who denied the theory of Long Range Penetration would . . . continue to deny it."[1] Secondly, he pointed out that the brigade was now at the very top of its form and a long postponement would have an adverse effect on its military value. Thirdly, British ignorance of Japanese jungle warfare methods would " remain profound " unless men went out and challenged them. His fourth argument was a very cogent one. There was one British outpost, and only one, within Burma. This was Fort Hertz which lies sixty miles south of the northern Chinese-Burma frontier. In September of 1942 a small parachute group[2] occupied the fort and the village of Sumpra-bum with its airfield forty miles south. Thereafter they maintained the fort and its environs as a centre of resistance with a garrison hastily raised from the local people, and known as the North Kachin Levies. By February of 1943 the situation at Fort Hertz was extremely

---

[1] Wingate Burma Report.
[2] Commanded by Lieut.-Colonel Gamble of the Australian Army.

The first expedition. Wingate with Major Anderson

A photograph taken on Wingate's return to England, August 1943

precarious. The Japanese appeared to be closing in. If there was no military diversion within Burma (so Wingate argued), this solitary redoubt, which contained the only British airfield in the country, would be left to its doom with fatal results to Burman morale and interior support. Such was his fourth and best argument. His fifth argument (doubtful in retrospect), was that unless we asserted our determination to cross the Chindwin the Japanese would seize the initiative in the lightly-held jungle country on both sides of the river. His last argument was an elaboration of the fifth. In his own words, without "the serious interruption of enemy plans and confusion in his military economy throughout Burma," such as 77 Brigade would bring about, the Japanese would be "free to develop offensive intentions."[1] The enemy were known to be massing troops in the Mandalay and Maymyo area.

No minute was made of the conversation but this was the order in which Wingate remembered his arguments. It was like him to think of Staff officers first.

Sir Archibald Wavell wanted to be persuaded against cancellation. He described his conflicting thoughts and feelings as follows : " I had to balance the inevitable losses—the larger since there would be no other operations to divide the enemy's forces—to be sustained without strategical profit, against the experience to be gained of Wingate's new method and organisation. I had little doubt in my own mind of the proper course, but I had to satisfy myself also that Wingate had no doubts and that the enterprise had a good chance of success and would not be a senseless sacrifice : and I went into Wingate's proposals in some detail before giving the sanction to proceed for which he and his brigade were so anxious."[2]

He gave the sanction after asking the opinion of General Somervell who said, " Well, I guess I'd let them roll."[3] It has never been explained why, with the cancellation of the British and Chinese advances in the centre and north, Wingate's expedition was not redirected in a south-easterly direction so as to attack in the rear the Japanese forces resisting and gradually seizing the initiative from the Arakan expedition. There is no evidence that such a project was discussed. It may have been believed that the relief of Fort Hertz was more important, or it may merely have been that there was now no time to replan any expedition which had to be out of Burma before the breaking of the monsoon.

On the day after his conference with Wingate, the Commander-in-Chief, accompanied by Somervell, inspected the seven columns of 77 Brigade. The units " were lined up in a grassy depression by a

---

[1] Wingate Burma Report.   [2] Rolo.
[3] Information obtained at the War Office. Colonel Walter Scott D.S.O., M.C.

stream between two hills,"[1] and the parade ended with an address by the ever tongue-tied Field-Marshal. He is remembered as saying something as follows : " This is a great adventure. It is not going to be an easy one. I wish you all the very best of luck."[1] Then searching for something more to say, but not finding it, he brought his right hand up to the salute, probably to ease an awkward interval.[2] Stirring tales were told afterwards of how the Commander-in-Chief, over-taken by a noble impulse to pay tribute, saluted the troops before they could salute him. It is much more likely that he was prompted by his habitual shyness, and it is typical of the man that his embarrassed motion of the hand made an impression as deep as the most dramatic gesture imaginable. The next day the brigade began to leave Imphal for the Chindwin.

The seven columns were now organised into two groups whose composition will be shown later. Following a plan of elaborate deception and secrecy, they marched from Imphal on the south-easterly road to Tamu so as to give spies a false idea of their intentions. The first two stages were accomplished by day and took them from Imphal to Palel, about forty miles, and as far as the two-way motor road reached at that time. From here on the road, winding into the Manipur hills, was a single track but still able to carry motor transport. The latter used it by day and the marching brigade by night as on the approach to Imphal a month before. They marched thus, in a long thin column which extended over several miles from end to end, and was sometimes visible in all its twisting length on successive sections of the mountain road, till they came to the staging camp at a place called Moreh near Tamu. Here they were on the Assam-Burma frontier, and here there was a parting of the ways, as the two groups were to operate separately from now on. Wingate therefore chose this moment to issue an order of the day to all the column commanders with instructions to com-municate it to officers and men immediately before the crossing of the Chindwin. The text was as follows :

" To-day we stand on the threshold of battle. The time of preparation is over, and we are moving on the enemy to prove ourselves and our methods. At this moment we stand beside the soldiers of the United Nations in the front line trenches throughout the world. It is always a minority that occupies the front line. It is a still smaller minority that accepts with a good heart tasks like this that we have chosen to carry out. We need not, therefore, as we go forward into the conflict, suspect ourselves of selfish or interested motives. We have all had the opportunity of withdrawing

[1] Rolo.   [2] Fergusson. A communication.

and we are here because we have chosen to be here ; that is, we
have chosen to bear the burden and heat of the day. Men who make
this choice are above the average in courage. We therefore have no
fear for the staunchness and guts of our comrades.

The motive which has led each and all of us to devote ourselves to what lies ahead cannot conceivably have been a bad
motive. Comfort and security are not sacrificed voluntarily for the
sake of others by ill-disposed people. Our motive, therefore, may
be taken to be the desire to serve our day and generation in the
way that seems nearest to our hand. The battle is not always to
the strong nor the race to the swift. Victory in war cannot be
counted upon, but what can be counted is that we shall go forward
determined to do what we can to bring this war to the end which
we believe best for our friends and comrades in arms, without
boastfulness or forgetting our duty, resolved to do the right so far
as we can see the right.

Our aim is to make possible a Government of the world in
which all men can live at peace and with equal opportunity of
service.

Finally, knowing the vanity of man's effort and the confusion
of his purpose, let us pray that God may accept our service and
direct our endeavours, so that when we shall have done all we shall
see the fruit of our labours and be satisfied.

O.C. Wingate.   Commander
77th Indian Infantry Brigade "

Before moving farther, Wingate held a conference of his column
commanders at Moreh, which was also the Headquarters of 23 Division,
the unit of 4 Corps to be most closely involved with the Long Range
Penetration. Here they went over the plan of operations together for
the last time.

The Japanese-held land before them was not wholly unexplored
by the army in Assam. Small patrols of 4 Corps had crossed the
Chindwin from time to time, and during late December and the early
part of January others from 77 Brigade under Captains Buchanan,
Griffiths, Bruce and Herring of the Burma Rifles had penetrated up to
thirty miles into the territory to the east, and returned safely. It
followed that the men of 77 Brigade knew that what they were about
to attempt was possible for small bands; but whether it was at all
possible for three thousand men and a thousand beasts was still
untested, and when the difficulties of the river itself and the jungle hills
on either side are remembered, the courage of the brigade's decision
remains beyond all praise.

387

The plan of entry was elaborately ingenious and depended on a complex system of deception and double bluff. It ran as follows: Number 2 group which was the main force and consisted of the Brigade- Burma Rifles- and Group-Headquarters, with five columns (numbers 3, 4, 5, 7, 8), was to cross at a place about forty miles down the river from Homalin, called Tonhe, while Number 1 group, consisting of its own headquarters and two Gurkha columns (1 and 2), was to cross at the village of Auktaung about fifty miles south of Tonhe. The crossings were to be so timed as to attract Japanese attention on to Number 1 group and away from the main force. The first crossing was to be made at Tonhe by the Burma Rifles Headquarters (150 all ranks) under Lieutenant-Colonel Wheeler. Thereafter there was to be no further crossing at Tonhe for twenty-four hours while the whole of Number 1 group (1,000 men and 250 beasts) under Lieutenant-Colonel Alexander crossed at Auktaung and then received supplies by parachute in broad daylight. By this time the Japanese were to suppose that the first crossing at Tonhe was a feint to distract attention from a main crossing at Auktaung. Further to convince them of error, Major Jefferies was to move south from Number 1 group with a " deception squad " to a village called Ta Nga where, dressed in Wingate's red tabs, and seemingly accompanied by a high-ranking headquarters, he was to order large quantities of food and supplies from the pro-Japanese headman, mentioning place names as though he was preparing a southward march, and otherwise acting the part of an indiscreet senior commander. In the meantime the rest of Number 2 group (about 2,000 men and over 800 beasts) was to cross at Tonhe and move swiftly inland undetected.[1] The plan may sound over-elaborate and dependent on too many assumptions to succeed. But it did succeed and showed an extraordinarily precise understanding of Japanese reaction.

At this last conference Wingate outlined in detail the whole subsequent plan as well. This will be shown, not now, but in the course of the narrative. One curious little episode occurred before the meeting broke up and should be noted. The commander of Number 7 column, Major Gilkes of the 13th King's, asked whether, in the event of the expedition having reached its utmost limit in Burma, and of return by the Chindwin having become prohibitively difficult, columns might attempt to reach safety by marching onwards to China. Wingate replied that there was no objection.

The groups separated. The remaining marches were done under cover of the dark. On the night of the 13th of February, before the arrival at Tonhe of the major part of Number 2 group, Colonel Wheeler

[1] Wingate Burma Report. Fergusson I. Rolo.

and his Burma Headquarters began crossing the four hundred yards breadth of the fast-flowing river Chindwin. Then the Southern Group began crossing at Auktaung the next night and continued from late on the 14th to early morning of the 16th, when, following the plan, they received parachuted supplies in the daytime for all to see.

In the night of the 14th, while the Auktaung crossing was in full progress, Wingate initiated the main crossing at Tonhe on which success or instant and total failure depended.

If one would imagine William Frith's masterly and disorderly picture of " The Railway Station " as a massed male nude study and enlarged many times to include not only vastly more numbers but more nationalities, the whole reset in a night landscape of outrageous and sinisterly grand romance, wherein a full moon shed its rays on dark mountains of jungle, and on a river which returned its light, then one may have some imperfect notion of what the first bold step by the Northern force in this enterprise looked like ; a scene of hurry, and rush, and ordering, and counter-ordering, and desperation, and foul language, as an elaborate administration broke down into hasty im-provisations when suddenly put to a test for which no one was adequately prepared. As soon as the advance party was over and had signalled an " All clear " by torch, lighting a fire at the same time to serve as a directional beacon, the first task was to get the power-ropes across and secured to trees on the east bank. This was very difficult because the ropes sank beneath the surface on the way over, fouled the river bottom, had to be released by divers, always to find it fouled a little farther beyond, until Wingate ingeniously found a method, and ordered the toiling parties to fasten the ropes stage by stage to river fishing stakes, plentiful on this stretch, until they reached the far bank, whereat boat parties having taken up the stakes one by one, the men on the shore were to tauten the ropes and lash them. This was done. Anti-tank guns had already been ferried across by Wheeler's men, and so now, with guns on either bank covering the water against a possible Japanese river patrol, the main crossing began in the last hours of the night. Men were ferried across in rubber dinghies alternately with strings of swimming beasts and soon, on account of the beasts, all was renewed pandemonium. Only two minorities among the pack animals had no fear of the river : the bullocks swam across with unquestioning obedience, and the half-dozen elephants (one lost by his load of ammunition slipping and immobilising him in midstream) pounded through the flood with a noble unhesitancy, bearing their mahouts and vast burdens with them ; but the beast majority, who were mules, fussed, refused, kicked, had hysterics, bolted if they could, and in the water showed a distracting tendency to turn back half-way over. When coaxing and beating had failed, men tried rushing them in herds with a haroosh down gangways made of bamboo sticks in the manner of the sheep dip, but this method often failed too, because one beast would suddenly break back and then the whole herd would stampede, with some of them vanishing into the jungle never to be seen again. The horses went over with less bother and sometimes gave confidence to the mules. The eight messenger dogs (equipped with message cases on the collar) sometimes did needed service as one or other swam by the head of a rebellious mule in order to scare it from turning, and to guide it sheep-dog fashion to the shore.[1] The men of the brigade meanwhile were continually ferrying across in the boats of Tonhe or in their own rubber dinghies or on makeshift rafts, each boatload or raftload towing other men swimming, and mules, and hauling onward by the ropes. When the sun rose the river showed " a fantastic scene, naked men fighting madly with plunging mules ; tiny boats, rocking precariously as shaven-headed little Gurkhas loaded them with precious cargoes of mortars, Bren guns, and rifles ; men inflating their rubber dinghies ; elephants . . . ploughing majestically through the water . . . long lines of mules tethered to trees waiting their turn to cross ; and down the mountainside stragglers who had lost their way in the dark hurrying so as not to be left behind."[2] The last column due to cross was Number 5, but seeing, when he arrived at Tonhe, how the columns before him were behind schedule the commander, Fergusson, obtained permission to cross independently about three miles north at a place called Hwematte. There he and his men faced a renewal of the ordeal by rope, boat, mule and broad treacherous water on their own.

In his report Wingate did not say when he himself landed on the east bank. This was probably because he crossed and re-crossed often. His final crossing was on the night of the 16th to the 17th, when Brigade Headquarters followed Columns 4, 3 and 8 over, and left Group Headquarters, and Number 7 Column under Major Gilkes to cross after them, during the following day and night. At dawn on the 18th " the signal light on the east bank blinked for the last time and went out." Everything imaginable had gone wrong except for the only thing that mattered : the main force had crossed the Chindwin without being discovered by the Japanese.[3]

According to plan, number 1 group, to the south, were two days

---

[1] See Appendix B for details of these dogs.
[2] Rolo, based on information by Group-Captain Robert Thompson.
[3] Wingate Burma Report. Fergusson I. Rolo. Halley.

in advance of the Northern schedule and by this time they had reached a point about twenty miles inland. But soon they fell behindhand owing to the difficulties of the ground and various strokes of bad luck. On the 15th Major Jefferies had set out for Ta Nga where he duly acted the commander's part with convincing pomp and relish, while the two columns and Headquarter body of the main group moved to the south-east, approaching a place called Maingnyaung[1] on the 18th. They had news of a Japanese garrison here, two hundred and fifty strong, and went forward to ambush them. They succeeded in doing so but, straightaway, this first battle action of 77 Brigade in Burma went wrong. This is what happened. Three Gurkha platoons met an enemy patrol in the afternoon. There was an exchange of shots in which six Japanese were killed. The enemy patrol went back, alerted their head-quarters who opened a bombardment with mortar. Thereupon the Gurkha transport officer ordered the pack animals to safety, and at this the muleteers, seized with panic, ran away back to the Chindwin, and in their terror stampeded many of the animals. A large part of the mules were missing for several days, many were lost for good, supplies were thus drastically and suddenly cut down, and the chance of dealing a surprise blow was lost. In the hope of retrieving the advantage, Major Dunlop, the commander of Number 1 column, went southwards in pursuit through country so difficult that the men needed to hack out pathways and cut steps for the pack animals. He and his column reached a village called Ywatha where they found food supplies but no sign of the ambushed garrison.

The failure of the action and the deviation from the plan caused by the panic cost Number 1 group a delay of three days. Then, on the 22nd, the plan was taken up again with a fresh diversion. Major Jefferies and his deceivers again went southwards, this time towards Lesser Indaw,[2] till the going proved intolerably difficult, whereon, after making his impression and collecting food in the villages on the way, he turned east for a rendezvous with Dunlop on the railway. While he was thus drawing attention from the main body of Number 1 group, the latter made their slow way from Maingnyaung out of the hill country east of the Chindwin. It was hard work by the account of Dunlop : " Manhandling loads, wading through streams for miles, and short rations kept down the day's march. Some of the mules were badly galled and all were very thin. They ate large quantities of bamboo leaves but these had little nourishment. The loss of the grain (at the action of the 18th) was telling. Eventually we reached the

[1] Pronounced Mine-Jung.
[2] So described in order to differentiate it from Indaw on the Rangoon-Myitkyina railway.

summit of the escarpment and saw the Mu valley laid out in front of us."

While these things were happening Number 2 group, by now renamed Northern Force,[1] made their way to Myene, about five miles inland from the Chindwin. Here the first columns of the main body and Number 5 column under Fergusson met in drenching rain on the morning of the 17th. Myene is in a valley formed by a Chindwin tributary and here the first supplies were dropped on Northern Force by parachute on the nights of the 15th, 16th and 17th. The first supply had been gathered by the Burma Rifles Headquarter column who had immediately moved due eastwards towards Tonmakeng[2] and the nearby townlet of Sinlamaung, about forty miles away. They went off with bullocks and mules, and such was the skill of these Burmans in jungle movement that they could travel faster with their lumbering cattle than others could with mules.[3] While they were on their way the rest of Northern Force reassembled from the Chindwin and picked up their rations and equipment every night in the paddy fields round Myene. The supply drops (as the provisionings were called) went forward smoothly enough except for that of the 16th. A thunderstorm forced one of the aircraft to turn back, but the pilot dropped his load before recrossing the river. One of his packages contained mail addressed to Brigade- Burma Rifles- and Group-Headquarters and as bad luck would have it he dropped it near a Japanese post on the eastern bank. It cannot be shown what use the enemy made of this intelligence windfall. It ought to have given them the measure of the brigade but it is doubtful whether it did so.

On the afternoon of the 19th Lieutenant Toye, a young man who had recently joined the Burma Rifles, rode in from Tonmakeng, (having covered forty miles of jungle country in sixteen hours), with news of Wheeler's arrival there and of the enemy dispositions. There were two hundred Japanese in Sinlamaung, but none in Tonmakeng from where enemy troops had moved north-westwards to a concentration in Homalin. Wingate believed (mistakenly it seems) that the Japanese were going to Homalin as the first step in an invasion of Assam. If this was so, as he was convinced, it provided him with a classic test of his often-asserted principle that the answer to penetration (or invasion) must be a yet deeper counter-penetration. The news from Tonmakeng forced him to consider two alternatives : either to thrust ahead past the garrison at Sinlamaung to the Mu valley, or to go to Tonmakeng, despite the proximity of the Japanese, and wait there for

[1] Wingate Burma Report.
[2] Pronounced Tonmacheng. Most Burmese names, and all those ending in " ng " have the accent on the last syllable.
[3] Wingate Burma Report.

a supply drop before pressing on to the railway. Either course was extremely dangerous. He set out eastwards undecided. He had already sent Number 3 column under Calvert ahead the day before. The march of the main body began on the 19th with Fergusson's column leading, followed in order by Brigade Headquarters, Number 8 and 4 columns, Group Headquarters and Number 7 column.[1]

The first part of their road lay through flat teak forest " very pleasant marching "[2] in late February when the leaves are still on the trees and form a canopy from the sun or an umbrella from the rain. The men in these agreeable conditions (which lasted only a short time) soon began to grow overconfident. They had crossed the Chindwin, marched inland to Myene, taken up quantities of supplies, were now marching through easy country, all without encountering a single enemy, and so in the myopic way of the battle zone, they forgot their dangers and behaved as if they did not need to bother any longer about enemies in Burma. Their brigadier looked with mounting wrath at abundant and cumulating evidence that officers and men were neglecting all his teaching and all the march discipline he had dinned into them in the merciless camps at Saugor. He noticed them dawdling about their bivouacs instead of making them swiftly and silently, and neglecting all security precautions ; he noticed that their path through the jungle was marked by a litter of " cigarette cartons and other packings that would have been too liberal for a paper chase." He dwelt in his mind on the " abysmal ignorance " and the " poor standard of intelligence that prevails among wartime infantry officers," and he decided that the only remedy was frequent fiery harangues. " Whenever opportunity occurred," he related after, " in the course of the approach march to the railway I personally lectured all officers. . . ."

He believed that what the brigade needed in its sudden easy-going relaxed mood was a fight. A chance for that was reported back from Calvert's column which, as said, was marching a day ahead of the main group. He had reliable information that a Japanese garrison was established in a village called Metkalet about ten miles south of Tonzi, a gold-mining village on the track from Myene to Tonmakeng. Wingate ordered Calvert and Fergusson to move down to an attack. Then further news about Metkalet reached him, two days later, that there was in fact no Japanese garrison there. He ordered the columns to return to the line of march. Fergusson in the meantime had marched his column into swamp country not marked on the official maps, and was struggling by improvised causeways out of this place of despond, when Wingate's message reached him and nearly drove him to tears of frustrated wrath.[3] In fact, Calvert's information had been near the

---

[1] Deducible from Fergusson I. [2] Fergusson I. [3] Fergusson I.

truth. Fergusson arrived at Metkalet to discover from the evidence of recent " mountainous " elephant droppings and still burning camp fires, besides what he could learn from the headman, that a body of fifty enemy soldiers had left hurriedly a few hours before. But unless valuable time was to be wasted there was no purpose in seeking battle with these elusive Japanese, and Calvert and Fergusson obediently led their columns, not without much to be tholed across country, back to the Tonmakeng track where the brigadier, cursing all within sight but never now doubting his venture, was leading his men on to the still distant North-South Railway.

On approaching Tonmakeng Wingate had finally to make up his mind whether to take in new supplies at this place, according to the original plan, or thrust on to the Mu valley and take them there. By his own account, he found decision difficult. The main argument for thrusting on was that with Northern Force's slow rate of progress from Myene, at ten miles a day instead of fifteen, the Japanese garrison at Sinlamaung was likely to know something about them from spies and their own patrols. The argument for stopping at Tonmakeng nevertheless was that nothing was yet known of Japanese dispositions in the Mu valley. There was an additional reason for risking a supply drop. From here to the Mu valley there was a way through the jungle, supposedly unknown to the Japanese, called " Casten's track,"[1] but for the hacking party to make it passable for the columns and their beasts and baggage would take time. So Wingate decided to stop at Tonmakeng. He said after that if the Japanese had regarrisoned this place and remained to fight here and at Sinlamaung, Northern Force could never have reached the railway and the expedition must have ended in early failure.

They reached the neighbourhood of Tonmakeng late on the 22nd of February.[2] This was the plan. Numbers 3, 7 and 8 columns were to form battle groups under Calvert and attack the Japanese at Sinlamaung, while Fergusson and Number 5 column and men not included in the battle groups were to defend the dropping zone at Tonmakeng and take charge of the gathering operation. The supply drop was to be a massive one taking place on three successive days till

---

[1] So called after a forestry officer in Burma Government employ who reconnoitred the track in 1942. There were three main types of road in Burma : motor roads, Government tracks through the jungle maintained as open passages, and jungle tracks which were blazed but not maintained and needed hacking. Casten's track was one of this kind.
[2] The dates given in different authorities conflict between the 13th and 24th when the supply drop at Tonmakeng began. Unless 24 hours have been inadvertently dropped in Wingate's report and other main authorities, Lieutenant Toye's ride would seem to have been accomplished at the speed of light. To resolve the problem the writer has devised a new time-table not directly supported by first-hand accounts. After the 24th the dates present no difficulty.

the 26th. After the first drop Number 4 column was to set out in advance to hack out a passage along Casten's track. Sinlamaung and Tonmakeng are only ten miles from each other and the Fergusson and Calvert parties could therefore act as mutual protection.

This hazardous operation succeeded by boldness and luck. The supply drop was carried out on the 24th, 25th and 26th in accordance with the plan, but the action to the south ended feebly. Calvert went forward on a reconnoitring sortie but could not find Sinlamaung.[1] In the afternoon of the 24th he met Group Headquarters and the battle groups marching south to join him and together they continued the reconnaissance without success. They met villagers towards evening who said that the garrison had left Sinlamaung for the east. Calvert attempted a pursuit, got near to some of the Japanese eastward positions, but by this time the moon had set and he and his party lost their way in the dark. Calvert ordered men to smoke so as to retain contact. Bearings were lost nonetheless and the night raiders marched in circles. Then at dawn on the 25th Calvert found the way to Sin-lamaung in which he was followed by the rest of the assault parties, but there was no battle. The Japanese had left, as reported, but so recently that the rearguard tea was still hot in the canisters and was drunk by the raiders. They destroyed the Japanese stores and hutments and returned to Tonmakeng with loot which included an elephant and his mahout. While these things were happening two Japanese patrols passed from south-east to north-west through the brigade area, avoiding a fight. All the indications were that the Japanese stationed in the hill country east of the Chindwin were bewildered and even in a state of panic at the invasion. Wingate purposed to keep them thus in all Burma, and he succeeded.

On the 26th when the supply drops were completed Wingate called a conference of his commanders in the monastery of Tonmakeng and outlined the next stage. All the columns except Number 3 were now to march over the mountain tops to the east, along Casten's track to the Zibyutaungdan[2] escarpment twenty miles away. Number 3 column, at their commander's request, was to take a separate route to the south-east going along another clandestine track of which Calvert had been told at Sinlamaung. Before dawn on the 27th he and his column set out. The rest of Northern Force began their march on the same day.

Casten's track, when hacked out by Number 4 column, was so narrow and so closely surrounded by jungle that the troops could only march along it in single file. It was the most dangerous progress they

[1] The reason was that the maps were out of date and Sinlamaung in the manner of Burman villages had moved on a mile or two since last surveyed. Fergusson. A communication.
[2] Pronounced Zibyoo-Tung-Don.

made at any time between the Chindwin and the Irrawaddy because the Japanese could easily seal off both ends of the track, and then destroy the imprisoned force by bombardment or starvation. Even to the most confident it was an alarming situation. It was as they were making their way along this track that Wingate showed, as he had showed at Agibar, the full power of his leadership, but here he showed it in a way so improbable (though very typically), that the bare recital of the facts may sound incredible. He called a conference by radio signal of all his officers. When Fergusson received the signal he assumed that he had it in corrupt form, and he asked for it to be repeated as he did not like to leave his column without any officers at all at the approach to dangerous country. He was given the signal again. There was a bare space in the shape of an amphitheatre in the course of the track, and this was the rendezvous. It took some hours for the officers to assemble here. They expected to be told some news about the enemy, or of some drastic change of plan. They were quite unprepared for what in fact did happen. For when they were all gathered together, Wingate told them nothing new about the enemy, nor gave them fresh tactical instructions, nor did he lecture them this time about their shortcomings. What he did was to address them for upwards of an hour on what he scornfully referred to as "the so-called miracle of Dunkirk." He heaped abuse on the spirit which liked to see a great national achievement in the shameful defeat and flight from the battle-field of 1940; he declared that the rejoicing over Dunkirk manifested a degenerate state of mind which had lured on aggressive nations to plunder and war, and could still delay the triumph of the just cause. He illustrated what he had to say with quotations from the Bible. Then he sent the officers back to their posts and three hours later the march was resumed.

As they made their difficult way back none of the officers felt any inclination to smile at this strange encounter. It was not till some time afterwards that the men realised how strange an encounter it had been.[1]

One of Fergusson's junior officers, Philip Stibbe, left a vivid first-hand record of this march. "Our way ran along the top of a ridge and our packs were especially heavy after the dropping. Marching along a watershed . . . has many advantages, but all I knew about that track was that it never remained on the level for more than a few yards. Every time we had struggled to the top of a rise we saw a dip and another rise in front of us. Many . . . were so steep that the only way the mules could get up them was at a run. The muleteers did wonderful work throughout the campaign, but I never admired them more than

[1] Fergusson. A communication.

I did during those two days. . . . We followed [a] river for several miles, wading along it and then going along the bank for a bit, then wading again and so on. . . . By this time our feet were so hard that it was unlikely that they would blister through marching with boots full of water. . . . I told myself that if I had not been an officer I would have fallen out at the side of the track and told everyone to go to hell. But nobody gave in. . . . Wingate . . . issued . . . unpopular orders that nobody was ever to brew up tea before starting off in the morning. . . . This was a great blow to most of us. . . . Rumour had it that Wingate himself did not like tea, and that on the rare occasions when he did take it he always strained it through a sock."[1]

On the 1st of March they came to the end of Casten's track, and out on to the Zibyutaungdan escarpment. They descended to the Mu valley[2] and went into a bivouac near Pinbon which held another Japanese garrison. Here Wingate called a conference of commanders to go over the next part of the plan. The plan was this : the columns would now disperse to separate tasks to meet again at a rendezvous which would be signalled and which was previsaged as beyond the Irrawaddy. Number 4 column was to move due east towards Pinbon with orders to ambush the road running between Mansi and Pinlebu, their purpose being to distract attention from the main objective which was the railway. A similar purpose was to be followed by Numbers 7 and 8 columns who would make a demonstration attack on Pinlebu. In the meantime Numbers 3 and 5 columns would move to the railway and carry out simultaneous demolitions. There was to be one other dispersion. One of the officers of the Burma Rifles, whom Wingate described as " the redoubtable Captain Herring," was to go far to the east straightway, across the Irrawaddy to the Kachin highlands south of Bhamo, north-east of Mandalay. He was to take a platoon composed of Kachins and his purpose was to rally the highland population who were correctly believed to have remained loyal to the British. He was given orders for a rendezvous with Number 1 group to take place on the 24th of March at Mong Mit.

The day after this conference, at dawn, the whole of Northern Force, except for Number 4 column who stayed behind in the Pinbon area, and Number 3 column who were still following their own path, marched southwards down the motor road, led by Wingate. They marched throughout the day and covered about twenty miles till they reached their bivouac area about ten miles north-east of Pinlebu in the forest off the road. Such a daylight march was in defiance of all

---

[1] *Return via Rangoon* by Philip Stibbe. Referred to subsequently as Stibbe.

[2] So called here for the sake of simplicity. In fact the point of descent was near the junction of the Chaunggyi valley (running into the Chindwin) and the Mu valley. The watershed is low and the effect is of a single valley. Fergusson I.

Wingate's own teaching. When he came to relate these things after he asserted that he had incurred little danger by this march because in the torrential rain of that day motor transport could not use the road and, as a safeguard, the rearguard column (Number 7 under Gilkes) blew up all bridges after Northern Force's passage. He said also that it was necessary to get out of the Mu valley quickly and added, in a convincing final note, that sometimes a commander has to break his own most cherished rules.

During the first week of March the shape and intention of Wingate's plan began to appear in a succession of predicted results. The whole thing depended on an astonishingly well-designed sequence of feint and thrust. Number 1 group's crossing of the Chindwin had drawn attention away from the main effort to the north. When the latter operation was recognised, the Japanese, too late, made a preventive move west to Homalin while Wingate thrust on in an easterly direction to the Mu valley. And now at last the Japanese might have imagined they had solved the riddle : the southern movement of Number 1 group to the railway, and the siege operations in the north on Pinbon and Pinlebu, could reveal the whole enterprise as an enormous offensive patrol in depth whose purpose was only secondarily to breach the railway line south of Wuntho, and primarily to seize the garrison towns of the Mu valley. The Japanese were obedient to these suggestions. While they reinforced Pinbon and Pinlebu, Fergusson led Number 5 column and Calvert Number 3 column eastwards to the railway north of Wuntho.

In spite of setbacks and mistakes, the operation was by now proving its strategical merit in abundance. Then, on the 3rd and 4th of March, the brigade suffered two shattering disasters.

Number 1 group to the south entered the Mu valley where the railway runs parallel to the river to its eastward at an average distance of ten miles. They had progressed slower than Northern Force, and by the time they reached the railway they were expected. In the late afternoon of the 2nd of March Number 2 column and the deception squad under Jefferies were at a place on the line called Kyaikthin[1] about thirty miles south of Wuntho. They were too late. They had hardly moved out of bivouac to the attack at midnight when they heard Japanese orders screamed from a well-laid ambush. There was confused fighting in the dark till the dispersal call was sounded by the bugler, but by now the commander was surrounded, and believing that he would never be able to reach the agreed rendezvous at Hinthaw near the Irrawaddy, he shouted orders for a change of rendezvous, but only a few heard him. In the action the wireless, the ciphers, and the

[1] Pronounced Chikesin.

bulk of the equipment were lost. The column was scattered. Of those who went to Hinthaw many, not finding their commander, turned round and struggled back through the jungle to the Chindwin, while others wandered hither and thither in the Irrawaddy country till they found other columns of the brigade. The commander himself and the remnant who followed him to the new rendezvous to the west of the railway, finding themselves bereft of the wherewithal to continue the fight, or to communicate with the brigadier, or call for more supplies, made their way to the Chindwin and back to India. Number 2 column no longer existed.

Such was the disaster in the south.[1] A similar one occurred in Wingate's own group, Northern Force, the day after. Early in the morning of the 4th, Number 4 column set out southwards in obedience to an order to join Wingate. In accordance with his policy of feint, they had been conducting an offensive reconnaissance around Pinbon, and had had several small encounters with the Japanese in which they had given a reassuring account of themselves. Then in this early morning they had their first serious encounter. Two miles west of Pinbon near a place called Kyaungle[2] a Japanese ambush party attacked them, skilfully directing their fire and surprise on the centre of the column where Headquarters were marching with the men of 142 Commando Company. They beat off the attack easily but in the course of the rapid close-quarter fusillade some of the young Gurkhas, men in their first action, broke in disorder and in doing so (as at Main-gnyaung) they stampeded the mules. The column was split and their commander gave the dispersal signal. He collected them at the operational rendezvous, but on their way from here southwards to meet Wingate they were attacked again. They beat off this second attack, dispersed again, reformed again, but by the time they reached the meeting place Wingate and 7 and 8 columns had gone. The commander was in the same case as his colleague of Number 2 column. He had no wireless set, no food, only a few animals, and only ten rounds of ammunition left for each man. He took his men back to India.[3] Before the end of the first week of March Wingate had lost two of his seven columns.

At first this black news looked worse than it was, especially with regard to Number 1 group. Wingate was told that the whole of it had been destroyed. In fact, the disaster in the south was the less damaging

[1] See Rolo and *Wingate's Phantom Army* by W. G. Burchett, referred to subsequently as Burchett, for considerable and interesting detail of this disaster.

[2] Pronounced Chunglay.

[3] " I have no adverse comment to pass on (the commander's) conduct which showed judgment and courage throughout." Wingate Burma Report. The journey back to Assam took Number 4 Column two weeks.

of the two. It even helped the group's subsidiary task because among things lost were the badges of rank worn by Jefferies on his deception tours, and examination of these trinkets made the Japanese believe that they had destroyed Brigade Headquarters and the leadership of the whole campaign : Jefferies's last and unwitted deception was greatly to increase Japanese misunderstanding of the brigade's dispositions and their own situation with regard to it. The elimination of Number 2 column had not, in fact seriously interfered with the main southern group task beyond delaying it, and on the night of the 3rd of March men of Number 1 column under Major Dunlop destroyed a railway bridge by means of " a lifting and twisting charge," about three miles north of Kyaikthin. In the early hours of the 4th they moved eastwards to Hinthaw.

Two days later, on the 6th of March, Fergusson and Calvert were within striking distance of the railway between Wuntho and Indaw. Little has been said of Calvert, since his independent progress through the jungle, entirely typical of the man, takes him somewhat away from Wingate's story, but he had already added to Wingate's achievement. All that was lost in the disasters to the two columns was compensated by the fierce and swift passage of Number 3 column by the Namza route. As a master of the jungle Calvert was without any equal even among the Burmans. He had a macabre sense of humour. He never passed a track through the forest without plentifully mining it, and increasing confusion by pinning up warning signs in Burmese or Japanese supposedly signed by the enemy Commander-in-Chief.[1] From beginning to end a chief stratagem of the expedition was to perplex the Japanese so that they should never be the least sure as to what was happening to them, and from beginning to end Calvert's widespread lethal practical jokes kept the enemy in chronic bewilderment. In only one respect had he failed so far. Since crossing the Chindwin he had sought an engagement in vain, and he longed for one. Calvert had considerable eastern experience. He had learned hatred of the Japanese.

In the first week of March he was at last to find a chance of battle. On the 4th he arrived two miles west of a place called Nankan on the railway, about eighteen miles north-east of Wuntho. He stayed there two days, resting his men and waiting for the 6th. On the evening of the 5th Fergusson reached Tatlwin about eight miles west of a river gorge section of the railway called the Bonchaung, a few miles up the line from Nankan. The two columns were now poised for a swift destructive raid on the Burma railway. While they moved into their hidden positions and waited, Major Scott led Number 8 column

[1] Burchett.

southwards from Wingate's Headquarters and the main Northern group, for the demonstration assault on Pinlebu.

The Pinlebu garrison numbered around eight hundred. Wingate's plan resembled that of the Tonmakeng operations, but with far more hazard. While Scott's column attacked Pinlebu and its neighbourhood a large supply drop was to take place to the north-east, the party attacking the garrison and the party defending the dropping zone to act as mutual protection.

What happened roughly was this. On the 4th Pinlebu was raided by the R.A.F. Early in the morning of the 5th Scott occupied some villages north of the town, and this enabled him to establish road-blocks on all ways north and east leading to the dropping zone. The Japanese were convinced, by Scott's movements and by the air-raid, that Pinlebu was being invested by a large force, a supposal heightened by an overnight visit to the evacuated town by two of Scott's men on the night of the 4th. There were a few encounters, notably between one of the road-block parties and the enemy nearest them. By the 6th the Japanese believed that the British had occupied Pinlebu, and they laid down a heavy barrage on the empty town and on Scott's vacated bivouac where he had cunningly left smoking fires. The enemy were never given a chance of discovering the dimensions of the attacking force. The feint was one of the most successful of the campaign : for the loss of six men in battle, and ten others lost in the jungle, Number 8 column covered a large-scale supply drop, confused yet further the Japanese speculations about the meaning of the invasion, proved (what few even now believed possible) the superiority of British over Japanese skill in jungle movement, and, most important of all, succeeded in drawing attention from Number 3 and Number 5 columns.[1]

The attack on the north-south railway line, the main economic artery of Upper Burma, and the brigade's principal objective, took place on the afternoon and evening of the 6th. The demolitions by Number 3 column were carried out first, after a battle in which Calvert showed all his fierce brilliance. He set ambush posts on the northern and southern roads leading to Nankan. Too late, Japanese troops arrived from Indaw for the protection of the railway, but though these troops were mercilessly ambushed a mile or so from Nankan, they succeeded, by weight of numbers, in pushing through to the station and village. They were only just too late to prevent the demolitions. The battle developed in Nankan village and in the course of it one of the railway bridges was mined under Japanese fire. Calvert was in his element, leading men into the thickest of the fight between the station and the bridge to its west. Amid the noise of mortar and weapon-fire

[1] Burchett. Wingate Burma Report. Information obtained at the War Office.

and the crash of the explosions the Japanese were seized with what can best be called heroic panic, and at one moment a party of them came yelling across open country to be shot down to the last man. At the end of the action Calvert and his men had slaughtered nearly a third of the force opposed to them, had destroyed three bridges and cut the railway in numerous places, without the loss of a single man of his own or any important item of equipment.[1] After this astonishing achievement he led his men swiftly to the east.

The demolition by Fergusson's column at the Bonchaung went through without what military men primly call " enemy interference," though there was a short fight in a nearby village called Kyaik-in.[2] This happened on the morning of the 6th. A platoon under Lieutenant John Kerr surprised, and killed all but one of a lorry load of Japanese, but these had not come with orders to mount any special guard on the railway, and the two demolition parties worked unhindered. (Kerr was gravely wounded in the fight and had to be left with three others.) The charges were ready by nightfall. The first explosion was set off at nine o'clock at night on the bridge just south of Bonchaung railway station. The column commander was supervising in person and afterwards set down a first-hand record of what he saw.

" The flash illumined the whole hillside. It showed the men standing tense and waiting, the muleteers with a good grip of their mules ; and the brown of the path and the green of the trees preternaturally vivid. Then came the bang. The mules plunged and kicked, the hills for miles around rolled the noise of it about their hollows and flung it to their neighbours. Mike Calvert and John Fraser heard it away in their distant bivouacs ; and all of us hoped that John Kerr and his little group of abandoned men heard it also, and knew that we had accomplished that which we had come so far to do."

The second explosion came about two hours after. The charge was laid in the cliff face of the gorge, and when it was set off it brought hundreds of tons of earth and rock down on to the line. Number 5 column then moved to the east.

During these days Wingate and his Headquarters were established in hills called the Bambwe Taung ten miles north of Wuntho. With great success, despite the loss of two columns, the first phase of the campaign, what might be called the Chindwin phase, was over. Wingate was now facing the most critical decision of the whole campaign : whether or not to cross the Irrawaddy. What happened as a result of his deliberations belongs to the next chapter. In the

[1] Calvert's account quoted in Wingate Burma Report.
[2] Pronounced Chike-in.

meantime another question which lay on his mind may be briefly considered at this point of the story.

In this account of the 1943 expedition to Burma, the reader may have noticed the absence of a consistent feature of Wingate's life. In the ventures in which he had proved himself hitherto, he had always been driven forward by the stimulus of his belief in great causes "making for rightness": the return of the Jewish people to the promised land, the liberation of enslaved Ethiopia. It will be remembered that in his early days he declared that he was "fated to lead a country" and that he knew no other way of "fulfilment." How did these deep enthusiasms find a place in his present mission?

From remarks scattered in what he wrote at Delhi and in the Saugor days, and from a few political references in his subsequent report, it is evident that when he first took up his assignment with 77 Brigade he saw himself in a new version of his favourite rôle : that of the liberating knight-errant, in this case rescuing Burma from Japanese tyranny. As said, his delight in his Burma riflemen, though before all things based on their military virtue, was probably connected with just such a characteristic vision of chivalry. None of this can be said with any certainty, and for a significant reason. The old fire is not there to illumine his thoughts : nothing that he wrote on Burman political matters is comparable with his impassioned and assertive pleadings on behalf of Ethiopia and Israel. This is not in the least surprising, for the truth is that in Burma there existed no political opening for his romantic spirit : there was no Haile Selassie, no Hagana, no patriot movement within, no heart-stirring rallying cry. In so far as a national movement existed at all it was on the enemy side and found expression in a small ill-conditioned force known as the Burmese Independence Army, led by Aung San, a jackalish youth in Japanese employ. In 1942 this young man had earned Japanese approval by harrying some broken remnants of the retreating British army and attacking civilian refugees in the last stages of privation.[1] In 1944, he was to curry favour with the British authorities by doing the same to his Japanese promoters. Except for great cleverness and a Hitlerine fixity of purpose there was nothing to admire in him. With no national leader and movement other than Aung San and the Burmese Independence Army, Wingate had no way of playing his Ethiopian part again in Burma.[2]

[1] Mr. Hugh Tinker has said, writing in a Chatham House publication : " It is not easy for an Englishman to see the achievement of this young man free from all prejudice." (!)
[2] The anti-Japanese and pro-British tribal movements to the east and north could not be called national because they were largely separatist in character.

There was another obstacle. Although the inhabitants of that multi-racial land are among the most naturally intelligent in the world they are among the least politically conscious. Even nationalism meant little to them in 1943. As a people they had no notion what the war was about, and did not care. Most of them only wanted to be left alone. In tracing Wingate's story, it has been necessary in past chapters to tell in some detail about the affairs of Palestine and Ethiopia. To do the same now in the case of Burma would be an unpardonable digression. He appeared there as a soldier, and not, as he would have liked to do, as the liberator-in-arms who would open the way to independence.

When the brigade crossed the Chindwin Wingate took a public relations unit with him. To the end he made efforts to rally the people, sending Aung Thin (whom he used to call " The Patriot "), and other Burmese-speaking officers, into the villages on the way " to make propaganda." These efforts were not rewarding, and Wingate kept them up more as a matter of principle than from hope of their efficacy. He recognised the situation early on. Following the experience of Ethiopia, the public relations unit had been furnished with short-range broadcasting machinery and the wherewithal for producing leaflets under the direction of Aung Thin and Sao Man Hpa, but by the time Northern Force was thirty miles beyond the Chindwin all this equipment was at the bottom of a watercourse. Thirteen years later, in Rangoon, the present writer once asked Aung Thin which of the watercourses between the Chindwin and Tonmakeng had been the scene of this abandonment. Aung Thin replied without a moment's hesitation : " The first."

CHAPTER XVIII

THE IRRAWADDY

WINGATE'S DECISION to cross the Irrawaddy was the most difficult, the most dangerous, and the most expensive in men, of any which he took at any time. Of all the deeds of his professional career it is the most blamed, but it is also open to a defence which, if accepted, gives him his surest title to be considered as a great soldier. He did not live long enough to learn what that defence was, and it was not of a kind that he, or anyone, could have guessed at the time these things happened.

In the second week of March his whole existing force, with the exception of Number 7 and Number 8 columns, Brigade and Northern Force Headquarters, were marching towards the Irrawaddy. Wingate himself, in the temporary safety of the Bambwe Taung hills, was slowly reaching the decision to cross. He remained long in a state of painful doubt. He made his state of mind quite clear in his account, and the fact that, in the course of what he wrote, he returned frequently to the subject of his ultimate decision to cross, that he defended his decision first on one ground and then on another, sometimes with strong arguments, sometimes in pursuit of tortured ones ; these tell-tale literary evidences surely prove that he was never easy in his mind, either at the time or later, about a bold military stroke which cost hundreds of lives.

The difficulty of decision lay in this : that after Calvert and Fergusson had delivered their attacks on the railway the moment arrived, according to all military teaching, for an entirely new second phase to open, in fact for that broad offensive into Burma by the army in Assam which had been originally laid down as a condition of the Wingate venture, and had been cancelled in February. As things were Wingate had to make his own second phase. He saw the danger of continuing eastwards. He also saw a way of initiating a new phase which would avoid the Irrawaddy, and give safety to his men. This new plan was as follows : to turn the country where he was at the moment (the Bambwe Taung) into another Fort Hertz so that, con-centrated in this strongly defensible country, the brigade could remain supplied from the air till a limited incursion from Assam relieved them.

In the meantime, while waiting for the incursion, they themselves could make sortie after sortie from their fastness on to the roads around them and the railway, forcing the Japanese to give up Indaw and the Irrawaddy towns immediately north and south of it. By this means all northern Burma west of the Irrawaddy might be reclaimed. It was a masterly solution, and bore a close resemblance to what Wingate was to contrive the next year. There was only one strong argument against it, namely, that since the attacks by Calvert and Fergusson the Japanese had organised patrols in the country between the Bambwe Taung and the Meza valley east of the railway. The question therefore was whether a return progress by a column through jungle country, with Japanese patrols on the roads and main tracks, would be more hazardous than crossing the Irrawaddy into country that was unknown, and where the Japanese could seize the whole brigade in a constricted territory surrounded by rivers. The choice was between these two policies.

Wingate recoiled from the responsibility of making the choice. This is not to say that he refused his responsibility or acted other than as a commander should. But at this moment of supreme and fatal danger he behaved in a most uncharacteristic fashion; he left the initiative to others; he allowed himself to be led to the decision by his forward commanders, Calvert and Fergusson. What happened was this: he signalled the two commanders on the 8th giving the situation in outline and asking them if they considered it more prudent to retire to the mountains above Wuntho, or to go on eastwards across the river. Both of them reacted to this in the same way: they regarded it as a test of virtue, and both replied that they wanted to press on, stressing that if they were to cross the river unopposed they must make the attempt without delay.[1]

Before he had time to send definite orders Wingate received news that made him reject his new Bambwe Taung plan entirely, and revert to the original one. For it was now, not before, that he learned that the southern disaster was less than he had been told, that only one column of Number 1 group had been routed, and that Group Headquarters and Dunlop's column had actually made the crossing, in accordance with their instruction, at a place called Tagaung. To Calvert and Fergusson he then signalled orders in the sense they had asked for.

Having made this fateful decision Wingate was immediately confronted with the necessity of making another. In his report he insisted (so often and so variously as to raise in his reader's mind all the doubts that were once in his own), that the country beyond the

[1] Wingate Burma Report and a Fergusson communication.

Irrawaddy was better suited to his expedition than that which 3 and 5 columns were leaving, but he could not hide from himself the fact that even if this was the case (and it was not), it would be a wise precaution to retain some of his force west of the river. Common sense urged that Wingate should stay behind with his two headquarters groups, and the two columns with them. When accounting for himself, he gave many plausible reasons why he should not remain behind ; but he never mentioned what was so obviously one overriding reason : namely, that he quite literally could not have borne to stay in relative safety while his subordinates did the precise opposite.

He did not make up his mind till the 16th. On that day, at first light, he ordered the force under his immediate command to follow him to the Irrawaddy, and he thus committed the whole brigade to the terrible second phase of the expedition.[1]

After tracing these ten crucial days of Wingate's life from the 6th to the 16th of March, one question is still insistent : why did Wingate *not* settle, after all, for his "Wuntho-hill plan," which bore all the marks of his most brilliant and successful improvisations ; why did he prefer instead to stand by the cruder, less original, manifestly less workable plan to cross the Irrawaddy ? No simple answer suggests itself except one which is not open to proof. He wanted to be the leader of such an expedition as would alter the whole tide of affairs in the most distressed and unhopeful British military theatre. If it was true that a great ambition drove him on, here, as everywhere in his life, it was an ambition in which self played little part. In the incalculable way of war Wingate's decision, for all its defiance of ordinary sense, and for all the suffering it entailed, was the right one.[2]

The remains of Number 1 group were the first to cross. Their forward party of four men led by Lieutenant Bruce went into Tagaung on the 6th to find themselves confronted by a company of Aung San's army. Bruce harangued them, scared them into believing that he was in telepathic touch with the R.A.F., and shamed them into helping him. He assembled a fleet of river craft. The group arrived on the

---

[1] The foregoing, from the beginning of the chapter, is written after close study of Wingate Burma Report in conjunction with information obtained from the War Office, and after consultation with Bernard Fergusson and Brigadier G. M. Anderson O.B.E.

[2] An opposite view, with which the writer is not in agreement for reasons indicated in a later chapter, is expressed in the official history of *The War against Japan vol. II.* referred to subsequently as *Official History*.

9th and crossed unhindered. Jefferies and his party crossed independently at the same time. The depleted group were all across by the 10th.

Number 5 column under Fergusson reached Tigyaing[1] on the same day. Captain Fraser had gone forward with an advance party and the main column came into Tigyaing about eleven o'clock, marching in columns of threes and with arms at the slope, " showing the flag " as best they might in their tattered state, Fergusson at their head with eye-glass glittering.[2] He and his officers had already seen disquieting evidence that the Japanese knew where they were ; smoke signals had been observed ascending in a wide ring round their bivouac ; and even before they marched in, a Japanese observation plane flew over Tigyaing and its neighbourhood, dropping leaflets. Fergusson established pickets on the main roads leading out of the town and one of these stopped a man travelling with suspicious speed towards Tawma, the nearest Japanese garrison.

The situation was not an easy one to understand. The people of Tigyaing received the column with a moving loyalty whose worth was proved by their giving the British invaders massive provisions, placing all the boats of the town at their disposal, and manning the boats expertly. Fergusson read the leaflets to the populace amid their loud and loyal merriment, and when he gave them a vigorous address he was received with renewed demonstrations. The crossing began in the afternoon. But in the meantime a Japanese column of two hundred and fifty was moving towards Tigyaing from Tawma, the Japanese commander having been alerted not only by the observation plane, but also by a message sent to him by the Tigyaing town council. The latter did not act treacherously, but in accordance with a puzzling sense of obligation ; they owed allegiance to the British, on which account they provisioned them and gave them the boats ; they had promised the Japanese to inform them of any British troops they saw, on which account they sent the message. The war had never been explained to them and was not understood by them.[3]

By nightfall Fergusson's men were across the river. The commander himself was in the last party to leave the western shore, and as

---

[1] Pronounced Tee-Jung.

[2] An eye-witness account given to the writer by Mr. Hyi, a Chinese resident of Tigyaing, who gave Fergusson lunch on this day.

[3] In February of 1956 the writer was in Tigyaing and with the aid of Fergusson I, went over the ground and received an exhaustive account of these events from people who remembered them. The information about the messenger from the town council was given at a meeting at which he met the persons who had sent him. There was no suggestion of embarrassment in the occasion except on the part of one town elder who indicated that he had rather the matter had not been raised before an Englishman. His objections were not supported or, it seemed, understood by the others.

they were leaving, the first shots were heard from the approaching Japanese.[1]

The most difficult crossing was that of Number 3 column led by Calvert. It took place five miles down the river from Tigyaing where the west shore of the Irrawaddy is divided into islands stiff with elephant grass. After a swift and efficient supply drop on the 11th, Calvert and his men reached this place in the dark in the first hours of the 13th. The garrison of Tawma was on the prowl by now and ambushed some of the column in the early morning. The rearguard was on the west bank, the main body on an island. If the Japanese had pressed the attack nothing could have saved the column from complete destruction. But they were saved by Japanese bewilderment, Calvert's energy, and a remarkable stroke of luck. Before the Japanese had time to discover the size and dispositions of the column, Calvert had reorganised the rearguard, inspired them anew with his own wild courage, and effectively counter-attacked. The crossing began at noon in boats and rafts from the neighbouring hamlets. Then, early in the afternoon, a convoy of sailing boats was seen coming upstream. The men waiting on the sandbanks of the island hailed them and pressed their owners into ferrying service. Calvert now had an adequate fleet. The crossing went on till midnight. The last duty of the column on the west bank was to destroy abandoned equipment, to kill mules which could not be brought across, and to leave the wounded in the care of a local headman.[2] The column had lost seven men and much equipment, but it was still a fighting unit, and a supply drop could restore it to its full efficiency again.[3] To have crossed the mile-wide Irrawaddy in the face of opposition was a great feat.

Wingate with the main body of Northern Force, numbering about twelve hundred men, left the Bambwe Taung while Calvert was crossing, and made for a point on the river north of Tigyaing. " I relied on my own jungle-craft," he related after, " to lead the Brigade group across the railway and the Meza river without meeting the enemy." By the 17th they were on the shores of the Irrawaddy opposite the little town of Inywa[4] just below the point where the great river is

---

[1] Fergusson I, Stibbe, Burchett, which all contain considerable and interesting detail.

[2] The wounded were five Gurkhas and one Burma Rifleman. Calvert left them with the headman of a village called Mahlainggyon. He also left a note for the Japanese commander as follows : " These men have been fighting for their King and Country just as you have. They have fought gallantly and been wounded. I leave them confidently in your charge, knowing that with your well-known traditions of Bushido you will look after them as well as if they were your own." The commander at Tawma seems to have been exceptional and these men were treated in a humane manner. Information obtained at the War Office.

[3] Rolo. His account is first-hand, having been given by Group-Captain R. Thompson. It contains numerous interesting details omitted here.

[4] Pronounced as though written : " In you are," in English.

joined by its principal northern tributary, the Shweli. Nowhere is the Irrawaddy more magnificent than at this confluence, where on the west bank the Gangaw range descends to the water.

On this crossing, power ropes could not be used owing to the breadth of the river which is rarely less than a mile at any place between Katha and Mandalay. The crossing could only be done in boats, not in rubber dinghies, and the usual procedure was to attach dinghies and mules to boats and then strenuously paddle the latter over. As the Irrawaddy south of Katha is markedly slower than the Chindwin, the actual operation of crossing was markedly easier, but it was always much more dangerous. The shores are nearly everywhere open paddy country without any cover at all. The need for boats meant that the crossing had to be attempted either at a large inhabited place, or after a long delay elsewhere, while boats were collected in the neighbourhood. Either of these procedures meant the likelihood of news of the attempt being spread, and the luck of Calvert (the only commander to cross from uninhabited ground), in finding a sufficient fleet, was enormous.

On the west shore opposite Inywa there are a number of little riverside villages, Mehin, Hlebo, Thagaya, Anawk-Inywa (or West Inywa), and from these the Brigade group set out for the eastern shore. Their bivouac before crossing was near Hlebo. The town of Inywa on the east shore was reported to be held by the enemy, but on investigation this only meant that elements of the Burmese Independence Army were there. Wingate decided that before the crossing was under way an attempt should be made to win over or neutralise these allies of the Japanese, so he sent Aung Thin across with a small escort of Burma Riflemen. This was not the first time that the Burmese captain had gone ahead of Wingate's force to test local loyalties, but this time between him and protection there was the whole breadth of the river. He was received in friendly fashion by the people of Inywa. The soldiery of Aung San thereon took fright. Some ran away, others shut themselves up in their billets. In either case they were no more heard of.[1]

Sao Man Hpa, in the meantime, had succeeded in explaining the arrival of the Brigade group to the people on the western shore, and they responded with co-operation similar to that of Tigyaing, but without the latter's complications of conscience. They gave all their boats and all their labour. The crossing began at nightfall and was continued till sunset of the 18th.

The operation passed off with relative smoothness. The greatest difficulty in this, as in all crossings, was with the mules, and forty had

[1] For this service Aung Thin was justly recommended for his D.S.O.

to be left behind. Those that did cross swam tethered behind boats, manned by skilled paddlers, and drawing them and rubber dinghies. Each separate journey from shore to shore and back took an hour.

There are differing accounts of Wingate himself during the twenty-four hours of the crossing. To this day he is remembered by the people of the western shore. His grotesque sun-helmet caused him to stand out from a crowd of European officers and men, all of whom, despite beards and tan, looked much alike in feature and porcine colouring to the eyes of these villagers. He is not remembered as the wild enthusiast of Ein Harod and Ethiopia, but as watching proceedings with a stern calm, meeting headmen and other local dignitaries with quiet good manners, and spending much time with Lieutenant Spurlock the signals officer, a young man to whom he was evidently attached. But this memory of Wingate in a classic attitude, as the fateful crossing went forward, is strangely contradicted by another. One of his officers, Captain Hastings, came up to him to report something or other which had gone amiss. Wingate was standing apart at this moment seen by no one else. On receiving this news, whatever it was, he suddenly seemed to feel the whole weight of exhaustion and responsibility that was on him; suddenly for a few seconds he lost his strenuous self-control and with a cry of exasperation he flung himself to the ground. The other quickly withdrew. There is no reason to doubt either account.

His own record of how he crossed the Irrawaddy is regrettably meagre, one among a hundred evidences of his impersonality at continual variance with his egotism. He did not even tell when and where he made the crossing, but local memories supported by others say that he left the west shore at Thagaya, north of Hlebo, and landed on the eastern shore about three miles south of Inywa. This he did in the early morning of the 18th.

When the last boat had crossed and gone back empty to Hlebo, and the whole Brigade group had moved east to a bivouac in the forest reserve country of Indaung, a sergeant of the 13th King's reflected, that, despite much to be complained of, things had gone well with 77 Brigade ; they had crossed the Chindwin, severed the railway, crossed the Irrawaddy, all at trifling loss to themselves. " There must," he felt, " be a catch somewhere."[1] And there certainly was.[2]

[1] Halley.

[2] This account of Wingate's crossing is taken from Wingate Burma Report, Burchett, Rolo, Halley. The writer visited the scene of the crossing in February, 1956, and interviewed people of Hlebo and Inywa with the invaluable aid of U Khin Maung of Inywa, and U Thein Ohn of Katha. Their account of what happened is supported by G. M. Anderson. As given here the incident of Wingate's sudden access of rage follows an account by Bernard Fergusson as the latter remembered hearing it from the late Captain Hastings.

The dangers of taking the whole brigade across the Irrawaddy had never been regarded lightly. For all that they had been underestimated. They proved to be much greater than anyone had supposed. The intelligence gathered in Imphal before the expedition set out had been faulty as regards this remote part of Burma. On the 16th Wingate had issued a special order of the day to all ranks in which he held out promises of better days. Anticipating (perfectly correctly as it turned out) that Herring's mission to the Kachin hills would be successful, he had told his men that they were about to enter on a "more fruitful phase of operations," with the advantage that they would have periods of rest "among the friendly tribesmen east of the Irrawaddy." All this was most misleading. In Wingate's own words "none of us realised that between us and these hypothetical friends lay a dry hot belt of waterless forest freely intersected by motorable tracks heavily patrolled by the Japanese." With his own abnormal strength developed to the limit, he was reluctant to recognise the main disadvantage under which his force now began to labour, and in the end laboured almost, as it seemed, in vain. To quote the understating language of a war diary : "At this period a number of officers and men showed signs of losing their physical fitness and energy and the . . . marches had strained them to the utmost."[1] Unknown to itself or its commander the brigade was rapidly reaching the end of its strength and would soon be unable to fight.

A complicated situation had developed beyond the eastern shore. It can be described in simple terms thus : Number 1 group to the south were moving towards Mong Mit by an indirect route in obedience to orders from Wingate to meet him on the way in an area called Tagaung Taung. This took them north of their directest line of march, and as a result they found themselves around the 15th in proximity to Number 3 and Number 5 columns. In Wingate's words Number 1 group's movement "had the effect of funnelling the columns together both in space and time. Instead of being stretched out in width and in depth, they were concertina'd within fifteen miles of each other. Instead of the enemy being dispersed over a wide area looking for them, the Japanese were able to concentrate around the base of the triangle formed by the Shweli and Irrawaddy rivers." The country was not jungle, in the ordinary sense, being for the most part open and flat. On the afternoon of the 15th Number 5 column was seen by a hovering Japanese observation plane, as they marched over paddy. Their discovery could mean discovery of the whole of the brigade's whereabouts, and the likely counter-action was easily guessed. The enemy had only to man the roads from Myitson to Male on the Irra-

[1] War Diary Number 8 Column.

waddy to trap the whole brigade. Wingate's immediate need was to get as many men as he could out of the " Shweli loop," as they came to call this fearful place where the Shweli bends round to form a peninsula surrounded by the two rivers. On the 17th he issued orders for Numbers 3 and 5 columns to move south under Calvert with the object of demolishing the Gokteik viaduct on the main Maymyo-Lashio road, and for Number 1 group to move to Mogok and thereon to Mong Mit. The next day he changed the orders to Number 5 column ordering Fergusson to remain where he was so as to cover the southward advance of the brigade group.

These plans were frustrated, chiefly because of the increasing slowness of the march, and the increasing difficulty of supply dropping. Of these handicaps, the lessening pace under the stress of hunger and thirst and disintegrating boots was the most immediately fatal to Number 1 group. When they reached Mong Mit they were too late for their rendezvous with Herring. Number 5 column suffered most from lack of supply dropping. They had to go for periods of forty-eight hours without food and almost without drink. On one occasion Fergusson sent Wingate a signal referring him to a verse of Psalm 22 : " I may tell all my bones : they look *and* stare upon me." With grim humour Wingate replied by referring him to the Gospel of St. John. " Consider that it is expedient that one man should die for the people, and that the whole nation perish not."[1]

The day after the crossing at Hlebo Wingate took his force to a bivouac twelve miles south-south-east of Inywa. The next day he reached a point ten miles farther. By the third day, the 21st, he was thirty miles away from Inywa, always going in the same direction. Here, at a bivouac on a seasonal river called the Salin Chaung, he stopped for two days in order to concentrate his straggled columns and rest the men. The force that he was leading was more than two battalions in size, gigantic for supply purposes in this hot dry country. But they suffered less than some of the others. They had to endure continual hunger, but not to the intolerable extent imposed on Number 5 column, because they had had a supply drop before crossing. They had one great advantage, that of being able to find water, in only " adequate " quantities, it is true, but enough to keep down raging thirst. The Burma Riflemen with them knew how to dig for the precious stuff, and Wingate himself had his own extraordinary, instinctive and now closely trained faculty in such things.

It seems that during the two days of rest and reassembly in the Salin Chaung Wingate recognised that in taking all 77 Brigade east of the Irrawaddy he had tempted fate to the utmost, and he began the

[1] Fergusson I.

413

undoing of the deed. The initiative came from India. As early as the 14th, Eastern Army Headquarters had asked 4 Corps about Wingate's intentions. It was now, about the 23rd, that 4 Corps demanded a precise answer. Wingate told the Corps Commander in reply that he proposed to lead the brigade towards the Kachin hills below Bhamo, their objective from there to be the Lashio-Bhamo road. In answer 4 Corps told Wingate that, so far afield as the Kachin hills, supply dropping might become impossible except rarely. They suggested instead an operation against Shwebo on the main line, west of the river. By his own account Wingate was without news of Captain Herring, and was with only too plentiful news of the dwindling strength of his two main fighting columns, Numbers 3 and 5, news which was confirmed by what he could see of the state of his own men. He replied that, since the crossing, Japanese patrols on the river had seized all boats, so that the Shwebo operation could not be counted on. 4 Corps then decided to bring the expedition to an end and ordered Wingate to organise a withdrawal to India. He did not resist. In fact, he had already anticipated these instructions by ordering Calvert to return to the Chindwin, unless he was near Gokteik.[1] From now on he had one purpose : to get the best of his officers and men out of the Shweli loop and back to India so that, with their unique experience, they could organise a greater and victorious long range penetration in the next year. The evidence of his own account and of people who were with him indicates that in his wretched bivouacs in the isolated and hourly more dangerous country between the Irrawaddy and the south-bending Shweli, Wingate began to lose interest in his present venture. His thoughts were concentrated on matters of military theory and need : on how to perfect and use afresh his technique of penetration with the knowledge he had gathered. If it is beyond question that he had some of the cold harsh faults that go with high ambition, it is also easy to understand why, when all seemed lost, men followed him with all the old confidence, and told each other that " he'll get us out of this."

He did get the brigade out, but with heavy loss.

While Wingate was debating in his own mind what should be his next move, Calvert, on the 23rd, not yet having received his orders to withdraw, made a brilliant assault on the enemy near Sitton. Early on that day one of his officers captured a Burman courier with messages which showed that a Japanese battalion were moving to patrol stations on roads leading from Myitson towards the Irrawaddy. He immediately organised an ambush in three phases, each to lead to the next. The

[1] The message was sent on the 21st but owing to a wireless failure did not reach Calvert till the 24th. 3 Column War Diary.

action was entirely successful. For the loss of one Gurkha N.C.O. a hundred enemy were killed, and the outgoing patrols were withdrawn to the depleted Japanese battalion huddled in Sitton.[1] This was the twelfth battle encounter of Number 3 column, and their last major action. On the 24th Calvert received his orders to return to the Chindwin urging him if possible to make his way to Lake Indawgyi, sixty miles north of Katha, where Wingate hoped to organise a brigade rendezvous.

The day before this, on the 23rd, Wingate signalled Fergusson (who had been joined by Jefferies and his party), to meet him at his supply-dropping rendezvous two miles or so west of Baw. These orders astonished Fergusson and (with the orders to Calvert) remain a matter for criticism, for they meant calling Number 5 column back into the Shweli loop just as they were breaking free of it. The column immediately began their march and, after many misadventures, met the brigade group eight miles north of Baw a day late. The delay in the meeting was chiefly due to the fact that at Baw the brigade group fought their last battle under adverse conditions.

The plan was the same as at Tonmakeng and Pinlebu: battle groups attacking the garrison village were to act as defence of the dropping zone, but on this occasion, owing to the weariness of the troops and a measure of bad luck the plan misfired. The first move was to block all the roads leading to Baw, but two of the blocking parties misjudged distance in the dark, one halting farther off than they should have done (an error for which Wingate very severely punished their officer), the other blundering in too far and alerting a sentry. Surprise was lost, there was a confused battle in the jungle, and the pilots of the supplying aircraft, seeing that something was amiss, flew off after dropping only a third of their packages. Wingate quickly withdrew the force northwards to the rendezvous which was in a river bed called the Shaukpin Chaung. It was here that Fergusson and Jefferies met him on the 25th.

He was downcast. Jefferies found him pacing up and down in the river bed, and as soon as greetings were over, for they had not met since before the Chindwin, Wingate gloomily outlined the present position to him. He was remembered saying something as follows : " Just put yourself in the position of the Jap commander. Your one aim will be to prevent anyone from getting out alive. You've been made to look very stupid. There's only one way you can save face, and that's by annihilating the whole expedition. We can take it for granted that from now on the Jap commander is going to do every-

---

[1] Burchett. Information obtained at the War Office. Accounts of the action were later used as text-book illustrations in British and American military manuals.

thing in his power to wipe us out. And the first thing he'll do is to make a strong effort to prevent us recrossing the Irrawaddy."[1]

On the next day, the 26th, Wingate called a conference of his column commanders. He told them some of his plan for defeating Japanese intentions. Like all his plans it was an extraordinary mixture of simplicity and ingenuity, and was centred on a policy of bluff. He proposed that the whole body should march straight back with him to Inywa, arguing that the Japanese would never expect him to make the recrossing at that place. Before moving over the river to the western shore they would abandon all but the most necessary equipment and kill all their beasts. On the far side they would disperse into small groups again, and on their way back to Assam attack Indaw and the railway over the Meza river south-west of it, if possible.[2] He invited comment. Fergusson made a counter-suggestion, that the brigade group as now constituted, numbering over twelve hundred, should stay together as a fighting unit, cross the Shweli, and move north, reaching India by a wide circular movement, going east of Bhamo, north of Myitkyina, and entering Assam by the Hakawng valley. He argued that if they kept their beasts they could also keep their support weapons, and that, though they would suffer losses in action, they would have a decisive advantage wherever they chose to cross out of the Shweli loop. Wingate refused the suggestion on the grounds that supply dropping would become prohibitively difficult as they moved east of the Shweli and become impossible after the breaking of the monsoon.[3] The decision was taken for Inywa and the march back to India began on the 27th.

Wingate's conduct of this phase of the expedition is difficult to follow. The sudden swift unexpectable return to Inywa is all in Wingate's style, and very nearly succeeded. The difficulty does not lie there but in his ordering Number 5 column to go back into the Shweli loop, and his orders to Number 3 column which resulted in Calvert taking the same fatal step. For on the 24th Calvert had sent a reply to Wingate's belated signal in which he told his commander that he would cross the Irrawaddy between Bhamo and Katha.[4] His direct route lay through the loop and across the Shweli. Wingate did not warn him against re-entering the loop, and in the event Calvert did this and narrowly escaped disaster. It is difficult at first to see why Wingate did not arrange for the two columns to be substantially supplied south of the loop, with orders to march straight back to India.

Some of the enigma is dispelled, however, by the rest of Wingate's

[1] Jefferies quoted in Rolo.   [2] Wingate Burma Report.
[3] Fergusson I and Fergusson's Interim Report on the Expedition.
[4] Number 3 Column War Diary.

plan for the withdrawal of his force. Unknown to his column commanders he arranged for the R.A.F. to make false supply drops south of the Shweli loop. This succeeded in misleading the Japanese as to the whereabouts of the columns, and caused them to concentrate their patrols away from the enclosed country in the north. To this feint another seems to have been added. On the 24th Wingate had sent one of his Biblical messages to Number 1 group : " Remember Lot's wife. Return not whence ye came. Seek thy salvation in the mountains. Genesis xix." They assumed this to mean that they must continue their slow and difficult march towards the mountainous country of Mong Mit and the now missed rendezvous with Herring. They were told nothing about the withdrawal. They had a hope of reaching safety in the Kachin country but it was slender. Among men who have studied this campaign, either from documents or from experience, there is a consensus of opinion that Wingate intended Number 1 Group to act as a decoy from the main part of the brigade.[1] Such deeds are not to be blamed on commanders. They have to be done by all commanders. They are of the essence of warfare. It can at least be said that the sacrifice of these men was not in vain.

The march back to Inywa began at one o'clock in the morning of the 27th. Number 5 column brought up the rear. Fergusson recorded afterwards that " Wingate's uncanny instinct for cross-country marching—his sense of watersheds, good gradients, thinner jungle and suchlike—was apparent even from my place far down the long procession." He describes the character of " that miserable march " as " a slow business, with frequent halts, and with the knowledge of the Irrawaddy stretched like a barrier between ourselves and the free country beyond." Whenever a column descended into a river bed some of its mules would be led off and shot, and the men who had tended the poor beasts all the way from the Central Provinces wept over them.[2]

The officers and men had no doubt that the Japanese were following them. At midday on the 27th they had proof. A man of Number 5 column was shot at, whereon Fergusson organised a diversion by the rearguard with the object of putting the Japanese patrols off the track of the brigade. Preceded by elaborate feints, purposely littered tracks and false bivouacs, he led his men to an attack on the village of Hintha, about half-way between Baw and Inywa, before daybreak of the 28th. This was the last battle of Number 5 column and worthily concluded their fighting record in the expedition.[1] They succeeded in their purpose and the bewildered Japanese did not afterwards succeed in

---

[1] See *Official History* Chapter XVIII.
[2] Fergusson I. Rolo. Burchett. Stibbe. Halley.

closing with the main body in the interior of the Shweli loop. It was in this action that Lieutenant Philip Stibbe was wounded and, according to the bitter exactions of this kind of war, was left behind with one noble-natured Burman Rifleman who, at the cost of his life, volunteered to stay with him. Stibbe was inevitably taken prisoner and inevitably subjected to the abominations of Japanese custom when he came to be interrogated. He pretended to break down and divulge the brigade plan, and it is possible that his false confession sealed the success of Hintha and saved countless men. After this action Number 5 column struggled forward to the rendezvous near Inywa, but, through various misadventures, they never again joined the main body.

After a march in which they had covered fifty miles in as many hours, the main body, worn out with hunger and marching, reached their bivouacs in the country round Inywa at four o'clock in the afternoon of the 28th. The bivouacs were spread over several miles, a circumstance which in earlier phases of the expedition hardly affected rendezvous, but made a difference now with everything they did losing speed and efficiency through exhaustion. No reconnaissance was made of the river before dark, and patrols in mutual search were not sent out by the main brigade group or the Burma Rifles Headquarter group. It may be supposed that when at length the separating parties came on their bivouacs, and at long last could count on a halt of a few hours, sleep came down on them as though it were some devouring beast of prey. The imprisonment of the Shweli loop was more than geographical. In the escape, any temporary advantage over time had to be paid for in new disadvantage in movement.

At three o'clock in the morning of the 29th Wingate and the Brigade Headquarter column went to Inywa. They expected to meet a patrol of the Burma Rifles but none came.[1] This added considerably to the difficulties of crossing, because without the Riflemen he had only two officers, Aung Thin and Sao Man Hpa, who could speak Burmese and organise the collection of boats. Soon the Headquarter column was joined near the shore by Number 7 column who were to cross first. By six o'clock Aung Thin and Sao Man Hpa had collected twenty country boats from the Shweli (the Japanese having taken away or destroyed most of those on the main river), but with insufficient oars. Towards six o'clock Number 2 Group Headquarter column arrived with Number 8 column, the latter taking up rearguard defence positions. With inadequate river transport, and with the certainty of Japanese forces not far away, the signal for crossing was given as

---

[1] In his report Wingate takes some of the blame for the failure of the Burma Rifles to meet him. He suggests that he should have sent a patrol to their bivouac at Pynlebin.

daylight began breaking and they could see again the huge dun volume of the river.

The operation was commanded by Jefferies. "After nine years in the navy," Wingate growled at him, "you ought to be able to get us over the Irrawaddy." The first boats were more than half-way to the western shore when the Japanese began to attack. They fired on the boats with mortars, light automatics and rifles, and sank one boat. The brigade mortars and machine-guns opened up in reply, and this caused the enemy to raise their sights and fire on the eastern shore while the rest of the boats made a landing. The men of Number 7 column took up battle positions and succeeded in thrusting the Japanese back from the landing area. The enemy were in small numbers, and without heavy machine-guns. Wingate was standing on a sandbank, "looking" according to the description of Jefferies, "like some minor prophet with his huge beard and a blanket wrapped around his shoulders."[1] He needed to make up his mind quickly. By a stroke of luck he had at the last moment found an extra boat which he had requisitioned from a surprised family of river traders. (They had arrived on the scene as the crossing began.) To offset this small advantage he had just heard from Aung Thin that the people of Inywa reported two Japanese companies in one of the west shore villages opposite. He called Jefferies to him and said something as follows : "They are in some strength just behind us to the east. They are in considerable strength on the other side. We've got to make ourselves scarce, and pretty quickly." He could almost certainly have forced a crossing, at considerable loss, but, wisely or not, he decided against making the attempt. It is impossible to say which was his right course.[2]

The men on the west shore were left to find their way back, and did. Wingate called off the crossing between eight and nine in the morning, and summoned his principals to a rendezvous. What happened then is best described in his own words : "I held a short and sad meeting with my column commanders and Colonel Cooke. I told them I intended to withdraw at once to a secure bivouac in the forest and that they were to follow suit. Supply drops would be arranged individually. I then bade them good-bye and marched my Headquarters away. . . . At that moment, I must confess it seemed to me that the enemy stood an excellent chance of pinning the force down before it could disperse, and I do not think that I exerted myself sufficiently to instil the necessary confidence into my subordinates.

[1] Rolo.
[2] This account of the attempted crossing follows Wingate Burma Report, Burchett, Rolo, Halley and an Anderson communication.

Colonel Cooke, Major Scott, and Major Gilkes, however, behaved throughout with complete cheerfulness, and it was their quiet steady work that saved the majority of the Brigade Group."

After a meeting with some of the officers of the Burma Rifles later that day, Wingate moved with the Brigade column to his "secure bivouac" which was about ten miles (by direct distance) east-south-east of Inywa, and ten miles south of the Shweli at the top of the loop. Here at two o'clock in the afternoon of the 30th he was supplied from the air and the column, numbering two hundred and twenty, was then divided into five "dispersal groups." "I assembled the whole Headquarters," Wingate recorded afterwards, "and addressed the men for the last time. I explained what they had accomplished, why we were best advised to separate, what the plan was, and how they should behave under various circumstances. I expressed full confidence in their leaders and their ability to reach India, warned them to take their time, thanked them for their devoted services, and bade them God speed."

Wingate's own dispersal group was forty-three strong. Besides himself it included Jefferies and eight of his men, the Brigade-Major, Anderson, Lieutenant Spurlock, an R.A.F. detachment of two officers and two flight-sergeants, Captain Katju an Indian officer from the public relations department, Aung Thin, an officer and four men of the Gurkhas, an officer and six men of the Burma Rifles, four British beast-tenders and a remainder who were officially described as "followers," and among whom one should be mentioned, Wingate's Indian bearer who was called Bachi Ram. This man had joined him in the early days of the brigade. By oversight or caprice he seems never to have been enlisted in the army. He was, according to the accounts of those who knew him, a somewhat exasperating person, but his master, stern, harsh, and sometimes cruel to others, showed a continual and sometimes even absurd forbearance in his dealings with this devoted servant.

While the rest of Number 2 group dispersed to cross the Shweli or the Irrawaddy by the east, north, south and south-west, and while Number 1 group went forward with their hopeless mission, Wingate and his forty-two took an unusual course of action. They remained in the neighbourhood of the supply drop of the 30th for a full week, changing their bivouac only once and by less than a mile. They settled down to a régime of sleep and food in preparation for the rigours of the long and the perilous march back to the Chindwin. Wingate has been much criticised for this. It has been urged against him that while the rest of his men faced the dangers of the river crossings while the hunt was up, and without any advantage of preliminary rest, he took an easier way out. The criticism is understandable enough, but ridiculous all the same. There can be no doubt what Wingate's answer to these strictures would have been : that the commander of so singular an exploit as this had become a precious asset to military counsels, and that if this was the easier way out, so much the more was it his duty to follow it. (He blamed Calvert in his report for leading the most dangerously placed of the dispersal groups of Number 3 column.) But, however sound this argument, a more readily acceptable one is implicit in the facts. The hunt was up along the rivers, but this did not mean that the pack had been drawn off in the territory of the Shweli loop. To stay was as dangerous as to leave. Wingate's decision was typical of his thinking : he did not wish to commit all his force to the same hazard, and he took advantage of the fact that there were two sorts to choose from. In the event his own choice was the most hazardous of all in Northern Force. When he came to make his crossings Japanese patrols were still active on the Irrawaddy, and had been intensified on the Chindwin.

The week in this bivouac was a strange time. Men who were there look back on those days as happy ones. For the first time since the Bambwe Taung they could rest, and a whole week's rest was a luxury they had not known since Imphal. They could eat plentifully for the first time in nearly two months, though here again the daily slaughter of their faithful mules and horses often cast a gloom over their feasting. They no longer killed the beasts by shooting, but, in accordance with the rules of this secret life, by cutting their throats after haltering them tightly, with their heads fastened high up so that they could not scream. But this grisly routine could not take much away from their strangely found enjoyment. They forgot their dangers and built up their physical and mental vigour once more. Wingate himself had sunk to a great depth of fatigue of body and mind during the marches and counter-marches in the Shweli loop, and he confessed afterwards that on the return to Inywa he had felt as though he was near the end of his strength.[1] His resilience took a familiar form. Never a taciturn man (strength and silence are a rare combination), he now became not only talkative but almost fantastically so. He is variously remembered as arguing and monologising on Plato's dialogues, the works of Shaw and Wells, the future of the cinema, English and French painting of the eighteenth century, the merits of the symphony as opposed to the concerto, the psychological significance of strip-cartoons with special reference to Popeye the Sailor, Jane, and Wimpy, the place in literature of detective fiction, the failure of the League of Nations, the use of military forces under a system of world government, and the art,

[1] Anderson. A communication.

mind, and character of Leonardo da Vinci. Major Anderson had a copy of Palgrave's *Golden Treasury* and from this he gave numerous readings, especially of Gray's Elegy. He used to return to the present to talk about his future plans. Sometimes he found occasion to talk about his past. One day when he had been denouncing Army officers with more than usual vehemence, Aung Thin put to him a question which must often occur to anyone who studies his life. " If," asked Aung Thin, " you find soldiers so contemptible, and the military life so abhorrent, why did you choose to become a soldier yourself ? " To this he replied somewhat as follows : " It has never entered my head to be anything else. It was in my family tradition. When I was a little boy I spent all my time playing soldiers, and when I grew up I found, in that respect, that my habits did not change." And then he told him something about Lodolf. During this week of inaction Wingate found light and urgent labour with which to occupy his forty-two companions. Everyone was ordered to toil at the manufacture of paddles out of bamboo, for he was determined not to be caught again as he had been at Inywa.

This week in bivouac was one of the very few occasions when they needed to take account of the wild life of the jungle. In reading of 77 Brigade, or of the events in Burma of 1944, one may be surprised at how little mention there is of perils from jungle animals in this country containing elephants, rhinoceros, tigers, panthers, leopards and snakes in abundance. It seems that all other living things avoid man, a fact which Wingate had impressed on the brigade in training, notably on an occasion when a private of the 13th King's had met a tiger while relieving nature in the Saugor jungle. ("Why did you run away ? " he had thundered at the man. "Don't you know that when you find yourself face to face with a tiger all you have to do is to stare him out ? ") But now they were in some danger from the wild elephant which roam these little-inhabited forest-lands. To protect themselves they built up large fires to scare the great beasts away, and they often had to stand by for an ignition signal while herds wandered near. The danger was not so much of being trampled as of being betrayed through flame and smoke. But they never needed to light the fires and the elephants, after much threatening, left them unharmed. The only creatures of the jungle that continually and murderously attacked Wingate's men were mosquitoes, and, in the second expedition of 1944, when they were in the monsoon, the leeches.

On April the 7th they set out south-west for the Irrawaddy. They had no mules by now, and before leaving the bivouac they destroyed their precious transmitting set. Wingate believed that the journey to

India would take him a fortnight.[1] It took him eight days longer than that.

They reached the Irrawaddy south of Tigyaing the same day. The hunt was up along both shores still.

Throughout two days and a night they tried to find a crossing point, always to be frustrated by fleeing boatmen and Japanese patrols. At last on the 10th they came to the same place between Tigyaing and Tagaung where Calvert had crossed on the 13th of March. There was a little village nearby on the eastern shore called Satsa. Here Wingate found some dugout canoes and a bamboo fence capable of conversion into rafts. Aung Thin was sent to ask the headman for the use of these things, and momentarily the luck changed. The headman turned out to be a friend in need. He gave them two large boats with rowers. They planned to go over in three parties but as the boats were going back for the last journey over, Japanese arrived on the eastern shore. The boatmen fled. Wingate had then to decide whether to wait for the remainder or to go on westwards while the going was good. He went on. Most of the commanders had to make this agonising decision in the course of the retreat. There can be no question but that Wingate's decision was the right one.

They soon found that they were not on the western shore after all. They were on a big island, the same one on which Number 3 column had nearly been trapped when moving eastwards. But their luck still held. There was a village on the island and the good folk ferried them across the last piece of the river.

They marched on in a north-westerly direction, and next day came to the Meza river. Wingate tried to repeat the Irrawaddy routine : Aung Thin was sent to a village to find boats and rowers, but by now the luck was out again. In furious panic the villagers surrounded Aung Thin and demanded his surrender, brandishing swords at him. When Wingate and others came to Aung Thin's support, the villagers changed their tune, piteously explaining that there were Japanese patrols a short way off and that if they helped the British some of them would be shot and all of them have their houses burned down. In the end these poor people did consent to guide them to a ford where they crossed the Meza on foot.[2] By dusk of the 11th they had marched seventy miles with two river crossings and about eight hours' sleep, and still they had to go on.

They continued to hold a west-north-westerly course. They were

[1] Rolo. He and Burchett contain first-hand authority, the former recording the account of Major Jefferies, the latter that of Brigadier Anderson. Unfortunately, in his report Wingate himself gave no account of his return, remarking only that " From this moment on, my own story is merely one of many similar ones."
[2] Burchett.

now aiming for the railway. Between it and the Meza was a country of rocky hill, precipitous on the eastern side. They were in the driest season of the year before the monsoon rains. They were hungry and thirsty and tormented by mosquitoes, having lost their protection equipment of veils and ointment. Strange to relate, even in these conditions, Wingate used to spend much of the brief rest periods in ardent discussions on Beethoven, and the Italian Renaissance, and readings from the *Golden Treasury*. Aung Thin was puzzled as to what this might mean. He concluded that it was partly a device to keep the others from surrendering to fatigue, and partly perhaps prompted by a noble vanity—if this was to be the end of Wingate's life on earth, then someone would remember how majestically he had occupied his mind in his last days![1]

The approach to the railway was through teak forest, pleasant marching earlier in the year, but not after the great leaves have fallen in the dry season. To move through it then is like walking through crockery. Vainly Wingate tried to diminish the noise. For a while a man was sent ahead of the column on all-fours to clear a path, but this made progress so slow that they reverted to ordinary marching with what discretion they could. He found by experiment that the noise of teak leaves underfoot was audible three hundred yards away. But there was nothing for it but to trust to luck, and, regardless of the crash of leaves (a noise that sounds to the maker as though it could drive him mad), they marched through the forests of descending foothills and plains to where the railway runs on even ground between Wuntho and Indaw. Their luck was back. The teak stopped a hundred yards from the railway or they could never have crossed without being heard on the approach. It was midnight. Since the attacks by Calvert and Fergusson the whole length of the railway was closely patrolled, and nowhere more so than at this point where Calvert had fought and laid waste. Wingate collected his men close together, whispered, " Here we go," and led the column over the railway and into the teak forest on the other side.[1] They moved some way into the jungle and lay down to rest. Wingate said to Jefferies : " That was bad patrol work. The Japs should never have let us through."

While they were resting they heard the puffing of an engine and the clank of wheels on rails. They debated among themselves what this noise signified. It could mean that the railway was repaired, or it could mean merely that a train was running between stations. They hoped it meant the latter.[2] They could not stop and organise another

[1] Aung Thin.
[2] Anderson. In fact their hopes were vain. With the help of forced labour the line was restored in four weeks from the time of the demolitions on the 6th of March.

demolition in this country where they were expected. After a few hours Wingate roused them and they thrust on.

Between the railway and the Mu valley they had to cross the Mingin range. Sometimes the going was so difficult that they had to make mountaineering ropes out of rifle slings. They had come to the end of their rations of biscuit and dates and relied now on what they could get on the way. The Burma Riflemen with them could find out and kill the elusive beasts of the jungle and they were glad to eat python.[1] This was their best jungle meat. The roots which they often made into soup were sometimes pleasing to the taste but always wanting in sustenance. They never rested more than three or four hours. They had continual evidence that the Japanese were never far behind them. At one village Aung Thin was able to buy some rice, but after, as they marched on, and while they were still near enough to hear, the drums and gongs rang out in summons to the Japanese patrols. At another village farther on the way Aung Thin bought a bullock which on arrival turned out to be a buffalo. They wanted to take it with them but the buffalo was immovable. They pushed and pulled in vain. They could not afford time to coax it. As in their restful bivouac, they could not risk a shot being heard, so Wingate slaughtered the beast. Then they butchered the meat and carried it away to cook and eat it in the jungle.[1] They enjoyed their first full meal in many days. But this moment of relief ended in tragedy.

The signals officer, Lieutenant Spurlock, had been suffering from dysentery since the Irrawaddy. The sudden and irresistible meal of buffalo worsened his state, and twenty-four hours later he could not go on. He asked to be left. Wingate could not bear to be true to his teaching at this moment. As said, he was attached to the young man, and he could not bring himself to leave him to the certainty of capture if not of dying miserably, while the column went on. There are many instances of Wingate showing excessive harshness, but now he erred, if it should be said he erred at all, in the opposite sense. To save Spurlock he halted the column for forty-eight hours. The sacrifice of time was in vain. The young man was too ill to move. Wingate stayed with him to the end. The moment of parting came on a moonlight night. As the commander left his side Spurlock staggered to his feet and saluted him, and the column went on, grief in every heart.[2] The sick and the wounded could not be allowed to jeopardise the safety of their more numerous, more fortunate and more valuable comrades. They were a minority without rights in the hateful democracy of war.

Through the dry uplands of the Mingin range they marched on with the least possible pause. Wingate imposed merciless water drill

[1] Burchett.   [2] Aung Thin. Anderson. Burchett.

on them so much so that, quite fatuously as it seemed on one occasion, he forbade them to stop at a lime tree to collect its ripe fruit. He was acting on an instinct that the area was dangerous, and it so happened, as they learned afterwards, that a Japanese patrol was near the place at the time and would probably have come up with them if they had stayed. Not for one moment during the march between the Irrawaddy and the Mu were they more than a few hours away from the enemy. They were near the end of their strength when again their luck turned. They came to a monastery and when Aung Thin had conducted his usual embassy the abbot and his monks gave them five sucking pigs, chickens, bananas, tomatoes and rice.[1] They had at last come to water again on the slopes leading to the Mu valley. They went on to the river and crossed it at night. Before them was the Zibyutaungdan escarpment, a rock wall fifteen hundred feet high. It was unlikely that any of the passes to its western heights had been left unguarded. But they marched towards it with the courage of men without any alternative.

On their way from the river to the escarpment they had the most extraordinary of all their strokes of good luck. Aung Thin tried to buy food at a village, with little success, but as the column was moving away an old man came running out of the village and joined them. He was a hermit, and he explained to Wingate, through Aung Thin, that he was convinced of a mission from God to rescue a party of strangers of whom he had been miraculously forewarned. Wingate and the rest suspected that he was in effect a Japanese agent, but Aung Thin believed him to be sincere. The situation of the retreating column was so desperate that, as men do in such straits, they decided to believe the man, if only for the sake of convenience. He said he could take them over the escarpment by paths unknown to the Japanese. And he was as good as his word. By animal tracks, remote woodcutters' paths, stream beds, and always by devious ways the old hermit took them safely up to the top of the range. By this time they had lost another of their party through sickness: a lance-corporal of the 13th King's who was suffering from sores in his legs. This brave man, seeing that he was retarding the pace of the column, deliberately lost himself in the jungle.[2]

On the 23rd of April they reached a height from which they could see successive green-clad ranges towards the west from one of whose north-east valleys clouds were rising. Wingate was seized with the drama of the moment. In solemn accents he exclaimed : " Behold the Chindwin. It is a poor heart that never rejoices."[3]

They were now only thirty miles away from the river, but these

[1] Burchett. Rolo. Anderson.   [2] Rolo.   [3] Anderson.

were among their worst miles, with man and nature against them. The hunt was up along the Chindwin as strenuously as ever it had been in the Shweli loop and along the Irrawaddy. Within the last fortnight Number 3 and Number 5 columns had crossed and every post between Homalin and Sittaung was manned and in exchange of patrols. To avoid inland pickets their strange guide on one occasion took them down eight miles of a flowing tributary. When at last they reached the Chindwin they found that (possibly because of the forty-eight hours' wait with Spurlock), the enemy were aware of their approach and had made all preparations in their power to kill or capture them. They arrived at the river on the 27th of April[1] about twenty miles south of the place where they had crossed ten weeks before. Wingate sent out scouts. They came back with gloomy news: all boats had been commandeered; there were no large British forces east of the river; the Japanese were everywhere.

The hermit, who was still with them, had a friend in the neighbourhood, and this friend brought them food and additional bad news. The Japanese had somehow discovered that the brigade commander himself, leading about thirty men, was seeking to cross the Chindwin, and they had trailed him. At the moment they were conducting an intensive search of the jungle around them, and the hermit's friend could tell them moreover exactly where the patrols had been in the course of the last twenty-four hours. Immediately and characteristically Wingate decided to attempt to cross where the patrols had last searched. He sent out his weary column to lay false clues of his path, and fixed the attempt for the next evening. The hermit and his friend promised to go to look for boats meanwhile. There then occurred the very strange parting of Wingate and his mysterious benefactor.

Someone in the column (perhaps Wingate himself), had caught a diminutive turtle. The hermit, after the departure of his friend before him, asked Wingate to give him the turtle, as a condition of help, and Wingate gave it. Through Aung Thin the holy man explained that he wanted the turtle as an augury of good luck, and then he motioned them both to come down with him to a tributary stream. The three men went down together. The hermit prayed over the turtle, let it run free into the water, and then departed. Turtle soup was not to be lightly denied to his men, yet Wingate was reluctant to interfere with the hermit's arrangements, and the turtle swam off to freedom and life. Afterwards Wingate said that, in his own opinion, the hermit was conveying by these mysterious actions that all was lost and only fate could now save them.

[1] There is a discrepancy between the accounts of Jefferies and Anderson. According to Jefferies they arrived on the 26th (Rolo).

In a bivouac away from water or paths they waited for the return of the two Burmans till about three in the morning of the 28th. Between snatches of sleep, and by the light of the moon, Wingate took the occasion to read the Platonic Dialogues in a whisper.[1] When it was clear that the hermit and his friend were not coming back, Wingate made a new plan.

It was simple. Opposite to them, on the west shore, was a British post, according to their latest information. Wingate divided his party in two : those who were strong enough swimmers to get across on their own, and those who needed to rely on boats. He himself would take charge of the swimmers, Major Anderson of the others. The party with Wingate were Jefferies, Aung Thin, Sergeant Wilshaw, Sergeant Carey, and Private Boreham. It should be said that the whole group knew how to swim, but that to swim the fast-flowing Chindwin, after what they had endured, was a considerable physical feat.

The Wingate party, having arranged a signalling rendezvous with the Anderson party, moved off from the last bivouac at about half-past five in the morning. They found a track leading to the shore, but soon they found it impressed all over with Japanese boot-marks, and between them and the river was a massive hedge of elephant grass. They looked at their maps. The elephant grass was marked as ending before a wide stretch of beach which would probably be under observation. To follow the track might mean to walk into a Japanese post. To cut a path through the elephant grass might be impossible. Wingate said to Jefferies, " Well, John, which shall it be ? " Jefferies preferred the elephant grass and Wingate agreed with him. He said : " We'll tear it apart, blade by blade."

Grass is a feeble name for this particular kind of jungle growth. The sharp wiry blades rise to more than twice a man's height, and at their base they are matted together in near-solidity. It took the five of them seven hours to hack through about seven hundred yards of these close-growing reeds. They became indifferent to noise, and went through on this snail's progress with the fury of men cheated at the last, for this was the worst of what they endured on that march. Afterwards they were to laugh at the journalist cliché-description of the jungle as " the green hell," but the term was apt enough for this last half-mile to the river. Suddenly at the end their luck turned again. Wingate was at the head of them when he stopped hacking, turned round, and beckoned to Jefferies. " Take a look at this, John," he said.

In their favour, for once, the map was at fault. There was no long beach. Within a few yards of them was the great river Chindwin.

[1] Aung Thin. Rolo.

It was three o'clock in the afternoon and broad daylight, but they were at their goal, and there was no question of staying and waiting for the dark. Wingate gave orders for them all to cut their trousers into shorts, to abandon all equipment except their rifles and packs, to tie boots to packs, to be ready to go at once at his signal. His last words of advice were : " Don't fight the current. When you get to the other side take cover."[1]

They did not have to wait long for the signal. When Wingate gave it, they rushed down the bank into the river. No one fired on them. They had about four to five hundred yards to cross. Almost immediately they felt weighed down by their weakness and the enormity of the seeming-easy undertaking. Not one of them but was nearly swept away to death except Sergeant Wilshaw who, through all the fatigues of the campaign, had preserved for himself that piece of swimming equipment named after Mae West. Buoyed up by his chest-girth lifebelt he could afford to go slowly and to rest and flounder here and there without danger of sinking, so by last minute plan he was last in, a rear party to help those in danger. All of them had to rest at moments by floating on their backs. Wingate was kept up on the surface by bamboo sticks thrust in his pack, and his topee slung back making a minute boat for his head and shoulders, and thus spinning round in the central current he regained the strength needed for the last strokes to the shore. Jefferies, the best swimmer, became caught up in the streaming rags of his shirt sleeves and would have been lost that way if he had not struck out so strongly at first that he had crossed the middle by the time he began to lose the use of his limbs, and was carried by the currents towards the western shore. Aung Thin had hurt his knee in a river bed a short time before and swam near Boreham and Carey and all three of them floated close to Wilshaw, and his Mae West gave them confidence and solace in a fearful moment. They would all have been drowned if their strength had been only a little less. When he had floated on his back for the time needed to be able to move again Wingate turned over for the last effort. He passed Jefferies and said, " Keep going, you're nearly there."[2] A few seconds later he began to sink and his feet touched uncertain, slithering, treacherous ground, but ground nonetheless. With what might have seemed his last strength on earth he clambered up to the river's edge, followed by Jefferies. The other four were still in the water but slowly reaching grounding level. He rallied Jefferies saying : " Come on, the Japs may be here, run to cover."[3] But neither of them could move for some moments. They watched the others struggling to the shore.

The crossing had been made. They were back. But the final

---

[1] Rolo.   [2] Burchett.   [3] Rolo.

dramatic moment was marked by a wild touch of farce. When he had recovered his breath sufficiently to go inland from the shallow water where he was sitting with Jefferies, Wingate rose up and began to make his way up the long sand beach. Suddenly he let out a yell of pain and began to leap hither and thither, then dashed back into the water. The men still in the river, now crawling up to the shore, and Jefferies, thought that he had been shot by a silenced gun or a rifle whose noise had been lost in shrieks and howls of agony. Jefferies was the first to realise what had happened. The sunbaked sand had burnt Wingate's bare feet, whence the screams and panic leaps and the rush back to water. He had lost his boots in the crossing. He wrapped his trousers round his feet and, dressed only in his short bush shirt and the topee, Wingate, bearded and unbreeched, hobbled clownishly into safety from the most successful and astounding of his exploits.

The others understood what had happened and covered their feet before crossing the sand between the water and the trees.

When they were assembled again in the jungle they went in search of help. They met a fisherman who told them there were no Japanese on the western shore. He brought them to a village where they sat down to the utterly unaccustomed pleasures of a meal eaten in freedom from all danger. One of their hosts then guided them to the nearest British post and they were received by a company of the Gurkha Rifles. There are certain meetings whose joy remains a continual refreshment for the rest of a man's life.

Their first care was to find boats to cross that night to the eastern shore to rescue Anderson and the remaining men. Boats were collected and all preparations made for the attempt, but things had gone wrong with the other party. Japanese patrols came back to the area of the rendezvous and Anderson had to move as much as a mile south of it. Their signal was a feeble one. By now they had no electric torches that worked, and instead Anderson used a match held in a cooking pot with a hat passed before it. A mile off-target, this was not seen by Wingate and the waiting party on the other side. In deep gloom Anderson led his men back to their last bivouac as dawn began to show. It was their belief that Wingate and the others were all dead. The next day Captain Motilal Katju volunteered to seek boats in a neighbouring village. He took with him a Burman non-commissioned officer who, after a preliminary reconnaissance, warned him that there were Japanese troops in the place. Overbold Katju went in. A volley of rifle fire was heard, and this must have signalled his death for he was never seen by friendly eyes again. He had joined Wingate's brigade at the last moment and without any specialist training, having fought with the Army of India in Libya where he earned the Military Cross. He had endured all the terrors and fatigues of the campaign with the best, and his death at this time was a bitter blow to the lost men on the eastern shore. He was a cousin of Jawaharlal Nehru.

During the next day four of Anderson's men tried to cross by swimming. Two succeeded, one turned back, one was drowned. If the men on the eastern shore could have known that two of them were across they could have thrown off a great part of their anxiety, for the two swimmers were in time to tell of the change of rendezvous. That night the signal was answered. It was perhaps sent too soon, before night had wholly set in, for a Japanese patrol saw the boats. They opened fire with mortars and machine-guns as Anderson's men were leaving. The Gurkhas retaliated with mortars and held the Japanese attack. The whole of Anderson's remaining party crossed the Chindwin without the loss of a single man.

Wingate's dispersal group was the fourth component of the brigade to regain Assam. Calvert's column had gone across on the 15th, Fergusson's on the 25th, and Colonel Cooke with sixteen of Northern Force Headquarters column had been flown out from a place called Amatgyon on the 28th.[1] Thirty-four of Wingate's forty-three had come through the ordeal. Of the other four dispersal groups of brigade Headquarters only one, the defence platoon, reached safety. A fortnight passed after the 29th before others made their way out of enemy-held Burma. On the 13th of May Number 8 column crossed the upper Chindwin at Tamanthi, and the Headquarter column of the Burma Rifles reached Fort Hertz. On this same day the remains of Number 1 group recrossed near the place where they had first seen the Chindwin exactly three months before. They had gone through the worst by far of these ordeals, and only two hundred and sixty returned of the thousand who had set out in February.[2] Others of Number 2 group Headquarter column came back on the 26th May. The last column of all to make harbour was Number 7 under the command of Major Gilkes. After failing to cross the Shweli Gilkes decided to

[1] The circumstances were remarkable. The Headquarter Column and Number 8 Column, marching together, sent a message that they would be near Amatgyon on the 28th for a supply drop. Here they found a piece of flat ground and spelt out, " Plane land here now," in large letters on the ground with the aid of maps and parachute-cloth, and a Dakota transport plane, after reconnaissance, succeeded in making the landing. Colonel Cooke though wounded was reluctant to leave but did so at the entreaty of Major Scott of Number 8 Column who said he would not face the responsibility of leaving him to certain capture by the Japanese for Cooke was beyond marching. To enable the overloaded plane to take off one wounded man volunteered to stay behind. Rolo. Information obtained at the War Office.

[2] The majority of the survivors owed their safety to the devotion of Lieutenant Chit-Ken, M.C., of the Burma Rifles.

avoid rivers and after a series of astonishing adventures he marched his column into the Chinese town of Paoshan on the 3rd of June. The General commanding the 71st Chinese Army entertained them in princely style and they were flown back to Assam on the 8th.

It was clear even as early as the end of April that the casualties were likely to prove extremely high. In the event the unit to suffer most were the 13th King's who lost well over a third of their men. Of seven hundred and twenty-one who went in, only three hundred and eighty-four came back to India in 1943. After the reconquest in 1945 seventy-one more of the 13th King's were found among those who had survived incarceration.[1] Of the whole three thousand of 77 Brigade who crossed the Chindwin between the 13th and 18th of March, 1943, two thousand one hundred and eighty-two came back to India that year. Only six hundred of these were fit for active soldiering again. Of the missing eight hundred the great majority had vanished for ever. The casualty figures would have been less appalling if the Japanese had moved to a state of civilisation in which they could understand how soldiers in advantage should treat prisoners of war. This is not the place to dwell on the horrible barbarism which the captors showed to the captured.[2]

[1] Lieutenant Spurlock was among the prisoners who survived.
[2] Figures based on information obtained at the War Office and a communication from Major-General S. A. Cooke, C.B., O.B.E.

CHAPTER XIX

FAME AND THE CHINDITS

AFTER A day's rest in the Gurkha post, and an easy march to the motor road-head, Wingate and his companions reached Imphal on the 3rd of May. He reported to the Corps Commander, General Scoones, who sent a brief résumé of the brigade's achievement to the Commander-in-Chief. At Wingate's request he picked out Fergusson, Calvert, and the R.A.F. elements with the force for particular praise.

In the later part of April news of the expedition had begun to spread with the return of the first men back. (One or two journalists had discovered about it as early as February but had shown exemplary discretion.) With the arrivals between the 15th and the 29th secrecy rapidly broke down, and when it was known that Wingate himself was in Imphal many people, prompted by official and private curiosity, travelled there to find out for themselves.

But it was some time before a communiqué could be issued. With the virtual cessation of their wireless links there was no way of knowing the ultimate fate of 77 Brigade with any precision, till more men were out. Scoones's résumé, though remarkably accurate, was admittedly based on Wingate's guesswork. Only one other report was to hand. It had been written by Bernard Fergusson immediately on arrival, and had been finished and handed to the Corps Commander on the first of May. It dealt in the main with the adventures of Number 5 column, but to some extent gave a history of the brigade in general, and contained criticisms, (expressed in the most respectful terms), of Wingate's handling of his force in the Shweli loop.[1] Wingate was very annoyed with Fergusson for having written this, but Fergusson pointed out that he felt it his duty to write a report with reference to the whole brigade while the events were fresh in his mind, in case Wingate should not come back. With some grumbling Wingate accepted his explanation. These were internal matters not suspected outside. What was becoming known to the world was that a valiant expedition had been successfully concluded, but with only fragmentary reports available, G.H.Q. knew little more than the rumour-mongers

[1] Copy of the report in W.P.I.

about the details. The curiosity increased and Imphal began to grow crowded.

On the 6th of May General Irwin, the Army Commander, arrived with the Army Group Commander Sir George Giffard. They went round Number 19 clearing station where many of the men of the brigade were recovering from wounds, malaria, exhaustion, jungle sores and other ailments of climate and deprivation. Irwin held a long consultation with Wingate, and the next day the two of them flew to Delhi. On the 10th of May the Viceroy, Lord Linlithgow, came to Imphal and did a round of the hospital wards and the brigade lines. In the meantime, with Wingate's arrival in Delhi, there began the opening stages of his last long struggle with authority.

Sir Archibald Wavell, Wingate's great and generous patron, was still Commander-in-Chief in name, but he had left India, and it was very generally known that he would not return to his post. Before leaving he had given Wingate his support in a valuable and strange manner, and the beneficiary looked on the legacy with mixed feelings. For while the expedition of 77 Brigade was still in the field, Wavell had ordered the formation of another Long Range Penetration Group, to be known as 111 Brigade. This was composed of the 1st battalion of the Cameronians, two battalions of the Gurkha Rifles, the 2nd battalion of the King's Own Regiment, under the command of Brigadier William Lentaigne, D.S.O., who, as a Gurkha commander, had made a name for courage and military skill in the retreat of 1942. Wingate had doubts about the composition of the new brigade and the qualifications of its commander, influenced by his lack of belief in Gurkha ability to master his own ideas of guerilla warfare. Yet this unexpected extension of his force could not be refused. He was pleased, worried, and puzzled.

The Assistant and now Acting Commander-in-Chief was Sir Claude Auchinleck. He was soon to take over. If Wingate ever supposed that this fair-minded man was prejudiced against him because of the events of July 1941, he was much mistaken. Auchinleck was no opponent of irregular formations. On the contrary he had been criticised in his own command in Egypt for his support of David Stirling and the freedom he had allowed to the growth of the Special Air Service units. But he never believed that Long Range Penetration Groups could accomplish more than an extension of patrol work. He became Wingate's opponent, never his enemy.

For more than a fortnight Wingate stayed in Maiden's Hotel, suffering reaction from what he had been through, but, in his own words, " kept going owing to the urgency of the work." He did not meet Auchinleck on this occasion, but he saw the Chief of the

General Staff with the Director of Military Operations and attended two meetings in the office of the Director of Staff Duties. He gave accounts of the expedition, elucidated his theories, and obtained satisfactory decisions (later altered) as to the immediate fate of his brigade. He was invited to lecture to American officers in Delhi on what he had done. He promised an early report. His purpose throughout these days was to lay the foundations for a second effort on bigger lines, to seize opportunity while it was fresh. His preaching met a critical audience. The casualties, which, imperfectly known, seemed then even higher than they were, made many people doubt the practicability of the long-range penetration method, and the idea that this wild brave man was an irresponsible maniac persisted in many minds. His success in Delhi was partial and doubtful. The foundations of his fame were being laid elsewhere, by other hands and unknown to him.

On the 12th of May the Press arrived in force at Imphal. They went among the men in the lines and the hospital and collected their stories ; they prompted Headquarters to issue a communiqué and to raise the censorship ban on this epic of British arms. The Acting Commander-in-Chief was on the side of the Press. He wanted publicity as soon as possible for the only British success to date in the Far East, all the more so as there was a recent British reverse to cover at Arakan. At length the story was released for the 21st of May. It made headlines in every British paper and all the English papers published in India and elsewhere in the East, while the B.B.C. broadcast a special communiqué on its Home and Overseas services. Journalist instinct had proved reliable. The story made an immediate and enormous impression, and from the 21st of May to the end of the war and after, there was a continual Press market for stories about the men who had crossed into Burma and fought the enemy behind their front line.

Wingate himself took no part in the initiation of the publicity campaign that made his name famous throughout the English-speaking world. For all his wide reading and wide experience, he retained a certain naïvety of character to the end, and it was only in the last months of his life that he even began to understand the enormous influence that Press publicity can exert on opinion and on events. What happened in May 1943 shows that at this time he was quite remarkably indifferent to what newspapers might want to say about his exploits, so much so that when the Press arrived at Imphal he was not there ! Correspondents sought him out later, but he made no attempt to satisfy their appetite for stories. William Burchett, then *Daily Express* war correspondent, has given a vivid description of his own endeavours to engage Wingate's co-operation.

" When I first called on him at his hotel in Delhi, I found him sitting naked on his bed, eyes buried deep in a book. He hardly glanced up as I entered, and rather gruffly asked what I wanted of him. . . . He wasn't interested in me or my requirements, but seemed most excited about the book he was reading. He put it down every few minutes and scribbled something on the margins. Then Bernard Fergusson came in and the two of them started an animated discussion about this book, which turned out to be a critical commentary on Emily Brontë and her work, liberally annotated with Wingate's acid comments on the commentator."

Among the numerous articles that now appeared one was to have considerable effect. It was by Graham Stanford and appeared in the *Daily Mail* on the 22nd of May. The headline read " Wingate—Clive of Burma ? "

Press articles on military affairs make frequent use of nicknames and of a service jargon peculiar to Fleet Street. Generals are referred to as " brass-hats," a term virtually unknown to the Army, and personalities are high-lighted by such endearments as " Mad Mike," a sobriquet now invented by correspondents in Imphal for Calvert. " Clive of Burma " did not stay for long, neither did the various comic titles most widely used at this time to describe 77 Brigade : " Wingate's Circus " (an authentic slang term of the men themselves), enjoyed a brief global circulation, as did " Wingate's Follies," " The Jungle Follies," " The Ghost Army," and other Press contraptions of the kind. One article of the 21st of May, however, used a term unknown to the men, but of genuine Wingate origin. Writing in the *Daily Express*, and referring to a conversation he had had with Wingate in February before the expedition, Alaric Jacob referred to the force as " The Chindits." The name caught on very slowly at first, but by the end of July it had driven out its rivals. It was at first reluctantly and then gladly accepted by the men themselves. In course of time it achieved a quasi-official status.

It has been said, notably by Field-Marshal Sir William Slim, that the Press excitement over Wingate's expedition was its only justification, and that if the truth is strictly to be told, the Arakan and the Chindit expeditions should be considered together as two costly fiascos. This opinion does justice neither to the Press nor to the Chindits. It is true that certain of the claims made for the Chindits in the Press have been subsequently proved fallacious and the result of imperfect military intelligence[1]. But these claims, such as that the Chindits caused the Japanese to cancel an expedition against Fort Hertz, were never extravagant, and had professional military acceptance at the

[1] Official History.

time. Indeed, it will be easy to show that history can make larger claims for Wingate and his men than made in any newspaper then. If the Press went to ridiculous lengths to glamorise Wingate it still did not give an essentially false picture of his achievement. Misrepresentation came in more respectable guise. When, much later, Sir William Slim came to write a book he asserted that the railway had only been put out of commission for a few days, and that nothing the Chindits did had the smallest effect on Japanese conduct of the war.[1] This was to ignore not only considerable railway evidence, but that of Japanese records, some of which had been published at the time of the Field-Marshal's book, and enough of which were accessible. During the first Chindit expedition Sir William Slim was commanding 15 Corps in whose area the frustrated attempt on Arakan had been made.

What is undoubtedly true, however, and gives a basis to Sir William Slim's view, is that the immediate and very important result of the 1943 Chindit expedition was more in the psychological than the military sphere. The news raised spirits and threw energetic confidence into a people and into an army who had come to think of themselves as utterly outclassed by the Japanese in all forms of jungle fighting. It put new heart into men. Nor should one only think of the British in this respect, and of the Army of India. There were millions of Indian men and women who had no quarrel with British rule and administration, but who had grown disturbed in their mind about their allegiance, and had come to ask whether, after such calamitous defeats as those of 1942 in Burma, the natural end of Britain as a great Eastern power had not come, and whether Indian loyalties ought to lie elsewhere. When the news reached them of Wingate's achievement they found their trust fortified.[2]

After a little less than three weeks in Delhi Wingate left for Calcutta. On the 29th he flew back to Imphal to supervise the temporary dispersal of his brigade, a complicated and muddled piece of administration (the muddle made by superior authority changing its mind more than once too often), and of which the details would tax the reader's patience, even if he happened to be a Chindit himself. At length the men of the 13th King's and 142 Company went to Bombay, the Gurkha Rifles to their regimental centre at Dehra Dun, and the Burma Rifles to Hoshiarpur and Karachi, all to enjoy five weeks' leave. " It was a period of hectic improvisation," recorded Major Bromhead, " in order to get the scattered columns of the brigade back to India down the

---

[1] Slim.
[2] This opinion was given to the writer by a number of Indians whom he met in Delhi in 1956.

line of communication which was precarious at all times and made worse by the early monsoon." By the 5th of June the exodus was over except for the end of Number 7 column's odyssey, and Brigade Head-quarters which, under the care of Major Anderson, remained in Imphal till June the 18th.

While all these lesser miseries of victory were going forward, Wingate felt the need, as perhaps he had never felt it before, to express the ideas and experience within him. He wanted to write a memo-randum. He also wanted rest. At this moment of his life he made a deep and curious friendship. The 19th Military clearing station at Imphal was under the direction of Matron Agnes MacGeary. She was a small, vigorous, efficient and altruistic Scotswoman. Her kindly nature was an eminently practical one, and she had found her vocation in nursing. Descriptions of Agnes MacGeary by people who knew her put one in mind of Florence Nightingale. She ran the hospital in Imphal with medical thoroughness and a natural power of leadership. She was a stern humanitarian, and like most proficient people in this sphere was without the sentimental " sensitivity " which often masquerades as the angel of charity. No military commander enjoyed a surer authority over men than this imperious woman. She needed to show sternness rather than indulgence in most cases, and for a strange reason. A danger which confronted many Chindits on their return to civilised life was of sinking into a fatal torpor when surrounded with the luxuries of cleanliness, a soft bed, and white cool sheets. One may think it a pleasant way to leave this life, but a description in Calvert's book of what happened under such circumstances makes one think again. A less expert nurse might have lost lives through kindly pampering. Matron MacGeary sometimes seemed cruel when she forced exhausted men out of bed, made them dress and walk about, and fairly threw them on their own resources. But she never seems to have made a false diagnosis or prescribed wrong treatment.[1] In the course of looking after invalids of 77 Brigade she learned what they had done. She was filled with admiration, and identified herself with these men. When their commander came back to Imphal at the end of May and called at the hospital to inquire after the patients from his brigade, Agnes MacGeary saw that he was endangering himself by excessive activity. He told her that he intended to settle down to work on his report. There were two empty rooms in a wing of the hospital. She ordered Wingate to install himself in these rooms and write his report while undergoing a regime of rest supervised by herself. He obeyed.

[1] This account of the late Matron MacGeary is taken from what the author has learned from Edward Jary and Michael Calvert.

The labour of composition occupied him from the last days of May till the 17th of June.[1] The result was the longest and best of his written things. It was very accurate and even to-day, with much new information (necessarily unknown to Wingate at the time) to modify what he wrote, it remains the best general record of what the intrepid three thousand Chindits did in their first expedition. The report was written without egotism, and the reader often wishes he had told much more about himself. It is the most entertaining thing he wrote, and the gravity of the theme is often lightened by sardonic humour. The same could be said of much of what he had written before, but in his Burma Report he expressed himself with an ease and flow that was new. It was as though, had he been a writer, (as he sometimes wished), he had at last found himself and produced his first mature work. In contrast to his Ethiopian report, there are in this one generous judgments on people who failed to achieve what he ordered. For all that, he erred occasionally in tact, as he had erred frequently before.

The report had a strange history. As he wrote it day by day the sheets were typed and submitted to General Scoones for his approval and criticism. Early on in this process the General pointed out to the author that to make its maximum effect his report should be " so worded that it could be read by our allies."[2] This advice was followed, " otherwise " related Wingate, " the Report would have drawn attention to a number of things which have been omitted." Yet in fact General Scoones's warning ought to have been taken more seriously, both by Wingate and the General himself. In its completed state it still contained expressions open to misrepresentation. It contained also strictures on some of his subordinates both in personal and collective terms, and on outside groups and persons such as the Military Training Directorate, G.H.Q. liaison officers, and other components of the hierarchy. After his experiences in Cairo two years before one may wonder at the obstinate spirit that made him repeat his mistake, albeit in inoffensive terms and a broad-minded spirit. However that was, the moral of the tale was not forthcoming. The more uncomfortably outspoken passages in the report did Wingate no harm at all, and may even have helped him forward to greatness of position.

When the report with its sixteen appendices was finished Wingate obtained General Scoones's approval for the whole. He took this approval as giving him the right to obtain a printing (which he arranged without reference to the competent authorities in G.H.Q.), and also to show it at his discretion, " where such was clearly in the

---

[1] Entry in a personal notebook : " 17 June. Report finished ! " W.P.I.
[2] *Note on the development of L.R.P.Gs.* W.P.I.

interests of the King's service."[1] One may legitimately wonder whether, stretching the argument a little, he showed it to Matron MacGeary. He found himself deeply in her debt for having restored him quickly to all his accustomed strength and vigour, and his gratitude prompted a deep affection. The two of them shared an important point of character; both were people passionately dedicated to their ideals. Wingate only to rely increasingly on her and her sturdy common sense, and he consulted her on every kind of subject, as becomes clear at a later stage in the story. On the 21st of June he said good-bye to her and left by air for Delhi.

On the way he noted a disturbing portent of trouble ahead. The first stop on the flight was at Calcutta, at the aerodrome of Dum-Dum. Here Wingate was informed that his passage onwards to Delhi had been cancelled by orders from General Headquarters, yet when the plane took off he saw that three seats were empty. This may merely have been the result of the thousand administrative muddles which inevitably afflict every military organisation in war, or it may have meant something worse. Needless to say, Wingate assumed that it meant something worse. However, apart from some inconvenience at Dum-Dum the incident made no difference to his movements as he quickly found an American army plane whose pilot was willing to take him. He arrived in Delhi only a day late.

Here he met Brigadier Lentaigne for the first time. They were very different men. Lentaigne was a soldier of the orthodox pattern; disciplined, unquestioning, reliable, a person of intelligence but not of outstanding imagination. He had no wish to lead a private army. He had admiration for, but no ardent belief in Wingate's long range penetration theory. Wingate and Lentaigne were not without mutual respect, but Wingate could rarely find a congenial companion in a man who did not share his ideas and enthusiasms. The two men were never close friends.

Wingate found Lentaigne at this first meeting " troubled about his own brigade, with good reason." He was troubled himself. The return to Delhi bore a distressing resemblance to the return to Cairo in 1941. There was no definite G.H.Q. movement against Wingate and his theories, or none that is discernible in records ; but there was plenty of suspicion of the real worth of the achievement, plenty of regret for the success of supposedly unsound ideas, often best deducible from the turn of phrase in official expressions of opinion.[2] The moment for G.H.Q. attack came with the printing of the report.

The sequence of dates is unusually illuminating in this part of the

---

[1] *Note on development.*
[2] Information obtained at the War Office and New Delhi.

story. From his arrival in Delhi on the 22nd, or possibly the 23rd, till the 6th of July, Wingate was mainly occupied in preparing " citations," organising printing and correcting proofs. On the morning of the 6th of July the copies were delivered to him by the Government of India official press. On the same day he sent copies to the office of the Director of Military Operations. Unwisely it would seem, he had sent copies of the typescript to 4 Corps and to General Irwin before this, and it appears that they had forwarded one or more of these to General Headquarters. At all events, from the swiftness of the proceedings thereon taken against Wingate, it would appear that his enemies were waiting for him.[1] For on the next morning, that of the 7th, Fergusson came to tell Wingate that the Chief of the General Staff had ordered all copies of the report to be withdrawn until they had been re-examined by 4 Corps, and approved by General Irwin. With sickening disappointment Wingate must have recognised once again a familiar manœuvre by displeased authority, that of organising delay by playing with time and scruple : 4 Corps and Eastern army could be kept in argument for some weeks, a reprinting could take some weeks more, and by the time the report came up for discussion, after numerous preliminaries, enough time would have gone by for a second Wingate expedition to be unpractical before the next monsoon.

If there was such a plan, it was frustrated by events not envisaged by staff officers in India. The 7th of July was an ironical date for the withdrawal of the report : the Press which had gone to all lengths in making Wingate's name known, (including the inevitable misreported " interviews " with his wife and relations), was in need of new material, and first-rate material was given to them in time for publication on this very day. There had been a long delay by the censorship over the release of photographs, but in the first week of July the ban was lifted, and on the 7th almost every large daily paper in the British Isles appeared with photographs of haggard bearded men in tattered tropical uniform and Australian bush hats, of Colonel Cooke's party of wounded flying from Amatgyon, of Bernard Fergusson sporting a monocle in his right eye (with further tales of the monocles which had supposedly rained to him from the skies),[2] and, most prominently of all, photographs of the brigade commander in thick dark beard and over his brooding eyes the talismanic sun-helmet. The excitement started anew.

---

[1] In the files of the Ministry of Defence in New Delhi there is a typescript of the report with blue pencil marks indicating with precision the passages later removed in the expurgated edition.

[2] The truth of this matter is distressingly mild. Before the expedition Fergusson had ordered from Calcutta a monocle-carriage which did not reach him before he set out, so the package was delivered to him with other personal mail in one of the supply drops. Fergusson. A communication.

The men who wanted to prevent further Wingate ventures had to recognise that their opponent was a national hero.

He had received many letters from England, among which were moving messages from his wife and family, but also some less personal congratulations. There was a letter from Buckingham Palace conveying the personal interest of the King, another from the Viceroy-designate Lord Wavell, and another from "the father of the Army", Lord Birdwood. Yet it seems that Wingate did not draw the conclusion from this evidence that his position was now so strong as to be unassailable, for the moment at least. One of his letters contained the congratulations of Mr. Amery, and this crossed a communication from Wingate. Breaking service rules in characteristic fashion, and assuming permission to show his report to people " when such was clearly in the interests of the King's service," he had sent one copy direct to the Secretary of State for India.[1] By this action he had completely out-manœuvred his opponents, but he did not yet know it.

He had a cousin living in Simla, Doctor Esther Wingate, and about this time he went to stay with her for a few days' rest in that pleasing refuge. He had as well an official reason for the visit. The late Governor-General of Burma, Sir Reginald Dorman Smith, wanted to see him. It is characteristic of Wingate that he insisted to Sir Reginald's aide-de-camp that the Governor's car should be sent to fetch him to the appointment, not that he was concerned with his own dignity but that of the body he represented.

In Simla he had an odd encounter. Aung Thin was there on leave and one day he sought out Wingate to unburden himself on a matter which was troubling him. Their conversation as remembered later went somewhat as follows :

" Well, Patriot, what's the matter ? "

" I am in an awkward position. I am now on Sir Reginald's staff and I have been taken to task by his experts."

" What do you mean ? "

" Well, sir, the papers are beginning to describe the brigade as 'The Chindits.' They say that you call them that after the griffins outside the pagodas."

" What if I do ? "

" Sao Man Hpa and I were supposed to be your Burman experts and now everyone in the Secretariat laughs at me and says I don't even know my own language. They say I must have told you that the pagoda griffins are called Chindits."

<hr>

[1] The late L. S. Amery. A communication.

"Well, that's all right, isn't it ? "

"No. They are called *Chinthé*. I told you so when you asked."

Wingate received this reminder with a gasp of horror. He said "*chinthé*" to himself over and over again and then, "Good heavens ! " he cried out. "I gave the Press the wrong word. What on earth can I do about it now ? This is frightful ! "

Aung Thin had only intended to register a mild protest to safeguard his reputation. He was astonished at the effect of his words on the other, but when, hoping to mollify him, he said, "Oh, I don't suppose it matters really." Wingate flew into a passion. He leaped across the room and seized Aung Thin by the coat and began shaking him, crying out : "Doesn't matter ! It matters a great deal ! Don't you see what I've done, Patriot. I've made utter fools of my men. I've made a fool of you and myself. I've called the brigade after an animal that doesn't exist ! It's frightful ! What the hell can we do about it ? "

Aung Thin tried to pacify him again by saying : "Well, if the animal does not exist, why not say that we've created him ? "

Wingate exclaimed, " Boh ! " and retired muttering. But he made no subsequent effort to stop the growth of his brigade's new title, and never referred to the matter again with Aung Thin. Few people know Burmese, Chindit is a good word, and in the end Burmese speakers of Burma accepted this addition to their language.[1]

Back in Delhi, Wingate faced a grim situation, without allies in the hierarchy, and with his report withdrawn. Furthermore, he believed that there was disaffection within his own ranks. Colonel Cooke was appalled at the scale of loss in the 13th Kings. As said, the choice of this battalion for the Chindit expedition was the result of man-power shortage ; they were not naturally suited, as the Burma Rifles were, to their jungle task, a fact which makes their performance the more marvellous. It was agreed that, except for a few of the officers, they would not be called on again. Colonel Cooke, bitterly conscious of humane responsibilities to his men, made it clear that his own military duties must lie with his battalion, whatever rôle was given to it. Wingate wanted this able and experienced man as a brigade commander in the new ventures he was planning, and with blameable narrowness he regarded Cooke's insistence on remaining with the 13th Kings as disloyal. In judging Wingate's actions at this time it should be remembered that by the withdrawal of the report he had been placed at a serious disadvantage which might easily have seemed fatal. He would have been more tolerant perhaps if he had known the extent of his new strength. How great that was appeared in the course of the next month.

[1] Aung Thin.

Mr. Amery received his copy of the banned report in the middle of July. It delighted him not only as a vindication of his support of Wingate in a dark hour, but of ideas which he himself had put forward at the end of April when the success or otherwise of 77 Brigade was not ascertainable. In a memorandum addressed to the Prime Minister he had already urged the need to secure an allied base behind the Japanese lines so as to threaten Japanese communications from Bangkok. He had said : " This would at once cut off all Japanese forces in Malaya, and if carried out far enough north threaten Bangkok and Japanese communications with Burma from the air . . . [we should] keep the Japanese as busy as we can in North Burma by a vigorous expansion of the guerilla war as now waged by Wingate's brigade." Mr. Amery concluded his memorandum by admitting his amateur status in grand strategy, adding, however, that "a fresh eye may sometimes see an opening which the most spirited practised eyes have overlooked." When Mr. Amery found many of his ideas expressed independently in a well-written report by a professional soldier, he took an obvious course and sent the report to his friend and chief, Mr. Churchill.

Mr. Churchill was at that moment in the middle of a strenuous debate, to express the matter mildly, with his service chiefs and with General Auchinleck, over their proposals to put into effect certain decisions of the Trident Conference. This had been held in Washington in May, and had been the scene of difficult debate between the British and American staffs and leaders. In simple terms, the Americans aimed at a more vigorous prosecution of the war against Japan, at the expense, in the British view, of efficient conduct of the war against Germany. Thanks to pertinacious negotiation on the British side the Americans had come a long way round towards the British view,[1] but without in any way losing their Far Eastern preoccupations. On these the Americans, in the British view, needed reassurance. To meet any objections that the war on the Far Eastern British front was being waged with lack of offensive, some Trident decisions were taken on the subject of Burma. The main ones were these : to concentrate available British resources on the Assam front ; to enlarge the volume of airborne supply to China and increase American forces there ; to initiate aggressive land and air operations against the Japanese in Burma, from Imphal and Ledo, in conjunction with the Chinese Army in Yunnan ; to capture Akyab and Ramree island, and to harry Japanese sea communications in the Bay of Bengal and the Andaman Sea. On receiving their instructions the military in India pointed out the difficulty of carrying out this programme in 1943 and proposed that it should be deferred till 1944, and some of it to the dry season of

[1] *The Turn of the Tide* by Sir Arthur Bryant, referred to subsequently as Bryant.

1944-45. At this Mr. Churchill was moved to protest in the plainest terms at what he considered overcaution.[1] Hardly had he done so than Wingate's report reached him. The effect was instant, dramatic, enormous. It brought Mr. Churchill's discontent with India to a head, and he drew a contrast between the young brigadier's achievement and the culpable hesitation, as he saw it, of the India Generals. On the 24th of July he wrote the following astonishing letter to Sir Hastings Ismay.

"See how these difficulties are mounting up and what a vast expenditure of force is required for these trumpery gains. All the Commanders on the spot seem to be competing with one another to magnify their demands and the obstacles they have to overcome.

"All this shows how necessary it is to decide on a commander. I still consider he should be a determined and competent soldier, in the prime of life and with the latest experience in the field. General Oliver Leese is, I believe, the right man, and as soon as the fighting in Sicily is over he should come back to this country for consultations. I consider Wingate should command the army against Burma. He is a man of genius and audacity and has rightly been discerned by all eyes as a figure quite above the ordinary level. The expression "The Clive of Burma" has already gained currency. There is no doubt that, in the welter of inefficiency and lassitude which have characterised our operations on the India front, this man, his force and his achievements, stand out, and no mere question of seniority must obstruct the advance of real personalities to their proper stations in war. He too should come home for discussions here at an early date."

On the 25th of July Wingate was sent for by signal, and he received his orders on that day or the next. He did not know what the summons meant, but he was glad of it. Out of favour in India, he had much to gain from a swift visit home, if only because his most potent ally to date, Mr. Amery, was in England. He did not know yet that he had another potent ally in 10 Downing Street.

The story of Wingate's return and his sudden elevation is very well known. It is one of the most attractive of the Second World War, and the reader should be immediately reassured that in the main it is true. It was a drama right enough, but not quite the melodrama of popular taste and legend, so the biographer is under duty to subdue some rose-colour.

At the time of his summons to England Wingate kept a notebook in which, amid much doodling (usually of ears) he set down appointments and things to be borne in mind at various meetings. From this cryptic record it is clear that he was scheduled to leave Delhi on the

[1] Information obtained at the War Office.

445

31st of July or the 1st of August, but in fact left on the 30th of July, and this may explain why he made the journey wearing his tropical clothes complete with bush-shirt and sun-helmet : a sudden change of timetable may have defeated even Indian tailoring speed. From a jotting he evidently intended to buy a suit of battledress in Cairo. He flew by land-plane to Karachi, whence by flying-boat to Basra the same evening. Twenty-four hours later the flying-boat stopped at Kallia on the north shore of the Dead Sea. As soon as Wingate knew his route in detail he had signalled Bernard Fergusson to meet him at Kallia, but the rendezvous failed. Fergusson had been invited by the Middle East Commander, Sir Maitland Wilson, to give a series of lectures on the Chindit expedition, and at this time he was in Syria. He could not meet Wingate without breaking his programme, so he sent his regrets. Wingate was extremely annoyed.[1]

He found yet graver cause of annoyance at Kallia. Here he was in Palestine, once more, and he wanted to take a car to Jerusalem, but the people in charge forbade him. Of course he discerned here the hand of anti-Zionist malignance ![1] There was probably none of this : it is much more likely that since the hour of departure was uncertain, as usual with wartime transport, the officer in charge refused to allow the passengers to disperse. This was the last time Wingate was in the land he loved more than any in the world, and he was condemned to spend it in empty hours confined to Palestine's emptiest and dismallest corner. The flying-boat was destined for South Africa and flew on to Cairo the next morning, and here Wingate left it. He was given a room in Shepheard's Hotel.

One of his first actions in Cairo was to try to get in touch with his Zionist friends. Shertock was in Cairo but was unable to meet him for a reason that had some irony in it. He had to go to Ismailia to inspect a company of the Jewish Brigade group, and that group was all that ever came of the long and devoted efforts of Jewish and Gentile Zionists to raise a Jewish army to fight Nazi Germany. Wingate spoke on the telephone to him, and the latter promised to send Akavia, now a lieutenant in the Palestine Buffs, to Cairo. In the evening Akavia arrived at Shepheard's Hotel and met Wingate in the entrance hall. He ran up to him and greeted him. With solemnity Wingate said, " Shalom Avram ! " Akavia went on talking in English till Wingate with a laugh said, " Shalom Avram ! " again, and then the other took the hint and replied in Hebrew. Akavia noticed that Wingate was looking well, fully recovered from his ordeal, and brimful of confidence. (He had not seen him since the calamities of July, 1941.) He noticed, too, that he had not lost his eccentricities. Wingate was not wearing

---

[1] Fergusson. A communication.

an alarm clock strapped to his wrist, but in its place there was a small locked blue bag which, he told Akavia, he kept secured to his wrist by day and night. It contained copies of the suppressed report. The two friends talked in Wingate's bedroom till a late hour, and Wingate told Akavia how his ambition was unchanged since the day when they first met at Ein Harod : to work for the restoration of Israel in Palestine.[1]

The next day, the 2nd of August, Wingate left from Cairo West aerodrome. On the morning of the 4th of August he arrived in England. He was met by a personal representative of the Chief of the Imperial General Staff, and he learned that he was to report to the Chief personally in the afternoon. Sir Alan Brooke recorded afterwards : " I was very interested in meeting Wingate. . . . [He had] turned out a great success and originated the Long Range Penetration Forces which worked right into Japanese-held territory. In the discussion I had with him he explained that he considered that what he had done on a small scale could be run with much larger forces. He required, however, for these forces the cream of everything, the best men, the best N.C.O s, the best officers, the best equipment and a large air lift. I considered that the results of his form of attacks were certainly worth backing within reason. I provided him with all the contacts in England to obtain what he wanted, and told him that on my return from Canada I would go into the whole matter with him to see that he obtained what he wanted."[2]

As a first move in this campaign to found a large-scale Chindit force, Wingate made appointments for the 5th and 7th of August with the Director of Military Operations, and with one of Sir Alan Brooke's assistant chiefs, a man whose name has figured in the story already, Major-General John Evetts.[3] These appointments were not kept, as a result of later events that day.

Before leaving the C.I.G.S., the latter instructed Wingate to report his arrival at number 10 Downing Street. Wingate obeyed, not knowing, beyond the fact that the C.I.G.S. was going to Canada, the supreme state secret of the hour, that on the 5th of August the Prime Minister and the Chiefs of Staff were to sail to Quebec to meet President Roosevelt and the American chiefs of staff at the Quadrant Conference.

The gates of opportunity opened wide now. What happened in Downing Street is best described in Sir Winston Churchill's own words : ". . . Wingate, who had already made his mark as a leader of irregulars in Abyssinia . . . had greatly distinguished himself in the jungle fighting in Burma. These new brilliant exploits won him in some circles of the Army in which he served the title of ' The Clive of Burma.' I had

[1] Akavia.   [2] Bryant   [3] Personal Notebook. W.P.I.

447

heard much of all this, and knew also how the Zionists had sought him as a future Commander-in-Chief of any Israelite army that might be formed. I had him summoned home in order that I might have a look at him before I left for Quebec. I was about to dine alone on the night of August 4th at Downing Street when the news that he had arrived by air and was actually in the house was brought to me. I immediately asked him to join me at dinner. We had not talked for half an hour before I felt myself in the presence of a man of the highest quality. He plunged at once into his theme of how the Japanese could be mastered in jungle warfare by long range penetration groups landed by air behind the enemy lines. This interested me greatly. I wished to hear much more about it, and also to let him tell his tale to the Chiefs of Staff.

" I decided at once to take him with me on the voyage. I told him our train would leave at ten. It was then nearly nine. Wingate had arrived just as he was after three days flight from the actual front, and with no clothes but what he stood up in. He was of course quite ready to go, but expressed regret that he would not be able to see his wife. . . ."[1]

Before this meeting with the Prime Minister Wingate had telephoned to Lorna in Aberdeenshire. By the time he received the invitation to Quebec she had caught a night express to London. The Prime Minister instantly decided that she should come to Quebec too[2] and, as he recorded in his history, " the resources of my Private Office were equal to the occasion." Without explanation she was taken off the express at Edinburgh at a quarter past eleven that night by a Railway Transport Officer who knew as little of the matter as she. Accommodation was found for her in Edinburgh. Wingate left King's Cross at one minute to midnight on the 4th, and met his wife on a suburban platform of Waverley Station the next morning.[3]

From Edinburgh they travelled across Scotland to the berth of the *Queen Mary* on the Clyde. The great liner sailed on the 5th, and, in Sir Winston Churchill's words, " drove on through the waves, and we lived in the utmost comfort on board her, with a diet of pre-war times. As usual on these voyages, we worked all day long."

The Prime Minister had said that he " wished to hear much more about it," and one morning Wingate received the expected summons to

---

[1] *The Second World War Volume V* by Sir Winston Churchill. Referred to subsequently as Churchill V.

[2] In *Gideon Goes To War* it is asserted that Mrs. Wingate was taken to Quebec as a result of Mrs. Churchill's last minute entreaty on board the *Queen Mary*. This is not supported by Sir Winston's account or the evidence of Quadrant administration papers in W.P.I.

[3] Mrs. Lorna Smith.

the great man's cabin. A refreshingly lucid page of Wingate's notebook indicates the subjects of the discussion, and may be quoted without embellishment :

"Points for P.M.

"Illustrate on map ops past and future.

Unless done next time on conquering scale *better not done* as will blow gaff and expend patriot potential.

Summarise steps taken : too few and too bad troops. No control by . . . ? . . . of any steps—consulted usually after the event.

Suppression of Report.

Giffard's plans.

The Japanese problem and reaction—methods—how to defeat.

The time factor.

Indaw communications.

The Manipur road.

Tamu—Tiddim L. of C.

The enemy's L. of C.

The air arm and R.A.F. Co-op.

Airborne troops.

Lease-lend air transport."

When he entered the cabin, Wingate found Mr. Churchill with a copy of his report. The Prime Minister invited the other to sit down and then opened the conversation with some such words as this : " I have read your report carefully. It is very good. Yet I will say that there are some phrases in it which are not to my liking—nay, more, I will aver that they are not to the liking of our language. For example——" And here he indicated some crudities and solecisms. Then he turned to the other and after humming to himself for a moment, added, " You know, similar mistakes are to be found in the dispatches and letters of the first Duke of Marlborough." This meeting was the crucial one, for it was now that Wingate needed to substantiate in detail before a formidable critic what the latter had initially accepted in a moment of uncritical enthusiasm. Wingate said afterwards that he was nervous before this meeting, and that no conventional essay in tact could have put him more perfectly at ease than Mr. Churchill's strictures on the other's vigorous, effective, but unprofessional prose.[1]

They got down to business. At the end of their talk the Prime Minister retained the whole of his conviction and he indicated what aspects of the Far East campaigns he wanted the other to discuss and

[1] Miss Monica Wingate. The story as she remembers it from her brother's account.

with whom. Opinions on Wingate are likely to differ for a long time, but Sir Winston Churchill never wavered in his own belief that here was a soldier of the highest capacity, and a man of great and valorous character.

As the *Queen Mary* " drove on through the waves," meetings of the British Chiefs of Staff were held on board towards the end of the voyage. At their first discussion on the 8th of August they examined forthcoming operations from Assam. By this time Wingate had seen Sir Alan Brooke again and the latter informed the meeting of the new Chindit proposal. It was agreed, he said, that future Chindit operations must precede an advance by the army, or the effort was wasted. Wingate had proposed a large-scale penetration on the lines of the last one, with the additional proposal that two thousand Chindits should be flown to Yunnan to act as the spearhead (and encouragement), to a Chinese advance southwards. It was noted that Wingate's plans, if carried out, would totally commit British arms in the Far East to Burma as the scene of the defeat of Japan. There was uncertainty as to the wisdom of this.[1]

The fifth meeting of the Chiefs of Staff was held late on the same day and Wingate was called in to explain his views at length and in person. It was on this occasion that he first put forward what he considered his requirement : six brigades. He said that he wanted three to operate in offensive rôles, and the remaining three to protect communications and airfields. His detailed propositions regarding strategy and tactics need not be considered here, but it is interesting to note that the six-brigade system that he proposed was very like what he eventually got. At this meeting he made some curious comments on Japanese reactions, and these show, once again in the story, his ever-active and ever-original power of observation. In planning offensives against Japanese, he said, a special time factor needed to be borne in mind, a time factor resulting from the slowness of the Japanese in organising counter-action. He explained that their mental tardiness could give the Japanese an unexpected advantage, in that by the time they were ready to strike back, the offensive against them was likely to have lost its momentum. Whatever offensive was next launched in Burma must maintain momentum until the monsoon of 1944. He made a good impression.[2]

The remaining meetings of the Chiefs of Staff on board the *Queen Mary* were concerned with other matters, notably operation "Overlord." Wingate had other private meetings with the principals, with Lord Louis Mountbatten and Sir Hastings Ismay among others,[3] but this

[1] Information obtained at the War Office. [2] Churchill V.
[3] Personal Notebook.

appearance at the fifth meeting of the British Chiefs of Staff was his only public performance before arrival at Quebec.

Since his dinner with the Prime Minister on the 4th of August Wingate had at last found an opportunity to apparel himself anew. In place of his bush-shirt, sun-helmet, and drill he was now wearing battledress, but of naval cut and colour, the only sort available to his measurement, it seems, aboard the liner. At the time of his journey from India to England, on the 2nd of August, the award of a second bar to his D.S.O. had been announced in the *London Gazette*. He wore no badges of rank with his naval battledress, and no ribbons except that of his triple D.S.O. Some of his fellow passengers, while admiring the greatness of the distinction, commented adversely on the oddity of the costume.[1] Such oddity was so very typical of Wingate that it is permissible to wonder whether he had purposely neglected to buy a conventional uniform in Cairo where such equipment was abundant in all sizes.

The two hundred and fifty people travelling in the *Queen Mary* to Quadrant and Quebec had been on this sort of business before[2] and consequently made something of a " set " from which the Wingates naturally sat apart. This was remarked and a Major-General, noted for jollity, was urged to make friends with the strange couple, and bring them into the shipboard convivialities. The General found his efforts quite fruitless and was somewhat daunted by the stern concentrated spirit which met him and shamed his frivolity.[3] The member of the mission whom Wingate met most frequently was Colonel Antony Head. His function was described as that of "representative with the Directors of Plans for Amphibious Operations," an assignment open to wide interpretation which in this case included the task of setting Wingate's long-range penetration proposals into a form acceptable to protocol. He and the Wingates usually dined together, and he saw Wingate frequently in the course of every day. They became friends, and Wingate told the other something about himself and how he had reached his ideas of strategy. He talked about the Ethiopian campaign and recalled, with unquenched bitterness, how on returning to Cairo his account of Gideon Force had been virtually suppressed. Though he evidently liked Antony Head, the latter was continually aware of a degree of withdrawal from ordinary life on the part of Wingate which seemed almost to exclude the possibility of friendship, as this is ordinarily understood. He felt that here was a man who would

[1] The Right Hon. Antony Head, P.C., M.C.

[2] With the exception of Wing-Commander Gibson, V.C., who was taken by the Prime Minister to give first-hand accounts to the Combined Chiefs of Staff.

[3] Lt.-General Sir Ian Jacob, K.B.E. A communication, but not an autobiographical one.

abandon any human tie, if he sincerely believed that such an act could further the things he believed in. Agreed this was fancy, yet such excessive terms, he was sure, best described the strange character before him, with his absolute dedication to purpose, his trust that to follow conviction was to be an instrument of God.[1] On the 9th of August the *Queen Mary* reached Halifax. On the evening of the 10th the British mission reached Quebec by train.

The Quadrant conference was chiefly occupied with the European theatre, and of that nothing much need be said here. All the discussions showed major differences between the British and the Americans. Those on the War in the Far East were complicated by further differences between Mr. Churchill and the British Chiefs of Staff. But throughout the debate, which was once so haeted that the room had to be cleared of all except the principals,[2] all parties found a point of agreement in Wingate. Although he had never attended a high-level political conference before, he understood his advantage and from Quadrant he obtained authority commensurate with his ambition.

The American mission did not arrive in Quebec until three days after the British party. This gave the British Chiefs of Staffs Committee, and the Joint Planning Staff, time to prepare and clarify. Sir Alan Brooke had told Wingate on the *Queen Mary* that he wanted him to expound his ideas to the Combined Chiefs of Staff, and had instructed him to furnish the British Joint Planning Staff with a memorandum as soon as they were settled in Quebec. He had his paper ready on the 10th. It was short and conclusive and contained no Biblical quotations. Of his many memoranda this was the most remarkable in immediate effect and ultimate result.

He began by outlining the principles of long range penetration, and in his second section detailed his present proposal, that three groups (each of eight columns), should invade Burma from the East and West. One was to operate from China, another from the area North of Tamu, and the third from the Chin hills. These operations were to be timed in conjunction with advances by the army in Assam, by Stilwell's Chinese-American force, and by the Chinese forces in Yunnan, for all three of which he did not hesitate to outline a strategic plan. He reiterated his views on slow Japanese reaction and the necessity to reach a climax before the 1944 monsoon. In the light of what happened after, perhaps the most remarkable thing in the memorandum was in the third section where Wingate spoke of a likely Japanese offensive on the Assam front, and

---

[1] Head.
[2] For the remarkable details see Churchill V p. 80-81 and Bryant p. 713.

proposed changes in his plan to meet such a circumstance. He concluded with a section entitled "Recommendations." They were four. The first was "a. Accept plan." The next two were concerned with organisation and the provision of troops "from the U.K." He insisted that a prime need was to establish machinery for the turning out of long range penetration groups at an increasing rate. His last recommendation was that India should be warned and he himself returned there as soon as possible. In the course of the memorandum he asked for a force totalling around twenty-six and a half thousand, all ranks.[1]

During the three days of exclusively British deliberation in Quebec the Joint Planning Staff and the Chiefs of Staff read this memorandum, after which the Service Chiefs decided to send three signals to the Commander-in-Chief in India : the first to announce that they had decided to use Wingate's long-range penetration scheme in a magnified form in forthcoming operations ; the second, to give the gist of his memorandum, but as coming from them, not him ; the third to give details of how he and they proposed to recruit the necessary men. The first drafts by the Joint Planners were considered by the Chiefs of Staff to be unnecessarily tentative in character ; the telegrams as finally sent insisted that there could be no doubt about the practical merit of what Wingate had achieved and of what he now proposed, and asserted the determination of the higher direction to continue his work. The telegrams were sent with a request for an answer by the 20th of August. In the statistics they followed Wingate precisely except in unimportant details.[2]

On the same day as these telegrams were sent, on the 14th, one arrived from India announcing bad news. The monsoon had caused floods in the country west of Calcutta, and the consequent havoc was thought likely to interfere gravely with future operations on the Burma front. In the event the disaster had no discernible influence on military operations from India, but it is worth noting that though here was a reason for not burdening India G.H.Q. administration with a large new organisation, no one at Quebec raised this point in opposition to Wingate's proposals. He was in an extraordinarily commanding position.

The Americans had arrived on the evening of the 13th; the combined British and American Chiefs of Staff began their meetings on the morning of the 14th, and held their first discussion on the Far Eastern theatre in the afternoon.[3] At this meeting Wingate's proposals were put before the American delegation. The latter were even less

[1] W.P.I. Official History.
[2] Wingate asked for 110 Jeeps and the request to India was for 100. This was the only difference in statistics.
[3] Bryant.

likely to oppose them than the British. As said, Wingate was a point of agreement. So far as the war against Japan was concerned there was dissension on all else, both on what the British intended to do and intended not to do. The Americans resisted British claims to a full share in operations against Japan after the defeat of Germany,[1] but at the same time they pressed for an early British offensive on the Assam front, underestimating, in the British view, the difficulties of attack with only jungle communications. At the end of the meeting on the 14th Sir Alan Brooke noted in his diary: " These floods look like affecting the Burma campaign drastically and put us in a difficult position in view of the pressure put on us by our American friends to carry out a Burma campaign."[2]

There was then a lull so far as Burma was concerned : between the 14th and the 17th the Conference was occupied with European matters, notably with Italy from where representatives had just arrived in Spain to seek more reasonable terms than unconditional surrender. While these things were under discussion Wingate was given important work to do, namely, to act as Far Eastern specialist adviser to Lord Louis Mountbatten in drafting a proposal which had originated with Mr. Churchill. This was known by the code name of " Culverin," and it put forward an operational plan to seize the Andaman Islands and the northern end of Sumatra, with the purpose of laying sea and air siege to Japanese-occupied territory from the Assam frontier to Singapore. This grand design, splendid in imagination, was vigorously opposed by Sir Alan Brooke, and was the cause of the difference between the Prime Minister and his Service Chiefs,[3] but Mr. Churchill would not let go, and the proposal was worked out in detail by Lord Louis Mountbatten with assistance. It will appear later by how strange and even tragic an irony Wingate, of all men, became a principal mover in " Culverin."[4]

He and Lorna, with most members of the two missions, were lodged in the Frontenac Hotel. He continued to wear his naval battledress. He met the American chiefs and their Staff officers and with them he quickly laid the foundations of the Anglo-American character of the second Chindit expedition. Antony Head, who saw more of him than did anyone else at Quebec, noticed a strange way he had of vanishing from the scene. For brief periods he would become " incommunicado," away from the bustle and lobbying of the conference, so that it was sometimes difficult to find him. No doubt he wanted to be by himself or with Lorna, and he probably still felt at moments the sudden

[1] Churchill V.   [2] Bryant.   [3] Bryant.
[4] Wingate's part in " Culverin " appears from a letter from him to Lord Louis Mountbatten of 10.2.44. W.P.I.

undeniable need of rest that seizes men after such fatigues as he had endured a short time before.

Wingate's first major appearance on the Quebec scene was on the afternoon of the 17th before the Combined Chiefs in session. It seems that the British principals, in expectation of a stormy discussion on the Mediterranean, kept Wingate in reserve for whenever the meeting was ready to move to the Far Eastern agenda, indeed, Sir Alan Brooke's personal record makes it fairly clear that he and his British colleagues hoped that Wingate, the " point of agreement," might resolve discords at the end of an angry debate. One must smile at the spectacle of this stormy petrel of a man, this merciless discomfiter of authority, finding himself in the rôle of " the little uniter," but those who would smile too much should remember what lay behind the part thrust upon him. On this occasion he acquitted himself well. He spoke quickly, rigidly to the point, and fixed the attention of this audience which was thoroughly used to and thoroughly weary of the arts of eloquent men. As usual he made no allowances for the eminence of his listeners and spoke with as much candour as though he were addressing his column commanders. At one point he referred (with doubtful loyalty) to the Army of India as " that system of outdoor relief," but the impropriety being strictly in context did not take away from the merit of the performance.[1] He earned the approval of the chairman. " Quite a good meeting," wrote Sir Alan Brooke in his diary, " at which I produced Wingate who gave a first-class talk on his ideas and his views on the running of the Burma Campaign."

On the same day Mr. Roosevelt arrived in Quebec from the United States. Mr. Churchill wanted the President to meet Wingate, and so a short private session was arranged for the following morning. Wingate received instructions to this effect late on the 17th, and he set to work, with the help of Antony Head, to prepare a presentation of the Chindit expedition and the present proposals in the light of the most recent discussions. This was a considerable task and occupied them till a late hour. Next morning President Roosevelt, wearing the unusual combination of a black jacket and white velveteen trousers, was wheeled into a room where Wingate was standing before a large map of Assam and Burma. The American statesman greeted the young brigadier with his usual cordial demonstrations. The only other persons present were the British Prime Minister, Lord Louis Mountbatten, and Colonel Head. Wingate excelled himself in a modest and stirring account, packed with matter, delivered with hardly one look at his notes. He was frequently interrupted by one or other of the two statesmen who wanted now to ask a question, now to refer

[1] Head.

Wingate's subject to some wide question of strategy. At the end Mr. Churchill said something to this effect : " Brigadier Wingate, we owe you our thanks. You have expounded a large and very complex subject with exemplary lucidity." Colonel Head half-expected that in acknowledgment of this rare tribute Wingate would make some reference to the help he had received in organising the lucidity of the occasion, but Wingate only replied : " Such is always my practice, sir."[1]

This was a high point of Wingate's good fortune and the last occasion in Quebec when he addressed an audience with a set piece, but he attended among the juniors at other British meetings and other meetings of the Combined Chiefs of Staff.[2] It was noted that he showed a skill in the art of committee work such as a politician of long experience might have envied. He had the mysterious ability to make his presence felt without insistence. He rarely asked to speak but waited till he was invited, and somehow, by the expression of his face or whatever goes to impress personality, he made it difficult for others to pass him over in the course of debate. Sometimes when his opinion was sought he paused for as much as fifteen seconds, (which can seem like fifteen minutes), before giving his answer.[3]

One day he had a curious encounter in the Château Frontenac. He was sitting in the restaurant, his elbows on the table and his chin resting on his hands as he harangued and argued with fellow members of the British delegation, when he caught sight of an elderly officer in air force uniform. Something about this man was familiar. Suddenly Wingate recognised that senior officer of his Sudan Defence Force days, the same who had once told him to keep his opinions to himself or he would be sent home. Wingate went over and introduced himself. The tyrant of his youth had of course no difficulty in remembering his now famous victim. He had nothing of the tyrant about him now. Wingate asked him about himself and the other told him that he was a King's messenger now for which reason he wore R.A.F. uniform, (though he did not explain how he contrived this irregularity), adding somewhat pathetically that he enjoyed his new duties as they gave him opportunities to meet " important people." Wingate was spontaneously glad to see someone who belonged to his early days in Africa, but the other was manifestly uneasy in the presence of the formidable being whom he had once tried to lick into shape, and the renewed acquaintance did not flourish.[4]

The 19th of August was marked by major political storms. It was on this day that the committee room of the Combined Chiefs of Staff had to be cleared of all except the principals, whereafter tempers were

[1] Head. [2] Personal Notebook. [3] Head.
[4] The Edinburgh Paper.

restored by the help of Lord Louis Mountbatten's experiments with ice blocks. Although the subject of the meeting was the war in the Far East Wingate does not seem to have been present. This may have been because he had urgent business within the British delegation. For it was on the 19th that the answer to the telegrams of the 14th came from India. The news that the Chiefs of Staff supported the long-range penetration scheme to maximum extent had been received with the utmost dismay in New Delhi. The decision was not only against much prejudice but against much serious conviction.

The achievement of 77 Brigade was never underestimated by Sir Claude Auchinleck and years afterwards, when it had been subjected to hostile scrutiny and Sir William Slim's denigrations, he thought and spoke of Wingate's meteoric act of defiance with complete admiration. It appealed to all in him that made him a natural leader of soldiers. But he was never an uncritical admirer of the strange man who had brought this marvel about. A few days after Mr. Churchill had urged Wingate's appointment to an army command, Sir Claude Auchinleck (unaware of Mr. Churchill's recommendation), wrote as follows to the C.I.G.S., " Wingate has exceptional power to organise and inspire personally officers and men engaged in these highly difficult independent operations . . . but the farther he is removed from personal contact with the troops employed, for example as Corps Commander, the less valuable he is likely to be."[1]

While the Quebec conference went forward, with Wingate as a point of agreement, a strenuous controversy on Chinditry in general had opened in India. The views of the Commander-in-Chief were moderate and even friendly compared to those of the majority on his staff, and the proposals of Quadrant had stirred G.H.Q. into a renewed opposition to Wingate such as made their earlier one seem mild.[2]

To enable him to resist his instructions the staff had furnished the Commander-in-Chief with cogent arguments. The main ones were these : that the expansion would require aircraft in large numbers, and that if such aircraft were supplied they could be far better employed in maintaining and conveying normal forces in the battle zone ; that any other large reinforcements to India should first be applied to the normal forces, and that the principle must never be overlooked or forgotten for a moment that long range penetration groups, like other irregulars, were army auxiliaries, " an aid not a substitute "; that the most important long range penetration tasks, notably the destruction of Japanese petrol and ammunition stores, were beyond the capacity of troops operating on the Wingate system ; that there was no time to train ; that no account had been taken of the ground transport require-

[1] Information obtained at the War Office.   [2] Tulloch. Head.

ment.[1] Wingate had asked for six brigades in the new Chindit organisation. The demand had then been augmented by him to eight, then reduced again to six by the Joint Planners and the Chiefs of Staff. It was to be noted, however, that in making the reduction the Chiefs of Staff had not refused Wingate's full demand, for in their telegram to India they explained that they required an immediate assignment of six brigades but with two more to follow. On receiving this proposition in Delhi the Commander-in-Chief had proposed to his advisers a reduction of the requirement to three. Even this modest move towards the policy of Quebec had been resisted in India and Sir Claude Auchinleck found himself in some conflict with his staff. He had intended to find the third Chindit brigade from the 81st West African Division, but numerous arguments against tampering with this unit, the first division to be raised in West Africa, had been voiced from within, forwarded to the staff and by them forwarded to the Commander-in-Chief who was counted on to make known deeply felt grievances.

Sir Claude Auchinleck sent a moderate and masterly reply to Quebec. He set out his case in three main sections, first dealing with the value of the long range penetration groups, secondly (and at length) with the possibility of an advance into Burma by the army in the winter, and thirdly, with the man-power question. In the first section he reiterated the principle that any use of irregulars must be governed by the capacity of the main forces to exploit the situation caused by irregular operations. He somewhat overstated the difference between normal troops and irregulars when he said that the irregular rôle was not to fight but evade and harass. In the second section he considered the date when exploitation might be practical. All plans for an offensive were conditioned by the state of communications in Assam, and in the present circumstances there was no possibility of these being established to needed capacity before March of 1944. General Auchinleck, having put forward this point with statistics, and having drawn attention to an air transport requirement of four squadrons, went on to consider the proposal to associate one long range penetration group with an advance by the Chinese army from Yunnan. He said he placed no reliance on Chinese promises that they would make this advance, and added that recent reports confirmed his doubts. He thought that this army, called " Yokeforce " in official code jargon, would never move into Burma before a general British offensive was in evidence, and such an offensive, he said, could not be ready before March of the next year. These arguments amounted to an assertion that the proposed expansion of the Chindits would prove a dispersal and waste of effort in the coming winter, though the second section contained one important

[1] D.M.O. papers of August, 1943, in Ministry of Defence Archives, New Delhi.

qualification of this opinion, namely, that the expansion might be of practical benefit if it was found necessary to use the groups " to counter a penetration into Assam by the enemy." As things fell out, this was in fact the circumstance in which they were used in 1944.

The third section on the man-power question contained the strongest criticism. If the instructions of the Chiefs of Staff were met in full this could only be done by serious disruption of the existing forces. It would be necessary before anything else to break up 70 Division, one of the most distinguished formations of the British Army. Number 1 Indian Division, being of the animal-and-motor-transport type, would have to be similarly dislocated, and the provision of three British battalions would disorganise a third division, quite apart from what would follow the provision of about three thousand five hundred R.A.F. personnel, army engineers, signallers and other specialist troops. This, the General remorselessly continued, was calculated on the assumption that 100 per cent of the troops provided would be found suitable for Chindit campaigning, whereas experience showed that only 60 per cent were likely to survive the test of training, and then further depredations would have to be made. The expansion would have a calamitous effect on the proposed advance of Stilwell's force from Ledo, the maintenance of the supply line to China, and the reserves of animal and motor transport in the army of Assam. The proposed capture of Ramree would have to be abandoned. He pointed out the confusion which could follow the establishment of an independent Force Headquarters. Having proposed the formation of a brigade from the 81st West African Division, the General urged that this should be the limit of expansion, and concluded with an eloquent plea for the withdrawal of a policy which would do grave harm to an army already suffering in morale from frequent reorganisations.[1]

The India hierarchy knew nothing of what was happening at Quebec. They could not guess that it was impossible for the British negotiators to withdraw support from the new Wingate proposal without provoking renewed differences with the Americans, just as these differences were at last being settled. It must also be remembered, (what was not known in India), that a new and enlarged Wingate campaign was a point of agreement not only between Americans and British, but between the British Chiefs of Staff and the British Prime Minister who was intent on a strategy in which the Burma campaign would be limited to the north, with an equal effort devoted to the establishment of an Allied base on Sumatra. Discussion between Mr. Churchill and Sir Alan Brooke on this subject reached a climax on the 19th.[2] From his own point of view General Auchinleck's telegram

[1] New Delhi Archives.   [2] Bryant.

could not have arrived on a less propitious day. It jarred on the political mood of the moment. In a private talk with Wingate Mr. Churchill commented on it with some freedom.

The telegram from India of the 19th was followed by another on the 21st. This went some way further towards meeting the original instructions of the Chiefs of Staff and proposed that the whole of 81 West African Division should be put to long range penetration usage but without breaking the formation, keeping it intact under its existing command and staff. This meant that the India proposal for three Chindit brigades was raised to five, only one less than the Joint Planners had asked for, and it is evident that the object of this new recommendation was to save 70 Division.

Before the arrival of the second telegram Wingate had launched his counter-attack. This took the form of a spirited memorandum over 3,000 words long. He contested every single point made by General Auchinleck. A few quotations can give a notion of the style of argument.

" (General Auchinleck) finds himself unable to recommend the formation and training of more than the existing L.R.P.G.s. The grounds on which he bases this opinion are that the creation of any more L.R.P.G.s will denude the Army in India of essential forces. There are in India to-day, and have been for a considerable time, something in the neighbourhood of a million men under arms.

" Since the fall of Singapore the war against the Japanese has in the main been conducted from India with second-rate troops. Better troops in the shape of certain veteran troops, armoured corps, assault brigades, etc., have been withheld from contact with the enemy. Everywhere, except in one instance, the troops given the task of fighting the enemy have been worsted and made fools of. It is not too bold to say that this is due to faulty methods. In the one case referred to[1] the methods employed were quite different. But General Auchinleck has not suggested that these methods should therefore be applied on a large scale.

" The statement that the object of L.R.P.G.s is not to fight but to evade the enemy is the reverse of the fact. The whole object of L.R.P.G.s is to fight. The only one we have so far seen fought continuously and a good deal harder than was convenient. It was unfit both as regards personnel and training to fight the Japanese. It was quite unsupported. Nevertheless, it had to fight and fight hard. Troops of these columns must have seen many more Japanese during the Chindit operation than normal infantry have seen of this enemy in years. Of course L.R.P.G.s seek to evade the enemy when there is no object in meeting him.

[1] 77 Brigade.

460

" As regards the necessity of a follow-up this is most certainly vital. Why the light forces required should not be ready I cannot conceive. The longer this war in Assam lasts, the less ready to advance the formations seem to become . . . as long as a year ago we were speaking with confidence of our intention to make these advances not in 43-44 but in 42-43 ! The longer the war goes on the further this prospect of an advance recedes."[1]

This referred only to the Commander-in-Chief's telegram of the 19th. In a second memorandum he dealt with the second telegram. He thought he detected a trap : by retaining divisional organisation, command and staff, 81 West African Division could be used to complicate and thereby diminish his own authority. He was also, judging by what he wrote, mindful of his unhappy experiences with Gurkhas. The West Africans had jungle training of their own and in division strength they might prove resistant to another school of teaching, even under Wingate's domineering leadership. Yet for all that, General Auchinleck's second telegram offered, in terms of numbers, most of what had been asked for, and it must have needed strength of mind to refuse. The strength was there ; Wingate looked at the gift horse in the mouth, and refused it utterly. Nevertheless, in his short, harsh, well-argued second memorandum, he consented, as though making a gesture of unusual generosity, to take one West African brigade, on a strictly experimental basis. His patron Field-Marshal Lord Wavell once said that no man could be a general unless he had something of the gambling impulse. Wingate had it.

On the 23rd of August the Joint Planning Staff, having considered the two telegrams from India and Wingate's two memoranda, gave their recommendations on the Long Range Penetration Groups. They fully supported the maximum demand for eight brigades but pointed out that this was not practical while uncertainty prevailed regarding the proposal for an attack on Sumatra. So instead they recommended that the expansion should be limited for the time being, but only for the time being, to six brigades, the reorganisation to be confined to the breaking up of 70 Division and one brigade of 81 West African Division. They supported Wingate's demand for specialist troops and for the establishment of his own Headquarters. The recommendations were acted on without further debate, and instructions were sent to Delhi. On the 25th the Conference formally set up the South-East Asia Command (which had been discussed since May) under the supreme direction of Lord Louis Mountbatten. This meant that Wingate's next expedition would be conducted under a commander who wholeheartedly admired and believed in him. His run of

[1] W.P.I.

good fortune was not yet finished; it continued in overwhelming profusion after Quebec. For when the Conference dispersed Wingate accompanied Lord Louis to Washington and there they had a meeting with General Arnold, the Commander of the United States Army Air Force. During Quadrant Wingate had opened negotiations with Arnold for American air co-operation with the Chindits, and one day in conference the American commander had replied to a question on the subject with what seemed at the time a facetiously lavish offer. In Washington Mountbatten reminded him of this promise, and thereupon, to his and Wingate's surprise, Arnold seriously confirmed the offer, and undertook to organise an aerial task force to work in association with any form of long range penetration scheme. He said that as soon as he had chosen a task force commander he would send him to London to discuss details.[1]

It is probably true to say that in the whole course of the Second World War, no junior military commander enjoyed a personal political success comparable to that of Wingate at Quebec. His enjoyment of it, very slight in sensual terms, was suddenly marred by a great personal grief. His removal from London to Quebec had been so hurried that when he left he had not yet made his arrival known to his family. They were anxious to get in communication with him at this moment, because on the 8th of August his mother had suddenly fallen gravely ill. After a few hours she died. His sister Sybil wrote to him to India on the 9th, but hardly had she done so than perplexing rumours that Wingate was in England reached her. The family made inquiries but could find out nothing. At length Sybil rang up Mr. Amery to ask him if he knew where her brother was, and in a guarded reply, he said that he would see to it that a letter or telegram reached him.[2] The news when it did reach Wingate, came as a shattering blow, all the more perhaps because he had few affections outside his family, and because he had missed seeing his mother for the last time, by so little.

The last letter of Mrs. Wingate to her eldest son had been written on the 3rd of July, and it contained a remarkable passage very characteristic of their family circle : " Where should I or any of us be without prayer. Stick to your praying, darling. I was much struck a week ago by the fact that David never took God's guidance for granted, nor made his plans first and expected God to endorse them afterwards. I was reading II Sam. 5, 19-25 and saw that David did not take it for granted that God had guided him to one form of attack at one time, and that He wanted David to follow that same method the second time.

---

[1] Information obtained at the War Office. *Back to Mandalay* by Lowell Thomas, referred to later as Thomas.
[2] Miss Monica Wingate.

5. 23 says, ' David inquired of the Lord and got different guidance to success.' God seems to have given you a great military genius for this special and dangerous form of war, and He will continue to prosper you if you continue to seek Him . . . you have made a great name for yourself with His help. You are bound (like David or Wellington or anybody !) to have setbacks as well, but avoid giving cause for jealousy, or bitterness."

From the United States he flew back to England, while Lorna returned in the *Queen Mary*.

CHAPTER XX

HARVESTING IN BAD WEATHER

HE ARRIVED in London early one morning, and a few hours later called on Mrs. Sieff. She was naturally very surprised to see him, and hastened to congratulate him on his success and fame. He looked at her in silence for a moment, and then with much solemnity he reminded her how she had introduced him to Harold Laski who had brought his case to the notice of the Prime Minister. He ended by saying something as follows : " I am going to be so busy while I'm in London that I won't be able to see many of my friends, and I shall be able to see no one for more than a few moments. But I had to see you, to tell you that if it had not been for your help when I was back from Ethiopia last year, none of this would have happened, and I would be a gunner in Dorset."

Monica came to share the flat in Hill Street while Lorna was on her way back by sea. She gave him an account of their mother's end, and he asked her to give him Mrs. Wingate's Bible, so that he might keep it in her memory. He saw much of his other two sisters, Rachel who was working in the Ministry of Information, and Sybil who was working in the Ministry of Production. He was disappointed not to see his brothers but they were both serving overseas, Nigel as a Lieutenant-Colonel in command of the 42nd Light Anti-Aircraft Regiment in the Eighth Army, Granville as commander of a battery in Northern Ireland. He met Kounine again. He is remembered as eagerly enjoying the little private life he could allow himself, for most of his time was spent otherwise in consolidating the gains of Quebec. He knew well enough that unless he did this now he would have little chance of doing it in Delhi.

His first official call was on the Assistant C.I.G.S., General Evetts. He showed at once by his manner that he was passing through the anxieties reserved for the fortunate : " I'm in a desperate situation," he said, " and only you can help me out of it." And he explained that he needed to find a staff, and order equipment, and obtain his establishment, and almost organise a division within a few days. He had asked for much, been given much, and now he had the crushing task of translating arguments into deeds and facts. In earlier days Evetts had often seen Wingate storming at men and fate because he had been refused what he wanted, and he could not help being somewhat amused now at a volcanic outbreak which was the consequence of his being given what he wanted in abundance. But he understood Wingate's predicament easily enough, promised his help and gave it with much effect. In London the foundations of the second expedition were laid.

The cross-Channel offensive from England, operation " Overlord," was in preparation, and as a result recognised military and administration talent in the army had long been closely booked. In these circumstances Wingate found himself hard put to it to find a first class principal staff officer. Suddenly he saw his solution. He remembered Derek Tulloch. He sent him a telegram on the 1st of September: " Am in London. Wish to see you immediately. Orde."

The telegram found Derek Tulloch partridge-shooting in Lancashire and enjoying the first day of a long-awaited fortnight's leave. He had noted his friend's sudden rise to eminence with excitement but quite without surprise. He was always an admirer of Wingate, though never a hero-worshipper. He always regarded him as a man of great and outstanding character and attainments, but he never blindly followed his enthusiasms, and sometimes opposed them strenuously. It is a most curious thing in Wingate's life that the only man with whom he enjoyed a long and indissoluble friendship had no part in his ardent Zionism and openly expressed himself as being on the other side. Tulloch had no hesitation about his next step, and on the same day as the telegram reached him, he and Mary Tulloch took the night train to London.

The two men met again the next morning in an office which Lord Louis Mountbatten had set aside for Chindit work in the Combined Operations Headquarters in Richmond Terrace. His friend was immediately impressed by the change in the other. He had last seen him before he left for India the year before, full of doubt as regards his appointment to the Far East, even wondering whether he should refuse it and try again for his Tibesti schemes. There was no hesitancy about him now, and the change wrought in him was not by alteration but intensification. His determination and singleness of purpose now seemed absolute. In his essay on Wingate Tulloch described their conversation together. " He sketched his plans roughly to me, related what had happened following his return from Burma, his visit to Quebec, and the subsequent decisions—all this in about twenty minutes. Then he said : ' I want your help. I cannot get the nucleus of Staff officers or commanders, the sort I want for this force, from

India. I must get the nucleus from home. Good Staff officers are rare in India and I probably won't get them anyway, as my scheme will not be popular—not at all. I have *carte blanche* up to a certain number and you must help me to select the right ones. I know no one at home now. Ensure that you get the best only. Remember that you have *carte blanche*.' "

The next days were spent in interviewing officers who wished to join the Chindits, in journeying to factories and stores, in conferring with technicians and specialists all over industrial England, and in ordering material to be sent to his Headquarters in the Central Provinces of India. He had already ordered much equipment from the United States during his brief visit, for with the support he had gathered at Quebec he was almost in a position to act as his own Minister of Supply. His observation in the first expedition had given him a precise idea of what he wanted, and he was quick, as always, to learn how to adapt his ideas to technical facilities. He seems to have made only one false estimate in his choice of equipment : he became an enthusiast for a type of flame-thrower called the Lifebuoy which was to prove of little use in the field. For the rest the second Chindit expedition was one of the most skilfully equipped of the war.

The most important of his encounters in the Combined Operations Headquarters were at two interviews with General Arnold's choice of aerial task force commander. This was Colonel Philip Cochran. He and Wingate had little in common except courage, remarkable war records, and the fact that both were victims of Press publicity. A great deal of bosh had been published about the Chindit commander by this time, and Colonel Cochran's career had been long embarrassed by a strip cartoon tracing the adventures of " Flip Corkin." It is doubtful, however, whether the Colonel felt the embarrassment very keenly. He was at this time an irrepressibly gay man who never took himself as seriously as he took his calling. He and Wingate did not get on well at their first meeting. Lowell Thomas reconstructed from the records of friends a remarkable caricature account by Cochran of what happened.

" I found out . . . that Wingate had a habit of making speeches. You might ask him a specific question requiring a one-word answer, and he would go off on a long harangue about a lot of things. You might ask a military question, like the average rainfall in Burma in March, and he would go off on a lecture about the effect of rainfall on Burmese monasteries and the Buddhist religion. In our first talk I said : " What do you intend to do ? " And he went into one of his orations. . . . He kept talking about ' long range penetration,' which meant nothing to me. He mixed everything up with scholarship and the history of war. I didn't know what he was talking about. A lot was about things that were over my head and that I didn't care about. I had trouble with British accents in general, and his was exaggerated. . . . We finally ended it by saying that I'd come back next day, I hoping for a better break."[1]

According to Lowell Thomas, Cochran was so allergic to English enunciation that throughout their close association he believed Wingate to be suffering from an impediment in speech. He was evidently, at this time at least, naturally suspicious of Englishmen and he seems to have had the idea that Wingate was an elaborate hoax. Then at their second meeting he was suddenly and permanently converted to belief in him. Wingate succeeded in conveying what he meant by long range penetration. To quote Lowell Thomas's reconstruction again :

" I suddenly realised that, with his radio direction, Wingate used his guerilla columns in the same way that fighter-control headquarters directs planes out on a mission. I saw it as an adaptation of air to jungle, an application of radio-controlled air-war tactics to a walking war in the trees and the weeds. Wingate had hit upon the idea independently. He knew little about air. In his own tough element he was thinking along the same radio lines that an airman would about tactics among the clouds. I realised that there was something very deep about him. . . . He was the kind to convince his men by saying, ' We're going to do this or that, and we're going to win,' in such a manner that there was no argument. . . . One of the things awfully upsetting in war is not to know what is going to happen. When I left him, I was beginning to assimilate some of the flame of this guy Wingate."

Colonel Cochran returned to Washington to study the requirement of the task force with Colonel John Alison. Before leaving he had assured Wingate that the Chindits had only to " dream up " ideas and he would put them into operation. He said : " We will do anything you ask us to do, but it is up to you to produce the ideas for us to carry out."[2]

There is evidence that in London Wingate was in some sort of negotiation with the organisation called S.O.E. which had refused his services the year before. S.O.E. were probably anxious for close co-operation with the Chindits now, and he in turn was probably anxious to have access to their supplies and to be allowed to accept volunteers from among their ranks. But he was chary, as always, of losing any part of his independence through association, and his notebook contains a curious item under the address of S.O.E.'s Baker

[1] Thomas.
[2] Personal record of the Second Chindit Expedition by Derek Tulloch, referred to subsequently as Tulloch II.

Street headquarters. A sentence written in Arabic characters reads, " Do not be caught by Keswick." Later he was to have uneasy relations with S.O.E. representatives in India, but the fact that he warned himself against being " caught " suggests a process of smooth relations and wooing, at this time. For the moment things were going his way.

With abundant Ministerial support, with the added personal approval of the C.I.G.S., with the active help of an assistant chief, and with enthusiasm for the Chindits prevailing as strongly in the official world as among ordinary citizens, Wingate in London enjoyed a fruitful honeymoon with authority. There was only one disagreement, and this concerned rank. As a divisional commander Wingate very reasonably asked to be appointed an acting Major-General. The military secretary was against this, not because he contested the claim but because he very reasonably thought that the appointment ought to be made on the initiative of India. Wingate knew Indian state of opinion better than the military secretary, and he persisted in his claim to immediate promotion, even to the point of " a slight fracas."[1] In the end the appointment was made on War Office initiative, but very late in the day.

He saw Mr. Amery and gave him an account of Quebec and his new plans. He saw Cousin Rex for the last time. One day when he could snatch an hour's leisure, he went for a walk with Mary Tulloch and he told her, what he later told Mr. Humphrey Trevelyan, that he would never feel free in his conscience from the thought of the suffering that he had brought on men under his command. As with other Chindit commanders, it was the recollection of abandoning ill or wounded men that lay heaviest on his mind, and, as appears later, this had a large influence on his military plans. On one of these last English days he went with his sister Sybil to buy books in the Charing Cross road. They discussed the relation of faith to action, and he said that deeds such as he had accomplished, and such as he intended to accomplish in the near future, were valueless unless they had some profound purpose. He said : " One must have faith, and by that I mean faith in God."[2] He heard that the Weizmanns were in London, and one day he appeared unannounced in their rooms at the Dorchester. They were much surprised to see him while he—laughing at himself so that they laughed too—said : " I wanted you to see me in General's uniform." He could only stay a short time, and when he left he embraced them both. They never met again.[3]

He left London with Tulloch and four staff officers on the afternoon of the 11th of September. They went by train to one of the R.A.F. stations of the west country where they were told that their aircraft

[1] Tulloch II.   [2] Miss Sybil Wingate.   [3] Mrs. Weizmann.

would not be ready till late. They had done all the work they could, and from now till the end of the journey Wingate was in a relaxed mood, partly through force of circumstances, partly no doubt because he was putting into effect that belief in systematic rest which had once made him a lie-abed in his Sheffield days, and which he never lost. While waiting for the scheduled time of departure he and Tulloch went to Marlborough for dinner, and for a long moonlight stroll on the hills behind the town. They remembered the days when they had both been at Larkhill together, and kept horses at Pyt House. They fell to reconstructing long happy muddy hunts with the South Wilts and the Portman and the Blackmore Vale, and when, adventuring farther afield, they had sometimes ridden over this very country. They gave themselves up to the sentimental joys of nostalgia as long as their time allowed. Then they drove back to the aerodrome and left at midnight.

On the 13th, after stopping at Lisbon for one night, the aircraft came down for a brief halt at Castel Benito on the way to Cairo. Something happened there which was to have consequences. The weather was oppressively hot, even in the early morning when they arrived, and the passengers were put into a rest-house on the aerodrome. They were all thirsty, but nothing was ready for their reception. Cold drinks were ordered, and in Moslem fashion these were a long time in coming. While he and the others were all miserably waiting, Wingate saw a flower vase on a table in the corner from which the flowers had been removed but not the water, and, with typical impatience, and forgetful of his hero Gideon's teaching in the matter of delicacy when drinking, he picked up the vase and drained it.[1]

On the afternoon of the same day they arrived in Cairo. That evening, as he and Tulloch walked up the street stairs into Shepheard's Hotel, Wingate saw his brother Nigel among the people sitting on that once-famous veranda. This was a great and joyous surprise, for the Eighth Army in which Nigel was serving was now hundreds of miles to the west.[2] The onward journey was due to start again at dawn on the 15th, and during their day and a half pause in Cairo the two brothers spent most of their time together. These were the last carefree days of Wingate's life and he was in unusually high spirits, inclined to foolery and fun. Tulloch recorded him as practising his Arabic anew in chaffing the hotel servants, and singing Arab songs in the room they shared together. They went to the incomparable Zoo on one evening.

[1] Tulloch II.
[2] Nigel Wingate was on sick leave from his regiment following an attack of jaundice. Family letters. W.P.I.

It will not be supposed that Wingate came so near the Promised Land without doing something for Zion. He rang up the Cairo branch of the Jewish Agency to find out the whereabouts of his Jewish friends. He met some of these (unspecified) in the course of the 14th, and he told them that he had taken a recent opportunity to press on Mr. Churchill and President Roosevelt in person the need for a Jewish army, and that both had replied in an encouraging sense.[1]

A minor calamity, which Wingate took very hard, distressed their departure at sunrise the next day. One article of their baggage was a bundle composed of Wingate's pith helmet wrapped in a white fleecy rug which he had bought in America, and in the confusion of embarkation this was lost, and never retraced. He was not a superstitious man, but he deplored the loss of the cork-lined monstrosity that he had worn throughout his campaigns and used as a boat over the Chindwin, and by which he was known to his men. As soon as he arrived in Delhi he hastened to buy a new one.

Then, as they approached India, Wingate fell into a more serious mood. He told his friend that he had evil forebodings about the kind of reception that awaited them, and he said that the second Chindit expedition would only be saved by the fact that Mr. Churchill had granted him the right of direct communication whenever he was in difficulties. Tulloch laughed at his fears, told him that he was exaggerating as usual, and that this was another case of imagining enemies all about him. Wingate assured him that however that might have been at other times, he was not imagining now. Tulloch was soon to recognise his mistake.[2]

On the 16th they arrived in Karachi where Wingate was entertained by the district commander. He was in doubt the next day whether to go straight to Delhi, or first to the Central Provinces to see Wilcox, for his training camps would again lie in his command. He knew that he was about to appear before an eagerly fault-finding audience, for which reason he could not decide which course to take till the last moment. In the end he went to Agra where he stayed for two nights with the General, going to Delhi on the 19th. There, true to form, his enemies accused him of want of straightforwardness in not having gone direct to the Commander-in-Chief, and it may be taken as certain that had he gone straight to Delhi, the same people would have complained that he showed some want of straightforwardness in not having consulted the regional commander before confronting Sir Claude Auchinleck with his plans. For Wingate's fears of a bad reception in Delhi had not been the least exaggerated. There was no welcome for this man who had been a major eighteen months before, and who had

[1] Magen Baseter   [2] Tulloch II.

now contrived to make himself a strategical adviser to the leading statesmen of the world.

On his first day in Delhi he went with Tulloch to that splendid complex of official buildings where the Viceregal staff was situated as the neighbour of G.H.Q. At the latter he asked what arrangements had been made for his accommodation. None had been made. He asked where his office was situated and was told that there were no rooms to spare, and that in consequence he had not got an office. While in Quebec he had asked for and been granted the right to a private reconnaissance aircraft. He was now told that there were no aircraft available for the purpose. He asked for a car and was told that he must inform the G.H.Q. transport officer on any occasion when he wanted a car (with reasons stated), and he might obtain a car when one was free. He asked for a stenographer and was told to apply to the pool.[1]

On the 20th he was summoned to a conference presided over by a Deputy Chief of Staff, and attended by heads of departments. He went with Tulloch. The latter had never before seen him as a member of a committee, and he watched his performance with amazement and admiration, tinged with some compassion for the unfortunate chairman. The sense of the meeting was clear to the new arrivals from the beginning. Wingate was regarded as a vulgar go-getter who had gone behind the backs of his superiors in India to indulge in audacious intrigue with politicians, on the strength of very questionable achievement. He must be humbled and made to realise his true position, after which he would receive support for operations on a scale suited to his status. It was an initial trial of strength. The meeting opened with the chairman asking him to state his intentions and requirements. Wingate stood up and gave them in full, without apology. He sat down. Then comments were invited. These all shared a common theme, and omission : stress on the difficulties, no suggestion as to how to overcome them. Wingate grew restless and presently began to interrupt speakers. Tempers rose and the chairman, (who was a believer in Wingate), strove with increasing difficulty to impose order and restore calm. A climax came when a senior officer was asked by the chairman whether he could meet that part of the requirement that concerned his department. He said : " Well, this is the first I have ever heard about all this. How can I say now ? I ought to have been told before." Wingate rose and called down the table : " Why should you have been told before—I am telling you now." There was an agonised silence. In Tulloch's words : " Several of those present obviously hoped, and expected, that the earth would open

[1] Tulloch Essay.

471

and swallow this upstart who was thus desecrating the Halls of Valhalla."

The meeting entered its short last phase when Wingate rose, (this time at the chairman's invitation), to give his comments on the views which had been expressed. He decided to play his ace of trumps. He said, in his harshest way, that though the decisions reached at Quebec had been conveyed to India, it was manifest that to date no effort had been made in India to implement them, and that unless this train of events was changed, and he received wholehearted support from all departments concerned in G.H.Q., he would be obliged to tell the Prime Minister, by the direct channel of communication allowed by Mr. Churchill, that there was no chance of the operations which he had promised, and with which he had been entrusted, meeting with success, and that he would therefore ask to be relieved of his present responsibilities.

His trump card took the trick and made the first rubber. The debate was brought to an end with assurances of further study and a future meeting at an early date.

This was the first of a series of conferences at all of which Wingate showed himself insistently determined to follow up the advantage he had from Quebec, and the advantage he had gained at the first critical encounter. At one meeting, shortly after the initial one, he asserted his right to be treated as a master-factor, in characteristic fashion. The conference had settled down to business in tolerable good humour when the chairman said that he would open the meeting but that in ten minutes he would have to vacate the chair, as he had to go to another one. Instantly Wingate swept up his papers and said: "Then we will all go and not waste our time. Please let us know when you are free to attend a conference." The chairman did not accept the challenge. He sent a message to his other expectants and remained. It may be taken as certain that he did not forget the humiliation.

It is not easy to decide how right or otherwise Wingate was in this kind of behaviour. It is arguable that thereby he not merely confirmed his enemies in their hostility, but alienated people who were prepared to be his supporters, given a chance. But on the other hand, there was no question at all of the hostility being imagined in this instance. To take only one incident in illustration. One of the seniors, a man close to the Commander-in-Chief, took Tulloch aside after a meeting and advised him to withdraw his loyalty from Wingate, urging that as a professional soldier, he, Tulloch, was unlikely to find promotion or success with the Chindits. Only in a conflict *à outrance* do men give themselves away so completely, and it is very arguable that if Wingate had shown a conciliatory spirit and conventional manners before such prejudiced opposition, the Chindit plan would have been rapidly lost in the smotherings of decent procrastination.[1]

His small immediate achievement was that by the 21st of September he was given a room, a car, and a stenographer, but only on loan, and only in a ration of one apiece. His staff had to work in the corridor, surrounded by vendors of tea, lemonade and sweets.

He spent only a few days in Delhi, all occupied with conferences at the end of which he had formulated his immediate demands. The main ones were that the hotel at Gwalior should be set aside for use as his Headquarters in the Central Provinces, that 70th Division should be moved from Bangalore to the training area, that he should be furnished with staff officers, transport, and clerical personnel in adequate numbers, and that R.A.F. officers should be directed to him for ground duty with the Chindit brigades.[2] On the 24th he sent a short memorandum to the Chief of Staff, Lieutenant-General Morris, putting forward a suggestion for the name of the new force. He pointed out that the name in such circumstances " is a matter of some importance as it has an effect on the members of the formation." He recommended that the Chindits should in future be known as " Gideon Force."[3] For some reason the proposal was not acceptable, and the Chindits were given instead the prosaic title of Special Force.

Fegusson was in Delhi at this time. From a temporary appointment as second in command in 111 Brigade he had first been ordered south with Captain Fraser and Major Anderson to organise training courses for the officers of 70 Division, and had then been given command (not yet effective) of one of the new brigades shortly to be formed. On the 19th of September he flew to Delhi with the Divisional General and some of the signals and administrative personnel, to meet Wingate, and it so happened that the first time he saw his commander on this occasion was in a street of New Delhi along which Wingate was walking in no good humour. As they talked together Fergusson presently noticed that Wingate's eyes were fixed rigidly on the other's left breast. On the space above the pocket there was to be seen, among lesser emblems, a new crimson and blue ribbon signifying the D.S.O. From his intent gaze, Fergusson expected that Wingate, though not much given to such courtesies, was about to say something charming about the award, but he awaited the little speech in vain. Then he noticed that the eyes of the other were not on the D.S.O., but another ribbon, that of the Palestine medal. Wingate presently growled in his

[1] Tulloch II and other notes by Tulloch made at the time. W.P.I. Information obtained at the War Office.
[2] Tulloch II.   [3] Correspondence in W.P.I.

gruffest voice : " A badge of disgrace !"[1] He was back to his old form.

From Delhi Wingate went south to meet 70th Division. On the way he stopped at Gwalior where he left Tulloch to reconnoitre training grounds in the Bundelkhand district, and then went on to Bangalore with the Divisional Commander, Major-General Symes. As told, the decision to break up 70th Division had been strongly resisted, and it remained the subject of more bitterness than any other instruction from Quebec. It was the deepest cause of personal rancour against Wingate himself. No one felt the bitterness of this reorganisation more than General Symes, but his character was instinct with loyalty and he never allowed his resentment to cloud his sense of duty to the new force. He was appointed second-in-command and as such became Wingate's faithful coadjutor in all the difficult times ahead. Wingate was grateful for such loyalty. With a delicacy of feeling that he did not always show in such matters, he was continually aware of the embarrassment of the other's position, and he behaved with consistent consideration to Symes. He liked and respected him but in the nature of things the two men could not become close friends.[2] The position was a very strange one. Wingate was the most junior Major-General in the army, and by the peculiar composition of Special Force his second-in-command was many times his senior.

On arrival at Bangalore Wingate found that very little had been done to implement the break-up, but he had the wisdom not to make one of his furious scenes. He met most of the officers, made a good impression, insisted that the move to Gwalior should be made immediately and this was done. The division went north in the first week of October.

In the meantime Wingate went on to Assam where he met General Scoones again and introduced himself to Major-General Stratemayer, the American Chief of Eastern Air Command which operated on the whole Burma Front.[3] He appears also to have seen General Stilwell, whom he had met at the Quadrant Conference. In the first week of October he was back in New Delhi, and, as he may have expected, he found that he had to begin his battles all over again. If he had won a rubber with his trump card, the match was still far off. Nothing had been done to meet any of his requirements. He still had no office in Delhi, no car, no stenographers. 70th Division were moving to the Central Provinces, but nothing had been done to secure his own headquarters in the hotel in Gwalior, the reason given being that this

---

[1] Fergusson. A communication.   [2] Tulloch II.

[3] In S.E.A.C. organisation the British and American Air Forces were integrated throughout the command under Air Chief Marshal Sir Robert Peirse as Allied Air Commander-in-Chief. General Stratemayer was Peirse's second-in-command throughout the whole S.E.A.C. area, besides being Air Commander in Burma.

would discommode the passengers of B.O.A.C.[1] He was back where he had been on arrival. It must be remembered that at this time G.H.Q. was occupied with a major reorganisation in the establishment of South-East Asia Command (known as S.E.A.C.), and the formation of the 14th Army, and this can explain a great deal of the delay. But for all that the evidence is strong that much of it was due to deliberate hostility. Wingate only saw the hostility.

But there was hope ahead. Lord Louis Mountbatten was due to arrive in Delhi in the first week of October. And then, two days before that event, Wingate fell ill.

On returning to Delhi from his reconnaissance Tulloch heard the news from Scott and went straightway to Maiden's Hotel. On entering Wingate's room he saw at a glance that his friend was very seriously ill. He found him being examined by a young R.A.F. medical officer who said that he ought to go to hospital without delay. But Wingate refused to do this, and furthermore he exacted a solemn promise from the medical officer to keep the fact that he was ill secret. It seems that he was fighting his illness, as men do, by refusing to admit it, and at the same time he was determined that, ill or not, he would meet Mount-batten on his arrival, if it was humanly possible to do so. The arrival was scheduled for the 7th, but on the 7th Wingate was no better, rather worse. Nevertheless, he forced Tulloch into agreement that he should get up and go to the aerodrome. He only wanted to make his presence known. After that, he said, he would put himself under medical care.

It was to be expected, after the events of Quadrant, that Wingate would receive an official invitation to be among the people selected to attend the historic moment when Mountbatten set foot on the soil of India, but the invitation did not arrive. In the name of " security " it was not sent. However, Wingate discovered the time of arrival through a friendly Press correspondent, and haggard, pale and shivering, he was on the airfield at the expected time. He was asked by some anxious person why he had come, and he gave a non-committal reply in a manner that invited no further questioning. His presence was noted, and not, he thought, with approval by those assembled by official appointment. Tactfully he stood aside from the gathered homage. The aeroplane landed. The Supreme Commander, with the grace of which he was master, emerged, saluted, descended the steps, shook hands and spoke with those officially congregated. Presently he noticed Wingate disposed at some, but not too great distance. The Supreme Commander went over and exchanged some

[1] Notes made by Wingate for Lord Louis Mountbatten (but not given to him), undated but evidently of the 5–7 October. W.P.I.

words with him too. Wingate told him that he was ill and must unfortunately go to hospital the next day. Mountbatten said that he wanted to discuss plans with him as soon as possible. He saw for himself how ill he was, and arranged that Tulloch should come and see him the next morning. The vital official contact had been made, after which Wingate resisted the counsel of his friends no longer. He willingly retired to bed again, and willingly consented to go to hospital and be looked after.[1]

He was moved to a military hospital where his illness rapidly entered a critical phase. (One may be reminded of a passage in *Candide*.) What happened next is best described in the words of Tulloch's essay : " I cabled to Lorna and then there began the most depressing weeks of my life. The hospital failed to diagnose the disease and thought it might be dysentery, or malaria, or malaria and dysentery combined, or it might be enteric. Orde was a better patient than I had expected, but he openly derided the hospital authorities to me. ' I told you so,' he would say, ' they are treating me for all kinds of diseases. I would have done better to stay at Maiden's Hotel.' " Even at the gate of death, he railed at the shortcomings of authority.

He nearly died. That he did not die was due, in large part, to the bold initiative of Lorna on receiving the telegram. The story is best told again in the words of Wingate's friend : " Lord Louis went over to Chungking shortly after his arrival, and while there received a telegram from Lorna Wingate suggesting that Matron MacGeary should be obtained to nurse Wingate. She had heard from Wingate what a splendid woman Matron MacGeary was, and how well she had looked after him and his men when they came out of Burma. . . . Lord Louis sent a message to me to try to arrange this immediately and I succeeded in doing so, with the help of the chief doctor in Delhi. He immediately gave his permission, and telephoned to Imphal for Matron MacGeary. . . . General Wedemayer diverted a Dakota which was returning from the Hump,[2] and which received instructions while in the air to pick up Miss MacGeary and bring her to Delhi at once. The Matron travelled through the night, sitting in the co-pilot's seat, and arrived at Delhi in the early hours of the morning." Thereafter the nature of the illness was quickly discovered. He was suffering from typhoid, contracted, with small doubt, when he drank from the flower vase at Castel Benito. Matron MacGeary introduced her vigorous efficiency into the case and nursed him through the crisis, under the direction of Colonel Cobbon, a specialist in typhoid cases whom Wingate grew to respect for his skill, in spite of his association

---

[1] Tulloch Essay. Tulloch II.
[2] The mountain ranges between North Assam and Chungking.

with the army medical service.[1] Wingate's delay in entering hospital, and the delay in making a correct diagnosis aggravated the illness. He came as near to death as one can do without losing life. He was in the hospital for nearly a month. Throughout his illness his door was guarded by Bachi Ram who had returned to his service. The crisis was over by November.[2]

This protracted and nearly fatal illness, which in the view of many people at the time signalled the natural end of the Chindits, proved to be of value to Wingate and his cause. At the time when India's disapproval of him had reached its full dimensions, his illness stirred approval of him in England to memorable expression. On the 17th of October a telegram arrived in G.H.Q. bearing this message : "Following from Prime Minister to General Wingate personal I am very sorry to hear of your illness and I hope you will be better soon, please do not repeat not hurry your convalescence ends." It would be a simplification of the complicated last chapter of Wingate's life to assert that this telegram and its successors changed the mental climate of G.H.Q. so far as Wingate and Special Force were concerned, but it undoubtedly made a difference. Doubtless there were many who regarded Wingate's talk of direct communication with the Prime Minister as a piece of exaggeration or even bluff, but here was the communication initiated from the London end. The hostility and obstruction continued, but not for a while with the same intensity and success.

In November another circumstance came to help Wingate in an indirect manner. The Viceroy, Field-Marshal Lord Wavell, observed the limitations of his office with strictness ; all the more because he was a soldier by profession he never interfered, or allowed occasion for people to say he interfered in military matters. But in November, when the time came for Wingate to leave hospital, he gave this man who already owed him much, a last and significant support. He decided to invite Wingate to spend his convalescence in Viceregal lodge as his guest.

Lady Wavell was not altogether pleased with the proposal when it was first put to her by her husband. Her mind went back to a not enjoyable lunch in 1942 when Wingate had been the guest of the Wavells on his return from his first fruitless mission to Burma. She had liked neither his disorderly clothes, nor his disorderly hair, nor the way he gobbled his food. Neither had she liked his conversation. There had been talk of the difficulties of waging a campaign in Upper

---

[1] Deducible from a letter to Lord Louis Mountbatten (referred to subsequently in footnotes as S.A.C.) 14.11.43. W.P.I.

[2] Letter from Wingate (19.11.43). W.P.I.

Burma, and she had said to her guest : " I have only seen the jungle in Assam, but I thought it was terrifying," whereupon he had replied in scornful reproof : " The jungle is your friend ! " After lunch she confided to her husband that if she had to go into a jungle she would not choose Wingate as her companion. He laughed and said nothing.

She did not resist her husband's argument when he put it to her now that people who necessarily lived in comfort, as they did, owed hospitality to men who endured hardship and risked their lives. She did, however, insist that their guest ought to have professional medical attention during his visit. It was at length arranged that Wingate should be accompanied by his friend and rescuer Agnes MacGeary. On the 2nd of November the strangely assorted couple, the haggard, brooding figure of the Chindit leader, and the small, erect, prim figure of the Matron, moved into the splendours of the palace which Lutyens designed for the residence of the last five Viceroys. Lady Wavell's fears were not realised. She found Wingate very different from the assertive and fierce-mannered man of the disastrous days of the year before. He was neatly dressed, quiet in behaviour, agreeably mannered, courteous, amiable. She liked him very much. She concluded that part of the transformation was due to the presence of Matron MacGeary. He obeyed her instructions as to treatment with scrupulousness, and seemed to stand in some awe of her.[1]

He stayed at Viceregal Lodge till the 17th when he moved to Faridkot House, the residence of the Supreme Allied Commander, for five days. On the 22nd he moved south to continue his convalescence as the guest of Mr. Humphrey Trevelyan, the political agent resident at Nowgong near the training grounds. Agnes MacGeary whom, against all the rules, he had appointed his personal assistant, accompanied him throughout these visits.[2]

Whether he wanted it or not, illness forced some private life on him at this juncture, and a result was some private correspondence. He wrote to Lorna on the 19th of November :

" I was grieved to hear you had got ill when you heard of my typhoid. You must not worry over such things or there will be no end to it. You must not go on thinking that I am obstinate and

[1] Lady Wavell. A communication. There is a well-known and widely believed story that Wingate went out driving in one of the splendid Viceregal open carriages, changed places with the coachman and lashed the horses into a furious gallop in the course of which they ditched the Commander-in-Chief's car. This is apocryphal. Mr. Peter Coates who was in charge of the Viceregal household, assures the writer that the State carriages were laid up throughout the war and that the only horse-drawn vehicle was a pony-cart. Doubtless Wingate drove this at speed.
[2] Sir Humphrey Trevelyan K.C.M.G.

foolish and act accordingly. I love you too much to be angry with you—otherwise I should be.

. . . The terrible bulletins were merely the doctors covering themselves just in case. Always in typhoid there's a danger of perforation full of possibilities.

I have been reading Feuchtwanger on Josephus. Interesting. Talked to Wavell on Eretz Yesrael. He said danger was to As from Js. I differed giving much chapter and verse from our experience. He is a likeable man—most kind to me.

Which reminds me, I am letting him have a short screed on the famine about which I know a good deal.[1] It is a ghastly thing to see.

Now do not fret yourself because of the ungodly. Don't worry over me. You have been worrying yourself and consequently me needlessly. And remember adopt a robust attitude to life. No coward soul—as has always been your way in all that concerns yourself—but you are a coward over me.

I feel optimistic—and what with the P.M.'s inquiries, etc., they thought it behoved them to be well on the right side. . . . I have plenty of friends as well as the expected foes and the latter are not doing too well at the moment. But, believe me, my own, I am quite philosophical over all my affairs and thoroughly cheerful. Interesting things are happening. . . . But my hope is that I may be used to do God's work in some measure. Don't praise me, love. I am a poor fish but I hope like the old beggar woman 'a struggler.'

. . . Derek has been a great standby in every way. He and Miss MacG. have really pulled me through so quickly. But I am embarrassed with kindness on every side. I feel rather like an ill-tempered dog when the world suddenly begins patting it."

The alarm felt by Lorna that he would throw himself back into his work without sufficient rest was shared by others. During November he received three messages from the Prime Minister enjoining a long convalescence.[2] His beloved sisters, Sybil, Rachel and Monica had written to him in the same sense. These admonitions were needed and without them he would have gone back to work much sooner than he did. He began to rebel against the Prime Minister's commands as early

[1] The Bengal famine of 1943 consequent on the floods. According to some Tulloch notes the " short screed " was not finished.

[2] Received in India on the 3rd, 12th, and 27th of November. The first paragraph of the last reads : " I am delighted to hear from Admiral Mountbatten that you are so much better. On no account throw away the advantage by premature effort to go back to ordinary duty. I have had this illness myself and had a most serious relapse through playing the fool." W.P.I.

as the 14th of November. On that day he wrote a memorandum to Mountbatten with the purpose of correcting "certain impressions which I notice are universally entertained about me and my state of health, which have no foundation either in fact or in medical science." In the same spirit, but with less serious expression, he registered some protest against family anxiety in the course of a letter written to Lorna on the 3rd of December. Like most of his letters it touched on a wide variety of subjects.

"I was glad to get a letter from you. . . . I miss you always as you me. This present ambitious phase of our lives may well end in obscurity. If so, beloved, I look forward happily to life together as peasants. Our life together has been a joy to me in spite of failings and faults on my own side.

. . . Thanks to the vigorous and sustained efforts both you and the entire connection have made to induce hypochondria into me, you have in some measure succeeded. I have my pulse taken frequently, eat quantities of food, and am generally pampered. I am now nearly normal in weight and feeling definitely better than when I fell ill. . . . Miss MacGeary is still with me but has nothing to do. Don't worry about anything or allow yourself to become ill.

I have at last got a really good A.D.C. He is Borrow—the man who went in with us last time with jaundice and came out with jaundice having been a help to all his party. He is a young lad —a schoolmaster in civilian life I believe.

I like Americans here very much and rely much on them— all but one who normally resides far away.[1] Carton de Wiart[2] is a real friend and will welcome me where he is. I am fond of the Chinese and hope to see something of them before all's over. The P.M. sends me messages of the kindest. . . . I am peaceful and happy in mind and only miss you."

As said already, the last of his convalescence was spent at the Agency at Nowgong. Mr. Trevelyan had met him a year ago during the training before the first expedition. Wingate had called on him one evening to ask for his official help in one of the exercises. Trevelyan had no idea who he was, had heard nothing of his exploits in Palestine or Ethiopia, and was instantly struck by the fierce strength of his personality. Later he and Mrs. Trevelyan made friends with this strange being, and the little relaxation Wingate could enjoy in India during

---

[1] Evidently a reference to General Stilwell.
[2] Sir Adrian Carton de Wiart V.C., K.B.E., C.B., C.M.G., D.S.O. At that time he was special military representative to General Chiang Kai-Shek.

Wingate briefs Air Force officers at Hailakandi. Colonel
Cochran is on the right

Wingate with Lord Louis Mountbatten

The Burma Railway. The track near Mawlu, where White
City was established in the second expedition

Tow ropes are attached to the gliders at Lalaghat before the
fly-in to Broadway

the last two years of his life was mostly spent in their house. He often astonished them, least agreeably when he took them or their children for nerve-testing drives in his jeep, most pleasantly when, against the petty conventions of ordinary conversation, he would without warning give passionate expression to his deepest feelings and ideas, would quote the Bible at great length, pouring out the splendours of the Authorised Version in illustration of some point in argument. Once when he called at the house with Calvert and Cochran, he recited Emily Brontë's " Last Lines " in entirety. Trevelyan said afterwards that extraordinary and sometimes fatiguing as these occasions were, they never struck him as ridiculous or as pieces of exhibitionism. On his side Wingate was drawn towards a family circle where he could find that intellectual refreshment which he needed, and of which army life starves a man.

During these convalescent days in late November Trevelyan noticed among much else two things that were new to him in Wingate's character. One was his humour, a quiet, inner, almost secret humour, expressed most often by a meaning glance and the shadow of a smile accompanying what he said and giving it irresistible comedy. The other was a premonition of early death. Wingate used to say such things as : " I don't know what happens—I can't imagine at all what *can* happen to a man like me in old age," and he often gave the impression that he believed that his right fate was death in battle and that he hoped for this. Trevelyan noted, as Lady Wavell had done, an anxiety not to disobey Matron MacGeary that seemed part affectionate and part fearful. Being near to his training camps he found the temptation to disobey too strong for him sometimes. He would go to his new Headquarters in the hotel at Gwalior for a night. On these occasions he would slip a razor into his pocket and say in an undertone to his host, " Don't tell Miss MacGeary, will you ? " On his return he would have some suitable story about being " unavoidably detained."[1]

It is easy but mistaken to see Wingate as mellowed during the last months of his life. He was not. The evidence of delightful letters home and agreeable behaviour in Viceregal lodge is deceptive. It must not be forgotten that during this time the struggle with G.H.Q. still raged on, Derek Tulloch doing most of the work on the Chindit side, with Wingate only occasionally emerging from convalescence to take a part himself. But he did not emerge to cast oil on troubled waters, but rather to ride a storm. He sometimes hit harder now than at any other time. One occasion can illustrate the character of several. There was much objection in the R.A.F. command to experienced air-trained personnel accompanying the brigades with the purpose of organising

[1] Trevelyan.

the reception of supply drops. In spite of higher agreement on this point, the command offered firm opposition. At length after a particularly bitter and long tussle on the subject Tulloch found himself unable to make further headway, and he reported to Wingate a senior air officer's final conclusion that, as he put it, " fifty R.A.F. men on the ground are fifty R.A.F. men wasted." Wingate, still weak at the time, roused himself from Viceregal lodge and made his way to air head-quarters and to the office of the senior in question. He pointed out that the subject of dispute was a decided matter, and that he was not demanding the seconding of R.A.F. personnel as a favour, but as a right. But there was no yielding, whereupon Wingate addressed the other in some such words as these : " Look here, you are a very able man, and so am I ; we both have plenty of brains and are both likely to go a long way. Are you going to co-operate with me or are you going to oppose me ? For I warn you that if you oppose me it will not be you who will win." The R.A.F. senior declared that his visitor had totally, and entirely, and completely, and laughably misunderstood him. After that he co-operated with Wingate—for a time.[1]

What can appear as a mellowed character in Wingate is in part a misreading of the fact that he now knew how to suit his conduct to the requirements of the time. As the year entered its last weeks, his circumstances, in spite of continual obstruction, remained extremely favourable to what he wanted to do. The trend of policy was essentially with him. In one of his personal telegrams to him Mr. Churchill went so far as to say : " All affairs in which you are interested are going very well here and January will be quite soon enough for you personally for full work."

In the event the affairs in which Wingate was interested fell apart in December. If he had protracted his convalescence till January he would have been too late.

[1] Tulloch Essay.

CHAPTER XXI

MOUNTING THE OPERATION

By December the organisation of Special Force was complete. In outline it was as follows: The original 77 Brigade was under the command of Michael Calvert. Of all the brigades it contained the largest nucleus of the original Chindits, though these were now a small minority, for relatively few men could undertake the training, let alone the type of operation, twice. The Burma Rifles were the principal element in this minority and as before they were distributed through different units. The main components of 77 brigade were drawn from battalions of the King's Regiment, the Lancashire Fusiliers, the South Staffords, and two battalions of the 4th and 9th Gurkha Rifles. One of the officers was Archie Wavell, the son of the Field-Marshal. He had never forgotten his meeting with the S.N.S. leader in a Palestine hospital, and had volunteered for Chindit service soon after Wingate's return to India.

There was among the smaller components of 77 Brigade one very peculiar one. In Hong Kong before the war Calvert had helped to raise a species of Home Guard called the Hong Kong Volunteers. A hundred of these men, Chinese, British and Portuguese, had found their way to India. They were put into a camp on arrival and, as is apt to happen to men in a time of mass migration, left to rot there in idleness. Their patriotism ignored, they were feeling " disconsolate and forgotten," till Calvert found them at Deolali near Bombay. He called a meeting and asked them " if they would like to join him and go into action." The answer was a shout of " Yes."[1]

111 Brigade had the largest component of Gurkhas, amounting to two battalions. This was a logical consequence of their commander, William Lentaigne, being himself a distinguished Gurkha officer. The brigade had besides a battalion of the King's Own Royal Regiment, and a battalion of the Cameronians.

The men of 70 Division were formed into three brigades. Bernard Fergusson, as said, was given command of one of these. It was known as the 16th Indian Infantry Brigade, and the main components were the 1st Battalion of the Queen's Royal Regiment, the 2nd Battalion of the

[1] Calvert.

483

Leicestershire Regiment, 51/69 Field Regiment of the Royal Artillery, and the 45th Reconnaissance Regiment of the Royal Armoured Corps.[1] The two other brigades of the division were known by the numbers 14 and 23. The former was commanded by Brigadier Thomas Brodie and the chief components were the 1st Battalion of the Bedfordshire and Hertfordshire Regiment, the 7th Battalion of the Leicestershire Regiment, the 2nd Battalion of the Black Watch, and the 2nd Battalion of the York and Lancaster Regiment. The 23rd Brigade was commanded by Brigadier Lawrence Perowne. The main components were the 2nd Battalion of the Duke of Wellington's Regiment, the 4th Battalion of the Border Regiment, and the 1st Battalion of the Essex Regiment.[2]

On the 4th of November the 3rd West African Infantry Brigade arrived in India. They joined Special Force in the Central Provinces on the 16th. Their principal components were the 6th, 7th and 12th Battalions of the Nigeria Regiment, and they were commanded by Brigadier Gillmore. This was the only formation of Special Force into which none of the Burma Rifles was drafted. There was also an American brigade described as 5307th Provisional Unit, which arrived in India in November and was commanded in the later stages of its training in the Central Provinces by Brigadier-General Joseph H. Cranston. Before the expedition, however, the unit was transferred from Wingate's command to that of Stilwell, where it became known as " Merril's Marauders." Its adventures lie outside Wingate's story. With the addition of Force Headquarters, and the large quantity of attached troops, Special Force (without the American brigade) numbered a little less than twenty-three thousand.

The training was on the familiar pattern of the previous year ; toil, hardship and specialisation, heightened now by a degree of professionalism from the experience of the first expedition. Three sentences in Calvert's book tell much about the character of gruelling weeks. " There followed long arduous training in marching, watermanship, mules, air supply, jungle shooting, air support with live bombs, digging, column marching, column bivouac, patrols, Royal Engineer Signal exercises, medical and veterinary tests. . . . Then came . . . talks and new plans, our introduction to Merril's Marauders, and Cochran's new Air Commando, glider training and airfield construction, the

[1] *The Wild Green Earth* by Bernard Fergusson referred to subsequently as Fergusson II.

[2] The brigades kept their original numbers from 70 Div. In the original re-organisation the brigades were of 3 battalion strength. This was contested by Wingate and the brigades increased to 4 battalion strength. The Director of Ordnance Services in India insisted on withdrawing artillery from the Division. Wingate contested this also but without success and (surprisingly enough) without rancour. (Tulloch II.) There were two transfers of battalions from their original brigades : 2 King's Own from 16 bde to 111 bde and 1.S. Staffords from 23 bde to 77 bde.

receipt of new weapons and equipment and its adaptation to our needs —all this before the final fifteen days' test under the eye of Wingate. Then away from the jungle for a week, to the trams and bright lights of Bombay."

Among the anomalies of this anomalous force one of the most remarkable was the American Air Commando. The manner in which it had been raised, and the fact that it was designed for Long Range Penetration work gave it the appearance of being a private air force under Wingate's command.[1] This was not so. The Commando had orders to operate "in support" of Long Range Penetration, but throughout it was under U.S.A.A.F. control and administration, and Wingate had no authority to command it in any way. As a further complication this small air force was under the immediate orders of joint commanders of equal rank, Colonels Philip Cochran and John Alison. All air-ground operations had to be determined by committee. Surprisingly enough this cumbersome arrangement worked smoothly,[2] and Wingate, Cochran and Alison acted in such close accord that the impression of a private air force was continually heightened. But for all that the Americans never abdicated their independence and there was to be one, but only one occasion, when Cochran rebelled against Wingate's disregard of his right to be consulted. He and Alison arrived in India in the second week of November.

Here is another point in the story on which legend has fastened. It has been represented that the two Americans found Wingate broken in body by illness, and broken in mind both by the shattering of his hopes at the hands of G.H.Q. opposition, and drastic changes in policy ; and the story goes on that Cochran and Alison roused him to his accustomed energy and determination by telling him that the new air unit contained gliders. At their utterance of the word "gliders," it is said, the old fire was rekindled in his soldierly breast.[3] But the event was more matter-of-fact. For one thing there was no need of rekindling for in November Wingate's prospects stood at their highest.

What happened was as follows. He had no professional knowledge of air matters and (a thing to surprise the student of his character), he had left all detail as to the composition of Number 1 Air Commando to Cochran. When the latter and Alison met Wingate in Delhi, they told him that they had included a certain number of gliders in the aircraft they had assembled for long range penetration purposes. The evidence shows that Wingate needed some persuasion regarding the practical value of the gliders, but was won round, and the moment of

[1] Strangely enough Sir William Slim falls into this mistake in his book. " 3 Indian Division had the unique luxury of its own air force." Slim, p. 217.
[2] Tulloch. A letter to the writer.   [3] Vide Thomas and *Gideon Goes To War*.

conversion can be dated with precision from a piece of correspondence. It so happened that General Stilwell was in Delhi on the 17th of November. Wingate met him at lunch at Mountbatten's house and they discussed Chindit aircraft needs in the proposed operation of flying a brigade to Yunnan. The plan raised a matter of controversy with Stilwell because, for this brigade flight, Wingate considered that he would, in addition to Number 1 Commando, need the use of aircraft normally employed in flying supplies to China over the big mountain barrier, known as " the hump," on the north-eastern frontier of Assam. Wingate evidently made this point to Stilwell. The latter is certain to have contested it because any diminution of supplies to China tended to complicate his own continually difficult position. Then by the evening of the 17th Wingate had changed his mind as a result of a talk with Cochran. He wrote to Stilwell as follows :

" Since our talk after lunch, I have had a good discussion with Colonel Cochran. . . . He has thrown a lot of fresh light on the problem of how to get the British Brigade into the Kachin Hills ; and I believe that . . . we can fly in the great bulk of this Brigade to a landing ground not far from the Shweli where it will be able to start operations at once on the Bhamo lines of communication *without having to call upon your over the hump aircraft*.[1] In addition, I suggest it will be necessary to fly in a token force, which can be kept to the minimum, to contact the Chinese and come in from the east. What it amounts to is that we need not put the strain on your Air Forces that I was suggesting this afternoon, but can, I believe, get it down to a fraction of this.

" I thought I would let you know this before you went back to China, the main point being that it seems if we get the full value out of the gliders, it will pay us best to put the Forces down in the area (east of the Shweli loop) rather than fly the whole lot to Paoshan to march them back to that area. Again, it will solve various problems of supply, and thus ease your problem."

This letter and Cochran's advocacy which caused it to be written are the origin of the melodramatic story of Wingate being roused from despondency by thoughts of gliders. The truth is that he was anxious to preserve his good relations with the American armed forces, and Cochran showed him a way to do so.

All the same, the glider legend should not be completely dismissed. Wingate's conversion to belief in this means of transport did result in an enormous change in his strategical ideas as to the right use of long range penetration groups, so great as to provide him with the means of overcoming his most intractable problems. But all that came later.

The fifteen-day exercise to which Calvert refers in his book was the

[1] Underlined in the original.

first one in which the new Chindits acted as a whole. It was preceded by stormy protests by Wingate against his faithful supporter General Wilcox. Central Command had evidently taken it for granted that Wingate would not be able to return to active duty before January, and on this assumption they set an exercise which they called "Wasp." Wingate examined the details in the last week of November, and found them unsatisfactory, but when he moved to substitute an exercise of his own, to be called "Thursday," he found to his anger that Central Command were unwilling to undertake the labour of fresh organisation, and attempted to assert their right to "Wasp." There followed an explosion from Special Force Headquarters addressed to General Giffard, and containing thunderous denunciation of General Wilcox and his staff, such as disposes of any lingering notion of a mellowing Wingate.[1] He got his way and his own exercise was used.

Pressed for time and exasperated by his long absence from active command, Wingate returned to work in something of the spirit of "a roaring lion . . . seeking whom he may devour." Matron MacGeary returned to Assam and with her went an influence of restraint. Derek Tulloch, drawing on memories still fresh, described Wingate as he was in late 1943 :

" The strain of trying to mount this operation with so little time tended to make him difficult. The air was full of imperious orders which had to be obeyed immediately and forthwith. He often asked the impossible, but frequently Neville Marks, his chief " Q " officer, managed to produce it. . . . Some of the staff got really frightened of him during this period and I told him so. He frankly did not believe me but agreed to try to get to know them better. The following day he visited every officer and every clerk in that huge H.Q. and had a word with each of them. He also addressed all the men in the front garden. A short address, and he rather barked at them, and they listened with respect but also with trepidation.

" He had the most shattering effect on nervous officers . . . he had no idea of the power of his personality over his juniors. One of our G.3s was foolish enough to pass the General's door on the way to tea. The General had just read a letter which enraged him and he could not get hold of me. He called this officer in, made him read the offending letter and then told him to take it away and see that it did not occur again. The G.3 came out feeling years older and gave up passing that dreaded door again. He was so frightened that he did not even dare say that the letter had nothing to do with his department. These spasms of temper were over as soon as they began."

When the exercise was finished Wingate arranged for all the officers

[1] Letter to Giffard of 29.11.43. W.P.I. and New Delhi Archives.

to meet for criticism and discussion in the cinema at Gwalior. It was a remarkable occasion. As his state of health had not allowed him to take much part in the exercise, he gave the meeting to Lentaigne. The latter began a methodical, well-reasoned but not inspiring commentary and before he had proceeded very far the attention of the audience was in danger of wandering. Wingate was with Lentaigne on the stage, and decided that this was not what was wanted. He got up and, with much courtesy, said that he would prefer to take the meeting himself. He then spoke for over an hour, examining every phase of the manœuvres, where they had succeeded, where they had shown mistakes, and throughout imparting anew to his audience his own ardent conviction that in long range penetration technique alone lay the secret of victory. Derek Tulloch declared that this was one of Wingate's most astonishing performances. There is no record of what was said because Wingate spoke without notes.[1] He had the confidence of assured success. He was still greatly in the ascendant. He did not know, and it seems that he was never perfectly to know of the great political changes that, about this time, undid half the work of Quebec.

During the late autumn of 1943 the Allied leaders held two conferences at which decisions were taken which affected the whole strategical plan in the Burma theatre. The first of these meetings was held in Cairo in late November and was called "Sextant." Generalissimo Chiang Kai-Shek met President Roosevelt and Mr. Churchill. In so far as Eastern affairs were concerned Sextant was a continuation of Quadrant, and was held in an atmosphere of some urgency because, during October, the Japanese had embarked on a forward policy on the Chindwin. They were reinforcing from Homalin to the southward on a 140-mile front, and in the south had had some success, seizing Fort White, and threatening Tiddim in the Chin Hills. Under these circumstances strategical discussion in Cairo was largely dominated by Mr. Churchill's proposal for amphibious assault. This plan had never been to the liking of Sir Alan Brooke and had by now been reduced to more modest dimensions : the seizure of North Sumatra was no longer contemplated, and the assault was to be confined to the Andaman Islands. The modified plan was called "Buccaneer." Sir Alan Brooke would have liked to have done with the thing altogether, but there was a complication. President Roosevelt was even more enthusiastic for this plan than Mr. Churchill, and he pressed it on the Generalissimo. The latter found in it the encouragement he had long sought from

[1] Tulloch Essay and a communication.

his allies, and Sextant concluded on the 26th of November with a decision to wage the war in the Burma theatre on a seven-point strategical programme. These in brief were the seven points :

1. The capture of the Andaman Islands.
2. An advance by 15 Corps on the Arakan front.
3. An advance by 4 Corps on the Central front.
4. An advance to Myitkyina and Mogaung by the Chinese-American force under Stilwell.
5. An advance by Yokeforce to Bhamo and Lashio.
6. A long range penetration by Special Force under Wingate.
7. The capture of Indaw by 50 Indian Parachute Brigade to be followed by the fly-in of 26 Indian Division.[1]

These operations, especially if undertaken simultaneously, looked as though they could result in the speedy reconquest of Upper Burma leading to the reconquest of the whole country after the 1944 monsoon. Chiang Kai-Shek made it clear that his own rôle in this programme depended on "Buccaneer." No one in Cairo saw any excessive difficulty in such a condition. The Generalissimo returned to China, Mountbatten to India, both in a state of high optimism. The President and the Prime Minister went to Tehran on the 27th. For the moment everyone seems to have reckoned without Stalin.

The Tehran conference was one of the most discordant of the whole war. President Roosevelt was anxious to cultivate Russian friendship even at some expense to the Anglo-American alliance, as was his custom, and Stalin was quick to notice Anglo-American differences and, by prizing the alliance apart, to get things going his way. The Russians were doubtful (as the Americans had been at Quebec), of British determination to undertake a full-scale attack across the English Channel, and to open an adequately wide-scale second front in operation "Overlord." There was much suspicion in Russia (to some extent shared by Americans) as to the wisdom or sincerity of the British system of dispersed attack. There had arisen a conflict of strategical opinion very similar to that between the "Westerners" and "Easterners" of the First World War. What needs to be recorded of the Tehran conference here is that Mr. Churchill preserved harmony by agreeing to so great a concentration of force in operation "Overlord" as denied essential requirements to the amphibious operation "Buccaneer" against the Japanese in the Andaman Islands. In exchange Stalin promised to enter the war against Japan—once he was satisfied as to the second front on the European mainland. By this arrangement the Burma theatre sank back into a third place.

[1] Churchill VI. Slim. Information obtained at the War Office.

The President and the Prime Minister returned from Tehran by way of Cairo. It was there that the President, at Mr. Churchill's persuasion, finally agreed to the cancellation of " Buccaneer." He does not seem to have recognised that he had made the cancellation inevitable. He agreed reluctantly. The Generalissimo was told by telegram on the 14th of December. His response to this news was expectable : he considered that he had been betrayed and in turn cancelled the advance of Yokeforce from Yunnan into Burma. He was offered another auxiliary operation in place of " Buccaneer ": an amphibious attack on Arakan. He remained obdurate. In London at the end of December, the Chiefs of Staff, seeing that no proposals for amphibious operations in place of " Buccaneer " could satisfy the Generalissimo, withdrew all landing craft from the Far Eastern theatre, for use in the West. The forward move on the Chindwin by the Japanese suggested a defensive policy to the Army in Assam, and after the withdrawal of landing craft the aggressive plans determined at Trident and Quadrant were reduced to a limited advance in Arakan, and advances down the Tiddim road and the Kabaw valley with the modest objective of establishing a firm front on the Chindwin. Hopes for the reconquest of Burma in 1944 were at an end.[1]

So far as Wingate was concerned these changes of plan removed in large part the rôle of his force. It was now arguable by his opponents that without the accompanying operations and the promised Chinese advance, his long range penetration effort, unsupported by any main army advance, would be a purposeless waste. Against such reasoning he could only have contended with the greatest difficulty, and in the course of the conflict he might have lost allies and been forced to accept defeat by the logic of events. What saved him in part was the very curious fact, for which there is recurrent evidence, that the decisions of Tehran were never communicated in a definitive shape even to the principals in the Far Eastern theatre. The events in fact were lacking in logic : the cancellation of " Buccaneer " was known to everyone, but not what the cancellation implied. This want of information, which Wingate shared with his opponents, kept the debate on uncertain ground over which he found his way skilfully. But this is not to suggest that his situation was not manifestly and radically weakened by what had happened. At the end of December he was as near to failure as at any time. How he avoided that failure nevertheless is the main subject of the last episode of his life.

In the world of the several headquarters and the planning com-

[1] Churchill VI. Slim. *The Stilwell Papers*. Information obtained at the War Office.

mittees in India, the buoyant hopes that Lord Louis Mountbatten had brought from Quebec were now seen to have been illusory, and with failing prospects tempers shortened. Hostility towards Wingate revived and found its usual outlet in obstruction. By the end of December he had less than a month before the beginning of his operation,[1] yet he was still without essential supplies. He had been promised mules and he was still waiting for them. His operations depended on air co-operation and he was still without supply-dropping aircraft, and the December exercise was carried out without a single aircraft although the Indian Parachute Brigade were exercising at the same time with sixty or seventy. The Parachute troops were to act as auxiliaries to the Chindits and yet the auxiliaries were being given facilities denied to the main body. He was still without the transport aircraft promised him at Quebec. Not one item of the equipment ordered in Washington and London had arrived. " It is a fact," he wrote to Mountbatten, " that Special Force is proposing to enter the theatre with the weapons of the last war, and that most of the lessons learned in the campaign of last spring have been ignored."[2]

On the 28th of December Mountbatten made a vigorous effort to restore the optimism of the post-Cairo days. Clearly influenced by discussion with Wingate, he circulated a minute to his staff with a copy to Wingate and General Giffard, Commander-in-Chief 11 Army Group in Assam. He evidently intended to provoke discussion of a con-structive kind in the hope that there would emerge a full alternative to the abandoned "grand design" which had depended on "Buccaneer." Among his suggestions was one to send Wingate as a special emissary to the Generalissimo with the object of pressing on him again the plan for a Chindit brigade to join Yokeforce ; he evidently hoped thereby to induce a Chinese advance despite Chiang Kai-Shek's angry cancellation. He proposed to strengthen Stilwell's force with a fully trained Chindit brigade,[3] and he put forward Wingate's idea of garrisoning airfields and kindred nodal points. " I wish to make it quite clear," he wrote, " that I have absolutely no intention of allowing the operations in northern Burma to fade away on account of the abandonment of ' Buccaneer.' " He asked that Wingate should be consulted on his propositions.

The response from 11 Army Group to this call to action was not encouraging. The minute did not accord with a prevalent taste for cold water, and a growing feeling that the day of the Chindits was over. The proposal to attempt a revival, by means of a Wingate mission, of

---

[1] Counting this from the first movement from the North by 16 Brigade under Fergusson.
[2] Draft letter (not sent) from Wingate to S.A.C. (27.12.43). W.P.I. Its contents were discussed with the S.A.C. Tulloch.
[3] " Merril's Marauders " had not yet left Wingate's for Stilwell's command.

the plan for a Chinese advance from Yunnan seems to have been scotched early on. It was not referred to in the answer which was dated 4th of January, and for the rest, the idea of garrisoning places captured by the Chindits was shown to be impractical in a lengthy parade of discouraging arguments. Wingate himself was not once mentioned in the course of this " Aide-Memoire."

On the 5th of January Wingate decided that he must stake everything if his plans were to survive at all. He wrote two memoranda on this day, one to Mountbatten, the other to 11 Army Group. The first of these was in the form of criticism of the Aide-Memoire. He dealt with debating skill, and in detail, with the many objections raised against Mountbatten's forward policy. The last sentence is all that needs to be recalled : " To sum up, 11 Army Group is opposed to taking any of the action proposed by the Supreme Commander to support L.R.P. operations, and no such action is in fact being taken."

The second memorandum, addressed to 11 Army Group, involved the greater risk to Wingate. It took the form of " Considerations affecting the employment of L.R.P. Forces Spring 1944 " and was sent with a request that it should be forwarded to the Supreme Commander. " In view of the fact," Wingate wrote in this covering note, " that the plan submitted by me at Quebec has now been abandoned, and that the Force under my command is at the moment committed to an operation which is not one for which it was designed, I desire to place on permanent record, both for my own protection and for the benefit of the Army, the reasons why the operation proposed by me has become impossible."

In the main paper he pointed out that the original long-range penetration plan decided at Quadrant had been in no way dependent on an accompanying amphibious operation, so that the cancellation of " Buccaneer " could not be held as a valid reason for second thoughts about the Chindits. The truth, he said, was that there had never been any intention of implementing the Chindit plan, and he added that he had " watched the process as it occurred." Moving to larger questions, he blamed 11 Army Group for abandoning a forward policy, showing how this course was not only against Quadrant directives but unwarrantably removed an essential condition from the agreed Chindit operation.[1] He inveighed against the amount of noncombatant troops maintained on the Assam front. Returning to his own affairs he went into a detailed description of his supply difficulties and what he called " the

[1] At this point in his memorandum Wingate showed misinformation. He argued that an amphibious operation in Arakan ought not to take away from an offensive in Upper Burma, unaware that the amphibious operation subsequent to Buccaneer, " Pigstick," had been cancelled some days before.

enormity of the withholding of equipment." He told how Agartala had been selected as the Chindit air base, with G.H.Q. agreement, but how no instructions to this effect had gone to the air authorities in Assam so that the base was not yet in working order. (The base was not to be ready even when operations began.)[1] He concluded by saying that unless he could be assured of a radical change of attitude by those who implemented policy, he wished to return to regimental duty, and resign his post.

The danger of offering resignation is that it may be accepted. But at the time he wrote this formidable memorandum, Wingate was in a position that was still strong enough, though only just strong enough, to allow him to threaten the fatal step with safety. Here again he was helped by the illogicality of events. For though he had become a continual occasion of discord among his countrymen, he still, and in defiance of his own nature, remained a point of agreement between the British and Americans, and although there were few Americans in the Burma theatre, these were at the moment playing a very important part. Stilwell and Major-General Frank Dorn (the head of the American Military Mission in Chungking) were, with some faint hope of success, still urging the Generalissimo to sanction the advance of Yokeforce after all.[2] To have disbanded the Chindits, the only remaining military allurement to Chiang Kai-Shek, would have been great folly in the midst of these negotiations. There was also Wingate's exasperating right of direct access to the Prime Minister, and the latter was known to have a way of taking Wingate's side.

These circumstances, liable to change, were quite enough to make it impolitic for Wingate's resignation to be accepted, and the storm had no alternative but to blow itself out—for the time being. Lord Louis Mountbatten exerted his authority and his charm with his customary adroitness, and peace was patched up between the contending parties—a peace that was broken within a week.

The breach occurred over a complicated technical question concerning wireless equipment. The R.A.F. asserted that there were no portable sets in India capable of exchanging messages with the Very High Frequency sets recently introduced into R.A.F. aircraft. Special Force questioned the truth of this and the matter was referred to the long-tried Supreme Commander. On the day of the meeting Wingate was represented by Tulloch who insisted that he had himself experimented with a portable set capable of V.H.F. communication, while the other side said this was impossible. An argument began and was brought to a sudden stop by the chairman striking the table. Mount-

[1] Tulloch II.   [2] The Stilwell Papers.

batten, who was growing restless, said, "Someone here is talking nonsense." In the ensuing silence he went over to a telephone, called his signals officer, gave him the facts as stated by both sides and told him to find out which version of them was true. The meeting turned awkwardly to other matters until the telephone rang five minutes later. Mountbatten took the call, spoke for a minute or so, and then replaced the receiver (as later remembered) with some violence. He informed the meeting that Tulloch had given the correct version. He then said : "Wingate has been promised certain things and while I am here I will see that he gets them. I want no more argument on the subject. His demands must be met so that his first three brigades can go in properly equipped. When that is done we can discuss things further."[1] After that scene the restored peace was not easier than the one that had been broken.

It is important in tracing the last stormy weeks of Wingate's life to avoid giving an impression that he was opposed by jealousy, malice and folly alone, as he sometimes believed. The opponents were ruthless and sometimes unscrupulous, but in most cases this was because they acted under an appalled conviction that the decision for a second Chindit expedition was a colossal military blunder which must be prevented at all costs, and when the cancellations of December gradually and increasingly made their effect, more and more people, including some of Wingate's admirers, came to share that opinion. Before long discontent with the weakened *raison d'être* of the force began to spread even to the Chindits themselves. On the 16th of January, Fergusson told Wingate that he felt bound to offer his resignation because, having learned that there was to be no offensive from Yunnan, and no adequate advance from 4 Corps in support of the penetration, he could not take the responsibility of leading his men, to whom he had promised better things, into a repetition of the ordeals of a year ago.

Wingate, not without anger, argued Fergusson into withdrawing his resignation,[2] and it should be stressed that this was no pied-piper act on the part of the spellbinder. For on the same day as Fergusson offered his resignation, Wingate submitted a paper from his headquarters to the Supreme Commander in which he outlined a new Chindit policy to meet the new circumstances. This was the beginning of the last constructive action of his life, and in it is the real answer to his critics. The inventive originality of his mind, though sometimes wayward when left to itself, never quailed before the challenge of

---

[1] Note for S.A.C. by Wingate. W.P.I. Tulloch II and a communication.

[2] Wingate-Fergusson-Tulloch correspondence, W.P.I., and a communication from Fergusson.

events in which he was involved. Never in his life did he meet a challenge with more certitude than now.

Like most of the other military ideas which gave him his reputation, the one by which he restored the Chindits to a practical rôle was extremely simple. It probably had one origin in his discarded 1943 plan to establish in the forests of the Bambwe Taung a defended place to which columns could retire for safety and from which they could set out on raids. It may have had another origin in Mr. Amery's curious memorandum of July to Mr. Churchill. Its main origin was in his own combination of commonsense calculation with inventive imagination. His present plan was to establish defended areas, as it were pockets of reclaimed land wherever his brigades were operating. Their entry into Burma would be made by aircraft and gliders, and the brigade positions would be made in two phases occupying two successive nights and one day. First a party of two columns would seize an unoccupied tract including paddy fields to serve as a landing strip ; secondly, the rest of the brigade would be brought on to the landing strip. Within thirty-six hours a brigade would be in battle formation in the middle of enemy country, ready for assault on enemy installations, concentrations, and lines of communications. The plan meant this : that in the absence of an enemy offensive the long range penetration groups would provide their own system of support and refuge. Given a system of relief, they could conduct an offensive on their own.

The proposal was formidable in itself, but Wingate found the wherewithal to make it irresistible. In his appreciation to Mountbatten of the 16th, he submitted cogent evidence that the Japanese move forward was the preparatory stage of an offensive against Assam. He went on to argue that the Chindits, assured of adequate security by his new plan, could operate with their greatest effect during an enemy offensive, while the Japanese Army was continually compelled to use the long bad vulnerable roads of Burma. He warned that the offensive would be strong and damaging and that before it was overcome 11 Army Group might have to face the temporary loss of all Manipur. If Wingate was not the first, (and he may have been), to give warning of the coming invasion, he was certainly among the first, and certainly among the most accurate. " The otter " had never been behindhand in drawing correct and unexpected conclusions.

The announcement of the new Chindit policy was coupled with some demands. He asked for the Supreme Commander's support in a request that the Dakotas then training with the Indian Parachute Brigade should instead train with his own men at Silchar ; that additional gliders should be " obtained . . . to a temporary and provisional total of 500 "; that towing gear sufficient for a hundred towing aircraft should be provided, and that six-pounder anti-tank guns should be allotted for positional defence. He proposed that 111 Brigade and 77 Brigade should enter Burma by glider operation, while 16 Brigade should enter by land from the Stilwell front based on Ledo. He asked Mountbatten to support his plan in the event of initial disaster and the loss of Manipur. He also asked that four battalions should be set aside from 11 Army Group for garrison duty.[1] Mountbatten gave Wingate the support he asked for and told him to discuss the matter with the authorities in Assam.

Sir William Slim had command of the 14th Army, a post for which, it will be remembered, Mr. Churchill had once recommended Wingate, a fact not then known to either of the two generals. As things were now, Slim was to be Wingate's commander during whatever Chindit operations were authorised for 1944. They had first met three years before, when Wingate commanded Gideon Force, and Slim the 10th Indian Infantry Brigade in the army of General Platt. The two men had not seen East African events with the same eyes. While Wingate had regarded the Ethiopian cause as sacred, Slim had looked on the campaign as part of the day's work, and remembering it, fourteen years after, he referred jocosely to Wingate and the patriots as "he with his Abyssinian partisans, whom in those days we impolitely called Shiftas or brigands." They were not made for each other. Their relations were to be strained and variable.

Slim in early 1944 occupied a position in the British Army that was somewhat analogous to that of Wavell in 1940, for as Wavell had impressed his character on the forlorn army of the Nile and restored it to health and vigour, so had Slim put heart anew into the army on the Burman frontier. Like Wavell he could arouse feelings of personal affection in every soldier under his command. He was to declare himself an admirer of Wingate, but the criticism with which he admixed his admiration was sometimes so harsh as to seem positively biased, as when he described the great services to morale rendered by the first Chindit expedition as "phoney propaganda."[2] Before Slim's appointment to 14th Army he and Wingate met several times in Delhi on easy terms; when Slim became Wingate's commander he was inevitably on less easy terms with this most intractable of subordinates. Early on in their official relationship Slim made it clear that he objected to Wingate availing himself of his right to communicate directly with the Prime Minister, except with his agreement, and though Wingate protested against this curtailment of his privilege, (which he had never abused), he could not but acknowledge that what Slim asked for was

[1] Appreciation (16.1.44). W.P.I.   [2] Slim.

reasonable.[1] By his insistence on the point Slim achieved what many in G.H.Q. had vainly wanted, but this did not mean that Slim was to be reckoned with the opposition. He was a man of far too educated and broad a mind to want to be rid of a subordinate of such fire, skill, and luck. His admiration was genuine ; so was his antipathy ; he showed himself ambivalent on the subject of Wingate both during these events and in his record of them. For that reason it is difficult to see this enigmatic figure as the plain man he depicted in his autobiographical memoirs of the Far Eastern war.

In accordance with Mountbatten's orders, Wingate went to meet Slim at Ranchi on the 18th of January. By now Wingate's new Chindit plan was complete in outline, but it still wanted details, and one detail took on great importance in his mind : he wanted a description, a name for his project such as would seize the imagination. The name came late in his deliberations, and thus probably at the end of a long search. What he found bore the mark of Lodolf. He decided that the new system should be known as that of " The Stronghold."

The Army Commander did not arrive in Ranchi till the morning of the 19th when he and Wingate went into conference for forty minutes. The meeting was highly successful. Wingate not only succeeded in persuading Slim of the merits of his new plan but obtained his collaboration : the Army Commander pointed out that 4 Corps had a system of defence, called the " floater model," in which every garrisoned base was served by a satellite mobile column trained to operate against the rear of an attacking enemy formation, and he recommended Wingate to study this method and incorporate it in his new system. Wingate did so.[2] As regards the necessary aircraft for the operation they disagreed on the best source of supply. Slim believed that these were best deducted from the hump traffic, Wingate that they should come from the Indian Parachute Brigade,[3] but there was no difference on the need to find the aircraft. Lastly, Slim agreed to set aside four battalions from 26 Division to garrison strongholds.[4] It appears from what was recorded at the time that Wingate was so relieved

[1] Information obtained at the War Office. Sir William Slim gives a detailed account of how the dispute was resolved in a manner very humiliating to Wingate at a private interview between them.

[2] Slim. In a sarcastic passage the Field-Marshal suggests in his book that Wingate claimed the idea as his own invention, but references to the floater columns in his Training Note 8 do not read in this sense.

[3] Wingate made many references to the uselessness of parachute troops in his last papers. Here he certainly generalised excessively from the particular, but experience in Europe showed that long range parachute operations were only feasible in places where the local population were armed and prepared for active co-operation. In Burma they had no such opening.

[4] W.P.I.

and rejoiced to find so much of his new plan accepted that he did not look closely at the conditions attaching to agreement. Slim made it clear in his instructions to his Headquarters, and in his report to Mountbatten, that the decision rested exclusively with him when these garrison battalions should be flown in, and whether they should be flown in at all.[1] Wingate reporting to Mountbatten on the 20th wrote as though the matter of the four battalions was settled definitely in his favour, indeed he only mentioned one point of difference which concerned their immediate location : he wanted the battalions to train under him with 77 Brigade, while Slim preferred them to remain where they were at Chittagong. Wingate saw nothing ominous here, and went to Comilla to meet Major-General Lomax the 26th Divisional Commander. He came to a further agreement with Lomax, or so he believed, and then went on a round of visits to acquaint Calvert, Lentaigne, and Fergusson with his new plan and with the glad news of the Army Commander's wholehearted support, especially in the matter of garrisons.[2]

As the time for the operation drew near the brigades had begun to move from the training area in the Central Provinces. 77 Brigade under Calvert were at a place called Hailakandi about fifteen miles across country from Silchar. 111 Brigade under Lentaigne were at Imphal where Wingate had again set up his Headquarters complete with map-room as in the former days.[3] 16 Brigade under Fergusson were in process of moving by train to Ledo, their commander flying ahead of them to General Stilwell's Headquarters which were at a place called Shingbwiyang, a few miles from the Chindwin and technically within Burma. At this time, at the hands of " Security," Special Force received a new title : 3 Indian Division, a description which did not please them and annoyed the Army of India.

A curious and very characteristic incident is remembered of Wingate's visit to 77 Brigade. He inspected the men of the 1st Battalion of the King's Regiment, and then addressed them. They expected, as the men on Casten's track had done, to be told something about forthcoming operations, and like them were told something else. On this occasion Wingate did not take the miracle of Dunkirk as his subject but the remoter events of the battle of Dunbar. He held forth on the character of Cromwell, and how by communicating his own faith to his army he had got the very best out of every man serving under him, so that at Dunbar he snatched victory from defeat, and he went into some details of the action. Most of his audience had no notion that

[1] W.P.I.   [2] Statement by Commander Special Force (25.1.44). W.P.I.
[3] To be scrupulous it should be mentioned that the H.Q. was set up by 4 Corps. " Scoones has . . . built me a Headquarters that compares favourably with Faridkot for comfort." Wingate to S.A.C. (27.1.44).

there had ever been a battle at Dunbar, and many of them had an imperfect notion as to the identity of Oliver Cromwell, yet Wingate succeeded in causing the impression he wanted, as he had done on Casten's track. The men felt their confidence renewed and their imagination stirred, though they might have been hard put to it to say why.[1]

From Imphal, where he saw Lentaigne, he went north to meet Fergusson at Shingbwiyang. Here he was to meet Stilwell also. Since Wingate had come to threaten the volume of hump traffic once more, Fergusson expected that there would be a clash between the two generals. It remains a matter for surprise that there was in fact none. Stilwell was, with the exception only of Wingate, the strangest character in South-East Asia Command. He had much of Wingate's driving inward energy, though apparently quite divorced from Wingate's noble idealism. He was devoured by two great passions at this time, one was to build a road from Ledo to Myitkyina, the other was hatred of the British. By his own candid account Vinegar Joe, as he was commonly known, entertained for British people the kind of feelings that a pious Nazi developed for Jews : a spiritual disapproval informed by acute physical repulsion. For him the British were always limeys. He regarded them as deceitful, effeminate, and extremely dangerous, if for no other reason than because, in his view, they were desirous of laying Imperial hands on the United States and her interests. But this odd sour man had redeeming features. He was a bold, intelligent and courageous leader of soldiers ; he was a superb writer of extreme American prose,[2] and he was capable of overcoming the violent prejudices that warped his judgment. For example, though senior to Sir William Slim he consented on a selfless impulse to serve under him.[3] Mountbatten laboured under the treble disadvantage, in his eyes, of princely blood, a lordly title and an English accent, yet Stilwell acted as his faithful deputy, and even went so far as to vote him " a good egg," though he retracted later. In his relations with Wingate he controlled his prejudices again. Perhaps because so many limeys disliked Wingate, Stilwell found it in himself to be a good colleague to the Chindit commander. Fergusson was present at their meeting at Shingbwiyang for some of the time and described it afterwards : " I sat for ten minutes and discussed our plans with those two very strong characters. Wingate, heavy-browed, broad and powerful ; Stilwell with his steel-rimmed spectacles, tallish, wiry and gaunt. Both had determined faces, with deep furrows about their mouths ; both could display atrocious

---

[1] Jary. An eye-witness account.
[2] His description, reproduced in *The Stilwell Papers*, of Roosevelt announcing the results of Tehran to him in Cairo is a masterpiece of comic writing.
[3] Slim.

manners, and were not prepared to be thwarted by anybody. Both looked like prophets, and both had many of the characteristics of prophets : vision, intolerance, energy, ruthlessness, courage."

Wingate had by now devised a three-brigade plan whose outline was as follows : 77 Brigade was to be flown in to the Kaukkwe valley north-east of Katha where they would establish a stronghold, a block on the Indaw-Myitkyina railway, and a block on the Bhamo-Lashio road ; 111 Brigade was to be flown in to the country south of Pinlebu from where they would establish a stronghold and attack communications to Wuntho and in the Mu valley ; in the meantime 16 Brigade would march overland from the Stilwell front, and after seizing Lonkin, would go on south to establish a stronghold north of Indaw from where they would attack the Bonchaung gorge, the Meza bridge and seize the Indaw airfield. The plan was to establish in the centre of Japanese communications three strongholds near enough for mutual support, and strong enough for constant and strategically damaging raids. With garrison troops assured, the Chindits had come into their own again, so it seemed.

At the end of his round of visits, and after a reconnaissance flight over the interior of Burma to pick out suitable landing grounds, Wingate arrived in Comilla on the 25th of January. He was confronted with a shattering disappointment. The Army Commander had changed his mind. Two days after his conference with Wingate, Slim had told Mountbatten of his agreement, but in terms that raised his own condition of support. From the first he had given his unconditional consent to one battalion for garrison duty, while the other three battalions were to be flown in at the Army Commander's discretion, but after reflection he made the condition that he would only add a brigade to the battalion " if genuine circumstances should appear such as render exploitation by 4 Corps remunerative." This was a new idea of the stronghold plan, or rather an old and discouraging idea revived in a new form : the garrisons were to be provided only if the " follow-up " offensive (already cancelled), should be forthcoming nevertheless. But by the 25th, Slim had changed his mind further, so as to reverse his earlier decision completely. He would now allot no battalions at all from 11 Army Group for stronghold garrisoning, and he proposed instead that the garrisons should be found from the West African Brigade in Special Force. When informed of these latest decisions Wingate saw that he was back at his starting point, back where he had been before he had obtained, or seemed to have obtained, Slim's agreement to what he asked. Once again, for the fourth or fifth time since his return to India, he was at a crisis in his career, and, as he usually did at such moments, he wrote a memorandum.

In detail he traced the course of his negotiation with the Army Commander, and then passionately condemned Slim's revocation of his decision to supply him with garrison troops. He gave one copy of the memorandum to Slim and forwarded another to Mountbatten with a covering letter in which he advised the cancellation of the operation and offered his resignation again. From the tone of the covering letter it seems likely that this time he was not manœuvring and meant exactly what he said; he was fully prepared for his resignation to be accepted. "The commanding British generals," he wrote, "are not at heart for it [the expedition]. . . . Not only has this already prejudiced . . . success . . . but who can tell its deadly effect in the future when at the height of some crisis I shall wish . . . to count on loyal support? It is a change of heart that is required and I cannot change their hearts. I believe that the cancellation of the operation will be disgraceful to our arms, but to court probable disaster might be still more disgraceful. . . . No time remains. I waste two days out of three in presenting unanswerable arguments to which the answer is silence."[1]

The point of view of Sir William Slim must never be lost sight of, if this strange piece of military history is to be understood. He had commanded the last effort to stem Japanese victory in Burma in 1942. He had the fullest experience possible of land war with the Japanese Army, and he had the enthusiastic confidence of his troops. He was conscious through personal experience, in a way Wingate could not be, that the army under his command, and of which Wingate formed a part, could not stand another defeat at Japanese hands without losing all belief in itself, and all ability to master its enemy. Only gradually was that army beginning to understand how to move and fight in this country. By his own admission Slim was determined that in any further engagement with Japanese, his own troops would be in a decisive majority.[2] For the time being, but only for the time being, he was "Maginot-minded," in the jargon of the day. Prejudice has made of Maginot a term of abuse, but it would be inept to blame an Army commander for such mindedness in the circumstances of the Far East theatre in early 1944, and strangely enough Wingate's story suggests Sir William Slim's justification. These are not matters for consideration here. What needs to be remembered here is that though the issue was never stated in such simple terms, Slim stood for a policy of caution and Wingate for one of the utmost audacity.

[1] Wingate to S.A.C. (26.1.44). W.P.I. A brief and entirely different version of the whole of this garrison-episode, in which Slim appears as a forthright strong man and Wingate as a pathetically weak blusterer appears in the Field-Marshal's book, pp. 218-219. The present version follows contemporary documents exclusively.
[2] Slim.

Peace was restored again. This time the olive branch was handled by Sir George Giffard. It was a peace of compromise, as most peaces are, and as usually happens in such cases, the peace was accepted with grumbling. As regards garrisons, Slim agreed to order a Gurkha battalion, complete with its supporting troops and guns, to join 77 Brigade for training in stronghold work. He agreed furthermore to a considerable allotment of artillery for the protection of each stronghold : four twenty-five pounders and six light anti-aircraft pieces, all manned. The rest of the needed garrison force was to be found, in accordance with Slim's recommendation of the 25th, from three battalions of the 3rd West African Brigade. Before consenting to this, the bitterest of the conditions, Wingate protested that such a use of the West African Brigade was to give a normal infantry task to a highly specialised unit and to limit the reserves which would be needed for an extension of the long range penetration. It was made clear to him that there was no intention of extending the Chindits. The second expedition was to be rigorously confined to the six Chindit brigades in existence. In acknowledging his agreement to General Giffard, Wingate made it clear that he accepted because he still hoped that, in the event of great Chindit success, British infantry from other sources would be made over to him for the stronghold garrisons, and he made the same point in reporting the agreement to Mountbatten. The only subject on which the negotiations seem to have gone with relative smoothness was, as before, in the matter of air transport. But the Pax Giffardica was uniquely successful in one important respect. It lasted.[1]

In the course of this January, Wingate had little time for private life, but in common with all men he had something resembling it despite the pressure of business ; despite his exacting command, his burden of overwork, his ceaseless negotiations, his constant and always uncomfortable journeys. On some of these he was accompanied by Calvert who has given a rare picture of him undergoing the ordeals of air travel. " There was an impish humour about everything that he did. When travelling by air, he always considered that he was being done down and not being allowed to take enough luggage. He would therefore invariably place his foot under the weighing machine as his luggage was being weighed. The weighing machines in India used to be the old-fashioned type in those days. He would glare at the weigher-in from under his topee, while sweat, due to the amount of clothes he had put on, poured down from his nose and chin. I used to laugh

---

[1] Wingate to Giffard (26.1.44). Wingate to S.A.C. (27.1.44). W.P.I. In his book Sir William Slim hints that Wingate only agreed because he had been threatened by Slim with court martial in the event of his refusing an order.

helplessly in a corner. My luggage was once overweight, and he gave me a long homily as to how to carry my luggage, finishing up with, 'It is all right as long as we are the only people to do it,' and a hint of a smile."

He corresponded with Matron MacGeary who to the delight of all Chindits had been awarded the M.B.E. in the New Year honours. She was transferred in January from the 19th Casualty Clearing Station to the 18th Indian General Hospital Centre, situated in the same area. Wingate also found time to correspond with the officer whom he had rescued from despair during his voyage from Durban to Glasgow three years before. In the late autumn he had received the joyous news that Lorna was with child. On the 21st of January, while touring his brigades after his encouraging meeting with Slim on the 19th, he wrote to her:

> "Beloved, I have had three letters from you in a bunch—the most recent dated 22-12. It relieved me of some anxiety. I continue to enjoy excellent health. I have just completed a tour with the Godfather.[1] He is a splendid person. Apart from him and a few others my reception generally in British Army circles is that of Pasteur at the hands of French medicos! Not so with the others concerned. I am hopeful of the future but time will show. . . . What a mercy it was that the P.M. recovered and is again on the war path. The difference it makes is very marked.
>
> I sometimes think my typhoid has deprived me of my mental force—that although placid, fat, and happy, I have lost some of the intellectual acuteness and force that I enjoyed before the renewal of my gut. However, I shall not worry too much about that. I spend much of my time in the air. My old dislike of flying is quite gone. I always carry two stenographers about with me but my literary output of late has not been too good. War is I suppose a necessary evil—as is a surgical operation. The drugging of one human being by another,[2] the hideous mutilation by the knife, are in themselves an evil but become good through the motive. Can one fight in war with good motives? If not one ought not to fight. I believe one can. I do not believe in carrying on war with hatred for one's enemy. On the contrary. It is a police operation which has in view the welfare of the criminal as well as of the community protected.
>
> Life would be easier for us if we had a dogma like the aunts.

[1] Lord Louis Mountbatten.
[2] He felt very strongly about drugs. One of Wingate's January orders to Special Force forbids the carrying of opium by columns as a means of currency in Burma. W.P.I.

But while I acknowledge the goodness of Christ and sweetness of His teaching and would be honoured beyond expectation to be described as a christian, yet I do not know the christian dogmas—Christ *is* God, blood redemption, operative only by expressing a belief in the resurrection and doctrine, new birth on this, etc.—to be necessary.

If it is may God guide us to that knowledge.

To-day I met one Zinder, correspondent of *Life* and *Time*. He had just come from Palestine with messages from Moshe and Reuben. What he told me of the infamous search and muster of settlers distressed me. What scoundrels those police are. I hope for a change though I believe we shall see fulfilment of Ha Tikvah. . . .[1]

You did not include the letter from Vera. You spoke of one from Chaim.

God bless you, my dear love, in 1944, and give you a safe delivery. I am very happy to be married to you. May we have many years together. I love you very much. Orde."

[1] The Hope.

CHAPTER XXII

THE SECOND CHINDIT EXPEDITION

NUMBER 16 BRIGADE concentrated in Ledo in the last days of the month and prepared for their march over the Paktai Hills to the Chindwin. An eye-witness account describes this beginning of the second expedition :

" Here we sat (at Ledo) doing nothing in the rain for several days. . . . The mules with their leaders were meanwhile dispatched down the famous Ledo road under construction by American engineers. They had a miserable walk for some seventy miles, in ten to twenty inches of mud. The remainder of us were lucky to do the journey in an American convoy of huge lorries driven by Chinese. . . . The road was a jagged scar torn through dense jungle. Hairpin bends over mountain ranges up to 5,000 feet, descents to semi-built bridges over roaring torrents, and bulldozers and American negroes working everywhere, were an unforgettable sight."[1]

Sir George Giffard came to Ledo to say good-bye to the brigade on the 1st of February, and on the 3rd Wingate joined Fergusson and left with him and the last men to see the beginning of the ascent of the Paktai. A day later they reached the roadhead and together marched the first ten miles of the climb. " We began," recorded Fergusson, " to clamber up a brown, muddy butter-slide. . . . To get up that first hill, less than a mile in length, unimpeded by packs or weapons, took us a full hour. Two or three hundred of my men were working on it, building steps and traverses with bamboo and other wood, felled by its side. . . . (When, two or three days later, the mules began to tackle the hill, they knocked the steps sideways in the violence of their struggles, so that they had to be rebuilt after every two or three animals had passed.) . . . Far below us in the valley, the roar of the traffic on the road continued, and the bulldozers pushed and pulled at the reluctant mountain : deep blue smoke rose from the wet fires of the Chinese labour camps. Sometimes for a few moments the rain lifted, and one saw out across the valley to the towering mountain on the other side. . . . Wingate had seen all he wanted to see. He refused to be daunted by the obvious difficulties which lay ahead. " That's all right," he kept

[1] T. V. Close in *The Queen's Own Royal Regiment Journal*, May, 1947.

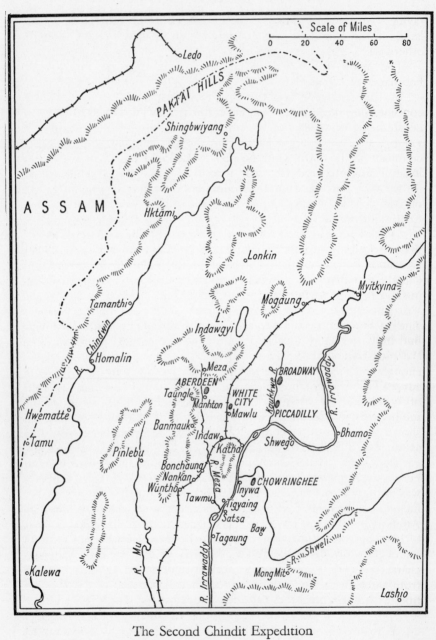

The Second Chindit Expedition

saying, " that's not too bad. You'll manage that all right." . . . Weeks later, at the Chindwin, he confessed that he had in fact thought otherwise.[1]"

The march from Ledo to the Chindwin took the brigade all February.

By the first week of the month 77 Brigade had completed their concentration near Silchar and were going through their final exercise before being flown into their stronghold area in the Kaukkwe valley ; 111 Brigade were concentrated at Imphal with a similar programme to culminate in their stronghold south of the Kaukkwe but of which the location was still unsettled. Both brigades were to be given the signal for the flight into action in the moon period occurring in the first days of March. The other three brigades were still training in the Central Provinces.[2]

On the 4th of February, General Slim and Major-General Strate-mayer issued " Fourteenth Army and Eastern Air Command Combined Operation Instruction 4." This was the official order for the second Chindit expedition. It defined the principal Chindit purpose as the maintenance of communications with China by the infliction of " maximum loss and confusion to enemy forces in North Burma." The operation was to be supported by an advance by Stilwell's army, but from the British Chindwin side no more was envisaged than " demonstrations and enterprises as strong as possible." Strangely enough, (in view of Tehran), hopes were still entertained of an early advance by Yokeforce from Yunnan, and it was laid down that one of Wingate's tasks was to " create a favourable situation " for the fulfilment of that slender hope. The decision that 77 and 111 Brigades should fly in to their stronghold points was endorsed but not specified as to place. The Gurkha battalion was allotted to 77 Brigade for garrison duty, West African battalions to 111 and 16 Brigades. Fergusson's march, now approaching the end of its first week, was also given the benefit of a metrospective order. The instruction included a programme of air action to be conducted by Strategic Air Force.

Among administrative instructions, there were details on the flying out of casualties from strongholds. As said, the harsh side of Wingate's character was never proof against the appalling moral shock he received from the experience of leaving the sick and wounded behind in the first expedition, and he had devised effective measures against a

[1] Fergusson II. On 7.2.44. Wingate reported to Slim : " There is even a possibility that the Brigade may not succeed in getting through along the track chosen. I think, however, that it can be done as a one-time effort, but we must be prepared for delays." W.P.I.

[2] Tulloch II.

repetition of those horrors. It was laid down that the casualty clearing station for the force would be on the Tamu airfield. One of the concluding paragraphs gave the operational code names of which the most important was Thursday. This had been used for Wingate's December exercise and was now used for the expedition itself.

The reader hardly needs to be told that this eminent document did not pass unquestioned by Wingate. Strangely enough, he raised no objection on the military side, and the reason is that after their preliminary differences, he and Slim were now working in close accord.[1] But it was otherwise with some of the air authorities, and the bombing programme seems to have been planned without much reference to the Chindit Commander. His main objection was against the strategic conception and timing. The instruction ordered support bombing around the stronghold areas during the effort to establish them. Wingate preferred a large-scale deception bombing plan before the expedition, to draw Japanese fighters away from the stronghold area by massive raids on Rangoon, Mandalay and Bangkok. Nothing came of this proposal.

Wingate had one other objection to his orders, and that was on the subject of code names. He had protested about them before this and was to repeat his complaints after. A tiresome habit had grown up in headquarters during World War II of attaching facetious names to operations : Staff officers sometimes sought popularity by imitating the front-line soldier's foul-mouthed cynicism about his own exploits. The expedition was given the dull but innocuous code name of " Thursday " which Wingate accepted, but one of the subsidiaries was " Fistula " to which he objected strongly, but in vain. Many people who risked their lives under silly private-joke code names will not think the less of Wingate for raising this relatively small point on the eve of a great and hazardous enterprise.

While these final negotiations were going forward an important event occurred in Arakan. It was two months now since 15 Corps, under Lieutenant-General Sir Philip Christison, had begun their advance southward with the purpose of securing the little port of Maungdaw and its eastwards communications. (This expedition was all that remained of " Culverin " and " Buccaneer.") Throughout January, Christison's three divisions "methodically pounded forward."[2] The Japanese were at the same time reinforcing on this front as along the Chindwin, and their counter-attack was certain. It came on the 1st of February, and although it had been expected it fell on 15 Corps nevertheless with complete surprise. Manifesting their jungle skill as never before, the Japanese had crept round the British positions and

---

[1] Tulloch II. Information obtained at the War Office.   [2] Slim.

on the 1st they attacked 7th Indian Division in the rear and in strength. They succeeded brilliantly in their first objective which was to divide the British forces and wreck their land communications. The situation from the British side was as alarming as any they had faced since 1942. But the outcome was different. The army was filled with a new spirit and had been well trained. They stood their ground wherever this was conceivably possible and relied on air supply. To counter this the Japanese concentrated their Burma air force on the Arakan front and built up a temporary air parity which they quickly lost to superior American and British skill. The first two weeks of February were a time of the utmost anxiety, but thereafter the battle, though slow as all battles were in this part of the world, was unquestionably with the British.[1]

The events of the second Arakan campaign lie outside Wingate's story, but not so the influences which formed them. When assessing imponderables opinion is as good a guide as any, and it is a very widely held opinion among men who were there that two main influences had given the British Army in Assam its new character. One was the vigorous leadership of the Army commander who, despite the toils of his post, had met almost every unit in 14th Army and thrown his own determination and confidence into his troops. The other influence, (which Sir William Slim was later at some pains to minimise), was the example of the first Wingate expedition, and with it a practical grasp of the method and the vital importance in jungle country of maintaining ground forces by parachuted material. If Wingate had had time to recognise and to reflect on what was being achieved here, thanks to him, he might have been easier in his relations with the over-complicated air organisation in Assam. But judging by what he wrote he made no allowance for the strain put on the air forces by the Arakan battle.

During February, against the background of this battle, Wingate continued with his training, his planning, his visits to his troops in their forward stations, and not for one moment did he abate, or did circumstances allow him to abate the long wrestle with authority. He conducted the struggle with his usual pertinacity but not with all his usual skill for, strangely enough, he failed to seize a great advantage which might have proved decisive. In January he had accurately forecast a Japanese offensive, but now that he and others were being proved right by the events in Arakan, he did not assert a logical conclusion. He seems to have entirely forgotten a very significant point in his favour, Sir Claude Auchinleck's assertion in August that a Chindit expansion could only be justified if the long range penetration

[1] Slim.

groups were used " to counter a penetration into Assam by the enemy." It had long been a maxim of Wingate that " the answer to penetration is counter-penetration." He had stressed this anew in January, but now that the actual circumstances of penetration were there, he did not press his point, (so far as anything written shows), nor did he remind the opposition that this point had been authoritatively conceded at the very beginning by themselves. Instead, and possibly influenced anew by Mr. Amery's July memorandum, he gave up his mind to vast projects for advancing by Chindit methods to the eastern shores of Indo-China, and the dimensions of his proposals began to arouse some anxiety in the mind of Mountbatten. At the moment when he needed all the support he could get, he endangered the most valuable support he had. On the 9th the Supreme Commander wrote to him privately in terms which indicate well enough this extraordinary and untimely debate :

" Scoones and Lushington and I," said Mountbatten in the course of a long letter, " had a talk about our discussion with you last night and all three of us agreed that we had been at a complete loss to understand why you were so worried when I told you what the world strategy for the defeat of Japan was likely to be. It was only at the very end that we all three realised that this affected future plans which you presumably hoped one day to put up to me for a continental advance through Burma to Hanoi. . . .

" My directive has always limited me to a recapture of that part of Burma north of the 23rd parallel which was needed to reopen land communications with China. . . .

" You question the justifiability of carrying out your L.R.P.G. operations with the limited objective of aiding Ledo Force to advance. I must know whether you adhere to this view since I should have to represent this to the Chiefs of Staff who are, after all, responsible for world strategy. . . .

" I am sure you had no intention of ' putting me on the spot ' last night but the fact remains that you suggested that your L.R.P.G. operations should not go on unless the present ideas of world strategy were changed by the Chiefs of Staff ! ! "[1]

This courteous rebuke was answered by Wingate in a long letter written the next day, a letter which was less clear as to purpose and subject than most of his writings, but which did convey nevertheless the desired assurance that he was fully prepared to go forward with Thursday. The recipient may have allowed himself a sigh of relief that

[1] S.A.C. to Wingate (9.2.44). W.P.I. In an omitted passage Lord Mountbatten referred to alternative strategies depending on whether or not Culverin was adhered to. This again suggests that no one in S.E.A.C. was fully informed of what had happened at Tehran and the post-Tehran Cairo conference.

the controversy was ended. But if he did so he was mistaken. On the 11th Wingate again wrote to Mountbatten, sending him another long paper, this time on the subject of " the prospect of exploiting Operation Thursday." This curious document reads like a repetition of what had been said at the conversation with Scoones and Lushington. Again Wingate urged vast schemes such as could only be operated after radical changes in the central conduct of the war. " If Operation Thursday is a complete failure," he wrote, " L.R.P. will lapse. If, however, it has any measure of success, another good division now in India should be turned over to L.R.P. . . . The best prospect for the India Command will be to concentrate on progressing to Hanoi and Bangkok by the use of Airborne L.R.P. Brigades. . . . A campaign of this nature would require some 20-25 L.R.P. Brigades in being, a total strength of 100,000 infantry of good calibre." He went on to propose that by means of " an L.R.P. thrust " the army in Assam could not only occupy the Indo-Chinese peninsula but go much farther and join hands with the Americans in the Pacific ; he seriously suggested that a whole army group turned Chindit would " carry a chain of defended airports across China to the coast where it would meet up with the seaborne forces."[1]

The receipt of such papers made it difficult for Mountbatten to defend Wingate against those who said that he saw the Chindits and Thursday as the centre of operations.[2] Why did Wingate send such letters? Nothing in his papers and nothing remembered of what he said gives the answer. It may be that he had returned too early from illness to strenuous physical activity, and that in putting a strain on his health, he had unknowingly damaged his power of judgment; but whether or not that was so the circumstances of February can suggest why he behaved as he did.

This is the suggested explanation. He had let his enthusiasm run away with him when visiting Fergusson in late January. On that occasion he had told the commander of 16 Brigade not only about the Stronghold plan and the garrison battalions, but of his wider hopes. There is strong evidence (though contested by Sir William Slim[3]) that in an enthusiastic or unguarded moment the Army Commander had told Wingate : " If you win your objectives and capture the Indaw area, I'll see you get a follow-up division to hold it—I'll get it some-how." (To do this would mean reverting to the discarded Sextant plan, but in the extraordinarily uncertain state of information among

---

[1] Wingate to S.A.C. (11.2.44). W.P.I.

[2] Lieut.-General Sir Henry Pownall, K.C.B., K.B.E., D.S.O., M.C. A communication. Slim.

[3] The evidence is that of Tulloch. A letter to the writer. Information obtained at the War Office.

men in India as to what had been discarded as a result of Tehran and what had not, there was nothing impossible in such a proposal at that time.) It seems from Fergusson's book that on his visit to Ledo Wingate told him what the Army commander had said, or was believed to have said, and he went further. He confided in Fergusson his expectation that a Chindit success at Indaw would not only compel a reversion to the original plan for 26 Division to fly to Indaw, but would make an expansion of the Chindits to double their size irresistible, and, as was his wont, he put forward what was in his mind with zest and certainty, with all the weight of that massive personality. As a result he caused an impression on the other that the mission of not one but two divisions to Indaw was not merely a matter of hope, but something that had been decided on. In that belief Fergusson led his men. When he came to write about these things later he suggested that Wingate had purposely misled him in order to get the best out of 16 Brigade, but this is to pass a very harsh judgment in the light of single evidence. It is at least possible that Wingate let promise beget optimism so that to his hearer one became confused with the other. It is also likely that when Wingate came back from Ledo to find that he had lost the four battalions that he had definitely been promised, he then strove not only for the restoration of his garrison, but for such an enlargement of the long range penetration force as would ensure the position of his command, and of men to whom he had confided his hopes, beyond all question. It is conceivable that it was to accomplish this purpose, in the face of a sudden and unexpected reverse, that he chose to put forward the most extreme proposals he could devise.

But if such a course led him to write extravagant papers during February, he did not in any way lose his fine and individual touch as a military writer in the field where he excelled. On the 20th he put out his last considerable essay on long range penetration technique. It was called "Training Memorandum Number 8. The Stronghold." It was an astonishing performance, typical of himself and of his origins. It was a skilful adaptation and enlargement of familiar military ideas to the particular needs of the Chindits in the spring of 1944. Among training notes it must be unique. It was manifestly the product of a widely read mind, and yet it was the kind of reading troops enjoy. It appealed to that disposition which makes the learned Sir Walter Scott a best-seller. It could be described as an adaptation of Lodolf to modern war needs. The central term was taken from the book of Zechariah : "Turn ye to the Stronghold, ye prisoners of hope," and this was printed at the beginning. Throughout it maintained this purpose : common-sense statement of a method, alternated with and

Wingate with Colonel Cochran

Wingate and Derek Tulloch

Colonel Alison shows the dramatic photograph of Piccadilly's obstruction to Wingate, Calvert (on Wingate's right) and other officers. Tulloch is on the extreme right

sometimes expressed in terms of romantic exhortation. One quotation can give the spirit of the whole :

" The ideal situation for a Stronghold is the centre of a circle of 30 miles radius of closely wooded and very broken country, only passable to pack transport owing to great natural obstacles, and capable only of slow improvement. This centre should ideally consist of a level upland with a cleared strip for Dakotas, a separate supply-dropping area, taxi-ways to the Stronghold, a neighbouring friendly village or two, and an inexhaustible and uncontaminatable water supply within the Stronghold. Such an area can then be organised in the manner indicated in the accompanying sketches.

" The motto of the Stronghold is ' No Surrender.' "

Bernard Fergusson well described the impact of this remarkable " note " on its audience. " I had known the idea," he wrote in his second book on the Chindits, " when it first burgeoned in Wingate's brain, but in nothing like the clarity in which it now blazed from his triumphant paper. The conception was masterly and daring ; the very word ' Stronghold ' was typical of his taste for the challenging word ; his sense of drama, his unashamed and flaunting use of archaic phrases[1] invested what might have been a drab life with a sense of history. The Army, on the Burma frontier as elsewhere, proclaimed the virtues of a ' firm base '; how much more inspiring and invigorating is a ' sally from a Stronghold ' than an ' offensive movement pivoting on a firm base ' ! . . . The quotation from Zechariah . . . flared across the top of the first page and blazoned itself on my mind ; its comforting rhythm and heavy beat fitted my step along many miles of jungle path."[2]

On the 20th of February, Fergusson was still nine days from the Chindwin. Wingate had underestimated the difficulties of this march. His intention had been for 16 Brigade to cross on the 16th of February, but after seeing the first ten miles of the Paktai he had reported the 25th as the likeliest date. In the event, Fergusson and his men reached the river bank on the last day of the month. The crossing was very different from that at Tonhe the year before. Although there were some breakdowns in the time schedule of this air-ground operation, the plan worked well. In Fergusson's words the 1944 crossing was " a twentieth century performance, whereas the earlier crossings had been Early Victorian." An elaborate programme was followed. On the 28th a Black Watch patrol was flown in, from another brigade, to make a demonstration south of the nearest Japanese garrison town, called Hktami, situated ten miles downstream from the crossing place.

[1] The immediate neighbourhood of a Stronghold was described as " the demesne."
[2] Fergusson II. Two extracts.

At the same time Captain Harman (formerly of Fergusson's Number 5 column) was flown in with a small party to form a road block between Hktami and Fergusson. The latter sent a prearranged signal to the air base in Assam for a glider flight carrying river-crossing equipment. There was a delay here and so, by the time the two gliders arrived in the evening, two columns of Leicesters had begun to cross in rubber dinghies. The gliders brought cargoes of assault boats with outboard motors. Within five minutes the first of these were launched and rapid crossing began. A whole column of The Queen's Regiment achieved their crossing in two hours and ten minutes. The operation went on all night. Fergusson himself crossed in the early afternoon of the 1st of March. Simultaneously with the crossing there was a supply drop, and the next day the two gliders were "snatched off" by Dakota and towed back to the base. (The aircraft returned five days later to carry off the motor boats.) The mules provided the only link with the wild Frith-like scenes of the year before.[1]

On the afternoon of the 1st of March, Wingate was due to arrive by air on a piece of reconnoitred flat ground near the south bank of the crossing place. Fergusson was expecting him eagerly, not only for his own sake but because he was expected to bring the Brigade's second-in-command, Colonel Cave,[2] and the base signals officer, for conference. The party arrived at about half-past four. It consisted of Wingate, his A.D.C., George Borrow, Colonel Cochran and four war correspondents. There was no Colonel Cave and no signals officer. Fergusson looked on "black with fury, while Wingate explained blandly how he thought it . . . desirable for our march and crossing to receive proper attention in the Press. . . ." Discussion on the point was acrimonious in the extreme, and calm was only restored by Colonel Gaty, the American pilot, offering to fly back to Imphal for the missing officers. The offer was gladly accepted. In this odd comedy of war it is easy to see Wingate acting a vain part, but a defence of his behaviour is not hard to find. He had now learned how much good Press publicity can do for success in military ventures. His enemies were at their most active, and he was determined not to neglect at this moment an important and proved ally. Nevertheless, he need not perhaps have brought as many as four correspondents! He was never inclined to moderation.

He stayed by the crossing place till the afternoon of the next day. He was pleased with what he had seen, but decidedly worried at the slow rate of progress. 16 Brigade had been scheduled to reach the neighbourhood of Indaw by the 5th of March. The Chindwin crossing would hardly be completed by that date, and they had promised

[1] Fergusson II.　　　[2] Colonel F. O. Cave, O.B.E., M.C.

Stilwell to attack Lonkin on the way. Fergusson said that he could not possibly be at Indaw before the 20th, and Wingate could only urge him to lose no time unnecessarily.

A curious episode, recorded by Fergusson, shows how Wingate to the last, indulged the White Knight interest in experiment such as eleven years before had made him explore the Libyan desert on a diet of dried dates. While walking together along the Chindwin shore he and Fergusson found a man engaged in the exotic trade of selling turtle's eggs. On the spot Wingate bought the whole of the man's consignment, and then pressed them, in a way not to make for refusal, on a passing group of Chindits, assuring them that the consumption of this rare nourishment was good for the health. Turtle's eggs are no more appetising than those of other reptiles, and their effects on digestion were found to be disagreeable.[1]

Before leaving, Wingate gave Fergusson copies of his Stronghold memorandum, and then on the 2nd he flew back to Imphal. Regretably he had told Fergusson nothing of the final garrison plan. The crossing of the Chindwin was completed by the 4th. The next day, the 5th, had been chosen for the first large airborne operation and the beginning of the second Chindit expedition in earnest.

The aerodrome chosen for the flight of 77 Brigade into Burma, the action which opened the central operation of Thursday, was at Lalaghat near Silchar. Calvert's final orders were as follows : his brigade was to be flown to the Kaukkwe valley to land on two flat stretches known by the code names Broadway and Piccadilly. Calvert was to make a stronghold at Broadway, the more northerly of the landing grounds. Once established, he would sally out with the purpose of stopping Japanese traffic on the railway and on the Irrawaddy east of Katha, seizing Katha as well if he could. The flight operation had been rehearsed and calculated to the last detail. On the morning of the 5th the Army commander and Sir John Baldwin came to Lalaghat to witness the event. The first Dakota was due to take off with its gliders at five o'clock. All day " men swarmed about the aircraft, loading them, laying out tow-ropes, leading mules, humping packs, and moving endlessly in dusty columns, for all the world like busy ants round captive moths."[2]

Half an hour before five o'clock a small aircraft flew into Lalaghat and was met by a signalled jeep. One of Cochran's team of photographers leapt out of the plane and into the jeep and drove at speed to where Wingate was standing with Tulloch. The photographer was called Lieutenant Charles J. Russhon. Against orders, and to Wingate's fury, Cochran had sent Russhon with Colonel Gaty to make a photo-

[1] Fergusson II.   [2] Slim.

graphic reconnaissance of the Kaukkwe valley in the early afternoon. But there was no time to discuss this breach of the plan not to fly over the operational area, for Russhon brought devastating evidence that the Japanese were in readiness to oppose the landings. The photographs he had taken that afternoon showed that the whole level space of Piccadilly was covered by teak logs neatly arranged in four lines. There could be no question of landing there, and it was inconceivable that the obstacle had not been organised by the enemy. Success depended on secrecy and it was horribly evident that the secret was out.

Air Marshal Baldwin came up and examined the photographs with Wingate, Tulloch, Calvert, Cochran and Alison. Someone took a photograph of the group of worried men. A decision had to be taken quickly, and the decision could only be between whether to risk the possibility of an opposed landing which would mean certain disaster, and whether to call off the operation altogether and thus almost inevitably bring an end to the whole second Chindit venture. The decision was reached in about twenty minutes. It is clear that at first everyone took the most pessimistic view, and Wingate told Slim and Baldwin that he believed that he had been betrayed by Chinese. He then said that he wanted to discuss the situation with the operational commander. This was agreed. He went over to Calvert, and said: "Well, Mike, it looks as though the Japanese have tumbled to our plans. I leave the decision as to whether we go on with it to you. Do you want to go on?" Calvert said: "Definitely yes."[1]

Wingate then went into conference with Baldwin, Cochran, Alison and Tulloch, while Sir William Slim withdrew a short way off. It was one of those moments when everyone knew the other's thought and looked desperately for a new one. No new thought presented itself. The evidence of the photograph almost proved Japanese alertness, and there seemed nothing for it but to postpone the operation. Wingate strenuously objected to postponement, but for once he could find no argument to sustain him, and the photograph at which they looked continually had a horrible eloquence of its own. Then someone had an idea for an optimistic explanation of the carefully laid rows of logs. Piccadilly was the place where, in the first expedition, the aeroplane had landed to carry off Colonel Cooke and his wounded. This operation had been photographed by a war correspondent, and thus pictures of the place had been widely published in the British and American Press. Was it not possible that, as a consequence, the Japanese had located the place and blocked Piccadilly merely as a routine precaution? Russhon had photographed Broadway and the landing ground destined

[1] Calvert.

for 111 Brigade east of the Irrawaddy, and there was no sign of these having been blocked. Everyone seized on this point and, at Wingate's suggestion, it was decided that the fly-in should be attempted at Broadway and 111 Brigade's trans-Irrawaddy landing ground, which had the code name Chowringhee. They went to inform Sir William Slim. He listened to the proposal, and then turned to Wingate and said that he would give the order if Wingate was fully prepared to take the risk. Wingate said that he himself was prepared, but before giving a definite answer he must consult Calvert again. Slim agreed to this. There then began a discussion between Baldwin and the Americans as to the practicality of rebriefing the pilots, while Wingate went back to Calvert.

Wingate explained to him what had been decided and then said: " Are you prepared to do it ? If we don't go now I don't think that we shall ever go as we shall have to wait for the moon, and the season is already late. Slim and the airmen are willing to go on now that everything is ready. What do you think ? I don't like ordering you to go if I am not going myself. At the moment I have told them that I will consider it because I want to hear your views." Calvert answered : " I am prepared to take all my brigade into Broadway alone and take the consequence of a slower build-up, as I don't want to split my brigade either side of the Irrawaddy."[1] Cochran, Alison and Baldwin came up and told Wingate that they had second thoughts about using Chowringhee, if only because of the difficulty of rebriefing aircrews at such short notice. Wingate accepted the decision. He was still worried. Slim came over and asked Calvert for his views, and Calvert repeated what he had told Wingate. It was then settled that the numbers of gliders leaving Lalaghat should be reduced from eighty to sixty-one and that they should all go to Broadway. At the end of this twenty minutes of conference and decision, Wingate rebriefed the officers of 77 Brigade, and Cochran rebriefed his pilots. The American colonel showed himself a master of the arts of propaganda. He sprang on to the bonnet of a jeep and began by saying, " Say, fellers, we've got a better place to go to." The first Dakota took off at twelve minutes past six, only seventy-two minutes behind schedule.

Two simple code words had been agreed between Calvert and Tulloch. If things went badly at Broadway, then Calvert would signal " Soya Link," indicating that no more aircraft were to make the landing. If things went well, he would signal " Pork Sausage." (The terms were chosen from the least and best liked items in rations.) But even before Calvert had arrived at Broadway things began to go wrong on this night of calamities. The estimates for the glider loads

[1] Calvert.

517

had been erroneous. Fourteen gliders broke away from their towing aircraft in full flight. Of these six crash-landed in Burma, the rest in Assam.[1] Every glider breakaway was immediately signalled to Wingate who, in Calvert's words " sat . . . wondering whether his plans were working, powerless to do anything about it—first tasting the real horror of high command." Derek Tulloch described the scene at Lalaghat : " The report centre tent was as macabre a setting as could be imagined. It was packed with people. Two Generals and an Air Marshal all looking ghoulishly at the controller by whose side I was sitting. Report after report of mishaps came in at intervals. . . . Then came the dreaded code word over the air from the landing area, ' Soya Link.' " . . . This, they concluded, meant that the Japanese had laid an ambush at Broadway. Seven aircraft with gliders were still on their way and these were instantly ordered back. Tulloch described " a grim silence " in the tent. Sir John Baldwin said that he would fly back immediately to Comilla in order to arrange fighter cover for the evacuation the next day. Except for the wireless operators the party in the tent dispersed.

It was four o'clock in the morning. As they walked back to their own quarters Wingate said to Tulloch : " Well, Derek, it looks as though we've failed. The operation is off."

Tulloch answered : " I don't believe it. Everything will be O.K. We have quite enough troops on the ground for the first night. Let's go and have a few hours' sleep and we shall get good news in the morning."

Wingate said, " You're a bloody optimist."[2]

A couple of hours or so later, while it was still early morning, Tulloch was woken up to be given a new signal from Calvert. It was the signal of signals. It consisted of the beautiful longed-for words " Pork Sausage." He ran over to Wingate's room but found him in deep sleep, so he decided to leave him to rest a little longer while he tried to find out by the wireless-link what had happened. He was able to speak to Calvert. He learned that there had been no Japanese ambush but some gliders had crashed badly on reaching the ground. There were ruts for timber-dragging across the level space which had caused the first crashes ; then some of the towing aircraft had come in too quickly and too close one behind the other, and the result had been a piling up of damaged gliders till the airfield was crowded with wreckage. Twenty-four men had been killed and thirty badly wounded out of a total of five hundred and forty men landed. The prospect was good. Among equipment safely brought in was a bulldozer. Later that day Calvert spoke to Wingate. It was now ten o'clock in the morning and he said that he could receive more Dakotas that evening. What this

---

[1] Calvert. Slim. Information obtained at the War Office.   [2] Tulloch II.

meant was that the central operation, despite a host of distracting accidents, had gone essentially according to plan. It was even to be found that the lost gliders helped the plan forward, since remains of these crashed aircraft, found in the most unlikely places between the Irrawaddy and Assam, utterly bewildered the Japanese as to British intentions, bewildered them more than any ordinary deception plan could have done. The enemy, in consequence, were slow to discover Broadway or its purpose.[1]

Contrary to what was believed on the 5th of March the Japanese had no notion of what was toward. The alarm, though so well grounded on evidence, was in fact quite needless. One of the most curious things about this part of the story is to be found in the air photographs of Piccadilly. The careful and symmetrical blocking of the level space had an unmistakable appearance of military arrangement, and the conclusion that the plan had been betrayed was not only inevitable, but any other conclusion would have been in the highest degree irresponsible. Yet in fact the conclusion was wrong and the alarming discovery by Russhon was of nothing more than of a most unfortunate coincidence. Investigators after the war ascertained that the teak logs had nothing to do with the Japanese military at all. They had been neatly laid out in the sun by ordinary Burman woodcutters.[2]

The next night, nine hundred men were flown into Broadway and the entire preliminary movement of 77 Brigade was completed by the morning of the 10th. In the meantime the movement of 111 Brigade had begun. On the night of the 7th their forward party was flown into Chowringhee in fourteen gliders. The location of this landing ground was within the Shweli loop, a few miles from the place where Wingate had sheltered with his escape party the year before. On the next night the main party of 111 Brigade under Lentaigne flew into Chowringhee in Dakotas. They were the third of the brigades to enter Burma in the second expedition. Their task was to sever the road and rail communications between Wuntho and Indaw, and the road communications east of this northwards from Nankan, in the land between the railway and the river. They were to establish a stronghold five miles south of Banmauk. Before beginning on their tasks two columns of

---

[1] This account of the fly-in of 5–6 March follows Calvert, Tulloch Essay, Tulloch II, letters from Tulloch at the time, a letter from Tulloch to the writer, an interview with Sir John Baldwin, and a letter from him, and an interview with Colonel Walter Scott who was probably the person to suggest a connection between the log-laying and the Press-photograph. The events at Broadway are fully described in Calvert. Sir William Slim gives an account which, as regards Wingate's behaviour and other details, is at such variance with all other evidence that it has not been used.

[2] New Delhi Archives. Slim. Tulloch. It should be added that Scott dissents from this opinion and believes that the Japanese, having been told of the 1943 evacuation by the headman of Amitsi Gaun, ordered loglaying. He heard this from local people.

the brigade under Lieut.-Colonel Morris were to cross the Shweli to meet a force from Broadway moving under Herring to the Kachins east of Bhamo.[1] The rest of the brigade were to cross the Irrawaddy to the west. "You have been allotted the hardest and therefore the most honourable task," wrote Wingate in his operational order to Lentaigne, and over his signature he put in his spidery handwriting, "For there is no restraint to the Lord to save by many or by few."

The whole fly-in of 111 Brigade went smoothly. They set off from Tulihal near Imphal. There is an excellent eye-witness account of what it was to be in one of the Dakotas on the second night. "The plane shudders and lurches and moves off slowly down the runway. It accelerates. Then there is a lift and a stillness as it takes the air. It circles the airfield and turns eastwards. Twenty minutes and we can see the Chindwin shining silver in the moonlight. . . . The journey lasts an hour and a half. We cross the Irrawaddy and are ordered to prepare to land. We put on our packs and equipment and the plane commander stations himself at the door. Far below we can see the lights on the flare path at the landing place, for all the world a great modern airport. The plane circles until it is ordered down by Aldis lamp. The lights appear to rise and suddenly we bump and pitch along the uneven strip and turn off to our dispersal point. The door opens, we jump down and run to our appointed places on the edge of the jungle. A great feeling of relief surges up within and quite overcomes any unpleasant feeling that one might have had at being two hundred miles behind the enemy's lines."[2]

After the 9th no more men were flown to Chowringhee and the rest of Lentaigne's men were diverted to Broadway. Their fly-in was completed there by the morning of the 11th. Tulloch had advised this change of plan as he believed that the Japanese air force at Katha could not remain unaware of Chowringhee for more than two days. His judgment was quickly proved sound. Five hours after the last men had left the camp with Lentaigne on the morning of the 10th, the Japanese bombed the place in strength. "Morrisforce" had already left on their eastwards mission, and the remaining three columns made their way to the Irrawaddy. In spite of their new equipment and new training they found the escape from the Shweli loop almost as difficult as the first Chindits had done the year before, and one column had to turn back. It joined Morrisforce. Lentaigne's own column and a Gurkha column under Major Dibbon succeeded, after many difficulties, in reaching Kyunbin ten miles south of Pinlebu. From here they made their first

[1] This column known as DAH force belonged to 111 Brigade and was originally intended to fly into the Kachin country direct. In the event DAH force was flown into Broadway on the 11th to make their way East.

[2] Major MacCutcheon in *The History of the 4th Prince of Wales's Own Gurkha Rifles.*

attack, a fortnight after leaving Chowringhee. But this is to run ahead of the story.

In a remarkably short space of time Calvert fully established the stronghold of Broadway. It came to realise the dreams of Lodolf, a modernised Norman fortress complete with a hospital, cultivated fields, a chicken farm, and even some shops, besides a well-regulated air strip within the demesne. Then, in the middle of the second week of March, Calvert took a force of five columns of the brigade out of Broadway, and with them moved westwards to the railway, leaving behind a garrison of two battalions under Colonel Claud Rome. His object was to make a subsidiary stronghold to block communications from the south to Myitkyina. After various changes of plan which need not be gone into, he took possession of the new stronghold site by assault. The place was a group of small hills by the little railway town of Henu, a mile and a half north of the station town of Mawlu, and here on the 18th was fought the first battle of the second expedition, a difficult and bloody contest whose horror is well described in an official eye-witness account. " The characteristic of this fighting was its savagery. It is difficult, indeed, to envisage it unless one has seen it. It was, at times, almost ' medieval ' as more than one person said after. Hand-to-hand combat was the order of the day and night, and this went on literally for hours on end ; rifle and bayonet against two-handed feudal sword, kukri against bayonet, no quarter to the wounded, while hand-grenades lobbed over the heads of the combatants incessantly."[1] Calvert led the opening bayonet charge himself. One officer of the South Staffordshires, Lieutenant Cairns, was attacked by a Japanese officer who hacked off his arm with his sword, whereon Cairns shot him, seized the sword and continued to lead his men to the attack till he dropped dying to the ground.[2] The Japanese were routed. Later the new stronghold came to be called " White City " from the parachutes hanging in the trees. Traffic on the railway from Katha and Indaw to Myitkyina was effectively held up from then on.

While these things were happening and 77 Brigade were proving themselves again, great events were taking place on the Chindwin. The day after the first fly-in of 77 Brigade on the 5th of March, the Japanese began the major offensive of which their advance in Arakan had been the preliminary stage. On the 6th they began to move north-north-eastwards from around Kalewa, on the 8th they followed this with a complementary advance from the Chin Hills, followed by a second advance from Kalewa. While a twenty-day battle was fought

[1] *Notes on the Road Block* issued by Wingate's Headquarters. There is also a detailed and admirable description in Calvert.
[2] Citation for the posthumous V.C. awarded to Cairns.

for the Imphal road, with initial reverses to the British, the Japanese invaded from north of Homalin on the 14th and from the centre of their Chindwin front on the 15th. They attacked in three-divisional strength. As soon became clear, their objectives were the capture of Imphal, Kohima and Dimapur, with the purpose of including all Assam in the defences of Burma. Their intention was not, as has been said, the conquest of India, but they knew that if they succeeded in extending their defences to the gates of India, the whole British position in the Indian theatre would become politically and militarily untenable. They were fighting for a great prize ! The Japanese carried out every phase of the attack with an unhesitating devotion which, however reluctantly, must be admired. The advance was not halted until the 20th April ; the tables were not turned until the middle of May. The army in Assam fought back with the new spirit that it had shown in Arakan. Even so, disaster sometimes appeared imminent. In spite of their improved training and their quicker minds and better education, British soldiers in the mass were still easily liable to surprise by their Japanese enemies when fighting in jungle country. Reinforcements from India arrived only just in time to save Kohima and Dimapur. When putting the events of these three months on record, Sir William Slim acknowledged his debt to his army with a stirring and modest generosity such as makes the tone of what he said about Wingate all the less understandable. " I was," he wrote in his book, " like other generals before me . . . saved from the consequences of my mistakes by the resourcefulness of my subordinate commanders and the stubborn valour of my troops."

Against a background of sudden invasion, and what seemed then the most terrible of all threats to the safety of India, there were played these first scenes of the second Chindit expedition and the last scene of Wingate's life. He had already flown into Broadway on the second night of 77 Brigade's fly-in, that is on the 7th and on the 8th he had flown from that stronghold to Chowringhee, returning to Lalaghat after dark. His impulse, of course, was to be forward with his men, but he allowed himself to be restrained by Tulloch,[1] staying most of the time at his Headquarters, mastering the grind and press of administration business which closes in on a headquarters at times of battle.

On the 11th he issued an Order of the Day to all ranks of 3 Indian Division. The text was as follows : " Our first task is fulfilled. We have inflicted a complete surprise on the enemy. All our columns are inserted in the enemy's guts. The time has come to reap the fruit of the

---

[1] " Orde of course went in himself, needless to say. My main preoccupation at the moment is keeping him from crossing the Rubicon more than is absolutely necessary." Tulloch to Mary Tulloch (16.3.44). W.P.I.

advantage we have gained. The enemy will act with violence. We will oppose him with the resolve to reconquer our territory of Northern Burma. Let us thank God for the great success he has vouchsafed us and press forward with our sword in the enemy's ribs to expel him from our territory. This is not a moment, when such an advantage has been gained, to count the cost. This is a moment to live in history. It is an enterprise in which every man who takes part may feel proud one day to say I WAS THERE." Congratulations came in from 11th Army Group and from the Supreme Commander, and on the 12th Wingate availed himself of his right to communicate with Mr. Churchill. He sent him a situation report to the effect that twelve thousand men of the Chindits were within fifty miles of Indaw ; in detail that 77 Brigade was marching towards Mawlu, that 111 Brigade was crossing the Irrawaddy towards the Wuntho-Indaw communications, that Morrisforce was moving east to the Mandalay-Bhamo communications, that Dah force was moving east to the Kachin country north of Bhamo, and that 16 Brigade after seizing Lonkin with two columns, were entering the Meza valley on their way to Indaw. He concluded by saying, " Enemy completely surprised. Situation most promising if exploited."[1]

When the success of 77 Brigade was evident Wingate found himself working in a more congenial atmosphere than he was used to. Numerous colleagues gave him to understand that they had always been on his side, and had believed in and helped forward the Chindit idea from the beginning. Slim found this amusing and of one of Wingate's suddenly self-proclaimed allies he said to Tulloch : " Why he didn't even know the show was on ! "[2] Mountbatten was frankly pleased by this turn of events. He said : " The more people who delude themselves, or think that they delude others, into the belief that they have been strong supporters, the better ! "[2]

There were two main occasions for discord, in spite of this remarkable change in the official climate, and on the first of these Wingate acted the peacemaker. When the airstrip at Broadway was completed the R.A.F. proposed to maintain six Spitfires there. The plan was put to Wingate who agreed but, evidently by an oversight in the press of work, did not consult Cochran. Nor did the R.A.F. The Spitfires were flown in on the 12th. Cochran was furious, all the more so as Number 1 Air Commando, as an additional injury, received instructions to transport the R.A.F. supplies to maintain the Spitfires in fighting condition. He found Tulloch at Lalaghat and flew with him to Imphal. Arrived at Chindit Headquarters he protested with an emphasis worthy of the Chindit commander himself. The airfield at Broadway was an American venture, he said, accomplished by American courage and skill, and

[1] W.P.I.   [2] Letter, Tulloch to Mary Tulloch (16.3.44).

Cochran insisted that he had been "bounced," before he could introduce his own Mustang fighters into the first Allied airfield established in Japanese-occupied Burma. He recalled other unhappy experiences with the British service and made some forthright comments on what he considered a morbid R.A.F. appetite for publicity. Wingate's headquarter house in Imphal was of flimsy construction, and anything said in one room was fully audible in the adjacent ones. It so happened that while Cochran was giving loud and far from delicate expression to his discontents, several R.A.F. officers were waiting in the next room, including a senior staff officer. "This," as Tulloch recorded later, "did little to help relations."

Before anything could be done to meet Cochran's protest, the Japanese, on the 13th, attacked Broadway with thirty aircraft. The Spitfires shot down four, the anti-aircraft gunners another, and the attack was thoroughly beaten off. Public-spirited man as Cochran was, and a model of Anglo-American co-operation, he did not find that this successful action softened his rage. He had a just grievance, and he was not the more easily appeased when, on the 16th, the forces' magazine *SEAC* gave an account of the action of the 13th with the customary gratifying comment. Since Wingate had some responsibility in not having consulted Cochran, (his only omission in this respect), he took a conciliatory course. He wrote to the officer in charge of R.A.F. publicity on Mountbatten's staff, and put forward Cochran's complaints with moderation and courtesy.[1]

The other quarrel was a ridiculous business. As with the affair of the Spitfires it began with a failure in co-ordination and concerned Press publicity. On the 16th (the same day as Wingate made peace between Cochran and the R.A.F.) the Press published an account of the beginning of the second expedition, in accordance with an official "handout" from Mountbatten's headquarters. There had been controversy, in which Wingate took no part, as to how much ought to be told. The Army commander thought it best that nothing should be said at all till much later,[2] but information officers, with hungry war correspondents to feed, felt otherwise. At length a compromise was reached, satisfying to "security" and, as it was supposed, to the men in the front line. The published account made no mention of the Chindits or of Wingate or of Number 1 Air Commando or of Troop Carrier Command, but told non-committally of "troops of the 14th Army" and the air force stationed in Assam. This was very exasperating. The Army commander himself felt the affront keenly and told Tulloch that

---

[1] Correspondence Wingate-Baldwin-Air Commodore Vincent-Air Marshal Joubert. W.P.I. Tulloch II. The account of this episode in Thomas appears to be mistaken.
[2] Slim.

it was a case of presenting *Hamlet* without the Prince of Denmark.[1] As for Wingate, once more he thought he detected treacherous and designed obstruction by his multitudinous enemies in G.H.Q., and he was beside himself. In great and reckless rage he sent a telegram to the same officer with whom he had made the peace for Cochran, protesting in extreme terms and on behalf of the Chindits, adding that he had forbidden copies of the magazine *SEAC* to be delivered to his men, and asking for his protest to be conveyed to Mountbatten personally. He followed the telegram with an official letter to Mountbatten in the same sense.

This was a most unwise course of action. He ought to have asked, before sending this angry-worded telegram, what the publicity policy of Supreme Headquarters regarding the Chindits really was. In fact the Press policy of S.E.A.C. was much in Wingate's favour : the plan was to put out colourless reports to begin with, followed by more detailed ones as public interest was excited, moving towards a sensational dispatch in the style of " It can now be revealed, etc." Mountbatten replied to Wingate in a coal-heaping style. He explained the policy ; he told him that accounts of the fly-in written by accredited war correspondents, (to be published at an early date), were being prepared for the King, the Prime Minister, Sir Alan Brooke, General Marshall, and General Arnold ; he told him further that the Air Commander-in-Chief Sir Robert Peirse had personally drafted a paragraph greatly lauding Cochran and the Air Commando in a telegraphic dispatch to Mr. Churchill ; he showed in other detail the great lengths that he and his staff had gone to in order to give the Chindits public due, and as regards Wingate's forbidding the distribution to his men of the forces' magazine, he asserted that he had full confidence in the merits of *SEAC* and of its editor, Frank Owen. " Your astounding telegram," he wrote, " has made me realise how you have achieved your amazing success in getting yourself disliked by people who are only too ready to be on your side."

The quarrel had reached its natural end but did not, however, quite die down.[2] It was to be heard once more.

On the 20th Wingate flew to White City before dawn and inspected the little stronghold. " He had sensible suggestions for everyone," recorded Calvert, " whether it was the siting of a machine-gun, the lie of a 3-inch mortar, a point of hygiene to the doctors, the means by

---

[1] Tulloch. A communication.

[2] Slim. Tulloch II. Wingate to S.E.A.C. S.A.C. to Wingate. W.P.I. In his book Sir William Slim says that when suppression of the news was found impolitic he favoured full Chindit publicity because " the Japanese were much more likely if Wingate's name were given to take this expedition as merely a repetition of his minor and ineffective raid of 1943, and not to be too urgent in concentrating strong forces against it." p. 266.

which Protestant and Roman Catholic padres could keep up morale, the places for burying the dead, setting up wireless aerials, etc." He told Calvert something of the general situation in Assam, and how in spite of the fact that the reinforcements from India would give the British Army decisive superiority, he still feared that the Chindits would be diverted from long-range to short-range operations. He told him that the next day Chindit Headquarters would be moved from Imphal back to Sylhet. He explained the odd strategical difficulty of the moment, how his mission was to help Stilwell primarily, but that his instructions were becoming vitiated by the fact that Vinegar Joe was slowing up his advance towards Myitkyina, "in case the Limeys ran away" in Assam. He showed Calvert a résumé of his immediate plans[1] for further airfields and Strongholds south of Indaw which were designed to help 14th Army rather than the progress of Stilwell's Chinese-American force from Ledo. When Calvert confessed himself puzzled by this change in the Chindit mission, Wingate said : "We have got to help 14th Army. We are all, including Stilwell, under 14th Army command, and in spite of my complaints at times, they have been very helpful on the whole, even if they did doubt the practicability of this operation. Now they are converted." He told him that Slim himself was a believer in the Chindit idea, but that among 14th Army staff there were many doubters.[2]

He and Calvert relaxed for a little together. It amused them to walk in safety along the railway to break which so many hazards had been taken a year ago, and again now. Wingate kicked the lines as he walked. "So this is the 18th Jap Division's rail communication," he said, laughing. (Later, in the same sort of mood, Calvert bought a return ticket to Mandalay from Mawlu station.) When it was time to leave for a rendezvous with Bernard Fergusson he told Calvert "to be of good heart," for he would see that he "lacked for nothing." He left with Colonel Gaty.

From White City Wingate flew to a landing ground prepared by 16 Brigade at a placed called Taungle[3] in the Meza valley, and here Fergusson was waiting for him in the afternoon. The long and finely accomplished march of 16 Brigade was in its last stages, and here in the Meza valley between Taungle and a place called Manhton, at the confluence of the Meza and Kalat rivers, Fergusson had chosen his Stronghold site, to be known by the name of Aberdeen. He and his forward headquarters party had not yet found a suitable level space to serve as an airstrip for Dakotas, and immediately on arrival, Wingate

[1] In a paper called *Forecast of Possible Developments of Operation Thursday* dated 13.4.44. W.P.I.

[2] Calvert.   [3] Pronounced Tunglay.

decided to make the reconnaissance himself. He took a pony and rode off eastwards towards Manhton and returned to the airstrip at Taungle having chosen a site north of the little town by the village of Naunghmi. There was a level space running twelve hundred yards north and south, and on to the strip subsequently made here seven hundred sorties were to be flown in the next eight weeks.[1] This was the last occasion when " the otter " put his eye for country to practical use.

When he and Fergusson were together again on the airstrip at Taungle they planned the next move which was to be the assault on Indaw, one of the principal missions of the force. They agreed that the main attack should be from the north-east, and then they had some dispute as to the timing. Only the two columns of the Leicesters had reached Aberdeen, while the remainder were still toiling through the last stages of the march from Ledo, and the two columns who had been detached for the successful seizure of Lonkin were more than ten days away. Fergusson urged the common-sense counsel that Wingate should rest the brigade before using it, but the commander was against this. He told Fergusson that he had news of large Japanese reinforcements arriving at Indaw and that with any delay the arrival of the brigade must become known to the enemy, after which the capture of the airfield would probably become impossible. He told him that he was planning to fly 14 Brigade to Aberdeen as soon as the airstrip was ready, and that these fresh troops would be able to attack Indaw from the west simultaneously with Fergusson's own attack from the north-east. He told him that he was determined to fly 14 and 23 Brigades into the interior quickly, because there were suggestions at 14th Army Headquarters that they should be used as ordinary infantry in the defence of Assam and not as long range penetration groups. With these arguments he overrode Fergusson's doubts and insisted that the southward march of 16 Brigade to the scene of action should begin early on the 24th. So it was agreed.[2] It is an open question whether Wingate made a mistake here or not.

Wingate then flew eastwards to Broadway where he spent the night, leaving Colonel Gaty with Fergusson to begin the organisation of the Aberdeen airstrip. The next day, the 21st, he flew back to Imphal. He was met with disturbing news. During his absence the Army commander had told Tulloch that, with the increasing menace of the Japanese advance, he was contemplating using 14 and 23 Brigades as normal infantry for the defence of Imphal. Wingate's fears were realised, and he was exasperated. He saw the whole of his great project being reduced to nothing at the last moment, saw that belief in his

[1] Fergusson II. Tulloch II.
[2] Information obtained at the War Office. Fergusson II and a communication.

theory of long range penetration had vanished again in a few days. He immediately flew to the Army commander's headquarters at Comilla.

Though he approached it in a state of towering rage, his meeting with Slim on this day passed off harmoniously. If the Army commander had decided to use Wingate's two reserve brigades in a normal rôle the day before, he had changed his mind by the 21st. He explained to Wingate that he had no intention of diminishing the scale of the Chindit expedition, but that he was forced by circumstances to obtain immediate relief for 4th Corps. He explained the situation on the central Chindwin front in detail. A compromise was reached. Wingate agreed that 14 Brigade (followed by the garrison troops of the 3rd West African Brigade) should fly into Aberdeen immediately, but that once arrived there the brigade would follow a new rôle, different to the one that Wingate had devised for them. Instead of joining in the attack on Indaw, they were to move by defined stages to a place about fifteen miles west of Wuntho and about sixty miles south-west of Aberdeen where their task would be to form a Stronghold and disrupt the communications from Wuntho and Indaw to the Chindwin. It was agreed that Wingate should draft orders to the brigade in the sense of these decisions. For some reason which remains obscure Fergusson was not told of the change of plan.[1]

This second large-scale airborne operation was calculated to put a strain on the heavily taxed air force in Assam. As things stood there was only one way of meeting the requirement and that was by diverting traffic from the hump. That meant jeopardising relations with the Americans, and Wingate was always reluctant to do this, especially (it may be conjectured) so soon after the Spitfire storm with Cochran and Alison. Taking aircraft away from the hump also meant irritating the Chinese and Wingate persisted in a wishful belief, (ultimately but too late proved valid), that the Chinese army would move from Yunnan into Burma when they saw some Allied success within the country. With these thoughts in mind, he decided to play his supreme trump card in earnest. . . . A day or two before, Mr. Churchill had sent a message of congratulations to the Chindits, and this gave Wingate a convenient opportunity to use his right of direct communication. He decided to appeal for an immediate allotment of four squadrons of Dakota transport aircraft.

He unconsciously timed his move well. After the experience of Arakan, and the present battle, the Army commander had also come

---

[1] This account of the change of 14 Brigade and the attendant circumstances is taken from correspondence between the War Office and Fergusson and discussed with the latter by the writer.

to the conclusion that more carrier aircraft were needed urgently. He wanted them for flying reinforcements hither and thither, for evacuating wounded, and not least for keeping the Chindits in the field. On the 21st Slim was actually in the course of drafting a letter to 11 Army Group to this effect. When Wingate asked for his support in his intended appeal, Slim naturally gave it.[1]

This was the only occasion on which Wingate is known to have used his right to communicate with the Prime Minister on a matter of policy. Stories that he sent him frequent messages are unfounded; he was extremely moderate in this matter. But for the very reason perhaps that he recognised that such communications must be infrequent, he took occasion now to say more than was politic or fair; for he not only asked for the four squadrons but also protested to Mr. Churchill, regardless of Mountbatten's explanations to him, against the publicity policy imposed on *SEAC*. He even spoke of " distorted accounts " and demanded that " the truth be told." Mountbatten, in forwarding the telegram, was obliged to challenge the imputations on his staff, and explain the policy afresh to the Prime Minister. If it is felt by any-one that in this odd incident Wingate did not show at his finest, two things should be remembered as checks to moralising: Mountbatten refused to take offence and remained to the end and after Wingate's most loyal supporter; and, secondly, it should be remembered that it is easier for men to show their mettle when they have an audience than when they are without it, and Wingate was thinking not of himself but of the men under his command.

The conclusion of this " affair of the four squadrons " was that the Prime Minister, after sounding Mountbatten again, made the request for the Dakotas, and the Chiefs of Staff agreed to the allotment.[2] As regards the publicity question the Prime Minister behaved with the utmost generosity and promised that in the course of his next broadcast to the nation, scheduled for the 26th, he would tell in person what part the Chindits and their commander were playing in Burma. Mr. Churchill's reply was sent from London on the 24th. It is unlikely that Wingate ever saw it.

During the events last related two important things happened with the Chindit command. One was simple and successful. On the 22nd six gliders were landed on the Taungle strip to convey a party of American engineers with their equipment. Their task was to make of the selected Aberdeen strip a second Broadway aerodrome, and they

---

[1] W.P.I. Wingate's telegram is dated the 21st and Sir William Slim's letter to 11 Army Group is dated the 22nd. In a telegram of 23.3.44 on the same subject from Sir William Slim to 11 Army Group he refers to " my letter which was independent of and written before Wingate's telegram."

[2] They were not used for Chindit purposes however. Tulloch.

quickly succeeded. The other thing occupied more time. On the 21st Wingate gave the order to move his headquarters. Since early January he had maintained an advance headquarters at Imphal, and a rear headquarters at Sylhet. He had already found the existence of two bases cumbersome to the discharge of business, but his forward one at Imphal was peculiarly vulnerable to any, even minor Japanese success on this front. As Wingate had stressed many times, his were a "wireless headquarters," and this meant that they depended on a number of radio installations, of which some were at a distance from the town : the smallest incursion into the perimeter might cut off communication between Chindit command and Chindit brigades and columns. So on the 21st the whole of Wingate's elaborate headquarter machinery was ordered to be concentrated on Sylhet. The operation of removal took almost a week, and this meant, among other things, that during the attempt on Indaw Fergusson was in feeble communication with his immediately directing authority. This may explain why Fergusson was kept so calamitously ill-informed.[1]

On the night of the 23rd the first party of 14 Brigade were flown in to the newly completed airstrip of Aberdeen. They were a column formed from the Black Watch. Fergusson, as a Black Watch officer, would have liked to have greeted them, (and perhaps to have ascertained their orders), but he and the forward party left the Stronghold in the first hours of the 24th. There was little time for courtesies, and so he could only leave a written note for their commanding officer, Lieutenant-Colonel George Green. The attack on Indaw had begun. The Leicesters had bivouacked and rested beyond Aberdeen, but none of the others had, and most of 16 Brigade went forward into action without any halt at the Stronghold at all.[2]

On the morning of the 24th Wingate flew to Broadway, arriving there about half past nine. He changed aircraft and flew by light plane to White City where there had been another battle from the 21st to the 23rd. The action had been as hazardous and fierce as the original one for the seizure of Henu, and had been opened by a determined Japanese effort to oust 77 Brigade from their position. During one phase of the fighting the Japanese had established themselves at two points within the White City defences. The brigade had suffered thirty-four killed and forty-two wounded, and inflicted at least twice as many casualties on the attackers. By the 24th all was quiet again and the Japanese had retired. Wingate inspected the stronghold, and he was "on the whole well pleased."[3] He showed Calvert the messages of

[1] Tulloch II. Fergusson II.
[2] Fergusson II. Information obtained at the War Office.
[3] Calvert.

congratulation that had come from the Prime Minister and the President. Before leaving he told him that Lieutenant-Colonel Scott had been awarded the D.S.O., and then added, " Oh, by the way, you have a bar to your D.S.O. Let it go to your heart and not your head."

From White City he flew to Aberdeen to see the new arrivals and inspect the airfield. He was in good humour and was remembered saying to Colonel Green, " I would like to congratulate your men on belonging to the first Scottish regiment to land at a Scottish airport in Burma." From Aberdeen he returned to Broadway where he changed his light plane for the Mitchell bomber that had brought him out that morning. He flew back to Imphal.

CHAPTER XXIII

THE END

ON THE 23rd of March Sir John Baldwin wrote to Wingate on the subject of the removal of Chindit Advance Headquarters from Imphal. He was not in agreement with what had been done as he considered that the choice of Sylhet placed the Chindit staff at too great a distance from his own or any other air headquarters, and since the move was still in early stages, he hoped that Wingate might be able to make other arrangements. Such was the drift of his letter. On the 24th news came to him that Wingate was expected in Imphal, and, knowing that he was an irregular correspondent, he decided that he would fly there himself to meet him and get an answer in person. He flew from Comilla in a Lockheed plane. He landed on the airstrip at Imphal shortly before the other arrived from Aberdeen in his Mitchell bomber.[1]

Wingate's Imphal headquarters still existed in part, and as soon as he had landed he went there to read his correspondence among which he must have found Baldwin's letter with his message that he requested a meeting that day. He sat at his table and began to deal with this and other matters. It was the last time that those who were in the Headquarters that day saw Wingate, and they remembered afterwards that his behaviour had been quiet and reflective, like that of a man composed and at peace with himself. He did a somewhat strange thing. At one moment he rose and went over to his personal clerk, Sergeant Foreman, and laid a hand on his shoulder saying, "I have given you a difficult time, Foreman, but you have done splendid work for me, and I want you to know that I am very grateful indeed." He spoke almost as though he was saying good-bye.[2] Before leaving the building, he seems to have found time to begin a letter home to Lorna, for among his papers there is an undated one to her which runs as follows : "I have been reading the life of Madame Curie by her daughter Eve. It is a good account. Both she and Pierre seem to have led saintly lives, if without acknowledgment. Who do you think I have had with me— Sigmund.[3] He signalled to say he was in India so I got hold of him. Just at that moment arrived the letters from Chaim and Vera, long

---

[1] Sir John Baldwin. A communication. [2] Tulloch Essay.
[3] Sigmund Gestetner, a prominent British Zionist.

delayed. I had a good talk with S. He will probably get home by end April and can give you my news up to now.

" Miss MacGeary made a beautiful cake for my birthday and I had the unexpected pleasure of a visit from her on that day. I only see Derek now once in a while. He is working hard and does well. I hope to see him to-morrow.[1] I am on the whole suffering from too great placidity these days. I wish I . . ." The letter breaks off here.

He went to Baldwin's headquarters and together they discussed the contents of the R.A.F. commander's letter. The move had gone too far by now to allow Wingate to make a further change of location from Sylhet without loss of efficiency, and so instead the two men drew up a scheme for air-liaison under the new organisation. Their meeting might have been a difficult one. A few days before this Wingate, through touchy misunderstanding, had taken offence at a signal from Baldwin, and there had very nearly been another rupture with the R.A.F.[2] But by the time he met Baldwin, Wingate must have recognised that he had put himself in the wrong by his hastiness, a fact which probably explains why, in discussing their present and more serious difference of opinion, he showed himself conciliatory and easy. After friendly talk for an hour or so, they came to an agreement satisfying to both of them, and by the time they had finished their discussion they were both anxious to be on their way before dark. Baldwin planned to fly back to Comilla in his Lockheed, while the other, who still had the use of the Mitchell bomber that had brought him from the Stronghold, decided to visit Number 1 Air Commando at Lalaghat. His intention, in all probability, was to tell Cochran what had been decided in the course of the meeting. Wingate and Baldwin left air headquarters together and went to alert the crews of their two aircraft. It was now about five o'clock in the afternoon. As was usual on all airfields in the war, they found a number of people waiting for the chance of a lift. Among these were two war correspondents, Stuart Emery of the *News Chronicle* and Stanley Wills of the *Daily Herald*. They came up to Wingate and asked him if he would take them with him, and he said that he would. The other people in his party were his A.D.C. George Borrow, Lieutenant Brian Hodges, the pilot, 2nd Lieutenant Stephen Wanderer, and three American Air Force sergeants, Frank Sadoski, James Hickey and Vernon MacInninch.

---

[1] This with the " end April " reference and the fact that there is no other letter later than his birthday (26th February) strongly suggests 24th March as the date.

[2] Wingate had signalled Baldwin direct on an administration matter connected with the Spitfires on Broadway, and Baldwin replied asking him to route his signals through the Wing-Commander concerned. Wingate considered this an affront but Baldwin explained that his request was only intended to facilitate liaison. W.P.I.

Baldwin proposed that the Mitchell bomber should take off first as it was the faster of the two machines.

Stories were told afterwards that Wingate was advised against flying because of storms, and that with characteristic impetuosity he overruled his American pilot, Lieutenant Hodges.[1] All this is imagined. There was no reason to fear a difficult journey either to Lalaghat or Comilla. There were isolated storms but in the main the weather was fine.[2] Wingate's party clambered into his machine, his A.D.C. and the two passengers disposing themselves with familiar discomfort in its interior, while Wingate himself sat in the co-pilot's seat. He and Hodges exchanged a few words with the R.A.F. commander before the pilot moved the bomber across the field to the runway. They took off, swiftly followed by the Lockheed. The last that Sir John Baldwin saw of the Mitchell, it was flying over the Bishenpur hills. What happened between there and Lalaghat can never be known beyond the bare fact that on the westward slopes Wingate's aircraft plunged down into the earth and burst into flames with everyone aboard killed instantly.

For some days hope was desperately maintained, even after Squadron-Leader Norris had observed the wreckage while making a reconnaissance flight on the 25th over the Lushai and Bishenpur district.[3] The next day, Sunday the 26th, there was still no news, though the worst news was so nearly certain. Under these circumstances Mr. Churchill, in his broadcast to the nation, did not make the promised announcement of the Chindit flight into the interior of Burma, but instead referred to the Far Eastern campaign in general terms. Two days later the story of the opening of the second Chindit expedition was made known by ordinary means, but the Press-release for which Wingate had so furiously striven, contained no mention of the lost aircraft and his likely death. By tragic necessity his family, friends and admirers were allowed to rejoice over his wonderful second fame without any idea of what had happened a few days before. On the 29th, in Assam, a party from Chindit Headquarters, led by Major Frank Barnes, succeeded in making their way on foot to the wreckage reported by Norris. So violent had been the destruction, with the shattered machine dug eighteen feet into the ground, that identification was not easy, but among recognisable things they found

[1] " There was certainly no question of the pilot being overruled." Sir John Baldwin. A letter to the writer.
[2] " It was . . . quite a good flying day and the isolated storms could be avoided." Baldwin letter. The same point is made in a letter from General Alison to Mrs. Walter Bell.
[3] Wing-Commander Stanley Norris, D.F.C. A communication.

the remains of the famous sun-helmet. Barnes returned with his evidence to Sylhet. In the critical state of things in Assam, it was decided to postpone Christian funeral to when there would be time for such decencies. The news was conveyed to Lorna with the formal dignity of British official procedure on the 30th of March and announced in the Press two days later. On the same day it was announced by wireless message to the Chindits in the training camps, the forward stations, and the Strongholds in Burma. Throughout the force that he had commanded and formed, the shock was felt with the amazement and pain of sudden personal grief. Men who had only seen him for a moment felt that a potent factor in their lives had been taken away, and those who had worked close to him knew, despite their hopes, that a great adventure had come to an end. Even his enemies, according to the testimony of Sir William Slim, were oppressed with " a sense of loss that struck like a blow."[1]

There was a debate as to who should succeed him. Wingate himself seems to have favoured different choices at different times, but the idea that he made definite and conflicting promises is not well evidenced. The arrangement at the time of his death was that Tulloch should take command with the right of appointing another successor should he wish to. General Symes as the senior officer in the force had a substantial claim which was not accepted. Tulloch himself hesitated to take command because he believed that he lacked the essential qualification of field experience with the Chindits, and after much self-questioning he proposed and obtained the appointment of Lentaigne.

The new commander took over at a difficult time because the attack on Indaw by 16 Brigade had failed. Fergusson's troops were in need of rest ; the approach to Indaw was found to be impossibly difficult from the north-east because of the lack of water, and, most fatally of all, parties of 111 Brigade moving south-west from Broadway, and passing near Fergusson, (of whose mission they were ignorant), tried to throw the Japanese off the scent by telling the villagers on their way that they were marching to an attack on Indaw from the north. As a consequence when 16 Brigade did indeed attack from the north, they could not seize the town and airfield because the Japanese were in readiness, and the Chindit troops, weakened by their long marches, were in no state to fight against them. Wingate's impetuousness in sending the brigade in immediately is easily and perhaps rightly blamed, though this is a very difficult matter to judge in a campaign in which everything depended on surprise. 16 Brigade did in fact seize Indaw on the 27th of April, but the capture was not exploited. The airfield at Indaw was only a fair-weather strip and not a great military asset

[1] W.P.I. Press Files. Major Peter Taylor. Slim. Tulloch Essay. Tulloch II.

as had been imagined. Nevertheless, the subsequent withdrawal of the Chindits from the scene of success had the appearance of an abandonment of Wingate's plan and was for long a source of bitterness to many of his men.

Lentaigne has been blamed for not grasping opportunity more vigorously, for not insisting on the privileged treatment that his predecessor had received, especially in the matter of direct access to the Supreme Commander and the Prime Minister, but it is very questionable whether any such assertion of rights would have shown results. The anomalous status of Wingate had been much resented, and it is not easily imagined that a revival of it in favour of his successor would have been tolerated. Lentaigne was wise not to try to imitate a character that could never be his. He acquiesced in the logic of events, and his course was, so far as anyone can see, much the same as Wingate would have had to follow in the end. At the beginning of May, 16 Brigade was evacuated by air, and the Aberdeen Stronghold closed down. Under the circumstances of the battle for Assam, 23 Brigade was never used as a long-range penetration group, but it operated at short range, (with success), on the 14th Army front. The Strongholds of Broadway and White City went the same way as Aberdeen a few days later in May. This again caused bitterness but Calvert recognised that the time had come to open a new Chindit phase, and in the event he and his men escaped an annihilating attack by one day. After the closure of the central Strongholds, 77, 14 and 111 Brigades operated on Stilwell's front in accordance with the original Chindit plan. Another Stronghold was established in the north under the two names of Blackpool and Clydeside. Stilwell proved a hard task master, to an extent that leaves an ugly stain on his reputation. The last major action of the Chindits was the capture of Mogaung, completed by Calvert, after a long battle, on the 27th of June.[1]

The Chindits no longer operated as a coherent force after 1944. They might have played a great part in the reconquest, such as might have shortened the war in Burma, but without Wingate's inventive mind to devise a rôle for them in new circumstances, they gradually ceased to exist after the summer. Without the Chindit commander to lead them, this appears the result of a right decision. In one way the force had accomplished all its purpose and more : the whole army was now "Chindit-minded."[2] But if their disappearance is easily

[1] Tulloch II. Calvert. Information obtained at the War Office.
[2] Mountbatten quoted in Calvert.

defensible on grounds of strategy and common sense, nothing of the kind can be said of the manifestations of mean spirit that accompanied the change of policy. There are stories, not all of which can be dismissed, of how one or two of those who had opposed him received the news of Wingate's death with indecent glee, and when the Chindit operations were concluding, some of Wingate's officers, who believed they had things of interest to tell the authorities, were received in Delhi with contemptuous airs of superiority. But of all the revenges contrived by paltry-minded people against their dead and formidable enemy the most detestable was directed against Agnes MacGeary. It seems from what happened that her immediate superiors had for some time regarded her as a dangerous person. In March Wingate had arranged for her to manage a Special Forces Hospital in Sylhet, and there were complaints, possibly justified, that in this post she was apt to use Wingate's high-handed methods in obtaining medical supplies.[1] However, it was not on any respectable grounds that an attempt was made to transfer her from the operational theatre, but because she brought deficiencies in the medical service to the notice of the high command. At the end of April or the beginning of May, Lord Louis Mountbatten inspected her new hospital. He asked her if there was anything she needed and she was unwise enough to tell him the truth, and in front of witnesses she said that there was an X-ray apparatus lying idle in Silchar which she had applied for, and which she had been promised, but which was still there. The Supreme Commander issued a personal order for the apparatus to be transferred, and this was done. Authority took umbrage. Her superiors told the Matron that she was never again to raise such questions with such people as the Supreme Commander except through the usual channels. She said that she could not tell untruths, even by implication, and offered her resignation. The authorities refused to accept her resignation and instead appointed her to a post on the then tranquil North-West Frontier of India, out of harm's way. In the event this ridiculous order was not acted on because shortly after receiving it Agnes MacGeary fell ill with typhoid, and being unable to take up active duty again in the war, she was eventually posted to the Medical Directorate in Delhi.[2] The story ended innocuously, but what needs to be remembered is that this woman was one of the most able and remarkable nurses in the whole medical profession, and that at a time of battle and heavy casualties, conventional-minded people tried to relegate her to a post of minor usefulness, out of dislike of the man with whom she had been associated. This repulsive episode can almost persuade the student of Wingate's life that he was fully justified throughout the long

[1] Lady Wavell.   [2] Tulloch II. and correspondence in W.P.I.

rebellion which occupied nearly the whole of his days, and in which there was no lasting truce from his early youth to the day of his death.

The character of Orde Wingate was one of close concentration, of fixed purposes, of few, ardent and narrow passions. At the same time he had the great variety that goes with a potent and restless mind. He made some very different impressions on the people he knew. Many who admired him and gave him devoted service found little to love in him. He was not a man who craved affection or often encouraged it, and he once explained to Anderson his belief (characteristic of his extremism) that a popular officer was a bad officer. His behaviour was in keeping with this sombre conviction, and some who worked with him found his continual solemnity, and his sleepless preoccupation with the objects of his faith, and his proselytising habit, oppressive things to live with. Lord Wavell put it on record that he found him a man hard to know, and added, as though in explanation, that he could detect in him none of the irrepressible humour which had enchanted him in his famous kinsman. Other accounts written in the same spirit can tempt one to suppose that Wingate was a joyless sobersides, but William Allen and Michael Calvert both show a man who was no stranger to a sense of fun, and Calvert is not alone in suspecting a boisterous strain which he purposely held in check. Among his Jewish friends these two contradictory elements were visible in their most natural conjunction. As a military commander he ruled his squadsmen by fear and trust rather than affection, but as a Zionist among Zionists in the Kibbutzim he was " Hayedid," the friend.

This chiaroscuro contrast showed yet more clearly in those matters which belonged to the centre of his being. His unrelenting harshness, and the merciless discipline with which he conducted all his exploits, repelled many people, but many others who met him were impressed by a gift of ready sympathy. The case of the unhappy man with whom he made friends on the journey from South Africa is not an isolated incident. Among similar things, there is a record of him throwing all the energy of his personality into an effort to rally one of his men who was failing through exhaustion after the first Chindit expedition, and saving his life. He was " *dur aux grands*," and often needlessly unrelenting to the strong whether above or below him, but never to the weak or to people broken in spirit. He only knew happiness spasmodically, and he could often understand, as a contented man could not, what unhappiness means. In larger contexts he could give imaginative sympathy to those whose whole fate was one of misfortune, and there was in him an instinctive grasp of what an inheritance of suffering can do to men. From this came his zeal for Ethiopian independence, and in part for Zionism. If he was frequently indifferent to the niceties of social intercourse, he had all the instinctive generosity on which social intercourse is founded.

This contrast between his inner beliefs and his surface conduct indicates what was perhaps one of the strangest things about him. Principles interested him more than men. He could and often did outrage people, sometimes quite indefensibly as in his treatment of Sandford, but he would never knowingly outrage a principle to which he had given his allegiance. In every phase of his life, from his early struggles to the triumphs of his maturity, the same strange note of impersonality is always unmistakable. He sincerely thought of himself as the instrument of fate and often saw other people in this light. From this came some of the mistakes in his dealings. He did not appreciate that other people were likely to have very different ideas about themselves. He was genuinely surprised that his description of British generals in Ethiopia as "military apes" had occasioned offence damaging to his career, because he considered his attack logical, and he assumed that his opponents would recognise the justice of his insulting words and hasten to alter what they were doing. He believed his severe criticisms of his men were a necessary piece of thanklessness to improve the system of recruitment to the ventures he led, and he assumed that his men would feel this too. Likewise if he praised himself he did so in order to forward a needful principle of warfare. He was sometimes wanting in gratitude to those who helped him, but he was always wanting in rancour to those with whom he disagreed, once the disagreement was passed, and the principle settled. His coldness of feeling led to another paradox : this intensely ambitious and touchy man was deficient in the small vanities, and he could never rightly estimate the large part they play in human affairs. But if there was a flaw in his understanding it was that he never learned that a disregard of people is own brother to a disregard of principle. He never fully understood that injustice to men is an affront to that principle of justice to which he gave himself with noble dedication. It is only in extenuation that one can say that he was often prepared to disregard himself for the sake of a cause.

Though his variety meant that he made some conflicting impressions, he made one master impression on all but a very few who met him after his early years. He was unquestionably a man of genius, using that term in its original and stricter sense. There was in him an inner and active impulse which gave him continual energy with a sense of obeying unseen powers, a driving force such as the ancient idea of the attendant daemon well describes. The deep-seated religious faith which told him to give his powers to the service of God could only increase his sense of mysterious influences shaping the course of his life, and the fact that his religion, for all its passion and unquestioning faith in the Scriptures, was undefined, gave to his religious disposition the ardent character of a search for the truth. If the most striking contrast in him was between his impersonality and his egotism, there was an explanation to be found in the inner impulse of which he was intensely conscious. In all sincerity, and in a spirit that may be called humble, he guarded his fortunes for the sake of the unknown force of which he believed himself to be the earthly habitation. The belief was extravagant but it was not mere delusion. The power was there. It accounts for every one of his achievements, for none of them was open to a man with less than gigantic force of character. Equally, the presence of a mysterious and inherent power makes intelligible much of his private life; the intimations of his youth concerning beckoning visions and fears of unfulfilment; his early proneness to ravaging melancholia; his constant passion to explain himself during the course of his active life, as though to clear away a besetting mystery, and, for all the incisiveness of his mind, his frequent inability to do so. It explains the violence of his delight in great literature and music, because he was conscious of sharing a disposition with the master spirits of poetry and composition, and though there may be something in Aung Thin's comical interpretation of Wingate's sudden recourse to poetic masterpieces in a moment of great peril, the real cause probably lay much deeper.

The possession of genius does not make for personal happiness, if we are to judge by the lives of men so endowed; least of all does it do so in a society which is sceptical of that supreme quality. In spite of numerous efforts to reform, the society of England remains firmly bourgeois in morals, ideas and taste. It does not provide a propitious atmosphere for a man of extreme originality and unusual upbringing, who manifestly regards himself as driven by hidden forces; and this fact can explain much of Wingate's chronic and sometimes puzzling rebelliousness. If we imagine him as a character in one of the great Russian novels he does not seem in the least fantastic, but his path lay not only in a society opposed to all excess, and devoted to the middle way and the virtues of compromise, but in that section of it where correctitude and convention are most respected. It is to the great credit of the army that despite Wingate's aversion to all its cherished ways he advanced far in its service, but his progress could at no stage have been other than grievously painful.

Such in outline, in the writer's opinion, was the character of this man. It remains to say that human nature is mysterious and at the core of every human being there is that which eludes all search and all study, no matter how long and minute. This is especially true of such a man as Wingate who held often, and perhaps more often than he knew, to the esoteric and little frequented path of his spiritual ancestors of Puritan England and Scotland. In the end he like them maintains his secret, even from those who knew him best. None, even among his closest associates and friends, either know him or believed it was possible to know him in entirety.

His place in our history, a thing likely to have been of more interest to him than estimates of his personality, may not be determined for a long time. It will depend on the considered criticism and consensus in opinion of military historians. The writer is not such a being and can only tentatively indicate possible lines along which a judgment may be made.

Wingate has been accused of narrowness in his military ideas, of seeing the type of operation with which he was associated as the only means to military victory. This is to judge him superficially. He first found himself as a soldier in circumstances where he could put his early Sudan training as a patrol leader to practical and brilliant use. All his subsequent appointments, with the exception of Sidcup, were to theatres where he could emulate that first success, but there is no reason to suppose that his talents lay in only one field, and Sidcup offers strong evidence of his versatility. He was never slow to learn or excessively conservative of method. He made it clear in his Burma report that he regarded the long range penetration method as a means of attack only in circumstances of air superiority and ample wireless facilities. He was perfectly capable of adopting quite other methods in other circumstances. He cannot be called narrow because he obeyed instructions to specialise.

Of the four principal military actions of his life only the last two can provide material for a definitive opinion on Wingate's historic merits as a soldier. The operations in Palestine were too small in scope for such a purpose, and his enemies in Ethiopia were so inept as to detract from the achievements of their conqueror. The real test did not come till the war in the Far East.

In his time Wingate's exploits in Burma were the subject of enthusiastic praise, and so far as the public was concerned this was due to the romantic nature of the two expeditions rather than to serious military considerations. Against the high estimate in which he was generally held in 1943 and 1944, there was an inevitable and perhaps necessary reaction. The extravagant claims made for Lawrence of Arabia were remembered, and it appeared to later opinion at the end of the war and the years immediately after, that here was another case of a gallant enterprise which had been exciting to the imagination, passing as a great military accomplishment. Wingate came to be thought of as a man who had had the short-lived luck to be vastly overrated. Sir William Slim's account of him is largely a reflection of an official change of mind.

But there were a few people in high places who maintained throughout that Wingate's operations had more significance than that of a morale-raiser for the readers of newspapers. Among these was Lord Wavell. He was impressed by evidence in captured Japanese documents that Wingate's first expedition had had a considerable influence on Japanese strategy.[1] Other reasons for believing so appeared independently. From an interview in January 1946 with two Japanese generals, and a Japanese Staff officer all of whom had served in Burma, General Symes reported that the first Wingate expedition had unquestionably resulted in a Japanese decision to attack due west over the Chindwin.[2] The details and conclusions deduced at the time from this evidence, and from the documents quoted by Lord Wavell, seem to have been faulty, and were certainly contradictory. This allowed the reaction against Wingate and the Chindits to persist undismayed. But deeper research into Japanese documentation, (a feat to which the writer can make no claim), tends to confirm the main proposition put forward by the witnesses examined by General Symes, namely, that the courage and scale of the first Wingate expedition prompted the enemy command in Burma to commit a blunder of enormous consequence.

The sequence of events on which Wingate exerted influence was very roughly as follows : by 1944 the Japanese Government and high command knew that they could not be victors but they had substantial hope that by staying on the defensive in the redoubt of Burma they might obtain conditions. This was sound reasoning and sound policy, but Wingate's irruption unsettled both. It caused the Japanese to question the strength of their line of defence. At the same time it caused them to underestimate the difficulties of a direct attack westwards. They were led to the belief that if the British whom they had defeated were capable of such actions, then they themselves could move forward without fear to a direct assault on the 14th Army and establish an impregnable line in Assam. If, as now seems incontestable, Wingate was a main influence on this trend in Japanese military thinking then there is no need to question the value of what he did, and even the crossing of the Irrawaddy and all that followed

[1] Letter—Wavell-Under Secretary of War (18.7.43).
[2] New Delhi Archives.

from that, can be justified, the action added to the scale of what was done, and the scale produced the effect by which the British plan for reconquest could at last enter a final and active phase. For the decision of the Japanese to attack Assam due west was fatal to them. In the course of their three-pronged attack they lost 65,000 men, nearly half their number, and much more than half of their battle material. After so great a disaster to the enemy the reconquest of Burma[1] under Slim's masterly leadership was possible and even inevitable.

No such result was or could have been in Wingate's intention, and it is at least highly doubtful if the other major effect of the first expedition was consciously intended by him either. This was the influence of Chindit practice on the method of supply by aircraft and of air-infantry co-operation as employed by 11 Army Group in the campaign of 1944-1945. According to some of the best informed opinion, what was learned in the field from Wingate's theory, training and conduct of operations was absolutely decisive for victory.[2] These two Chindit consequences, confusion of Japanese policy and reform of British method, were Wingate's greatest achievements, but in them one can easily discern one reason why he is likely to remain a subject of dispute : both of them were indirect achievements and for that reason are not fully open to a neat interpretation of cause and effect. To some extent he must remain mysterious in his public career as in his private character.

This is especially true of his part in the events of 1944. The active stage of Operation Thursday was less than three weeks old when Wingate was killed, and nothing is known for certain of his immediate plans ; furthermore, the whole of the great undertaking in which he lost his life has a perplexing character. The second expedition, like the first, depended on an advance by the army, and, like the first, it went in with no prospect of such an advance to exploit what it might accomplish. The Stronghold system was Wingate's brilliant improvisation wherewith to use Chindits effectively without an advance, but this did not transform them from guerilla troops nor absolve them from the need to change their location rapidly and frequently. When surprise was lost the Strongholds could always be destroyed by first-class Japanese troops, as Broadway, Aberdeen and White City would have been if Lentaigne had not ordered a quick move north. It is idle to speculate on what Wingate himself would have done in circumstances that were only gradually becoming clear at the moment of his

[1] For details of the process whereby the Japanese altered their policy the interested reader should consult *Official History*, chapter XXVI, pp 426-434.
[2] Sir John Baldwin.

death, but there can be no doubt that he, too, would have had to initiate a new phase.

The main, and it seems unchallengeable, theory on which Wingate acted in planning and mounting the second expedition was that in the circumstances of Burma in 1944 there could be no victorious army offensive, (as the term is normally understood), until the opposing army had first received a mortal wound. Wingate's purpose was to deliver that wound. But in the event the Japanese inflicted it on themselves by attempting the impossible, and on a scale beyond any calculations. The main purpose for which he raised his six Chindit brigades was accomplished by different means, and he could never know that he was a cause of those different means. The deeds of his fame were at the last obscured by the great dimensions of what he brought about. Fitting and strange fate of a man through whose whole nature there ran so much enigma.

There remains the brief epilogue. Three weeks after his death, on the 14th of April, a memorial service was held at St. Margaret's, Westminster, at which Leopold Amery read a brief panegyric in honour of the man whose career he had vitally influenced. He described him as one who, " in his upbringing, in his fundamentally religious and almost mystic temperament, as in his way of handling men of all races . . . was very like his fellow countrymen and fellow pilgrims of an earlier generation, David Livingstone and General Gordon. . . ." He said that, "his greatness as a leader lay in qualities beyond mere intellectual grasp of war, or swift daring ; it lay in a deep, compelling faith."

The son he had longed for, and who had been so often in his thoughts during the last months of his life, was born on the 11th of May. He was christened Orde Jonathan.

In July, a second party, this time under the leadership of the principal chaplain of Special Force, Christopher Perowne, set out from the Sylhet Headquarters for the scene of the obscure disaster. Their purpose was to pay last honours to the untended remains of Wingate and his eight companions. They reached the place on the 6th. Those to be buried belonged to different religions, so Colonel Perowne used an improvised form of consecration, memorial and blessing in the place of the Anglican office of the dead. The grave was marked by a cross made in the military workshops of Sylhet and inscribed with the nine names.

On August 2nd, Winston Churchill paid the most famous of all tributes to Wingate. In the course of a speech in the House of

Commons he said, "We placed our hopes at Quebec in the new Supreme Commander Admiral Mountbatten and in his brilliant lieutenant Major-General Wingate who, alas, has paid a soldier's debt. There was a man of genius who might well have become also a man of destiny. He has gone, but his spirit lives on in the long range penetration groups, and has underlain all these intricate and daring air operations and military operations based on air transport and on air supply." When he came to write the fifth volume of his history of the Second World War the august author referred to Wingate in terms of the same admiration and also of personal affection.

In 1947 Wingate's remains were exhumed with those of the other victims of the disaster and reinterred in Arlington cemetery in the United States. His family protested that his tomb should be in some more fitting place, and one that had association with his name, but though Mr. Churchill interested himself in the matter personally, no exception was allowed in this case to the rules governing the siting of war graves. Authority had the last word.

There are three main memorials to Wingate. One has been mentioned already, the handsome tablet in the porch of the school chapel at Charterhouse which was ceremonially unveiled by Lord Louis Mountbatten in 1946. In Addis Ababa his name is commemorated in the Wingate School for boys. In the State of Israel there is a "children's village," a settlement devoted to the care of young people who have lost their parents, standing in the hills a few miles south of Haifa. It is named after him as Yemin Orde. Here in 1948, during the Arab-Jewish war, Lorna (who was in the country at the time) arranged for the Bible which he had carried in his campaigns to be dropped to the settlers with other supplies. He is remembered in Israel with an affection given to no other Englishman except Arthur Balfour.

There is a temptation to say of any man that he died at the best time, and it is strong in the case of Wingate who fell in the midst of great achievement, and " as the meteor falls, sudden, swift, unaccountable."[1] But to believe in the rightness of an early death must often amount to gross injustice ; it implies that he who died was incapable of further development. In Wingate's life there remained, without doubt, another fierce, stormy, uncompromising chapter to be filled in the years that followed the war, and saw a settlement by strife of the long-perplexed Palestine question. It is easily imagined that he would have embroiled himself in the politics of that conflict with an intemperateness that would have put him beyond the help of his friends, but to assume that is to assume that he was incapable of mastering political

[1] Wavell. Introduction to Rolo.

skill. To be fair to his memory one should not forget the immense progress as a politician that he did make between his crusade for Ethiopian rights and his performance in Quebec, though certainly he is not likely to have acted as a cool political tactician when Palestine was in debate. However that may have been, rashness need not necessarily have stood in the way of action, and it is clear what action he would have sought. The hope of his life was to lead a Jewish army and it can be said, on the authority of the present leaders of Israel, that if he had survived the war he would in the end have commanded the small Zionist force which kept at bay, and then routed the Moslem armies which tried to extirpate the revived Jewish nation.

If he was happy in his death it was not because life had little more to give him, but rather because life was at that moment giving him gifts reserved to men who stand above their fellows, and giving in abundance. But fate may have stinted him of that which he most wanted, and the fulfilment of his supreme ambition.

APPENDIX A

In Mr. Leonard Mosley's biographical study of Wingate, *Gideon Goes To War*, the dinner-party at Emmanuel Wilenski's house is described on page 75 as follows :

"Wilenski . . . informed Wingate that a meeting would be held the following day in his home. Most of the Hagana leaders, including Golomb, would be present.

"The Hagana leaders were waiting when Wingate arrived. Mrs. Wilenski remained in the hall of the house, keeping watch in case there should be a raid by the British police. Wingate looked very pale and ill, and his eyes were burning. He walked to the head of the table and immediately began to speak about Zionism. He talked for half an hour about the Jewish State. He was speaking to professional Zionists who had probably heard everything that had ever been said on the subject, but such was his zeal and passion and enormous driving enthusiasm that they were enthralled by his words.

"Abruptly he changed the subject. 'To be practical,' he said : 'Members of Hagana, the White Paper has turned you down. There will be no Jewish State unless you fight for it, and it is the English you will have to fight. The time has come to declare war on the English. I have come to ask you to make that declaration to-night, and to plan your first action.'

"He paused, but no one asked questions. They were all waiting. 'Your first attack, if you will take my advice, will be against the great oil refinery in Haifa. Its destruction would be a grave blow to the British Empire.'

"One of the Hagana leaders protested. 'That's impossible. We'd never get inside, for one thing.'

"'You will,' replied Wingate, 'if you allow me to lead the operation. I know the refinery. I can get you inside.'

"Said another Hagana leader : 'You ? A British Officer ? How could you do it ? What about your military career ? '

"Wingate looked at him coldly. 'There are times when a man must make a decision. Now, comrades, are you with me—and am I to lead you ? '

"The leaders of the Hagana went into consultation, and turned him down. 'This is no time,' they said (it was 1939) 'to embarrass the British, even for the sake of a Jewish State.' "

When this account appeared, first in the *Sunday Express*, and then in Mr. Mosley's book, it passed without any authoritative challenge. At this time I was in early stages of my Wingate researches. I made inquiries from people who had known him, from members of the Wingate family and from Mrs. Lorna Smith. They could tell me nothing. None of his friends had ever heard about any such criminal proposal, and Mrs. Lorna Smith, not having been present at the meeting in question, was in the painful position of lacking any evidence to disprove the allegation.

The fact of Mr. Mosley's account remaining unchallenged, despite names of living people having been mentioned, gave me the idea that there must be some basis of fact to what he said. During a visit to Israel in March, 1956, I made as thorough an examination as I could of Wingate's Palestine career in the thirties. Among the great mass of information given to me I could never find any evidence relating to this episode either in substantiation or disproof. I found that people such as David Hacohen, Chaim Laskov, Yeheskiel Sachar, Israel Carmi, Leo Cohen and Moshe Sharett who had either been members of Hagana or in the inner councils of the Jewish Agency, knew nothing about this arresting incident. It occurred to me after a while that this complete absence of positive or negative evidence in itself threw suspicion on the reliability of the sources consulted by Mr. Mosley. If such a proposal had ever been made it must have become known in Jewish circles in Palestine, and these are not always above taking delight in gossip of a scandalous nature. It was pointed out to me by several witnesses that the original story was evidently not told at first hand. Wingate had a very individual style of speech and his appeal to the Hagana leaders as " comrades " was quite out of character. Some of the detail pointed to the fact that the teller of the tale was not familiar with pre-war Palestine. To visit a Jewish house in Haifa was not a risky proceeding. Police raids were not to be feared on such occasions. Mrs. Wilenski was not likely to spend her time in the hall of her house while guests were present, nor on her own evidence did she do so. Mr. Mosley's informant was evidently thinking of the Palestine of 1946 and 1947.

I found it surprisingly difficult to discover who had been at the meeting in question. This suggested, among other things, that the story came from a confusion of several different occasions. I will indicate presently what I believe them to have been.

Professor Rattner was particularly illuminating on the subject. In 1939 he was as near to being Field Commander of Hagana as was possible under that body's committee system of rule. He assured me that no such major action as blowing up the Haifa refinery could have been discussed in any way at all without his being consulted, and he never heard of any such project. He examined Mr. Mosley's record with me (not having read it before), and made two comments of interest. First he pointed out that the originator of the story (or Wingate if the record was authentic), knew little about Hagana and the Jewish position in Palestine at that time. The majority of the workers in the refinery were Jews all of whom, with no exceptions that he could recall, were Hagana members, and so Wingate's boast that he alone could introduce Jews into the works, and the Hagana protestation that to enter them was beyond their powers, made no sense. Wingate, without doubt, knew a great deal about Jewish life in Palestine. The writer seems to have been misled.

Professor Rattner's second comment tickled me. I reproduce his words as precisely as I can remember them. " You must have noticed," he said, " that Zionists have never been behind-hand in making propaganda for themselves and I cannot imagine that a story which does so much credit to Jews at the expense of any British officer, even Wingate, would not have been given an enormous circulation."

The facts of the case began to emerge. It is true that there was a meeting at Wilenski's house (very different from the one described in *Gideon Goes To War*), at the time of the publication of the White Paper. One of the guests was Yakov Dori who in March 1956 was principal of the Technical College at Haifa. I visited him and in a candid talk with me he said he remembered the occasion very well. He read the passage from *Gideon Goes To War* in my presence—as with Professor Rattner for the first time. He said that Mr. Mosley's description of Wingate as " very pale and ill, and his eyes burning " was apt enough. He also remembered Wingate giving a long harangue on Zionism, which was listened to with deep interest, and he agreed that in the course of it Wingate emphasised that Zionists would come into conflict with their one-time friends and protectors, the British. But Mr. Dori strenuously denied that there had been any talk about practical measures, and certainly none on the subject of the enormous sabotage operation mentioned by Mr. Mosley. He remembered Eliahu Golomb being present. He remembered the evening as having passed calmly.

Shortly after meeting Mr. Dori I spent a long session with Mr. and Mrs. Yolan, the Wilenskis of 1939, in their house in Haifa, the scene of the meeting in May, 1939. It is their account of the evening, influenced by what I had heard previously from other people, that forms the basis of the record I give. I have not attempted to do anything more than give an account of how this occasion is remembered.

People remember treacherous proposals placed before them under dramatic circumstances. Nothing like this is remembered by the people to whom the proposal was allegedly made. I think that Wingate may be taken, on that fact alone, as absolutely cleared beyond question, of the charge of encouraging an act of major destruction in Haifa.

What was the origin of the story ? The possibility that it came from a confusion of several incidents with one fancied episode has been mentioned. Two incidents which can be established on evidence bear a feeble but definite resemblance to the story in Mr. Mosley's book : they are Wingate's advice to pursue a " tough line " in negotiations conveyed through a friend to Dr. Weizmann (page 182), and his conversation with David Hacohen which seems to have been one of two or possibly three other similar conversations with Jewish friends. Both these incidents are somewhat shocking but both are separated by a difference in kind from the criminal proposition supposed to have been made at Haifa Nevertheless, it is easy to imagine how even slight exaggeration or distortion of the incidents could make them appear infinitely worse than they were. Wingate himself who retained a fond and youthful taste for violent expression calculated to shock more conventional people, may have helped distorted versions to become known. It is to be noted, however, that the scandal is not widespread.

An additional explanation was suggested to me by Colonel Rivlin of the Israel Ministry of Defence. It is his opinion that there *was* a plan to destroy the refinery at Haifa with which Hagana would have been closely associated. But this plan, he believes, belongs not to 1939 but to 1941 and 1942 when Allied fortunes were at so low a pitch that a British evacuation of Egypt and Palestine was not outside calculations that had to be made Certain secret British organisations were in charge of demolitions aimed at denying the installations of Haifa to the enemy in the event of evacuation, and it was part of their design to employ the resources of Hagana whose illegal position was so qualified and anomalous (as appears in the story of the S.N.S.), that it remains hardly definable. Their employment in those days by an irregular but official British organisation is not in itself an impossible or even improbable proposition. A leakage of information may have occurred, (it usually does occur), and men of Hagana who remembered Wingate's enthusiasm for a Jewish army thought they saw his hand here. Thence a legend began and suffered the distortions to which legends are liable. I find this an ingenious explanation but without definite evidence of such a plan it cannot be considered more than plausible.

There is a last point to be cleared up. In a passage anterior to his account of the meeting with Hagana leaders, Mr. Mosley represents Wingate as being drunk when presenting his gift of whisky to the

APPENDIX A

Wilenskis. This might suggest that when he made his proposal to blow up the refinery he had taken to drink and was not clear as to the enormity of what he was saying. But Mr. and Mrs. Yolan deny that he was drunk at the time of the gift. He was not prudish about drinking, and, as is mentioned on page 129 was capable of "indiscretions." But such lapses were so rare as to be negligible in his life.

APPENDIX B

MOST ACCOUNTS of the crossing of the Chindwin by 77 Brigade in 1943 make reference to the messenger dogs, but thereafter little is heard of them. They faded from notice after the first hazard, and few people seem to remember their later history. As with former difficulties, I have consulted Bernard Fergusson, who gives me the following information.

The idea of messenger dogs was not of Wingate origin, and he did not have any particular belief in it, but in spite of his doubts he agreed to try it out in the first expedition. The dogs were trained on a logical system. Each individual dog was taught to know and recognise and be attached to two men. When Man A said " Go," the dog, carrying a message in his satchel, ran to Man B, with whom he would remain till Man B ordered him back to Man A by the same procedure. There was one dog to each column. The normal function of a dog was to run a two-way messenger service between a Column Headquarters and an outpost. They were taught to trail their handlers long distances. Training was strict, and it was a major offence for a person outside messenger-dog society to pet, or feed, or talk to, a messenger-dog, and equally for a person within that society to talk to any dog other than his own. The dogs were of various breeds ; Bernard Fergusson's was a Staffordshire terrier bitch, by the name of Judy.

In the event, the dogs were not a military success, though this was due to lack of opportunity rather than to faulty theory. Fergusson's Judy was used only once with success in her proper rôle. In the later stages of the expedition both her handlers were killed, but on one occasion after this she rendered a useful and touching service. The day after the remnants of Number 5 column had crossed the Irrawaddy in three dispersal groups, on their homeward journey, Judy suddenly made an appearance out of the jungle on to Fergusson's path. Efforts were made to attract her, but she instantly ran off, and was not seen again by any of Fergusson's own party until after they had reached Imphal some weeks later. She had, however, delivered a message since, after the death of her handlers, she had attached herself to Flight-Lieutenant Sharp, Fergusson's R.A.F. officer, and her behaviour on the jungle path made it clear to Fergusson that Sharp's party had successfully crossed the river. Fergusson concludes his note on Judy as follows : " She celebrated her arrival at Imphal by producing a litter of puppies, having evidently misunderstood the purpose of the expedition."

ACKNOWLEDGMENTS

The author and publishers gratefully acknowledge permission to include passages from the following books : —

THE TURN OF THE TIDE : Sir Arthur Bryant.

GIDEON GOES TO WAR by Leonard Mosley : Arthur Barker Ltd.

WAR IS PEOPLE by Lorna Lindsley : Houghton Mifflin Co. Boston, U. S. A.

PRISONERS OF HOPE by Michael Calvert : Jonathan Cape Ltd.

THE SECOND WORLD WAR by Sir Winston Churchill : Cassell and Co. Ltd.

GUERILLA WARFARE IN ABYSSINIA by William Allen : Penguin Books Ltd.

BACK TO MANDALAY by Lowell Thomas : Frederick Muller Ltd.

RETURN VIA RANGOON by Philip Stibbe : Newman Wolsey Ltd.

AFRICAN AFTERTHOUGHTS by Sir Philip Mitchell : Hutchinson and Co.

BEYOND THE CHINDWIN : Brigadier Bernard Fergusson.

THE WILD GREEN EARTH : Brigadier Bernard Fergusson.

WINGATE'S RAIDERS by Charles Rolo : A. M. Heath and Co. Ltd.

WINGATE'S PHANTOM ARMY by W. G. Burchett : Frederick Muller Ltd.

INDEX

INDEX